grokking
Bitcoin

Get the eBooks FREE!

(PDF, ePub, Kindle, and liveBook all included)

We believe that once you buy a book from us, you should be
able to read it in any format we have available. To get electronic
versions of this book at no additional cost to you, purchase and
then register this book at the Manning website.

Go to https://www.manning.com/freebook and follow the
instructions to complete your pBook registration.

That's it!
Thanks from Manning!

grokking
Bitcoin

Kalle Rosenbaum

Foreword by David A. Harding

MANNING
SHELTER ISLAND

For online information and ordering of this and other Manning books, please visit
www.manning.com. The publisher offers discounts on this book when ordered in
quantity. For more information, please contact

    Special Sales Department
    Manning Publications Co.
    20 Baldwin Road, PO Box 761
    Shelter Island, NY 11964
    Email: orders@manning.com

 Manning Publications Co   Development editor: Christina Taylor
20 Baldwin Road   Technical development editor: Ozren Harlovic
Shelter Island, NY 11964   Review editor: Ozren Harlovic
     Production editor: Lori Weidert
     Copy editor: Rebecca Dueul-Gallegos
     Proofreader: Tiffany Taylor
     Technical proofreader: Jan Goyavaerts
     Typesetter: Kevin Callahan
     Cover designer: Leslie Haimes
     Illustrator: Chuck Larson

ISBN 9781617294648
Printed in the United States of America

• •

To the love of my life, my wife, Linnéa. Smart, faithful, real.
And to all awesome Bitcoiners everywhere.

Contents

foreword

What is the difference between Bitcoin and the various monies used in multiplayer games? Each is defined by software, is created out of nothing, and can have prices comparable to traditional currencies. To a casual observer, they seem much the same.

But there is an important difference in how they're designed that affects every aspect of their respective systems: whereas game currencies try to stop cheating by reactively banning users suspected of abuse, Bitcoin proactively prevents various types of cheating by making them impossible, impractical, or less profitable than honest behavior.

Grokking Bitcoin describes exactly how Bitcoin accomplishes that. As you learn about hash functions, digital signatures, proof of work, and many other technical concepts, you'll see over and over that Bitcoin effectively prevents cheating without requiring the global banning of any user.

The book then demonstrates the many benefits of this key feature. As you learn about addresses, wallets, miners, and nodes, you'll discover that if no one can cheat effectively, it's safe to allow everyone to participate in every part of the protocol, leaving no one in a trusted position of authority over the system. And with no one holding a trusted position, there's no need for identities in the first place. *Grokking Bitcoin* goes on to show how it's possible for anyone to use the public Bitcoin blockchain with a degree of privacy.

A decentralized system that doesn't use identities or depend on trust is quite different from the everyday systems with which most of us are familiar. Author Kalle Rosenbaum turns this liability into an asset by starting the explanation of each part of Bitcoin using a centralized, trusted, or identity-dependent system that any reader can intuitively understand. He then transforms that basic system step-by-step into the decentralized, trustless, and pseudonymous system implemented in Bitcoin. With each step filled with clear explanations and many excellent illustrations, even the most highly technical topic is made accessible to the interested layperson.

Bitcoin needs books like *Grokking Bitcoin,* but it also needs an active group of users who read those books and come to understand the technical principles on which Bitcoin is built. During these early days of what I hope will be the long history of Bitcoin, users are often asked to evaluate proposed changes to the system—changes that may affect the security and privacy of their bitcoins. Those who have read this book will understand how the system prevents cheating and will be able to help ensure that future changes preserve that essential feature and its many benefits.

—David A. Harding
Contributor to Bitcoin documentation

preface

Bitcoin is changing the world.

The world has seen many major improvements to human life, among which are vaccines, electricity, radio, automobiles, and the internet. Some of these technologies start out as rich people's games, but eventually they trickle down to the general public and bring huge benefits to Earth's population. Bitcoin will soon be right there among them. This is what makes me super-excited about Bitcoin.

Luckily, I'm fortunate enough to live in a pretty functional society. When conducting financial transactions, I never have to worry that someone will come knocking on my door. I've never felt that I need to spend my money immediately because otherwise hyperinflation will eat my lunch. But that also makes it harder for me to grok why Bitcoin is important. Bitcoin is mostly theoretical to me, but when I hear reports from less fortunate people living under oppressive or incompetent regimes about how Bitcoin makes their lives better, it becomes very real. Bitcoin will give people an opportunity to opt out of the system that's holding them hostage.

Satoshi Nakamoto, a pseudonym for a person or a group that wants to remain unknown, published a scientific paper on a cryptography-oriented e-mail list in October 2008. The title of the paper was, "Bitcoin: A Peer-to-Peer Electronic Cash System" (see web resource 1 in appendix C). Nakamoto's paper described the vital parts of Bitcoin, the first digital money system where there's no central authority to issue money or process transactions. In January 2009, Nakamoto published the first software program to implement the described system. Bitcoin didn't get much attention then, apart from within a very limited set of cryptography experts. Gradually, as the system proved itself to be working, more people became interested. But the resistance against Bitcoin was and is still far bigger and louder than the adopters, as is the case with all groundbreaking new technology. As of 2019, hundreds of millions of people are aware of Bitcoin, and tens of millions of people are using Bitcoin.

When I started exploring Bitcoin in 2013, it took me a long time to acquire a decent understanding of the technology. That's not because I'm remarkably stupid; it's because Bitcoin is a complex system. It's not just a fancy database—it's a mishmash of economy, mathematics, technology, and anthropology.

I started a technical blog about Bitcoin in 2015, and I guess Manning liked my content, because the company sent me an email asking if I was interested in writing a book about "blockchain." Since my passion is Bitcoin—not only the blockchain, an overly hyped word for Bitcoin's database—I replied and thanked Manning and said I'd be interested in writing a book about Bitcoin. I've struggled a few years trying to find a place in the Bitcoin community, and this opportunity seemed like a great fit. The project started, and it turned out to be far harder and far more time-consuming than I expected.

This book began as a typical technical description of Bitcoin, but it was difficult to teach one topic without the full context. The cognitive load at the beginning of the book would be too overwhelming. It became clear that I needed to do something else. I discussed it with my wife, and we came up with the idea of conceptually building Bitcoin from the ground up. The book starts with a really simple spreadsheet system that anyone can understand, and that system evolves into Bitcoin. Each chapter points out some problems with the current system, and we fix them by adding the technology covered by that chapter.

The manuscript for *Grokking Bitcoin* will be released under the Creative Commons Attribution-NonCommercial-ShareAlike 4.0 International (CC BY-NC-SA 4.0) license shortly after its print publication. Releasing a version under an open license was a requirement I had in writing this book. It is my way of giving back to the Bitcoin community that has given me so much over the years. It is my, and Manning's, hope that those who can't afford to buy this book will benefit from the open source version. There are, of course, less philanthropic reasons. We also hope that open sourcing this book will give it more visibility, as potential readers browse through it. Please buy the beautifully typeset version if you can afford it. Manning and I have spent an enormous amount of time and effort in producing this book, and we would greatly appreciate the income!

I hope you enjoy reading *Grokking Bitcoin* as much as I suffered writing it!

acknowledgments

I have a lot of people to thank for making this book possible.

First, I'd like to thank my wife, Linnéa, for all our valuable discussions and your consistent encouragement. You are absolutely fantastic.

Christina Taylor at Manning, my dear development editor: thank you for keeping me busy. Work work work. Thank you also to Bert Bates for your very valuable input on the pedagogy.

I'd like to also thank everyone else at Manning who contributed with their professionalism, including Ozren Harlovic, Rebecca Rinehart, Candace Gillhoolley, Ana Romac, Michael Stephens, Erin Twohey, Christopher Kaufmann, Matko Hrvatin, and Greg Wild. A special thanks to the fantastic production team: Chuck Larson, illustrator; Rebecca Deuel-Gallegos, copy editor; Kevin Callahan, typesetter; Tiffany Taylor, proofreader; and Lori Weidert, production editor.

I'd also like to thank Jonathan Jogenfors and Pontus Lindblom for reviewing some chapters covering their respective fields of expertise.

A lot of people on various internet forums were very helpful during my research. The ones that stand out the most are David A. Harding, Pieter Wuille, and Mark "Murch" Erhardt. Thank you for all our Twitter conversations and great answers on Bitcoin Stack Exchange (see web resource 2 in appendix C).

I got help from Andreas M. Antonopoulos when negotiating the open source terms for this book. Your encouragement during that process was gold. Thank you! In addition, thanks for the "vegetarian restaurant" analogy used in chapter 11. Thank you also for your amazing talks; you are a major source of inspiration for me.

I wrote this book using Asciidoctor, which is a text markup language. Thank you, Dan Allen, for your hard work on Asciidoctor; it's fantastic.

The book went through three review rounds, with several reviewers in each round. Those reviews were extremely useful in vetting ideas and finding gaps in the learning path. Thank you to Jan Goyvaerts, Max Humber, Iryna Romanenko, Jean-François Morin, Al Krinker, Joel Kotarski, Markus Beckmann, Christopher Bailey, Viton Vitanis, Paolo Freuli, Tomo Helman, Marcello Seri, Maciej Drozdzowski, Cicero Zandona, Barnaby Norman, Frances Buontempo, Glenn Swonk, and Sergio Fernandez Gonzalez.

Thank you also to all the Manning Early Access Program (MEAP) readers who contributed their thoughts, corrections, and questions on the Manning Forum, and to Aruna Surya for providing feedback via email.

If I left someone out, I'm terribly sorry; thank you, too.

about this book

The primary goal of this book is for you to be able to decide for yourself whether you trust Bitcoin. On the way to that goal, you'll learn a number of Bitcoin concepts—such as digital signatures, proof of work, and peer-to-peer networks—on a pretty deep level. Some secondary goals fall out naturally:

- Install and use a Bitcoin wallet on your phone and understand what you're doing.

- Engage in technical Bitcoin discussions.

- Make informed decisions about how to store your private keys depending on the number of bitcoins stored and the required level of security and convenience.

- Run a full Bitcoin node to engage in financial transactions without trusting a third party.

- See through extraordinary claims made by scammers, deceivers, and conmen who are piggybacking on Bitcoin's success. Be careful out there!

Who should read this book

This book is intended for technically interested people who want to understand Bitcoin on a deep technical level. The book doesn't require any programming skills, but a basic understanding of some technical concepts is beneficial—for example, databases, computer networks, computer programs, and web servers. A little math background can be useful too, but it's certainly not required.

How this book is organized: A roadmap

This book consists of 11 chapters and 3 appendices:

- Chapter 1 is an overview of Bitcoin. You'll learn what Bitcoin is, why it matters, and roughly how it operates.

- Chapter 2 discusses cryptographic hash functions and digital signatures. These are the fundamental building blocks needed for the rest of this book. I also lay the groundwork for a fictive money system, the cookie token spreadsheet, that we'll build on in chapters 2–8.

- Chapter 3 covers addresses. When you send bitcoins, you send them to the recipient's Bitcoin address. What are Bitcoin addresses, why are they needed, and how are they created and used?

- Chapter 4 goes through how a Bitcoin wallet keeps track of your secret keys and how multiple secret keys can be generated from a single huge random number called a seed. Backups are also discussed in detail.

- Chapter 5 explores the anatomy of a Bitcoin transaction and how transactions are digitally signed and processed.

- Chapter 6 discusses the blockchain: the database where transactions are stored. We walk through how the blockchain is structured and how it enables the use of so-called lightweight wallets.

- Chapter 7 covers proof of work, which is used to select who gets to add new transactions to the blockchain. This process, called mining, is what keeps your bitcoins secure in the blockchain.

- Chapter 8 explores the Bitcoin network. Bitcoin has no central point of control, and you'll see how that's possible with a peer-to-peer network. I also explain how to take active part in the Bitcoin network by running your own node.

- Chapter 9 revisits transactions. We circle back to discover some bells and whistles that are important for various applications.

- Chapter 10 introduces segregated witness. Bitcoin was upgraded with major improvements to transaction reliability, verification efficiency, and blockchain capacity in 2017, and this chapter gives you all the details.

- Chapter 11 goes through soft forks and hard forks and how Bitcoin can be safely upgraded using a soft fork together with a careful deployment plan.

I suggest that you read chapters 2–8, where we'll build the cookie token system from the ground up, sequentially. Each chapter adds a technology to the system to solve a specific problem, and by chapter 8, we'll have built Bitcoin. Chapters 9, 10, and 11 can be read out of order, but I recommend reading chapter 11 carefully, because it covers the essence of Bitcoin. If you get chapter 11, you're grokking Bitcoin.

I reuse some overview figures from chapter 1 every now and then throughout the book to help you with orientation, both in chapter intros and embedded in the chapters. It's easy to lose track of the big picture and the goal of the current topic; look for the periscope and section headers like "Where were we?"

Each chapter, except chapter 1, contains exercises. They're there for you to assess your skills. Each batch of exercises is divided into an easier section called "Warm up," used for shorter fact checks; and a tougher section, "Dig in," that requires more thinking. Some of the exercises in the "Dig in" sections are dreadfully difficult, so if you get stuck, please consult appendix B for answers.

Code conventions

There's not much code in this book. None, actually. But there are some Linux commands in chapter 8 and appendix A. A command is prefixed by a dollar sign and a space, as follows:

```
$ cd ~/.bitcoin
```

When a command is too long to fit on a single line, we break the line with a backslash \ and indent the next line by four characters, as follows:

```
$ ./bitcoin-cli getrawtransaction \
    30bca6feaf58b811c1c36a65c287f4bd393770c23a4cc63c0be00f28f62ef170 1
```

Backslashes can be used to write commands across multiple lines in most Linux command-line interpreters, so you can copy and paste such commands into your terminal. Lines of output from commands aren't broken with backslashes; they're instead wrapped as needed using a line break arrow as follows:

```
{"result":"000000000019d6689c085ae165831e934ff763ae46a2a6c172b3f1b60a8ce26f",
↳ "error":null,"id":"1"}
```

Throughout the book, data is written in a `fixed-width` font: for example, `7af24c99`. I usually don't explicitly write out what encoding is used (decimal numbers, hexadecimal strings, base64 strings, base58 strings, and so forth), because it's often obvious from the context.

liveBook discussion forum

Purchase of *Grokking Bitcoin* includes free access to a private web forum run by Manning Publications where you can make comments about the book, ask technical questions, and receive help from the author and from other users. To access the forum, go to https://livebook.manning.com/#!/book/grokking-bitcoin/discussion. You can also learn more about Manning's forums and the rules of conduct at https://livebook.manning.com/#!/discussion.

Manning's commitment to our readers is to provide a venue where a meaningful dialogue between individual readers, and between readers and the author can take place. It is not a commitment to any specific amount of participation on the part of the author, whose contribution to the forum remains voluntary (and unpaid). We suggest you try asking the author some challenging questions lest his interest stray! The forum and the archives of previous discussions will be accessible from the publisher's website as long as the book is in print.

Other online resources

If you have specific questions about Bitcoin that you didn't find the answer to in this book, I recommend Bitcoin Stack Exchange (web resource 2 in appendix C), which is a platform for questions and answers where good answers are up-voted by readers.

I also recommend the Bitcoin Developer Reference (web resource 3), for more comprehensive documentation of Bitcoin.

The Bitcoin Core source code (web resource 4) is the most accurate source of information. It's the reference implementation of the Bitcoin protocol, and reading that source code is sometimes the only way to find answers to questions.

If you want to search the contents of this book online, I recommend working with the source code available at web resource 5. It will be released at the latest 90 days after the book is published.

about the author

Kalle Rosenbaum has worked as a software developer for 20 years. His passion for Bitcoin began in 2013 and has continued uninterrupted. Kalle started a Bitcoin consultancy company in 2015 and has worked in the Bitcoin industry since then. He also writes a technical blog that explains various technical Bitcoin topics, such as block-propagation improvements, sidechains, and replace-by-fee. The purpose of the blog is to teach himself and let others benefit, too.

This chapter covers

- Getting to know Bitcoin

- Following a Bitcoin payment

- Problems solved by Bitcoin

The goal of this book is to teach you enough about Bitcoin to make informed decisions about how you can use it to improve your private life or business. My hope is that you'll learn enough to make up your own mind whether you trust Bitcoin or not (with any luck, the former). To get you off the ground, I'm going to assume you know roughly what the following terms mean:

- Computer program
- Database
- Computer network
- Web server

If you're unsure of any of these terms, don't worry. Either look them up or go ahead anyway—I think you'll manage.

What is Bitcoin?

Bitcoin is a digital cash system. It allows for people to move bitcoins, the currency unit of Bitcoin, between each other without using a bank or any other trusted third party. It resembles traditional bank notes and coins, but it's purely digital and used over the internet. The Bitcoin currency isn't tied to any specific *fiat currency* like the US dollar or the Chinese renminbi; it has free-floating exchange rates against most fiat currencies. You can buy and sell bitcoins for fiat currencies online using one of several exchanges, such as kraken.com, bitstamp.net, or localbitcoins.com.

> **Bitcoin or bitcoin?**
>
> The system is named *Bitcoin* with a capital B. The currency unit is called a *bitcoin* with a lowercase b. Commonly used symbols for bitcoins are ₿, BTC, and XBT. We'll mostly use BTC in this book.

No government or company controls Bitcoin. Instead, thousands of computers around the globe—the *Bitcoin network*, shown in figure 1.1—collectively keep the system working 24/7. You don't need to register or sign up anywhere to use Bitcoin, you just need internet access and a computer program, like a mobile app, to use it.

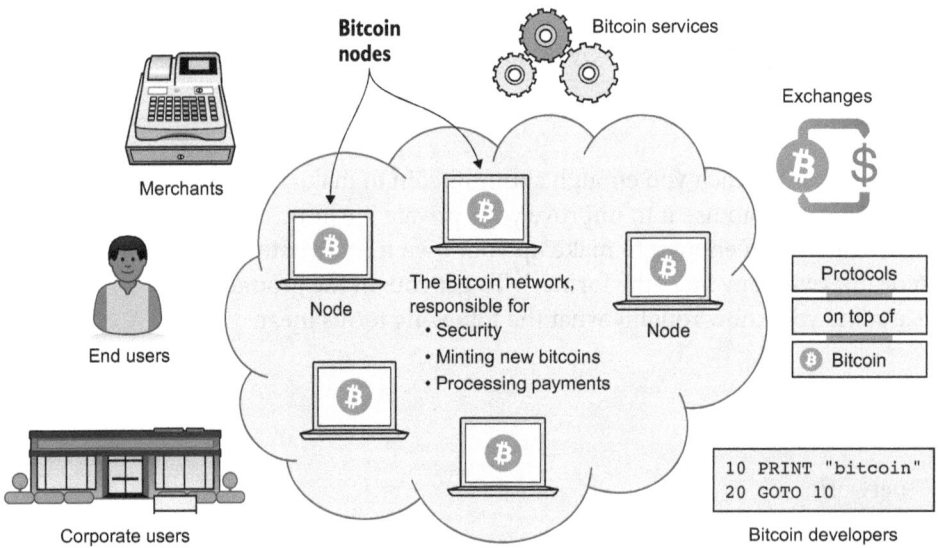

Figure 1.1   The Bitcoin network and its ecosystem

Anyone can use or participate in the Bitcoin network without special permission from a bank or similar institution. Thanks to Bitcoin's *permissionless* nature, a lot of Bitcoin-related technology has emerged over the years. We can roughly categorize participants in this Bitcoin ecosystem into several groups:

- *End users*—People using Bitcoin for their day-to-day needs, such as savings, shopping, speculation, or salaries

- *Corporate users*—Companies using Bitcoin to solve their business needs, such as paying wages internationally, or use cases similar to those of end users

- *Merchants*—For example, a restaurant or a bookstore accepting Bitcoin payments

- *Bitcoin services*—Companies providing Bitcoin-related services to customers, such as topping up mobile phones, anonymization services, remittance services, or tipping services

- *Exchanges*—Commercial services people can use to exchange their local currency to and from bitcoins

- *Protocols on top*—Systems that operate "on top" of Bitcoin to perform certain tasks, such as payment network protocols, specialized tokens, and decentralized exchanges

- *Bitcoin developers*—People working, often for free, with the open source computer programs that participants of the Bitcoin network use

Bitcoin doesn't care

The Bitcoin network doesn't distinguish between users. No user is more important than any other user. It doesn't matter who they are or what they do; everyone participates on the same terms.

The Bitcoin network's job is to process Bitcoin payments, secure the ledger of who owns what from unauthorized modifications, and get new bitcoins into circulation at the predetermined rate. The network consists of thousands of computers around the world. We call these computers *Bitcoin nodes*, or just *nodes*. Any of the actors mentioned previously can also participate actively in the Bitcoin network by running their own Bitcoin node. You must run your own node if you don't want to trust others to provide you with correct financial information.

The big picture

The Bitcoin network is a network of computers running Bitcoin software. This network verifies and confirms payments between Bitcoin users.

Suppose Alice wants to make a payment of 1 BTC to Bob. The payment starts with Alice creating a transaction and sending it to the Bitcoin

network, as shown in figure 1.2. I outline the process's four steps here
and explain each step further in the following subsections. Figure 1.2
will appear in the introduction of chapters 2 through 8, where I'll point
out which part of the figure we'll cover in the chapter.

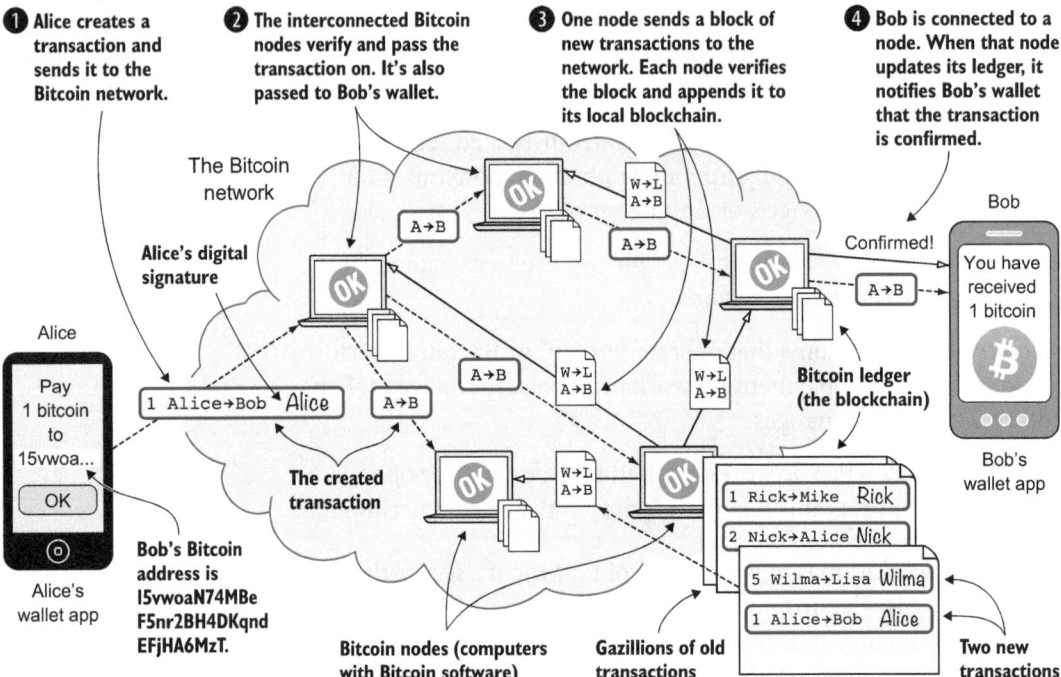

Figure 1.2   A Bitcoin payment. The payment is processed in four steps.

Now, let's follow Alice's payment from Alice to Bob:

❶ Alice creates and signs a transaction that moves 1 bitcoin from her
to Bob. She then sends the transaction to the Bitcoin network.

❷ The computers in the network—the Bitcoin nodes—check that
Alice actually has the money to spend and that the transaction
is authentic. They then pass the transaction to their neighbors,
called *peers*.

❸ Each computer updates its own copy of the *Bitcoin blockchain*, or the
ledger, with the new payment information.

❹ The network notifies Bob that he has received 1 bitcoin.

> **I thought Bitcoin was anonymous!**
>
> Bitcoin doesn't use names or any other personal information, but I use names in this first example for simplicity.

Note how Alice does not really *send* 1 bitcoin to Bob, but asks the Bitcoin network to move 1 bitcoin from Alice to Bob in the Bitcoin blockchain.

The Bitcoin blockchain is a database that each computer in the Bitcoin network has a copy of. Think of the blockchain as a ledger of all transactions ever made.

We'll go through these steps in more detail in the next four sections, one step per section.

Step ❶: Transactions

Step ❶ of the process (figure 1.3) is when Alice asks the network to move 1 bitcoin to Bob. She does this by sending a Bitcoin transaction to the Bitcoin network. This transaction contains instructions on how to move the money and a digital signature that proves it's really Alice requesting that the money be moved.

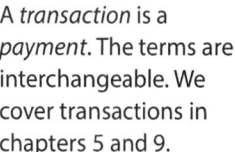

Transaction

A *transaction* is a *payment*. The terms are interchangeable. We cover transactions in chapters 5 and 9.

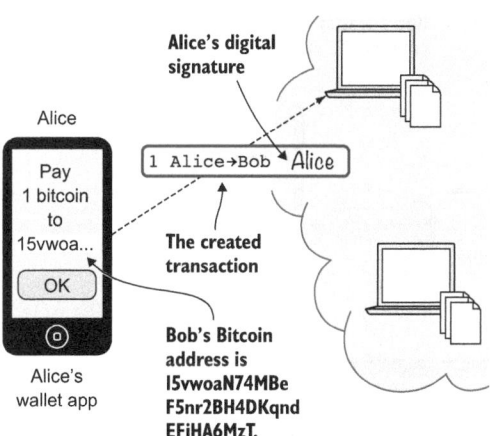

Figure 1.3 Alice creates a transaction, signs it, and sends it to one or more Bitcoin nodes in the Bitcoin network.

The Bitcoin *transaction* is a piece of data specifying

- The amount to move (1 bitcoin)

- The Bitcoin address to move the money to (Bob's Bitcoin address, `15vwoaN74MBeF5nr2BH4DKqndEFjHA6MzT`)

- A *digital signature* (made with Alice's private key)

The digital signature is created from the transaction and a huge secret number, called a *private key*, that only Alice has access to. The result is a digital signature that only the private key's owner could have created.

Alice's mobile wallet app is connected to one or more nodes in the Bitcoin network and sends the transaction to those nodes.

<aside>
Digital signatures

We'll discuss digital signatures in depth in chapter 2.
</aside>

Step ❷: The Bitcoin network

Alice has sent a transaction to one or more Bitcoin nodes. In step ❷ of the process (figure 1.4), each such node checks that the transaction is valid and passes it on to its peers. It does this by consulting its local copy of the blockchain and verifying that

- The bitcoin that Alice spends exists.

- Alice's digital signature is valid.

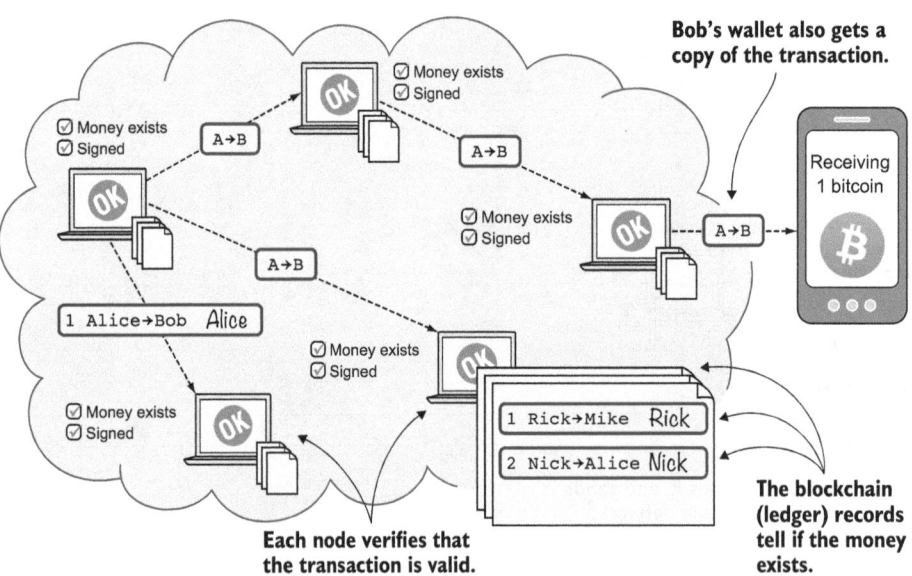

Figure 1.4   Alice has sent her transaction to a node in the network. The node verifies the transaction and forwards it to other nodes. Eventually, the transaction will reach all nodes in the network.

<aside>
Invalid transactions

Invalid transactions are dropped. They won't reach further than the first node.
</aside>

If all checks pass, a node forwards the transaction to its peers in the Bitcoin network. This is known as *relaying*. Alice's transaction will shortly have traveled the entire network while each node verifies it along the way. The blockchain hasn't been updated yet; that's the next step.

Step ❸: The blockchain

In step ❸, nodes update their local copies of the Bitcoin blockchain with Alice's transaction. The blockchain contains historic information about all previous transactions; new transactions, such as Alice's, are appended to it every now and then.

Updating the blockchain with Alice's transaction isn't as straightforward as it might seem. Alice's transaction isn't the only one going on in the Bitcoin network. Potentially thousands of transactions can be in flight at the same time. If all nodes updated their copy of the blockchain as they received transactions, the copies wouldn't remain copies for long because transactions can come in different orders on different nodes, as figure 1.5 shows.

The blockchain

The name *blockchain* comes from how the ledger is structured. It uses blocks that are chained together in such a way that modifications to the blockchain can be detected. I'll have more on that in chapter 6.

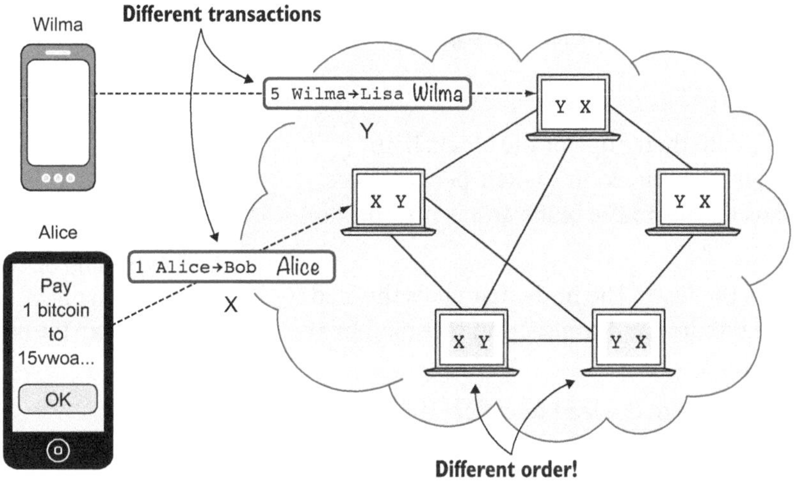

Figure 1.5 Transactions arrive in different orders at different nodes. If all nodes wrote their transactions to the blockchain in order of arrival, the different nodes' blockchains would differ.

To coordinate the ordering of transactions, one node takes the lead, saying "I want to add these two transactions to the blockchain in the order Y, X!" This message, known as a *block*, is sent out on the network by that leader (figure 1.6), in the same way that Alice sent the transaction.

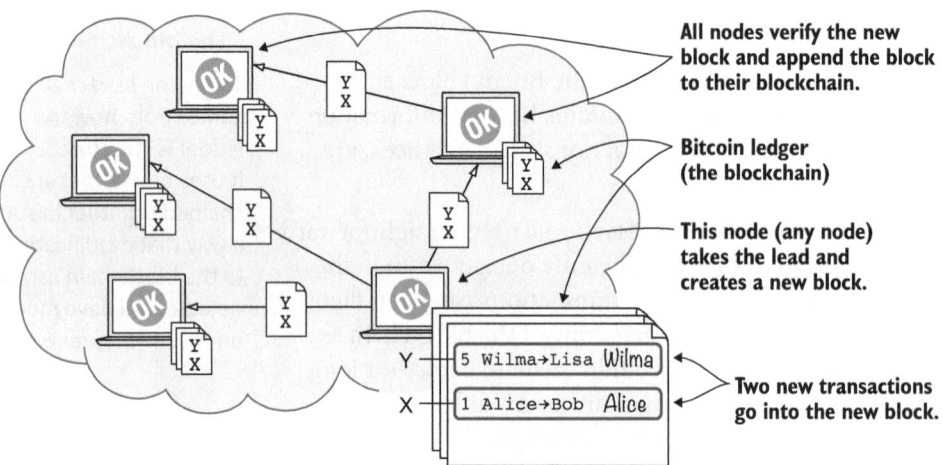

Figure 1.6   One node takes the lead and tells the others in what order to add transactions. The other nodes verify the block and update their blockchain copies accordingly.

As nodes see this block, they update their copy of the blockchain according to the message and pass the block on to their peers. Alice's transaction was one of the transactions in the block and is now part of the blockchain.

Why would a node want to take the lead? The node that takes the lead is rewarded with newly minted bitcoins and transaction fees paid by the transactions it includes in the block.

But wouldn't every node constantly take the lead to collect the rewards? No, because to take the lead, a node must solve a hard problem. This requires the node to consume considerable time and electricity, which ensures that leaders don't pop up often. The problem is so hard that most nodes in the network don't even try. Nodes that do try are called *miners* because they mine new coins, similar to a gold miner digging for gold. We'll discuss this process further in chapter 7.

The blockchain is append-only

New transactions are added to the end of the blockchain only—it grows only from the end.

Step ❹: Wallets

Bob and Alice are Bitcoin network users, and they both need a computer program to interact with the network. Such a program is called a *Bitcoin wallet*. Several types of Bitcoin wallets are available for different devices, such as mobile phones and desktop computers, and there are even specialized hardware wallet devices.

Before step ❹ of the payment process, the nodes in the network update their local copy of the blockchain. Now, the network needs to notify Alice and Bob that the transaction went through, as figure 1.7 shows.

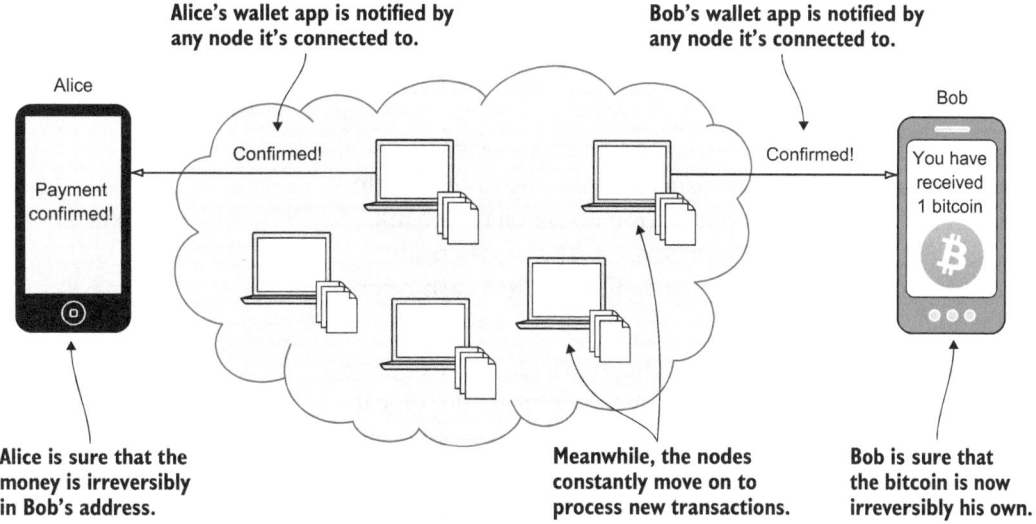

Figure 1.7   Bob's wallet has asked a node to notify the wallet upon activity at Bob's Bitcoin address. Alice pays to Bob's address, and the node has just written the transaction to the blockchain, so it notifies Bob's wallet.

Bob's wallet is connected to some of the nodes in the Bitcoin network. When a transaction concerning Bob is added to the blockchain, the nodes that Bob's wallet is connected to will notify Bob's wallet. The wallet will then display a message to Bob that he received 1 bitcoin. Alice also uses a wallet. Her wallet will be notified of her own transaction.

Besides sending and receiving transactions, Bob's and Alice's wallets also manage their private keys for them. As described earlier, a private key is used to create digital signatures, as well as to generate a Bitcoin address. Alice created her digital signature with one of her private keys. When Bob later wants to spend the money he received at his Bitcoin address, which he generated from his private key, he needs to create a transaction and digitally sign it with that private key.

Wallet duties

A typical Bitcoin wallet will

- Manage keys
- Watch incoming/ outgoing bitcoins
- Send bitcoins

Problems with money today

Bitcoin wouldn't be this widespread if it didn't solve real problems for real people. Bitcoin solves several problems inherent to the traditional financial system. Let's look at some commonly discussed problem areas.

Segregation

People with bank accounts and access to banking services such as online payments or loans are privileged. According to the World Bank, about 38% of the world's population doesn't have a bank account (see web resource 6 in appendix C). The numbers are slowly improving, but many people are still stuck in a cash-only environment.

Without a bank account and basic banking services, such as online payments, people can't expand their businesses outside their local communities. A merchant won't be able to offer goods or services on the internet to increase its customer base. A person living in a rural area might have to travel half a day to pay a utility bill or top up their prepaid mobile phone.

This segregation between banked people and unbanked people is driven by several factors:

Problems

☐ Segregation

- Banking services are too expensive for some people.

- To use banking services, you need documentation, such as an ID card, that many people don't have.

- Banking services can be denied to people with certain political views or those conducting certain businesses. People might also be denied service due to their ethnicity, nationality, sexual preferences, or skin color.

Privacy issues

When it comes to electronic payments such as credit cards or bank transfers, traditional money poses several privacy problems. States can easily

- Trace payments
- Censor payments

- Freeze funds
- Seize funds

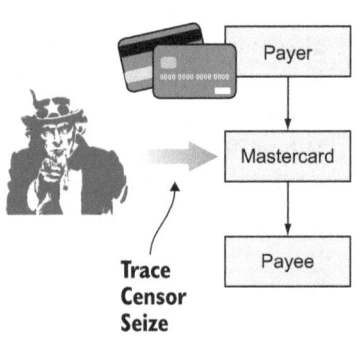

You might say, "I have nothing to hide, and the government needs these tools to fight crime." The problem is, you don't know what your government will look like in five years and how that government defines crime. New laws are just an election away. After the next election, your government could pass a law that allows it to freeze the funds of people with your political view. In some parts of the world, this is already happening.

We've seen lots of examples in which these powers are abused to disable someone's ability to transact. For example, the nonprofit organization WikiLeaks was put under a blockade in 2010 in which all donations through traditional channels were blocked after pressure from the US government on the major payment networks, such as Visa and Mastercard (see web resource 7). We've also seen how Cyprus seized 47.5% of all bank deposits exceeding 100,000 € as part of a financial rescue program in 2013 (web resource 8).

> **Problems**
> ☐ Segregation
> ☐ Privacy issues

Note that bank notes and coins usually aren't affected. As long as there is cash, people can trade freely and privately. In some parts of the world—for example, Sweden—cash is being phased out, which means soon you won't be able to buy chewing gum without someone recording your transaction.

Inflation

Inflation means the purchasing power of a currency decreases (figure 1.8).

Today   Tomorrow

Figure 1.8   Inflation

Most currencies are subject to inflation, some more than others. For example, the Zimbabwean dollar inflated nearly 10^{23}% from 2007–2008, peaking at 80 billion percent per month during a few months in 2008. That's an average daily inflation rate of nearly 100%. Prices roughly doubled every day.

> **Problems**
> ☐ Segregation
> ☐ Privacy issues
> ☐ Inflation

Extreme cases of inflation like this are called *hyperinflation*, and are usually driven by a rapid increase in the money supply. Governments sometimes increase the money supply as a tool to extract value from the population and pay for expenses such as the national debt, warfare, or welfare. If this tool is overused, the risk of hyperinflation is apparent.

A rapid increase in the money supply will most likely lead to a depreciation of a country's currency. This, in turn, pushes people to exchange their local currency for goods or alternative currencies that better hold value, which further drives down the value of the local currency. This can spiral to extremes, as in Zimbabwe. The result is devastating for people as they see their life savings diminish to virtually nothing. Table 1.1 shows examples of recent hyperinflations.

Table 1.1   Some modern hyperinflations. Source: Wikipedia

Country	Year	Worst monthly inflation (%)
Zimbabwe	2007–2008	4.19×10^{16}
Yugoslavia	1992–1994	313×10^{6}
Peru	1990	397
Ukraine	1992–1994	285
Venezuela	2012–	120

Zimbabwe is one of the most extreme cases of inflation throughout history, but even today, some countries suffer from very high inflation. One is Venezuela, where its currency, the bolívar, experienced an 254% inflation rate during 2016 and suffered from about a 1,088% inflation rate in 2017. A staggering 1,370,000% inflation rate is forecast for 2018.

Borders

Moving value across national borders using national, or *fiat*, currency is hard, expensive, and sometimes even forbidden. If you want to send 1,000 Swedish crowns (SEK) from Sweden to a person in the Philippines, you can use a service like Western Union for the transfer. At the time I investigated this, 1,000 SEK was worth 5,374 Philippine pesos (PHP) or 109 US dollars. See table 1.2.

Table 1.2   Cost of sending 5,374 PHP from Sweden to the Philippines

Send from	Receive to	Received by recipient	Fees	Fees %
Bank	Bank	5,109 PHP	265 PHP	4.9%
Bank	Cash	4,810 PHP	564 PHP	10.5%
Credit card	Cash	4,498 PHP	876 PHP	16.3%

If the recipient has a bank account that can receive an international money transfer, you can get away with a 4.9% fee. But a typical remittance recipient will be able to receive only cash, which doubles or triples the cost to 10.5% or 16.3%, depending on how quickly or conveniently they want it.

In contrast with international transfers, moving fiat currency within a nation state's borders is usually convenient. For example, you can hand over cash directly to the recipient or transfer money using some mobile app made specifically for the currency. As long as you stay within one country and one currency, fiat currencies usually do a good job.

Problems
☐ Segregation
☐ Privacy issues
☐ Inflation
☐ Borders

The Bitcoin approach

Bitcoin offers a fundamentally different model than traditional financial institutions. Let's explore the major differences one by one.

Decentralized

Instead of a central organization such as the US Federal Reserve controlling the currency, control of Bitcoin is distributed among thousands of computers, or nodes. No single node or group of nodes has more privileges or obligations than any other. This equality between nodes makes Bitcoin *decentralized*, as opposed to *centralized* systems, such as banks or the Google search engine (figure 1.9).

In a centralized system, the service is controlled by a single entity, such as a bank. This single entity can decide who gets to use the service and what the user is allowed to do. For example, an online video service can choose to provide a video only to people in a certain geographical location.

Centralized   Decentralized

Figure 1.9   Centralized and decentralized services

With a decentralized system such as Bitcoin, which has several thousands of nodes spread around the globe, it's extremely hard to control who uses the system and how. No matter where or who they are, or to whom they're sending money, the Bitcoin system will treat all users equally. The Bitcoin system has no central point that can be exploited to censor payments, deny users service, or seize funds.

Problems fixed

☑ Segregation
☑ Privacy issues
☐ Inflation
☐ Borders

As mentioned, Bitcoin is permissionless, which means you don't need to ask anyone for permission to participate. Anyone with a computer and an internet connection can set up a Bitcoin node and take an active role in the Bitcoin network—no questions asked, no registration required.

Changing the rules of Bitcoin is nearly impossible without broad consensus. If a node doesn't obey the rules, the rest of the nodes will ignore it. For example, one rule is that Bitcoin's money supply is limited to 21 million bitcoins. This limit is nearly impossible to change because of decentralization; there's no one you can threaten or bribe to change these rules.

Limited supply

Because Bitcoin's money supply won't exceed 21 million bitcoins, people can be sure that if they own 1 bitcoin, they will *always* own at least one 21-millionth of the total supply of bitcoins. This feature isn't found in any fiat currency, where decisions on supply are made every so often by a company or state. Bitcoin is resistant to high inflation because you can't increase the money supply at will.

Problems fixed

☑ Segregation
☑ Privacy issues
☑ Inflation
☐ Borders

Bitcoin's money supply isn't fixed today. It's increasing, at a diminishing rate, according to a *predetermined* schedule and will eventually stop increasing around the year 2140. See figure 1.10.

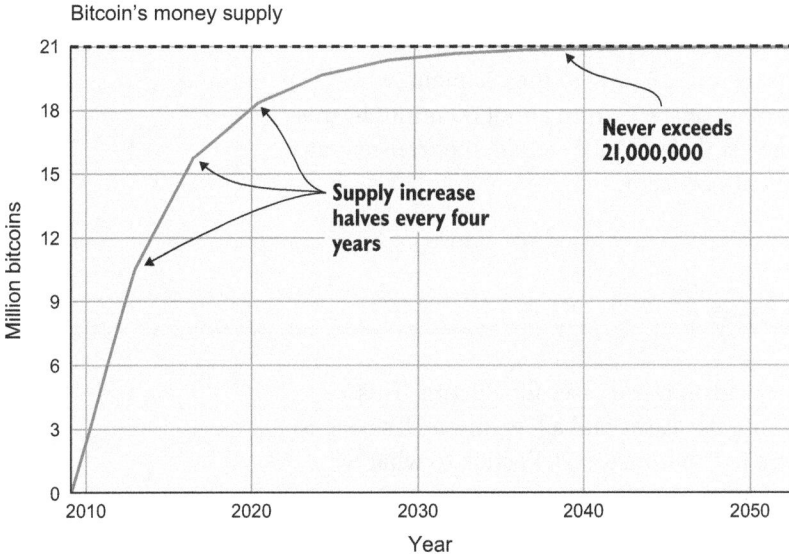

Figure 1.10   The supply of bitcoins approaches 21 million over time. The increase is barely visible during the last 100 years before 2140.

As of this writing, the money supply is about 17 million bitcoins, and the current yearly increase is at roughly 4%. This increase is halved every four years.

Borderless

Because Bitcoin is a system run by ordinary computers connected to the internet, it's as global as the internet. This means anyone with an internet connection can send money to other people across the world, as figure 1.11 illustrates.

Problems fixed

☑ Segregation
☑ Privacy issues
☑ Inflation
☑ Borders

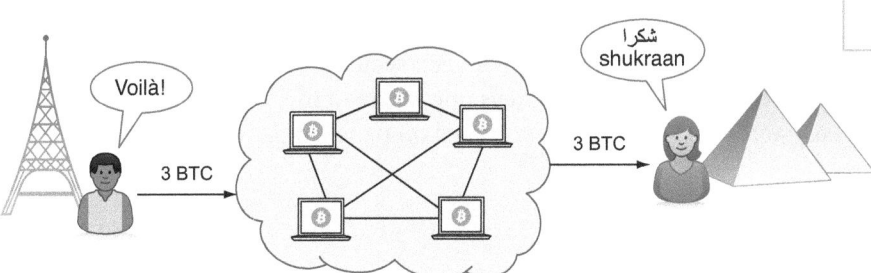

Figure 1.11   Bitcoin is borderless.

There is no difference between sending a bitcoin to someone in the same room or sending it to someone on another continent. The experience is the same: money is sent directly to the recipient, who sees the payment nearly instantaneously. Within about 60 minutes, this recipient can be *sure* the money is theirs. Once settled, the transfer can't be reversed without the recipient's consent.

How is Bitcoin used?

So far, we've touched on a few common use cases for Bitcoin. This section will dig deeper into those use cases and a few others. It's hard to predict what use cases we'll see in the future, so let's stick to what we know now.

Savings

One interesting Bitcoin feature is that you keep your money safe by storing a set of private keys: the secret pieces of information you'll need when you want to spend your money. You choose how those private keys are stored. You can write them on paper, or you can store them electronically with a mobile app to have easy access to them. You can also memorize your private keys. These keys are all anyone needs to spend your money. Keep them safe.

Savings is an attractive use case for Bitcoin. A simple way to save is to create a private key and write it down on a piece of paper that you store in a safe. This piece of paper is now your savings account, your savings wallet. You can then send bitcoins to your wallet. As long as your private key is kept safe, your money is safe. You can choose from a lot of different saving schemes to find the right balance between security and convenience. For example, you can keep your keys unencrypted in your mobile phone for easy access or store them encrypted on paper in a vault with armed guards.

Cross-border payments

As noted, moving money from one country to another is expensive (say, 15%), especially if you move money to a poor country, and the recipient doesn't have a bank account. It's becoming increasingly popular to use Bitcoin to circumvent this expensive and slow legacy system. It's usually cheaper to exchange Swedish crowns for bitcoins in Sweden and transfer the bitcoins to your friend in the Philippines. Your friend will then exchange the bitcoins locally for Philippine pesos.

Some companies offer services so that you pay Swedish crowns to the company and the company pays out Philippine pesos to your friend (figure 1.12). You won't even know that Bitcoin is used under the hood. Such companies typically charge a few percent for the service, but it will still be cheaper than traditional remittance services.

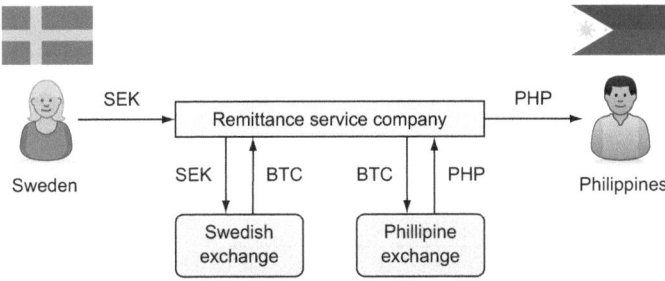

Figure 1.12   A remittance company uses Bitcoin to transfer money from Sweden to the Philippines.

Of course, if recipients can make good use of Bitcoin where they live, there's no need for a middleman that takes a cut of the money. You can send bitcoins directly to your friend. This is what Bitcoin is all about. Exchanges and other such service companies are just bridges between the old legacy world and the new Bitcoin world.

Shopping

The most obvious use case for Bitcoin is shopping. Bitcoin's borderlessness and security make it ideal for online payments for goods and services.

In traditional online payments, you send your debit card details to the merchant and *hope* the merchant will withdraw as much as you agreed on. You also *hope* the merchant handles your debit card details with great care. They probably store the details in a database. Think about that: for every debit card purchase you make, your card details will be stored in that merchant's database. It's likely that *one* of the databases will be hacked and your card details stolen. The more merchants store your details, the higher the risk.

With Bitcoin, you don't have that problem because you don't send any sensitive information to the merchant, or anyone else. You transfer the amount of money you agreed on and nothing more.

Speculation

The world is full of people wanting to get rich quick. Bitcoin can be alluring to them because of its price *volatility*, or tendency to change. Looking at the history of bitcoin's price, as shown in figure 1.13, it's tempting to try to buy when it's low and sell when it's high.

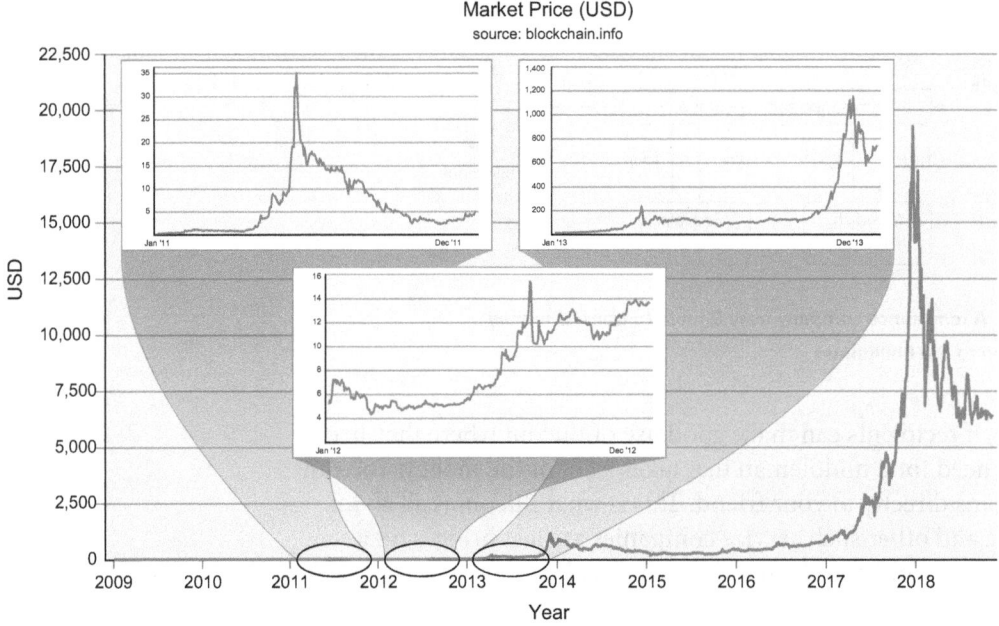

Figure 1.13   Price in USD since the beginning of Bitcoin

In November 2013, the price climbed from about $100 USD to more than $1100 in a few weeks. This was clearly a so-called *bubble*, in which people were afraid of missing out on a great rise, so they bought in, driving the price further up, until it eventually started dropping again. The drop to 50% of its peak value was just as quick as its rise. The same pattern repeated in late 2017 but at a greater magnitude. This has happened many times already. Fluctuations like this are rarely driven by any specific news or technological advancement, but usually arise from speculation. Speculation can be fun, if you can afford to lose, but it's more like a lottery than something to make a living from.

Sometimes a government or big corporation makes a negative statement about Bitcoin that creates fear in the market, but those events tend to have a limited effect on bitcoin's value.

Bitcoin's price volatility seems contradictory to the claims of it having a non-inflationary property; a 50% drop in market value appears pretty inflationary. Bitcoin is still relatively new, and lots of short-term speculation causes this volatility. But as Bitcoin grows and more people and institutions start using it to store their wealth, it will probably stabilize in the long run, and its deflationary property will emerge over time.

Noncurrency uses

Bitcoin is digital cash, but this form of cash can be used for things beyond money. This section covers two common uses, but there are others, including those not yet invented.

Ownership

Bitcoin lets you embed small pieces of data with payments. This data can be, for example, a chassis number of a car. When the car leaves the factory, the manufacturer can make a small Bitcoin payment to the new car owner, containing the chassis number. This payment will then represent the transfer of ownership for that car.

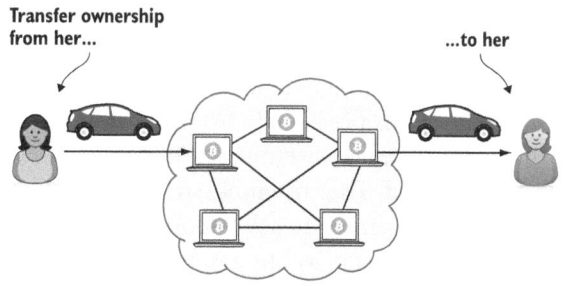

Transfer ownership from her...   ...to her

Bitcoin payments are public records, but they aren't tied to people in any way. They're tied to long strings of numbers called *public keys*, explained in detail in chapter 2. The car manufacturer has made its public key available on its website, in newspapers, and in advertisements to tie the key to the manufacturer's identity. Anyone can then verify that the manufacturer has transferred ownership of the car to the new owner. The new owner can show that she owns the car by proving that she owns the private key belonging to the public key to which the manufacturer has transferred ownership.

The new owner can sell the car to someone else and transfer ownership by sending the same bitcoins she got from the manufacturer to the new owner's public key. The general public can follow the car's ownership from the manufacturer through every owner's public key up to the current owner.

Proof of existence

Using the same technique to store data in a Bitcoin payment to transfer ownership of a car, you can prove that a document existed prior to a certain point in time.

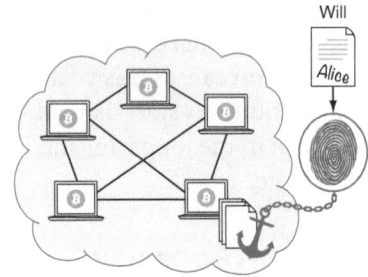

A digital document has a *fingerprint*: a cryptographic hash that anyone can calculate from that document. Creating a different document with the same fingerprint is practically impossible. This fingerprint can be attached to a Bitcoin payment. Where the money goes is irrelevant; the important thing is that the fingerprint is recorded in the Bitcoin blockchain. You "anchor" the document in the blockchain.

Bitcoin payments are public records, so anyone can verify that the document existed before the time of the payment by taking the document's fingerprint and comparing it to the fingerprint stored in the blockchain.

How is Bitcoin valued?

As you read in the section "Speculation," a bitcoin's price can fluctuate dramatically. But where does this price come from? Several Bitcoin exchanges exist, most of them internet-based. They resemble stock markets, where users wanting to sell bitcoins are matched with users wanting to buy bitcoins.

Different markets can have different market prices depending on the supply and demand in that market. For example, in countries such as Venezuela, where the government tries to hinder the Bitcoin market, the supply is low. But the demand is high because people want to escape their hyperinflating currency. These factors drive the Bitcoin price up in that market compared to, for example, the US and European markets, where people can trade more freely.

When not to use Bitcoin

Bitcoin is nice and all, but it's not suitable for all financial activity. At least, not yet.

Tiny payments

A Bitcoin transaction should usually include a processing fee. This fee isn't related to the amount sent but to how big the transaction is in bytes. This is because the Bitcoin network's cost for processing a transaction depends mostly on how big (in bytes) the transaction is. High-value transactions aren't bigger (in bytes) than low-value transactions, so the fee is about the same for both kinds of transactions. The fee required for a transaction also depends on supply and demand for available space in the blockchain. The blockchain can't handle more than roughly 12 MB of transactions per hour, which means miners sometimes have to prioritize transactions. Paying a higher fee will probably give your transaction a higher priority.

If the fee is a significant share of the actual payment you want to make, it isn't economically viable to pay with ordinary Bitcoin transactions (see table 1.3).

Table 1.3   Feasibility of different fee levels

Amount to transfer	Fee	Fee %	Feasible
2 BTC	0.003 BTC	0.15%	Yes
0.002 BTC	0.001 BTC	50%	Probably not
0.001 BTC	0.005 BTC	500%	No

But promising emerging technologies are being built on top of Bitcoin. One example is the Lightning Network, which allows for cheap, instantaneous micropayments of tiny fractions of a bitcoin. Using the Lightning Network, you could potentially pay just 100 satoshis (where 1 satoshi = 0.00000001 BTC) at a fee of as little as 1 satoshi.

Instant payments

Bitcoin payments take time to confirm. The recipient sees the payment immediately but shouldn't trust the payment until the Bitcoin network confirms it, which typically happens within 20 minutes. Trusting an unconfirmed transaction can be risky; the sender can *double spend* the bitcoins by sending the same bitcoins in another transaction to another Bitcoin address—for example, the sender's.

The confirmation time can add friction in brick-and-mortar shops because customers don't want to wait 20 minutes before getting their coffee. This might not be a big issue in some online shops, where the shop can wait 20 minutes before sending the goods to the customer; but some online services, such as pay-per-view, could find the confirmation time problematic.

This limitation can also be fixed by systems built on top of Bitcoin—for example, the Lightning Network—especially when the payment amount is small.

Savings you can't afford to lose

Bitcoin is probably the most secure money there is, but it's still in its infancy. Things *could* go bad with Bitcoin, as in the following scenarios:

> **Bitcoin security**
>
> You are in charge of the security of your bitcoins. Only you. Be careful!

- You lose your private keys: the secrets you must have to spend your money.

- Your private keys are stolen by some bad guy.

- The government in your location tries to crack down on Bitcoin users by imprisonment or other means of force.

- The price of Bitcoin swings down dramatically due to rumors or speculation.

- Software bugs make Bitcoin insecure.

- Weaknesses arise in the cryptography Bitcoin uses.

Although all these risks are *possible*, most of them are unlikely. This list is somewhat ordered with the most likely at the top. Always weigh the risks before putting money on the line, and select your security measures accordingly. This book will help you understand the risks and how to secure your money.

Other cryptocurrencies

This book will cover Bitcoin, but several other so-called *crypto-currencies* exist, and new ones pop up all the time. Cryptocurrencies other than Bitcoin are often referred to as *alt-coins*, meaning *alternative coins.* I'll list a few alt-coins along with their purpose and market capitalization, or *market cap* (table 1.4). The market cap is the product of the money supply (number of coins) and the current market price per coin. Note that the market cap will most likely have changed a lot by the time you read this. I include this information only to give you a glimpse of Bitcoin's position relative to other cryptocurrencies.

Table 1.4   Market capitalization of a few cryptocurrencies as of 11 November 2018

Currency	Purpose	Market cap (billions of dollars)
bitcoin	Global money; included for reference	111
ethereum	Running software on a decentralized abstract computer	22.4
MONERO	Privacy	1.7
CASH	Privacy	0.8
namecoin	Naming system; complements the domain name system (DNS)	0.008

I encourage you to look up these cryptocurrencies, because they all provide interesting new features beyond Bitcoin. Hundreds of other alt-coins exist. Some, such as those in the table, provide unique features that aren't available in Bitcoin, and others provide little to nothing innovative. Some alt-coins may even be outright scams. Stay vigilant.

Anyone can create an alt-coin by taking existing cryptocurrency software and modifying it to their needs.

Let's say Sheila wants to start an alt-coin, Wowcoin. She takes the Bitcoin software and changes the maximum money supply to 11,000,000, instead of Bitcoin's 21,000,000 coins. When she starts Wowcoin, Sheila will be lonely because no one else is using her alt-coin. If she wants Wowcoin to have some real value, she must convince other people to begin using it. If she's not providing anything innovative, she's going to have a hard time getting other people on board, because they're pretty happy with what Bitcoin already provides. Everybody else is using Bitcoin, so why would you use Wowcoin? Think of it as starting a new internet that you call Wownet. People on Wownet won't be able to use services on the internet. Conversely, people on the internet won't be able to use your service if you're on Wownet. So why would anyone use Wownet? We call this the *network effect* (see figure 1.14)—people tend to go where other people are.

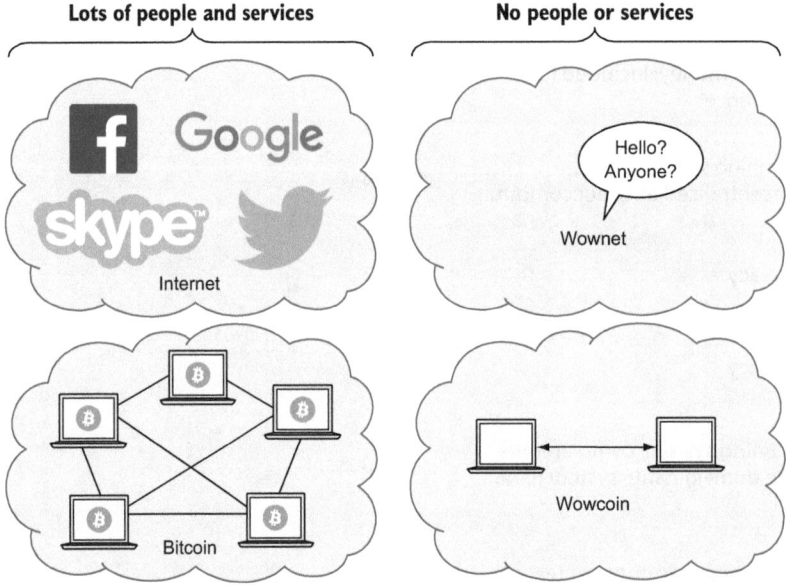

Figure 1.14   Network effect

Although some interesting alt-coins are out there, it's hard to tell which of these will survive long-term. Also, picking one or a few alt-coins to cover in this book would be an arbitrary choice. Consequently, I focus solely on Bitcoin.

Summary

- Bitcoin is global, borderless money that anyone with an internet connection can use.

- Many different actors use Bitcoin, including savers, merchants, and traders for various purposes, such as payments, remittances, and savings.

- A network of computers, the Bitcoin network, verifies and keeps records of all payments.

- A transaction goes through the following steps: send transaction, verify transaction, add transaction to the blockchain, and notify the recipient and sender wallets.

- Bitcoin solves problems with inflation, borders, segregation, and privacy by providing limited supply, decentralization, and borderlessness.

- Several alternative cryptocurrencies exist apart from Bitcoin, such as Ethereum, Zcash, and Namecoin.

- A (crypto)currency becomes more useful as more users use it. This is called the network effect.

cryptographic hash functions and digital signatures | 2

This chapter covers

- Creating a simple money system: cookie tokens

- Understanding cryptographic hash functions

- Authenticating payments using digital signatures

- Keeping your secrets secret

I'll start this chapter by setting the stage for the rest of this book. We'll look at a simple payment system that we can improve on using Bitcoin technologies. By the time we get to chapter 8, this simple system will have evolved into what we call Bitcoin.

The second part of this chapter will teach you what you need to know about cryptographic hash functions. These are so important to Bitcoin that you really need to understand them before learning anything else. You'll see how a cryptographic hash function can be used to verify that a file hasn't changed since a previous point in time.

The rest of the chapter will solve the problem of the *imposter*: a bad guy claiming to be someone else to pay money from that someone's account. We solve this problem by introducing digital signatures (figure 2.1) into the simple system.

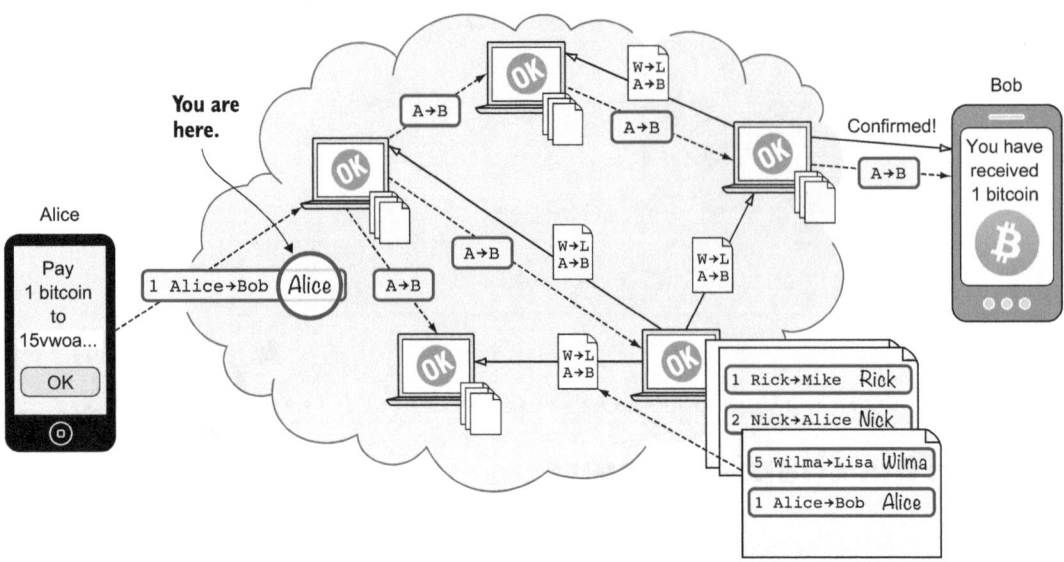

Figure 2.1   Digital signatures in Bitcoin

The cookie token spreadsheet

Suppose there's a cafe in the office where you work. You and your coworkers use a spreadsheet to keep track of *cookie tokens* (figure 2.2), which use the symbol CT. You can exchange cookie tokens for cookies in the cafe.

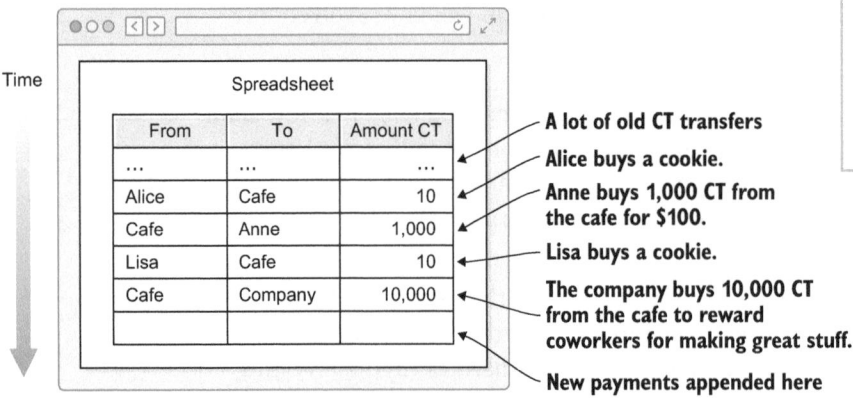

Figure 2.2   The cookie token spreadsheet has a column for the sender, a column for the recipient, and a column for the number of cookie tokens transferred. New cookie token transfers are appended at the end of the spreadsheet.

> **Bitcoin, the currency**
>
> A cookie token corresponds to a bitcoin, the currency unit of Bitcoin. Bitcoin got its first price point in 2010, when someone bought two pizzas for 10,000 BTC. That money would get you 6,000,000 pizzas as of November 2018.

Lisa stores this spreadsheet on her computer. It's shared read-only for everybody on the office network to open and watch, except Lisa. Lisa is very trustworthy. Everybody trusts her. She has full access to do whatever she likes with the spreadsheet. You and all the others can only view the spreadsheet by opening it in read-only mode.

Whenever Alice wants a cookie, she asks Lisa, who sits right next to the cafe, to transfer 10 CT from Alice to the cafe. Lisa knows who Alice is and can verify in the spreadsheet that she owns enough cookie tokens; she'll search for "Alice" in the spreadsheet, sum all the amounts with Alice's name in the To column, and subtract all the amounts with Alice's name in the From column. Figure 2.3 shows the complete search result; three transfers involve Alice.

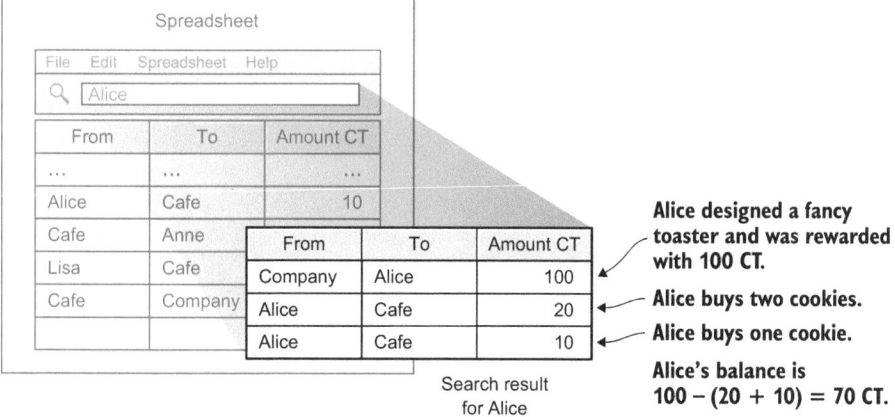

Figure 2.3 Lisa calculates Alice's balance. The sum of her received cookie tokens is 100, and the sum of her withdrawn cookie tokens is 30. Alice's balance is 70 CT.

Lisa calculates that Alice has 70 CT, enough for Alice to pay 10 CT to the cafe. She *appends* a row at the end of the spreadsheet (figure 2.4).

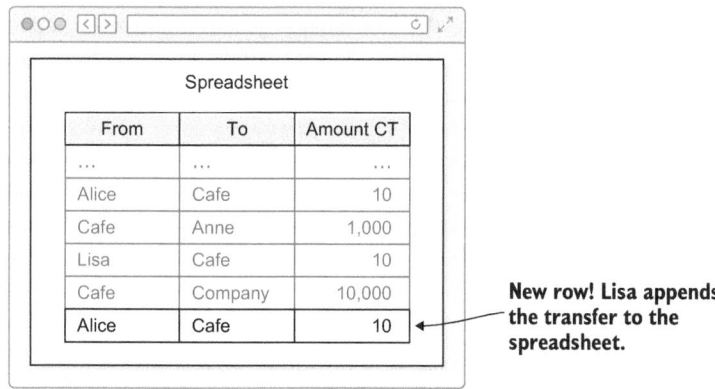

Figure 2.4 Lisa adds Alice's payment for a cookie. The payment is appended last in the cookie token spreadsheet.

The cafe sees this new row in the spreadsheet and hands a cookie over to Alice.

When you run out of cookie tokens, you can buy tokens for dollars from someone who is willing to sell you some—possibly Anne or the cafe—at a price you both agree on. Lisa will then add a row to the spreadsheet accordingly.

Lisa has promised never to remove or change anything in the spreadsheet, just add to it. What happens in the spreadsheet, stays in the spreadsheet!

Lisa, who is performing valuable work to secure this money system, is rewarded with 7,200 newly minted cookie tokens per day (figure 2.5). Every day, she adds a new row to the spreadsheet that creates 7,200 new cookie tokens with Lisa as the recipient.

From	To	Amount CT
...	...	...
Cafe	Company	10,000
Alice	Cafe	10
NEW	Lisa	7,200

Spreadsheet

Lisa is rewarded for her valuable work to secure the spreadsheet.

Figure 2.5   Lisa is rewarded with cookie tokens.

This is how all the cookie tokens in the spreadsheet are created. The first row in the spreadsheet is a reward row—like the one in the spreadsheet just shown—that creates the very first 7,200 CT ever. The plan is that Lisa is rewarded with 7,200 CT per day during the first four years, and then the reward is halved to 3,600 CT/day for the next four years, and so on until the reward is 0 CT/day.

Don't worry, for now, about what happens when the reward approaches 0—that's far in the future. We'll discuss that in chapter 7. This reward halving makes the total money supply—the total number of cookie tokens in circulation—approach 21 million CT, but it will never exceed 21 million.

Money supply curve

Bitcoin uses the same schedule for issuance as the cookie token spreadsheet. All new bitcoins are created as rewards to the nodes securing the Bitcoin ledger—the blockchain—just as Lisa is rewarded for securing the cookie token spreadsheet.

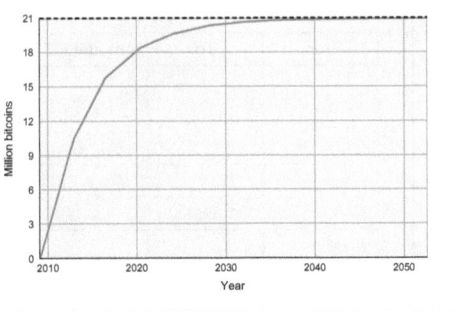

What Lisa does with the new cookie tokens she earns is up to her. She can buy cookies or sell the cookie tokens. She can also save them for later. The spreadsheet system works well, and everybody eats a healthy number of cookies.

Lisa basically performs the same work as miners in the Bitcoin network. She verifies payments and updates the ledger, the cookie token spreadsheet. Table 2.1 clarifies how the concepts in the spreadsheet correspond to concepts in Bitcoin.

Table 2.1 How key ingredients of the cookie token system and the Bitcoin system relate

Cookie tokens	Bitcoin	Covered in
1 cookie token	1 bitcoin	Chapter 2
The spreadsheet	The blockchain	Chapter 6
A row in the spreadsheet	A transaction	Chapter 5
Lisa	A miner	Chapter 7

This table will follow us throughout the book. It describes differences between the cookie token system and Bitcoin. I'll delete rows from it as I introduce various Bitcoin stuff. For example, the row "The spreadsheet" will be deleted in chapter 6, when we use a blockchain to store transactions. I'll also add a few rows as I introduce new concepts for the cookie token system that differ from those in Bitcoin.

At the end of chapter 8, this table will contain only the first row, mapping 1 cookie token to 1 bitcoin. This will mark the end of this cookie token example, and from that point, we'll talk only about Bitcoin itself.

Table 2.2 is your starting point for learning how Bitcoin works, which we can call version 1.0 of the cookie token spreadsheet system.

Table 2.2 Release notes, cookie tokens 1.0

Version	Feature	How
NEW 1.0	Simple payment system	Relies on Lisa being trustworthy and knowing everyone's face
	Finite money supply	7,200 new CT rewarded to Lisa daily; halves every four years

We'll add a lot of fancy stuff to this system and release a new version in every chapter. For example, at the end of this chapter, we'll release version 2.0, which uses digital signatures to solve the problem of imposters. Every chapter will take us closer to the end result: Bitcoin. But please be aware that this isn't at all how Bitcoin evolved in reality— I'm just using this made-up system to help explain each important topic in isolation.

Cryptographic hashes

Cryptographic hashes are used everywhere in Bitcoin. Trying to learn Bitcoin without knowing what cryptographic hashes are is like trying to learn chemistry without knowing what an atom is.

You can think of a cryptographic hash as a fingerprint. A person will produce the same fingerprint of her left thumb every time it's taken, but it's extremely hard to find another person with the same left thumb fingerprint. The fingerprint doesn't disclose any information about the person other than that particular fingerprint. You can't know what math skills or eye color the person has by looking at this fingerprint.

Digital information also has fingerprints. This fingerprint is called a *cryptographic hash*. To create a cryptographic hash of a file, you send the file into a computer program called a *cryptographic hash function*. Suppose you want to create a cryptographic hash—a fingerprint—of your favorite cat picture. Figure 2.6 illustrates this process.

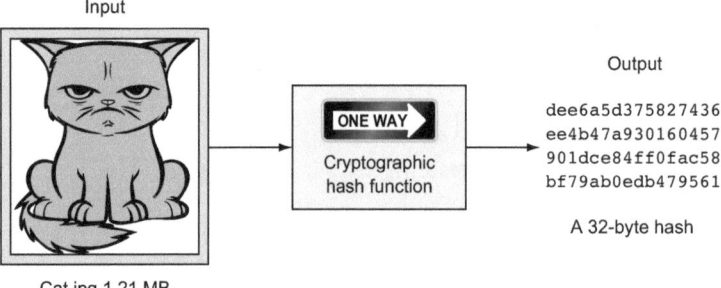

Input

ONE WAY

Cryptographic
hash function

Output

```
dee6a5d375827436
ee4b47a930160457
901dce84ff0fac58
bf79ab0edb479561
```

A 32-byte hash

Cat.jpg 1.21 MB

Figure 2.6   Creating a cryptographic hash of a cat picture. Input is the cat picture, and output is a big, 32-byte number.

The output—the hash—is a 256-bit number; 256 bits equals 32 bytes because 1 byte consists of 8 bits. Thus, to store the number in a file, the file will be 32 bytes big, which is tiny compared to the size of the 1.21 MB cat picture. The particular cryptographic hash function used in this example is called SHA256 (Secure Hash Algorithm with 256-bit output) and is the most commonly used one in Bitcoin.

The word *hash* means something that's chopped into small pieces or mixed up. That's a good description of what a cryptographic hash function does. It takes the cat picture and performs a mathematical calculation on it. Out comes a big number—the cryptographic hash—that doesn't look remotely like a cat. You can't "reconstruct" the cat picture from just the hash—a cryptographic hash function is a *one-way function*. Figure 2.7 shows what happens when you change the cat picture a little and run it through the same cryptographic hash function.

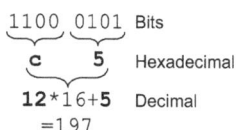

Bits? Bytes? Hex?

A *bit* is the smallest unit of information in a computer. It can take either of two different values: 0 or 1. Like a lightbulb, it can be either on or off. A *byte* is 8 bits that together can take 256 different values. We often use *hexadecimal*, or *hex*, encoding when we display numbers in this book. Each byte is printed as two hex digits each in the range 0–f, where a = 10 and f = 15.

$$\underbrace{1100}_{c}\ \underbrace{0101}_{5}\ \text{Bits}$$

c 5	Hexadecimal
12*16+**5**	Decimal
=197	

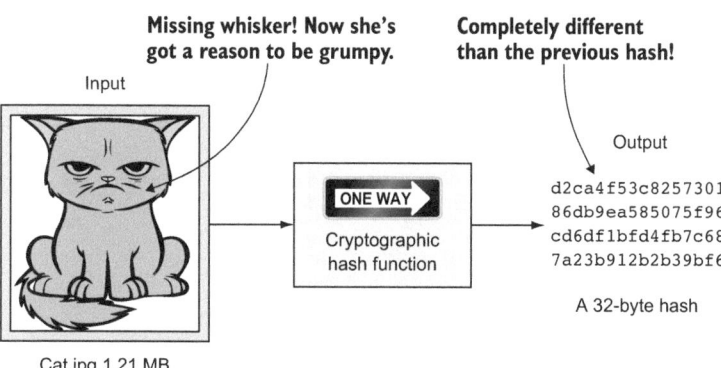

Missing whisker! Now she's got a reason to be grumpy.

Completely different than the previous hash!

Input

ONE WAY
Cryptographic hash function

Output

d2ca4f53c8257301
86db9ea585075f96
cd6df1bfd4fb7c68
7a23b912b2b39bf6

A 32-byte hash

Cat.jpg 1.21 MB

Figure 2.7 Hashing a modified cat picture. Can you spot the difference? The cryptographic hash function certainly did.

This hash turns out completely different than the first hash. Let's compare them:

- Old hash:
  dee6a5d375827436ee4b47a930160457901dce84ff0fac58bf79ab0edb479561

- New hash:
  d2ca4f53c825730186db9ea585075f96cd6df1bfd4fb7c687a23b912b2b39bf6

See how that tiny change to the cat picture made a huge difference in the hash value? The hash value is completely different, but the length of the hash is always the same regardless of input. The input "Hello" will also result in a 256-bit hash value.

Why are cryptographic hash functions useful?

Cryptographic hash functions can be used as an integrity check to detect changes in data. Suppose you want to store your favorite cat picture on your laptop's hard drive, but you suspect the stored picture might become corrupted. This could happen, for example, due to disk errors or hackers. How can you make sure you detect corruption?

First, you calculate a cryptographic hash of the cat picture on your hard drive and write it down on a piece of paper (figure 2.8).

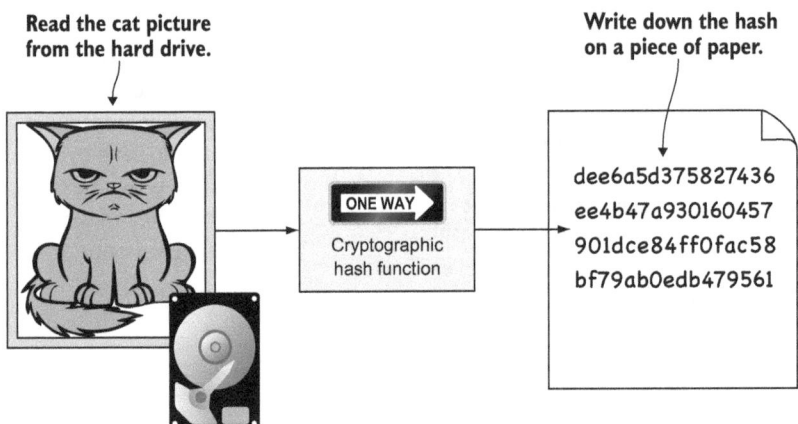

Figure 2.8   Save a hash of the cat picture on a piece of paper.

Later, when you want to look at the picture, you can check if it's changed since you wrote the hash on that paper. Calculate the cryptographic hash of the cat picture again, and compare it to the original hash on your paper (figure 2.9).

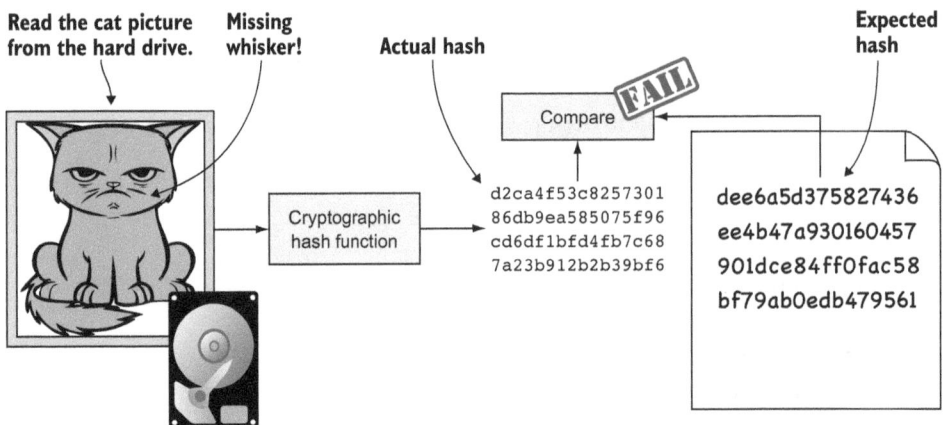

Figure 2.9   Check the integrity of the cat picture. You detect a change.

If the new hash matches the one on paper, you can be sure the picture hasn't changed. On the other hand, if the hashes don't match, the cat picture has definitely changed.

Bitcoin uses cryptographic hash functions a lot to verify that data hasn't changed. For example, every now and then—on average, every 10 minutes—a new hash of the entire payment history is created. If someone tries to change the data, anyone verifying the hash of the modified data will notice.

How does a cryptographic hash function work?

The real answer is complex, so I won't go into exact detail. But to help you understand the operation of a cryptographic hash function, we'll create a very simplistic one. Well, it isn't really cryptographic, as I'll explain later. Let's just call it a hash function for now.

Suppose you want to hash a file containing the six bytes `a1 02 12 6b c6 7d`. You want the hash to be a 1-byte number (8 bits). You can construct a hash function using *addition modulo 256*, which means to wrap around to 0 when the result of an addition reaches 256 (figure 2.10).

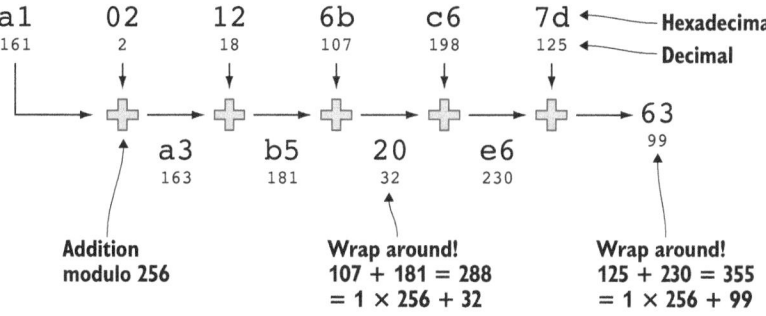

Figure 2.10   Simplistic hash function using byte-wise addition modulo 256

The result is the decimal number 99. What does 99 say about the original input `a1 02 12 6b c6 7d`? Not much—99 looks just as random as any other single-byte number.

If you change the input, the hash will change, although a chance exists that the hash will remain 99. After all, this simple hash function has just 256 different possible outputs. With real cryptographic hash functions, like the one we used to hash the cat picture, this chance is unimaginably small. You'll soon get a glimpse of this probability.

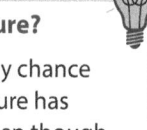

How sure?

There's a tiny chance the cat picture has changed even though the hashes match. But as you'll see later, that chance is so small, you can ignore it.

Modulo

Modulo means to wrap around when a calculation reaches a certain value. For example:

- 0 mod 256 = 0
- 255 mod 256 = 255
- 256 mod 256 = 0
- 257 mod 256 = 1
- 258 mod 256 = 2

258 mod 256 is the remainder of the integer division 258/256: 258 = 1 × 256 + 2. The remainder is 2.

Properties of a cryptographic hash function

A cryptographic hash function takes any digital input data, called a *pre-image*, and produces a fixed-length output, called a *hash*. In the example with the cat picture on your hard drive, the pre-image is the cat picture of 1.21 MB, and the hash is a 256-bit number. The function will output the exact same hash each time the same pre-image is used. But it will, with extremely high probability, output a totally different hash when even the slightest variation of that pre-image is used. The hash is also commonly referred to as a *digest*.

Let's look at what properties you can expect from a cryptographic hash function. I'll illustrate using SHA256 because it's the one Bitcoin uses most. Several cryptographic hash functions are available, but they all provide the same basic properties:

1. **The same input will always produce the same hash.**

2. **Slightly different inputs will produce very different hashes.**

3. **The hash is always of the same fixed size. For SHA256, it's 256 bits.**

4. **Brute-force trial and error is the only known way to find an input that gives a certain hash.**

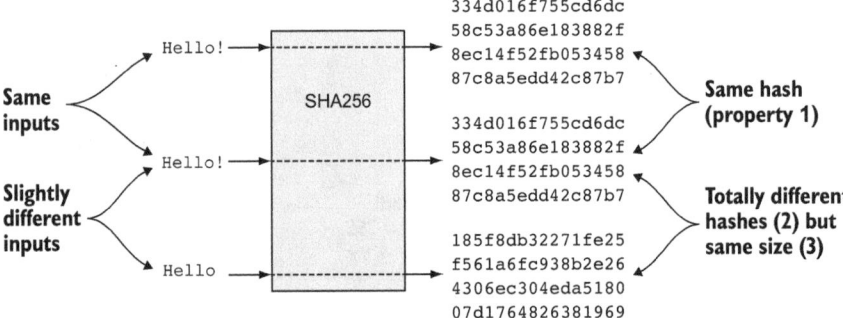

Figure 2.11   A cryptographic hash function, SHA256, in action. The input "Hello!" will give you the same output every time, but the slightly modified input "Hello" will give you totally different output.

Figure 2.11 illustrates the first three properties. The fourth property of a cryptographic hash function is what makes it a *cryptographic* hash function, and this needs a bit more elaboration. There are some variations to the fourth property, all of which are desirable for cryptographic hash functions (figure 2.12):

- *Collision resistance*—You have only the cryptographic hash function at hand. It's hard to find two *different* inputs that *result in the same hash.*

- *Pre-image resistance*—You have the hash function and a hash. It's hard to find *a pre-image of that hash.*

- *Second-pre-image resistance*—You have the hash function and a pre-image (and thus the hash of that pre-image). It's hard to find *another pre-image with the same hash.*

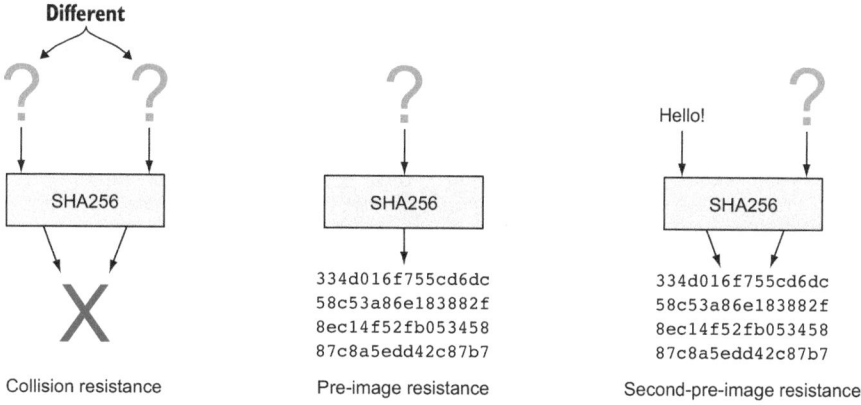

Figure 2.12   **Different desirable properties for cryptographic hash functions. For collision resistance, X can be anything, as long as the two different inputs give the same output X.**

Illustration of "hard"

The term *hard* in this context means astronomically hard. It's silly to even try. We'll look at second-pre-image resistance as an example of what *hard* means, but a similar example can be made for any of the three variants.

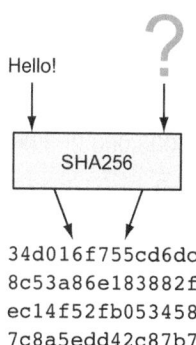

Suppose you want to find an input to SHA256 that results in the same hash as "Hello!":

```
334d016f755cd6dc58c53a86e183882f8ec14f52fb05345887c8a5edd42c87b7
```

You can't change the input "Hello!" just a little so the function "won't notice." It *will* notice and will output a totally different hash. The only way to find an input other than "Hello!" that gives the hash 334d016f...d42c87b7 is to try different inputs one by one and check whether one produces the desired hash.

Let's try, using table 2.3.

Table 2.3   Finding an input with the same hash as "Hello!" is nearly impossible.

Input	Hash	Success?
Hello1!	82642dd9...2e366e64	Nope
Hello2!	493cb8b9...83ba14f8	Nope
Hello3!	90488e86...64530bae	Nope
...	...	Nope, nope, ..., nope
Hello9998!	cf0bc6de...e6b0caa4	Nope
Hello9999!	df82680f...ef9bc235	Nope
Hello10000!	466a7662...ce77859c	Nope
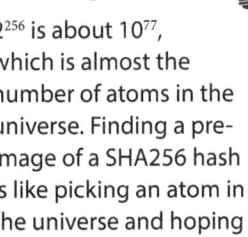	dee6a5d3...db479561	Nope
My entire music collection	a5bcb2d9...9c143f7a	Nope

As you can see, we aren't very successful. Think about how much time it would take for a typical desktop computer to find such an input. It can calculate about 60 million hashes per second, and the expected number of tries needed to find a solution is 2^{255}. The result is $2^{255} / (60 \times 10^6)$ s $\approx$ 10^{68} s $\approx 3 \times 10^{61}$ years, or about 30,000,000,000,000,000,000,000,000, 000,000,000,000,000,000,000,000,000,000,000 years.

I think we can stop trying, don't you? I don't think buying a faster computer will help, either. Even if we had 1 trillion computers and ran them concurrently, it would take about 3×10^{49} years.

Pre-image resistance, second-pre-image resistance, and collision resistance are extremely important in Bitcoin. Most of its security relies on these properties.

How big is 2^{256}?

2^{256} is about 10^{77}, which is almost the number of atoms in the universe. Finding a pre-image of a SHA256 hash is like picking an atom in the universe and hoping it's the correct one.

Some well-known hash functions

Table 2.4 shows several different cryptographic hash functions. Some aren't considered cryptographically secure.

Table 2.4   A few cryptographic hash functions. Some old ones have been deemed insecure.

Name	Bits	Secure so far?	Used in Bitcoin?
SHA256	256	Yes	Yes
SHA512	512	Yes	Yes, in some wallets
RIPEMD160	160	Yes	Yes
SHA-1	160	No. A collision has been found.	No
MD5	128	No. Collisions can be trivially created. The algorithm is also vulnerable to pre-image attacks, but not trivially.	No

Generally, when a single collision has been found in a cryptographic hash function, most cryptographers will consider the function insecure.

Recap of cryptographic hashes

A cryptographic hash function is a computer program that takes any data as input and computes a big number—a cryptographic hash—based on that input.

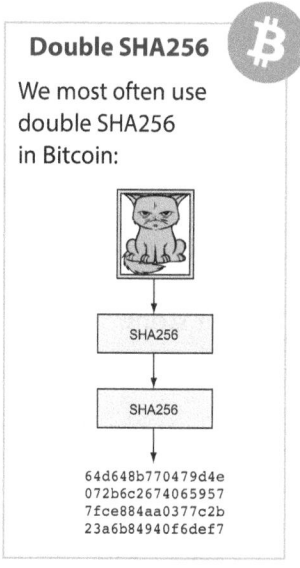

Double SHA256

We most often use double SHA256 in Bitcoin:

SHA256

SHA256

```
64d648b770479d4e
072b6c2674065957
7fce884aa0377c2b
23a6b84940f6def7
```

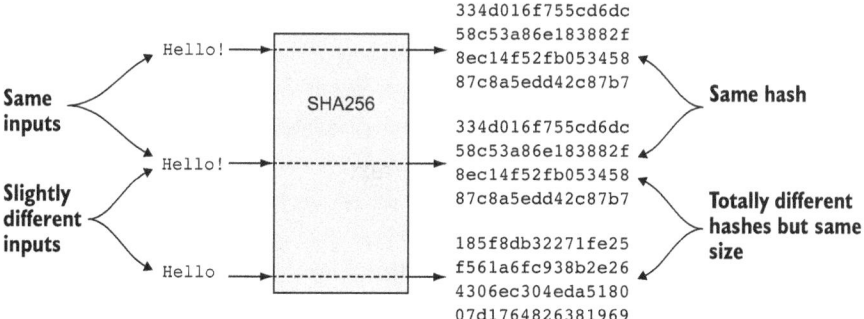

It's astronomically hard to find an input that will result in a specific output. This is why we call it a *one-way function*. You have to repeatedly guess different inputs.

We'll discuss important topics throughout this book. When you've learned about a specific topic, like cryptographic hash functions, you can put a new tool into your toolbox for later use. Your first tool is the cryptographic hash function, which is represented here by a paper shredder; the cryptographic hash is represented by a pile of paper strips.

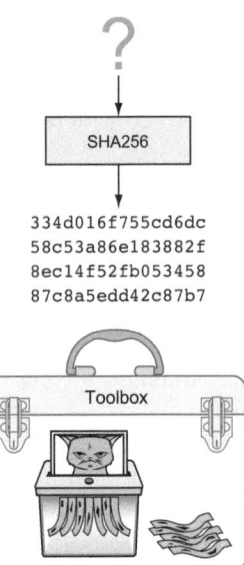

From now on, we'll use these tool icons to represent cryptographic hash functions and cryptographic hashes, with some exceptions.

Exercises

Warm up

2.1   How many bits is the output of SHA256?

2.2   How many bytes is the output of SHA256?

2.3   What's needed to calculate the cryptographic hash of the text "hash me"?

2.4   What are the decimal and the binary representations of the hexadecimal data `061a`?

2.5   Can you, in practice, modify the text "cat" so the modified text gets the same cryptographic hash as "cat"?

Dig in

2.6   The simplistic hash function from the section "How does a cryptographic hash function work?", repeated for you as follows, isn't a *cryptographic* hash function. Which two of the four properties of a cryptographic hash function is it lacking?

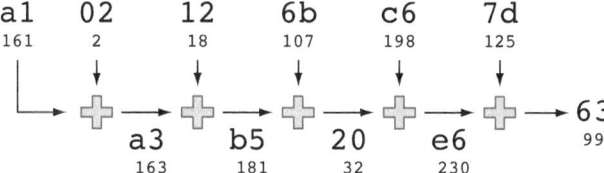

The four properties are also repeated as follows:

1. The same input will always produce the same hash.

2. Slightly different inputs will produce very different hashes.

3. The hash is always of the same fixed size. For SHA256, it's 256 bits.

4. Brute-force trial and error is the only known way to find an input that gives a certain hash.

2.7   Let's go back to the example where you had a cat picture on your hard drive and wrote down the cryptographic hash of the picture on a piece of paper. Suppose someone wanted to change the cat picture on your hard drive without you noticing. What variant of the fourth property is important for stopping the attacker from succeeding?

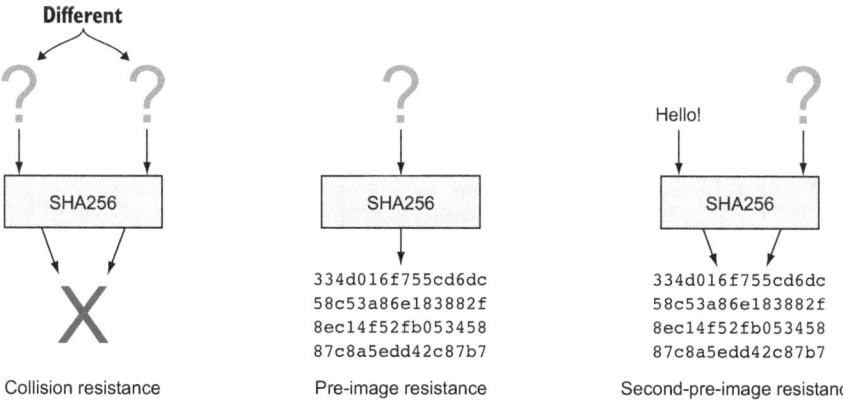

Digital signatures

In this section, we explore how you can prove to someone that you approve a payment. To do that, we use *digital signatures*. A digital signature is a digital equivalent of a handwritten signature. The difference is that a handwritten signature is tied to a person, whereas a digital signature is tied to a random number called a *private key*. A digital signature is much harder to forge than a handwritten signature.

Typical use of digital signatures

Suppose you want to send your favorite cat picture to your friend Fred via email, but you suspect the picture might be, maliciously or accidentally, corrupted during transfer. How would you and Fred make sure the picture Fred receives is exactly the same as the one you send?

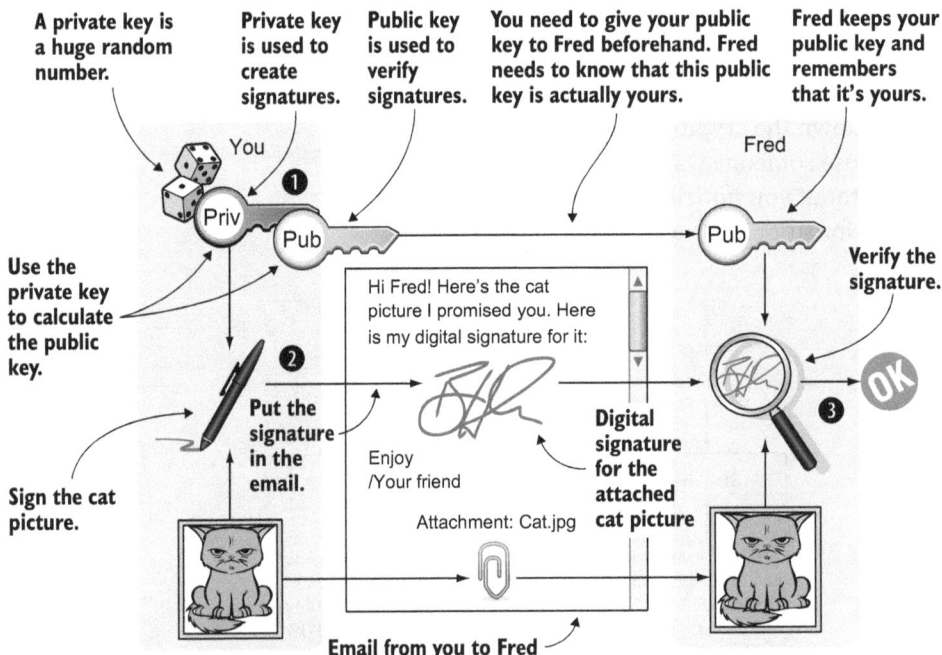

Figure 2.13 You send a digitally signed cat picture to Fred. Fred verifies the signature to make sure he's got the same cat as the cat you signed.

You can include a digital signature of the cat picture in the email. Fred can then verify this digital signature to make sure the cat picture is authentic. You do this in three different phases, as figure 2.13 shows.

Step ❶ is *preparation*. You create a huge random number: the private key. You can use this to create digital signatures. You then create the *public key*, which is used to verify the signatures the private key creates. The public key is *calculated* from the private key. You hand the public key to Fred in person so Fred is sure it belongs to you.

Step ❷ is *signing*. You write an email to Fred and attach the cat picture. You also use your private key and the cat picture to digitally sign the cat picture. The result is a digital signature that you include in your email message. You then send the email to Fred.

Step ❸ is *verifying*. Fred receives your email, but he's concerned the cat picture might be corrupt, so he wants to verify the signature. He uses the public key he got from you in step ❶, the digital signature in the email, and the attached cat picture. If the signature or the cat picture has changed since you created the signature, the verification will fail.

Improving cookie token security

It's time to return to our cookie token spreadsheet. The company is growing, and Lisa has a hard time recognizing everyone. She notices that some people aren't honest. For example, Mallory says she is Anne, to trick Lisa into moving cookie tokens from Anne to the cafe, instead of from Mallory to the cafe. Lisa thinks of requiring everybody to digitally sign their cookie token transfers by writing a message and a digital signature in an email, as figure 2.14 shows.

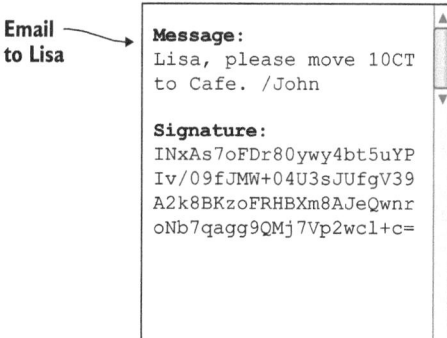

Figure 2.14 John needs to digitally sign his payment request and include the signature in the email.

Suppose John is the new guy at the office. The company gave him some cookie tokens as a welcome gift when he started. Now, John wants to buy a cookie in the cafe for 10 CT. He needs to digitally sign a cookie token transfer. Figure 2.15 shows what he has to do.

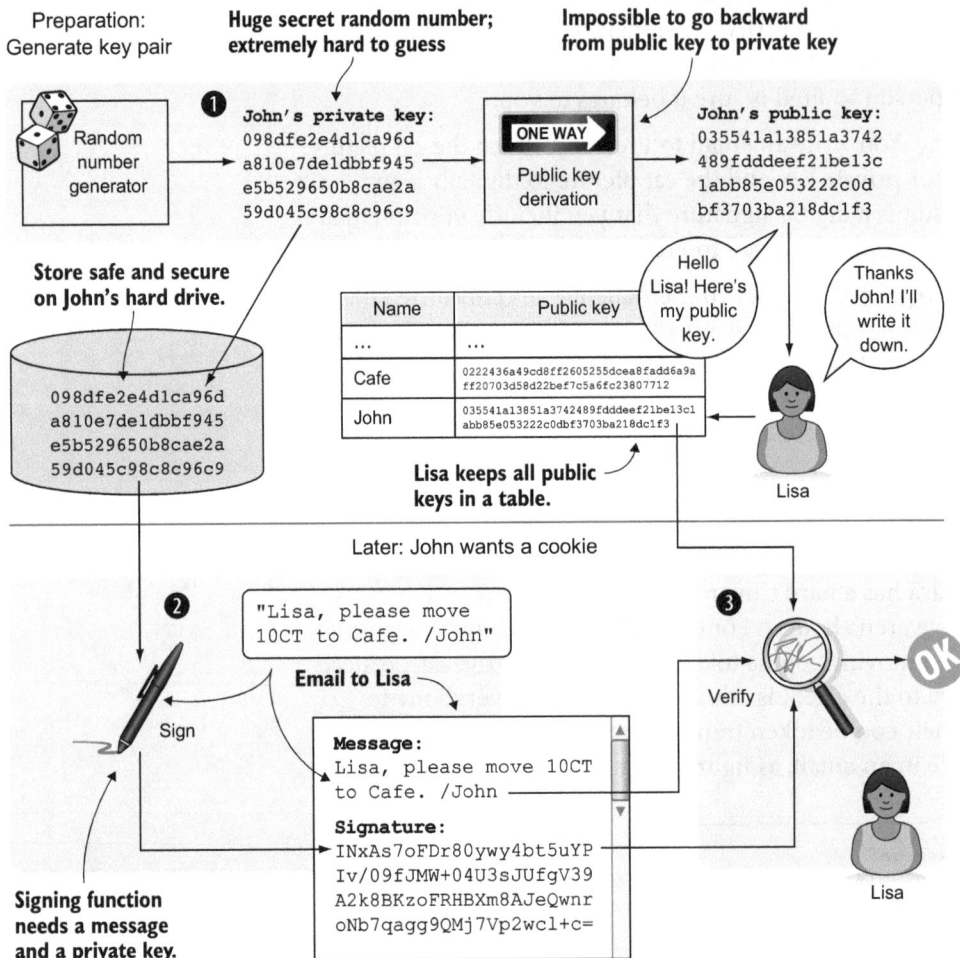

Figure 2.15   The digital signature process. ❶ John creates a key pair and gives the public key to Lisa. ❷ John signs a message with the private key. ❸ Lisa verifies the message is signed with the private key belonging to the public key she got from John.

Just as with the email to Fred in the previous section, there are three phases in this process (please compare with the steps in figure 2.13 to see the similarities):

❶ John prepares by generating a key pair. John keeps the private key secret and hands the public key over to Lisa. This is a one-time setup step.

❷ John wants a cookie. He writes a message and signs it with his private key. He sends the message and the digital signature in an email to Lisa.

❸ Lisa verifies the signature of the message using John's public key and updates the spreadsheet.

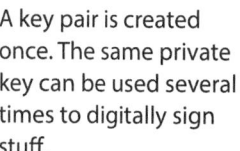

Key pair reuse

A key pair is created once. The same private key can be used several times to digitally sign stuff.

Preparation: John generates a key pair

The signing and verification processes are based on a key pair. John needs a private key to sign payments, and Lisa will need John's public key to verify John's signatures. John needs to prepare for this by creating a key pair. He does this by first generating a private key and then calculating the public key from that private key, as figure 2.16 shows.

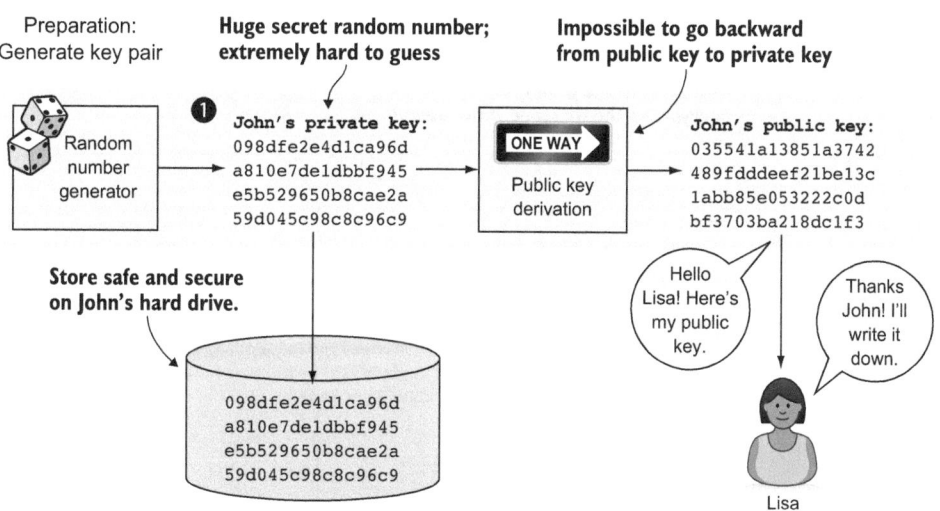

Figure 2.16   John creates a key pair. The private key is a huge random number, and the public key is derived from that random number. John stores his private key on his hard drive, and the public key is handed to Lisa.

John will use a random number generator to generate a huge, 256-bit random number. A random number generator is available on almost all operating systems. The random number is now John's private key. The private key is then transformed into a public key using a public-key derivation function.

Public-key derivation is a one-way function, just like cryptographic hash functions; you can't derive the private key from the public key. The security of digital signatures relies heavily on this feature. Also, running the private key through the public-key derivation function multiple times will always result in the same public key.

The public key is 33 bytes (66 hex digits) long. This is longer than the private key, which is 32 bytes (64 hex digits) long. The reason for the "extra" byte and how the public-key derivation function works is a hard topic, covered in chapter 4. Luckily, you don't have to be a cryptography expert to understand how signatures work from a user's perspective.

Two ways to use the key pair

Keys are used to encrypt and decrypt data. Encryption is used to make messages unreadable to everybody but those who hold the proper decryption key.

We can think of the private and public keys as a pair because they have a strong relationship: the public key can be used to encrypt messages that only the private key can decrypt, and the private key can encrypt messages that only the public key can decrypt (Figure 2.17).

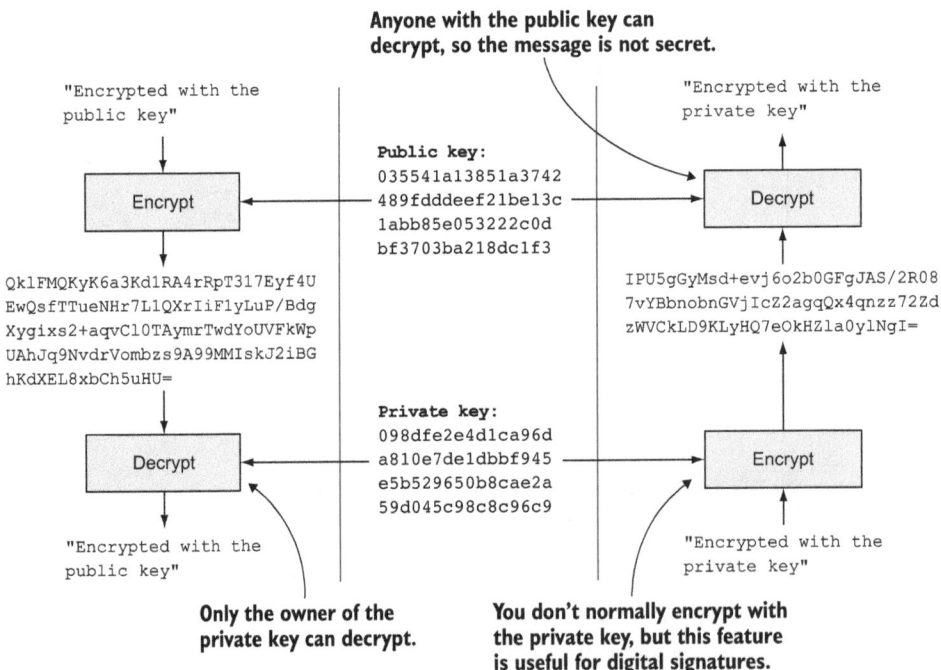

Figure 2.17 Encrypting and decrypting with the public and private keys. Left: Encrypt with the public key, and decrypt with the private key. Right: Encrypt with the private key, and decrypt with the public key.

Following the left side of figure 2.17, only John would be able to read the encrypted message because he's the only one with access to his private key. Bitcoin doesn't use this feature of public and private keys at all. It's used when two parties want to communicate in private, as when you do your online banking. When you see the little padlock in the address bar of your web browser, then you know the process shown on the left side of the figure is being used to secure your communication.

> 💡 We'll use the right side of figure 2.17 to make digital signatures. We won't use the left side at all in this book.

Following the right side of the figure, Lisa can decrypt the message because she has the public key belonging to John's private key. This feature is used for digital signatures. Using the private key to encrypt secret messages isn't a good idea because the public key is, well, public. Anyone with the public key can decrypt the message. Digital signatures, on the other hand, don't need any secret messages. We'll explore digital signatures deeper soon. But first, some recap and orientation.

Recap of key pairs

Let's summarize what you've learned about public and private keys. You create a key pair by first creating a private key. The private key is a huge, secret random number. The public key is then calculated from the private key.

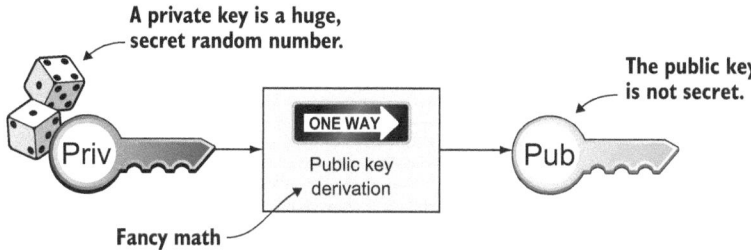

You can use the private key to encrypt a message that can be decrypted only using the public key.

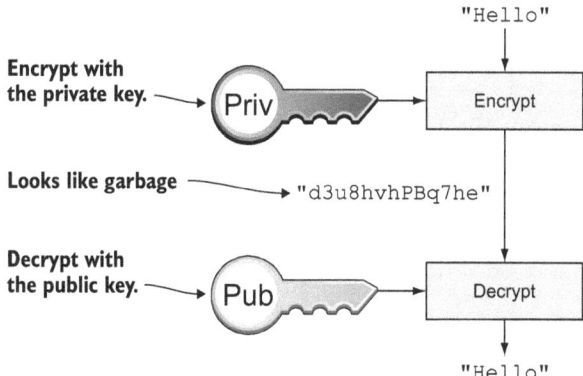

The encryption and decryption in this figure are the foundation for digital signatures. This process is *not* suitable for sending secret messages because the public key is usually widely known.

The reverse process is also common, in which the public key is used to encrypt and the private key is used to decrypt. This process is used to send secret messages. Bitcoin doesn't use it.

Where were we?

Digital signatures were briefly mentioned in chapter 1, where Alice signed her Bitcoin transaction of 1 BTC to Bob using her private key (figure 2.18).

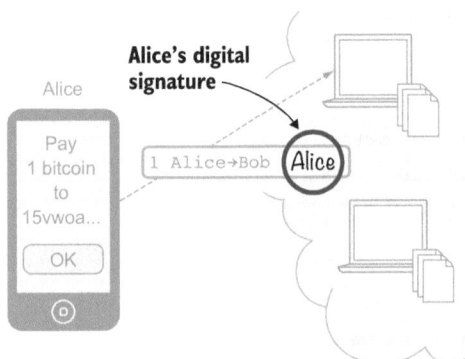

Figure 2.18   Digital signatures in Bitcoin

John has created a pair of keys and is about to digitally sign his payment to the cafe with his private key so Lisa can verify that it's actually John making the payment. Lisa verifies this using John's public key.

John signs his payment

Let's have a close look at how the signing really happens (figure 2.19).

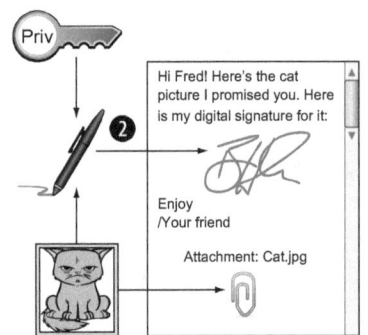

The message John wants to sign is, "Lisa, please move 10CT to Cafe. /John". The signing function will hash this message with SHA256, whose output is a 256-bit number. This hash value is then encrypted with John's private key. The result is a digital signature that looks like this:

```
INxAs7oFDr80ywy4bt5uYPIv/09fJMW+04U3sJUfgV39
A2k8BKzoFRHBXm8AJeQwnroNb7qagg9QMj7Vp2wcl+c=
```

John wants a cookie

```
"Lisa, please move
10CT to Cafe. /John"
```

Email to Lisa

**Keeps the signature
short no matter the
length of the message**

SHA256

Message:
Lisa, please move 10CT
to Cafe. /John

Signature:
INxAs7oFDr80ywy4bt5uYP
Iv/09fJMW+04U3sJUfgV39
A2k8BKzoFRHBXm8AJeQwnr
oNb7qagg9QMj7Vp2wcl+c=

**John reads this from
his hard drive.**

John's private key:
098dfe2e4d1ca96d
a810e7de1dbbf945
e5b529650b8cae2a
59d045c98c8c96c9

Encrypt

**Only John could have
created this signature.
He's the only one with
access to his private key.**

```
INxAs7oFDr80ywy4bt5uYP
Iv/09fJMW+04U3sJUfgV39
A2k8BKzoFRHBXm8AJeQwnr
oNb7qagg9QMj7Vp2wcl+c=
```

**Figure 2.19   John digitally signs the transfer of 10 CT to the cafe. The message to Lisa is
first hashed and then encrypted with John's private key. The email to Lisa contains both
the message in cleartext and the signature.**

**The signature is an encrypted hash of a message. If John had used
another private key to sign with or a slightly different message, the
signature would have looked completely different.**

For example, using the input message "Lisa, please move 10CT to
Mallory. /John" would generate this signature:

```
ILDtL+AVMmOrcrvCRwnsJUJUtzedNkSoLb7OLRoH2iaD
G1f2WX1dAOTYkszR1z0TfTVIVwdAlD0W7B2hBTAzFkk=
```

This isn't remotely similar to the previous signature. This is good for
John, because he knows his signature can't be used for messages other
than his specific message.

John has now composed an email to Lisa. This email contains
a message and a signature of that message. John finishes by sending
the email to Lisa.

**Signatures in
Bitcoin**

Bitcoin uses this type
of signature for most
payments today, but
it isn't the only way to
authenticate a payment.

Lisa verifies the signature

Lisa looks at the email and sees it claims to be from John, so she looks up John in her table of public keys (figure 2.20).

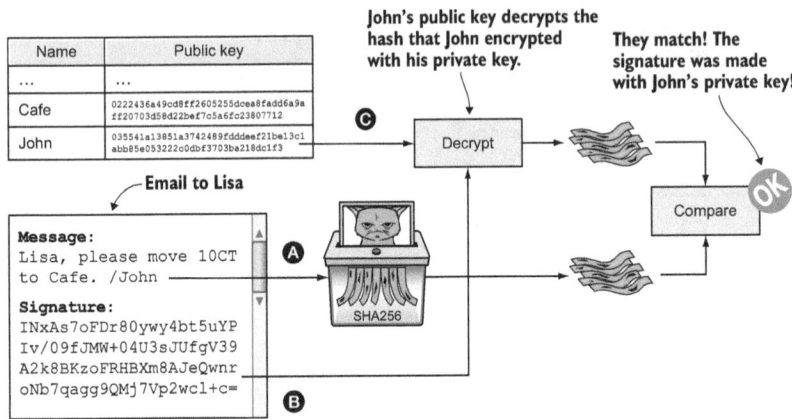

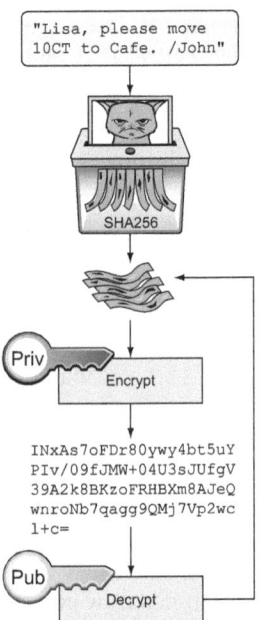

Figure 2.20   Lisa uses the message Ⓐ, the signature Ⓑ, and John's public key Ⓒ to verify that the message is signed with John's private key.

Lisa's actions in this figure aim to determine that the cookie token transfer was signed by the private key it claims to be signed with. The message *says* it's from John. She received John's public key the other day and put that public key in her table of public keys. The things she has at hand are

A signature is an encrypted hash

Ⓐ   The message "Lisa, please move 10CT to Cafe. /John"

Ⓑ   The signature `INxAs7oFDr8…`

Ⓒ   John's public key that she just looked up in her table

John encrypted the message's hash with his *private* key. This encrypted hash is the signature. If Lisa decrypts the signature Ⓑ with John's *public* key Ⓒ, the result should be a hash that equals the hash of the message Ⓐ in the email.

Lisa takes the signature Ⓑ and decrypts it with the public key Ⓒ she looked up in her table of public keys. The decryption outputs a big number. If this number is equal to the hash of the message Ⓐ, it proves John's private key was used to sign the message. Lisa takes the message Ⓐ, exactly as written, and hashes that message just like John did when he created the signature. This message hash is then compared with the decrypted signature. The message hash and the decrypted signature match, which means the signature is valid.

Note that this process works only if John and Lisa use the exact same digital signature scheme. This must be agreed on beforehand, but it's usually standardized. In Bitcoin, everyone knows exactly what digital signature scheme to use.

Lisa can now be sure no one is trying to fool her. She updates the spreadsheet with John's transfer, as shown in figure 2.21.

From	To	Amount CT
...	...	...
Anne	Cafe	30
John	Cafe	10

New row! John has signed a transfer and Lisa verified it. She checks his balance and adds the transfer to the spreadsheet.

Figure 2.21 Lisa has added a row for John's cookie token transfer after verifying the signature of John's message.

Private key security

John is in control of his cookie tokens because he owns the private key. No one but John can use John's cookie tokens because he's the only one with access to his private key. If his private key is stolen, he can lose any and all of his cookie tokens.

The morning after John's transfer, he comes to the office, takes his laptop from his desk, and goes straight to the cafe to buy two morning cookies. He opens his laptop to write an email to Lisa:

Good morning Lisa! Please move 20 CT to Cafe. /John
Signature:
```
H1CdE34cRuJDsHo5VnpvKqllC5JrMJ1jWcUjL2VjPbsj
X6pi/up07q/gWxStb1biGU2fjcKpT4DIxlNd2da9x0o=
```

He sends this email containing the message and a signature to Lisa. But the cafe doesn't hand him any cookies. The guy behind the desk says he hasn't seen an incoming payment of 20 CT yet. Lisa usually verifies and executes transfers quickly.

John opens the spreadsheet—he has read-only access, remember—and searches for "John." Figure 2.22 shows what he sees.

From	To	Amount CT
Company	John	100
John	Cafe	10
John	Melissa	90

— Total balance 100 CT
— This was yesterday's cookie. Balance is 90 CT.
— What? John did NOT send 90 CT to Melissa!

Figure 2.22   Someone stole money from John. Who is Melissa, and how was this possible? John didn't sign any such transfer.

John steps into Lisa's office, asking for an explanation. She answers that she got a message signed with John's private key, asking her to send money to a new coworker, Melissa. Lisa even shows him the message and signature. Of course, there is no Melissa at the office, even though several new employees have started at the company. Lisa doesn't care about names anymore, only public keys and signatures. But she needs the name to look up the correct public key in the table.

The explanation to all this is that Mallory has

1. Managed to copy John's private key. John's laptop has been on his desk all night long. Anyone could have taken the hard drive out of the laptop to search for his private key.

2. Created a new key pair and sent the new public key to Lisa, with the following message:

    Hi Lisa. My name is Melissa, and I'm new here.
    My public key is
    `02c5d2dd24ad71f89bfd99b9c2132f796fa746596a06f5`
    `a33c53c9d762e37d9008`

3. Sent a fraudulent message, signed with the stolen private key, to Lisa as follows:

    Hi Lisa, please move 90 CT to Melissa. Thanks, John
    Signature:
    `IPSq8z0IyCVZNZNMIgrOz5CNRRtRO+A8Tc3j9og4pWbA`
    `H/zT22dQEhSaFSwOXNp0lOyE34d1+4e30R86qzEbJIw=`

Lisa verified the transfer in step 3, concluded it was valid, and executed the transfer. John asks Lisa to revert the—according to him—fraudulent transfer. But Lisa refuses to do so. She thinks the transfer is perfectly valid. If John let someone see his private key, that's his problem, not Lisa's. That's part of why she's so trusted in the company—she keeps her promises.

John creates a new key pair and asks Lisa to add his new public key under the name John2. How can John secure his new private key and still have it readily available when he wants a cookie? John is pretty sure he won't have more than 1,000 cookie tokens on that key.

The security of the spreadsheet has shifted from a system in which Lisa knows everyone's face to one in which she knows everyone's public key. In a sense, the security could be worse now, because it might be easier for Mallory to steal John's private key than it is for her to trick Lisa into thinking Mallory is John. This depends on how John protects his private key. An important thing to note is that the security of John's private key is totally up to him. No one will be able to restore John's private key if he loses it. And Lisa sure isn't going to reverse "fraudulent" transfers just because John is sloppy with security.

If John stores his private key in cleartext in a shared folder on the company's intranet, anyone can easily copy it and use it to steal his cookie tokens. But if John stores the private key in an encrypted file, protected by a strong password, on his own laptop's hard drive, getting a copy of his key is a lot harder. An attacker would have to

- Get access to John's hard drive

- Know John's password

If John never has more than 50 CT on his private key, he might not be that concerned with security. But the cafe, which manages about 10,000 CT daily, might be concerned. John and the cafe probably need different strategies for storing their private keys.

A trade-off exists between security and convenience. You can, for example, keep your private key encrypted on an offline laptop in a bank safe-deposit box. When you want to buy a cookie, you'll need to go to the bank, take the laptop out of your safe-deposit box, decrypt the private key with your password, and use it to digitally sign a message to Lisa that you save to a USB stick. Then, you'll have to put the laptop back into the safe-deposit box, bring the USB stick back to the office, and send the email to Lisa. The private key never leaves the laptop in the safe-deposit box. Very secure, and very inconvenient.

On the other hand, you can store your private key in cleartext on your mobile phone. You'll have the key at your fingertips and can sign a

You are responsible

You have full responsibility for the security of your private keys.

message within seconds of when the urge for a cookie starts to nudge you. Very insecure, and very convenient.

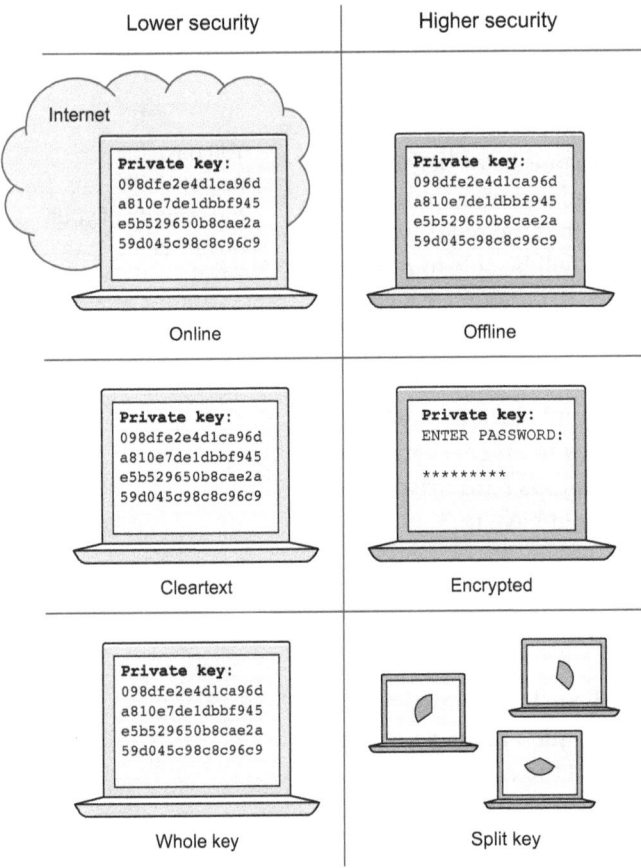

Figure 2.23   Security considerations against attackers. Note how the more secure options are also more inconvenient.

Some of the different trade-offs, as illustrated in figure 2.23, are as follows:

- *Online vs. offline*—Online means the private key is stored on a device with network access, like your mobile phone or general-purpose laptop. Offline means the private key is stored on a piece of paper or a computer without any network access. Online storage is risky because remote security exploits or malicious software on your computer, such as computer viruses, might send the private key to someone without you noticing. If the device is offline, no one can take the private key without physical access to the device.

- *Cleartext vs. encrypted*—If the private key is stored in cleartext in a file on your computer's hard drive, anyone with access to your computer, either remotely over a computer network or physically, can copy the private key. This includes any viruses your computer might be victim to. You can avoid many of these attacks by encrypting your private key with a password that only you know. An attacker would then need access to both your hard drive and your secret password to get the private key.

- *Whole key vs. split key*—People usually store their entire private key on a single computer. This is convenient—you need only one computer to spend your cookie tokens. An attacker must get access to your hard drive to steal the private key. But if your private key is split into three parts (there are good and bad schemes for this—be careful), and you store the three parts separately on three different computers, then the attacker must get access to the hard drives of three computers. This is much harder because they must know what three computers to attack and also successfully attack them. Making a payment in this setup is a real hassle, but very secure.

You can use any combination of these methods to store your keys. But as a rule of thumb, the greater the security against attackers, the greater the risk of you accidentally losing access to your key. For example, if you store the private key encrypted on your hard drive, you risk losing your key due to both computer failure and forgetting your password. In this sense, the more securely you store your key, the less secure it is.

Recap

Lisa has solved the problem with people claiming to be someone else when they make a payment. She requires all payers to digitally sign the cookie token transfers. Every spreadsheet user needs a private key and a public key. Lisa keeps track of who owns which public key. From now on, a payment must be written in an email to Lisa, and the message must be digitally signed with the person's private key. Lisa can then verify the signature to make sure she isn't being fooled. The gist is that as long as John keeps his private key to himself, no one will be able to spend his money.

Preparation: Generate key pair

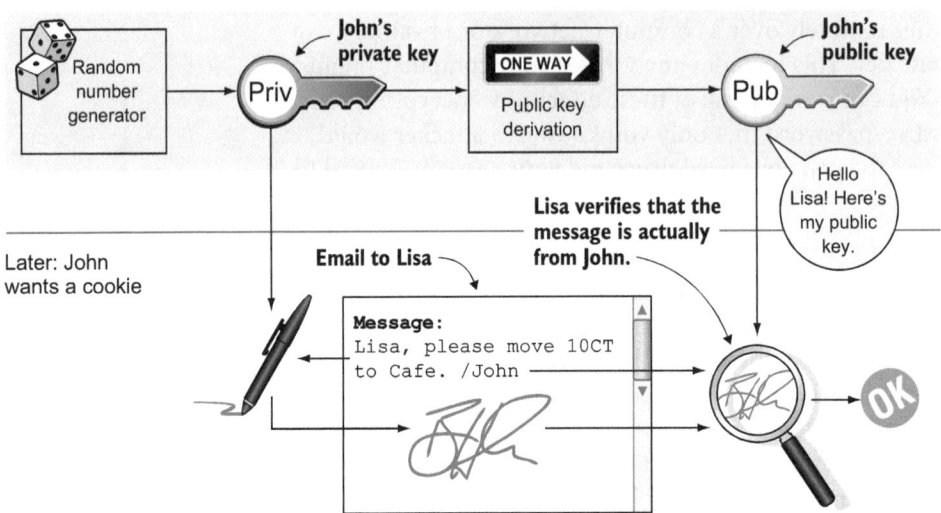

We need to add "Email to Lisa" to our concept table (table 2.5).

Table 2.5   Adding "Email to Lisa" as a key concept

Cookie tokens	Bitcoin	Covered in
1 cookie token	1 bitcoin	Chapter 2
The spreadsheet	The blockchain	Chapter 6
Email to Lisa	**A transaction**	**Chapter 5**
A row in the spreadsheet	A transaction	Chapter 5
Lisa	A miner	Chapter 7

The email to Lisa will be replaced by transactions in chapter 5. Transactions will replace both the email to Lisa and the row in the spreadsheet. It's time to release version 2.0 of the cookie token spreadsheet system (table 2.6).

Table 2.6 Release notes, cookie tokens 2.0

Version	Feature	How
NEW 2.0	Secure payments	Digital signatures solve the problem with imposters.
1.0	Simple payment system	Relies on Lisa being trustworthy and knowing everyone's face
	Finite money supply	7,200 new CT rewarded to Lisa daily; halves every four years

Everybody still trusts Lisa to not change the spreadsheet in any way except when executing signed cookie token transfers. If Lisa wanted to, she could steal anyone's cookie tokens just by adding a transfer to the spreadsheet. But she wouldn't do that—or would she?

You now have a lot of new tools to put in your toolbox for later use: key-pair generation, digital signing, the signature, and the verification.

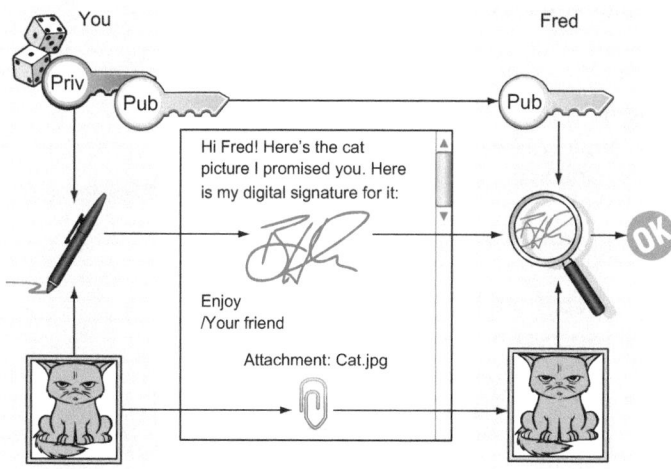

Exercises

Warm up

2.8   Lisa is currently rewarded 7,200 CT per day for her work. Why won't the supply increase infinitely over time? Why don't we have 7,200 × 10,000 = 72 million CT after 10,000 days?

2.9   How can coworkers detect if Lisa rewards herself too much or too often?

2.10   How is the private key of a key pair created?

2.11   What key is used to digitally sign a message?

2.12   The signing process hashes the message to sign. Why?

2.13   What would Mallory need to steal cookie tokens from John?

Dig in

2.14   Suppose you have a private key and you've given your public key to a friend, Fred. Suggest how Fred can send you a secret message that only you can understand.

2.15   Suppose you (let's pretend your name is Laura) and Fred still have the keys from the previous exercise. Now you want to send a message in a bottle to Fred saying,

> Hi Fred! Can we meet at Tiffany's at sunset tomorrow? /Laura

Explain how you would sign the message so Fred can be sure the message is actually from you. Explain what steps you and Fred take in the process.

Summary

- Bitcoins are created as rewards to nodes securing the blockchain.

- The reward halves every four years to limit the money supply.

- You can use cryptographic hash functions to detect changes in a file or in a message.

- You can't make up a pre-image of a cryptographic hash. A pre-image is an input that has a certain known output.

- Digital signatures are useful to prove a payment's authenticity. Only the rightful owner of bitcoins may spend them.

- Someone verifying a digital signature doesn't have to know *who* made the signature. They just have to know the signature was made with the private key the signature claims to be signed with.

- To receive bitcoins or cookie tokens, you need a public key. First, you create a private key for yourself in private. You then derive your public key from your private key.

- Several strategies are available for storing private keys, ranging from unencrypted on your mobile phone to split and encrypted across several offline devices.

- As a general rule of thumb, the more secure the private key is against theft, the easier it is to accidentally lose the key, and vice versa.

This chapter covers

- Basic privacy

- Replacing names with public key hashes

- Protecting against expensive typing errors

By the time you reach the end of this chapter, the cookie token spreadsheet will no longer have personal names—you'll be replacing these names with hashes of public keys. This is useful from a privacy perspective. No one can easily see who's paying whom, making it harder for others to extract information from the spreadsheet and see how many cookies any of your coworkers eat. Lisa also finds this useful because she doesn't have to maintain a table of names and public keys.

When switching to public key hashes in the spreadsheet, coworkers will no longer use names in their emails to Lisa. They will instead use strings of hex code representing public key hashes. This means it will be easy to make typing errors. If you make a typing error, your money may end up digitally burned!

Some coworkers invent cookie token addresses (Bitcoin addresses) that protect them from losing money due to typing errors (figure 3.1). Cookie token addresses are used between users to pay each other, pretty much like an email address, but they aren't used in the spreadsheet.

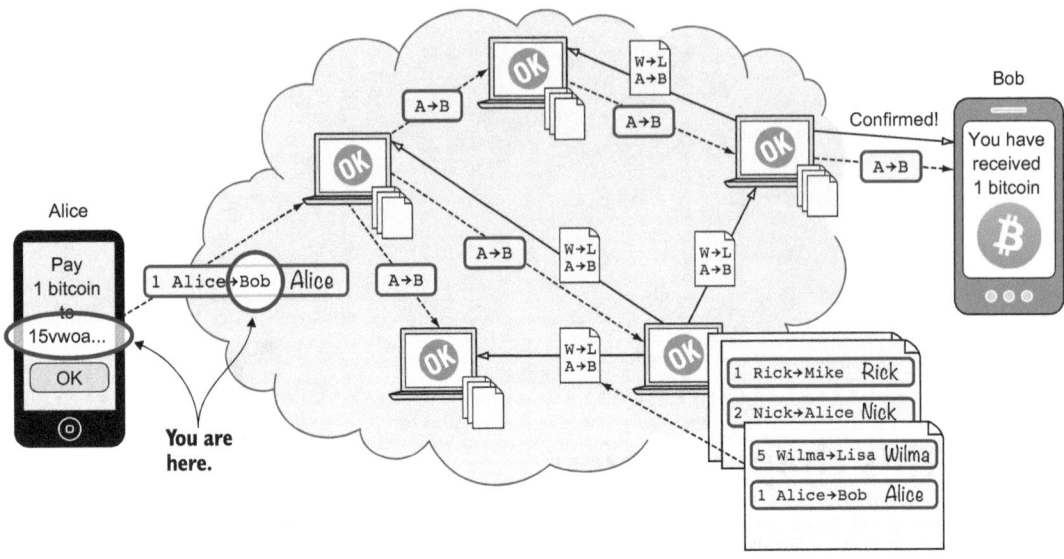

Figure 3.1 Cookie token addresses are exactly the same as Bitcoin addresses. They're used mainly by wallet software.

Cookie-eating habits disclosed

You and many of your coworkers have health insurance with Acme Insurances. Acme has persuaded John to give it a copy of the spreadsheet. Acme figures it can adjust premiums or hold workers' cookie-eating habits (figure 3.2) against them in an eventual insurance dispute.

Acme Insurances

This highly unethical insurance company will make serious attempts to spy on your habits, to "adjust" your premium.

From	To	Amount CT	
Cafe	Chloe	1,000	
Chloe	Cafe	10	← Chloe buys a cookie.
...	...	...	← Chloe buys lots of cookies.
Chloe	Cafe	40	← Chloe buys four cookies.
Chloe	Cafe	20	← Chloe buys two cookies.
Chloe	Cafe	20	← Chloe buys two cookies.

Search result for Chloe

Figure 3.2   Acme Insurances keeps an eye on Chloe's cookie-eating habits.

Another disturbing fact about the spreadsheet is that every coworker can easily look up other coworkers' balances, as well as their cookie-eating habits.

The coworkers have asked Lisa to come up with a solution to these problems. Otherwise, they'll stop using the spreadsheet.

Replacing names with public keys

Lisa has kept the table of names and public keys updated at all times since the coworkers started using digital signatures. She's sick of doing this, so she comes up with an idea that will benefit both her and her coworkers: Lisa will replace all names in the spreadsheet with their respective public keys (figure 3.3).

Name	Public key
...	...
Cafe	0222436a49cd8ff2605255dcea8fad ff20703d58d22bef7c5a6fc23807712
John	035541a13851a3742489fdddeef21be13c1 abb85e053222c0dbf3703ba218dc1f3

From	To	Amount CT
...	...	...
Cafe	Anne	1,000
Lisa	Cafe	10
Cafe	Company	10,000
Alice	Cafe	10
John	Cafe	10

From	To	CT
...	...	...
0222436a49cd8ff2605255 dcea8fadd6a9aff20703d5 8d22bef7c5a6fc23807712	02b33f40f80812ae832404 e97e039eaa92e6993a6d14 7c8854c09281be1292e920	1,000
036c4f8ed456142a75724d 57ab7f6c358850ee9a79dc 444fe5e754496c7cfa3371	0222436a49cd8ff2605255 dcea8fadd6a9aff20703d5 8d22bef7c5a6fc23807712	10
0222436a49cd8ff2605255 dcea8fadd6a9aff20703d5 8d22bef7c5a6fc23807712	037e944a7b778d190c05b5 9325c58eed069205148fa0 a2998273af0ffe36de9496	10,000
0317828d04ebd6d120e423 6bc0cf0cce12ebfdfa106c 7bf744deb547fcc52e768d	0222436a49cd8ff2605255 dcea8fadd6a9aff20703d5 8d22bef7c5a6fc23807712	10
035541a13851a3742489fd ddeef21be13c1abb85e053 222c0dbf3703ba218dc1f3	0222436a49cd8ff2605255 dcea8fadd6a9aff20703d5 8d22bef7c5a6fc23807712	10

Figure 3.3 Replacing names with public keys. The spreadsheet is now more unreadable, which is good from a privacy perspective.

It's now hard to see how many cookies Chloe has eaten without knowing her public key. If Acme Insurances receives this new spreadsheet, it won't be able to see who the senders and recipients are. It will see only the sender and recipient public keys of each payment.

Lisa can now delete her cumbersome table of names and public keys. But when she does this, users should no longer use names when making payments. They must instead use the sender's public key and the recipient's public key (figure 3.4).

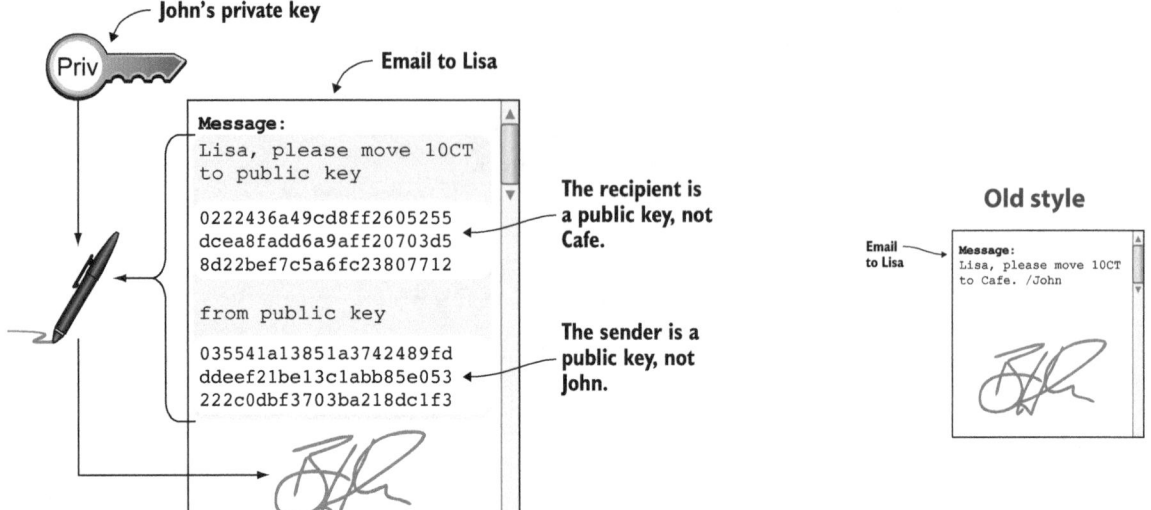

Figure 3.4   New-style payment using public keys instead of names

The email to Lisa contains a few vital parts:

- A message containing the

  - Amount

  - Sender public key

  - Recipient public key

- A signature made with the sender's private key

The essential difference is that the payment is now pseudonymous: names are replaced with the corresponding public keys. Otherwise, the payment looks the same as before.

New payment process

Suppose a new coworker just started at the company. Her name is Faiza. The company wants to send her 100 CT as a welcome gift. How can the company send 100 CT to Faiza?

First, the company needs the recipient's—Faiza's—public key. Faiza hasn't used cookie tokens yet, so she needs to create a key pair and give the public key to the sender—the company—as figure 3.5 shows.

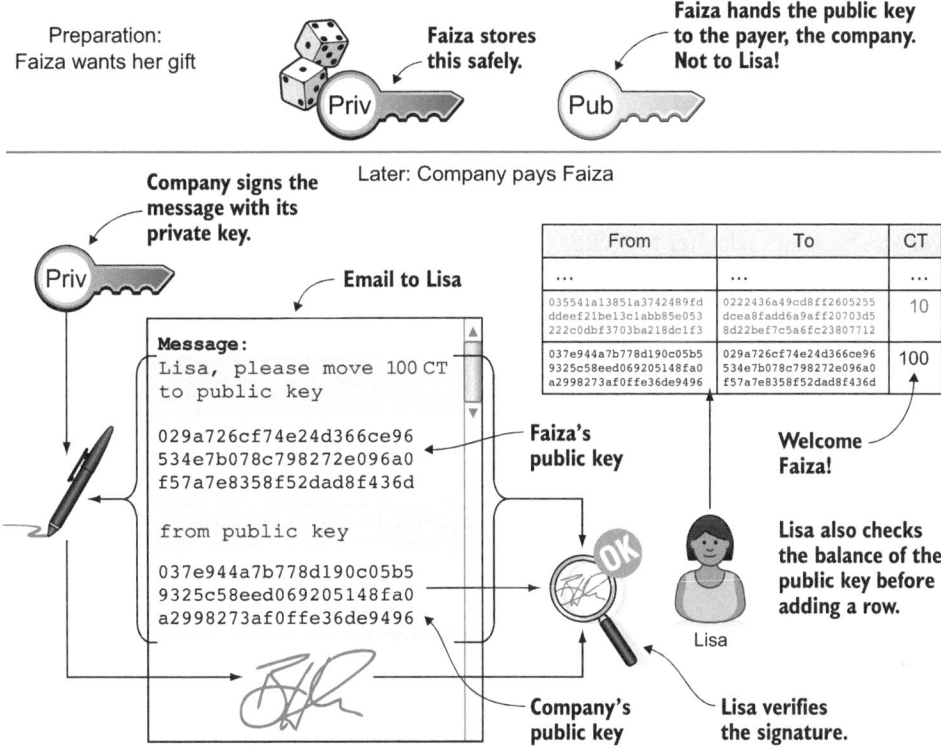

Figure 3.5 Faiza creates her public key and gives it to the company. The company creates a payment with Faiza's public key as the recipient.

Faiza creates a private and a public key, following the same process described in chapter 2's section "Improving cookie token security," but she doesn't give her public key to Lisa. Now that Lisa doesn't have the table of names and public keys, there's no longer any point in giving her the public key. She doesn't need it. Instead, Faiza gives the public key to the entity that wants to pay her cookie tokens—the company.

The company creates a message asking Lisa to move 100 CT from `037e944a…36de9496` to `029a726c…ad8f436d`. It then digitally signs the message and sends it to Lisa. Lisa uses

- The message
- The sender's public key
- The signature

to verify that the message is signed with the private key belonging to the sender's public key. She also verifies that the sender's public key has enough funds in the spreadsheet. She does this the same way she did when the spreadsheet contained names—she searches for the sender's public key and calculates the balance.

Lisa has never seen the recipient's public key before, but she doesn't care. She cares only that the sender has the money to spend and that the message is correctly signed. She'll write into the spreadsheet's recipient column whatever the message asks her to write.

> **Lisa In Bitcoin**
>
> Lisa is performing the same duties with cookie token payments that a Bitcoin miner would do with Bitcoin payments.

Faiza sees the new row with her public key in the To column. It gives her a warm, fuzzy feeling. She can now spend her cookie tokens as she pleases. Faiza didn't have to bother Lisa with her public key, saving Lisa a lot of work.

From	To	CT
...	...	...
037e944a7b778d190c05b5 9325c58eed069205148fa0 a2998273af0ffe36de9496	029a726cf74e24d366ce96 534e7b078c798272e096a0 f57a7e8358f52dad8f436d	100

Let's summarize what's happened so far:

• Names have been replaced with public keys in the spreadsheet.

• Lisa has thrown away the table of names and public keys.

• Payments are made using public keys instead of names to denote sender and recipient.

These changes have improved privacy and simplified Lisa's work. At the end of this chapter, we'll discuss more about how to further improve privacy.

The email to Lisa in this example probably reveals, *to Lisa*, who the sender is (the company, in this case) because of the From field of the email. For now, we can assume Lisa doesn't reveal or use this personal information in any way. We use email in this example in place of Bitcoin's peer-to-peer network. The Bitcoin network, discussed in detail in chapter 8, doesn't use any personal information.

Please take a moment to think about what Acme Insurances can now figure out from the spreadsheet. What information can it get if it figures out the name of the sender or recipient of *one* payment? It will be able to identify all payments that person has made.

Shortening the public key

Using public keys in the spreadsheet improved privacy, but such keys take up a lot of space compared to names. The name "John" takes 4 bytes in the spreadsheet, whereas a public key takes 33 bytes. Keeping the spreadsheet as small as possible is important because a smaller spreadsheet means faster downloading for coworkers wanting to check their balance; it also takes less space on Lisa's hard drive.

Hashing the public key to 20 bytes

Among the coworkers, some developers think they can replace 33-byte public keys with something shorter while still preserving enough security. They suggest replacing each public key in the cookie token spreadsheet with a cryptographic hash of the public key. This shortens senders and recipients in the spreadsheet but also protects users' money in the event of a flaw in the public key derivation function, as we'll see later. The hashing isn't made with a single cryptographic hash function but with two different cryptographic hash functions, as figure 3.6 illustrates. We'll discuss the reason for using two hash functions in the next section.

From	To	CT
...	...	...
035541a13851a3742489fd ddeef21be13c1abb85e053 222c0dbf3703ba218dc1f3	0222436a49cd8ff2605255 dcea8fadd6a9aff20703d5 8d22bef7c5a6fc23807712	10
037e944a7b778d190c05b5 9325c58eed069205148fa0 a2998273af0ffe36de9496	029a726cf74e24d366ce96 534e7b078c798272e096a0 f57a7e8358f52dad8f436d	100

From	To	CT
...	...	...
5f2613791b36f667fdb8 e95608b55e3df4c5f9eb	87e3d1692022a7744bf2 406a963c656c8393b1cc	10
bc27a2f538aa6a796e4b 2197f150ae0f667870eb	bea73261a7499c22f8e1 e57bdb0e41ffc35ce56a	100

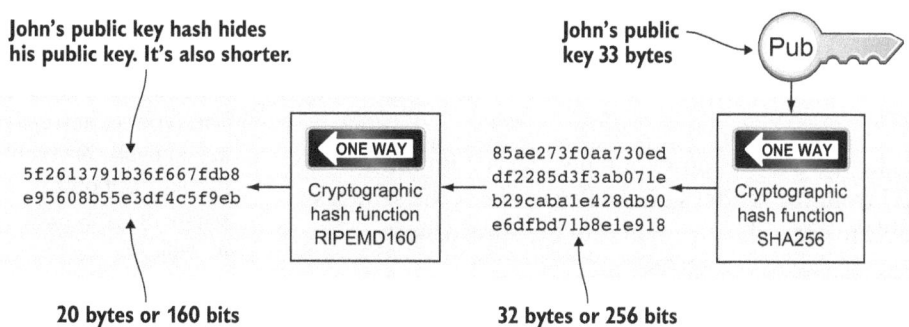

Figure 3.6 Replacing the public keys with the RIPEMD160 hash of the SHA256 hash of the public key

The public key is first hashed with SHA256, which you should be familiar with from the previous chapter. The output of this cryptographic hash function is then hashed with RIPEMD160, a cryptographic hash function that outputs a 160-bit (20-byte) number. We call this final hash the *public key hash* (PKH). All public keys in the spreadsheet are replaced with their respective PKHs.

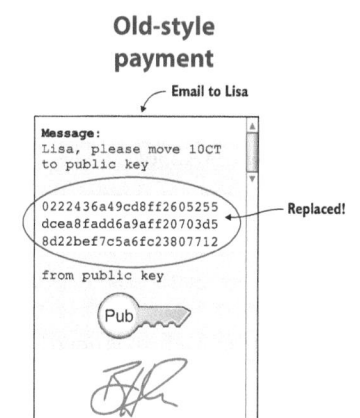

The payment process now differs from when Faiza received her 100 CT from the company. Suppose John wants to buy a cookie (figure 3.7).

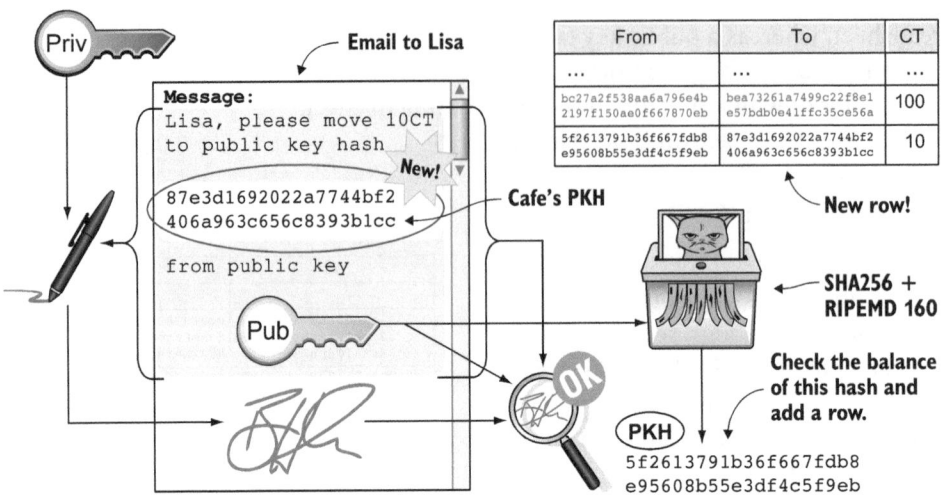

Figure 3.7   John buys a cookie. The sender is still a public key, but the recipient is a PKH instead of public key. Lisa needs to create the PKH from the sender's public key to verify the balance and execute the payment.

First, the message to Lisa is changed a bit. John must use the cafe's PKH—which was previously a public key—as the recipient. The sender is still a public key in the message because that public key is needed to verify the signature. Lisa doesn't keep people's public keys around anymore.

Second, because the spreadsheet now contains PKHs, Lisa must calculate the PKH from the sender's public key to check the sender's balance and be able to enter the payment into the spreadsheet.

> **p2pkh**
>
> Most payments in Bitcoin are made with a PKH as the recipient. This type is often called *pay-to-public-key-hash* (p2pkh), but other payment types exist as well.

Why SHA256 and RIPEMD160?

Using RIPEMD160 as the last cryptographic hash function is a deliberate choice to make the PKHs shorter. Compare the output from SHA256 with the output from RIPEMD160:

- SHA256:
  `85ae273f0aa730eddf2285d3f3ab071eb29caba1e428db90e6dfbd71b8e1e918`

- RIPEMD160:
  `5f2613791b36f667fdb8e95608b55e3df4c5f9eb`

It's a well-balanced trade-off between security and size.

But why have two different cryptographic hash functions? We don't really know why this scheme was chosen for Bitcoin because its inventor, Satoshi Nakamoto, has stopped corresponding with the Bitcoin community. We can only speculate. Instead, let's discuss some of the scheme's properties.

If either hash function isn't pre-image-resistant, the other still is. This means if you can calculate an input to RIPEMD160 that gives a certain PKH output, you still need to pre-image attack SHA256 (with about 2^{255} guesses) to find the public key. Likewise, if you can calculate an input to SHA256 that gives a certain output, you first need to pre-image attack RIPEMD160 before you can use that pre-image to calculate the public key.

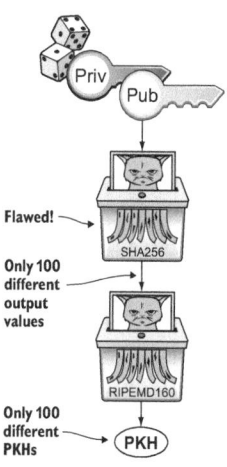

On the other hand, if it turns out that the output set of either cryptographic hash function is smaller than anticipated, then the security of the combined hash-function chain suffers. To make this clearer, pretend SHA256 has only 100 possible output values. You can steal money from anyone by trying different random private keys and calculating the corresponding PKHs. If a PKH matches your target, you've found a private key you can steal the money with. On average, you'd only have to test 50 different private keys to steal from one PKH. This property gives the worst of both worlds: if either of the two functions is weak, then the whole chain is weak. The probability that any function has this flaw is small. If any such flaw exists, the reduction in the output set likely isn't significant enough to endanger security in practice. Remember, we've yet to find one single collision in any of these cryptographic hash functions.

Another thing to note is that different organizations developed the two cryptographic hash functions. RIPEMD160 was developed at a European university in open collaboration with a broad community of cryptographers. SHA256 was developed by the US National Security Agency (NSA). Both are considered secure, and both have been subject to scrutiny from a large number of people.

Now that we've strengthened the security of the cookie token spreadsheet, let's think about privacy again. Has this improved privacy? Is it harder for Acme Insurances to figure out information about who's paying whom now compared to when we used public keys in the spreadsheet?

Has privacy improved?

No.

The answer is no. There is practically a one-to-one correspondence between the public keys and the PKHs. Using PKHs doesn't hide personal information any more than using plain public keys.

Avoiding expensive typing errors

When Lisa verifies a payment before executing it, she doesn't care who the recipient is or if it's even an existing recipient. She'll put into the recipient column of the spreadsheet whatever the payer asks her to. She can't even know if a recipient is valid or not, because she no longer knows everyone's public keys.

This is convenient for Lisa, but it can cause people to lose money if they aren't careful. Imagine once again that John wants to buy a cookie. This time, he's not careful enough when writing the message, as figure 3.8 shows.

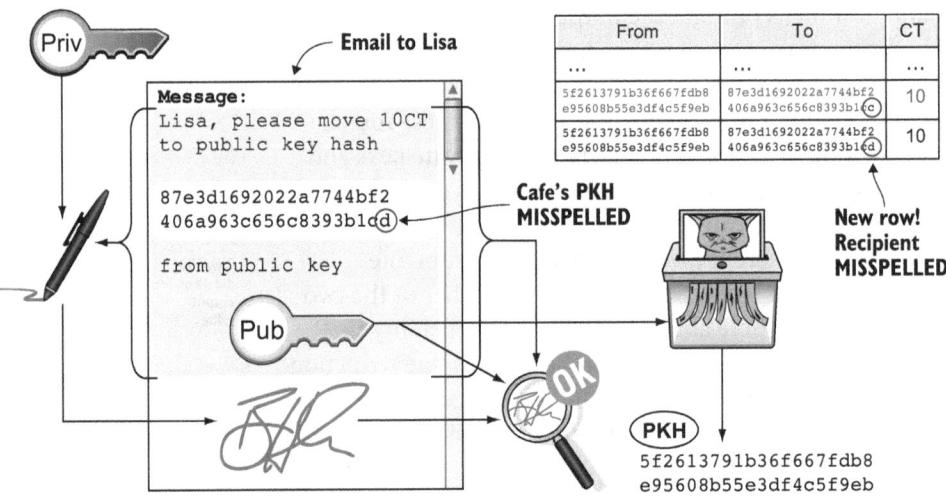

Figure 3.8   John makes a typo in the recipient in the email to Lisa. What now?

He makes a typing error in the recipient PKH. The last character is d when it should have been c. What happens now?

John doesn't notice the error and happily signs the message and sends the email to Lisa. Lisa verifies the signature, which verifies fine, and calculates the sender's PKH. She doesn't care about the recipient. She inserts a new row in the spreadsheet paying from 5f261379...f4c5f9eb to 87e3d169...8393b1cd.

Then she considers herself done, moving on to other interesting tasks. The cafe owner, who is searching for his PKH in the spreadsheet, doesn't see an incoming payment. John stands at the counter in the cafe

Any recipient goes

There is no "wrong" recipient PKH. Lisa adds any recipient as long as the signature is valid.

yelling at the cafe owner that he *did* send money, so "Give me the freakin' cookie!" The cafe owner refuses. John takes a close look at the spreadsheet and searches for his PKH. He finds the one he just made and realizes his spelling mistake.

John has sent money to a "public key hash" for which there is no known private key. No one will ever be able to spend those 10 CT— not the cafe, not John, nobody. John has just digitally burned 10 CT.

Unfortunately, this will probably happen again and again in the future if nothing is done to prevent it. The problem can happen at any point from when the cafe owner reads his own PKH to give to John to when John writes his message before signing it. You could argue that Lisa could also make this mistake when she updates the spreadsheet, but she's so thorough that this would *never* happen. She's just too good at what she's doing. Lisa will never cause someone else's funds to be burned.

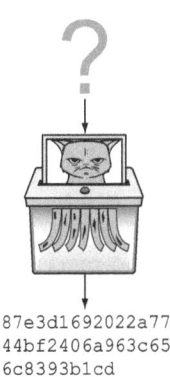

```
87e3d1692022a77
44bf2406a963c65
6c8393b1cd
```

Where were we?

This chapter deals with Bitcoin addresses. To remind you where this all fits into Bitcoin, remember the diagram from chapter 1, shown again in figure 3.9.

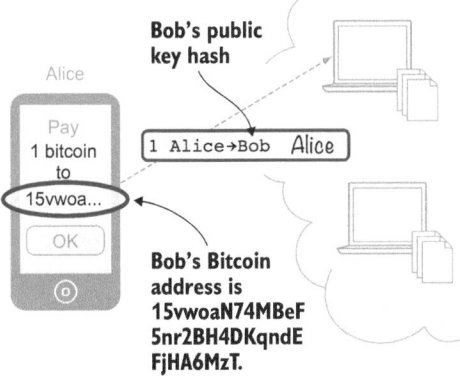

Figure 3.9   Bitcoin addresses

Toward the end of this chapter, we'll end up with Bitcoin (cookie token) addresses. We've just replaced the names in the spreadsheet with PKHs. We'll now get to *Bitcoin addresses*. A Bitcoin address is a *converted*

PKH—that is, it's a PKH written in a way more suitable for human users and safe against spelling errors. The PKH is sent to Lisa (or Bitcoin nodes), but the address is what users see and give to each other.

Base58check

Among the coworkers, the security-oriented people discuss the problem with typos and come up with the idea of *cookie token addresses*. A cookie token address is a PKH *encoded* to detect typing errors. The PKH can be converted back and forth between this encoding and plain byte format.

Suppose Faiza feels sorry for John and wants to give him 20 CT from her 100 CT to ease his pain. She doesn't want to make the same mistake John did, so she asks him for his cookie token address. John creates this by encoding his PKH with a function called *base58check* (figure 3.10).

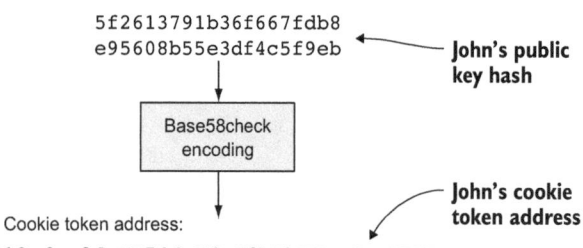

```
5f2613791b36f667fdb8
e95608b55e3df4c5f9eb  ◄──── John's public
                              key hash

        ┌──────────────┐
        │  Base58check │
        │   encoding   │
        └──────────────┘
                │          John's cookie
                │          token address
Cookie token address: ▼
19g6oo8foQF5jfqK9gH2bLkFNwgCenRBPD
```

Figure 3.10   Overview of base58check encoding, which transforms a PKH into a cookie token address

The result is John's cookie token address: `19g6oo8f…gCenRBPD`. John hands this address to Faiza, who then makes a payment following the process in figure 3.11.

The payment process changes for the payer, but nothing changes for Lisa. Faiza will base58check *decode* John's address into a PKH. This decoding ensures that no typing errors were made in the address.

Who uses cookie token addresses?

Cookie token addresses are employed only between users to safely transmit a PKH. Lisa never sees them.

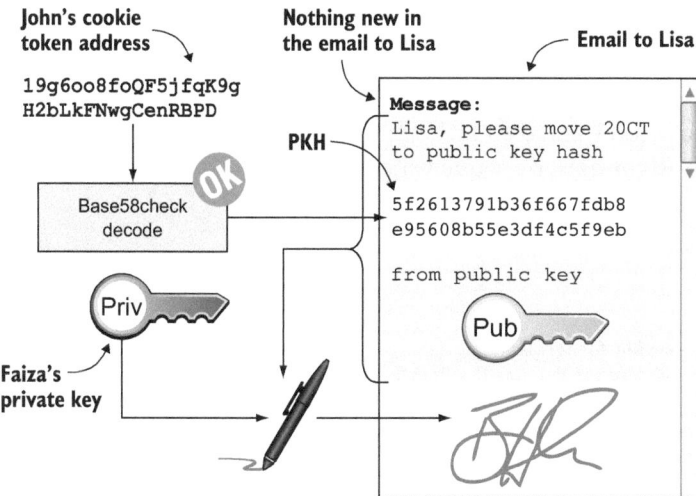

Figure 3.11 Faiza makes a payment to John's cookie token address. She decodes the address into a PKH, verifying that the address isn't misspelled.

As mentioned previously, a PKH can be converted to an address and back to a PKH. It is *not* a one-way function. It's just different ways to *represent* the PKH, either as a series of bytes or as an address (figure 3.12).

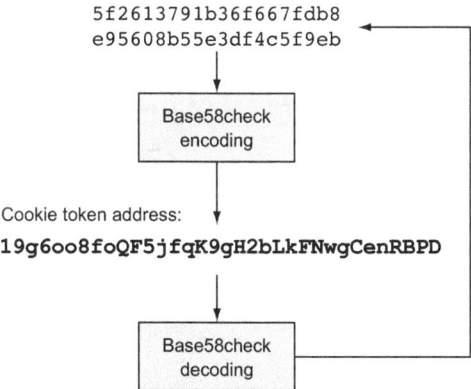

Figure 3.12 The PKH can be encoded into an address and decoded back into the PKH.

The email to Lisa is exactly the same as before. Only users employ the cookie token address. It isn't part of Lisa's validation process or the spreadsheet in any way.

Base58check encoding

Let's see how this mysterious base58check encoding works (figure 3.13). First, a version is added before the PKH. The people who came up with the idea of cookie token addresses wanted to make future upgrades to the address format easy. Right now, only one version of cookie token addresses is available. This version is a single 0 byte.

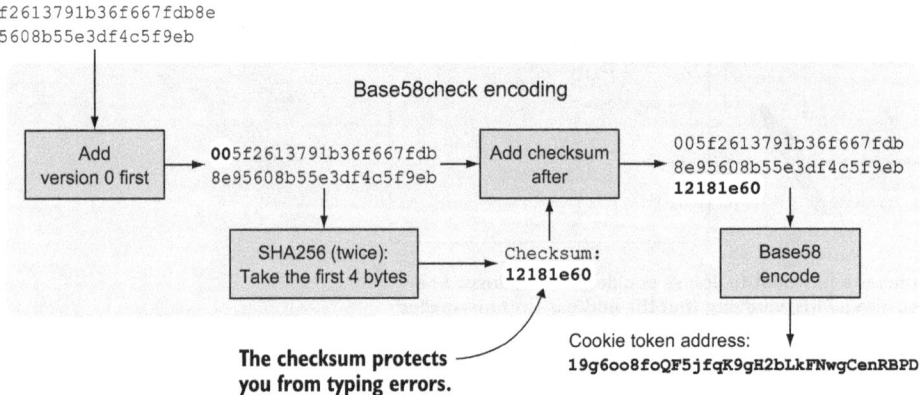

Figure 3.13   Base58check encoding John's PKH. A version is added to the hash, and then a checksum is created and appended to the versioned hash. Finally, the checksummed, versioned hash is base58 encoded.

To detect typing errors, a *checksum* is added. This checksum is calculated from the versioned PKH. To create a checksum, base58check hashes the versioned PKH with double SHA256. This means it's first hashed with SHA256, and the resulting hash is hashed again with SHA256. Take the first 4 bytes of the second hash, and let those 4 bytes be the checksum. This checksum is then appended to the versioned PKH. You'll soon see how this checksum protects users from typing errors. Be patient!

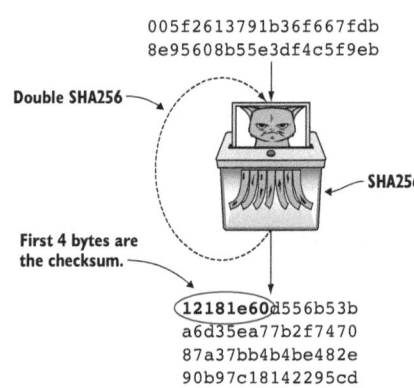

You started with a PKH of 20 bytes (40 hex characters). But now that you've added a version and a checksum, you have 25 bytes (50 hex characters). To make up for this increase, you'll encode the 25 bytes in a more compact way than hexadecimal encoding.

Using a more compact encoding

Hex encoding is an inefficient way to represent data bytes. It requires 2 characters for each byte. We use only 16 characters, where each character represent 4 bits, `0000` to `1111`.

Many encoding schemes exist that use more characters to represent data. The most widely known is base64, in which each character represents 6 bits of data; to do this, the scheme needs more characters than just letters and digits. Base64 uses the following alphabet:

`ABCDEFGHIJKLMNOPQRSTUVWXYZabcdefghijklmnopqrstuvwxyz0123456789+/`

The character `A` represents the bits `000000`, `B` represents `000001`, and the character `/` represents `111111`. This is a nice, easy, compact way to represent data with human-readable characters. I've already used base64-encoded data several times in this book to represent signatures.

But base64 doesn't quite fit the bill for cookie token addresses. We need an encoding that doesn't just detect typing errors when they happen but minimizes the risk of making them. Notice how some characters look similar in some fonts, like `lI` (lowercase L, capital I) and `0O` (zero and capital O). We also need a format that users can easily copy and paste, meaning special characters such as `+` and `/` shouldn't be allowed—they'll prevent us from marking the whole address by double-clicking it. Removing those six characters reduces the possibility of typing errors. But now we have only 58 characters left, so we need another type of encoding.

```
005f2613791b36f667fdb
8e95608b55e3df4c5f9eb
12181e60
```

```
Base58
encode
```

**19g6oo8foQF5jfqK9gH
2bLkFNwgCenRBPD**

```
Base58
decode
```

This new way to encode data is called *base58* because the alphabet is the following 58 characters:

`123456789ABCDEFGHJKLMNPQRSTUVWXYZabcdefghijkmnopqrstuvwxyz`

WARNING!

If you feel put off by this low-level base58 mumbo jumbo, you can skip to "Base58check decoding" and just accept that base58 is a way to encode and decode data. For the rest of you, please continue. It's fun.

In base64, each character represents exactly 6 bits, which makes it straightforward to encode and decode data. But with base58, each character represents slightly less than 6 bits but more than 5 bits. We need to encode data differently.

Let's get back to the example in which John creates his address. He's just added a version and a checksum. Now it's time to encode the 25 bytes into the final result: the address (figure 3.14).

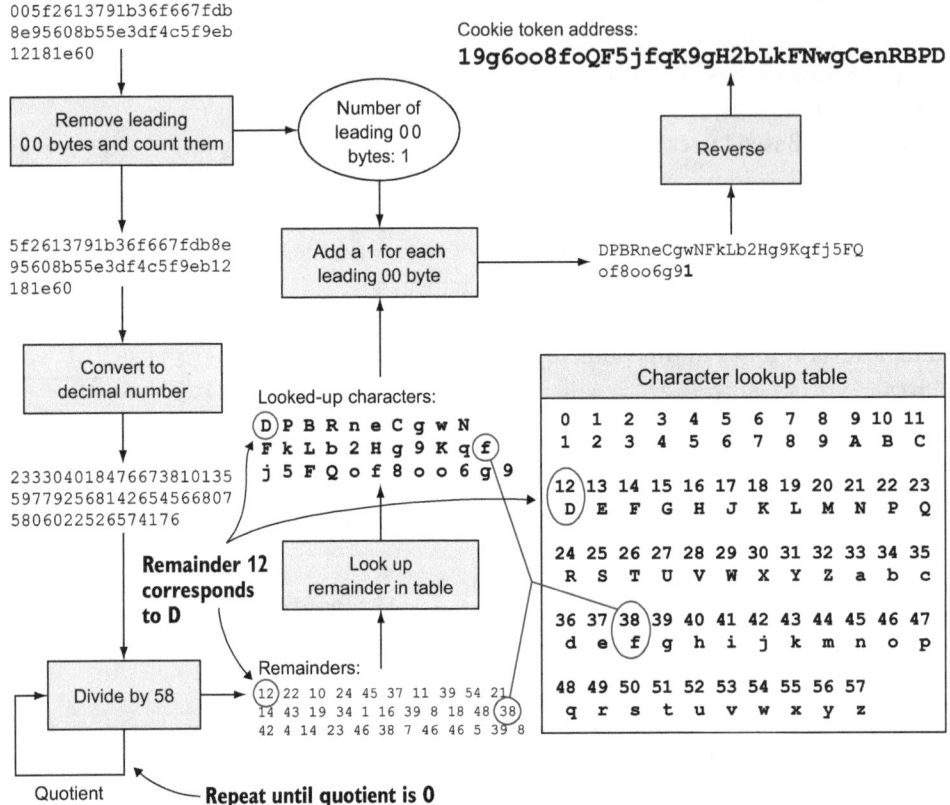

Figure 3.14   Encoding John's versioned and checksummed PKH with base58. The essential part is where you divide the number by 58 and keep the remainders, which are then mapped one by one in the lookup table.

The overall strategy of base58 is to treat the data as a huge number that you divide by 58 over and over until the quotient is 0; you keep the remainders of every division. You look up each remainder in the lookup table and append a 1 last for each leading 0 byte in the input. The string is finally reversed, and the result is John's cookie token address. Note that all cookie token addresses, not just John's, will start with a 1. This is because the version byte is 0, which is encoded by the character 1.

You can decode base58-encoded data such as John's address back to the original input of the base58 encoding. I'll leave this as an exercise for the interested reader.

Note that base58 encoding is nothing new. It's a generic way to convert a decimal number to any other base. You can use the same algorithm to convert to base3, instead—divide by 3 instead of 58. Maybe you'd also like to change the lookup table to map 0 to 0, 1 to 1, and 2 to 2 to get the characters you're used to. For example, write 17 in base 3:

$$17 = 5 \times 3 + 2$$
$$5 = 1 \times 3 + 2$$
$$1 = 0 \times 3 + 1$$

Then, look up the remainders in the lookup table (same digits as the ones you convert), and you'll get `2 2 1`. Reverse that to get the final result: `1 2 2`. Verify that it's correct as follows:

$$1 \times 3^2 + 2 \times 3^1 + 2 \times 3^0 = 9 + 6 + 2 = 17$$

Base58check decoding

John has just created his cookie token address by base58check encoding his PKH. He's given the address to Faiza so she can send him 20 CT. Now, Faiza needs to write a message to Lisa. To do this, she needs John's PKH. The great thing about base58check encoding is that the process can be reversed so you can get the PKH from the address while simultaneously checking for typing errors (figure 3.15).

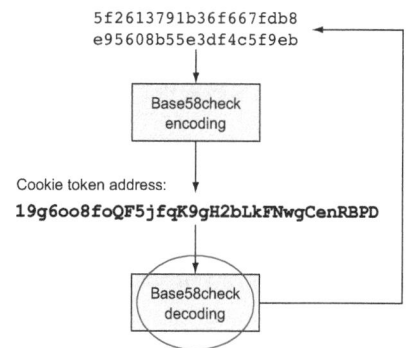

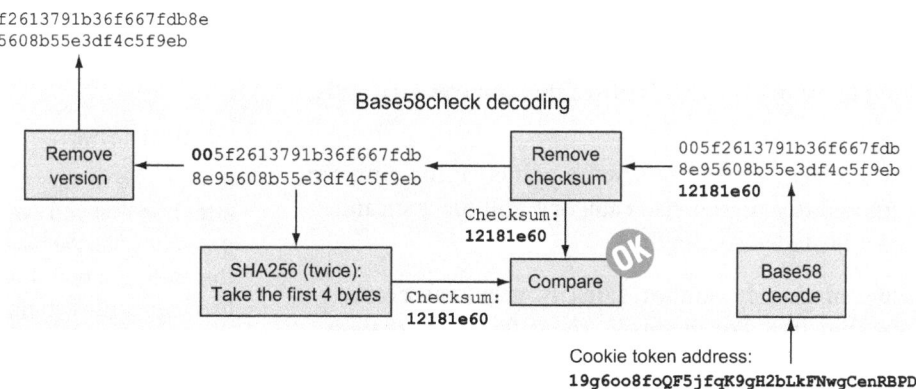

Figure 3.15 Base58check decoding is basically done by reversing the base58check encoding. Typing errors are detected when the checksums don't match.

Faiza takes John's cookie token address and base58 decodes it. Then, she removes the checksum and uses the remaining part, the versioned PKH, to calculate the checksum again. The newly calculated checksum and the just-removed checksum must match. Otherwise, a typing error has occurred, in which case Faiza won't create the message. She'll know the address was corrupted somewhere along the way and refrain from sending an email to Lisa. She'll verify that she entered the address correctly and that John gave her the correct address to learn where it went wrong.

How safe is the checksum? Suppose a typing error occurred in an address. What's the probability that the checksum won't detect the error? The checksum is 4 bytes, which corresponds to $2^{32} \approx 4.3$ billion values. The chance is about 1 in 4.3 billion that base58check fails to detect the typing error. It's pretty safe.

Back to privacy

Although privacy improved when we replaced names with PKHs, the spreadsheet still reveals some information that Acme Insurances finds useful.

For example, Acme can probably figure out the cafe has the PKH `87e3d169...8393b1cc` because a lot of 10 CT payments have been made to this PKH. From this, Acme will be able to see which PKHs are making the most 10 CT payments to that PKH. Let's say Acme talks to Faiza and asks her for information about her recent payments. She's made only one payment so far, the one to John. Faiza, unaware of why Acme is asking these questions, discloses that the transaction is for John.

A week later, John receives a letter from Acme politely informing him that he's been promoted to a higher risk category, and his insurance premium has been adjusted accordingly.

Some privacy issues obviously remain. Luckily, users can create as many addresses they like. For example, the cafe could create a unique address for every incoming payment. And John could create a brand-new cookie token address the next time he accepts cookie tokens from Faiza.

> **Forensics** 🅱
>
> This technique is often used in Bitcoin—for example, during crime investigations.

Dear John,

It has come to our attention that you live an unhealthy life. We have therefore promoted you to a higher risk category. Congratulations.

Sincerely,

Acme Insurances

Using unique addresses for each payment will make it harder for Acme to extract information from the cookie token spreadsheet, because they won't be able to tell which payments belong to the same person.

Recap

This chapter started with replacing the names in the spreadsheet with users' respective PKHs.

From	To	CT
...	...	...
John	Cafe	10
Company	Faiza	100

From	To	CT
...	...	...
5f2613791b36f667fdb8 e95608b55e3df4c5f9eb	87e3d1692022a7744bf2 406a963c656c8393b1cc	10
bc27a2f538aa6a796e4b 2197f150ae0f667870eb	bea73261a7499c22f8e1 e57bdb0e41ffc35ce56a	100

Then, we used base58check to create an address from a PKH. Let's put the pieces together and look at the whole cookie token address-creation process from random number generator to the address.

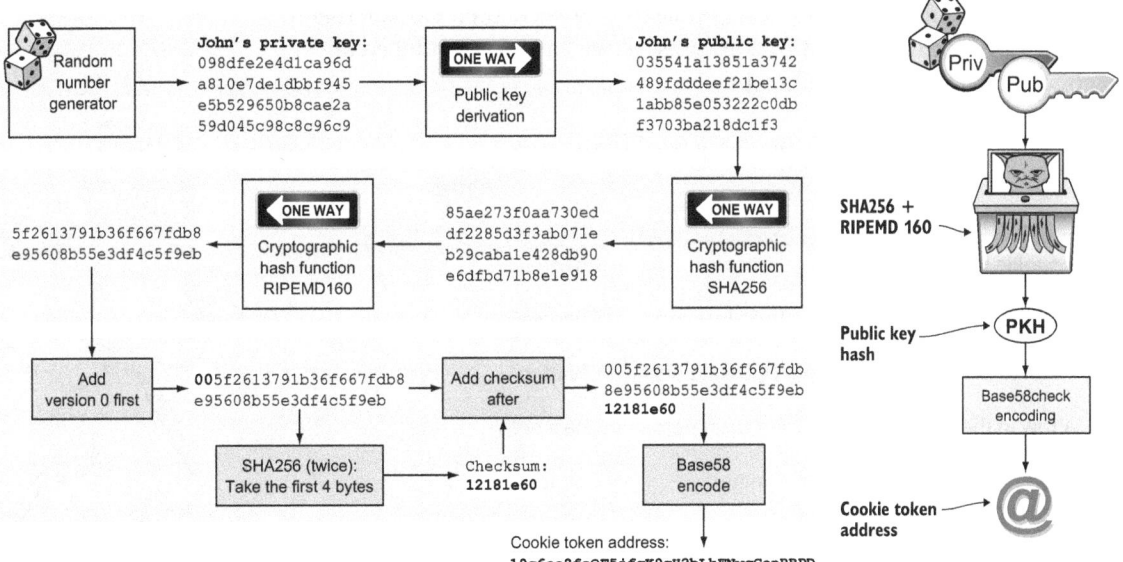

Faiza makes sure no typing errors happen by base58check decoding the address before signing the message.

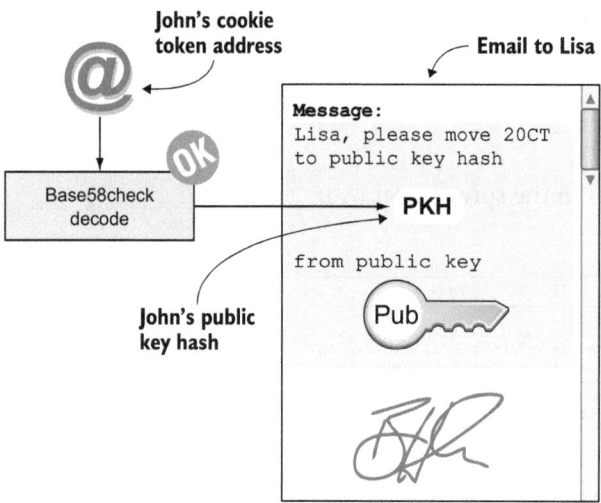

System changes

The concept table (table 3.1) isn't updated in this chapter. Cookie token addresses are exactly what Bitcoin uses, so we haven't introduced any concepts that differ from Bitcoin.

Table 3.1   Nothing new in the concept table

Cookie tokens	Bitcoin	Covered in
1 cookie token	1 bitcoin	Chapter 2
The spreadsheet	The blockchain	Chapter 6
Email to Lisa	A transaction	Chapter 5
A row in the spreadsheet	A transaction	Chapter 5
Lisa	A miner	Chapter 7

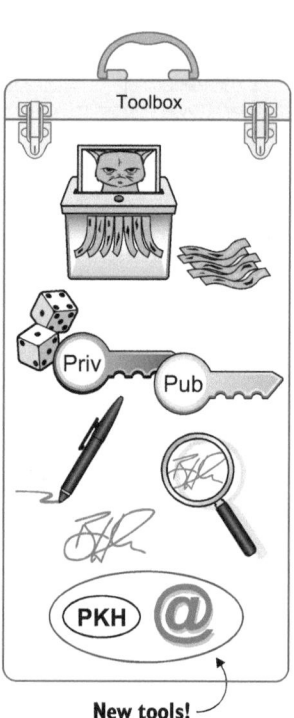

Thanks to PKH and cookie token addresses, Lisa can ditch her table of public keys. You can add PKH and addresses to your toolbox for later use, and we release version 3.0 of the cookie token system (table 3.2).

Table 3.2 Release notes, cookie tokens 3.0

Version	Feature	How
NEW 3.0	Safe from expensive typing errors	Cookie token addresses.
	Privacy improvements	A PKH instead of a personal name is stored in the spreadsheet.
2.0	Secure payments	Digital signatures solve the problem with imposters.
1.0	Simple payment system	Relies on Lisa being trustworthy and knowing everyone's face.
	Finite money supply	7,200 new CT are rewarded to Lisa daily; the amount halves every four years.

Exercises

Warm up

3.1 The PKH is shorter than the public key—only 160 bits. We made it shorter using RIPEMD160. Why do you want it to be shorter? There are two good reasons.

3.2 Base58check encoding is used to create a cookie token (Bitcoin) address from a PKH. Is it possible to reverse this process to create a PKH from an address?

3.3 When is base58check decoding used, and by whom?

3.4   Base58 encode the two hex bytes 0047. Use the following diagram. You may skip this exercise if you didn't read the section on base58 encoding.

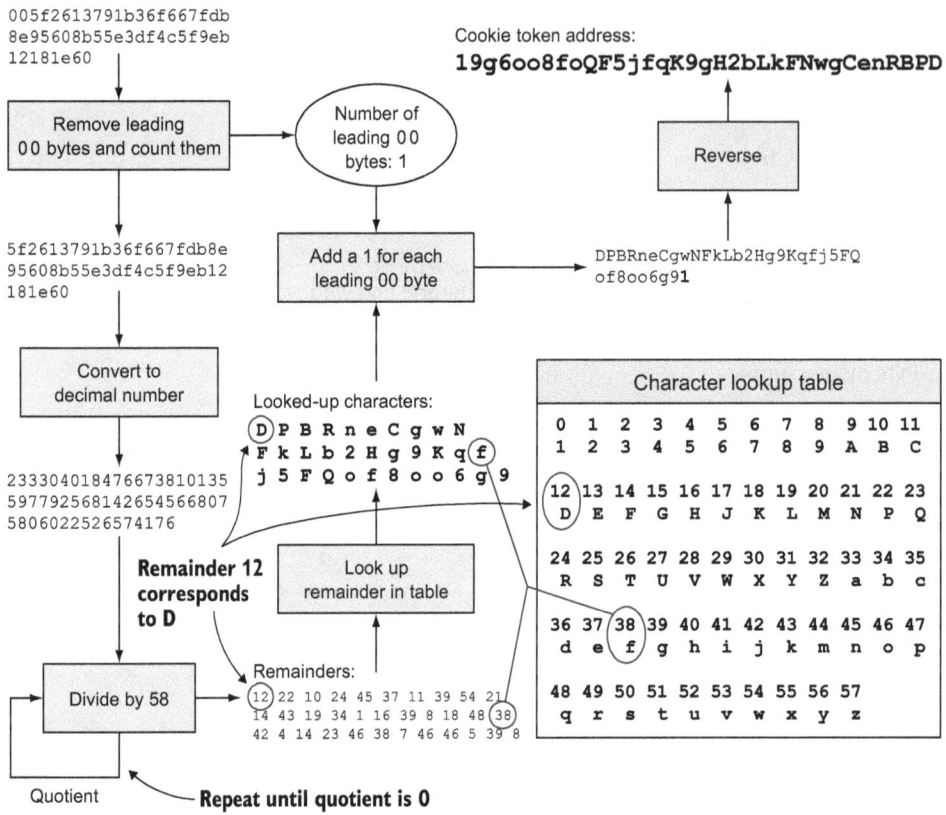

3.5   What in an address makes it mostly safe from typing errors?

Dig in

3.6   Imagine that John wants a cookie from the cafe. He has two addresses: $@_1$ with a balance of 5 CT, and $@_2$ with 8 CT. His total balance is 13 CT, so he should be able to afford 10 CT for a cookie. Give an example of how he could pay 10 CT to the cafe.

5 CT   8 CT

3.7   Is it possible to deduce what cookie token addresses were involved in a certain payment by looking at the following spreadsheet?

From	To	CT
...	...	...
5f2613791b36f667fdb8 e95608b55e3df4c5f9eb	87e3d1692022a7744bf2 406a963c656c8393b1cc	10
...	...	...

What addresses?

3.8   Is it possible to deduce what public keys were involved in a certain payment by looking at just the spreadsheet?

3.9   Suppose everybody always used unique addresses for each payment. What information from the spreadsheet could Acme use to roughly identify the cafe's addresses?

3.10   Suppose there was a serious flaw in the public key derivation function, so anyone could calculate the private key from a public key. What prevents a bad guy from stealing your money in this scenario?

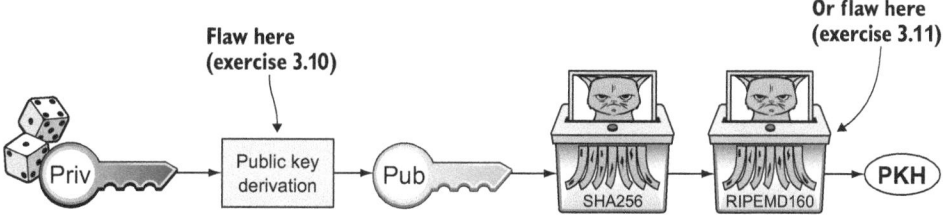

3.11   Suppose there was a serious flaw in RIPEMD160, so anyone could easily figure out a 256-bit pre-image of the PKH. This would mean it wasn't pre-image resistant. What prevents a bad guy from stealing your money in this scenario?

Summary

- Privacy is important for you, not just for criminals.

- Using PKHs instead of personal names as recipients for payments is important for privacy and more secure.

- Encoding a PKH as a Bitcoin address, or cookie token address, reduces the risk of sending money into the void, thanks to the checksum in the address.

- Only users care about Bitcoin addresses. The Bitcoin network, or Lisa, deals with plain PKHs.

- You can have as many Bitcoin addresses as you like. Using multiple addresses, preferably one per received payment, improves your privacy.

This chapter covers

- Automating payments

- Creating and managing keys

- Making simple, secure key backups

So far, we've done nothing to improve the user experience for the company's coworkers using the cookie token spreadsheet. The situation has become worse for users because emails to Lisa now need more information than in the beginning. On top of this, users should take extra steps to use multiple addresses to preserve their privacy.

In this chapter, we'll build a mobile app, called a *wallet* (figure 4.1), that handles many of the common tasks users want to perform. This wallet will create new addresses, store private keys, simplify how addresses are transferred between users, and automate the payment process.

We'll discuss different approaches to wallet backups. We'll also look at a new way to generate keys, called *hierarchical deterministic wallets* (HD wallets), so backups become dead simple; you only need to back up a

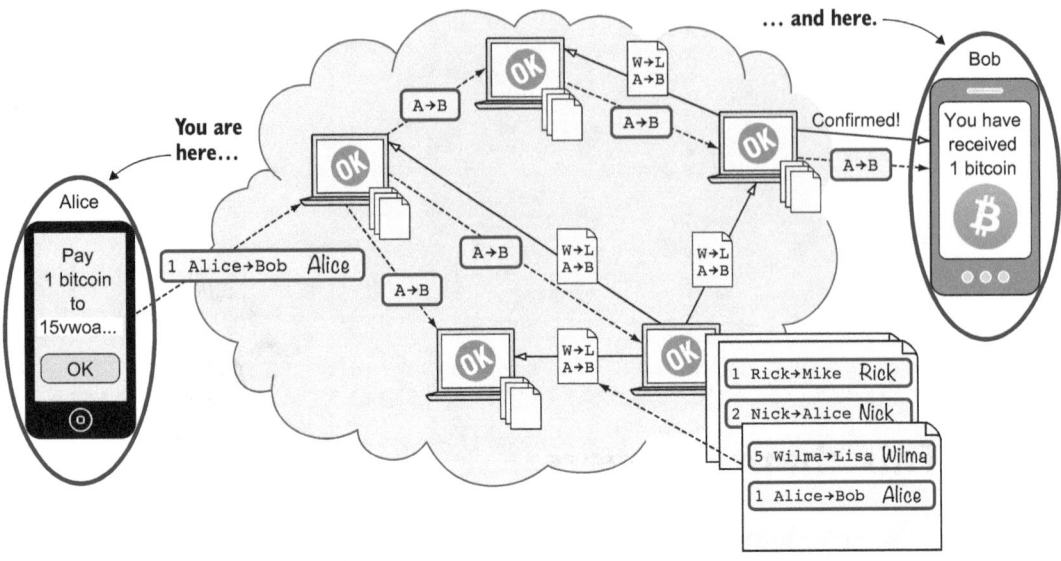

Figure 4.1   Using a Bitcoin wallet

single random number, called a *seed*, once and for all. We'll finish the chapter with an optional deep dive into the math behind public key derivation.

This chapter won't change anything regarding Lisa's work or the spreadsheet. We focus only on users here.

First wallet version

Among you and your coworkers, a group of software developers builds a mobile app called a *wallet* to simplify common tasks for themselves and other users. The group identifies the following tasks as the most common:

Bitcoin wallets

Several different wallets are available for Bitcoin. Some popular ones are
- Bitcoin Core
- Electrum
- GreenBits
- BRD (Bread)

See web resource 10 in appendix C for a comprehensive list.

- *Create new addresses*—Users must create new cookie token addresses every now and then. They might want to use different addresses for different purposes or even different addresses for all payments for privacy and security reasons.

- *Manage private keys*—For each address created, the wallet needs to store and manage the corresponding private key. Keeping private keys safe from intruders is a delicate task.

- *Transfer payment details from payee to payer*—When John wants to buy a cookie, he needs to get the cafe's address and the payment amount into his app. Writing it by hand is cumbersome and error-prone, so it would be nice if John could scan the details with his camera instead.

- *Make a payment*—The app should be able to send an email to Lisa with the digitally signed payment details.

- *Keep track of funds*—Users want to know how many cookies they can afford. The app should display the total number of cookie tokens a user has.

- *Back up private keys*—When private keys are created in the app, they only exist in the app. If the mobile phone is lost or broken, the private keys are gone. You know by now what happens when you lose your keys, don't you? You need a backup facility for private keys.

The development team builds an initial version of the app and calls it the wallet. The term *wallet* isn't perfect because the app doesn't really contain money. It contains the keys needed to spend money. The actual money is stored in the spreadsheet. The app is more akin to a physical keyring; but the term *wallet* is widely used in the Bitcoin world for all things that store private keys, so we should get over it and move on. Let's go through this wallet's features.

Suppose, once again, that John wants to buy a cookie in the cafe (figure 4.2). Both John and the cafe are using this new app.

The process goes through several steps:

QR codes

Quick response (QR) codes are a way to make text scan-able. This QR code says "Hello":

❶ The cafe asks its wallet to create a new address and request 10 CT to that address. This new address and the amount are displayed on the screen as a QR code. The QR code contains information on how much to pay, so John doesn't have to type that in manually.

❷ John points his phone's camera at the QR code to scan the payment details. It scans the *payment URI* (uniform resource identifier, a general specification on how to identify stuff; a web URL is an example of a URI):

```
ct:19UzNFW4Fq8wm8mtWmoPZAzE3tcB9tZVtN?amount=10
```

This tells John's phone to launch the cookie token wallet (`ct:`) and pay 10 (`amount=10`) cookie tokens to the address `19UzNFW4Fq8wm8mtWmoPZAzE3tcB9tZVtN`.

❸ John's wallet displays the payment details to John, who checks that they're reasonable and clicks OK.

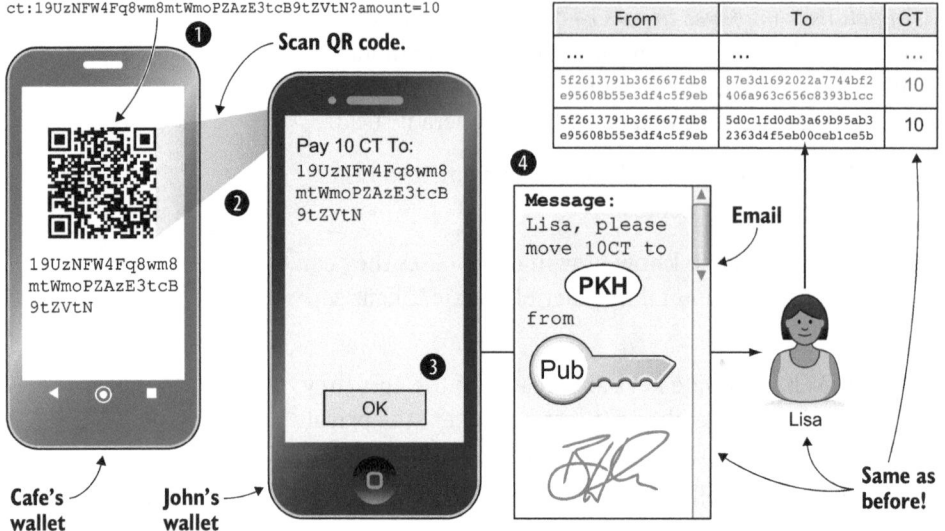

`ct:19UzNFW4Fq8wm8mtWmoPZAzE3tcB9tZVtN?amount=10`

❶

— **Scan QR code.**

❷

19UzNFW4Fq8wm8
mtWmoPZAzE3tcB
9tZVtN

Pay 10 CT To:
19UzNFW4Fq8wm8
mtWmoPZAzE3tcB
9tZVtN

❸

OK

Cafe's → **wallet**

John's → **wallet**

From	To	CT
...	...	...
5f2613791b36f667fdb8 e95608b55e3df4c5f9eb	87e3d1692022a7744bf2 406a963c656c8393b1cc	10
5f2613791b36f667fdb8 e95608b55e3df4c5f9eb	5d0c1fd0db3a69b95ab3 2363d4f5eb00ceb1ce5b	10

❹

Message:
Lisa, please
move 10CT to

(PKH)

from

(Pub)

Email

Lisa

Same as before!

Figure 4.2   John buys a cookie using the wallet app. The cafe generates a key and displays to John a QR code with payment details. John scans the payment details and taps OK to approve the payment. John's wallet sends an email to Lisa.

❹ John's wallet creates an email to Lisa that looks the same as before. The wallet automatically selects an address to send from and signs the message with the correct private key. On Lisa's side, nothing has changed. She verifies and executes the payment exactly as before.

Let's take a closer look at what John's wallet does in step 4 (figure 4.3). The wallet does the same thing a user would do manually in the earlier examples.

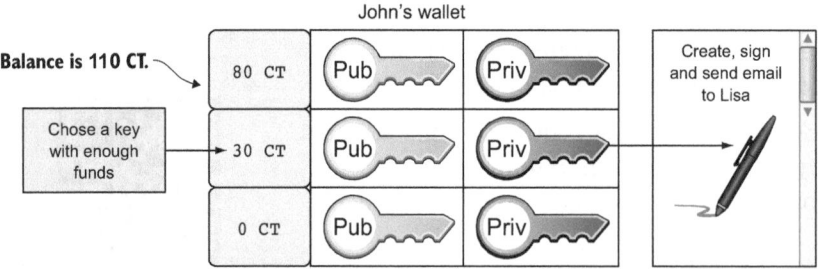

John's wallet

Balance is 110 CT.

Chose a key with enough funds

80 CT	Pub	Priv
30 CT	Pub	Priv
0 CT	Pub	Priv

Create, sign and send email to Lisa

Figure 4.3   John has just clicked OK in his wallet to approve the payment. The wallet takes care of the rest. It selects a key with enough funds and signs a message to Lisa. It then automatically emails the signed message to Lisa.

> **BIP21**
>
> BIPs (Bitcoin Improvement Proposals) are used to communicate ideas among developers. Some BIPs are adopted in Bitcoin software projects; others aren't. All BIPs are available at web resource 9 in appendix C.
>
> Bitcoin adopted BIP21 as a way to transfer payment details from one wallet to another using a URI. Bitcoin URIs start with `bitcoin:` instead of `ct:`.

Notice that the wallet manages three key pairs: two with funds and one with no funds. With this new wallet, users can have as many addresses as they want, which is good for privacy. The wallet will keep track of them for the user.

The cafe's wallet, as well as John's wallet, will check the spreadsheet every now and then to see if there are any new payments concerning any of the wallet's keys, as a sender, a recipient, or both (figure 4.4).

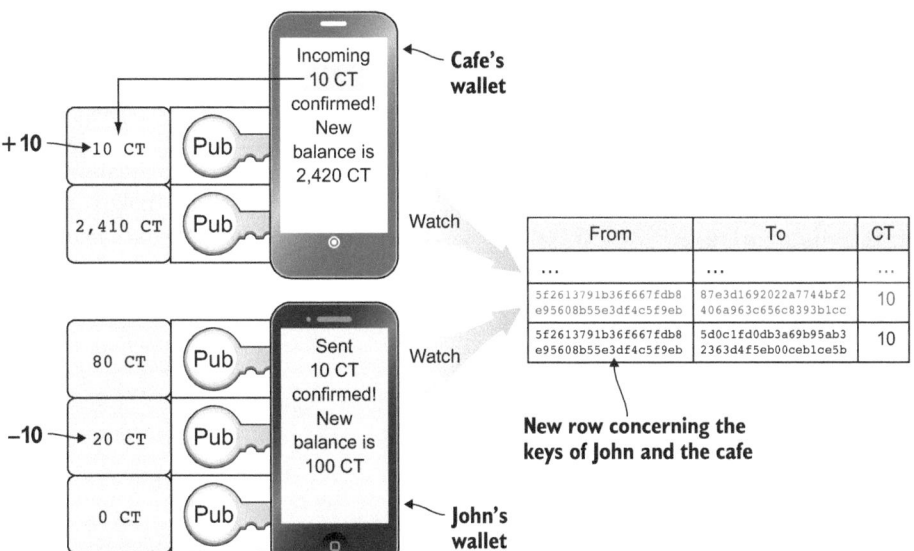

Figure 4.4 John's and the cafe's wallets check the spreadsheet every few seconds. If a new payment, either incoming or outgoing, is found, the wallet updates the balance of the concerned keys and notifies its user.

Even though John knows about the payment before Lisa confirms it in the spreadsheet, his wallet won't update the balance until it's confirmed. Why? Lisa might not approve the payment. Maybe the payment became corrupted during transfer, or the email ended up in Lisa's spam folder, so she doesn't see it.

If the wallet updates the balance without first seeing it in the spreadsheet, it could give false information to John. The wallet could, of course, be kind enough to inform John that a payment is pending confirmation.

Unconfirmed transactions

Unconfirmed means a transaction is created and sent to the Bitcoin network, but it isn't yet part of the Bitcoin blockchain. You shouldn't trust a payment until it's part of the blockchain. The same goes for cookie token payments—don't trust payments that aren't in the spreadsheet.

Private key backups

The development team creates a feature to back up the wallet's private keys. The idea is that the wallet creates a text file, the backup file, with all private keys in it and sends this file to an email address the user chooses.

Imagine that John wants to back up his private keys. The wallet collects all the keys it has ever created and writes them into a text file (figure 4.5).

Why back up?

Your keys hold your money. If you lose your keys, you lose your money. A proper backup is *not* optional. You must take immediate, active steps to make sure your keys are backed up; otherwise you will sooner or later lose your money.

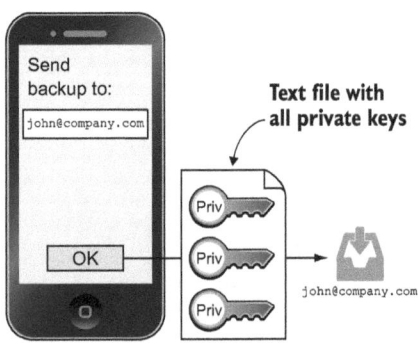

Figure 4.5   John backs up his private keys. They're sent in a text file to his email address.

The text file is emailed to John's email address. Can you see any problems with this? Yes, the biggest problem is that the keys have left the privacy of the wallet application and are being sent into the wild. Anyone with access to the email server or any other systems involved might be able to get the private keys without John noticing.

But another problem exists. As soon as John creates a new address after the backup is made, this new address isn't backed up. John must make a new backup that includes the new key. For every new key, he must make a new backup. Doing backups for every address becomes tiresome for the user.

Problems

- Risk of theft
- Excessive backups

Let's look at a few simple solutions to these two problems:

1. Automatically send a backup when an address is created. This increases the risk of theft because you send more backups.

2. Pre-create 100 addresses, and make a backup of them. Repeat when the first 100 addresses are used. This also increases the risk of theft, but not as much as solution 1.

3. Encrypt the backup with a password. This will secure the backed-up keys from theft.

A combination of solutions 2 and 3 seems like a good strategy; you seldom need to do a backup, and the backups are secured by a strong password.

The process is similar to the previous process, but this time John enters a password that's used to encrypt the private keys (figure 4.6). If John loses his phone, he needs the password and the backup file to restore his private keys.

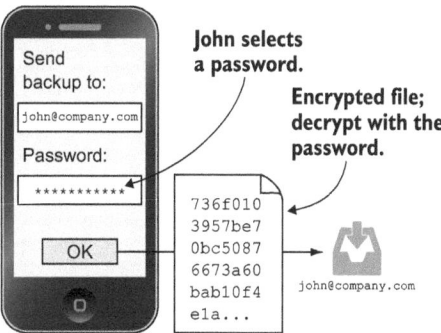

Figure 4.6   John backs up his private keys.
They're sent in a file encrypted with a password
that John enters into his phone.

If John loses his phone, he can easily install the wallet app on another phone. John sends the backup file to the app and enters his password; the keys are decrypted from the backup file and added to his wallet app.

A few words on password strength

A password's strength is measured in *entropy*. The higher the entropy, the harder it is to guess the password. The word *entropy*, as used in information security, comes from thermodynamics and means disorder or uncertainty. Suppose you construct a password of 8 characters from among the following 64 characters:

```
ABCDEFGHIJKLMNOPQRSTUVWXYZabcdefghijklmnopqrstuvwxyz0123456789+/
```

Each character in the password would then represent 6 bits of entropy because there are $64 = 2^6$ possible characters. If you select the 8 characters randomly (no cherry-picking, please!), say `E3NrkbA7`, the eight-character password will have $6 \times 8 = 48$ bits of entropy. This is equivalent in strength to 48 coin flips.

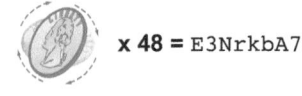

Suppose instead that you select random words from a dictionary of $2^{11} = 2{,}048$ words. How many words do you need to use to beat the 48-bit entropy of your eight-character password? Four words wouldn't be enough because $4 \times 11 = 44$ bits of entropy. But five words corresponds to 55 bits of entropy, which beats the password's entropy.

Flip coin–1 bit entropy

Random word from 2048-word dictionary–11 bits entropy

$2^{11} = 2{,}048$ words.

A password's real entropy also depends on what an attacker knows about the password. For example, suppose an attacker, Mallory, steals John's encrypted backup file and tries to perform a brute-force attack on it. A *brute-force* attack means the attacker makes repeated password guesses, over and over, until they find the correct password. If Mallory knows the password's length is exactly 8 and the characters are chosen from the 64 characters mentioned, the entropy is 48 bits. If she happens to know that the second character is `3`, the entropy drops to $6 \times 7 = 42$ bits. On the other hand, if Mallory doesn't know how many characters the password has, it will be harder for her, meaning the entropy will be higher.

11 flips = 1 word

This is true only if password selection is truly random. If John uses cherry-picking to select the password `j0Hn4321`, the entropy decreases dramatically. Typical password brute-force attack programs first try a lot of known words and names in different variations before trying more "random-looking" passwords. John is a well-known name, so an attacker will try a lot of different variations of that name as well as many other names and words. For example:

```
butter122 … waLk129 … go0die muh4mm@d
john John J0hn J0Hn J0HN j0hn j0Hn
j0hn j0Hn j0HN … john1 …
… john12 J0hn12 … j0Hn321 …
j0Hn4321
```

Bingo! Suppose there are 1,000,000 common words and names, and each word can come in 100,000 variations, on average. That's 100 billion different passwords to test, which corresponds to about 37 bits of entropy; 100 billion tries will take a high-end desktop computer a few days to perform. Let's say, for simplicity, that it takes one day. If John uses a truly random password, the entropy for the attacker is around 48 bits. It would take around 2,000 days, or about 5.5 years, to crack the password.

Problems with password-encrypted backups

The process for password-encrypted backups works pretty well, but it also introduces new problems:

- *More things to secure*—John now needs to keep track of two things: a backup file and a password. In the first version, only a backup file was needed.

- *Forgotten password*—Passwords that are rarely used, as is the case with backup passwords, will eventually be forgotten. You can write them down on paper and store them in a safe place to mitigate this issue. You can also store them using password-manager software, such as LastPass or KeePass.

- *Technology advancements*—As time passes, new, more advanced hardware and software is built that makes password cracking faster. If your eight-character password was safe five years ago, it's not good enough today. Passwords need more entropy as technology improves. You can re-encrypt your backup files every two years with a stronger password, but that's a complicated process that few users will manage.

- *Randomness is hard*—Coming up with random passwords is really hard. When the app asks John for a password, he needs to produce one on the spot. He doesn't have time to flip a coin 48 times to produce a good password. He will most likely make up something with far less entropy. One way to deal with this is to have the wallet give John a generated password. But this password is likely harder to remember than a self-invented password, which will increase the likelihood of a forgotten password.

It seems you haven't yet come up with a good way of dealing with backups. Let's not settle for this half-bad solution—there are better approaches.

Hierarchical deterministic wallets

One of the brighter developers at the company, a cryptographer, comes up with a new way to handle key creation to improve the backup situation and bring totally new features to wallets.

She realizes that if all private keys in a wallet were generated from a single random number called a *random seed*, the whole wallet could be backed up by writing down the seed on a piece of paper and storing it in a safe place (figure 4.7).

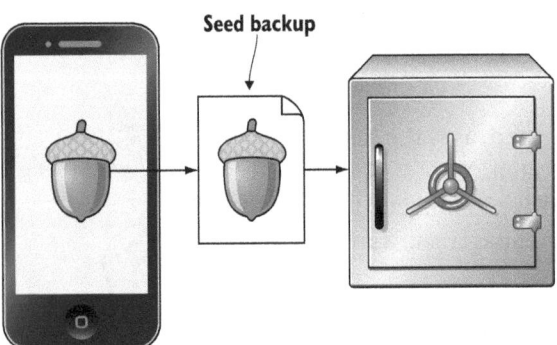

Figure 4.7   Backing up a seed. This is how you want to make backups.

She talks to some other cryptographers, and they decide on a strategy. They're going to make an HD wallet. Basically, keys are organized as a tree, in which one key is the root of the tree, and this root can have any number of child keys. Each child key can in turn have a large number of children of its own, and so on.

Suppose Rita wants to organize her keys based on their purpose and generate five keys to use for shopping at the cafe and another three keys to use as a savings account. Figure 4.8 shows how her keys could be organized.

The keys are organized as a tree, but it's a tree turned upside down because that's how computer geeks typically draw their trees. Anyway, the root key of the tree (at the top) is called the *master private key*. It's the key from which all the rest of the keys are derived. The master private key has two *child keys*: one that represents the shopping account (left, in figure 4.8) and one that represents the savings account (right). Each of these children has, in turn, its own children.

BIP32

This section describes a standard called BIP32, which is widely used by various Bitcoin wallet software. The BIPs are available online from web resource 9 in appendix C.

BIP44

BIP44, Multi-Account Hierarchy for Deterministic Wallets, describes which branches of the tree are used for which purposes. For now, let's use Rita's chosen key organization.

The shopping account key has five children, and the savings account key has three children. These eight children have no children of their own, which is why they're called *leaves* of the tree. The leaves are the private keys Rita uses to store cookie tokens, so an address is generated from each of these eight private keys.

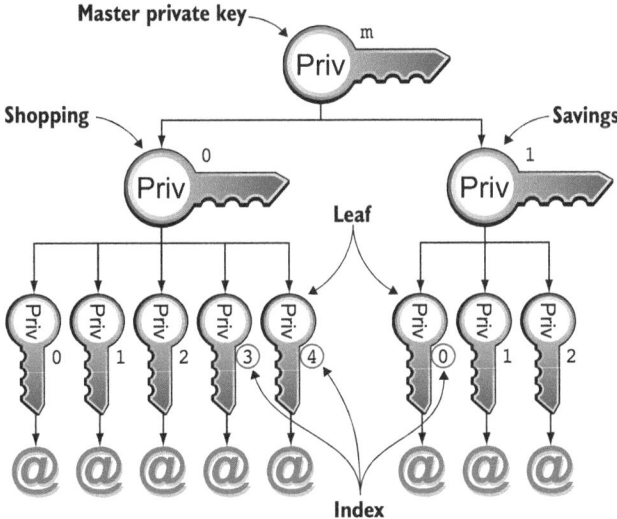

Figure 4.8 Rita creates two accounts, with five addresses in the shopping account and three addresses in the savings account.

Note how the keys in the tree are numbered. Each set of children is numbered from 0 upward. This gives each key a unique identifier. For example, the first savings key, *index* 0, is denoted m/1/0—m is special and refers to the master private key.

How is a tree structure like this accomplished? Let's look closer at the creation of some parts of the tree.

Three important processes are performed to create the tree, as figure 4.9 shows:

1. A random seed of 128 bits is generated. This seed is what the whole tree grows up (um, down) from.

2. The *master extended private key* is derived from the seed.

3. The descendant *extended private keys* of the master extended private key are derived.

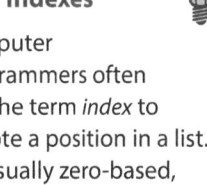

Indexes

Computer programmers often use the term *index* to denote a position in a list. It's usually zero-based, meaning the first item in the list has index 0, the second item has index 1, and so on. We'll use zero-based indexes throughout this book.

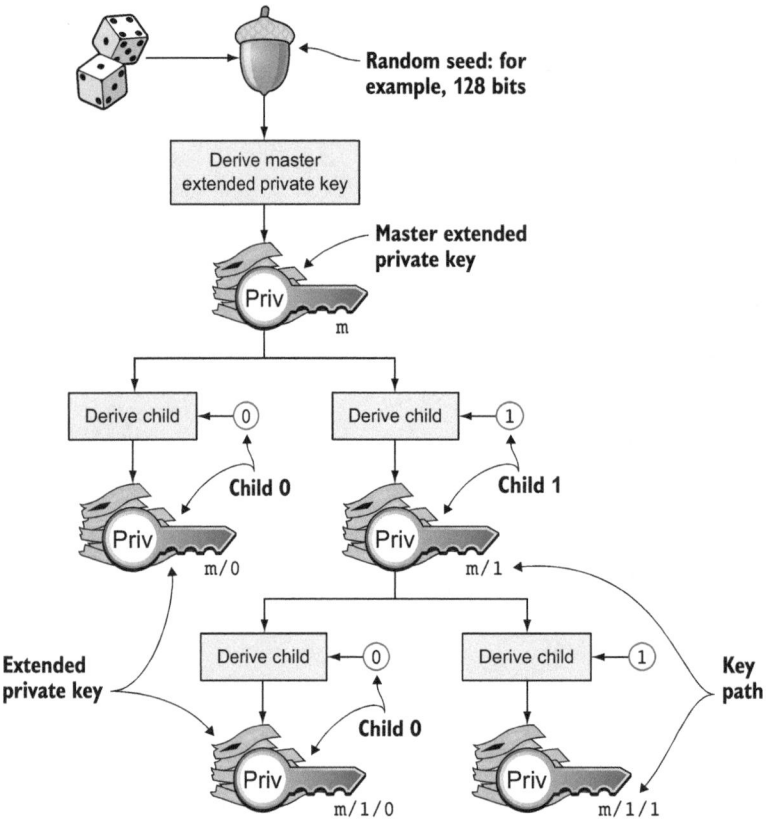

Figure 4.9 Creating the first two of Rita's three savings keys. A random seed is used to create a master extended private key, which is then used to create child extended private keys.

An *extended private key* (xprv) contains two items: a private key and a chain code (figure 4.10).

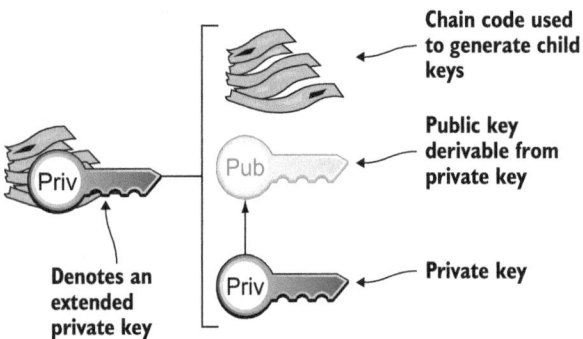

Figure 4.10 An xprv consists of a private key and a chain code.

The private key is indistinguishable from an old-type private key generated directly from a random number generator. You can use it to derive a public key and a cookie token address. You usually make addresses only out of leaves, but you could use internal keys as well. The other part of the xprv is the chain code. A chain code is the rightmost 256 bits of a 512-bit hash, hence the right-half hash icon in the figure. You'll see soon how that hash is created. The chain code's purpose is to provide entropy when generating a child xprv. The master xprv doesn't differ from other xprvs, but we give it a special name because it's the ancestor of all keys in the tree. It is, however, created differently.

In step 1, the random seed is created in the same way as when you created private keys in chapter 2. In this example, you generate 128 bits of random data, but it could just as well be 256 bits depending on the level of security you want—128 bits are enough for most users. You'll see later how the choice of seed size will affect the backup process; a longer seed means more writing on a piece of paper during backup. We'll get back to this in "Back to backup."

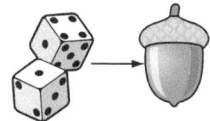

Steps 2 and 3 deserve their own subsections.

Deriving a master extended private key

Let's look deeper into how to generate the master xprv (figure 4.11).

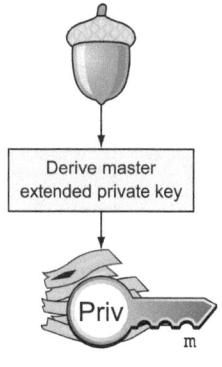

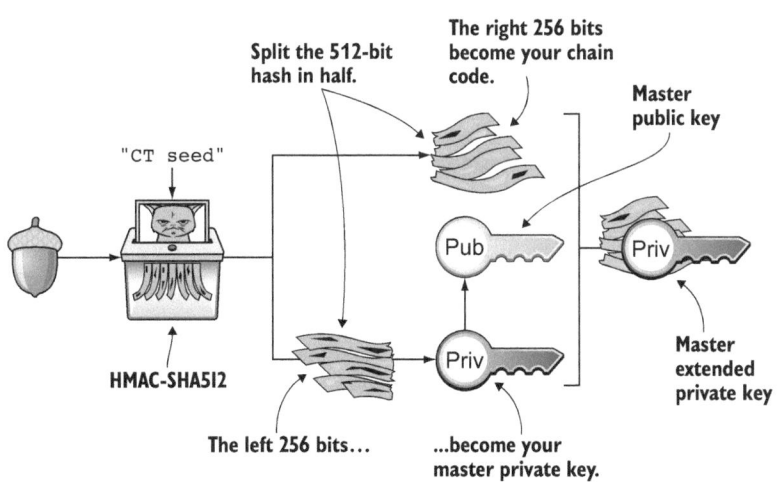

Figure 4.11 Deriving Rita's master xprv. The seed is hashed with HMAC-SHA512. The resulting hash of 512 bits is split into the left 256 bits, which become the master private key, and the right 256 bits, which become the chain code.

To create the master private key, the seed is hashed using HMAC-SHA512 (HMAC is short for Hash Based Message Authentication Code), which produces a 512-bit hash value. HMAC-SHA512 is a special cryptographic hash function that, besides the normal single input, also takes a key. From a user's perspective, you can regard HMAC-SHA512 as a normal cryptographic hash function but with multiple inputs. The hash value is split into the left 256 bits and the right 256 bits. The left 256 bits become the master private key, which is a normal private key; it's called the *master* private key because all other private keys are derived from this single private key (and the chain code). The right 256 bits become the *chain code*, used in the next step to derive children from the master xprv.

Deriving a child extended private key

You just created Rita's master xprv. It's time to derive the child xprv that groups together her three savings keys. The direct children of an xprv can be derived in any order. Let's derive the savings account key, m/1, first. The process for deriving a child xprv from a parent xprv is as follows (figure 4.12):

"CT seed"?

An HMAC needs two inputs: a value to hash and a key. You don't have or need a key for the master xprv because you have all the entropy you need in the seed. In figure 4.11, you input `CT seed` to give the HMAC *something*. A key is needed later, when you derive children of the master xprv.

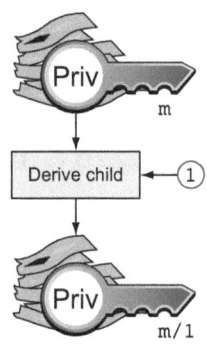

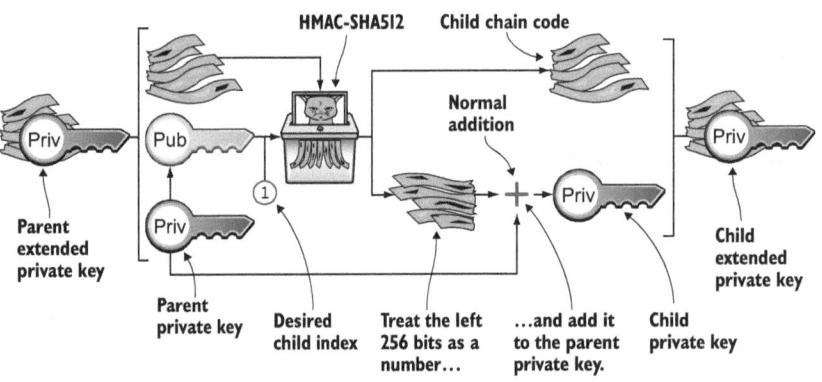

Figure 4.12 Deriving a child xprv from a parent xprv. The parent's public key and chain code and the desired index are hashed together. The parent private key is added to the left half of the hash, and the sum becomes the child private key. The right half becomes the child chain code.

1. The desired index is appended to the parent public key.

2. The public key and index become the input to HMAC-SHA512. The parent chain code acts as a source of entropy to the hash function. To simplify, think of it as three pieces of data are hashed together.

3. The 512-bit hash value is split in half:

   - The left 256 bits are added, with normal addition (modulo 2^{256}), to the parent private key. The sum becomes the child private key.

   - The right 256 bits become the child chain code.

4. The child private key and the child chain code together form the child xprv.

This same process is used for all children and grandchildren of the master xprv until you have all the keys Rita wanted in her wallet.

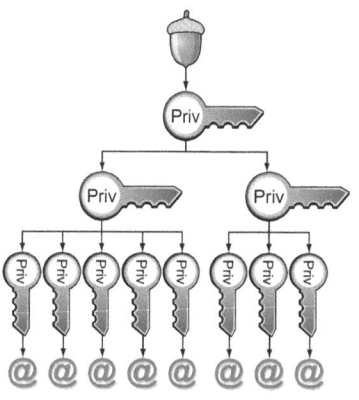

You might be wondering why you need the addition—why not use the left 256 bits as the child private key? The 512-bit hash is calculated from the public key and the chain code—collectively called the *extended public key* (xpub)—and an index. You'll see later how to use the xpub in less secure environments, such as a web server, to generate a corresponding tree of *public* keys. You need to add the parent private key to the left 256 bits to make it impossible for someone with the xpub to generate child private keys.

Where were we?

Let's recall why you're here: to create a wallet app that makes life easier for end users (figure 4.13).

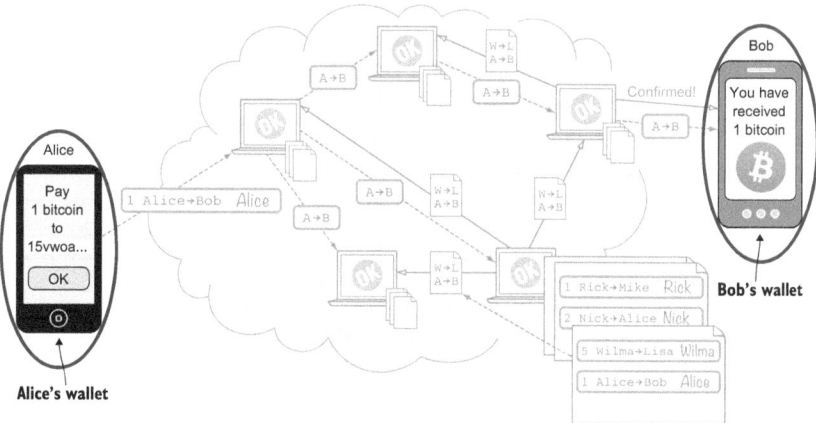

Figure 4.13 You're working on making a great wallet for users.

The main duties of a wallet are to

- Manage private keys
- Create new addresses
- Transfer payment details from payee to payer
- Make a payment
- Keep track of funds
- Back up private keys

We've covered the first five items, but we aren't quite finished with backups. We just looked at xprv derivation, which is the groundwork for better backups.

Back to backup

You want a safe, easy way to back up private keys. You've created an HD wallet to generate any number of private keys from a single seed. What's the minimum Rita needs to back up to restore all keys in her wallet, should she lose it? Right: the seed (and the tree structure, see margin). As long as her seed is safe, she can always re-create all her keys.

Suppose Rita's 128-bit (16-byte) seed is

```
16432a207785ec5c4e5a226e3bde819d
```

It's a lot easier to write these 32-hex digits on a piece of paper than it would be to write her eight private keys. But the biggest win is that Rita can write this down once and lock it in a safe. As long as that paper is safe, her wallet is safe from accidental loss. She can even create new keys from the same seed without having to make another backup.

But it's still difficult to write this down without any typos. What if Rita makes a typo and then loses her wallet? She won't be able to restore any of her keys! You need something even simpler that's more compatible with how humans work.

But the key paths?

To restore keys, you also need their paths. In Bitcoin, those paths are standardized in BIP44. If a wallet uses that standard, you implicitly know the keys' paths.

Backup

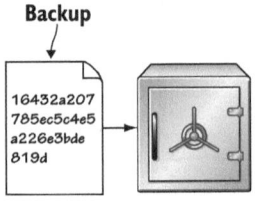

16432a207 785ec5c4e5 a226e3bde 819d

Mnemonic sentences

Recall that the seed is a sequence of bits. For example, Rita's seed is 128 bits long. What if you could encode those bits in a more human-friendly way? You can!

Rita's wallet used a random number generator to create a seed in the most straight-forward way possible. But if it had been done it in a slightly different way, it could display her seed as a sequence of 12 English words, called a *mnemonic sentence*:

Mnemonic: `bind bone marine upper gain comfort`
`defense dust hotel ten parrot depend`

BIP39

Most Bitcoin wallets use mnemonic sentences for backup. This is standardized in BIP39. Before that, wallets typically used password-protected files with all keys, which caused a lot of headache.

This mnemonic sentence presents the seed in a human-readable way. It's much more approachable to write down 12 words than it is to write down cryptic hex code. If Rita loses her wallet, she can install the wallet app on another phone and restore the seed from those 12 words. Rita can regenerate all her private keys from that seed.

This is a three-step process as shown in figure 4.14.

Backup

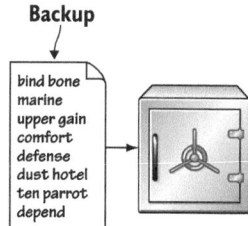

bind bone marine upper gain comfort defense dust hotel ten parrot depend

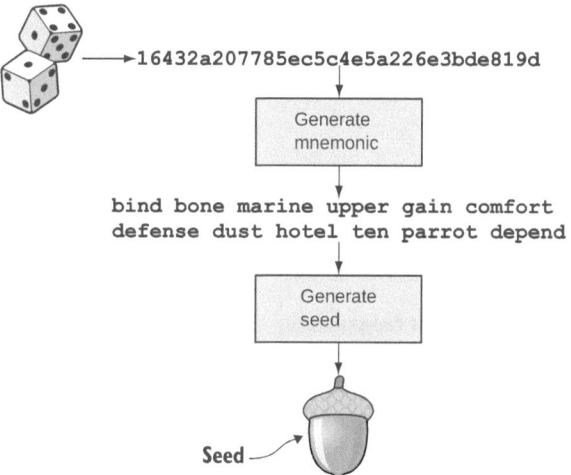

Figure 4.14   The three steps involved to create a seed from a random number generator.

First, a random number is generated. Second, the mnemonic sentence, that can be used for backup, is generated from the random number. In the last and third step, you generate a seed from the mnemonic sentence. The last two steps are discussed more in detail in the next two subsections.

Generating a mnemonic sentence

WARNING!

We're going to explore how the mnemonic sentence and seed generation works. It's really fun, but if you think this section goes too deep, you can accept the previous section and skip to to the section "Extended public keys."

The encoding starts with the random number, as shown in figure 4.15. The random number is hashed with SHA256, and the first 4 bits of the hash—in this case, 0111—are appended to the random number. Those 4 bits act as a checksum. You then arrange the bits into 12 groups of 11 bits, where each group encodes a number in the range 0 to 2047. Eleven bits can encode $2^{11} = 2{,}048$ different values, remember?

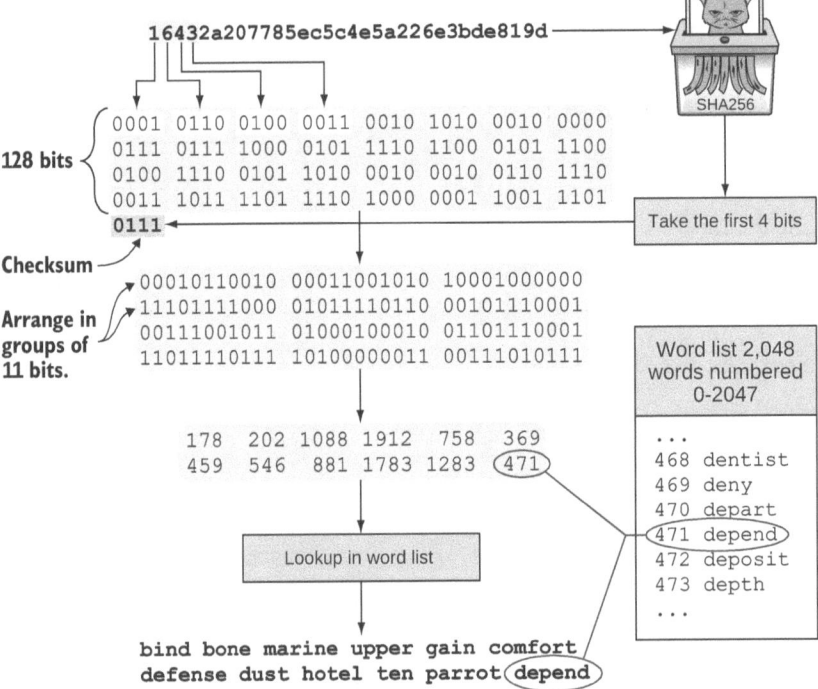

Figure 4.15   Generating a 12-word mnemonic sentence from a random number. The random number is checksummed, and every group of 11 bits is looked up in a word list of 2,048 words.

The 12 numbers are looked up in a standardized word list of 2,048 words numbered from 0 to 2047. You can find this list in BIP39 from web resource 9 in appendix C; it contains commonly used

English words. After looking up all 12 numbers, the result is the mnemonic sentence.

The sentence doesn't mean anything in particular. It's 12 random words, just like the hex-encoded seed is 32 random hex digits.

Rita's wallet shows the mnemonic sentence to her, and she writes the 12 words down on a piece of paper. She puts the paper in a safe place and gets on with her life.

Generating a seed from a mnemonic sentence

Rita's wallet doesn't stop there. It has yet to generate a seed that it can use to generate addresses for Rita. The wallet will generate the seed in many steps (figure 4.16).

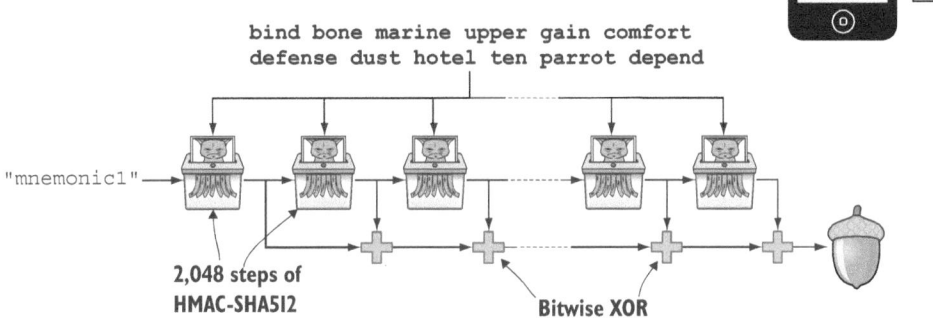

Figure 4.16 A seed is generated from a mnemonic phrase in 2,048 steps.

The mnemonic sentence is used as the main input for each of the 2,048 HMAC-SHA512 functions. This is the same function as we used in the "Deriving a master extended private key" section to generate a master xprv from the seed. The other input, which is called the key, is mnemonic1 in the first, leftmost, function. For subsequent functions the key input is the output of the previous function.

The output from each function is added using bitwise XOR (exclusive or) to form the final result, which is our 512 bit seed. In bitwise XOR, two numbers are compared bit by bit, and if the bits are equal the resulting bit is 0, otherwise 1. This seed is then used to generate a master xprv as described in the "Deriving a master extended private key" section.

You're probably wondering why the seed generation uses 2,048 steps of HMAC-SHA512. This process is called *PBKDF2* (Password-Based Key Derivation Function 2), which is a standardized way to achieve so-called key stretching. Key stretching makes brute-force attacking the mnemonic sentence harder because each try becomes slower due to the many steps involved.

The next day, Rita drops her phone into the ocean, and it disappears into the deep. She lost her wallet! But Rita isn't very concerned. She buys a new phone and installs the wallet app. She instructs her app to restore from a backup. The wallet asks her for her mnemonic sentence. She writes

```
bind bone marine upper gain comfort
defense dust hotel ten parrot depend
```

into the wallet app. The app uses the 4-bit checksum discussed in the previous section to make sure it's correct. It does that by running the mnemonic sentence generation backwards as figure 4.17 illustrates.

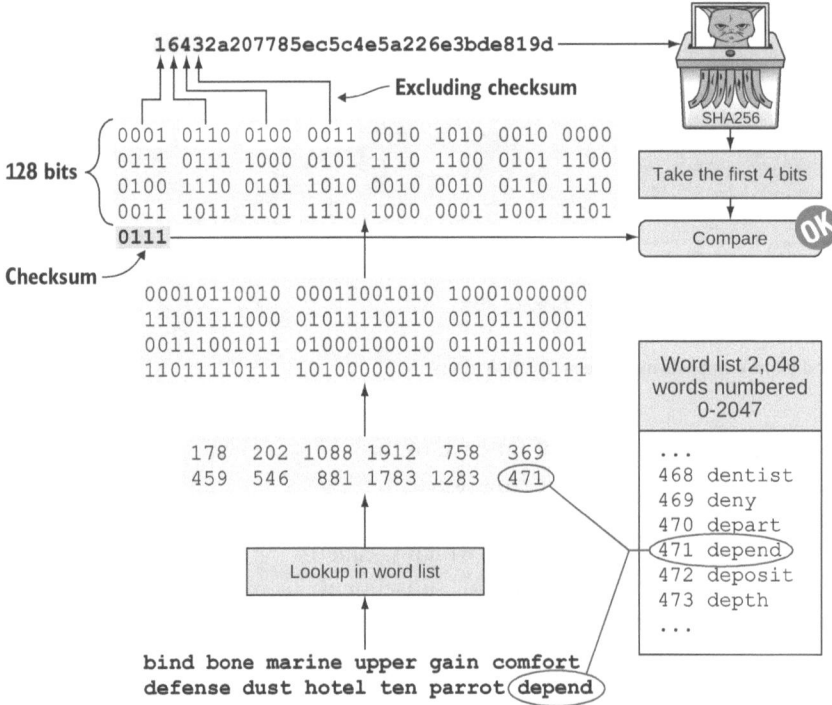

Figure 4.17   Verifying the checksum of a mnemonic sentence

If Rita accidentally writes the last word as deposit instead of depend, the checksum check will probably fail because she wrote the wrong word at the end. If she types depends instead of depend, the decoding will definitely fail because there's no word depends in the word list.

The checksum is pretty weak—4 bits make only 16 possible checksums. A wrongly written mnemonic sentence, in which all words exist in the word list, would have a 1/16 probability of not being detected. This seems bad. But the probability that you'd write such a sentence is small, because your misspelled words have to exist in the word list. This reduces the risk of an invalid mnemonic sentence being restored.

After the checksum has been verified, the app regenerates the seed as shown in figure 4.16 and all of Rita's private keys can be restored from that seed.

Extended public keys

Rita created her wallet from a random 128-bit seed, which she backed up with a 12-word mnemonic sentence. Her wallet can create any number of private keys from that seed. She can organize them into different "accounts" as she pleases. Very nice. But HD wallets have another feature: you can create a tree of public keys and chain codes without knowing any of the private keys.

Suppose the cafe uses an HD wallet. It wants to start selling cookies on its website and delivering those cookies to coworkers' cubicles.

For privacy reasons, the web server needs to be able to present a new cookie token address for every sale, but where does it get the addresses? The cafe could create an xprv for an *online sales* account in its HD wallet and put that xprv on the web server, as figure 4.18 shows.

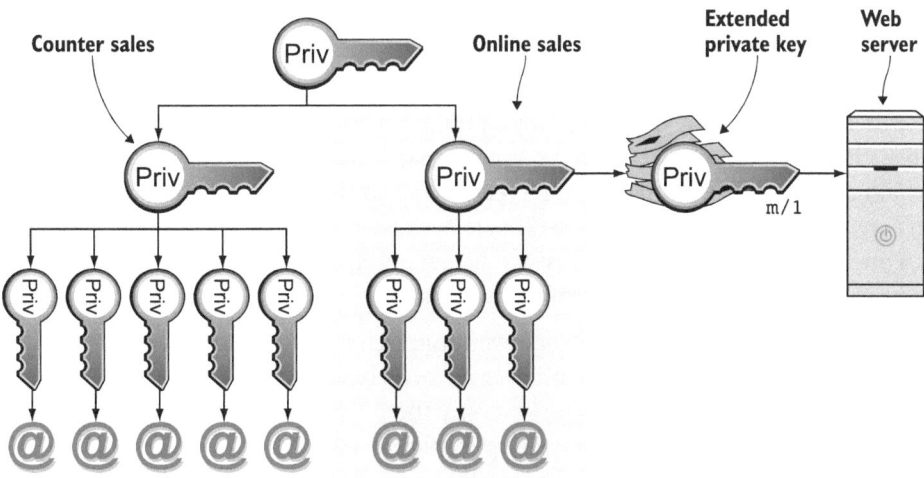

Figure 4.18   The cafe copies its online sales xprv to the web server.

The web server can now create new addresses as the orders pour in. Great! But what if Mallory, the gangster, gains access to the web server's hard drive? She can steal all the money in any of the addresses in the online sales account. She can't steal from any other addresses in the tree. For example, she can't calculate any key in the *counter sales* account because she doesn't have access to the master xprv, which is needed to calculate the counter sales account key and all its children.

Typical web servers are prone to hacking attempts because they're usually accessible from anywhere in the world. Storing money on the web server would probably attract a lot of hacking attempts. Sooner or later, someone would succeed in getting access to the web server's hard drive, and steal the xprv.

For this reason, the cafe wants to avoid having any private keys on the web server. Thanks to the HD wallet, this is possible by using xpubs (figure 4.19).

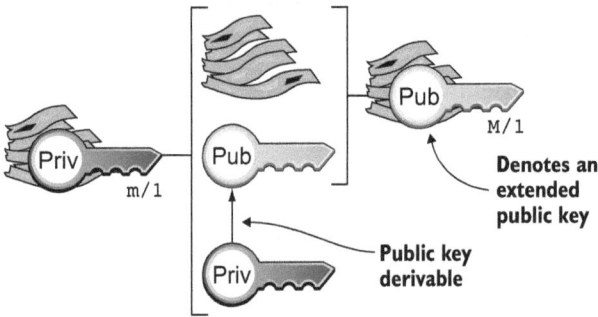

Figure 4.19   An xpub consists of a public key and a chain code.

An xpub is similar to an xprv, but the xpub contains a public key and a chain code, whereas the xprv contains a private key and a chain code. An xprv shares the chain code with the xpub. You can create an xpub from an xprv, but you can't create the xprv from the xpub. This is because public key derivation is a one-way function; a public key can be derived from a private key, but a private key can't be derived from a public key.

The cafe puts the xpub M/1 on the web server. By convention, we use M to denote an xpub path and m to denote an xprv path. M/1 and m/1 have the same chain code, but M/1 doesn't have the private key, only the public key. You can create the whole xpub tree from the master xpub (figure 4.20), which means you can generate any and all addresses without any private key. You can create addresses, but not spend money from those addresses.

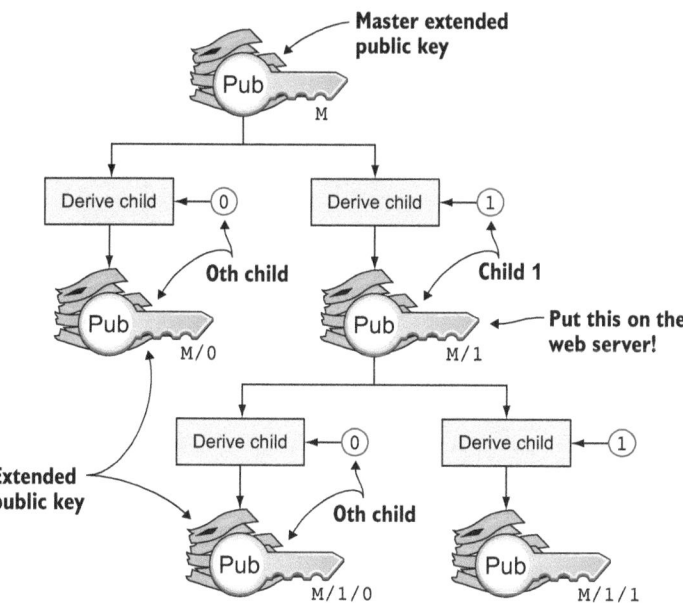

Figure 4.20 Generating the tree of xpubs from the master xpub.
The general pattern is the same as when generating xprvs,
but the child-derivation function differs.

This looks exactly like when you generated the tree of xprvs. The difference is that you have no private keys. As figure 4.21 shows, the xpubs are generated differently than the xprvs. Please compare this to the xprv derivation.

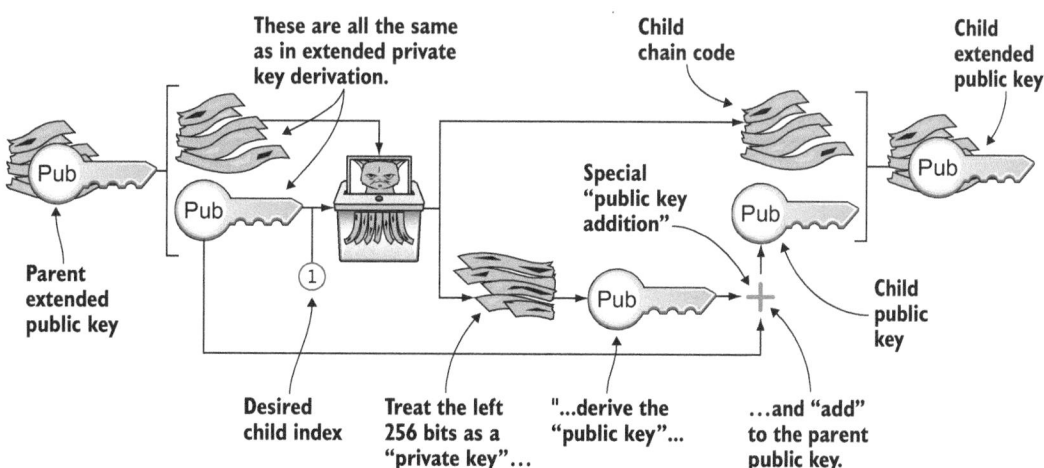

Figure 4.21 Xpub derivation. The private key addition from the xprv derivation is
replaced by public key "addition."

This resembles xprv derivation. The difference is what you do with the left 256 bits of the 512-bit hash. To calculate the child public key, you treat the left 256 bits as if they were a private key and derive a public key from them. This public key is then added to the parent public key using the special *public key addition* operation. The result is the child public key. Let's compare the child public key derivation to the child private key derivation (figure 4.22) from the point after generating the left 256 bits of the HMAC-SHA256 hash.

xprv derivation

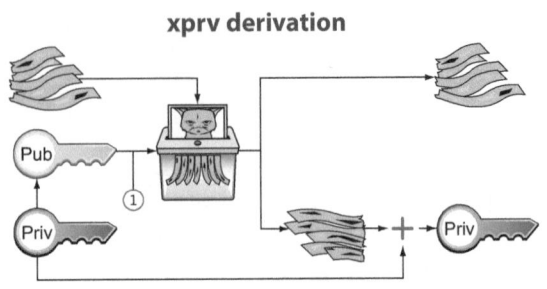

The left 256 bits of the hash are used for both private and public child key derivation.

Normal addition

Public key derived from the left-half hash

Special "public key addition"

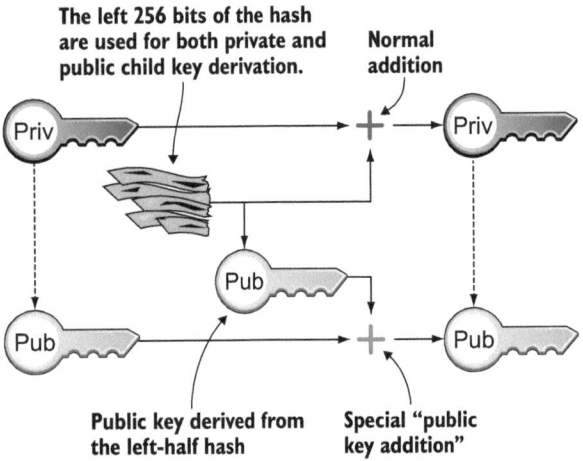

Figure 4.22　The plus on the private side has a corresponding plus on the public side. The parent private key plus some value is the child private key. The parent public key plus the public key derived from the same value is the child public key.

Normal addition is used for the private key. You add a 256-bit number to the parent private key to get the child private key. But to keep the result within 256-bit numbers, you use addition *modulo 2^{256}*.

The addition used to derive the child public key isn't exactly what most people (including me) are used to. For now, let's just say this addition works. We'll dig deeper into that in the "Public key math" section.

Deriving hardened private keys

This section will explain how to prevent a potential security issue with normal xprv derivation.

The cafe's online business works well. People are ordering cookies like crazy! The online sales account grows, with a new public key for every order. The xpub for the online sales account sits on the web server, and the xprv is present only in the cafe's wallet (and in a locked-away mnemonic sentence).

Suppose Mallory somehow steals the private key m/1/1, which contains only 10 CT. This might seem harmless because that private key has so little money in it. But it could be worse than that. If Mallory has also managed to get the xpub for the online sales account from the web server, she can *calculate the online sales xprv*, as figure 4.23 shows.

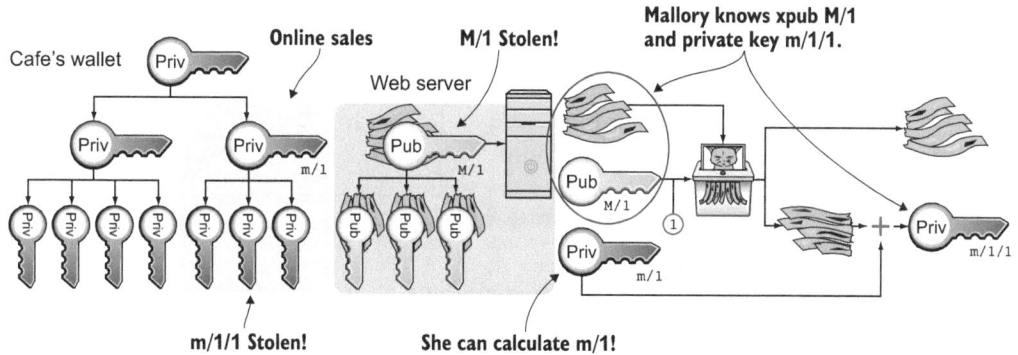

Figure 4.23 Mallory has stolen the private key m/1/1 from the cafe and the parent xpub from the web server. She can now steal all the money in the online sales account.

Remember how the xprv derivation function used normal addition to calculate a child private key from a parent private key?

m/1 + left half hash of index 1 = m/1/1

You can write this just as well as

m/1/1 − left half hash of index 1 = m/1

Mallory has everything she needs to calculate the left-half hash for any child index of M/1 she pleases, but she doesn't know which index her stolen private key has, so she starts testing with index 0:

m/1/1 − left half hash of index 0 = a private key

She derives the public key from this private key and notices that it doesn't match M/1, so 0 wasn't the correct index. She then tries index 1:

m/1/1 − left half hash of index 1 = another private key

This private key derives to the public key M/1. Bingo! She has calculated the private key m/1 for the online sales account. The xprv shares the chain code with the xpub, so she also has the xprv for m/1, and she can calculate the private key tree for the account. Mallory steals all the money from the online sales account. Not good.

Now think about what would happen if Mallory had the master xpub. She could use the same technique to derive the master xprv from the master xpub and m/1/1. Mallory can re-create all the private keys of all accounts in the entire wallet. Can you do something to prevent such a catastrophic scenario? Yes, with *yet another key-derivation function*! This new key-derivation function is called *hardened xprv derivation*.

Normal child xprv derivation

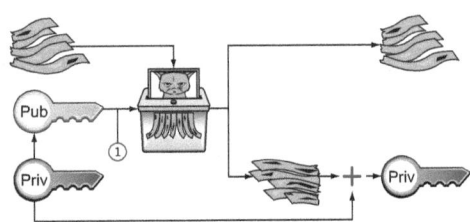

Suppose the cafe wants to prevent Mallory from accessing the master xprv, even if she got the master xpub and a private key in the online sales account. The cafe can generate the xprv for the online sales account using hardened xprv derivation, as figure 4.24 shows.

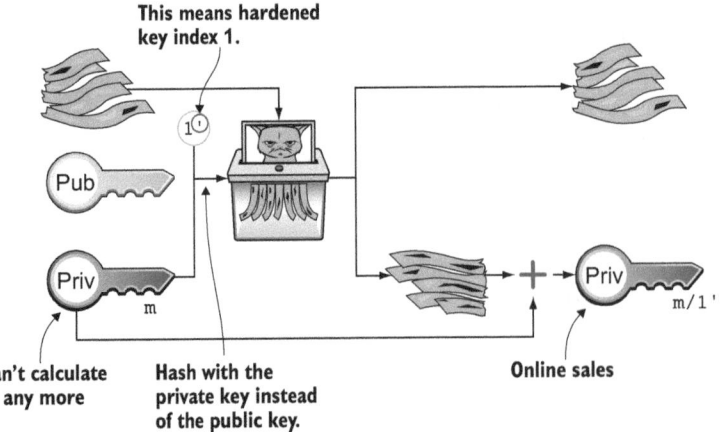

Figure 4.24 Deriving a hardened child xprv for the online sales account. You use the parent private key as input to the hash function instead of the public key.

The apostrophe in m/1' isn't a typo: it's used to denote hardened key derivation. The difference is that with hardened key derivation, you hash the *private* key instead of the public key. An attacker can't do the "minus" trick anymore because the hash is derived from the parent private key. Mallory can't calculate the left-half hash to subtract from the child private key because she doesn't have the parent private key. Figure 4.25 illustrates the result.

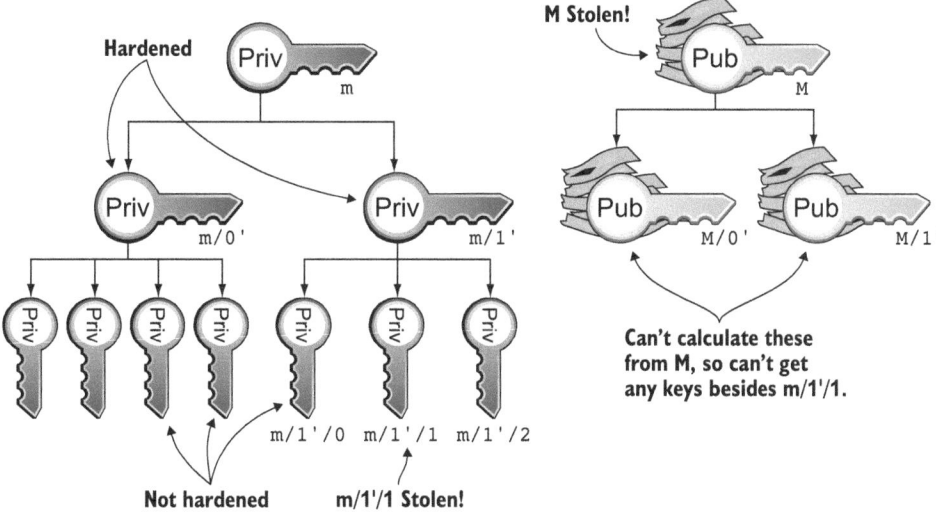

Figure 4.25   The master xpub can't be used to generate any child keys because m/0' and m/1' are hardened keys.

This also means you can't derive a hardened child xpub from a parent xpub. You must have the parent xprv to generate any children, public or private. The children of m/1' can't be derived as hardened private keys because that would require the cafe to put the private key m/1' on the online sales web server, which would be insecure. Using nonhardened leaf keys in the online sales account makes the cafe vulnerable to an attacker stealing m/1'/1 and M/1'. If that happens, all funds in the account will be stolen. With hardened xprv, you solve the case of a stolen M and m/1'/1 but not the case with a stolen M/1' and m/1'/1.

Public key math

This section digs deeper into the math behind public keys. We'll start by looking at how a public key is derived from a private key using *public key multiplication*. Later subsections will show why child xpub derivation, using *public key addition*, works, and how public keys are encoded in Bitcoin.

Public key multiplication

WARNING!

I'll try to explain this topic in simple terms, but if you think it's too much, you can skip this section and jump to "Recap."

Think back to when you derived a public key from a private key in chapter 2. I didn't really tell you *how* the public key was derived. I'll make an attempt here instead.

A public key in Bitcoin is a whole-number solution to this equation:

$$y^2 = x^3 + 7 \bmod (2^{256} - 4294968273)$$

Many such solutions exist, about 2^{256} of them, so let's simplify by using the solutions to $y^2 = x^3 + 7 \bmod 11$ instead (figure 4.26).

Normal public key derivation

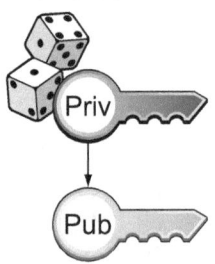

Bitcoin uses this curve

This specific elliptic curve is called *secp256k1* and is used in Bitcoin. Plenty of other curves have similar properties.

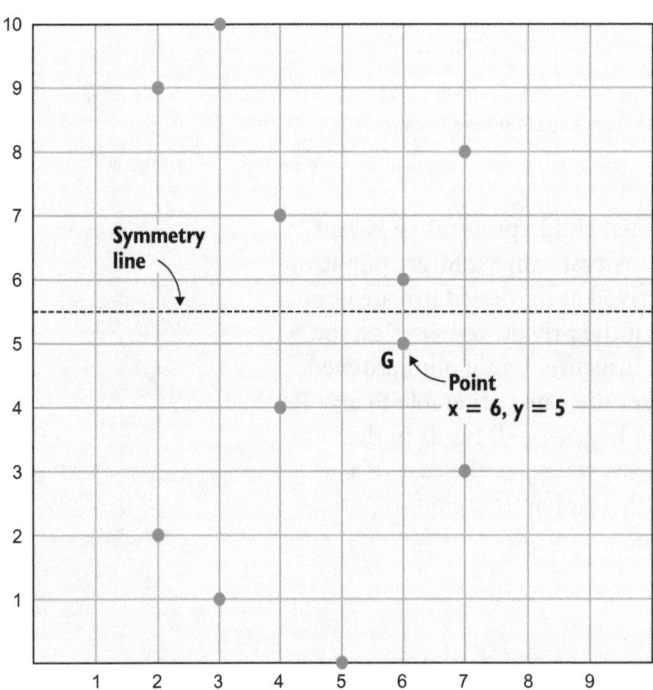

Figure 4.26 Whole-number solutions to the elliptic curve $y^2 = x^3 + 7$ mod 11. Each such solution is a public key.

The previous equations are examples of a class of equations called *elliptic curves*, and a solution is often referred to as a *point on the curve*. You can now calculate a public key, which is a point on the curve, from a private key. To do this, start at a special point, $G = (6,5)$, on the curve. G is somewhat arbitrarily chosen, but it's widely known by everybody to be the starting point for public key derivation. *The public key is the private key multiplied by G.*

Suppose your private key is 5. Then your public key is 5G.

To calculate this multiplication, you need two basic public key operations: addition and doubling, where doubling can be seen as adding a point to itself.

To add two points (figure 4.27), you draw a straight line that "wraps around" the edges of the diagram and that intersects your two points and one third point. This third point is the negative result of the addition. To get the final result of the addition, take the symmetric point at the same x value.

Curve? I see only dots.

It's called a *curve* because in the continuous, real-number world, the solutions form a curve like this:

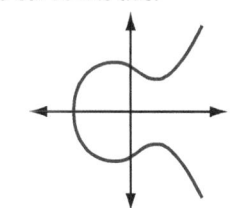

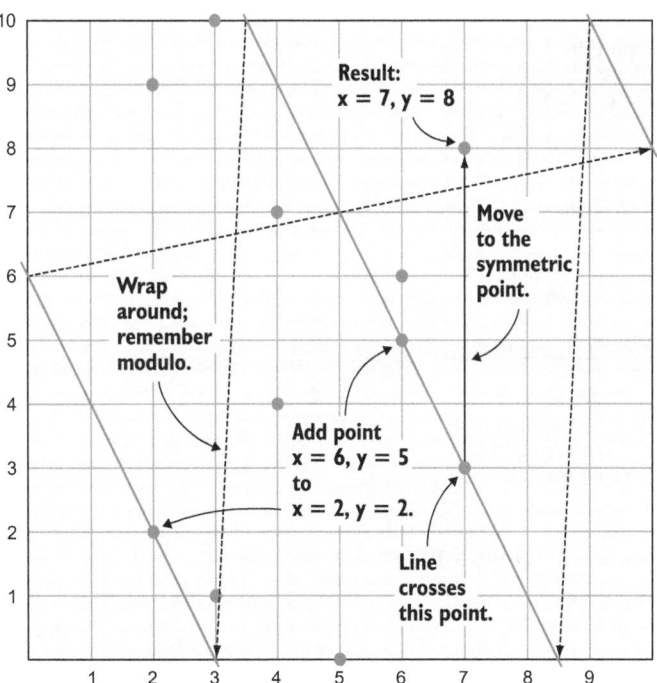

Figure 4.27 Point addition. You add $(x, y) = (6, 5)$ to $(2, 2)$ by drawing a straight line through them that will intersect a third point.

The result of (6, 5) + (2, 2) is (7, 8). The straight line between the two points crosses the point (7, 3). The complement point to (7, 3) is (7, 8), which is the result of the addition.

To double a point (figure 4.28) is to add it to itself, but there's no slope to be calculated from a single point. In this special case, you calculate the slope from the single point $P = (6,5)$ as $3 \times x^2 \times (2y)^{-1} \bmod 11 = 2$. The process is almost the same as adding two different points, but you calculate the slope of the line differently.

Is there always a third point?

Yes, there's always a line that intersects a third point. It's one of the curve's important properties.

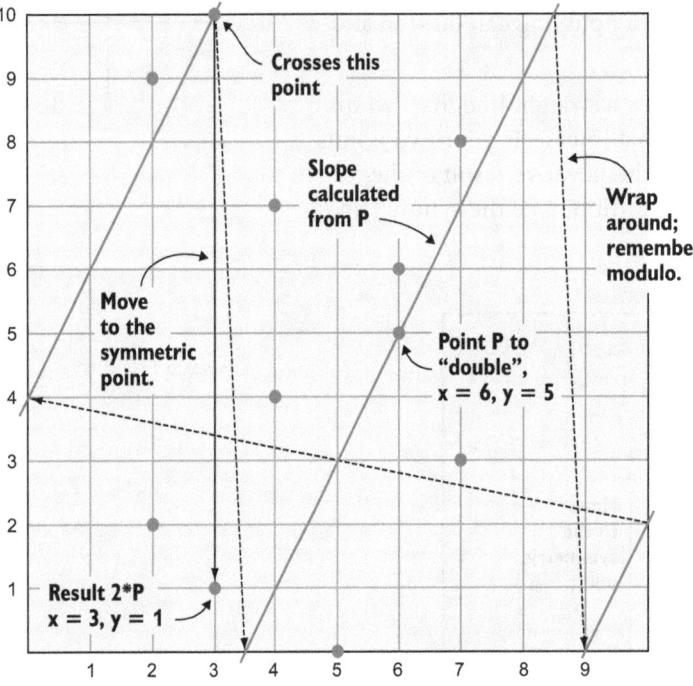

Figure 4.28   Point doubling. To double a point P, draw a line through P with a special slope that's calculated from P. The line crosses another point, (3,10). The complement point (3, 1) is the doubling result.

Using these two basic operations, adding and doubling, you can derive the multiplication of 5 and G. In binary form, 5 is

$$101_{binary} = 1 \times 2^2 + 0 \times 2^1 + 1 \times 2^0$$

Your public key is then

$$5G = 1 \times 2^2 \times G + 0 \times 2^1 \times G + 1 \times 2^0 \times G$$

Start in G and calculate the resulting public key point by taking terms from right to left:

1. Calculate $2^0 \times G = 1 \times G = G$. Easy. Now remember this point.

2. Calculate $2^1 \times G = 2 \times G$. This is a point doubling of the previously remembered point G from step 1. Remember the point. Because there is a 0 in front of $2^1 \times G$, you don't do anything with it—just remember it.

3. Calculate $2^2 \times G = 2 \times 2 \times G$, which is a doubling of the previously remembered point $2 \times G$. Because there is a 1 in front of the $2^2 \times G$ term, you add this result to the result of step 1.

In short, multiplication is performed by a sequence of adding and doubling operations.

Elliptic curve calculator

There's a nice elliptic curve calculator at web resource 11 in appendix C that you can play with to get a better feel for how this works.

Why is this secure?

The multiplication process is pretty easy to complete; it takes about 256 steps for a 256-bit private key. But to reverse this process is a totally different story. No known way exists to get the private key by point "division" (for example, point (6,6) "divided by" G). The only known way is to try different private keys and see if the public key is what you're looking for. This is what makes public-key derivation a one-way function.

Xpub derivation

You've seen how an ordinary public key is derived from a private key through public-key multiplication. But how can adding the parent public key with the public key derived from the left 256 bits make the child public key? See figure 4.29.

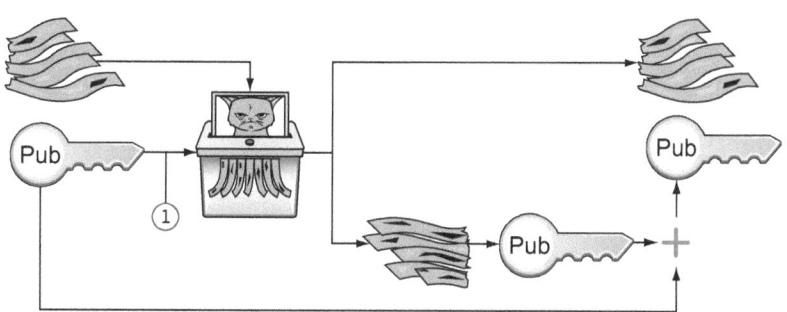

Figure 4.29 The child public key is derived by adding the parent public key with the public key derived from the left 256 bits.

You can convince yourself that it works by looking at both normal public-key derivation and child public-key derivation in the same picture: see figure 4.30.

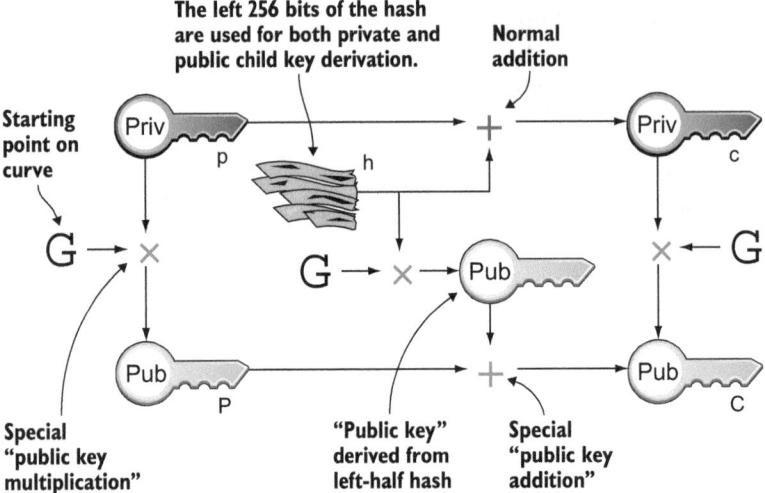

Figure 4.30   Xpub derivation and normal public-key derivation. A normal public key is the starting point G multiplied by a private key. A child public key is the parent public key added to the public key derived from the left-half hash.

The nice thing with elliptic curves is that the special public key "add" operation works a bit like normal add. The same goes for the special public key "multiplication." You can thus solve some equations:

$$c = p + h$$
$$C = Gh + Gp = G(h + p) = Gc$$

The result, $C = Gc$, is exactly how to derive the public key C from the private key c.

Public key encoding

Do you remember how John's public key looked like a big number?

```
035541a13851a3742489fdddeef21be13c1abb85e053222c0dbf3703ba218dc1f3
```

That doesn't look like a pair of coordinates, does it? The public key is encoded in a certain way. Because of the symmetry, exactly two points exist for every value of x, one with an even y value and one with an odd y value (figure 4.31).

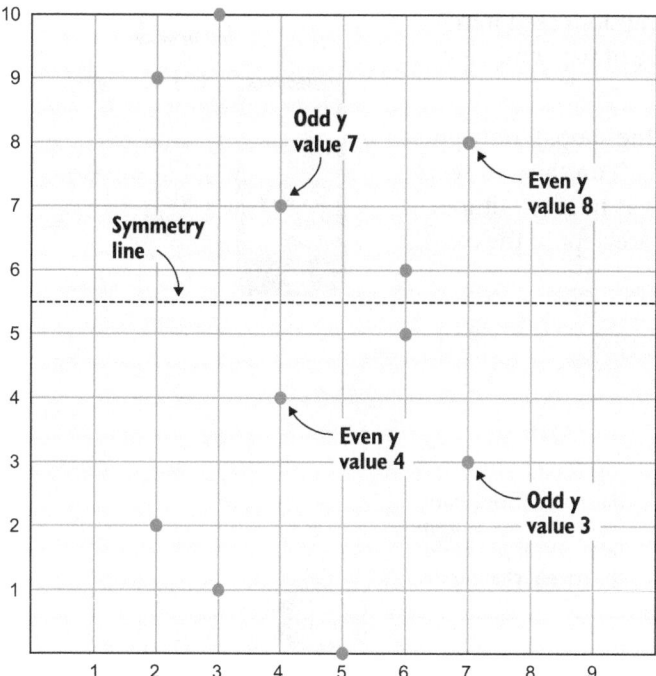

Figure 4.31   Each point on the curve has a symmetric point at the same x value.

You don't need to store *y* values, only whether the *y* value is even or odd. You do this by prefixing the *x* value with 02 (even) or 03 (odd). In John's case, the *y* value happens to be odd, so the prefix is 03.

This is why public keys are 33 bytes and not 32 bytes. It's a 256-bit number—the *x*-coordinate—prefixed by a byte specifying the odd/even property.

The curve in the figure has a single point $x = 5$, $y = 0$. This doesn't look symmetric, but it's a so-called *double-root* to the curve—it's two points with the same *y* value 0. They're symmetric because they're at equal distance 5.5 from the symmetry line. In this special case, both these points will use 02 because 0 is even.

Recap

Let's look back at what you've learned in this chapter. An HD wallet generates a tree of keys from a random seed. It can use key hardening to isolate different branches of the tree from each other.

Users back up their keys by writing the random seed in the form of 12 to 24 English words on a piece of paper and lock it up safely.

The cafe accepts cookie tokens in its online shop. It only puts the xpub for the online sales account, `M/1'`, on the web server, which can now create as many addresses as needed without using any private keys. The private keys are kept in the cafe's wallet and never touch the web server.

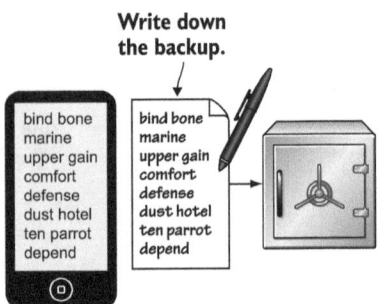

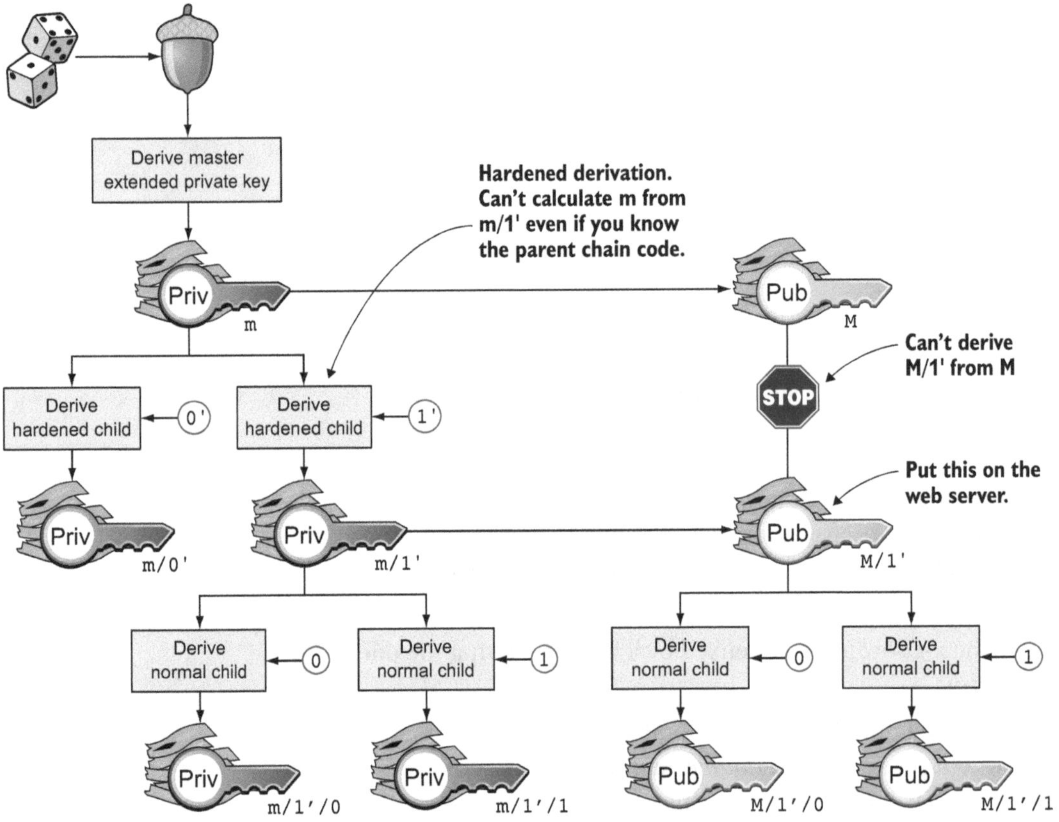

Write down the backup.

Hardened derivation. Can't calculate m from m/1' even if you know the parent chain code.

Can't derive M/1' from M

STOP

Put this on the web server.

System changes

Our concept table (table 4.1) isn't updated in this chapter. The wallets described in this chapter work basically as they do in Bitcoin, but they send an email to Lisa instead of sending a transaction across the global Bitcoin network. We'll get to that in the next chapter.

Table 4.1 Nothing new in the concept table

Cookie tokens	Bitcoin	Covered in
1 cookie token	1 bitcoin	Chapter 2
The spreadsheet	The blockchain	Chapter 6
Email to Lisa	A transaction	Chapter 5
A row in the spreadsheet	A transaction	Chapter 5
Lisa	A miner	Chapter 7

Let's have a release party! Cookie tokens 4.0, fresh from the lab!

Table 4.2 Release notes, cookie tokens 4.0

Version	Feature	How
NEW 4.0	Easy to make payments and create new addresses	Mobile app "wallet"
	Simplified backups	HD wallets are generated from a seed. Only the seed, 12 to 24 English words, needs to be backed up.
	Creating addresses in insecure environments	HD wallets can generate public key trees without ever seeing any of the private keys.
3.0	Safe from expensive typing errors	Cookie token addresses
	Privacy improvements	A PKH is stored in the spreadsheet instead of a personal name.
2.0	Secure payments	Digital signatures solve the problem with imposters.

Exercises

Warm up

4.1   Suppose you use a bitcoin wallet app and want to receive 50 BTC from your friend to your Bitcoin address `155gWNamPrwKwu5D6JZdaLVKvxbpoKsp5S`. Construct a payment URI to give to your friend. Hint: in Bitcoin, the URI starts with `bitcoin:` instead of `ct:`. Otherwise, they're the same.

4.2   How many coin flips does a random password of 10 characters correspond to? The password is selected from a 64-character alphabet.

4.3   Name a few problems with password-protected backups. There are at least four.

4.4   How is the seed created in an HD wallet?

4.5   What does an xprv consist of?

4.6   What does an xpub consist of?

Exercises 4.7 and 4.8 assume that you read the section "Deriving hardened private keys." If you skipped that section, you can skip these exercises, too.

4.7   Suppose you want to make a hardened xprv with index `7` from `m/2/1`. What information do you need to create `m/2/1/7'`?

4.8   Can you derive xpub `M/2/1/7'` from `M/2/1`? If not, how would you derive `M/2/1/7'`?

Dig in

4.9 Suppose you're a bad guy and have the master xpub of a clueless victim. You've also stolen the private key `m/4/1` that contains 1 BTC. Assume you also know this private key has this specific path. Describe how you'd go about calculating the master xprv. Use these hints:

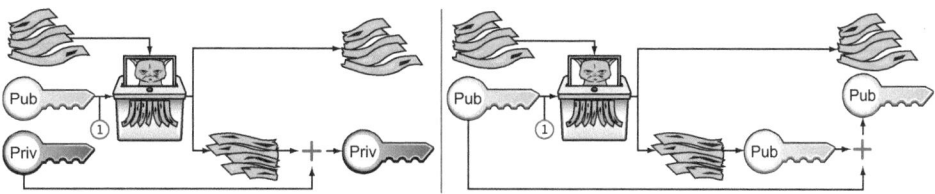

4.10 Suppose instead that your clueless victim had 0 bitcoins on the private key `m/4/1`, but plenty of money on other addresses under the same xprv. Would you be able to steal any money?

If you didn't read the section "Deriving hardened private keys," you can skip exercise 4.11.

4.11 Suggest a better approach your victim could have used to prevent you from stealing all the money.

4.12 Say the cafe owner wants employees to have access to the counter sales account because they must be able to create a new address for each sale. But they must not have access to the private keys because the owner doesn't trust the employees to handle them securely. Suggest how to achieve this. Hint: a wallet can import an xpub.

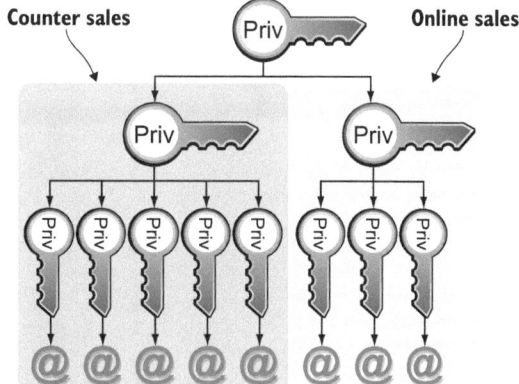

4.13 Suppose you work at the cafe and have loaded an xpub into your wallet. Your colleague Anita has loaded the same xpub into her wallet. You can both request payments from customers that go into the same account. How would you notice when Anita has received money into a previously empty key? Hint: you can create keys ahead of time.

Summary

- You usually use a mobile app, called a wallet, to send and receive money—cookie tokens or bitcoins.

- The wallet creates and stores keys, scans or shows payment details, sends payments, shows your balance, and backs up keys. You don't have to do any of this manually.

- Backups are hard to do right. Password-protected backups suffer from problems with forgotten passwords, technology improvements, and humans being lousy random number generators.

- With HD wallets, you back up your random seed and store that seed in a safe place. Do it only once.

- The seed can be encoded using a mnemonic sentence, which makes it easier to write down the seed.

- HD wallets generate multiple private keys from a seed and organize them in a tree structure to improve privacy.

- The tree of public keys—or any of its branches—can be generated from an xpub. This is useful for insecure environments such as web servers.

- Hardened private key derivation keeps "accounts" compartmentalized. It confines an attacker to a single account.

This chapter covers

- Bitcoin, or cookie token, transactions

- Creating, confirming, and verifying transactions

- Programming money

The cookie token payments you and your coworkers have been making so far have some serious problems. The worst is that Lisa can steal, which worries some new people. They're hesitant to use the system if they know Lisa can steal from them.

This chapter will focus mainly on *transactions* (figure 5.1): pieces of data that formalize how users send payments to Lisa. Transactions replace the old email to Lisa. They'll be stored as is in the spreadsheet instead of using the current To, From, and CT scheme. This will make it impossible for Lisa to steal other people's money because anyone can now verify all payments in the spreadsheet.

In this chapter, we'll go deep on transactions and explore how they're *programmable*, meaning they're flexible as far as what you can do with them. For example, multisignature transactions can require two signatures out of three possible signatures, to spend money shared among three people.

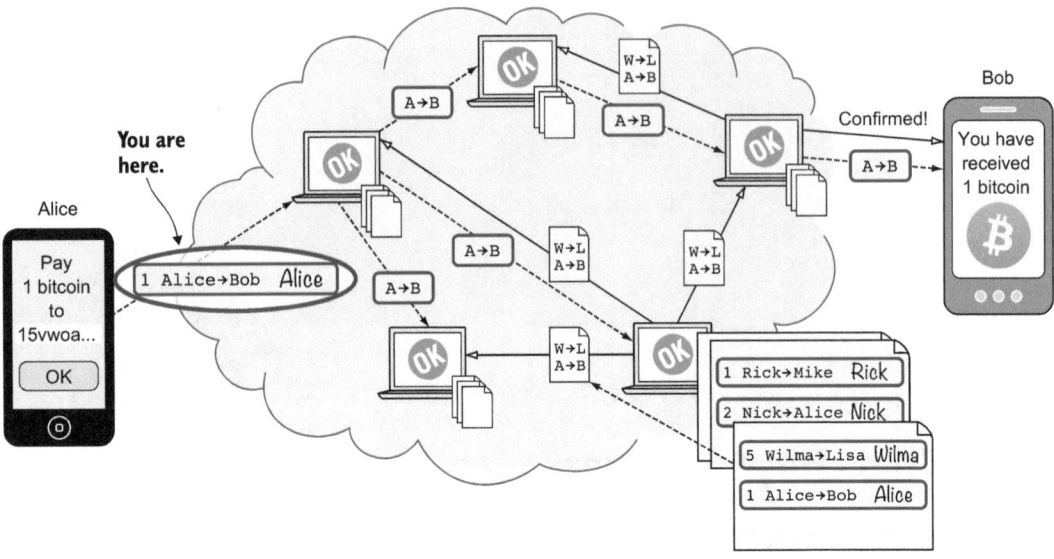

Figure 5.1   Bitcoin transactions

After this chapter, the system will have changed a lot—in how wallets create payments, how Lisa verifies payments, and how payments are stored. Most important, everyone will be able to verify payments in the spreadsheet.

Problems with the old system

Lisa is performing valuable work. She makes sure no one cheats by verifying digital signatures and checking public key hash (PKH) balances before confirming a payment. She confirms payments by adding them to the cookie token spreadsheet.

But this old approach presents several problems:

- Lisa is getting tired of calculating the balance before approving a payment. The ledger is growing, and each check becomes more time-consuming as new payments are added.

- If you have two addresses with 5 CT each, you must make two separate payments to pay 10 CT for a cookie. This lays an unnecessary burden on the sender as well as Lisa. It also bloats the spreadsheet with excessive rows.

- Because the company has grown and some people don't know Lisa well, trust in her begins to fade. Some people fear Lisa will steal cookie tokens from them in the spreadsheet. Only Lisa can verify signatures because only she sees the emails sent to her. So she *could* increase the CT column of a payment to her or add a row with a false payment from, say, John to Lisa (figure 5.2). No one could prove Lisa committed fraud. It doesn't matter that she's the most trustworthy human on earth. If people don't know that, they're going to assume Lisa is as greedy as everyone else.

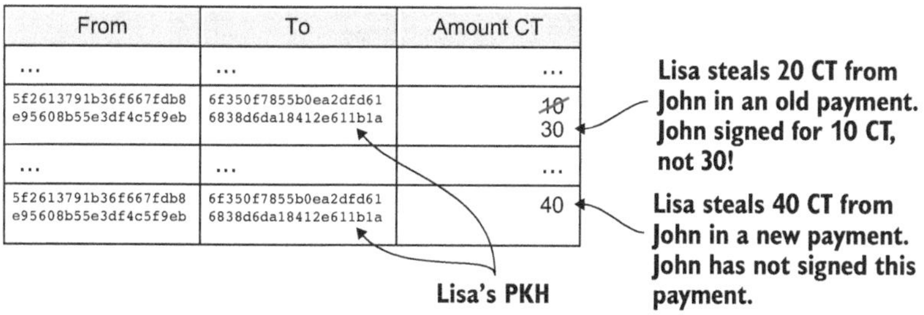

From	To	Amount CT
...	...	...
5f2613791b36f667fdb8 e95608b55e3df4c5f9eb	6f350f7855b0ea2dfd61 6838d6da18412e611b1a	~~10~~ 30
...	...	...
5f2613791b36f667fdb8 e95608b55e3df4c5f9eb	6f350f7855b0ea2dfd61 6838d6da18412e611b1a	40

Lisa steals 20 CT from John in an old payment. John signed for 10 CT, not 30!

Lisa steals 40 CT from John in a new payment. John has not signed this payment.

Lisa's PKH

Figure 5.2   Bad stuff Lisa could do. She wouldn't, but she could.

Note that Lisa can't create any new money, other than the 7,200 CT per day as agreed. Also if she tries to steal more than what's available on a PKH, someone verifying the spreadsheet will notice the total amount of money is becoming too big. Lisa will get busted.

Lisa hates that people distrust her. She knows there's not much she can do to change her coworkers' level of trust. An interesting alternative is to *minimize the trust needed*. She concludes that the best way to do this is to make the process super-transparent so everyone can verify payments. At the same time, she'll improve how she verifies that people don't spend money they don't have and how to spend from multiple addresses at the same time. She invents the *cookie token transaction* to solve the three problems outlined previously.

Minimize trust

Minimizing trust between people is what Bitcoin is all about. Transactions bring us one step closer to a trustless system in which everyone can verify everything.

Paying using a transaction

Transactions will replace both how a user's wallet sends a payment to Lisa and what's stored in the spreadsheet. They won't change how wallets behave from a user's perspective—the wallet app will *look* exactly the same.

Suppose John wants to buy a cookie in the cafe. He won't email Lisa the way he's done so many times before. The wallet software now uses transactions, so his wallet will create a transaction instead, as figure 5.3 shows. The transaction's purpose is to pay 10 CT to the cafe's cookie token address.

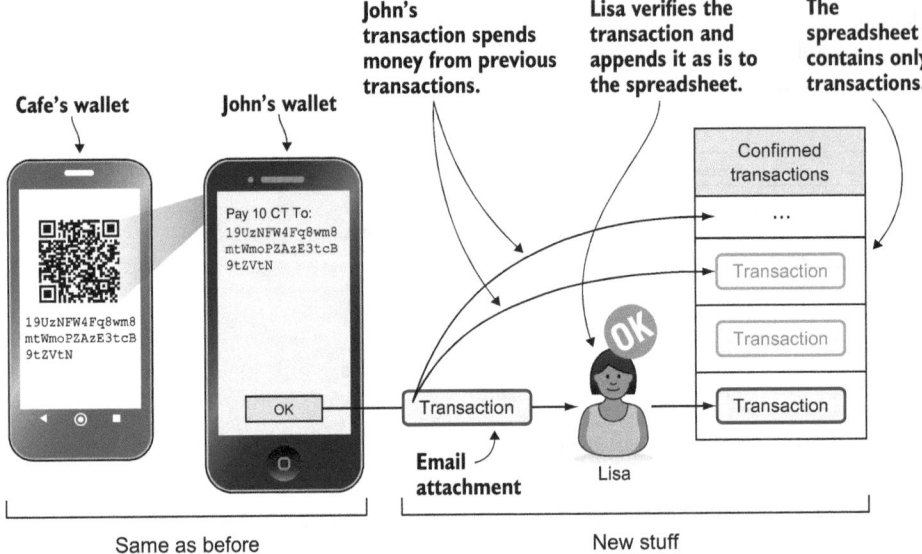

Figure 5.3   The payment process is the same for users, but it's different for Lisa and the spreadsheet.

John scans the cafe's payment URI, and his wallet creates a transaction and asks him to accept it. He clicks OK, and the wallet signs the transaction. John's wallet then sends the signed transaction as an attachment in an otherwise empty email to Lisa.

The transaction contains information about where to send money. But it also contains information about *what money* to spend by referencing specific "coins" called *unspent transaction outputs* (UTXOs) that John received in previous transactions.

Lisa verifies that the coins spent in the transaction exist and aren't already spent. She also verifies that the signatures—there might be several in a transaction—are valid. If all checks pass, Lisa confirms the transaction by appending it, exactly as she received it, to the end of the spreadsheet.

Once the transaction hits the spreadsheet, anyone can make the same verification of that transaction that Lisa did. They can do this to verify Lisa doesn't steal money from someone else or otherwise mess with other people's money.

In the next three subsections, we'll dig deeper into the three phases: create, confirm, and verify.

Creating the transaction

Let's dive in and look closer at how John's transaction is created.

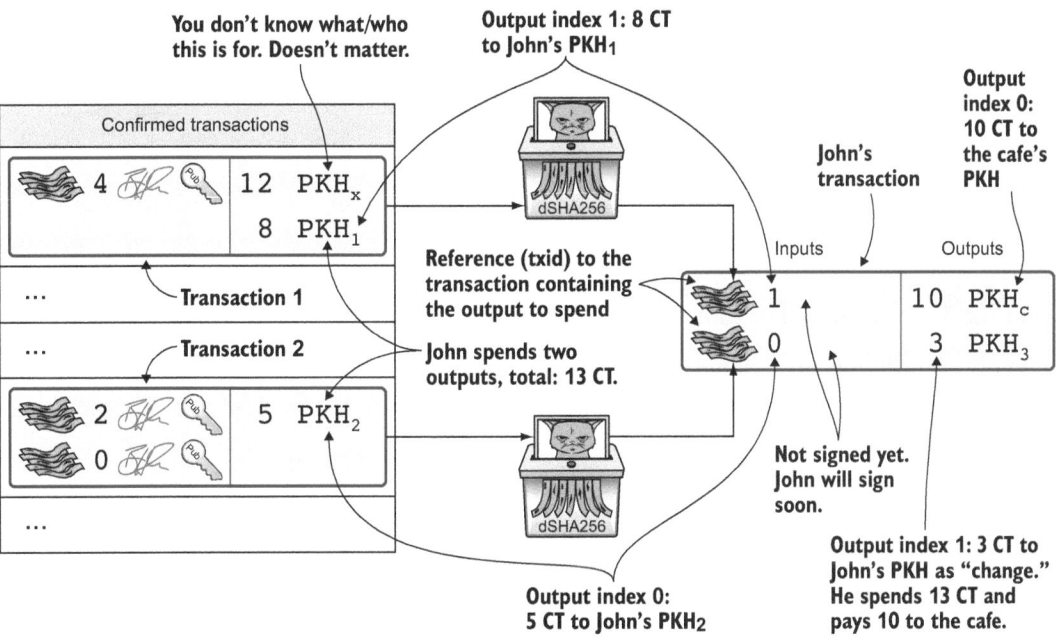

Figure 5.4 John's wallet prepares to pay 10 CT for a cookie. He uses two keys with funds to cover the cost. He pays himself the change of 3 CT to a fresh address. The transaction isn't yet signed.

John's wallet has created a new transaction (figure 5.4). It has two *inputs* and two *outputs*. Inputs specify which outputs of previous transactions to spend. Outputs specify where the money goes.

John's transaction

☐ Create (John)
☐ Confirm (Lisa)
☐ Verify (anyone)

Inputs

The inputs specify which transaction outputs to spend. John has two UTXOs, one with 8 CT and one with 5 CT. The unspent outputs belong to two previous transactions, transaction 1 and transaction 2, that paid money to John. Now, John wants to spend these UTXOs.

A transaction input references a previous transaction using the previous transaction's *transaction ID* (txid). The transaction's txid is its double SHA256 hash. It's called a transaction *ID* because this hash is often used to refer to the transaction, as in the case with inputs in figure 5.4.

NOTE

The rationale for using double SHA256 here isn't entirely clear, but doing so prevents something called a *length-extension attack*. Bitcoin's creator probably used double SHA256 as a security measure in order to not have to think about these kinds of attacks. For details, see web resource 12 in appendix C.

John's first input, with index 0, contains

- The txid of transaction 1
- The index, 1, of the output in transaction 1 to spend
- An empty placeholder for a signature

His second input, with index 1, contains

- The txid of transaction 2
- The index, 0, of the output in transaction 2 to spend
- An empty placeholder for a signature

John will fill in the signatures last, after the transaction is otherwise complete.

Outputs

A transaction output contains an amount and a PKH. John's transaction has two outputs. The output at index 0 pays 10 CT to PKH_C, the cafe, for the cookie. The output at index 1 pays 3 CT back to one of John's own keys, PKH_3. We call this *change* because it resembles traditional change, in which you pay $75 with a $100 bill and get $25 back: John pays with 13 CT and gets 3 CT back to his change address, PKH_3.

Change is needed because you can't partly spend a transaction output. You either spend it completely, or you don't spend it.

The outputs and inputs are a bit more advanced than just specifying a PKH in an output and a signature in the input. In reality, the output contains a computer program that will verify the signature in the spending input. We'll talk more about this later.

For a transaction to be valid, the sum of the input amounts must be greater than or equal to the sum of the output amounts. The difference, if any, is called a *transaction fee*, which we'll discuss in chapter 7. For now, John pays no transaction fee, so his output sum matches the input sum exactly.

> **Transaction fee**
>
> Normally, you need to pay a transaction fee for the Bitcoin network to process your transaction.

The transaction is now created, but it isn't yet signed. Anyone could have created this transaction because it's based completely on public information. The inputs just refer to transactions in the spreadsheet and indexes within those transactions. But only John will be able to sign this transaction, because only he has the private keys corresponding to PKH_1 and PKH_2.

Signing the transaction

John clicks OK in his wallet to approve signing the transaction. The wallet now needs to make two signatures, one for PKH_1 and one for PKH_2. This is because John must prove he has both the private key for PKH_1 and the private key for PKH_2. See figure 5.5.

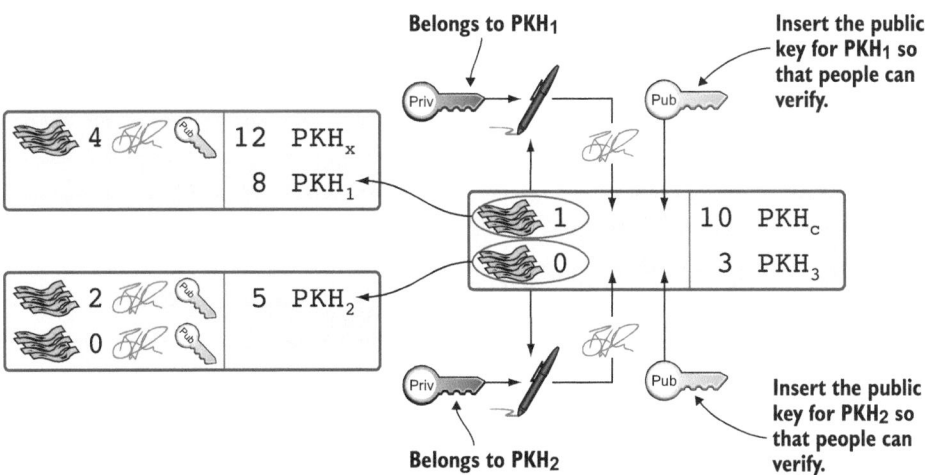

Figure 5.5 John's wallet signs the transaction. Each input gets its own signature. The public key is also needed in the inputs because anyone should be able to verify the signature.

Each input needs to be signed individually. The private key corresponding to PKH_1 must be used to sign the input at index 0 because that input spends money addressed to PKH_1. Similarly, the private key corresponding to PKH_2 must be used for the signature of the input at index 1 because it spends money addressed to PKH_2.

Each signature will commit to the entire transaction, which means the signing algorithm will hash the entire transaction, excluding signatures. If anything changes in the transaction, any signature made for this transaction will become invalid.

To make verification easier, you sign a cleaned version of the transaction, which means there are no signatures in any of the inputs. You can't put a signature in input 0 and *then* sign input 1. Verification would be difficult if the person verifying didn't know in what order the signatures were made. If you make *all* signatures from a cleaned transaction and *then* add all signatures to it, it doesn't matter in what order the signatures were made.

When the wallet has made all signatures, it adds them to the transaction. But one piece is still missing. How can someone verifying the transaction—for example, the cafe—know which public key to use to verify a signature? The cafe can see only the PKH in the spent output and the signature in the spending input. It can't get the public key from the PKH because cryptographic hashes are one-way functions, remember? John's wallet must explicitly add the corresponding public key to the input. The signature in input 0 that spends money from PKH_1 needs to be verified with the public key from which PKH_1 was generated. Similarly, input 1 gets the public key corresponding to PKH_2.

Lisa confirms the transaction

The transaction is ready to be sent to Lisa. John's wallet sends it as an attachment in an email. Lisa picks up the transaction and verifies that:

- The transaction spends outputs of transactions that actually exist in the spreadsheet and that they aren't already spent by some other transaction in the spreadsheet.

- The total value of the transaction outputs doesn't exceed the total value of the transaction inputs. Otherwise, the transaction would create new money out of thin air.

- The signatures are correct.

John's transaction

☑ Create (John)
☐ Confirm (Lisa)
☐ Verify (anyone)

Lisa doesn't have to calculate the PKH balance anymore, but she needs to check that the spent output exists and isn't already spent.

How does she check that an output of a transaction is unspent? Doesn't she have to search the spreadsheet to look for transactions that spend this output? Yes, she does. This seems about as cumbersome as searching through the spreadsheet to calculate balances. Don't worry: Lisa has a plan.

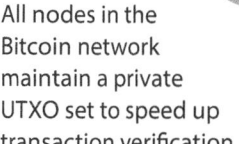

UTXO set

All nodes in the Bitcoin network maintain a private UTXO set to speed up transaction verification.

Unspent transaction output set

To make the unspent checks easier, she creates a new, private database that she calls the *UTXO set* (figure 5.6). It's a set of all UTXOs.

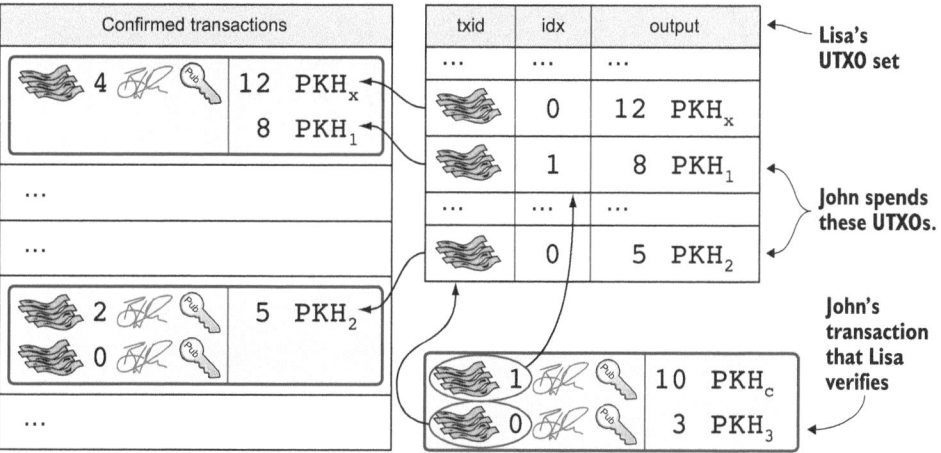

Figure 5.6   Lisa verifies that John doesn't double spend by using her UTXO set.

An entry in the UTXO set consists of a txid, an index (idx), and the actual transaction output. Lisa keeps her UTXO set updated while verifying transactions. Before Lisa adds John's transaction to the spreadsheet, she makes sure all outputs that the transaction spends are in the UTXO set. If not, then John is trying to spend money that either never existed in the spreadsheet or is already spent (usually referred to as a *double-spend attempt*).

For each input in John's transaction, Lisa uses her UTXO set to look up the txid and the output index. If all spent outputs are present in the UTXO set, no double-spend attempt or spending of nonexistent coins is detected. In this case, Lisa finds both outputs in her UTXO set and starts verifying signatures. Lisa needs to verify the signatures of both of John's transaction inputs.

Double spend

Double spend means to spend the same output twice. Lisa can prevent double spends by consulting her UTXO set.

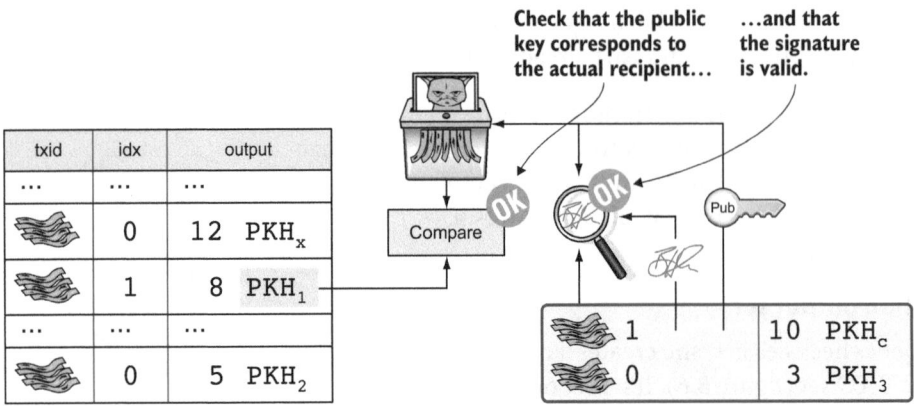

Figure 5.7   Lisa verifies the first signature of John's transaction.

She grabs the PKH from the output spent by the first input and verifies that it matches the hash of the public key in the input (figure 5.7). She verifies the signature in the input using the public key, the signature, and the transaction, and then verifies the second input's signature the same way. Both are good.

Lisa then adds the confirmed transaction to the spreadsheet. She must remove the newly spent outputs from the UTXO set and add the outputs of John's transaction to it (figure 5.8). This is how she keeps the UTXO set updated to reflect the transaction spreadsheet's contents.

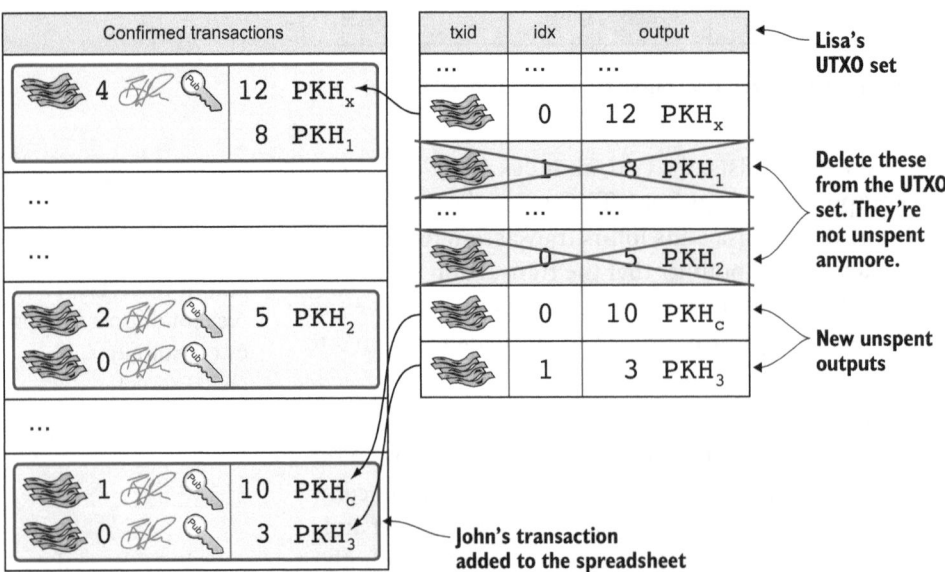

Figure 5.8   Lisa adds the transaction to the spreadsheet and removes the spent outputs from the UTXO set.

Lisa keeps the UTXO set up to date by updating it as figure 5.8 illustrates for every incoming transaction. If she loses the UTXO set, she can re-create it from the spreadsheet by starting with an empty UTXO set and reapplying all transactions in the spreadsheet to it, one by one.

It isn't only Lisa who can create a UTXO set. Anyone with access to the spreadsheet can now do the same. This is important in later chapters, when we replace Lisa with multiple people doing her job. It's also important for people who just want to verify the spreadsheet to convince themselves the information in it is correct.

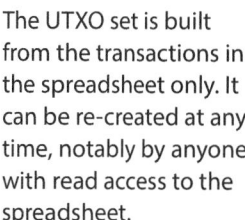

Rebuilding the UTXO set

The UTXO set is built from the transactions in the spreadsheet only. It can be re-created at any time, notably by anyone with read access to the spreadsheet.

Anyone verifies the transaction

Now that John's transaction is stored in the spreadsheet exactly as he created it, anyone with read access can verify it. Anyone can create a *private* UTXO set, work through all the transactions, and end up with the exact same UTXO set as Lisa.

This means anyone can make the same checks that Lisa does. They can verify that Lisa is doing her job. These verifiers are important to the system because they make sure updates to the spreadsheet obey the agreed-on rules.

In Bitcoin, these verifiers are called *full nodes*. Lisa is also a full node (a verifier), but she does more than a full node—she updates the spreadsheet. A full node is also called a *verifying node* or, more casually, a *node* in Bitcoin.

Lisa can no longer steal someone else's money, because doing so would make the spreadsheet invalid. For example, suppose she tried to change the output recipient of John's transaction from PKH_C to PKH_L. She effectively tries to steal 10 CT from the cafe (figure 5.9).

John's transaction

☑ Create (John)
☑ Confirm (Lisa)
☐ Verify (anyone)

John's transaction

☑ Create (John)
☑ Confirm (Lisa)
☑ Verify (anyone)

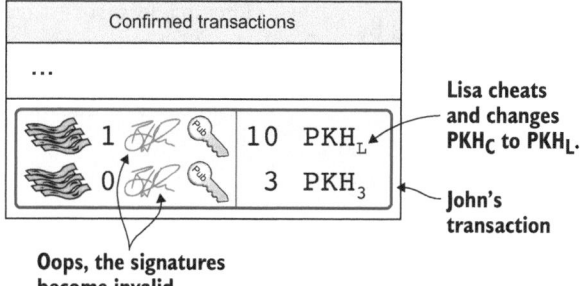

Lisa cheats and changes PKH_C to PKH_L.

John's transaction

Oops, the signatures become invalid.

Figure 5.9 Lisa can no longer steal someone else's money. If she does, the signatures will become invalid and disclose her immoral act.

Because Lisa has changed the contents of John's transaction, that transaction's signatures will no longer be valid. Anyone with access to the spreadsheet can notice this because everything is super-transparent.

Security consequences of public signatures

The good thing about public signatures is that anyone can verify all transactions. But there's a slight drawback.

Remember in chapter 3, when we introduced PKHs? When you used PKHs, the public key wasn't revealed in the spreadsheet. This protected money with two security layers: the public-key derivation function and a cryptographic hash function (SHA256 + RIPEMD160). If the public key was revealed somehow, the private key would still be protected by the public-key derivation function. It was like a belt and suspenders type of thing.

But using transactions, the public key is revealed in the spending transaction's input when an output is spent. Look at John's transaction again in figure 5.10.

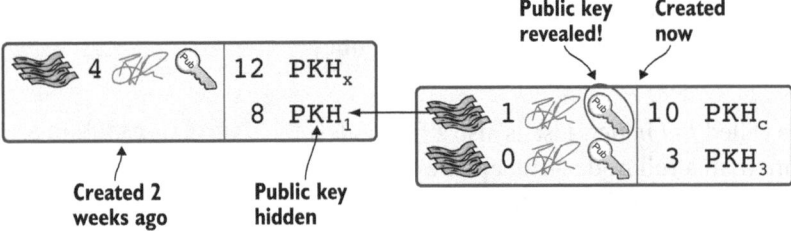

Figure 5.10   The input reveals the public key. We made an extra effort to avoid this in chapter 3.

The input contains the public key. But it only reveals the public key once the output is spent. This brings up an important point: don't reuse addresses! If John has other unspent outputs to PKH_1, those outputs are now less secure because they're no longer protected by the cryptographic hash function—only by the public-key derivation function.

Not only does address reuse degrade the security of your private keys, it also degrades your privacy, as discussed in chapter 3. Suppose again that John has other outputs to PKH_1. If Acme Insurances forces the cafe to reveal that it was John who bought the cookie, Acme would also know that all outputs to PKH_1 belong to John. This goes for change outputs, too.

Don't reuse addresses

Bitcoin addresses shouldn't be reused. Reusing addresses degrades both security and privacy.

Luckily, the wallets will automate key creation for you, so you usually don't have to worry about key reuse. Most Bitcoin wallets on the market today use unique addresses for all incoming payments.

Account-based and value-based systems

Let's reflect on the changes we've made. We've moved from an *account-based* system to a *value-based* system.

An account-based system keeps track of how much money each account has. This is the type of system we had before this chapter. Lisa had to calculate the balance of a PKH before deciding whether to allow a payment.

A value-based system keeps track of "coins" instead. In this chapter, Lisa needs to verify that the specific coins (UTXOs) exist before deciding whether to allow the payment. She doesn't have to verify the balance of any PKH. Bitcoin is also a value-based system.

Script

I haven't been totally honest about what a transaction contains. A transaction's output doesn't contain a PKH, but part of a small computer program that *contains* a PKH. This part of the program is called a *pubkey script*. The input that spends the output contains the other part of this program. This other part, the signature and the public key in John's transaction, is called a *signature script* (figure 5.11).

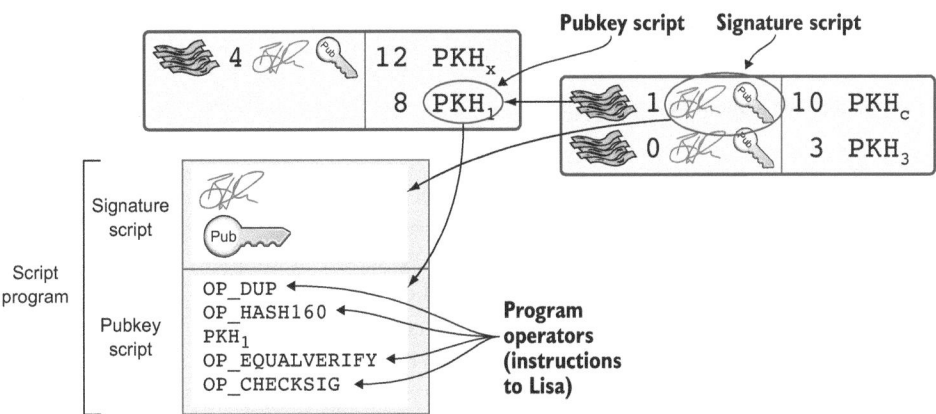

Figure 5.11 The signature script is the first part of a program. The pubkey script in the spent output is the second part. If the complete program results in OK, then the payment is authorized to spend the output.

This tiny program, written in a programming language called Script, contains the instructions to Lisa on how to verify that the spending transaction is authentic. If Lisa performs all the instructions in the program without errors, and the end result is OK, then the transaction is authentic.

The ability to write a computer program inside a transaction is useful for various use cases. We'll cover several use cases of customized programs throughout this book.

Suppose Lisa wants to verify input 0 of John's transaction. She'll run this program from top to bottom. A *stack* is used to keep track of intermediate calculation results. This stack is like a pile of stuff. You can add stuff on top of the stack, and you can take stuff off the top.

Let's start: look at figure 5.12. The first (top) item in the program is a signature, which is just data. When you encounter ordinary data, you'll put it on the stack. Lisa puts the signature on the previously empty stack. Then she encounters a public key, which is also just data. She puts that on the stack as well. The stack now contains a signature and a public key, with the public key on top.

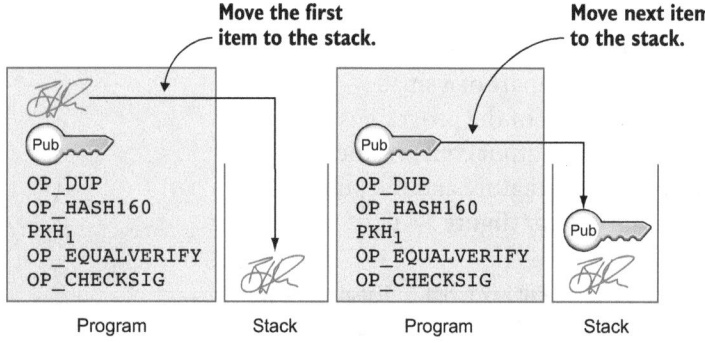

Figure 5.12   Adding a signature and a public key to the stack

The next item in the program is OP_DUP (figure 5.13). This isn't just data—this is an operator. An operator makes calculations based on items on the stack and, in some cases, the transaction being verified. This specific operator is simple: it means "Copy the top item on the stack (but keep it on the stack), and put the copy on top." Lisa follows orders and copies the public key on the stack. You now have two public keys and a signature on the stack.

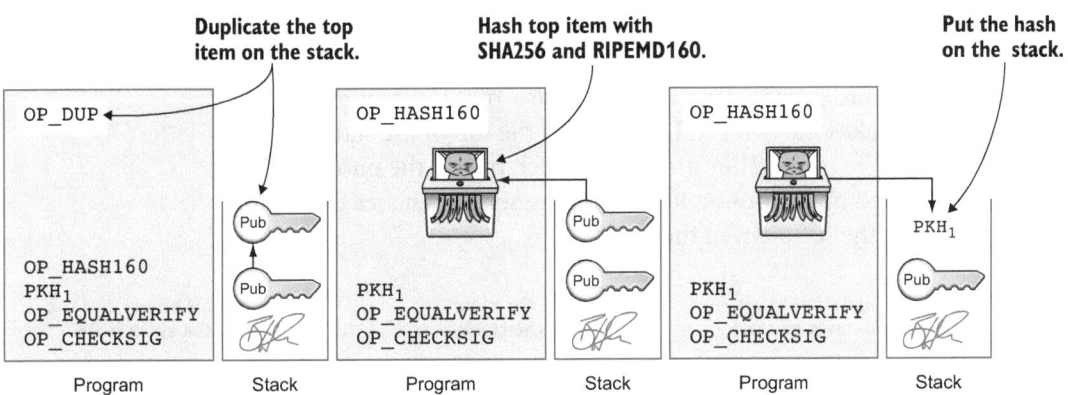

Figure 5.13   Copying the public key on the stack, and adding a PKH

The next item is also an operator, OP_HASH160 (also shown in figure 5.13). This means "Take the top item off the stack and hash it using SHA256+RIPEMD160, and put the result on the stack."

Cool. Lisa takes the top public key from the stack, hashes it, and puts the resulting PKH on top of the stack. This happens to be John's PKH_1 because it was John's public key that Lisa hashed.

The next item is just data (figure 5.14): it's PKH_1, which is the rightful recipient of the 8 CT. Lisa puts PKH_1 on the stack.

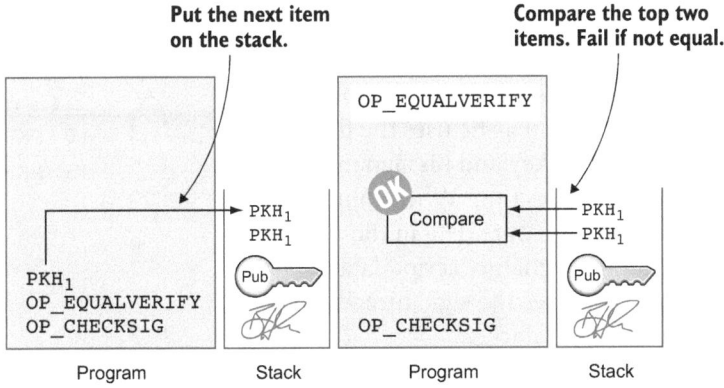

Figure 5.14   Adding PKH₁ to the stack and comparing the two PKH items

Next up is another operator, OP_EQUALVERIFY. This means "Take
the top two items from the stack and compare them. If they're equal,
continue to the next program instruction; otherwise, quit the program
with an error." Lisa takes the two PKH items from the top of the stack
and verifies that they're equal. They *are* equal, which means the public
key John has provided in his transaction's signature script matches the
PKH that was set as the recipient in the output.

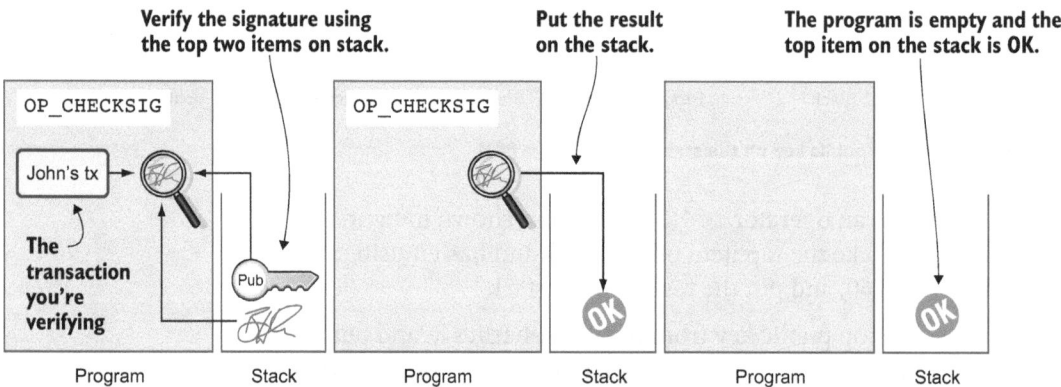

Figure 5.15 **Verifying the signature using John's transaction and the rest of the items
from the stack**

The last operator, OP_CHECKSIG (Figure 5.15), means "Verify that the
top public key on the stack and the signature that's next on the stack
correctly sign the transaction. Put true or false on top of the stack
depending on the verification outcome." Lisa takes John's transaction
and cleans out all the signature script from all inputs. She uses the top
two items from the stack, which are John's public key and his signature,
to verify that the signature signs the cleaned transaction. When John
signed this transaction, he did so without any signature data in the
inputs. This is why Lisa must first clean out the signature script data
from the transaction before verifying the signature. The signature was
good, so Lisa puts true, meaning OK, back on the stack.

**John's cleaned
transaction**

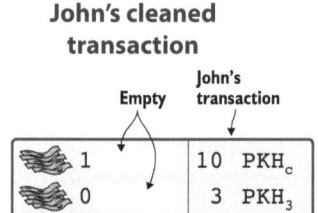

Look, the program is empty! Nothing is left to do. After running a
program, the top item on the stack reveals whether the spending of the
output is authentic. If true—OK—then the spending is authorized. If
false—not OK—then the transaction must be declined. Lisa looks at
the top item on the stack, and there's an OK. Lisa now knows that John's
input with index 0 is good (figure 5.16).

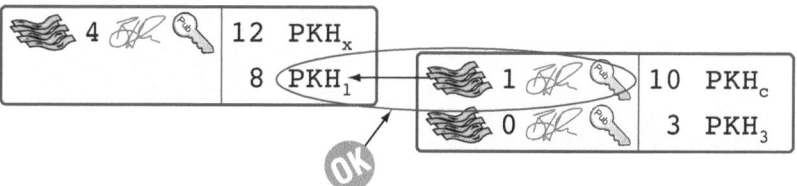

Figure 5.16 The first input is verified.

Lisa does the same checks for the other input, with index 1, of John's transaction. If this program also ends with OK, then the entire transaction is valid, and she can add the transaction to the spreadsheet.

Why use a program?

The pubkey script part of the program stipulates exactly what the spending transaction needs to provide to spend the output. The only way to spend an output is to provide a signature script that makes the program finish with an OK on top of the stack.

In the example I just presented, the only acceptable signature script is a valid signature followed by the public key corresponding to the PKH in the pubkey script.

Using a programming language, Script, in the transactions makes them very flexible. You'll see several different types of Script programs throughout this book. If the transactions didn't use a programming language, all use cases would have to be invented up front. The Script language lets people come up with new use cases as they please.

I've already mentioned that "pay to PKH" isn't the only way to pay. You can write any program in the pubkey script. For example, you can write a pubkey script that ends with OK only if the signature script provides two numbers whose sum is 10. Or, you can write a program that ends with OK only if the signature script contains the SHA256 pre-image of a hash. Consider this example:

Operators

A lot of useful operators can be used to create all kinds of fancy programs. Check out web resource 13 in appendix C for a complete list.

```
OP_SHA256
334d016f755cd6dc58c53a86e183882f8ec14f52fb05345887c8a5edd42c87b7
OP_EQUAL
```

This will allow anyone who knows an input to SHA256 that results in the hash 334d016f…d42c87b7 to spend the output. You happen to know from chapter 2 that the text "Hello!" will give this specific output. Suppose your signature script is

```
Hello!
```

Run the program to convince yourself that it works and that all signature scripts that don't contain a correct pre-image fail.

Why signature script and pubkey script?

You might wonder why we call the output script part *pubkey script* when it usually doesn't contain a public key. Likewise, the input script is called *signature script*, but it doesn't only contain a signature.

The pubkey script in Bitcoin transactions used to contain an actual public key, and the signature script used to contain the signature only. It was more straightforward then. A typical pubkey script looked like this

```
<public key> OP_CHECKSIG
```

and the signature script like this:

```
<signature>
```

> **Odd names**
>
> Bitcoin developers commonly use the term *scriptPubKey* for the pubkey script and *scriptSig* for the signature script because that's how they're named in the Bitcoin Core source code.

Things have changed since then, but the names *signature script* and *pubkey script* remain. Most developers today look at this more abstractly: the pubkey script can be regarded as a public key, and the signature script can be regarded as a signature, but not necessarily ordinary public keys and signatures. In a normal payment today, the "public key" is the script that needs to be satisfied by the "signature," the signature script. Of course, the "public key" here contains some operators and a PKH, but we can still view it as a public key on a conceptual level. The same goes for the signature script, which we can view as a signature on a conceptual level.

Where were we?

This chapter covers most aspects of transactions. Figure 5.17 is a reminder from chapter 1 of how a typical transaction is sent.

We've gone through the anatomy of the transaction and are now discussing different ways to authenticate, or "sign," transactions.

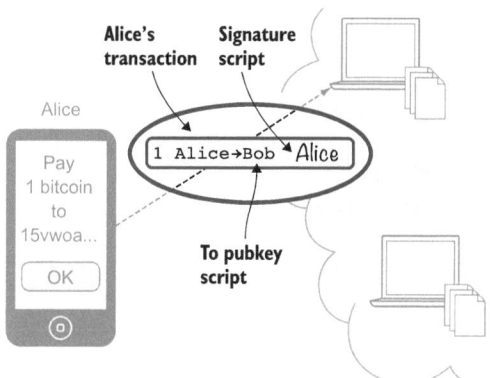

Figure 5.17 This chapter covers transactions. Right now, we're exploring different ways to authenticate transactions.

Fancy payment types

John's transaction just spent two *pay-to-public-key-hash* (p2pkh) outputs. But as noted earlier, other payment types are possible—for example, pay-to-hash, where you pay to a SHA256 hash. To spend this output, you need to provide the hash's pre-image in the spending input's signature script. We'll explore some more interesting and useful ways to authenticate transactions.

Pay to hash

```
OP_SHA256
334d...87b7
OP_EQUAL
```

Multiple signatures

In p2pkh, the recipient generates a cookie token address that's handed over to the sender. The sender then makes a payment to that address.

But what if the recipient would like their money secured by something other than a single private key? Suppose Faiza, Ellen, and John want to raise money for charity from their coworkers.

They could use a normal p2pkh address that their supporters donate cookie tokens to. They could let, say, Faiza have control over the private key, so only she could spend the funds. This approach has a few problems:

Please support us!

1BDQC9J2EkBt
5BY7PuenKQyH
QhFQnjcJTN

1. If Faiza dies, the money might be lost forever. Ellen and John won't be able to recover the funds.

2. If Faiza is sloppy with backup, the money might get lost. Again, no one will be able to recover the funds.

3. If Faiza is sloppy with her private key security, the money might get stolen.

4. Faiza might run away with the money.

A lot of risks seem to be inherent in this setup, but what if Faiza gives the private key to her two charity partners? Then, all partners can spend the money. This will solve problems 1 and 2, but problems 3 and 4 would be worse because now any of the three partners might be sloppy with private-key security or run away with the money.

This organization consists of three people. It would be better if these three people could *share the responsibility and the power over the money* somehow. Thanks to the Script programming language, they can accomplish this.

They can create one private key each and demand that two of the three keys must sign the transaction to spend the charity funds. (figure 5.18).

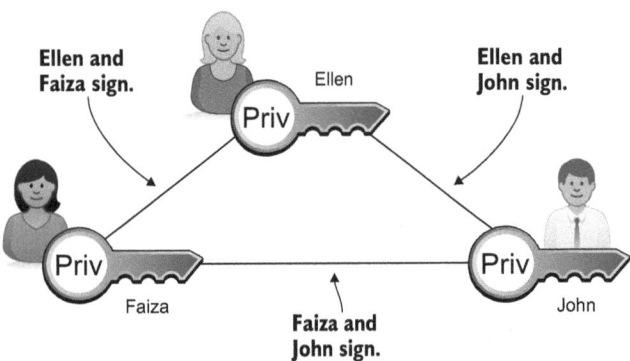

Figure 5.18   Multisignature setup between Faiza, Ellen, and John. Two of the three keys are needed to spend money.

This brings some good properties to the charity fundraising account:

- If one of the three keys is stolen, the thief can't steal the money.

- If one of the three keys is lost due to sloppy backups or death, then the other two keys are enough to spend the money.

- Out of the three partners, no single person can singlehandedly run away with the money.

Figure 5.19 shows a script program that enforces the two-of-three rule.

> **Bug**
>
> There is a bug in Bitcoin software that causes `OP_CHECKMULTISIG` to need an extra dummy item first in the signature script.

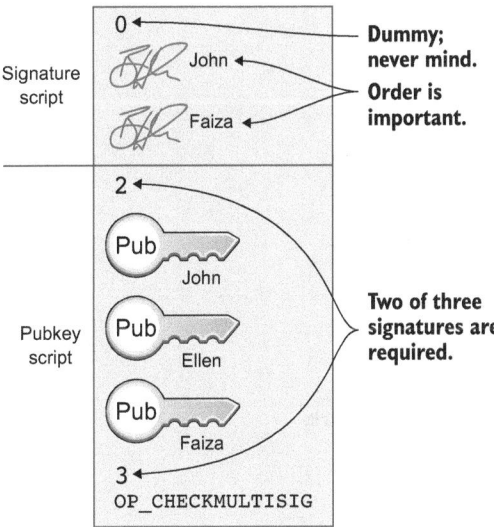

Figure 5.19   A program that enforces two signatures out of three possible keys. The secret sauce is OP_CHECKMULTISIG.

The OP_CHECKMULTISIG operator instructs Lisa to verify that the two signatures in the signature script are made with the keys in the pubkey script. Lisa runs the program in figure 5.20.

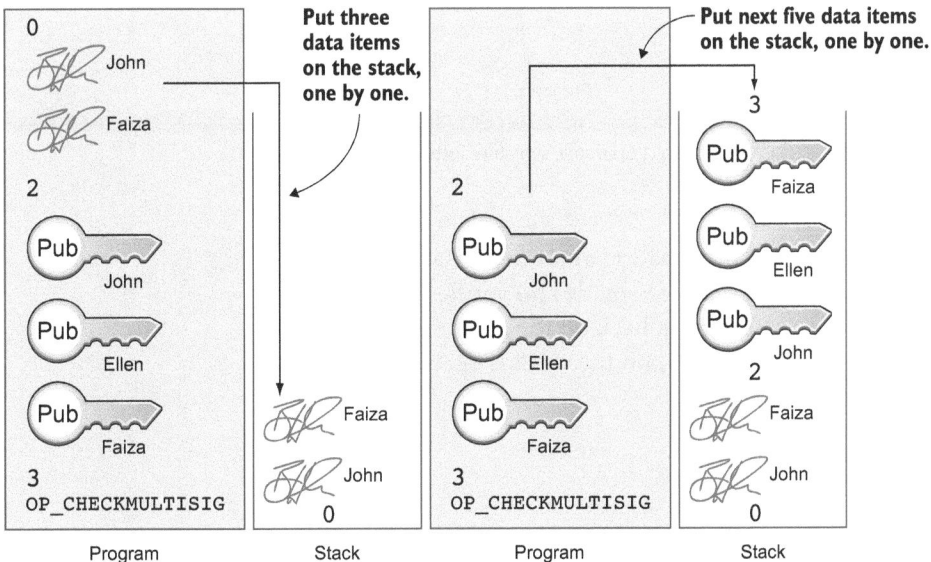

Figure 5.20   Moving some data items to the stack

The top eight data items in the program are put on the stack. Then the only operator, OP_CHECKMULTISIG, runs, as illustrated in figure 5.21. OP_CHECKMULTISIG takes a number, 3 in this case, from the stack and then expects that number of public keys from the stack followed by another number. This second number dictates how many signatures are needed to spend the money. In this case, the number is 2. Then, the operator takes the expected number of signatures from the stack, followed by the dummy mentioned earlier. You don't use the dummy item.

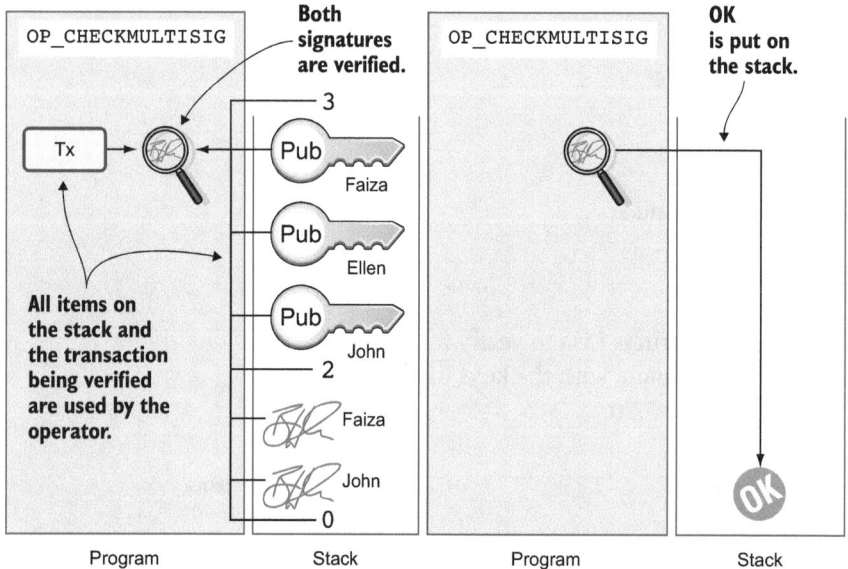

Figure 5.21   Executing the OP_CHECKMULTISIG operator, which results in OK this time

OP_CHECKMULTISIG uses all this information and the transaction to determine whether enough signatures are made and verifies those signatures. If everything is OK, it puts OK back on the stack. This is where the program ends. Because the top item on the stack is OK, the output spending is authorized.

A coworker who wants to donate cookie tokens to the charity needs to get their wallet to write the pubkey script in Figure 5.19 into the donation transaction's output. This presents a few problems:

Please support us!

Please pay to this pubkey script:

* The coworker's wallet knows how to make only p2pkh outputs. The wallet must be modified to understand multisignature outputs and include a user interface to make this kind of output understandable to users.

* A sender usually doesn't need to know how the recipient's money is protected. The sender doesn't care if it's multisignature, p2pkh, or anything else. They just want to pay.

* Transactions usually need to pay a fee to be processed (more on this in chapter 7). This fee generally depends on how big the transaction is, in bytes. A big pubkey script causes the sender to pay a higher fee. This isn't fair because it's the recipient who wants to use this fancy, expensive feature. The recipient, not the sender, should pay for this luxury.

You can fix all this with a small change to how the programs are run. Some developers among your coworkers invent something called *pay-to-script-hash* (p2sh).

Pay-to-script-hash

We've discussed how p2pkh hides the public key from the sender, who gets a hash of the public key to pay to instead of the public key itself.

p2sh takes this idea even further—it hides the script program. Instead of giving a big, complicated pubkey script to the sender, you give them just the hash of the script. The sender then makes a payment to that hash and leaves it up to the recipient to provide the script later, when the recipient wants to spend the money.

Suppose again that Faiza, Ellen, and John want to raise money for charity, and they want a multisignature setup to protect their money (figure 5.22).

BIP16

This type of payment was introduced in 2012 in BIP16.

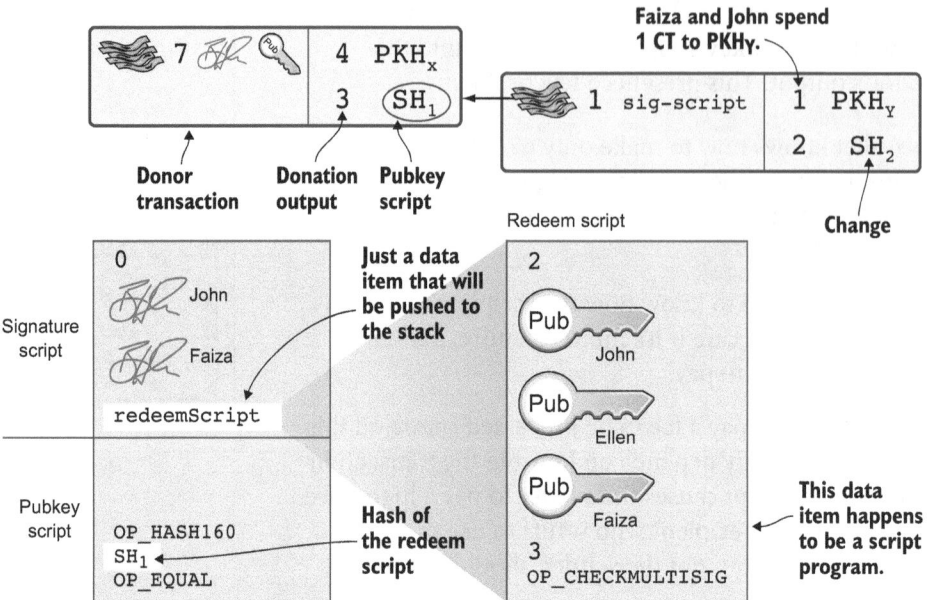

Figure 5.22   Overview of p2sh. The pubkey script is simple. The signature script is special because it contains a data item that contains a program.

To verify this transaction in full, you need new software. We'll talk about how this new software verifies this transaction in a moment. First, let's see how the old software would handle this transaction.

Old software

What if the person verifying the transaction hasn't upgraded their software to the bleeding-edge version that supports verifying p2sh payments? The developers made this forward-compatible, meaning old software won't reject these new transactions.

Let's pretend the cafe runs old software to verify this transaction in the spreadsheet (figure 5.23). Old software will do what it's always been doing—push the stuff in the signature script and then run the pubkey script.

When the program is finished, the top item on the stack is `true`, or `OK`. This means the payment is valid according to this old software.

You might recognize the pubkey script from the earlier example, when you could pay money to a pre-image of a hash. That's what happened here, too, but with a different cryptographic hash function.

> **Why verify?**
>
> The cafe isn't involved in this transaction, so why would the cafe want to verify it? The cafe wants to know whether Lisa is doing her job. It's in the cafe's interest to know if something fishy is going on.

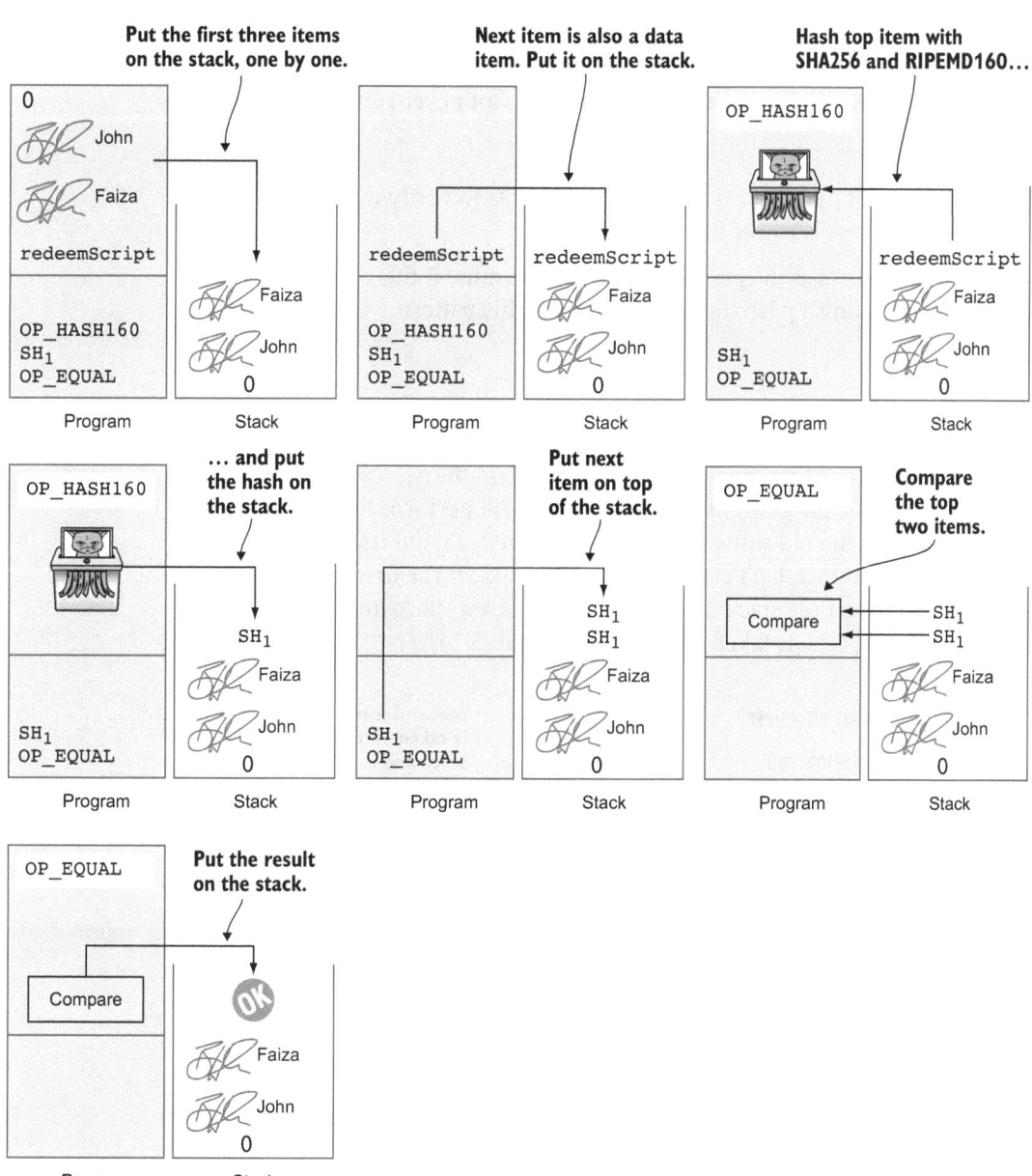

Figure 5.23   Verifying the p2sh transaction using old software

The old software interprets this program as a payment to a hash. Whoever can show a pre-image of this hash gets the money. The actual multisignature program contained in the redeem script never runs.

New software

Suppose the cafe just upgraded its software and wants to verify this transaction again. Let's see how that happens.

The new software looks at the pubkey script to determine if this transaction is spending a p2sh output. It looks for this pattern:

```
OP_HASH160
20 byte hash
OP_EQUAL
```

If the pubkey script has this exact pattern—the p2sh pattern—the software will treat the program differently. First, it will perform the same seven steps as the old software, shown in figure 5.23, but it will save the stack after step 2. Let's call this the *saved stack*. If the first seven steps result in OK, then the stack is replaced by the saved stack; and the top item, redeemScript, is taken off the stack (figure 5.24).

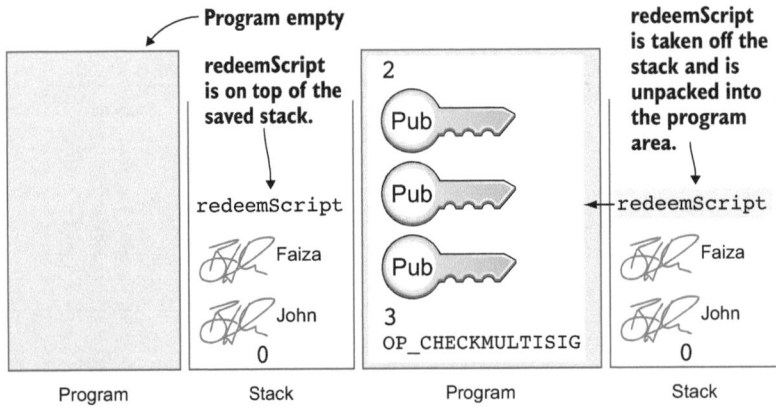

Figure 5.24 The stack is replaced by the saved stack, and redeemScript is taken off the stack.

redeemScript is a data item that contains a program, as previously described. This program is now entered into the program area and begins to execute. It executes from now on as if it was an old-style payment (figure 5.25).

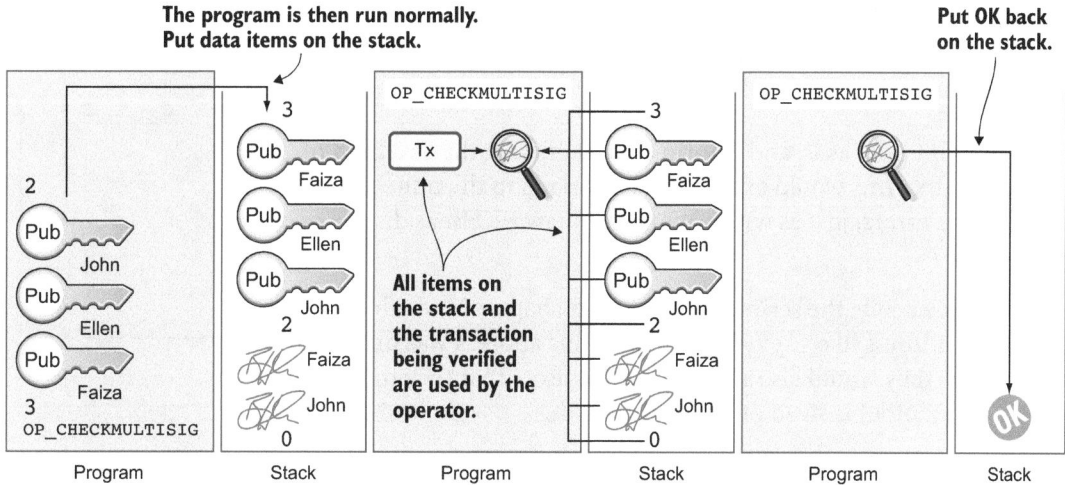

Figure 5.25   Executing the program contained in the redeem script

It's important for Lisa that she runs the latest software. If Lisa ran old software, she would verify only that the redeem script hash matches the script hash in the pubkey script. Anyone who happened to know the redeem script—for example, Faiza—would be able to take the money in the spreadsheet. Lisa would gladly confirm that transaction. This would cause problems if any verifying nodes ran new software. Those nodes wouldn't accept the transaction in the spreadsheet because it's invalid according to the new rules. The entire spreadsheet would then be invalid and unacceptable for new nodes from that point forward. We'll discuss this situation more in chapter 11.

Pay-to-script-hash addresses

Faiza, Ellen, and John have created their two-of-three multisignature redeem script:

```
2
022f52f2868dfc7ba9f17d2ee3ea2669f1fea7aea3df6d0cb7e31ea1df284bdaec
023d01ba1b7a1a2b84fc0f45a8a3a36cc7440500f99c797f084f966444db7baeee
02b0c907f0876485798fc1a8e15e9ddabae0858b49236ab3b1330f2cbadf854ee8
3
OP_CHECKMULTISIG
```

They now want people to pay to the redeem script's SHA256+RIPEMD160 hash:

```
04e214163b3b927c3d2058171dd66ff6780f8708
```

How do Faiza, Ellen, and John ask people to pay them? What do they print on the flyers so coworkers can pay to their script hash? Let's look at a couple of their options:

- Print the script hash as is, and inform coworkers that this is a hash of a redeem script. This would expose the coworkers to the unnecessary risk of typing errors, just as with payments to raw PKHs, as discussed in chapter 3.

- Base58check-encode the script hash just as in chapter 3, which would generate an address like 1SpXyW…RMmEMZ. If this address was printed on the flyers, they would also need to inform users that they must create a p2sh output instead of a normal p2pkh.

In both cases, if the donor erroneously makes a p2pkh payment using the printed hash or address, no one can spend the money because no private key corresponds to this false PKH.

These two options seem neither safe nor practical. Instead, let's introduce a new address format for p2sh, the *p2sh address* (figure 5.26). This format is similar to normal p2pkh addresses. It uses the base58check encoding scheme, just as normal addresses did.

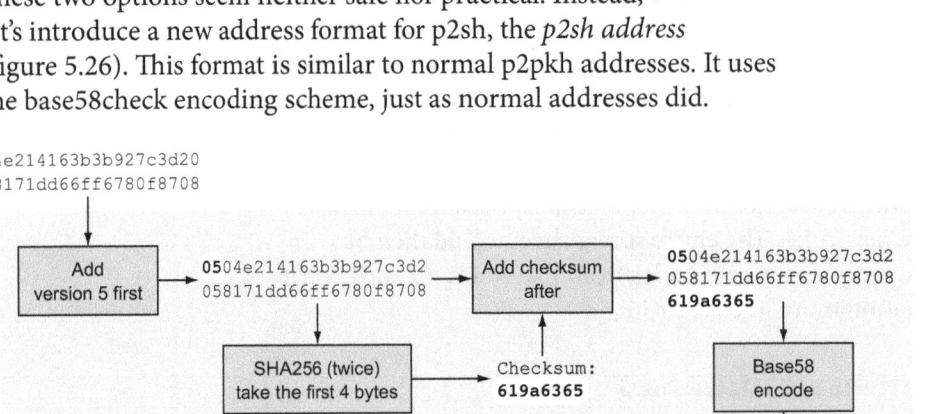

Figure 5.26   Creating a p2sh address. The difference from normal addresses is the version, which is 05 for p2sh addresses instead of 00.

This process is almost the same as for p2pkh addresses. The only difference is that the version is 05 instead of 00. This will cause the address to begin with a 3 instead of a 1.

Because of this change and how base58 works—using integer division by 58 successively—the last remainder will always be 2. If you're interested, figure 5.27 provides the base58 encoding of the versioned and checksummed script hash of Faiza's, Ellen's, and John's redeem script.

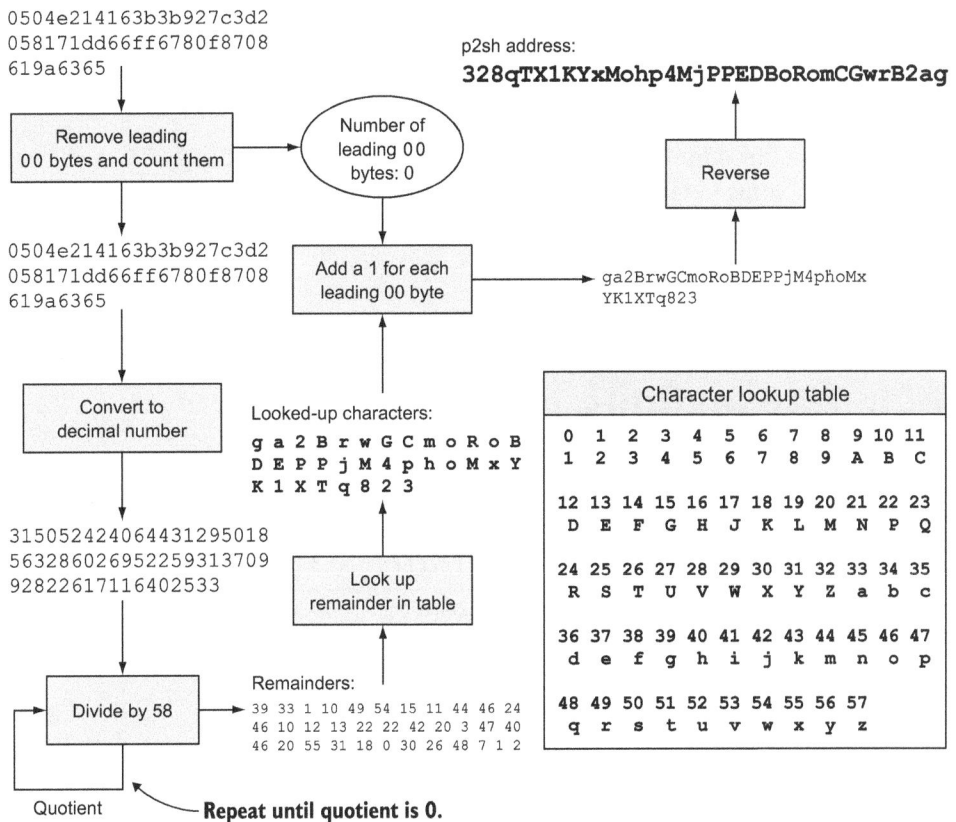

```
0504e214163b3b927c3d2
058171dd66ff6780f8708
619a6365
```

p2sh address:

328qTX1KYxMohp4MjPPEDBoRomCGwrB2ag

Figure 5.27   Encoding a versioned and checksummed script hash with base58. The result will always start with the character 3.

This last remainder 2 will translate to 3 in base58's character-lookup table. This 3 character will become the first character when the base58 process performs the reversing step. This causes all p2sh addresses to start with a 3. This is how users identify them as p2sh addresses and not, for example, p2pkh addresses.

Faiza, Ellen, and John can now print 328qTX…wrB2ag on their flyer. When a coworker scans this flyer's QR code, their wallet will recognize the address as a p2sh address because it starts with a 3. The wallet will base58check-decode the address and create a proper p2sh output:

```
OP_HASH160
04e214163b3b927c3d2058171dd66ff6780f8708
OP_EQUAL
```

This concludes our discussion of programmable transactions. You've learned that transactions can express a lot of different rules for how to spend money. Note that you can't constrain where spent money goes, only what's needed in the input to spend the money. The pubkey script makes the rules for what's required in the signature script. Later in the book, we'll revisit transactions to talk about more fancy stuff you can do with them, such as make spending impossible until a certain future date.

More stuff in transactions

We still haven't covered all the contents of a transaction. A few more pieces of information belong in transactions, including version, lock time, and sequence numbers:

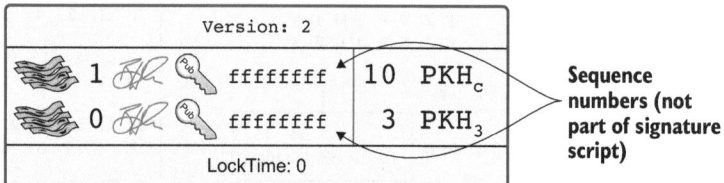

- *Version*—Each transaction has a version. As of this writing, there are two versions: 1 and 2.

- *Sequence number*—A 4-byte number on each input. For most transactions, this is set to its maximum value ffffffff. This is an old, disabled feature that's being repurposed for new functionality.

- *Lock time*—A point in time before which the transaction can't be added to the spreadsheet. If the lock time is 0, the transaction is always allowed to be added to the spreadsheet.

I include this sparse information here for completeness. We'll discuss these features more in chapter 9, when you know more about Bitcoin's fundamentals.

Rewards and coin creation

You might be wondering where all the cookie tokens come from in the first place. Remember in chapter 2, when I described how Lisa gets rewarded with 7,200 CT daily? She would insert a new row in the spreadsheet every day, paying 7,200 new CT to herself.

From	To	Amount CT
...	...	...
Cafe	Company	10,000
Alice	Cafe	10
NEW	Lisa	7,200

Now she still rewards herself with 7,200 CT per day, but in a slightly different way. Every day she adds a special transaction to the spreadsheet called a *coinbase transaction* (figure 5.28).

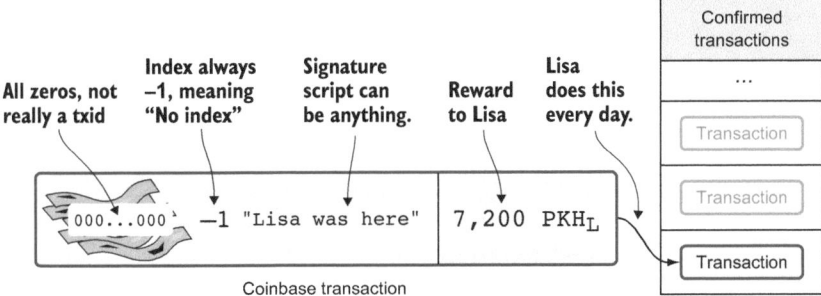

Figure 5.28   Lisa rewards herself every day with a coinbase transaction.

The coinbase transaction's input is called the *coinbase*. The only way to create new coins is to add a coinbase transaction to the spreadsheet. New coins are created as rewards to Lisa for performing her valuable work.

All transactions can be traced back to one or more coinbase transactions by following the txid references in transaction inputs. The transactions form a *transaction graph* (figure 5.29). They're interconnected through the txids.

Rewards

Rewards in Bitcoin are paid roughly every 10 minutes, using coinbase transactions, to the nodes securing the Bitcoin blockchain. I'll cover this in chapter 7.

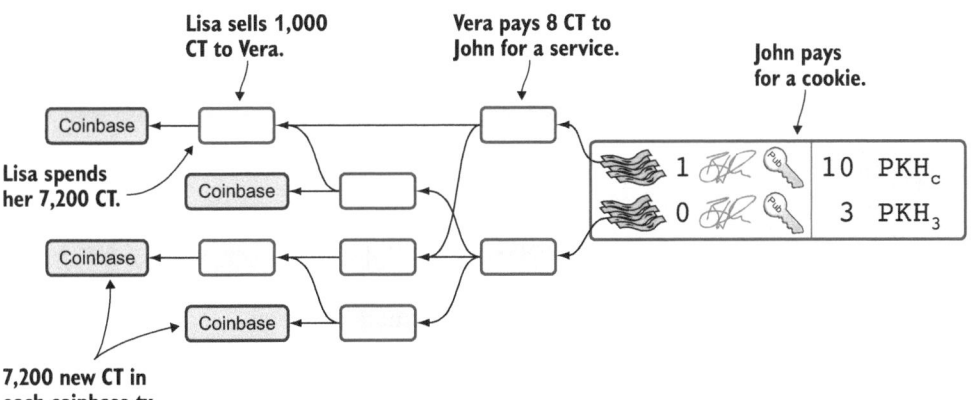

Figure 5.29   The transaction graph. All transactions descend from one or more coinbase transactions.

John's transaction stems from four different coinbase transactions. To verify John's transaction, you must follow all txids from John's transaction and verify all the transactions along the way until you've reached the four coinbase transactions. This is what the UTXO set helps verifiers with. It keeps track of all already-verified UTXOs. The verifiers only have to follow the txids (usually only one step) until it reaches an output that's in the UTXO set.

The coinbase transactions must also be verified so there is exactly one coinbase per 24 hours, and each coinbase creates exactly 7,200 new cookie tokens.

Transition from version 4.0

You might be wondering how the coworkers updated from the old spreadsheet—as it was in release 4.0—to the one that contains transactions. What happened to the already-existing cookie tokens in the spreadsheet?

They all agreed on a time slot when the upgrade would take place. During this time slot, Lisa created a single, huge transaction with one output per PKH in the spreadsheet. This transaction looks like a coinbase transaction but with a lot of outputs. Anyone can keep a version of the old spreadsheet and verify that this new transaction contains the exact same outputs as the old UTXO set. New verifiers can't be sure it went well, though—they'll have to trust Lisa with that.

Note that this isn't at all how it happened in Bitcoin, which was designed for transactions from the beginning. The "initial state" in Bitcoin was an empty UTXO set. No one had any bitcoins.

Trust in Lisa

In this chapter, we've formalized the payment process—for example, the transaction from the wallet must be sent as an attachment in an email to Lisa. Lisa can take advantage of this formal process to automate all her work. She writes a computer program that reads transactions from her email inbox and automatically verifies them, maintains the UTXO set, and adds transactions to the spreadsheet. Lisa can relax and just watch her computer program do the job for her. Nice.

But now you may wonder if she's still worth the 7,200 CT per day in rewards. She doesn't work actively with verification anymore;

she's just sitting there, twiddling her thumbs. Let's take a moment to reflect on what we're rewarding her for. She's rewarded not to perform boring manual work but to perform correct, honest confirmations of transactions and not censor them. That's what gives you and your coworkers value. If Lisa writes a computer program to do the heavy lifting, it doesn't make the payment processing less correct or honest.

Transactions solve the problem with Lisa arbitrarily changing stuff in the spreadsheet. The only things you have to trust Lisa with now are to

We trust that Lisa doesn't …

- Censor transactions
- Revert transactions

- *Not censor transactions*—She must add to the spreadsheet any valid transactions that she receives over email.

- *Not revert transactions*—To *revert* a transaction is to remove it from the spreadsheet.

If Lisa decides she doesn't like Faiza, and she also happens to know some of Faiza's UTXOs, she can refuse to process Faiza's transactions that try to spend those UTXOs. This means Faiza can't spend her money. Lisa is censoring Faiza's transactions.

If Lisa removes a transaction, whose outputs are all unspent, from the spreadsheet, it *might* be noticed by already-running verifiers. But verifiers that started after the reverting won't notice because the spreadsheet is still valid according to the rules.

Suppose Lisa reverts John's transaction from the "Paying using a transaction" section. Lisa removes John's transaction from the spreadsheet. No one has spent any of the outputs of John's transaction yet, so the spreadsheet doesn't contain any transactions that become invalid when John's transaction is deleted.

An already-running verifier—for example, the cafe—won't notice because it just watches the spreadsheet for added transactions at the end. It has already verified John's transaction and updated its private UTXO set. The cafe trusts Lisa to not delete transactions, so it never re-verifies the spreadsheet

Furthermore, suppose a new coworker, Vera, starts to build her own UTXO set from the spreadsheet, which now lacks John's transaction. This UTXO set will differ from the cafe's UTXO set. From Vera's viewpoint, John still has the money and hasn't paid 10 CT to the cafe. The outputs that John spent in his transaction appear unspent to Vera because they're in Vera's UTXO set.

We now have Vera, who thinks John still has the money; Lisa, who deleted the transaction; and the cafe, which thinks it got 10 CT from John. So far, no one has noticed Lisa's crime. It will remain unnoticed as long as nobody tries to spend an output from John's transaction. This could be the cafe spending its 10 CT or John spending his 3 CT change.

Let's say the cafe wants to pay its rent to the company. It needs to spend, among other outputs, the output of John's transaction. The cafe creates a transaction that spends the output, signs it, and sends it to Lisa. Lisa knows she's deleted John's transaction and her crime will now be noticed. If Lisa decides to confirm the cafe's transaction, then she'll make the entire spreadsheet invalid, and Vera and all other verifiers will reject the spreadsheet as a whole. Not good. If Lisa decides to reject the transaction, which is the more sensible thing for her to do, the cafe will notice because its transaction never confirms.

When the cafe notices, it can't prove that John's transaction was ever in the spreadsheet. Lisa can't prove that John's transaction was never in the spreadsheet. It's word against word. We'll solve this problem in chapter 6.

It isn't obvious why Lisa would delete John's transaction. Maybe John pays Lisa to do it. It would probably make more sense for Lisa to cheat with her own money instead. Let's say she buys a cookie in the cafe, and when the cafe has seen the transaction from Lisa to the cafe in the spreadsheet, it gives a cookie to Lisa. Yummy. Then Lisa walks back to her desk and removes her transaction. Now she's got a cookie *and* she gets to keep the money. This will, of course, be noticed when the cafe tries to spend the output from the removed transaction or the next time Lisa tries to double-spend the outputs spent by the removed transaction. But as with John's transaction, it's word against word. Lisa can claim the transaction was never in the spreadsheet, and the cafe can claim it was. No one can prove anything.

Recap

Transactions make it impossible for Lisa to steal cookie tokens from others. They solve the problem by making all signatures public in the spreadsheet. Users' wallets create and sign transactions that Lisa verifies and appends to the spreadsheet.

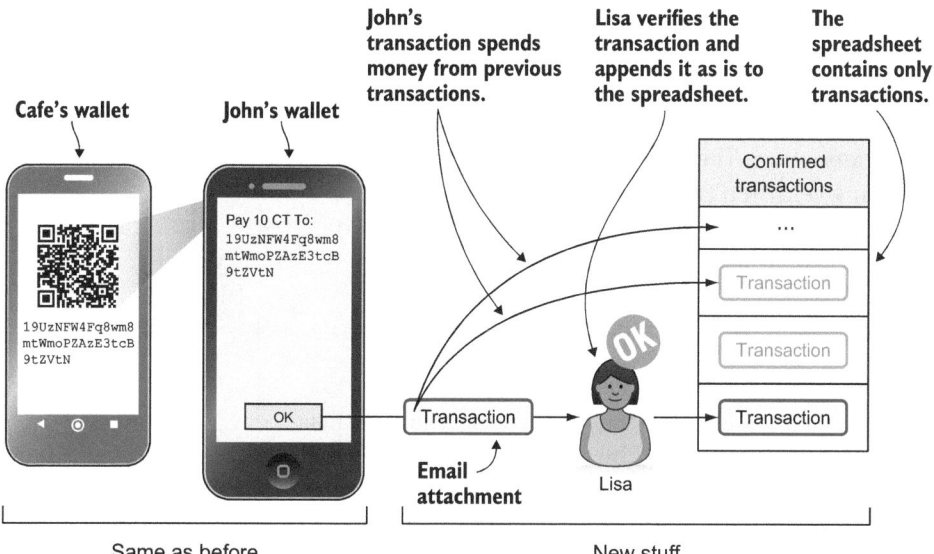

Transactions have inputs and outputs. An output of a transaction
contains the last part of a Script program. When the output is spent,
the input that's spending the output must provide the first part of
the program.

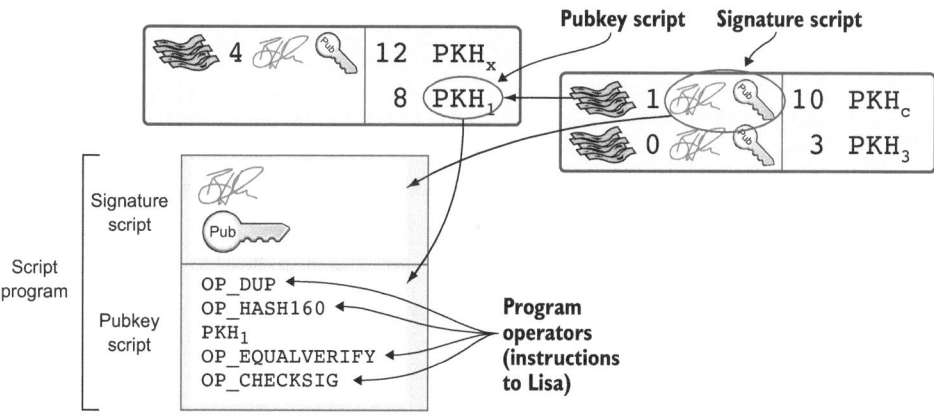

Lisa runs the program. If the program ends with OK, then the spending
of *that* output is authorized. If the programs of all inputs in a
transaction end with OK, the entire transaction is valid, and Lisa adds
the transaction to the spreadsheet.

Once the transaction is in the spreadsheet, anyone can make the exact same checks as Lisa did, because she added the transaction to the spreadsheet exactly as she received it. If Lisa makes changes to it, people will notice that the spreadsheet is no longer valid because it contains an invalid transaction. The only things you can't verify are if transactions are being censored (not added to the spreadsheet) or deleted from the spreadsheet. You have to trust Lisa with these two things for now.

System changes

Transactions and txid have been added to your toolbox. The concept-mapping table (table 5.1) shrinks by two rows: emails to Lisa and rows in the spreadsheet are replaced by transactions. Note that you still use email to send the transaction to Lisa, but the transaction has the same format as in Bitcoin. This is why we can remove the row.

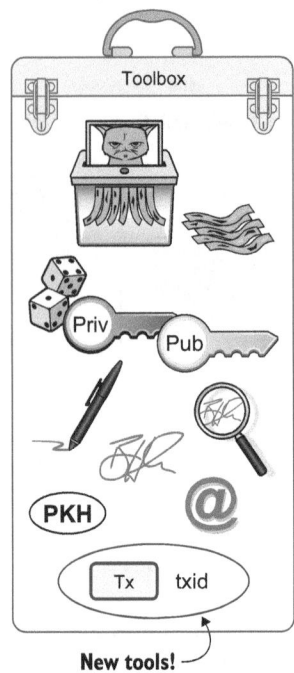

New tools!

Table 5.1   Transactions replace emails to Lisa and rows in the spreadsheet.

Cookie tokens	Bitcoin	Covered in
1 cookie token	1 bitcoin	Chapter 2
The spreadsheet	The blockchain	Chapter 6
~~Email to Lisa~~	~~A transaction~~	~~Chapter 5~~
~~A row in the spreadsheet~~	~~A transaction~~	~~Chapter 5~~
Lisa	A miner	Chapter 7

The next chapter will take care of replacing the spreadsheet, which now contains transactions, with a blockchain.

Let's release version 5.0 of the cookie token system (table 5.2).

Table 5.2   Release notes, cookie tokens 5.0

Version	Feature	How
NEW 5.0	Spend multiple "coins" in one payment	Multiple inputs in transactions
	Anyone can verify the spreadsheet	Make the signatures publicly available in the transactions
	Sender decides on criteria for spending the money	Script programs inside transactions
4.0	Easy to make payments and create new addresses	Mobile app "wallet"
	Simplified backups	HD wallets are generated from a seed. Only the seed, 12 to 24 English words, needs to be backed up.
	Creating addresses in insecure environments	HD wallets can generate public key trees without ever seeing any of the private keys
3.0	Safe from expensive typing errors	Cookie token addresses
	Privacy improvements	A PKH is stored in the spreadsheet instead of a personal name.

Exercises

Warm up

5.1   Suppose all your money is spread over three UTXOs: one with 4 CT, one with 7 CT, and one with 2 CT. Which of these outputs would you spend if you wanted to buy a cookie for 10 CT? What outputs would your transaction have, and what would their CT values be?

5.2   What are txids used for in a transaction?

5.3   Why do you usually need to add a change output in your transaction?

5.4   Where are the signatures located in a transaction?

5.5   Why is the public key needed in the input of a transaction if it spends a p2pkh output?

5.6   Why are the signature scripts of a transaction cleaned when your wallet signs the transaction?

5.7   Where are the pubkey scripts located in a transaction, and what do they contain?

5.8   What's required from a Script program (signature script + pubkey script) for an input to be considered authentic?

5.9   How can you recognize a p2sh address?

Dig in

5.10   Suppose you have 100 CT in a single output at index 7 of a transaction. You want to pay 10 CT to the cafe's p2pkh address $@_C$ and 40 CT to Faiza, Ellen, and John's charity's p2sh address $@_{FEJ}$. Construct a single transaction that does this. Please cheat by looking up the exact operators and program templates from this chapter. You don't have to sign any inputs.

5.11   The UTXO set contains all UTXOs. Suppose it contains 10,000 UTXOs, and you send a transaction to Lisa that has two inputs and five outputs. How many UTXOs will the UTXO set contain after the transaction has been confirmed?

5.12   Create a really simple pubkey script that allows anyone to spend the output. What would the signature script of the spending input contain?

5.13   Create a pubkey script that requires the spender to provide two numbers in the signature script whose sum is 10 in order to spend the money. An operator called `OP_ADD` takes the top two items from the stack and puts back the sum of those items.

5.14   Suppose you run a full node and receive money from Faiza in a confirmed transaction. Can you trust that the money from Faiza is real?

5.15   A public key is visible in the input that spends a p2pkh output. What's the drawback of this if you have multiple UTXOs for the same PKH? What can you do to avoid this drawback?

Summary

- Transactions have inputs and outputs, so you can spend multiple "coins" and pay multiple recipients in a single transaction.

- The outputs of transactions are "programmable." The sender wallet decides what program to put in the output. This dictates what's needed to spend the money.

- Anyone can verify the entire spreadsheet because all signatures are public. This greatly reduces trust in Lisa.

- Scripts can be used to enable multisignature capabilities—for example, three-of-seven capabilities. This is great for companies and charities.

- A new address type, a p2sh address beginning with 3, is used to simplify the payment process for a lot of fancy payment types, such as multisignatures.

- All transactions descend from one or more coinbase transactions. Coinbase transactions are the only way to create money.

- Money creation is verified by any coworker to make sure Lisa creates exactly as much as agreed: 7,200 CT per day and halving every four years.

- Lisa can censor and revert transactions. You still have to trust her with that.

the blockchain | **6**

This chapter covers

- Improving spreadsheet security

- Lightweight (SPV) wallets

- Reducing wallet bandwidth requirements

In chapter 5, we discussed transactions that let anyone verify all transactions in the spreadsheet. But there are still things verifiers can't verify—that Lisa doesn't remove or censor transactions. We'll handle censorship resistance in chapters 7 and 8. This chapter examines how to make it impossible for Lisa to remove or replace transactions without also making it obvious that she's tampered with the transaction history.

Lisa does this by replacing the spreadsheet with a *blockchain* (figure 6.1). The blockchain contains transactions that are secured from tampering through hashing and signing the set of transactions in a clever way. This technique makes it easy to provide cryptographic proof of fraud if Lisa deletes or replaces transactions. All verifiers keep their own copies of the blockchain, and they can fully verify it to ensure that Lisa doesn't remove already-confirmed transactions.

This chapter also introduces a lightweight wallet, or *simplified payment verification* (SPV) wallet, that will defer blockchain verification to someone else—a full node—to save bandwidth and storage space. This is possible thanks to the blockchain, but it comes at a cost.

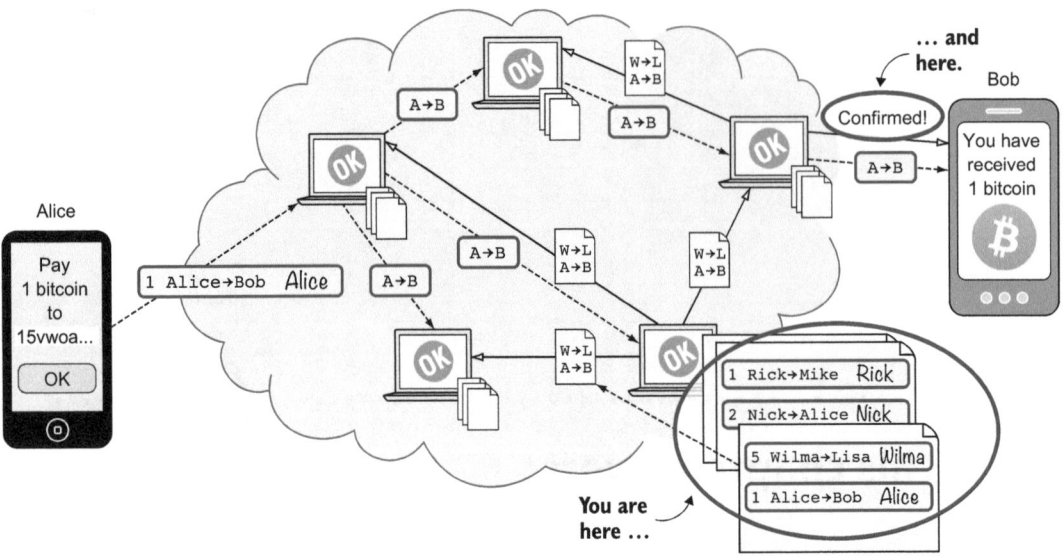

Figure 6.1   The Bitcoin blockchain

Lisa can delete transactions

As noted several times before, Lisa can delete transactions. For example, Lisa could buy a cookie from the cafe, eat it, and delete the transaction. Of course, she wouldn't do this because she's the most trustworthy person on earth, but not all her coworkers know or believe this. Suppose she does indeed delete a transaction, as figure 6.2 shows.

Later, when the cafe notices that the transaction has disappeared, it can't prove that Lisa's transaction was ever in the spreadsheet. And Lisa can't prove it wasn't there. This situation is troublesome. If it's word against word, you're in for a long and costly dispute, possibly involving lawyers, police, Acme Insurances, and private detectives.

How can you prove whether a transaction was confirmed? Lisa needs a way to publish transactions and their ordering such that she can't tamper with them.

Building the blockchain

Lisa can delete transactions because no one can prove that the list of all transactions has changed. What if we could change the system to make it provable that she's fiddled with history?

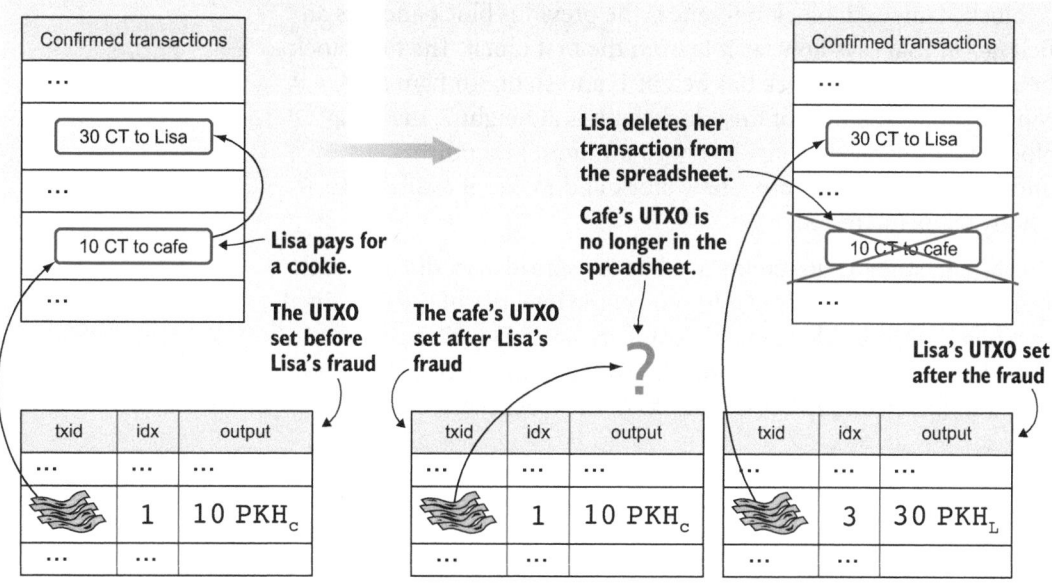

Figure 6.2 Lisa buys a cookie and then reverts the transaction. She just stole a cookie from the cafe! The cafe and Lisa now have different UTXO sets.

Among your coworkers, some developers suggest getting rid of the cookie token spreadsheet and replacing it with a blockchain (figure 6.3).

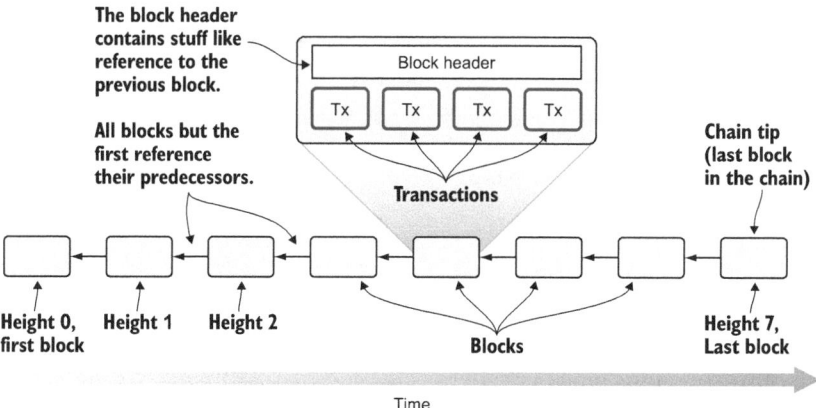

Figure 6.3 A blockchain is a chain of blocks. These blocks contain transactions, and each block references its predecessor.

In the blockchain, each block references the previous block and has an implicit *height* that says how far it is from the first block. The first block has height 0, the second block has height 1, and so on. In figure 6.3, the *chain tip*, or last block, of this blockchain is at height 7, meaning the blockchain is 8 blocks long. Every 10 minutes, Lisa puts recent unconfirmed transactions into a new block and makes it available to everybody who's interested.

The blockchain stores transactions just like the spreadsheet did. But each block also contains a *block header* to protect the integrity of the contained transactions and the blockchain before it. Let's say the blockchain in figure 6.3 has grown to contain 20 blocks, so the chain tip is at height 19. Figure 6.4 zooms in on the last few blocks of the blockchain.

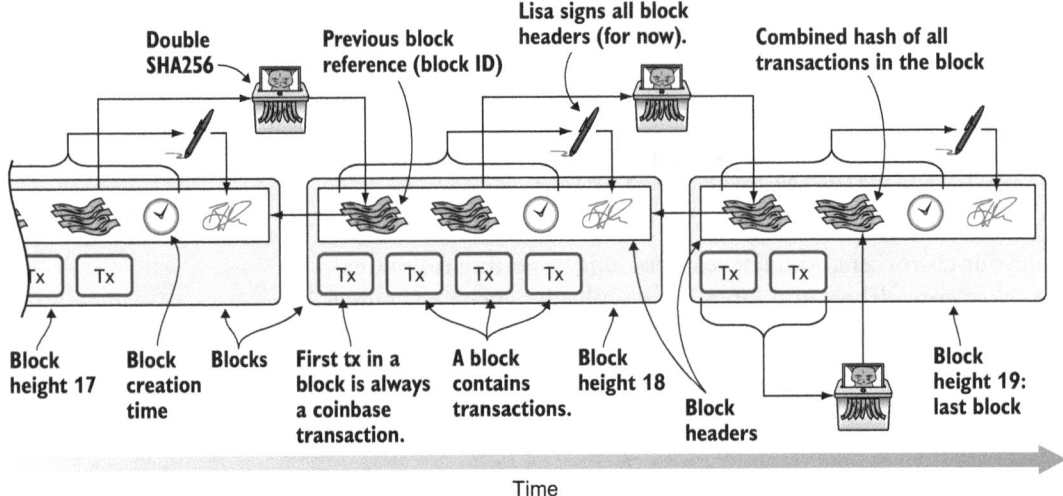

Figure 6.4 Each block header protects the integrity of the contained transactions and the blockchain before the block.

Each block contains one or more transactions and a block header. The block header consists of

- The double SHA256 hash of the previous block's header
- The combined hash of the transactions in the block, the *merkle root*
- A timestamp of the block's creation time
- Lisa's signature of the block header

Block header

Previous block reference (block ID) | Combined hash of the block's transactions | Block creation time | Block signature

The hash of a block header is an identifier for the block, just as a transaction hash, or transaction ID (txid), is an identifier for a transaction. I'll sometimes refer to the block header hash as the *block ID*.

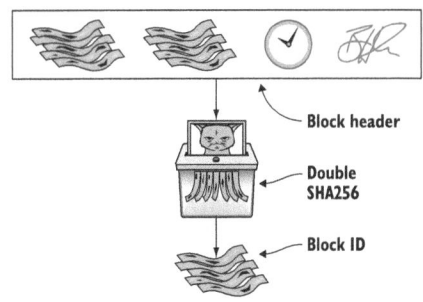

Block header

Double SHA256

Block ID

The leftmost part of the block header is the block ID of the previous block in the blockchain. This is why it's called a block*chain*. The previous block-header hashes form a chain of block headers.

The second part from the left is the combined hash of the transactions. This is the *merkle root* of a *merkle tree*. We'll talk about this in later sections of this chapter, but for now, let's just say that the transactions in the block are hashed together into a single hash value that's written into the block header. You can't change any transactions in the block without also changing the merkle root.

The third part from the left is the block's creation time. This time isn't exact and doesn't even always increase from block to block. But it's roughly accurate.

The fourth part is Lisa's block signature, which is a stamp of approval from Lisa that anyone can verify. Lisa's signature proves that she once approved the block, which can be held against her if she tries to cheat. You'll see how this works shortly. The digital signature in the block header introduces some problems, which we'll fix in chapter 7 by replacing these digital signatures with something called *proof of work*.

Lisa builds a block

Lisa creates a new block roughly every 10 minutes, containing unconfirmed transactions. She writes this block into a new file in a shared folder. Everyone has permission to create new files in the shared folder, but no one has permission to delete or change files. When Lisa writes a block to a file in the shared folder, she *confirms* the transactions in that block.

Suppose Lisa is about to create a new block at height 20. She'll do the following:

1. Create a block template.
2. Sign the block template to make it complete.
3. Publish the block.

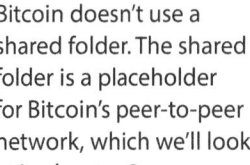

Shared folder? Really?

Bitcoin doesn't use a shared folder. The shared folder is a placeholder for Bitcoin's peer-to-peer network, which we'll look at in chapter 8.

Block templates

Lisa starts by creating the *block template*, a block without a signature (figure 6.5).

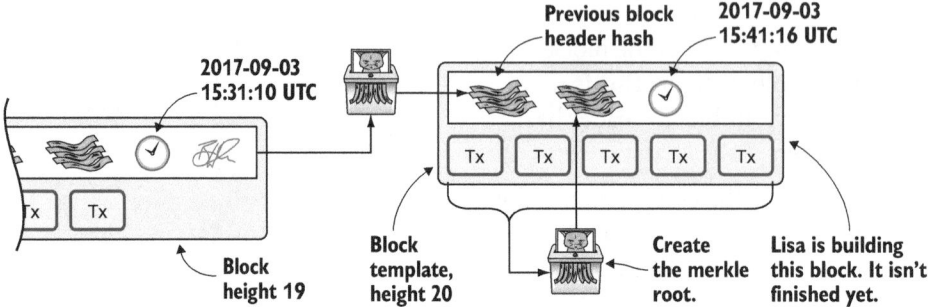

Figure 6.5   Lisa creates a new block. It's called a *block template* because it isn't yet signed.

She collects several transactions to put in the block. She then creates the block header. She creates the previous block ID by hashing the previous block header and putting the result in the new block header. The merkle root is built using the transactions in the block template, and the time is set to the current time.

The first transaction in her block is a coinbase transaction. Blocks' coinbase transactions create 50 CT per block instead of 7,200 CT as was the case in chapter 5. The idea is that Lisa produces a new block every 10 minutes, which means her daily 7,200 CT reward is spread out over 144 blocks: there are 144 blocks in 24 hours, and 144*50 CT = 7,200 CT. We'll talk more about block rewards and the coinbase in chapter 7.

> **Block rewards** 🅱
>
> In Bitcoin, the block reward covers more than just the newly created money. It also includes transaction fees, discussed in chapter 7. The newly created money in a block is called the *block subsidy*.

Signing the block

Before Lisa is finished with the block, she must sign it using a private key only she knows, as shown in figure 6.6.

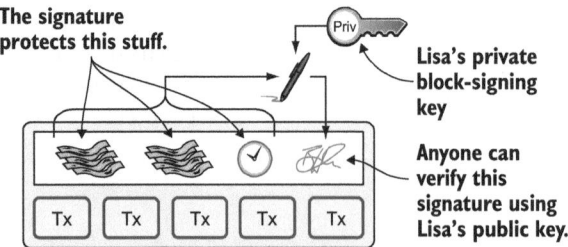

Figure 6.6   Lisa signs a block with her block-signing private key. The public key is well known among the coworkers.

Lisa uses her private block-signing key to sign the block header. This digital signature commits to

- The previous block ID, which means Lisa's signature commits to the entire blockchain before this new block

- The merkle root, which means the signature commits to all transactions in this new block

- The timestamp

If anything in the blockchain before the new block or in the transactions in this block changes, the block header's contents will have to change, too; consequently, the signature will become invalid.

The public key corresponding to Lisa's block-signing key must be made publicly available to all verifiers. The company can publish the public key on its intranet and on a bulletin board at the main entrance. The signature is required because only Lisa should be able to add blocks to the blockchain (for now). For example, John, can create a block and write it to the shared folder. But he won't be able to sign it correctly because he doesn't have Lisa's private key, so no one will accept John's block.

Using private keys to sign blocks can be a bad idea for two reasons:

- Lisa's private key can be stolen. If this happens, the thief can create valid blocks and write them to the shared folder. These blocks' coinbase transactions will of course pay the block rewards to the thief's PKH, and not to Lisa's.

- The sources containing Lisa's public key—for example, the bulletin board and the intranet—might be compromised and the public keys replaced by some bad guy's public key. If this happens, some verifiers will be tricked into accepting blocks signed by a key other than Lisa's block-signing key. The bad guy can fool some portion of the verifiers. A coworker shouldn't trust just the note on the bulletin board, because it's easy for someone to replace the note with a false public key. Coworkers need to get the public key from different sources, such as the bulletin board, the intranet, and by asking fellow workers. A single source is too easily manipulated by bad guys.

The way blocks are signed will change in chapter 7, from digital signatures to proof of work.

Proof of work

Bitcoin blocks aren't signed this way. They're "signed" with proof of work, described in chapter 7.

Lisa's public key

```
020fe0e27cb1
d913c71970fc
07d1ce541c25
35e0d2d46828
9e3ec2ac66c8
78fd75
```

Publishing the block

Once the block is signed, Lisa needs to make it available to verifiers. She uses the shared folder for this, creating a new file, block_20.dat, in which to save her new block (figure 6.7).

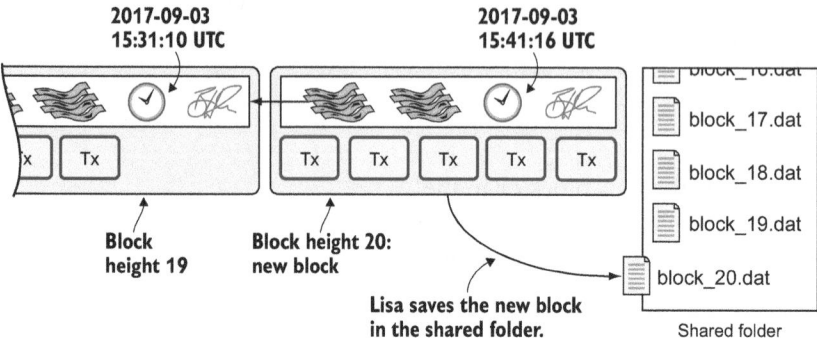

Figure 6.7   Lisa has signed her new block and saves it into a new file in the shared folder.

The block is now published. Anyone interested can read this block from the shared folder. Remember that no one can delete or alter this file due to restrictive permissions on the shared folder. Not even Lisa can change it. There is, however, a system administrator who has full permission to do anything with the shared folder. We'll get rid of the system administrator in chapter 8, when I introduce the peer-to-peer network.

Transaction selection

When Lisa builds her block, she picks transactions to include. She can select anything from zero transactions to all unconfirmed transactions. The transaction order isn't important as long as all transactions spend outputs already present in the blockchain or in the block being built. For example, the block in figure 6.8 is perfectly fine.

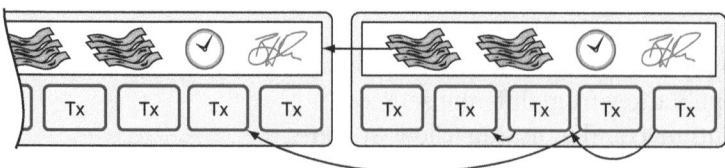

Figure 6.8   Transactions must be ordered in *spending order*. Otherwise, there are no restrictions.

All transactions in this block spend transactions already in the blockchain, meaning they all reference transactions to the left of themselves. But the block in figure 6.9 is invalid.

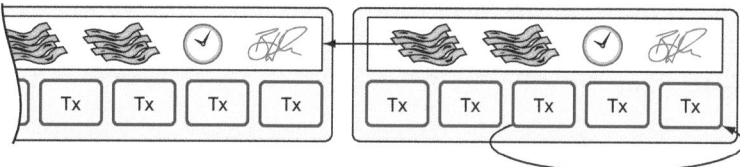

Figure 6.9   This block is invalid because a transaction spends an output that doesn't yet exist.

It's invalid because a transaction spends an output that's placed *after*— to the right of—the spending transaction.

How does this process protect you from deletes?

Suppose Lisa wants to eat a cookie without paying for it. She creates a transaction and puts it in the block she's currently working on, block height 21. She creates the block header, signs it, and writes the block to a new file (block_21.dat) in the shared folder (figure 6.10).

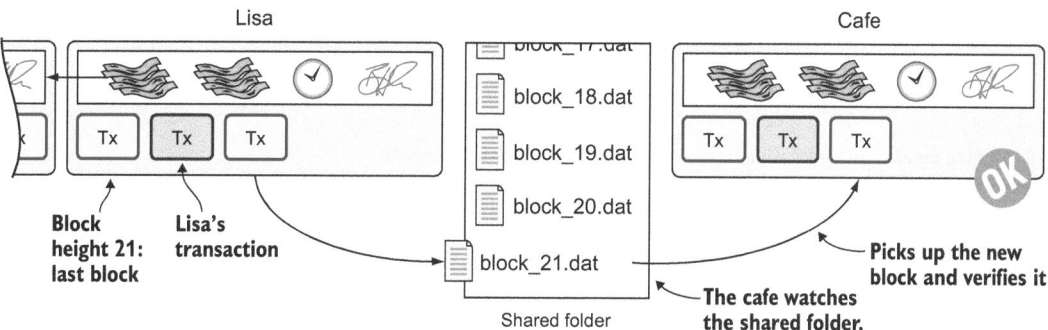

Figure 6.10   Lisa creates a block containing her payment for a cookie.

The cafe watches the shared folder for incoming blocks. When Lisa writes the block file into the shared folder, the cafe downloads the block and verifies it. Verifying a block involves verifying the following:

- The block-header signature is valid. The signature is verified using Lisa's public key obtained from the bulletin board or intranet.

- The previous block ID exists. It's block 20 in this case.

- All transactions in the block are valid. This uses the same verification approach as in chapter 5, using a private unspent transaction output (UTXO) set.

- The combined hash of all transactions matches the merkle root in the block header.

- The timestamp is within reasonable limits.

Lisa has paid for a cookie, and the cafe has downloaded the block that contains Lisa's transaction and verified it. The cafe gives Lisa the cookie, and she eats it.

Can Lisa undo this payment without being proven a fraud? Her only option is to make another, changed version of block 21 that doesn't include her transaction and to write this new block to the shared folder as block_21b.dat (figure 6.11).

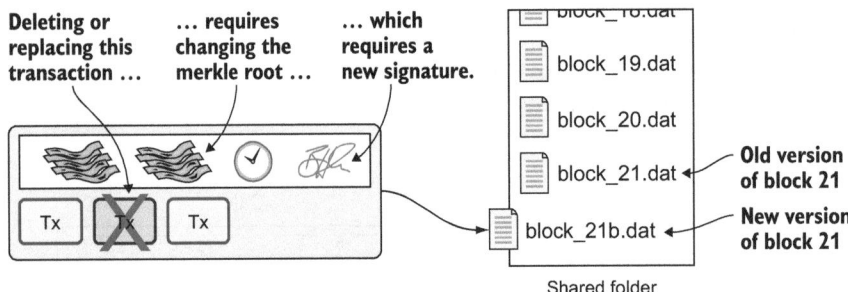

Figure 6.11   Lisa creates an alternative block at height 21 that doesn't contain her transaction.

The new version is like the old version but without Lisa's transaction. Because she tampers with the transactions in the block, she has to update the merkle root in the header with a merkle root that matches the new set of transactions in the block. When she changes the header, the signature is no longer valid, and the header needs to be re-signed. To make the changed block available to verifiers, she needs to put the block on the shared folder, for example using filename block_21b.dat.

The cafe has already downloaded the first version of block 21. When Lisa adds the new block file, the cafe will discover that there's another version of the block in the shared folder (figure 6.12).

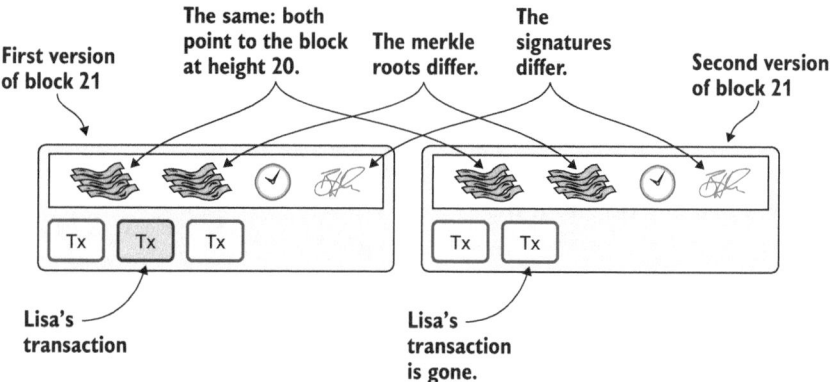

Figure 6.12 The cafe sees two versions of block 21, one with Lisa's transaction and one without.

Now the cafe sees two different blocks at height 21, one that contains the 10 CT payment to the cafe and one that doesn't. Both blocks are equally valid, and neither block is more accurate than the other from a verification perspective. But the good thing is that the cafe can prove Lisa is playing dirty tricks because she's created two different *signed* versions of the block. The signatures prove Lisa cheated, and you no longer have a word-against-word situation. Lisa will be fired or at least removed from her powerful position as a transaction processor.

What if there were other blocks after block 21 when Lisa cheated? Suppose blocks 22 and 23 were already created when Lisa decided she wanted to delete her transaction (figure 6.13).

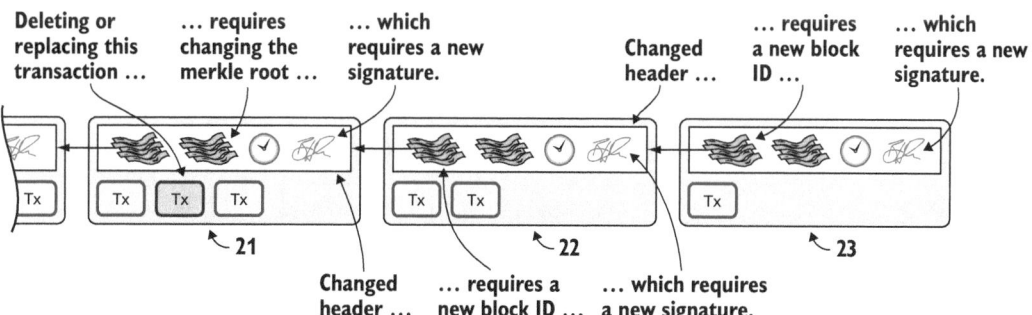

Figure 6.13 Lisa needs to create alternative versions of the block containing her transaction and all subsequent blocks.

Now she needs to make three alternative blocks: 21, 22, and 23. They must all be replaced by valid blocks.

Changing anything in a block makes that block and all subsequent blocks invalid. This is because each block header contains a pointer to the previous block—the previous block ID—which will become invalid if the previous block changes.

Make new versions of these blocks.

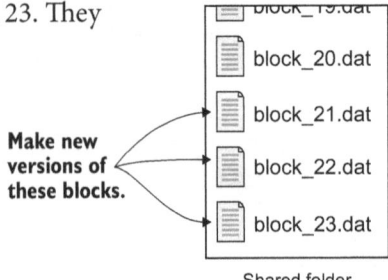

Shared folder

Why use a blockchain?

The blockchain is a complicated way to sign a bunch of transactions. Wouldn't it be much simpler if Lisa just signed all transactions ever made in one big chunk every 10 minutes? This would accomplish the same goal. But this approach has several problems:

- As the number of transactions grows, the time it takes for Lisa to sign the entire set will increase.

- The same goes for verifiers—the time it takes to verify a signature increases with the total number of transactions.

- It's hard for verifiers to know what's new since the last signature. This information is valuable when maintaining the UTXO set.

By using the blockchain, Lisa has to sign only the most recent block of transactions while still, indirectly via the previous block ID pointer, signing all historic transactions, as figure 6.14 shows.

This signature signs this block header ...   ... which is referenced in the next block ...   ... and thus indirectly signed again here ...   ... and here.

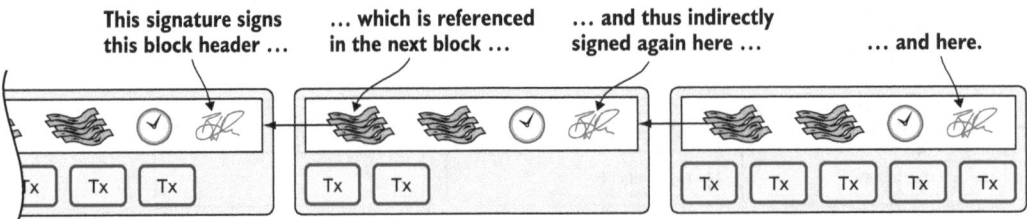

Figure 6.14   Each block signs all transactions ever made, thanks to the headers' previous block ID field.

Each block's signature reinforces the previous blocks' signatures. This will become important when we replace the signatures with proof of work in the next chapter.

The verifiers can also easily see what's new since the last block and update their UTXO sets accordingly. The new transactions are right there in the block.

The blockchain also provides some nice extra features that we'll discuss later, such as the merkle tree.

Lightweight wallets

Coworkers who want to verify the blockchain to make sure they have valid financial information use software that downloads the entire blockchain and keeps a UTXO set up to date at all times. This software needs to run nearly all the time to stay up to date with newly produced blocks. We call this running software a *full node*. A full node knows about all transactions since block 0, the *genesis block*. The company and the cafe are typical full-node users. They don't have to trust someone else with providing them with financial information: they get their information directly from the blockchain. Anyone is free to run this software as they please.

In chapter 4, I introduced a mobile app that coworkers can use to manage their private keys, as well as send and receive money. This wallet app has now been adapted to the new blockchain system.

Because most wallet users are on a mobile data plan, they don't want to waste bandwidth on downloading all—for them, uninteresting— block data. The overwhelming majority of the blocks won't contain any transactions concerning them, so downloading all that data would only make their phones run out of data traffic without providing useful information.

The full-node developers and the wallet developers cooperate to let wallets connect to full nodes over the internet and get relevant block data from those nodes in a way that doesn't require huge amounts of data traffic. Wallets are allowed to connect to any full node and ask for the data they need.

Suppose John's wallet contains two addresses, $@_a$ and $@_b$, and he wants to receive notifications from a full node about transactions concerning his wallet. He can make a network connection to any of the full nodes— for example, the cafe's. The wallet and the full node then start talking, as figure 6.15 shows.

> **Alternative names**
>
> A lightweight wallet is sometimes referred to as an *SPV client* or an *SPV wallet*. SPV stands for *simplified payment verification*.

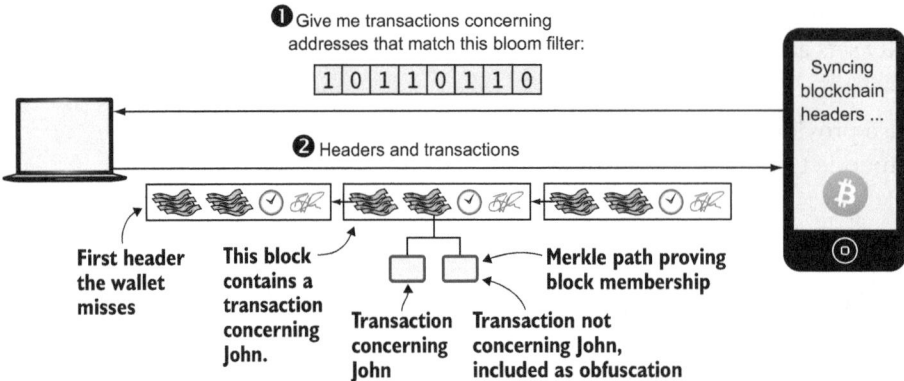

Figure 6.15   Information exchange between a lightweight wallet and a full node. The full node sends all block headers and a fraction of all transactions to the wallet.

We'll examine how this connection is made and how the wallet and node send information between each other more thoroughly in chapter 8. I only provide a high-level glimpse here, as follows:

❶ John's wallet asks the full node for all block headers since the wallet's last known block header and all transactions concerning John's addresses.

❷ The cafe's full node sends all requested block headers to the wallet and at least all transactions concerning John's addresses.

BIP37

This process is described in full detail in BIP37, found at web resource 9 in appendix C.

In step ❶, the wallet doesn't send the exact list of addresses in John's wallet. This would harm John's privacy because the cafe would then know that all John's addresses belong together and could sell that information to Acme Insurances. Not nice. John's wallet instead sends a filter to the full node. This filter is called a *bloom filter*. The full node uses it to determine whether to send a transaction to the wallet. The filter tells the full node to send all transactions concerning $@_a$ and $@_b$, but it also tells the full node to send transactions that aren't relevant to John's wallet, to obfuscate what addresses actually belong to the wallet. Although bloom filters don't have much to do with the blockchain, I still dedicate a subsection to them here because lightweight wallets use them extensively.

In step ❷, transactions and block headers are sent to John's wallet, but the complete blocks aren't sent (to save network traffic). John's wallet can't use just a transaction and the header to verify that the transaction is in the block. Something more is required: a *partial merkle tree* that proves that one or more transactions are included in the block.

The two steps are performed as a synchronizing phase just after the wallet connects to the cafe's full node. After this, as Lisa creates new blocks and the cafe's full node picks them up, the corresponding block headers are sent to the wallet together with all transactions concerning John's addresses in roughly the same way as described earlier.

We'll next discuss bloom filters. Merkle trees are explained in the "Merkle trees" section.

Bloom filters obfuscate addresses

John's wallet contains two addresses, $@_a$ and $@_b$, but John doesn't want to reveal to anyone that $@_a$ and $@_b$ belong to the same wallet. He has reason to be wary because he's heard rumors that Acme Insurances pays good money for such information, to "adjust" premiums based on people's cookie-eating habits.

Creating the bloom filter

To obfuscate what addresses belong together, John's wallet creates a bloom filter to send to the full node (figure 6.16).

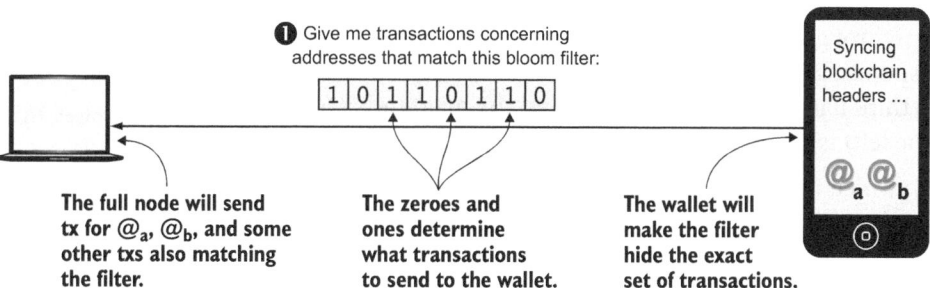

Figure 6.16 The client sends a bloom filter to the full node to obfuscate what addresses belong to the wallet.

The bloom filter is a sequence of bits, which, as mentioned in chapter 2, can have the value 0 or the value 1. John's bloom filter happens to be 8 bits long. Figure 6.17 illustrates how it was created.

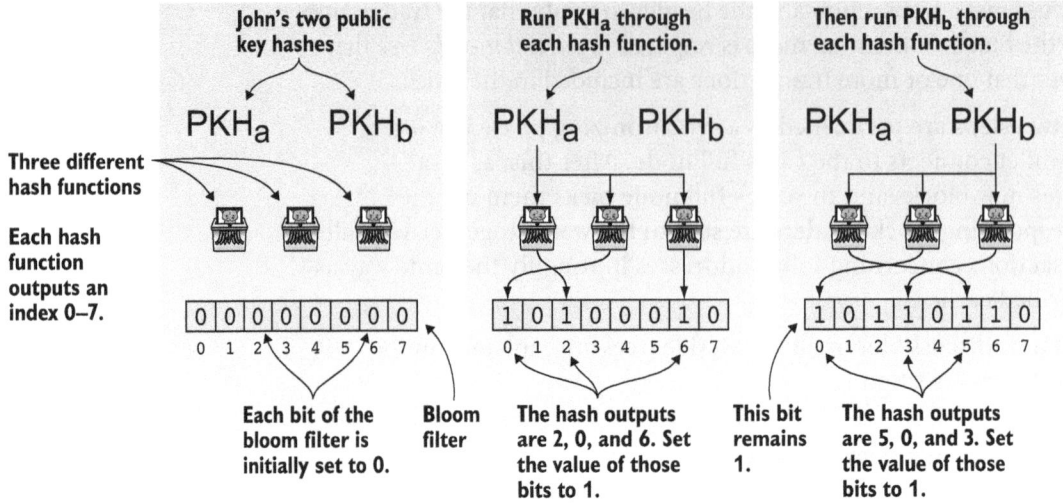

Figure 6.17 The lightweight wallet creates a bloom filter to send to the full node. Each address in the wallet is added to the bloom filter.

The wallet creates the sequence of bits (the bloom filter) and initializes them with zeroes all over. It then adds all John's public key hashes (PKHs) to the bloom filter, starting with PKH_a, the PKH for $@_a$.

It runs PKH_a through the first of the three hash functions. This hash function results in the value 2. This value is the index of a bit in the bloom filter. The bit at index 2 (the third from the left) is then set to 1. Then PKH_a is run through the second hash function, which outputs 0, and the corresponding bit (the first from the left in the figure) is set to 1. Finally, the third hash function outputs 6, and the bit at index 6 (seventh from the left) is set to 1.

Next up is PKH_b, which is handled the exact same way. The three hash functions output 5, 0, and 3. These three bits are all set to 1. Note that bit 0 was already set by PKH_a, so this bit isn't modified.

The bloom filter is finished and ready to be sent to the full node.

> **Why three hash functions?**
>
> The number of hash functions can be anything, as can the size of the bloom filter. This example uses three hash functions and 8 bits.

Using the bloom filter

The full node receives the bloom filter from the wallet and wants to use it to filter transactions to send to the wallet.

Suppose Lisa just published a new block to the shared folder, and the full node has verified the block. The full node now wants to send the new block's header and all relevant transactions in it to the wallet. How does the full node use the bloom filter to determine what transactions to send?

The block contains three transactions: Tx_1, Tx_2, and Tx_3 (figure 6.18).

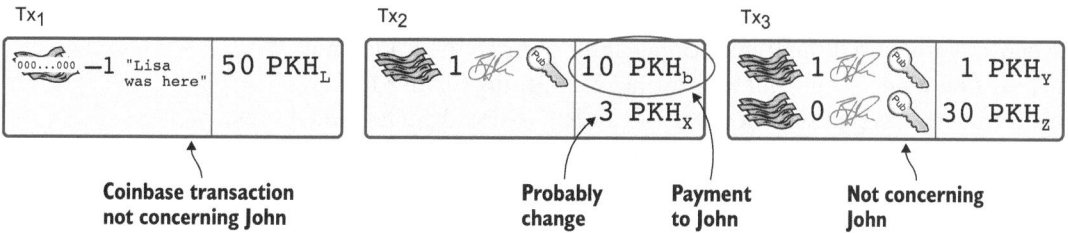

Figure 6.18 The block to send contains three transactions; only one concerns John.

Tx_1 and Tx_3 have nothing to do with John's addresses, but Tx_2 is a payment to John's address $@_b$. Let's look at how the full node uses the bloom filter (figure 6.19).

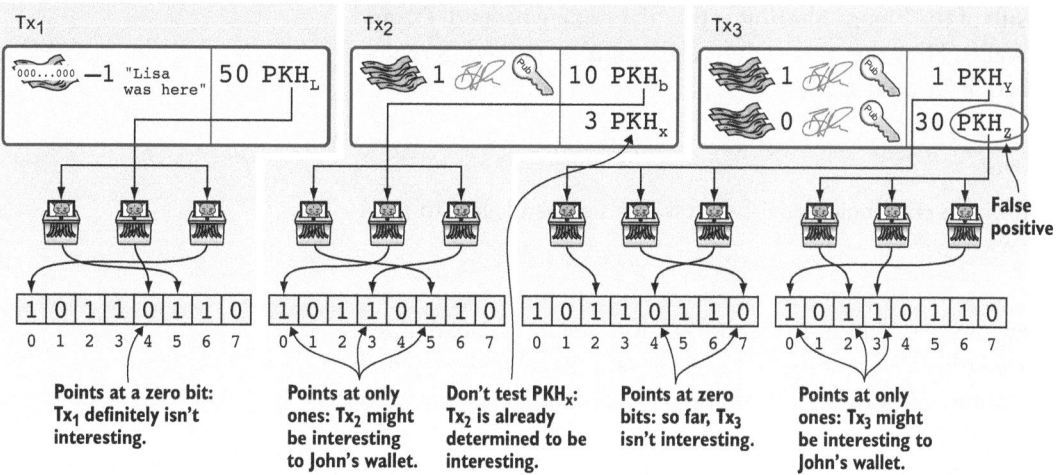

Figure 6.19 The full node uses the bloom filter to determine which transactions are "interesting" to the wallet.

For each output in a transaction, the node tests whether any PKH matches the filter. It starts with Tx_1, which has a single output to PKH_L. To test whether PKH_L matches the filter, it runs PKH_L through the same three hash functions as John's wallet did when the filter was created. The hash functions output the indexes 5, 1, and 0. The bits at index 5 and 0 are both 1, but the bit at index 1 is 0. A 0 bit means PKH_L definitely isn't interesting to John's wallet. If John's wallet was interested in PKH_L, the wallet would have added it to the filter, thus setting bit 1 to 1. Because PKH_L was the only PKH in Tx_1, John's wallet isn't interested in this transaction.

The next transaction is Tx_2. It contains two PKHs: PKH_b and PKH_x. It begins with PKH_b. Running this PKH through the hash functions gives the indexes 5, 0, and 3. All three bits have the value 1. This means the node can't say for sure if the transaction is interesting to the wallet, but it can't say that it's definitely *not* interesting. Testing any further PKHs in this transaction is pointless because the node has already determined that Tx_2 should be sent to the wallet.

The last transaction has two outputs to PKH_Y and PKH_Z. It starts with PKH_Y, which happens to point at 2, 7, and 4. Both bits 4 and 7 are 0, which means PKH_Y definitely isn't interesting to the wallet. Let's continue with PKH_Z, which results in bits 2, 3, and 0. All three bits have the value 1. This, again, means Tx_3 *might* be interesting to the wallet, so the node will send this transaction, too. John's wallet doesn't actually contain PKH_Z, but the bloom filter aims to match more than needed to preserve some degree of privacy. We call this a *false positive* match.

The result of the bloom filtering is that the node will send Tx_2 and Tx_3 to the wallet. How the transactions are sent is a totally different story, described in "Merkle trees."

WARNING!

The following is challenging. Feel free to skip this part and jump to "Where were we?"

The previous description is a simplification of what really happens. You tested only PKHs of the transaction outputs described, which would capture all transactions that pay cookie tokens *to* any of John's addresses. But what about transactions that are spending *from* John's addresses? We could argue that the full node doesn't need to send those transactions to the wallet because the wallet already knows about them, given that it created them in the first place. Unfortunately, you do need to send those transactions, for two reasons.

First, it might not be this wallet app that created the transaction. John can have multiple wallet apps that generate addresses from the same seed. For example, do you remember in chapter 4 how a wallet can be restored from a mnemonic sentence? This sentence can be used by multiple wallet apps at the same time. John might want to make a payment from one of the wallet apps and be notified of the payment in the other wallet app so he can monitor the total balance in that app.

Second, John wants to be notified when the transaction is confirmed. The wallet app might already have the transaction, but it's still marked as *unconfirmed* in the app. John wants to know when the transaction has been included in a block, so he needs the node to send him this transaction when it's in a block.

What the node really tests are the following items (figure 6.20):

- The txid of the transaction
- All transaction output (TXO) references in the inputs
- All data items in signature scripts
- All data items of the outputs

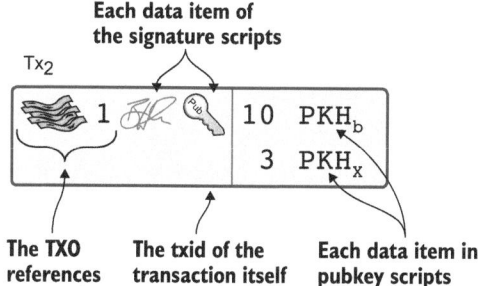

Figure 6.20 Several things in a transaction are tested through the bloom filter to determine whether the transaction is possibly interesting.

For John's wallet to be notified of spends, it needs to add either all its public keys to the bloom filter or all its UTXO references.

Throttling privacy and data traffic

The purpose of the bloom filter is to enhance user privacy. The level of privacy can be controlled by tuning the ratio between the number of 1s in the bloom filter and the bloom filter's size. The more 1s in the bloom filter in relation to the bloom filter's size, the more false positives. More false positives means the full node will send more unrelated transactions to the wallet. More unrelated transactions means more wasted data traffic but also improved privacy.

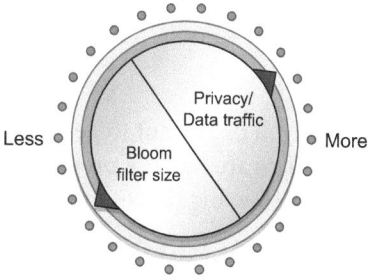

Let's do some back-of-the-envelope calculations. The bloom filter in the earlier example has 8 bits, of which five are 1s. A single hash function's output has a 5/8 probability of hitting a 1. For a single test, the probability that all three hash functions hit a 1 is then $(5/8)^3$. The probability that a single test is negative—at least one of the three hash functions points to a 0—is then $1 - (5/8)^3$. The full node will perform several tests on each transaction, typically nine for a transaction with two inputs and two outputs. Let's check this against the list of tests the full node performs:

* The txid of the transaction (1)

* All TXO references in the inputs (2)

* All data items in signature scripts (public key and signature × 2 = 4)

* All data items of the outputs (2)

The probability that all nine tests are negative is $(1 - (5/8)^3)^9 \approx 0.08$. So, almost all—92/100—transactions will be sent to the wallet. This shows that having only three 0s of 8 bits in the bloom filter won't help reduce the data much, but it protects your privacy better.

To get fewer false positives, John's wallet must use a larger bloom filter so the ratio (number of ones/bloom filter size) decreases.

Let's define some symbols:

t = Number of tests performed on a transaction (9)

p = Probability of a transaction being deemed uninteresting

r = Ratio of the number of 1s/bloom filter size

We can generalize our calculation as follows:

$$(1 - r^3)^t = p \Rightarrow 1 - r^3 = p^{\frac{1}{t}} \Rightarrow r^3 = 1 - p^{\frac{1}{t}}$$
$$\Rightarrow r = \sqrt[3]{1 - p^{\frac{1}{t}}}$$

Let's say you only want to get 1/10 of all transactions (given that all transactions are like the previous transaction, with two inputs and two outputs). How big do you have to make the bloom filter?

$$t = 9, p = \frac{9}{10}$$
$$r = \sqrt[3]{1 - p^{\frac{1}{t}}} = \sqrt[3]{1 - (\frac{9}{10})^{\frac{1}{9}}} \approx 0.23$$

This calculation means the bloom filter should be about 6/0.23 ≈ 26 bits to get only 1/10 of all transactions. The bloom filter size must be a multiple of 8 bits, so 26 bits isn't allowed. We can round upward to 32 bits.

Remember that these are rough calculations based on somewhat false assumptions regarding transaction characteristics. We also aren't considering that the number of 1s in the example isn't strictly six but can be anywhere from three to six, given that both John's addresses could have generated the same set of indexes. But this process should help you get an idea of how big a bloom filter must be.

Problems with bloom filters

Bloom filters have been broadly used by many lightweight wallets, but they have issues:

- *Privacy*—A node that receives bloom filters from a lightweight client can, with high precision, determine what addresses belong to a wallet. The more bloom filters collected, the higher the accuracy. See web resource 14 in appendix C for details.

- *Performance*—When a full node first receives a bloom filter from a lightweight client, the node needs to scan the entire blockchain for matching transactions. This scanning is processing and disk intensive and can take several minutes, depending on the full node's hardware. This fact can be used maliciously to attack full nodes so they become unresponsive, in a *denial-of-service* (DoS) attack.

New Bitcoin Improvement Proposals (BIPs), BIP157 and BIP158, have been proposed that aim to solve these issues, but they haven't been widely implemented and tested yet. The general idea is to reverse the process so a full node sends a filter to the lightweight wallet for each block. This filter contains information about what addresses the block affects. The lightweight client checks whether its addresses match the filter and, if so, downloads the entire block. The block can be downloaded from any source, not just the full node that sent the filter.

Where were we?

For the sake of orientation, figure 6.21 shows part of what I sketched out in "Step ❹: Wallets" in chapter 1, where Bob's wallet was notified of Alice's payment to Bob.

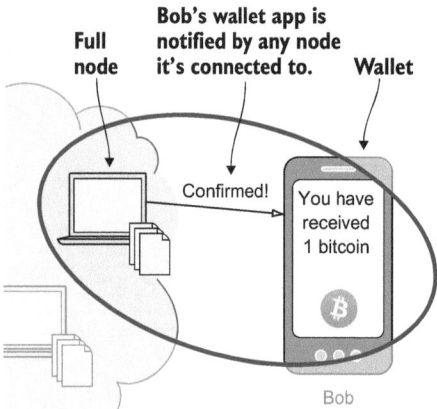

Figure 6.21   A Bitcoin wallet is notified of an incoming payment by a full node.

In the example in this chapter, John has sent a bloom filter to the cafe's full node to receive only information concerning him. The full node has received a block that contains two transactions that are interesting to John, at least according to John's bloom filter.

The next thing that happens is that the new block's header and the potentially interesting transactions are sent to John's wallet.

Merkle trees

Now that the full node has determined which transactions to send to the wallet, it needs to send the new block header and all transactions John's wallet might be interested in.

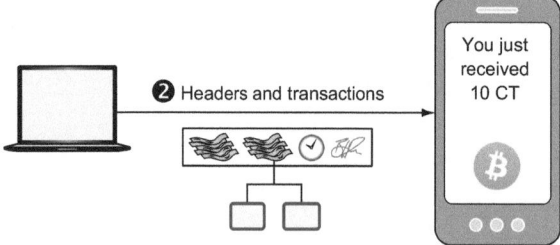

Figure 6.22   The full node feeds the lightweight wallet the block header and potentially relevant transactions.

The full node has determined that transactions Tx_2 and Tx_3 need to be sent to the wallet. If the node sends only the header and the two transactions, then John's wallet won't be able to verify that the transactions belong to the block. The merkle root depends on three transactions, Tx_1, Tx_2, and Tx_3, but the wallet only gets Tx_2 and Tx_3 from the full node. The wallet can't re-create the merkle root in the block header. It needs more information to verify that the transactions are included in the block. Remember that you want to save data traffic, so sending all transactions in the block isn't good enough.

Creating the merkle root

It's time to reveal how Lisa created the merkle root. Suppose Lisa is about to create the block header shown in figure 6.22. She needs to calculate the combined hash of all transactions, called the merkle root (figure 6.23). You calculate the merkle root by creating a hierarchy of cryptographic hashes, a merkle tree.

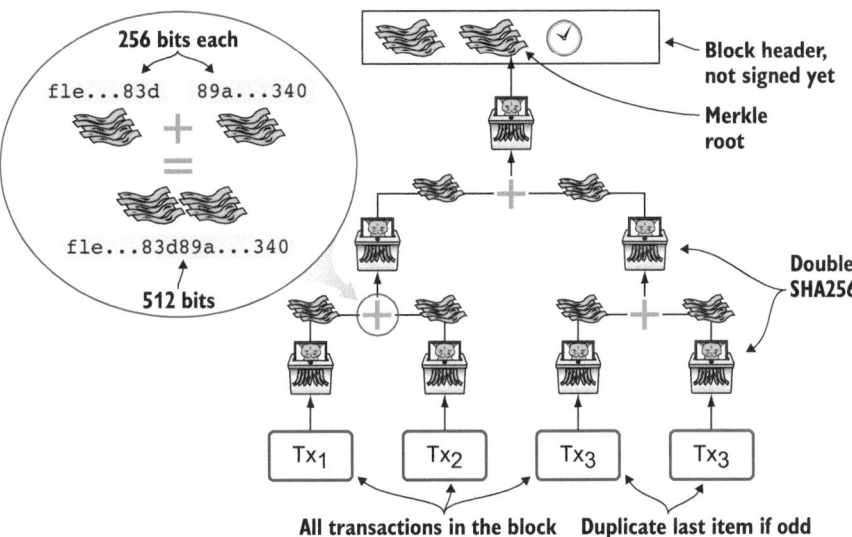

Figure 6.23   Lisa creates a merkle root from the transactions in a block.

The transactions are ordered the same way they are in the block. If the number of items is odd, the last item is duplicated and added last. This extra item isn't added to the block; it's only duplicated temporarily for the merkle tree calculation.

Each item (transaction, in this case) is hashed with double SHA256. This results in four hash values of 256 bits each.

The hash values are pairwise *concatenated*, meaning two hashes are merged by appending the second hash after the first hash. For example, `abc` concatenated with `def` becomes `abcdef`.

The four hash values have now become two concatenated values. Because two is an even number, you don't add an extra item at the end. The two concatenated values are each hashed separately, resulting in two 256-bit hashes.

These two hash values are concatenated into a single 512-bit value. This value is hashed, resulting in the 256-bit merkle root. This merkle root is written into the block header. If any transaction is added, deleted, or changed, the merkle root must be recalculated (figure 6.24).

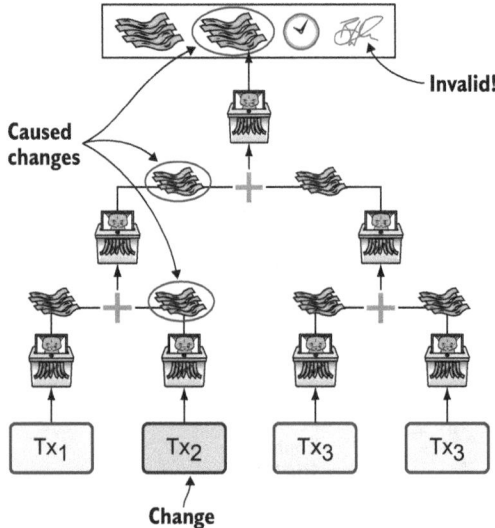

Figure 6.24   A change in the transactions will cause a change in the merkle root, making the signature invalid.

This is nice, because when Lisa signs the block header, you know that if someone tampers with the transactions in it, the signature becomes invalid.

Proving that a transaction is in a block

The full node wants to send Tx_2 and Tx_3 to John's wallet because it thinks those transactions might be interesting to John's wallet. The full node wants to prove to the wallet that both Tx_2 and Tx_3 are included in the block. But let's begin with proving only a single transaction, Tx_2. We'll look at a bigger, more complex example later in this chapter.

How can the full node provide proof to the wallet that Tx_2 is included in the block? It can provide a *partial merkle tree* that connects Tx_2 to the merkle root in the block header. The general idea is to send the bare minimum to the lightweight wallet—just enough to verify that Tx_2 is in the block. In this example, the node will send the stuff in figure 6.25 to the lightweight wallet.

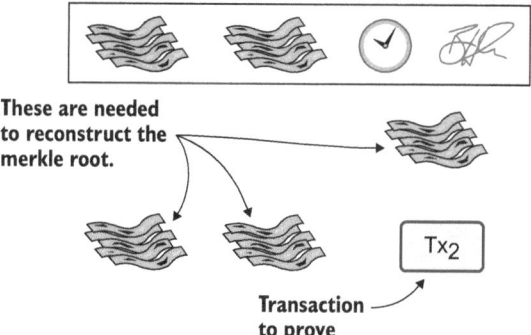

Figure 6.25   The bare minimum to prove Tx_2 is in the block. The full node sends this to the wallet.

The lightweight wallet will then use this information to verify that Tx_2 is in the block by calculating the intermediary hashes toward the root, and verify that the hash of Tx_2 is among the hashes provided by the full node (figure 6.26).

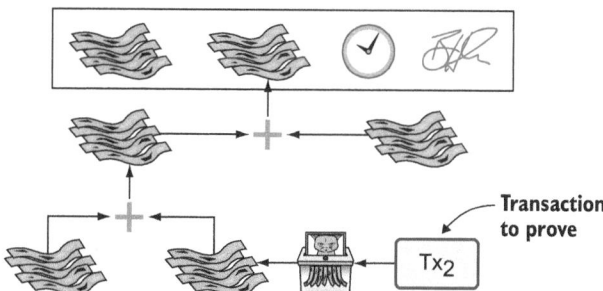

Figure 6.26   The lightweight wallet verifies that Tx_2 is in the block by reconstructing the merkle root.

The hash functions have been removed from the diagram to make it easier to read. The wallet can now be certain Tx_2 is in the block.

How it really works

WARNING!

The following describes in detail how to create and verify a partial merkle tree. If you want, you can skip this part and jump to "Security of lightweight wallets."

Creating the partial merkle tree

The partial merkle tree is a pruned version of the full merkle tree, containing only the parts needed to prove Tx_2 is part of the tree. The full node sends three things to the wallet:

- The block header

- The partial merkle tree

- Tx_2

Let's construct the partial merkle tree. The full node knows the number of transactions in the block, so it knows the merkle tree's shape. To construct the partial merkle tree, the full node examines the hashes in the merkle tree, starting at the merkle root and moving downward in the tree, left branch first (figure 6.27).

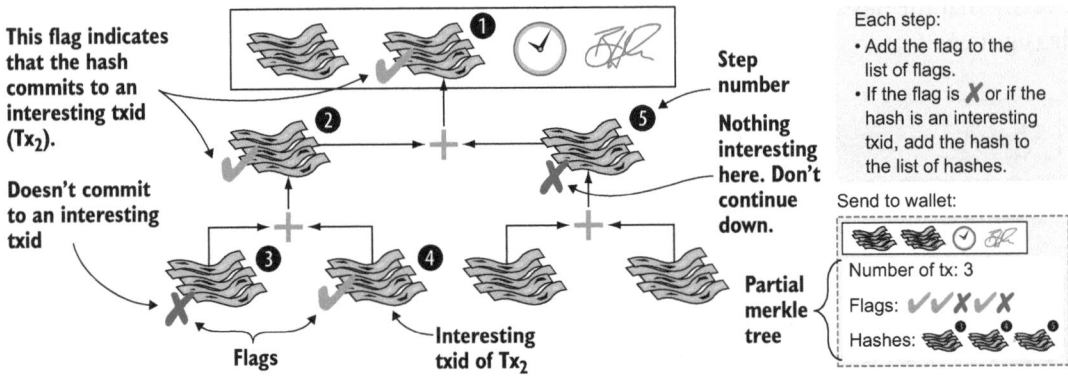

Figure 6.27   The full node constructs a partial merkle tree that connects Tx_2 to the merkle root in the block header.

The partial merkle tree consists of

- A number indicating the total number of transactions in the block

- A list of flags

- A list of hashes

At each step, you do two things with the current hash, as outlined in the following table:

1. Add the flag to the list of flags. ✘ means there's nothing interesting in this hash's branch; ✓ means this branch contains an interesting transaction.

2. If the flag is ✘, or if this hash is an interesting txid, add the hash to the list of hashes.

Step	Commits to interesting txid?	List of flags	Is flag ✘, or is the hash an interesting txid?	List of hashes
❶	Yes	✓	No	—
❷	Yes	✓✓	No	—
❸	No	✓✓✘	Yes	3
❹	Yes	✓✓✘✓	Yes	3 4
❺	No	✓✓✘✓✘	Yes	3 4 5

This ordering of the steps is called *depth first*, meaning you always move downward in the tree as far as you can before moving sideways. But you won't go down in tree branches that don't contain any interesting transactions. This is noted in the list of flags as ✘. You stop at ✘ because you don't want to send unnecessary data to the wallet, hence the term *partial* merkle tree.

Now that the full node has created this partial merkle tree, the node will send the block header and the partial merkle tree to the wallet, and then send the actual transaction Tx_2. The block header together with the partial merkle tree are often referred to as a *merkle proof*.

Verifying the partial merkle tree

The wallet has received a block header, a partial merkle tree, and the transaction Tx_2 from the full node. That's all the wallet needs to verify that Tx_2 is indeed included in the block. The goal is to verify that there's a way to "connect" Tx_2 to the merkle root in the block header. It starts with verifying the partial merkle tree (figure 6.28).

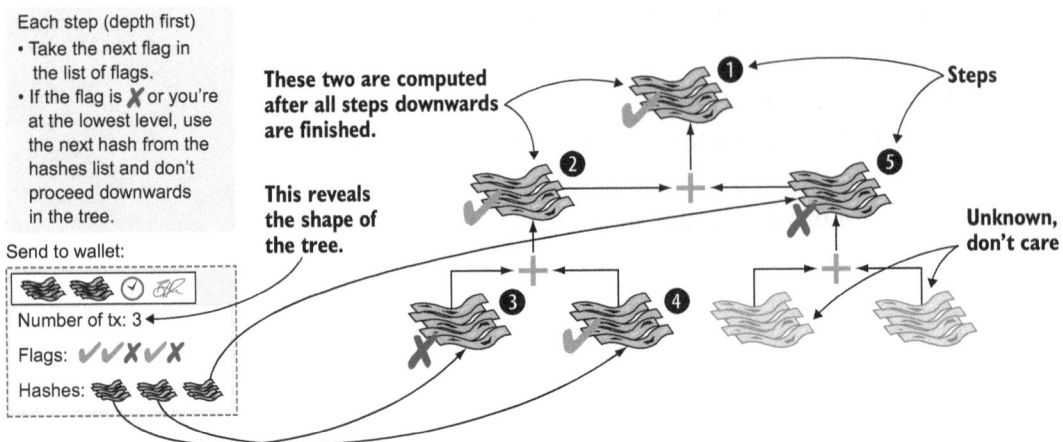

Each step (depth first)

• Take the next flag in the list of flags.
• If the flag is ✗ or you're at the lowest level, use the next hash from the hashes list and don't proceed downwards in the tree.

Send to wallet:

Number of tx: 3
Flags: ✓✓✗✓✗
Hashes:

These two are computed after all steps downwards are finished.

This reveals the shape of the tree.

Steps

Unknown, don't care

Figure 6.28   The wallet verifies the partial merkle tree.

Use the number of transactions (three) received from the full node to build the merkle tree's structure. The wallet knows how a merkle tree with three transactions looks.

Use the list of flags and the list of hashes to attach hashes to the merkle tree in depth-first order, as follows.

Step	Next flag from list	Remaining list of flags	Is flag ✗, or are you at the lowest level?	Attach hash	List of hashes
❶	✓	✓✗✓✗	No	—	3 4 5
❷	✓	✗✓✗	No	—	3 4 5
❸	✗	✓✗	Yes	3	4 5
❹	✓	✗	Yes	4	5
❺	✗		Yes	5	

The wallet has now attached enough hashes (❸, ❹, and ❺) to the merkle tree to fill in the blanks upward toward the partial merkle tree root. First, the hash of step ❷ is calculated from ❸ and ❹; then the root is calculated from ❷ and ❺.

Compare the calculated merkle root with the merkle root in the block header—the actual merkle root—and verify that they're the same. Also, check that the hash of Tx_2 is among the list of hashes received from the full node (figure 6.29).

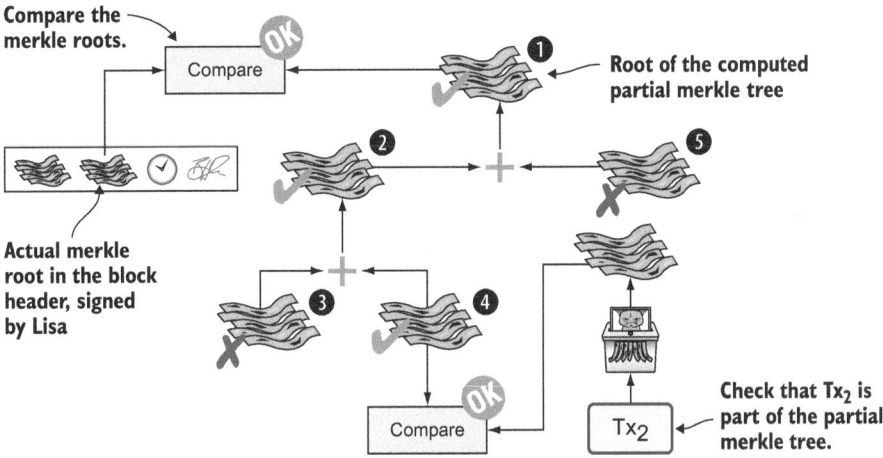

Figure 6.29 The wallet checks that the merkle roots match and that Tx_2 is included in the list of hashes. If so, Tx_2 is proven to belong to the block.

If the transaction turns out to match one of the hashes in the partial merkle tree, and if the partial merkle tree root matches the merkle root in the block header, the full node has proven that Tx_2 is part of the block.

But the full node wanted to send two transactions from this block. How would the merkle proof look with two transactions? Do you send multiple merkle proofs? No—we'll leave this as an exercise at the end of this chapter.

Handling thousands of transactions in a block

The block in the previous example contained only three transactions. You didn't save much space sending the header, the partial merkle tree, and Tx_2. You could just as well send all three txids instead of the partial merkle tree—that would be much simpler. But the gains with merkle proofs become more apparent when the number of transactions in a block increases.

Suppose the full node just verified a block containing 12 transactions. It has determined, by testing all transactions against the wallet's bloom filter, that two of the transactions are potentially interesting to the wallet. Figure 6.30 shows how this would look.

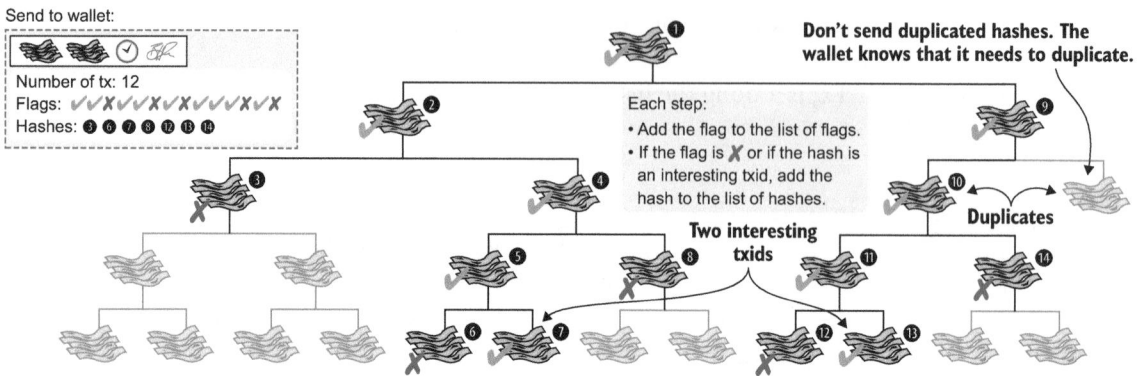

Figure 6.30   Constructing a partial merkle tree from 12 transactions and two interesting transactions

The full node has to send only the block header, the number 12, 14 flags, and seven hashes. This sums to about 240 bytes, far less data than sending the block header and all 12 txids (about 464 bytes).

Let's check some rough numbers to see how the merkle proof compares in size to the full block and the simplistic approach of sending all txids as the number of transactions grows (table 6.1).

Table 6.1   Size of merkle proofs compared to the block size and simple proof for different block sizes

Number of tx* in block	Block size (bytes)	Size of simple proof (bytes)	Size of merkle proof (bytes)	Length of list of hashes
1	330	112	112	1
10	2,580	400	240	5
100	25,080	3,280	336	8
1,000	250,080	32,080	432	11
10,000	2,500,080	320,080	560	15
100,000	25,000,080	3,200,080	656	18

*tx = transaction

Table 6.1 assumes that all transactions are 250 bytes and that you only want to prove a single transaction. The block size is calculated as the 80-byte block header plus the number of transactions times 250. The simple proof is calculated as the 80-byte block header plus the number of transactions times 32. The merkle proof is calculated as the 80-byte block header plus the length of the list of hashes times 32. Ignore the flags and number of transactions, because they're negligible.

The merkle proofs don't grow as fast as the simple proofs, because merkle proofs grow *logarithmically* with the number of transactions, whereas simple proofs grow *linearly* with the number of transactions. When the block *doubles* in size, the merkle proof size roughly increases *by a constant term* of 32 bytes, whereas the simple proof doubles in size.

> **80-byte header**
>
> Bitcoin's block header is always 80 bytes. The cookie token block headers are slightly bigger because of the signature. In the next chapter, you'll fix the block header to match Bitcoin's more closely; and in chapter 11, we'll talk about the version, which is also in the block header.

Security of lightweight wallets

Lightweight wallets seem like a nice touch for the cookie token system. They certainly are, but users should be aware of what they're missing out on compared to full nodes.

Full nodes verify the blockchain's complete history and know for sure that the money a transaction spends exists and that the signatures are valid.

A lightweight wallet knows the entire chain of block headers. It will verify that Lisa has correctly signed each block header. When the wallet receives a transaction and a merkle proof, it can check that the transaction is contained in the block and that Lisa signed that block. But it can't verify a lot of other things. For example:

* That the script programs in the transaction all return "OK," which usually means verifying the signatures of all inputs

* That the spent outputs aren't already spent

* That it receives all relevant transactions

The lightweight wallet also doesn't know what rules the full node is following. The full node might have adopted a rule that pays double the reward to Lisa. A typical full node would consider any block that pays too much to Lisa as invalid because that isn't a rule it signed up for, and would drop the block.

The lightweight wallet needs to trust the full node to verify those things on its behalf and that the full node is following the rules the wallet expects it to follow.

The full node can hide relevant transactions to the wallet. This means the wallet won't be notified about some incoming or outgoing transactions.

A lightweight wallet gives verification responsibility to the full node it's connected to. Suppose Lisa produces an invalid block—for example, a block that contains a transaction that spends an output that doesn't exist. When the full node receives this block, it should verify the block and drop it because it's invalid. But there might be occasions when the full node, deliberately or accidentally, doesn't detect the error. Perhaps the cafe is in cahoots with Lisa to fool John—who knows? The cafe and Lisa can, at least temporarily, make John believe he's received money that he didn't receive.

John can take at least two measures to reduce the risk of being fooled by a full node:

* *Connect to multiple full nodes simultaneously*—Most lightweight wallets in Bitcoin do this automatically. All full nodes that John's wallet is connected to must take active part in the conspiracy in order to fool John (figure 6.31).

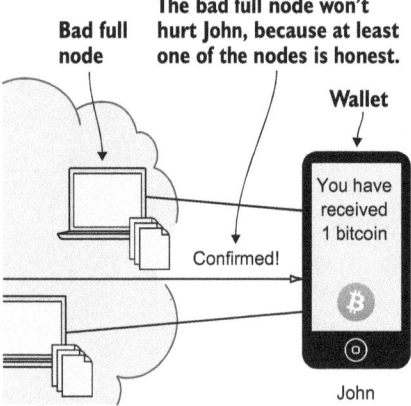

Figure 6.31   John's wallet is connected to multiple full nodes. Hopefully, they don't all collude to fool John.

- *Connect to a trusted node*—A *trusted node* is a full node that John runs himself on a computer he controls (figure 6.32). This way, John can use a lightweight wallet on his mobile phone to save data traffic while still being sure he receives correct information from his full node.

John's full node

John is sure that the full node won't lie, because the node is his.

Wallet

Confirmed!

You have received 1 bitcoin

John

Figure 6.32   John has set up a trusted node that his lightweight wallet connects to.

The last option is useful if John is concerned some full nodes might adopt rule changes he doesn't agree with. The only way to be absolutely sure you follow the rules *you want* is to run your own full node.

Recap

This chapter has described the blockchain and how it enables full nodes to prove if Lisa has tried to delete or change transactions. The blockchain is a sequence of blocks that are connected through cryptographic hashes.

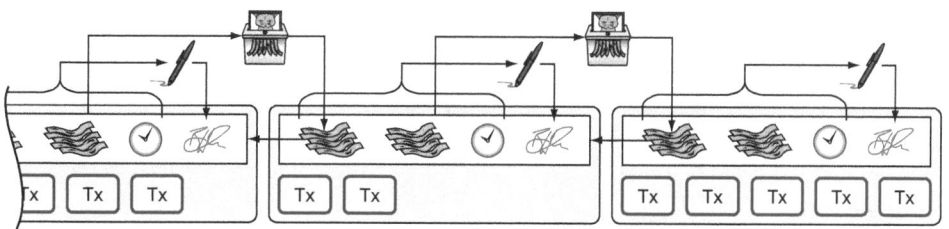

The merkle root in the block header is the combined hash of all contained transactions. This hash is created by hashing the transactions in a merkle tree structure. Hashes are concatenated pairwise, and the result is hashed to get one level closer to the root.

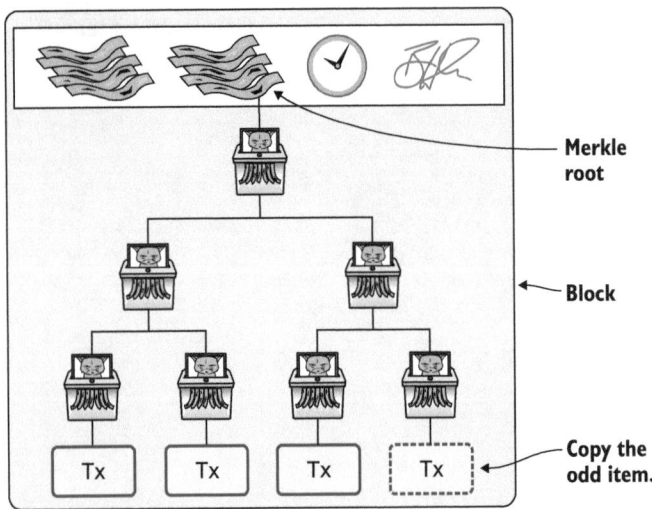

A full node can prove to a lightweight wallet that a transaction is in a block by sending a merkle proof to the wallet. The merkle proof consists of the block header and a partial merkle tree. The merkle proof grows logarithmically with the number of transactions in the block.

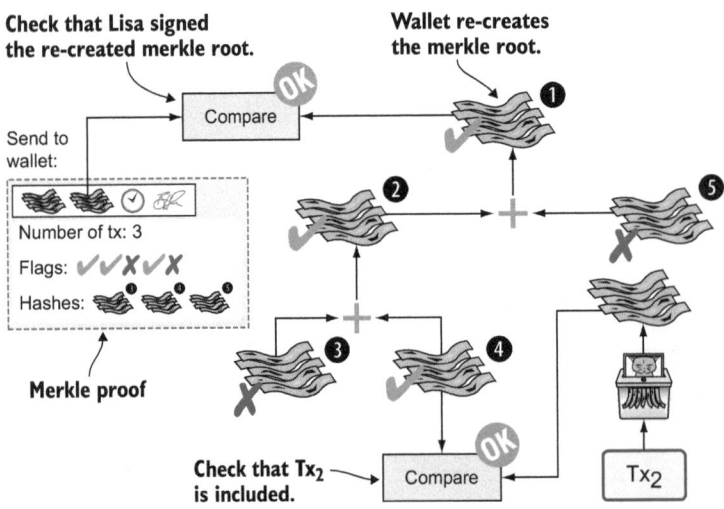

For privacy reasons, wallets don't want just the transactions they're actually interested in. To obfuscate what addresses belong to it, the wallet uses bloom filters to subscribe to more transactions than those that are actually interesting. It creates a bloom filter and sends it to the full node.

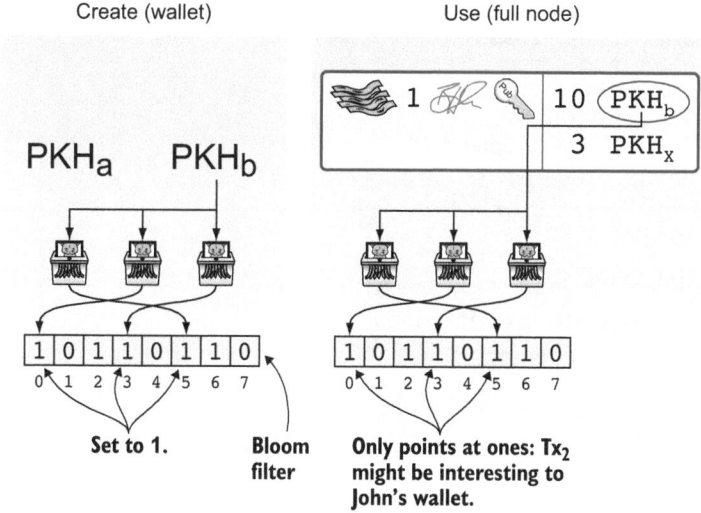

The full node tests various stuff from the transactions—for example, PKHs in outputs—using the three hash functions. If any such item hashes to indexes all containing 1, then the node will send the transaction. If not, it won't send the transaction.

This chapter has solved the issue with deleted or changed transactions. Lisa can't change the contents of the blockchain without being proven a fraud.

Lisa can still censor transactions. She can refuse to confirm transactions being sent to her. She has ultimate power over what goes into the blockchain and what doesn't. In chapter 7, we'll make it much harder for a single actor like Lisa to make such decisions.

System changes

We've introduced the blockchain, which replaces the spreadsheet on Lisa's computer (table 6.2). This chapter also introduced a new concept specifically for the cookie token system: the shared folder. This folder will be replaced by a peer-to-peer network of full nodes in chapter 8.

Table 6.2   The spreadsheet is replaced by the blockchain. We also introduced the shared folder, which acts as a placeholder for the Bitcoin network.

Cookie tokens	Bitcoin	Covered in
1 cookie token	1 bitcoin	Chapter 2
~~The spreadsheet~~	~~The blockchain~~	~~Chapter 6~~
Lisa	A miner	Chapter 7
Block signature	Proof of work	Chapter 7
The shared folder	The Bitcoin network	Chapter 8

This blockchain is close to how Bitcoin's blockchain works but with an important difference: Lisa signs the blocks using digital signatures, whereas in Bitcoin, they're signed using proof of work.

It's time again to release a new version of the cookie token system. Just look at the fancy new features in table 6.3!

Table 6.3   Release notes, cookie tokens 6.0

Version	Feature	How
NEW 6.0	Prevent Lisa from deleting transactions	Signed blocks in a blockchain
	Fully validating nodes	Download and verify the entire blockchain.
	Lightweight wallet saves data traffic	Bloom filters and merkle proofs
5.0	Spend multiple "coins" in one payment	Multiple inputs in transactions
	Anyone can verify the spreadsheet	Make the signatures publicly available in the transactions
	Sender decides on criteria for spending the money	Script programs inside transactions

Exercises

Warm up

6.1 How does a block in the blockchain refer to the previous block?

6.2 What information does the merkle root commit to?

6.3 What information does Lisa's block signature commit to?

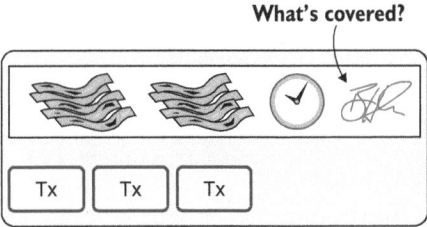

6.4 How are new cookie tokens (or bitcoins) created?

6.5 What transactions would match a bloom filter containing only 1s (1)?

6.6 What stuff from a transaction does the full node test when determining whether to send a transaction to the lightweight wallet? Skip this exercise if you didn't read the challenging parts on bloom filters.

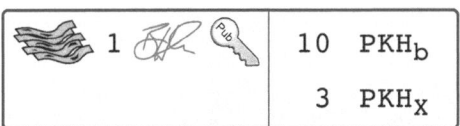

6.7 The hash functions used to create the bloom filter aren't *cryptographic* hash functions. Why not?

Dig in

6.8   Draw the structure of a merkle tree of a block with five transactions.

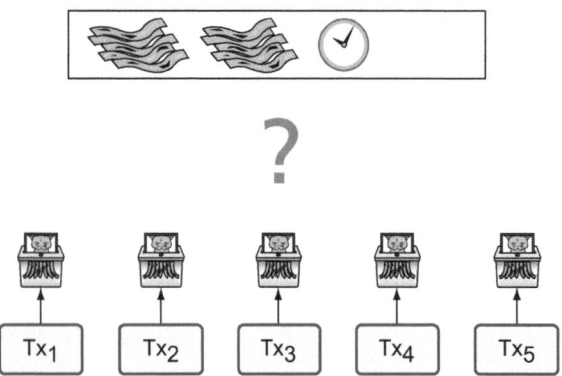

6.9   Lisa signs all blocks with her block-signing private key. The public key is made public through several sources, such as the intranet and the bulletin board. Name at least one security risk with this scheme. There are mainly two such risks.

6.10   There are two places where a single person can censor transactions or blocks. Which two places?

6.11   Suppose Lisa creates a block in the shared folder at the same height as another block. The new block contains the same transactions as the other block except that one transaction is replaced by another transaction spending the same money. She tries to pull off a double spend. Would this be detected by a full node that

a. Hasn't downloaded the original block yet?

b. Has already downloaded the original block?

WARNING!

Exercises 12–15 require you to have read the hard parts I warned you about earlier in the chapter.

6.12   Make a bloom filter of 8 bits of the two addresses @$_1$ and @$_2$, where @$_1$ hashes to the indexes 6, 1, and 7, and @$_2$ hashes to 1, 5, and 7. Then suppose a full node wants to use your bloom filter to decide whether to send the following transaction to the wallet:

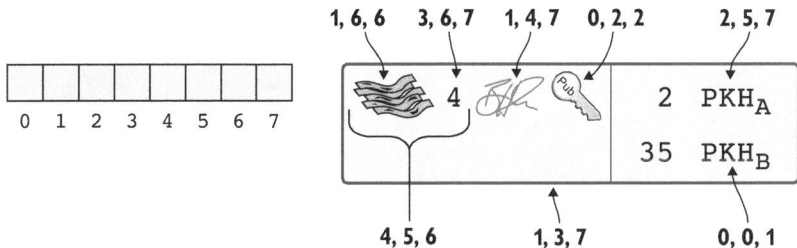

This image shows the hash function results for different parts of the transaction. Would the full node send this transaction to the lightweight wallet?

6.13   When we constructed the merkle proof in "Proving that a transaction is in a block," we only created the proof for a single transaction, Tx$_2$. In this exercise, construct a partial merkle tree for both transactions Tx$_2$ and Tx$_3$. The number of transactions in the block is three.

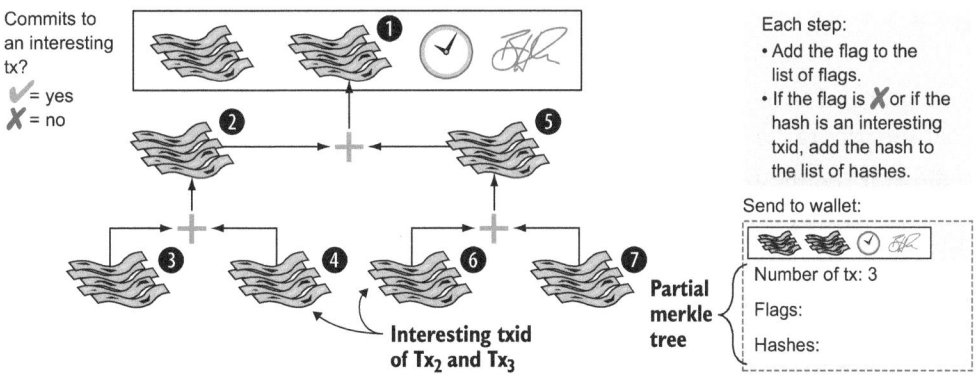

6.14   In "Handling thousands of transactions in a block," we constructed a partial merkle tree from a block with 12 transactions. What txids does the full node consider interesting?

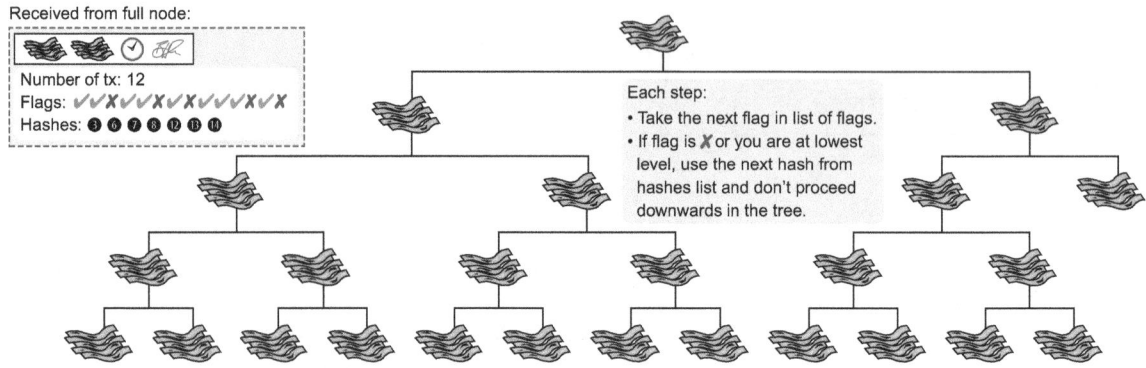

6.15   Suppose that you've calculated the root of a partial merkle tree, as in the previous exercise. What else do you need to do to verify that a certain transaction is included in this block?

Summary

- Transactions are placed in blocks that Lisa signs to hold her accountable if she tries to delete transactions.

- Each block signature commits to the transactions in that block and all previous blocks so history can't be tampered with without re-signing the fraudulent block and all subsequent blocks.

- The transactions in a block are collectively hashed in a merkle tree structure to create a merkle root that's written in the block header. This makes it possible to create a lightweight wallet.

- Lightweight wallets save bandwidth but at the cost of reduced security.

- Lightweight wallet security is reduced because such wallets can't fully verify a transaction and because a full node can hide transactions from them.

- The only way to be absolutely sure the block rules are followed is to run your own full node.

- The security of a lightweight wallet can be improved by connecting to multiple full nodes or a trusted node.

- Lisa can still censor transactions.

This chapter covers

- Making transactions censorship-resistant by allowing multiple "Lisas"

- Competing to produce the next block, or *mining*

- Understanding miner incentives

The previous chapter made it hard for Lisa to remove transactions by introducing a blockchain in which Lisa signs all blocks. This chapter will take this a step further and make the system *censorship resistant* so Lisa can't censor transactions.

To make the system censorship resistant, we'll replace the digital signatures in the block headers with *proof of work* (figure 7.1) to allow for any number of Lisas, or *miners*. These miners will compete to create the next block by trying to produce a valid proof of work. Miners can produce this proof by calculating a huge amount of cryptographic hashes. Wallets can now send their transactions to any or all of the miners to ensure that their transactions are being processed.

With the new proof-of-work system in place, miners want to make blocks as small as possible so they can upload them as quickly as possible to the shared folder. Miners have an incentive to exclude transactions, which was exactly what you wanted to avoid. To give miners an incentive to include a transaction, the transaction might pay a *transaction fee* that goes to the miner that produces a block that confirms the transaction.

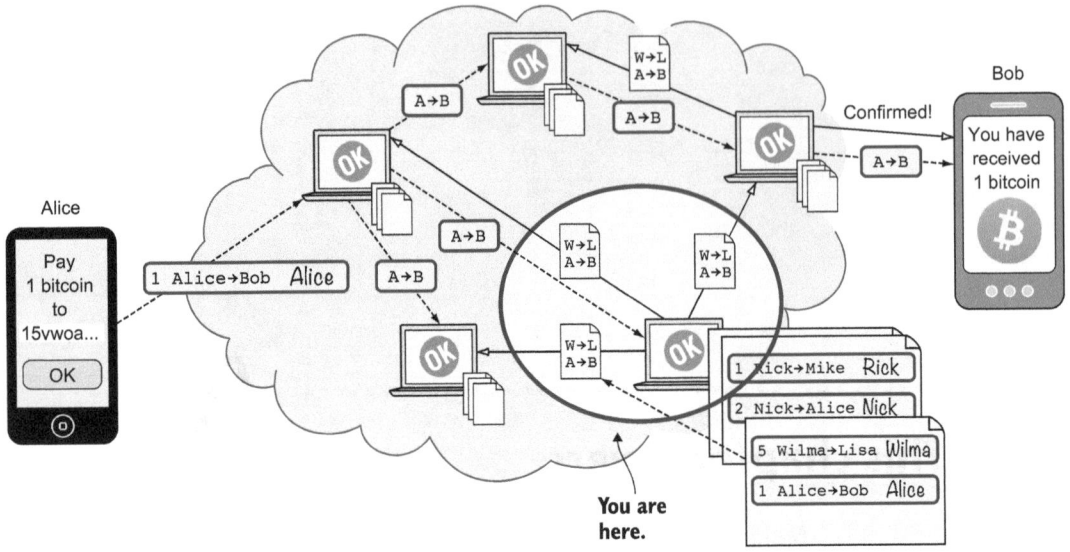

Figure 7.1 Proof of work

The proof-of-work system replaces digital signatures in the block headers. But digital signatures were introduced to prevent Lisa from deleting transactions. Don't worry—the proof-of-work system handles this too, but in a slightly different way. Instead of making it provable that Lisa cheats, you'll make it hard and expensive to cheat.

Throughout this chapter, we'll discuss miners' incentives. Why would they mine? Why wouldn't they delete transactions after being confirmed? What harm can a miner do if it controls most of the hashing computing power? We can discuss a lot of interesting dynamics regarding miner incentives.

Cloning Lisa

We discussed privacy a bit in the "Privacy issues" and "Decentralized" sections of chapter 1. I noted that in a system with a central authority, this authority has absolute power over who gets to use the service and for what purposes.

Lisa is a central authority who can censor any transaction she wants. Suppose Lisa just read a book by a famous dietitian, in which she

What about the shared folder?

Right: the administrator of the shared folder is also a central authority. The administrator can refuse to add certain blocks to it so nobody will ever see them. We'll fix this in chapter 8, when I introduce the peer-to-peer network.

learned that cookies are bad for you. She feels that she must take action against the cookie orgy going on at the company. She starts to refuse to process transactions she suspects are paying for cookies—for example, by looking for transactions with a 10 CT output (figure 7.2).

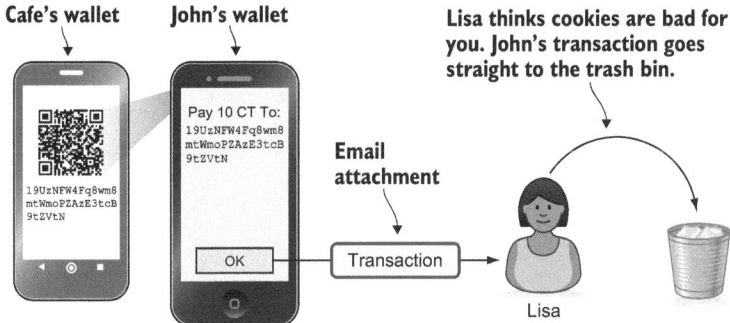

Figure 7.2   Lisa could censor transactions like a dictator. No cookies for John!

People wanting to pay for a cookie in the cafe will be denied service because their payments won't go through. Lisa might also filter out other transactions that don't have anything to do with cookies because she *suspects* they're being used to pay for cookies.

Another possibility for censorship would be that Acme Insurances forces or bribes Lisa to drop suspicious cookie-buying transactions because it doesn't want people to get ill from obesity. A sick person means huge losses for Acme.

Lisa is forced to censor transactions.

Acme   Lisa

What if you could have several people like Lisa so you don't rely on a single person being honest and available all the time? Suppose you let Tom and Qi also start doing what Lisa's doing. If wallets emailed all transactions to all three of them, the risk of a transaction being censored would decrease dramatically. But how would they produce the blocks in a controlled way so they didn't constantly produce conflicting blocks at the same height?

Block collisions

Suppose the current block height is 100. Tom and Qi have just published their block-signing public keys on the billboard and on the company's intranet. All wallets start sending transactions to all three block producers, or miners. Figure 7.3 illustrates what happens.

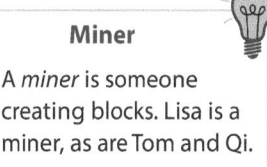

Miner

A *miner* is someone creating blocks. Lisa is a miner, as are Tom and Qi.

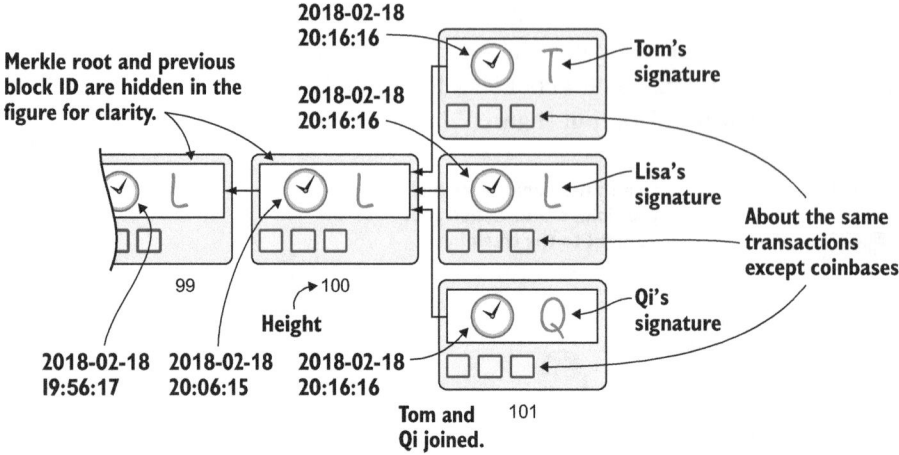

Figure 7.3   Tom and Qi begin creating blocks just as Lisa does, resulting in block collisions. The block headers have been simplified for clarity.

If they all just do what Lisa did, they'll produce a block every 10 minutes, resulting in three different blocks with roughly the same transactions. The major differences between the three conflicting blocks are the coinbase transaction and the signatures. The coinbase of Tom's blocks would pay the block reward to Tom's cookie token address, whereas the coinbase of Lisa's blocks would pay the block reward to Lisa's cookie token address.

Drawing lucky numbers

To avoid this problem, the miners must somehow decide which one produces the next block. They could take turns, but this would be complicated because Lisa's computer might be broken, or Tom might refuse to create a block for some reason. In such a scenario, the system would halt.

Let's try another naive approach (figure 7.4). Every second, each miner draws a random number between 0 and 999,999. If a miner happens to draw a number in the range 0 to 555, it will immediately sign and publish a block. The probability of drawing a lucky number on a single try is low—556/1,000,000, or roughly 1 in 1,800 tries. The miners draw one number per second, so each miner is expected to draw a lucky number every 30 minutes (1,800 seconds) on average. The three miners together will then produce on average 1 block every 10 minutes.

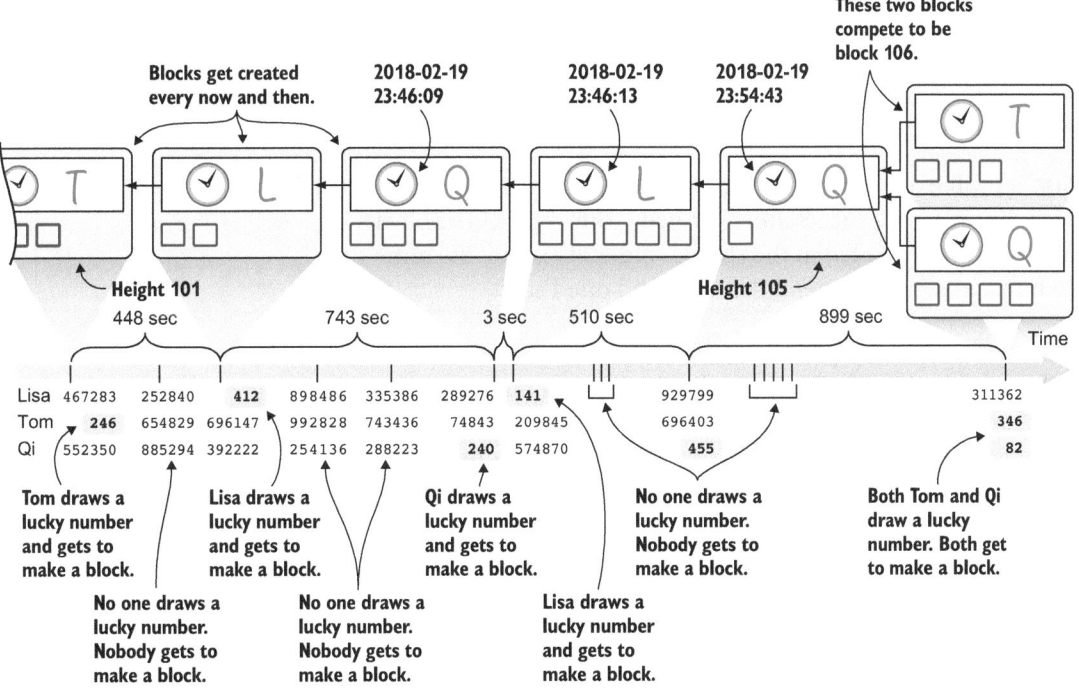

Figure 7.4   Three miners build blocks. Usually blocks are created nicely, one by one, but sometimes they will compete to become the next block, as at height 106.

When a miner draws a lucky number, chances are low that either of the other two miners also drew a lucky number at the same time. This means, usually, only a single miner will produce the next block.

The miners save their blocks as *<last-8-hexdigits-of-blockid>*.dat in the shared folder, so multiple blocks at the same height don't have to worry about file naming. An example of a filename is 9ce35c25.dat.

The system ticks on quite well, but once in a while, two miners draw a lucky number at the same time. They aren't aware that another miner also drew a lucky number, so they'll both produce a block at the same height. This situation is known as a *blockchain split* because the chain splits in two. Both branches are equally valid, so which one is "correct"? Which miner will "win" the block and collect the block reward of 50 CT?

You don't know the winner yet. It's up to the miners to decide which branch they want to extend with their next blocks. In figure 7.4, both Tom and Qi have created a block at height 106. The different miners would likely think as follows:

Honest miners

This approach is naive because we assume miners are drawing random numbers without cheating.

- *Tom*—I will extend my own block, because if I win the next block, I get rewards from 2 blocks.

- *Qi*—I will extend my own block, because if I win the next block, I get rewards from 2 blocks.

- *Lisa*—I will extend either of the 2 blocks, I don't care which. I'll just pick the first one I successfully verified: Tom's block. The blocks might not have landed in the shared folder at exactly the same time, so it makes sense to extend the first valid one I saw.

When the miners have picked a block at height 106 to extend, they build a new block at height 107 and start drawing numbers again. Several outcomes are possible from this situation, assuming everyone is honest: an immediate resolution, a delayed resolution, or a split of a split.

Immediate resolution

In the simplest and most common case, exactly one miner is the first to draw a lucky number. This time, it's Lisa who's lucky (figure 7.5).

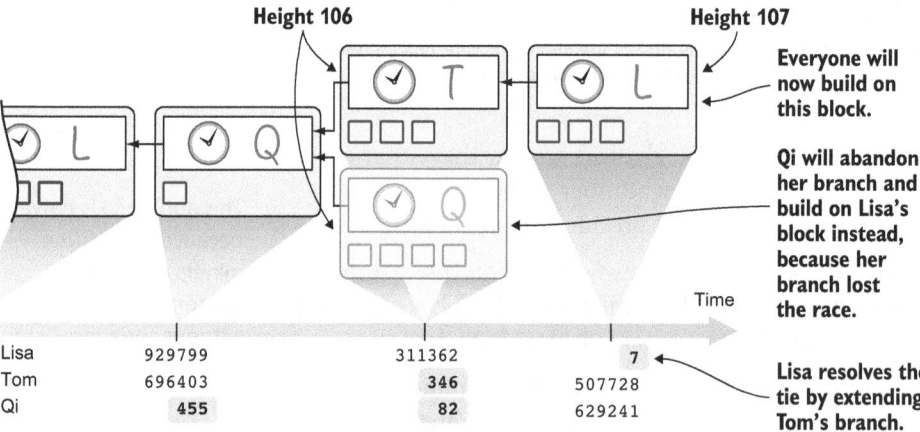

Figure 7.5 An immediate resolution: Lisa draws a lucky number.

Lisa extended Tom's block, so the branch Tom and Lisa were working on gets 1 block longer. A rule for this blockchain is that the *longest* chain is the correct one. This will change further along in this chapter, but for now, we follow the longest chain.

Qi, who was trying to extend her branch, notices that the other branch just got longer because Lisa published a block for that branch. Qi knows everyone else will follow the longer branch. If she stays on her short branch, she'll probably never catch up and become longer than the other branch. She's better off abandoning her short branch and moving over to the longer branch. Now, everyone is working on the same branch again, and the tie is resolved.

When Qi switches over to the new branch, she'll mark all transactions of her old branch (that aren't already in the new branch) as pending. They will be up for grabs for future blocks on the new branch. Nodes maintain a pool of pending transactions, generally called the *memory pool*, or *mempool*. To mark a transaction as pending means putting it in the mempool.

> The UTXO set is built from a single chain. It can't be built from multiple branches simultaneously. Full nodes must choose which branch to follow.

Because Qi abandoned her branch, she also abandoned her block reward. Her block will never be part of the longest chain, so she'll never be able to spend the block reward in her block. Only blocks on the longest chain will affect the UTXO set.

Delayed resolution

But what would happen if both Lisa and Qi happened to draw a lucky number at the same second (figure 7.6)? This would mean both branches would be extended by 1 block each. You still don't know which one is the correct branch. Miners will again pick sides and try to extend their branch of choice.

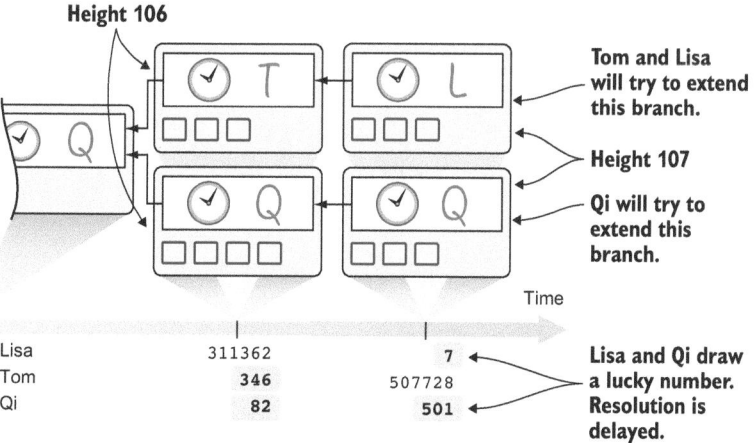

Figure 7.6   Both Lisa and Qi draw a lucky number at the same time. The situation isn't resolved yet.

Let's say Tom is the next to draw a lucky number. He builds the next block on his branch, which now becomes 3 blocks long. It becomes longer than the other branch, which is only 2 blocks long (figure 7.7).

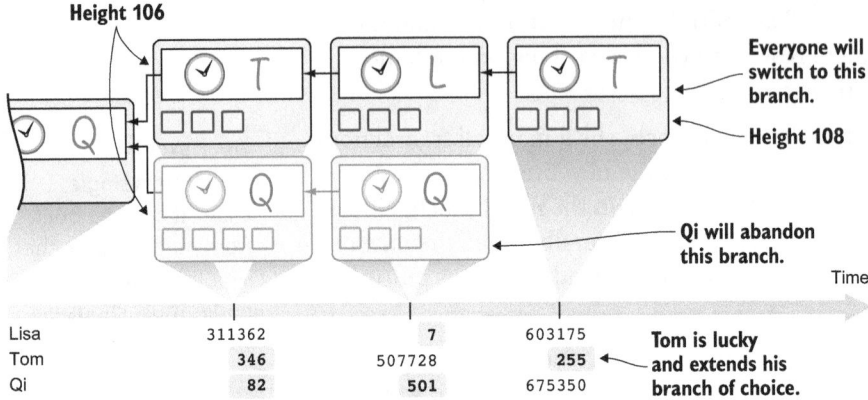

Figure 7.7   Tom is the next lucky miner, and he gets to extend "his" branch, which will now become the longest.

Every miner acknowledges this by switching to Tom's branch and moving on from there. You finally have a winning branch. Again, Qi happens to be the loser in this fight.

Split of split

Say instead Tom and Lisa both draw a lucky number at the same time. They would then both extend Tom's branch. The result would be a split of the split (figure 7.8).

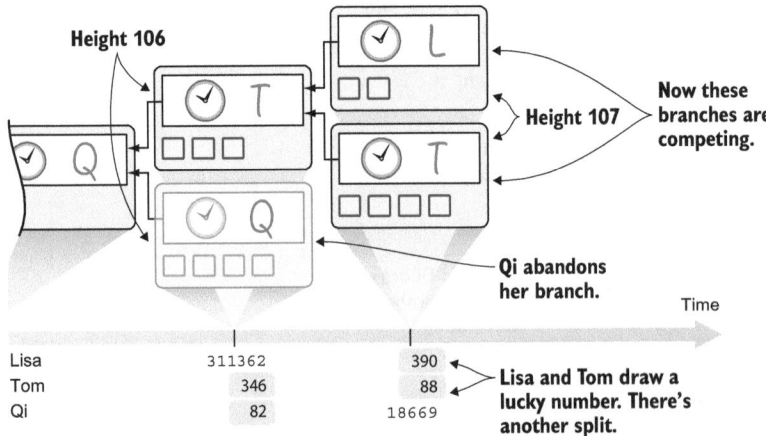

Figure 7.8   One of the branches experiences yet another split. This new split is resolved like the previous one.

You now have three branches. Qi's branch is probably abandoned because it's shorter than the two new branches, Lisa's branch and Tom's branch. This new competition will be resolved in the same way as the first split. It will be resolved

- Immediately by the next block

- After a delay because 2 blocks appear simultaneously, one on each branch

- When a new split is introduced on either of the two new branches

Probability of splits

Eventually, one branch of a split will win. The likelihood that two branches of length X happen next diminishes rapidly for increasing X:

Branch length	Probability	Happens about every ...
1	5.6e-4	2 weeks
2	2.1e-7	90 years
3	7.6e-11	250,000 years
4	2.8e-14	700,000,000 years

> **Scientific notation**
>
> 5.6e-4 = 0.00056
> 2.1e-7 = 0.00000021
> $Xe\text{-}Y$ is shorthand for $X \times 10^{-Y}$.

A split of branch length 1 is quite likely to happen, but a branch of length 2 probably won't happen during Lisa's lifetime (she's 45). No matter how long the splits are, eventually they'll resolve with a winner. This seems like a nice scheme. But it has its issues:

☐ You can cheat with lucky numbers. You can't prove you actually drew an honest lucky number.

☐ For every new miner, the system becomes more censorship resistant but also more vulnerable to private-key theft. More computers containing private keys means a higher probability that a key gets stolen. A stolen block-signing private key will let the thief create blocks by cheating with lucky numbers and collect the rewards for themselves.

☐ For each new miner, the risk that one miner cheats with lucky numbers increases.

> **Splits**
>
> Splits in Bitcoin occur less than once a month, and the trend is for them to become rarer over time due to more efficient verification and transport mechanisms.

☐ You can't just add new miners to the system. You need to lower the lucky-number threshold as more miners are added, to keep the average of 10 minutes per block and the money issuance at the desired rate.

Clearly, this system won't be able to increase the number of miners beyond a controlled group of highly trusted participants. You'll get a flood of blocks as miners start cheating, but you can't prove they're cheating. It's possible they're just really, really lucky.

Where were we?

This chapter is about *proof of work*. I haven't introduced that term properly yet, but I'll do so in the next section.

In the Bitcoin overview in chapter 1's section "Step 3: The blockchain," you saw that one miner takes the lead and decides which transactions go into the next block and in what order. Bitcoin uses proof of work to decide who gets to take the lead (figure 7.9).

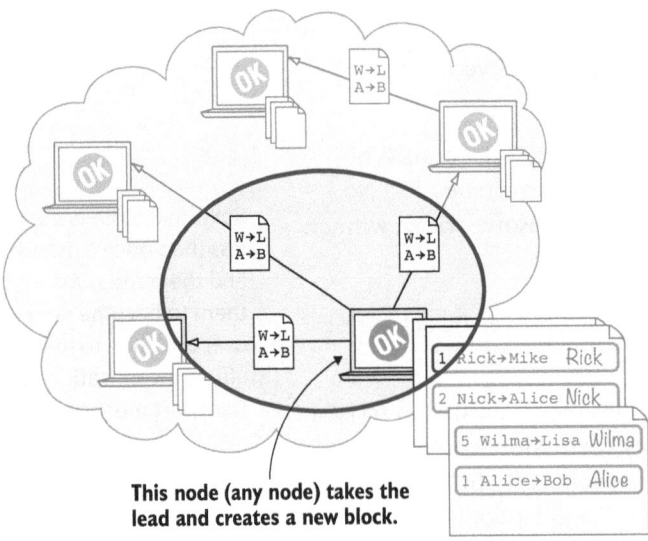

This node (any node) takes the lead and creates a new block.

Figure 7.9   Proof of work is how you select a leader without a leader.

Proof of work lets you randomly select a leader among all miners without using a central authority. Pay close attention to this chapter because this is the essence of Bitcoin. It's what makes Bitcoin truly *decentralized*. We want the system decentralized because this makes it censorship resistant. If the system has a central authority, then transactions can be censored.

Cloning Lisa was a first step toward decentralization, but it isn't perfect because you trust miners to draw honest lucky numbers.

Forcing honest lucky numbers

What if you could force miners to not cheat with lucky numbers? It turns out that you can! You can make them perform huge amounts of computations with their computers and have them prove they've performed the work. You can make them perform so much work that it takes each of the three miners about 30 minutes on average to produce a block, which will result in a 10-minute block interval, just as before.

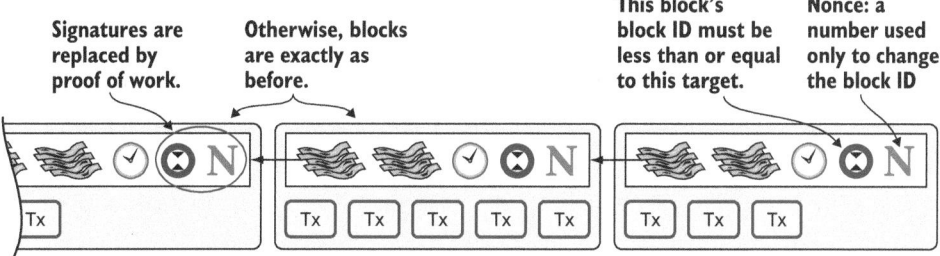

Signatures are replaced by proof of work.

Otherwise, blocks are exactly as before.

This block's block ID must be less than or equal to this target.

Nonce: a number used only to change the block ID

Figure 7.10 The block signatures are replaced by proof of work.

The trick is to replace the digital signatures in the block header with proof of work (figure 7.10). Suppose Qi just published a block, and the cafe's full node wants to verify that this block is valid. Besides verifying the usual stuff like transactions and the merkle root, the full node must verify that Qi's block includes a valid proof of work. The proof of work is valid if the block-header hash—block ID—is less than or equal to an agreed-on target that's written in the block header, as figure 7.11 shows.

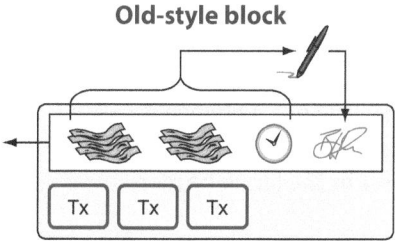

Old-style block

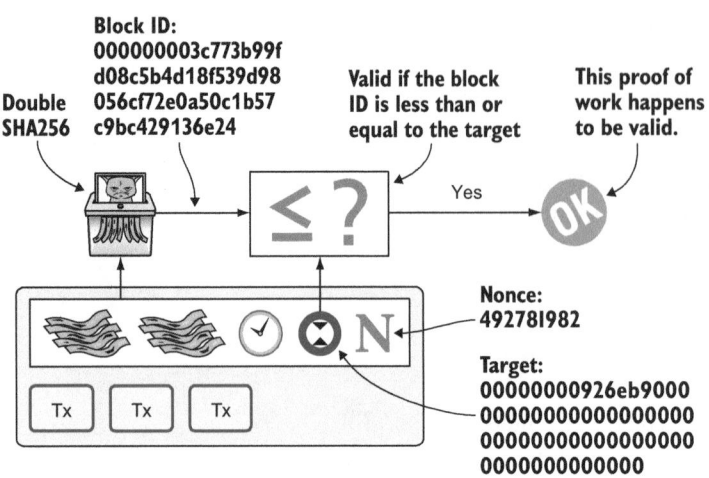

Block ID:
000000003c773b99f
d08c5b4d18f539d98
056cf72e0a50c1b57
c9bc429136e24

Double
SHA256

Valid if the block
ID is less than or
equal to the target

This proof of
work happens
to be valid.

Yes

Nonce:
492781982

Target:
00000000926eb9000
0000000000000000
0000000000000000
0000000000000

Figure 7.11   The block ID must be less than or equal to the target in the header. Otherwise, the block is invalid.

The nonce in this block header is 492781982. Qi selects this value using trial and error. The next section will explain how this works.

To determine whether a block's proof of work is valid, compare the 256-bit block ID to the 256-bit target written in the block header. In figure 7.11, the block ID and target are

```
block id: 000000003c773b99fd08c5b4d18f539d98056cf72e0a50c1b57c9bc429136e24
target:   00000000926eb9000000000000000000000000000000000000000000000000000
```

In this example, the block ID starts with 000000003…, whereas the target starts with 000000009…. The block ID is less than the target, which means this block's proof of work is valid.

The target is a number agreed on by all full nodes and miners. This target will change every now and then according to some common rules. Such a change is called a *retarget*, and I'll describe it in a later section. For now, you can regard it as a fixed number that must be set in the block header.

Producing a valid proof of work

To create a new block, a miner must produce a valid proof of work for the block before it's considered valid. To make a valid proof of work, the miner must create a block-header hash that's less than or equal to the target in the block header.

A block ID is a double SHA256 of the block header. As you learned in chapter 2, the only way to find a pre-image to a cryptographic hash function is to try different inputs over and over until you find one. The same goes here; the miner must try different block headers until it finds one that hashes to a value less than or equal to the target.

Input	Hash
Hello1!	8264…6e64
Hello2!	493c…14f8
Hello3!	9048…0bae
…	…

Let's go back in time and look at how Qi created her block. She creates a block, sets the target to `00000000926e…`, and sets the nonce to `0`. She then tests whether the proof of work is valid (figure 7.12).

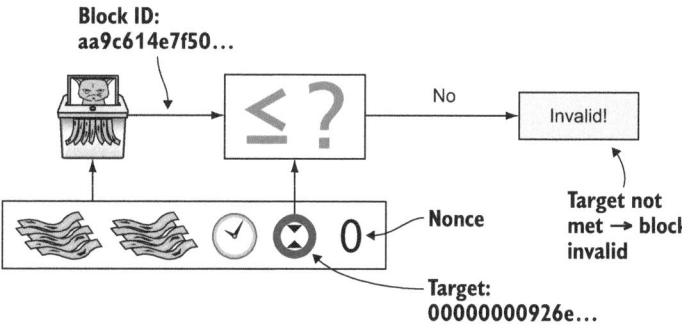

Block ID:
aa9c614e7f50…

No → Invalid!

Target not met → block invalid

Nonce

Target:
00000000926e…

Figure 7.12   Qi tests if her block is valid by verifying the proof of work.

She calculates the block ID by hashing her block header with double SHA256. In this case, the block ID is `aa9c614e7f50…`. This number is bigger than the target:

```
block id: aa9c614e7f5064ef11eedc51856cc7bfcdf71a1f2d319e56d4cc65bda939be79
target:   00000000926eb9000000000000000000000000000000000000000000000000
```

The rule is that the block ID must be less than or equal to the target for the proof of work to be valid. Qi fails miserably.

This is where the nonce comes in. A *nonce* is just a silly number that doesn't mean anything. It can be set to any value. Qi initially set the nonce to `0`, but she could just as well have set it to `123` or `92178237`. The nonce helps make a change in the block that will affect the block ID without changing any real data, like transactions or the previous block ID.

Nonce

The nonce is a 32-bit number, so there are "only" $2^{32} = 4,294,967,296$ possible different nonces to choose from.

Qi will now try again to make a valid proof of work. She increases the nonce from `0` to `1` and tests the validity again (figure 7.13).

When Qi changes the block header by increasing the nonce, the block ID changes—any tiny change in the header will result in a completely different block ID. This is the same property displayed in "Cryptographic hashes" in chapter 2, when we changed the cat picture (figure 7.14).

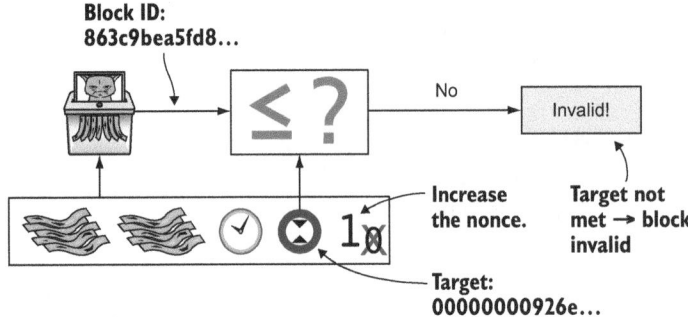

Figure 7.13   Qi increases the nonce and makes a second attempt at finding a valid proof of work. This also fails.

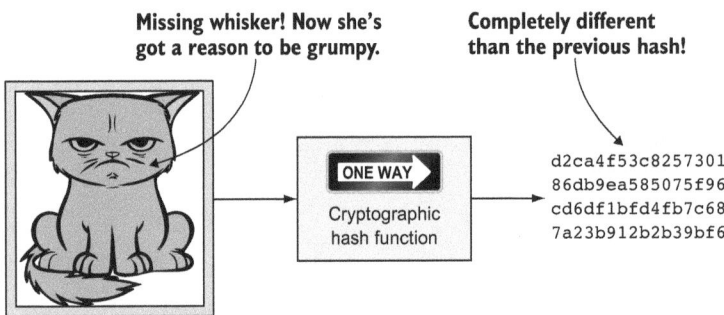

Figure 7.14   Changing the input of a cryptographic hash function results in completely different output.

The new block ID is 863c9bea5fd8... This is also bigger than the target. Qi fails again. I'm sorry, but there's no way around it—Qi must try once more. She increases the nonce from 1 to 2 and tests again (figure 7.15).

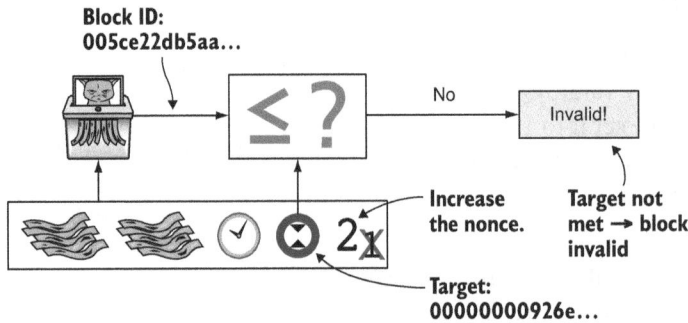

Figure 7.15   Qi's third attempt at finding a valid proof of work. She fails again.

The result is the same: miserable failure. The block ID was `005ce22db5aa…` this time, which is still bigger than the target.

She repeats this over and over. For example, figure 7.16 shows her 227,299,125th try. It was close, but close doesn't help. She has to keep trying (figure 7.17). And finally she gets the result shown in figure 7.18.

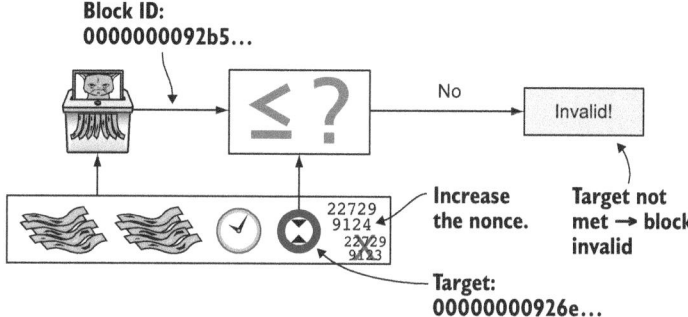

Figure 7.16 Qi's try with nonce 227,299,124. Close but no cigar!

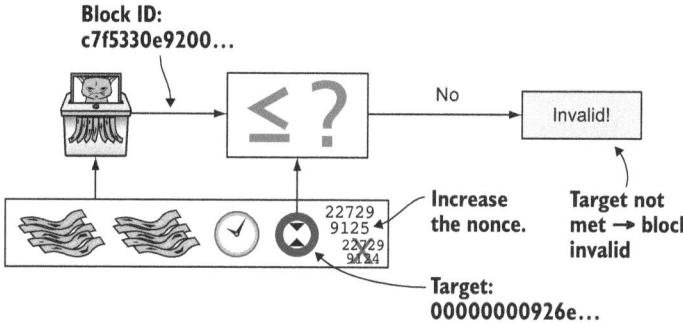

Figure 7.17 Qi keeps on working.

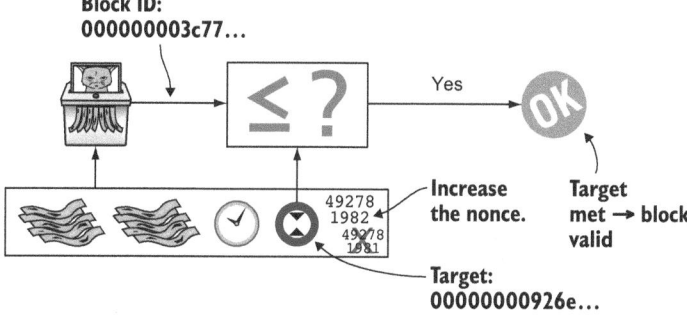

Figure 7.18 The nonce 492781982 is a winner!

The nonce 492781982 results in a block ID 000000003c77.... She compares this to the target:

```
block id: 000000003c773b99fd08c5b4d18f539d98056cf72e0a50c1b57c9bc429136e24
target:   00000000926eb900000000000000000000000000000000000000000000000000
```

Wow—this block ID is less than the target! Qi has performed a great deal of work to find a nonce that results in a block ID less than the target. She's created a block with a valid proof of work. Great, now she'll publish the block to the shared folder.

It's important to realize that all miners build their own unique blocks. For example, Tom is working on his own block concurrently with Qi (and Lisa), but his set of transactions is different than Qi's because his coinbase transaction pays the block reward to himself, whereas Qi's coinbase transaction pays the block reward to Qi. This difference will cause the merkle roots in their respective block headers to differ. If Tom sets Qi's winning nonce, 492781982, on his own block, he likely won't meet the target. Other things that probably differ between their blocks could be the timestamp or the selected list of transactions.

Why is this good?

Anyone can pick up the block from the shared folder and verify that the rule is met—the block ID is less than or equal to the agreed-on target. Block verification is now slightly different than before (figure 7.19).

Now

Previously

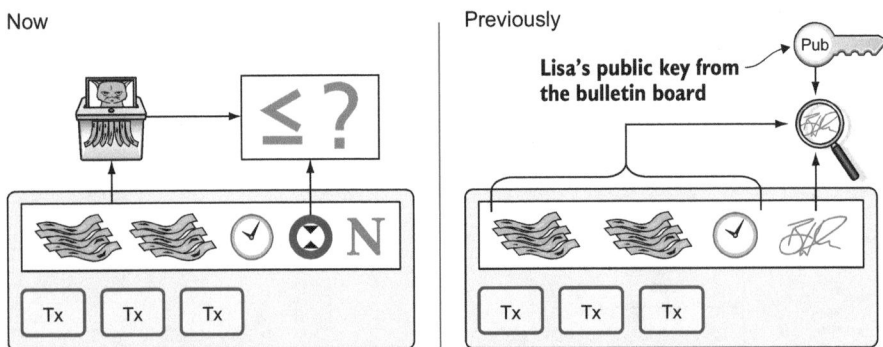

Lisa's public key from the bulletin board

Figure 7.19   Block verification has changed. The verifier no longer needs anything from outside the block.

The difference from verifying a digitally signed block is that the full node verifies the block producer has provided a valid proof of work instead of a valid digital signature.

Blocks are self-contained

You don't need anything from outside the blockchain to verify the block.

With proof of work, you don't need anything other than the blockchain itself to determine if the block is valid. You used to need stuff from outside the blockchain—the miner's public key from the bulletin board. This is a major leap forward toward decentralization. No central sources for public keys are left that can be manipulated.

Comparing with lucky numbers

The blockchain will grow the same way as before, but the drawing of lucky numbers is replaced by hashing the block header (figure 7.20). Table 7.1 compares the two systems.

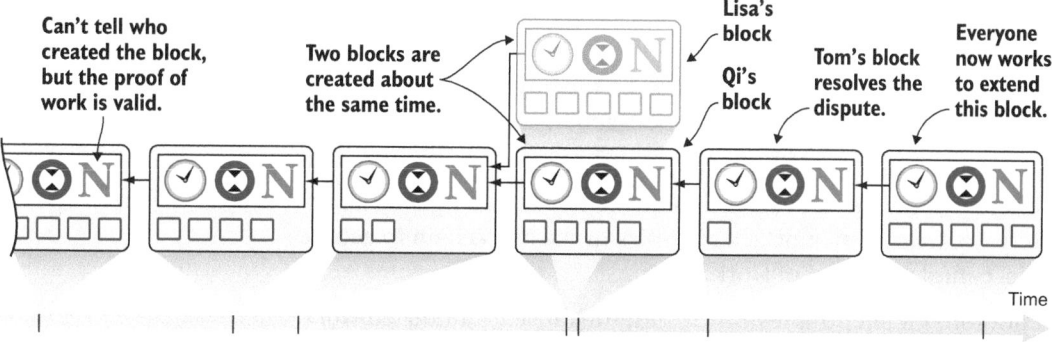

Figure 7.20 The blockchain works the same as when lucky numbers were used.

Instead of drawing a random number each second, the miners draw a number about every 0.02 microseconds through cryptographic hashing. At the same time, the lucky number limit, or target, is set to the 256-bit number 00000000926e…= $926eb9*2^{200}$ instead of just 555.

> 0.02 microseconds is just an example of how long a "try" can take. It varies from miner to miner.

Table 7.1 Comparing the lucky number system with the proof-of-work system

Idea	Target	Possible values	Draw every	Average block time	Best chain in a split
Lucky numbers	555	1,000,000	Second	10 minutes	Longest chain
Proof of work	$926eb9*2^{200}$	2^{256}	0.02 microseconds	10 minutes	Most work chain

A subtle but important difference is that with proof of work, it's the chain with the *most accumulated proof of work* that's considered the best branch to follow. In the lucky numbers case, nodes followed the longest chain. The accumulated proof of work for a blockchain is the sum of the difficulty of each individual block in the chain.

The *difficulty* of a block is a measurement of how many times harder it is to find a valid proof of work for that block compared to finding it for the genesis block.

More exactly, the *difficulty of block B* is calculated like this:

$$\frac{\text{target of the genesis block}}{\text{target of } B} = \frac{(2^{16} - 1) * 256^{26}}{\text{target of } B}$$

The target of the genesis block is divided by the target of *B*, which makes the difficulty of the genesis block exactly 1.

The gist of this is that the higher the target of a block, the lower the difficulty of that block, and the lower the target, the higher the difficulty. So, we sum all blocks' difficulties in the blockchain to get the chain's accumulated proof of work.

From now on, I'll refer to the branch with the most accumulated work as the *strongest branch* or *strongest chain*. Another commonly used term is *best chain*. The distinction between the longest and the strongest chain will become important in "Chain strength vs. chain length," when I've introduced *difficulty adjustments*.

Strongest chain

The strongest chain is the chain with the most accumulated proof of work.

What if you run out of nonces?

The nonce is a 32-bit number. This is pretty small. If a miner has tried all 4,294,967,296 possible numbers without success, they must do something else to change the block header. Otherwise, they'll redo the exact same tries they've already made. Several options exist for making a change (figure 7.21):

- Change the timestamp slightly.

- Add, remove, or rearrange transactions.

- Modify the coinbase transaction.

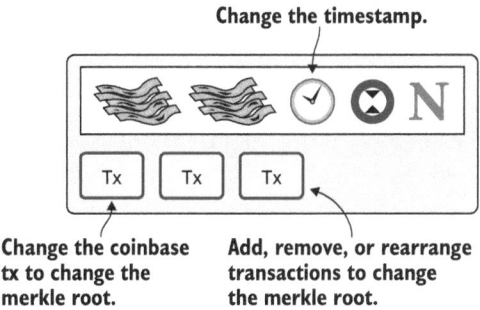

Change the timestamp.

Change the coinbase tx to change the merkle root.

Add, remove, or rearrange transactions to change the merkle root.

Figure 7.21   The block header can be changed in different ways.

Changing the timestamp is straightforward—just add a second to the timestamp, and the header will be different. If you use one of the other two options, you'll have to recalculate the merkle root because the transaction data has changed. When the merkle root is updated, the header changes.

Once you make any of these changes to the block, the header will change so the nonce can be reset to 0, and the miner can begin hashing again.

Miners have to move out

The company thinks the proof-of-work system is nice and all, but it doesn't want to pay for the electricity needed to perform all this work. Because computers run on electricity, the more calculations a computer makes, the more electricity it needs.

The company decides that miners must run their mining software elsewhere, such as in their own homes. This is fair. After all, miners are rewarded with 50 CT for each block they find. The electricity cost for them to produce a block is less than 50 CT. The current market value of 50 CT is five cookies in the cafe, and each cookie token is currently traded at about 20 cents. Each block gives a miner about $10 worth of cookie tokens, which isn't bad given that they each produce about 48 blocks per day.

Let's look quickly at the *hashrate* of our three miners. The hashrate is a measurement of how many hashes (tries) they can perform per second:

Miner	Hashrate (million hashes/s)	Expected blocks per day
Lisa	100	48
Tom	100	48
Qi	100	48
Total	300	144

This system will produce about 144 blocks per day, which is 1 block per 10 minutes on average.

Adding more hashrate

An interesting aspect of this system is that *anyone* can become a miner without asking for permission. They can just set up a computer at home and start building blocks. Blocks are no longer tied to a person but to an amount of computing work:

* *Lisa adds to her hashrate*—Lisa finds this business of mining at home lucrative. She decides to add another similar computer at her house, which effectively doubles her hashrate.

* *Rashid becomes a miner*—Rashid also wants to join the mining business. He sets up a computer at home that competes for new blocks. His computer is slightly faster than the competitors', so he expects to produce more blocks per day than, for example, Qi.

After Lisa's and Rashid's added hashrate, the total hashrate in the cookie token system has increased significantly:

Total Bitcoin hashrate

As of writing, Bitcoin's total hashrate is about 50 exahash/s. That's 50×10^{18} hash/s.

Miner	Hashrate (million hashes/s)	Expected blocks per day
Lisa	200	96
Tom	100	48
Qi	100	48
Rashid	150	72
Total	550	264

Look: we're producing more blocks per day than we designed for! The goal is 144 blocks per day, and 264 is significantly more than this. The *block rate* is too high, almost double the desired rate.

Problems with a high block rate

A higher block rate might seem beneficial because the confirmation time of transactions will decrease, but it comes with some problems.

Too-fast money creation

Remember the planned money supply curve from chapter 2? The plan was to issue half the money supply, 10.5 million CT, during the first four years; then, during the next four years, issue half of that, 5.25 million CT; and so on, until the issuance rounds down to 0. This whole process would take about 131 years.

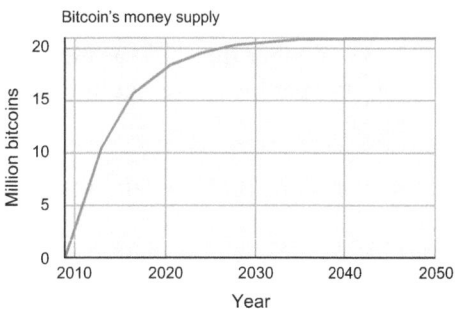

Now, because Lisa beefed up her mining and Rashid added his mining computer, the issuance is too fast. With this high block rate, it will take only half the time until all the cookie tokens are created.

This means the increase rate in money supply is 264/144 = 1.8 times the desired supply increase rate.

More splits

Splits happen naturally every now and then. But when the block rate increases, the risk of natural splits increases. Imagine if 3,000 people started mining in their basements. This would increase the block rate by 1,000 times. Each and every second, several miners would find a valid proof of work and publish a block. There would be splits on almost every block height. This makes transactions in recent blocks less reliable because those blocks can more easily be split off from the main chain.

This would also be problematic from a security perspective because if two branches have about 50% of the total hashrate on each branch, individual branch security is cut in half. We'll discuss blockchain security further in the "What harm can miners do?" section.

What's fixed?

We've fixed the hard problem of forcing "honest lucky numbers" in an interesting way. Let's see what issues from "Probability of splits" remain:

☑ You can cheat with lucky numbers. You can't prove you actually drew an honest lucky number.

☑ For every new miner, the system becomes more censorship-resistant but also more vulnerable to private key theft. A stolen block-signing private key will let the thief create blocks by cheating with lucky numbers and collect rewards for themselves.

☑ For each new miner, the risk that one cheats with lucky numbers increases.

☐ You can't just add new miners to the system. You need to lower the lucky-number threshold as more miners are added, to keep the 10 minutes per block average and the money issuance at the desired rate.

There's only one problem left in the list. We'll fix it in the next section.

Difficulty adjustments

Now that you've added more miners and more hashrate to the system, the block rate has increased. This is because the miners collectively make more tries per second than before, resulting in more blocks being produced per hour.

Everyone has agreed on the target in the block header, but you need to adjust the difficulty of mining a block to cater to increased or decreased total hash rate. The target is adjusted after every 2,016 blocks. This adjustment is called a *difficulty adjustment* or *retarget*, and the 2,016-block period is called a *retarget period*. Remember that each block contains a coinbase transaction that creates 50 new cookie tokens. You want 1 block per 10 minutes on average, to keep the pace of newly minted cookie tokens at the desired rate. That's two weeks for 2,016 blocks.

If the last retarget period was more than two weeks long, the target must increase to increase the probability that a block header hash will meet it. You decrease the difficulty. If the retarget period was less than two weeks long, you must decrease the target to decrease the probability of meeting it. You increase the difficulty.

The new target, N, is calculated as $N = O \times F$, where O is the old target and F is a target change factor that depends on the last retarget period, as figure 7.22 shows.

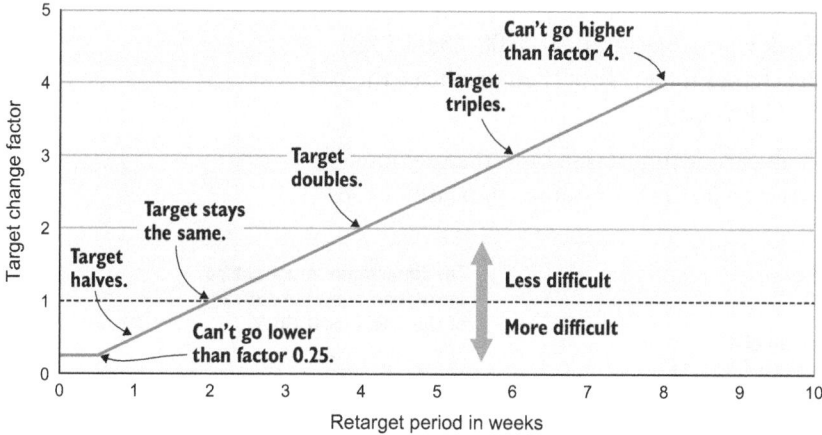

Figure 7.22   Adjusting the target based on the last 2,016 blocks. The goal is 2,016 blocks in two weeks.

Generally, we calculate the new target, N, from O and the duration, T, of the last retarget period as follows:

$$N = O * \begin{cases} \frac{1}{4} & \text{if } T < 0.5 \\ \frac{T}{2} & \text{if } 0.5 \leq T \leq 8 \\ 4 & \text{if } 8 < T \end{cases}$$

The target can't change by more than a factor of 4 or by less than a factor of 1/4 to limit the effect of certain double-spend attacks where someone isolates a victim's node from honest nodes to manipulate the difficulty in their favor. You can read about it at web resource 15 in appendix C.

Rules for timestamps

The block header contains a *timestamp*. Timestamps are important because you want the system to automatically adjust the target without human intervention so that, on average, 1 block is produced per 10 minutes. The block-creation rate is important because you want a predictable issuance of new cookie tokens.

Timestamps are also used by some bells and whistles in transactions. I'll have more about this in chapter 9.

The miner creating a block sets the timestamp to the current time before producing a proof of work. But because different full nodes run on different computers, their clocks might not be in perfect sync.

Suppose Lisa produces a block with timestamp 2017-08-13 07:33:21 UTC and publishes it on the shared folder. Tom then produces the next block, but his clock is behind Lisa's clock.

Tom produces a block with an earlier timestamp than the previous block. This isn't a problem as long as the timestamps don't differ too much (figure 7.23).

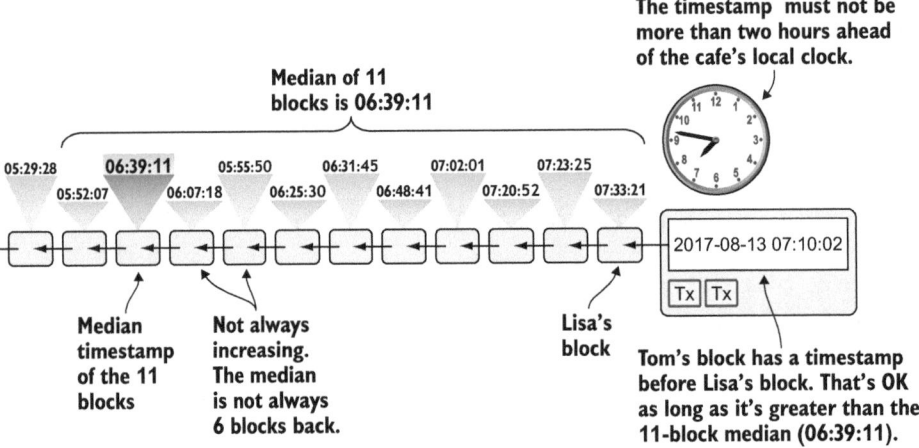

Figure 7.23   Two blocks are mined with decreasing timestamps. That's OK.

The timestamp must obey a few rules. Suppose the cafe's full node is about to verify Tom's block:

- The timestamp must be strictly later than the *median* of the previous 11 timestamps. This median is commonly referred to as the block's *median time past*.

- The timestamp must be at most two hours in the future according to the cafe's clock.

These rules ensure that no one manipulates their blocks' timestamps to influence the next target calculation. Imagine if the last block before the retarget had a timestamp six weeks after the current time. This would cause the next target to increase by a factor of 4, as table 7.2 shows.

Table 7.2 A bad miner manipulates the last timestamp of the 2,016 blocks before a retarget. H is the first block height of a retarget period. The new target will increase by a factor of 4.

Block height	Timestamp (ignoring seconds)	Elapsed timestamp time
H	2017-07-31 06:31	0
H + 1	2017-07-31 06:42	11:17
…	…	…
H + 2,013	2017-08-14 07:22	2 weeks and 51 min
H + 2,014	2017-08-14 07:33	2 weeks and 1h 2 min
H + 2,015	2017-09-25 08:51	8 weeks and 2h 20 min

The last timestamp is six weeks later than when the block was actually mined. All full nodes will reject this block because it violates the timestamp rules. Someone wants to manipulate the target. If this block had been accepted, the next target would be four times bigger than the current target, making it four times easier to find a valid proof of work. This kind of misbehavior is prohibited by the timestamp rules just described. Given that you can't lie more than two hours with your timestamp, the next target can't be manipulated more than marginally.

Chain strength vs. chain length

Let's get back to the discussion on chain strength and why it's important not to merely look at chain length. It intuitively seems reasonable that the harder it is to rewrite the chain's history, the better, so you should follow the strongest chain. But when do the strongest and longest chain differ?

They can differ for several reasons:

• Natural split right before a retarget

• Accidental splits due to incompatible software versions

• Deliberate splits as an attack against the honest chain

We'll look only at the first option here. Suppose a natural split occurs (figure 7.24).

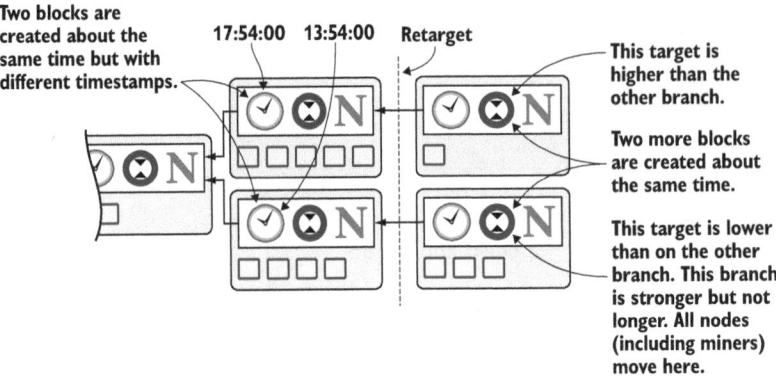

Figure 7.24   A natural split with differing timestamps between the branches will cause one branch to become stronger than the other in case of a retarget.

This is an unlikely scenario, but we need to consider it because it *might* happen. A split happens right before a retarget, and the 2 blocks' timestamps differ by four hours. Next, 2 new blocks are produced at the same time, one on each branch. These new blocks have been retargeted based on different histories. The last timestamps in the respective retarget periods differ by four hours, which causes the new targets to be different. Recall the retarget formula:

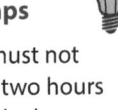

$$N = O * \begin{cases} \frac{1}{4} & \text{if } T < 0.5 \\ \frac{T}{2} & \text{if } 0.5 \leq T \leq 8 \\ 4 & \text{if } 8 < T \end{cases}$$

Because the new targets are different, the new difficulty of the last block on each branch is different. This means the chain strength differs because the branches now have different accumulated proof of work.

What harm can miners do?

In chapter 6, you made sure Lisa couldn't undo transactions without revealing her fraud attempt. You did this by requiring Lisa to digitally sign blocks so anyone can verify that Lisa has approved a block. If she later signs a competing block on the same height that replaces her own transaction with a transaction paying to herself instead, everyone will notice and hold her accountable.

Now the situation is different. Lisa doesn't sign her blocks anymore. The blocks are anonymous—nothing ties Lisa to a certain block. Doesn't this mean she can double spend again?

Well, yes, if she's very lucky.

Double spending

Suppose Lisa is about to pay for a cookie in the cafe. But at the time she pays, she also prepares a double-spend transaction (figure 7.25).

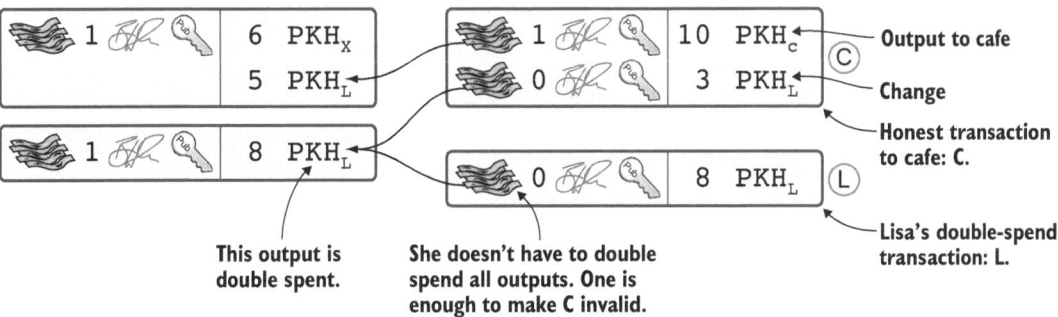

Figure 7.25   Lisa creates two transactions that spend one common output.

C is the transaction to the cafe. L is Lisa's double-spend transaction that she's going to use to snatch her money back. Both transactions are perfectly valid on their own, but both can't be valid at the same time because they both spend a common output. An output can be spent only once.

Lisa sends the honest payment, C, to all miners. While other miners try to add her honest transaction into a block and create a valid proof of work, Lisa secretly puts the double-spend transaction, L, into a secret block of her own and starts working on that block (figure 7.26).

Lisa's goal is to secretly find a valid proof of work for her fraud branch, containing L, that exceeds the honest chain's proof of work. If she succeeds, she'll publish all blocks in her branch, and all miners will switch over to her branch and start working to extend her branch instead. For simplicity, let's assume this all happens without any retargets (difficulty adjustments) happening; we're in the middle of a retarget period. This means all blocks have the same target (or difficulty), so we can strictly look at branch length instead of branch strength (accumulated proof of work).

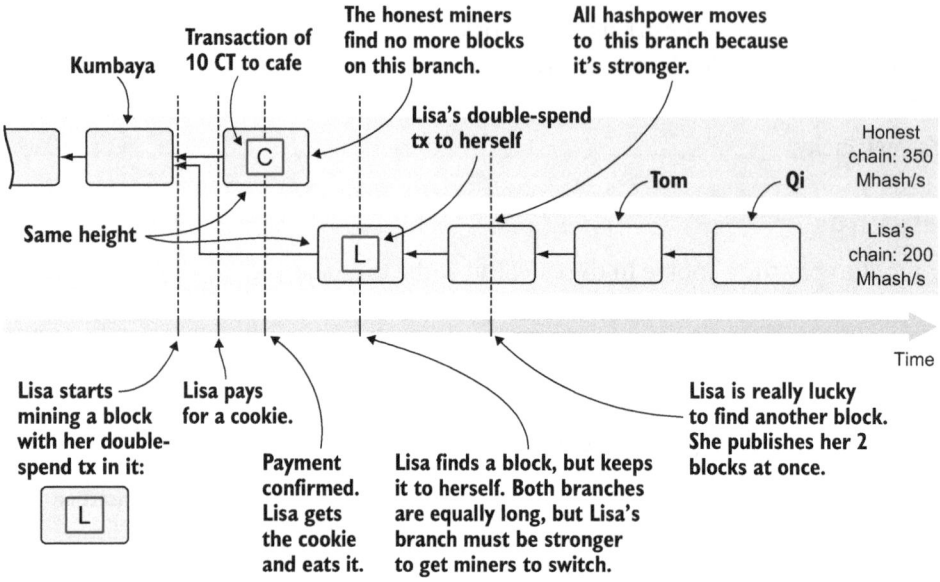

Figure 7.26   Lisa pulls off a double-spend attack—and succeeds despite her small hashrate.

A bunch of miners are trying to confirm Lisa's honest transaction, C, while Lisa works to find a valid proof of work for her block with the double-spend transaction, L. The cafe is waiting for a valid transaction before it hands out the cookie.

Eventually, the honest transaction will be confirmed on the honest chain. The cafe sees that block, verifies it, and gives the cookie to Lisa. Lisa eats it. While she swallows the last crumb, her computer happens to find a valid proof of work for her block. She doesn't publish her block yet because it won't help her. Miners are already mining on the honest branch because that's where they first saw a block.

The combined hashrate of all miners on the honest chain is 350 Mhash/s, whereas Lisa has only 200 Mhash/s. This means the honest chain should be able to find blocks more often than Lisa.

But everyone gets lucky once in a while. Lisa is lucky to find yet another block on her fraudulent branch. She now has 2 blocks on her branch, whereas the honest branch is only 1 block long. Lisa has more

Which branch to follow?

It isn't strictly necessary for a miner to always mine on the first seen block. But the most widely used Bitcoin software, Bitcoin Core, follows the first-seen block.

total proof of work on her chain than the honest miners have on their branch. Lisa publishes her 2 blocks to the shared folder.

Other miners will see those 2 blocks, see that Lisa's branch has more proof of work than the honest branch, and switch over to Lisa's branch. The miners that switch can't see that a crime is being committed or who create the blocks; they'll neutrally jump to the strongest valid chain.

The result is that transaction C to the cafe is effectively undone. It's no longer part of the chain with the most proof of work. The cafe has lost the 10 CT it thought it had when it gave the cookie to Lisa.

From this point forward, new blocks will extend Lisa's branch, and things will continue normally. The block with transaction C will become stale.

Protecting against double-spend attacks

Although the odds are against Lisa, she *could* get lucky and succeed in a double-spend attack, as in the previous example. Trying to pull off a double spend of 10 CT isn't economically feasible from Lisa's perspective. She risks spending lots of electricity and making her own blocks stale if she doesn't succeed. She'd lose out on the rewards from those stale blocks.

But what if she tried to double spend a larger amount than 10 CT: say, 100,000 CT? Then it might be worth it for Lisa to try to double spend. Just imagine if she could buy the whole cafe and pull off a double-spend attack. Then she would have a cafe and still have her 100,000 CT.

The cafe owner is willing to sell the cafe to Lisa for 100,000 CT. But the cafe is, of course, aware of double-spend attacks. So, the cafe owner tells Lisa that for this much money, he'll give her the cafe after six confirmations.

What does this mean? Lisa must pay the cafe owner 100,000 CT and then wait until the transaction is included in a block and 5 blocks have been built after that block. Only then will the owner hand the cafe over to Lisa.

To pull off a double-spend attack, Lisa must build an alternate branch in secret, just like in her previous attack, while the cafe awaits six confirmations. When the cafe owner has seen six confirmations and given the cafe to Lisa, she must at some point upload a stronger double-spend branch to the shared folder. This means Lisa must be lucky for a longer time period than in the previous example.

Let's see how it goes (figure 7.27).

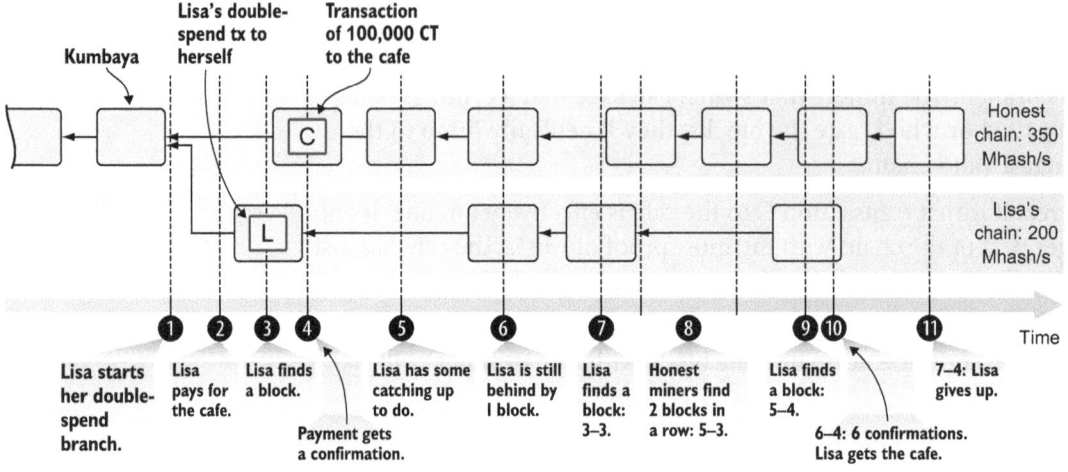

Figure 7.27   Lisa tries to double spend a transaction with six confirmations. She fails.

The outcome is as expected. Lisa couldn't produce more blocks than the honest chain in the long run. She gave up at 7–4.

The following table shows the sequence of events in this example:

Event	Score (C–L)	Comment
❶, ❷	0–0	Lisa starts mining on her secret branch containing her double-spend transaction. She also sends out a payment to the honest miners.
❸	0–1	Lisa finds a block but keeps it secret. She doesn't want the cafe to notice that there's a double-spend attack going on.
❹	1–1	The honest payment, C, gets its first confirmation. The cafe will wait for 5 more blocks before making the deal.
❺, ❻, ❼, ❽, ❾	5–4	Lisa keeps up OK, but she's 1 block behind and must create 2 blocks more than the cafe to succeed.
❿	6–4	The honest transaction has six confirmations. Lisa gets the cafe. The deed of transfer is signed. Lisa keeps trying to catch up.
⓫	7–4	Lisa thinks this stinks. The probability of creating 4 blocks more than the honest chain in the future is tiny.

Lisa gives up for several reasons:

- She realizes she doesn't have enough hashrate to catch up and surpass the honest chain. At any moment, the probability that Lisa finds the next block is 200/550 = 0.36. This means the probability that the honest miners find the next block is 1 − 0.36 = 0.64. Blocks are going to be found much faster on the honest chain.

- For each minute she keeps trying, her computer consumes electricity that costs money. If she doesn't succeed in her double-spend attempt, the electricity cost will have been in vain.

- For each block she mines on her own chain, she'll lose the 50 CT block reward if she fails.

The key here is that the cafe demanded six confirmations. The more confirmations needed, the harder it is for Lisa to build a stronger branch than the honest miners. She needs more luck.

When the cafe got its six confirmations, Lisa was 2 blocks behind. She would need to grow faster than the honest chain and become 1 block longer than the honest chain. Her chances are small. The more blocks she has to catch up with, the smaller the chances, as table 7.3 shows.

> **Confirmations**
>
> With six confirmations, you can be pretty sure no one will double-spend attack you. But the higher the transaction value, the more economically feasible it is to make a double-spend attempt.

Table 7.3 Probability that an attacker catches up, from the attacker's perspective

Catch-up blocks (z)	Probability, q_z, of the attacker catching up if they have q% of hashrate					
	1%	10%	18% (Tom)	36% (Lisa)	45%	50%
1	0.010101	0.111111	0.219512	0.562500	0.818182	1.000000
2	0.000102	0.012346	0.048186	0.316406	0.669421	1.000000
3	1.0e-06	0.001372	**0.010577**	0.177979	0.547708	1.000000
4	1.0e-08	0.000152	0.002322	**0.100113**	0.448125	1.000000
5	1.1e-10	0.000017	0.000510	0.056314	0.366648	1.000000
6	1.1e-12	1.9e-06	0.000112	0.031676	0.299985	1.000000
10	1.1e-20	2.9e-10	2.6e-07	0.003171	0.134431	1.000000

The probability, q_z, is calculated as

$$q = \text{attacker's hashrate}$$
$$p = \text{honest hashrate}$$
$$z = \text{blocks to catch up}$$
$$q_z = \begin{cases} 1 & \text{if } p \leq q \\ (\frac{q}{p})^z & \text{if } q > p \end{cases}$$

Look at the column for a 36% hashrate, which is what Lisa has. When she's 3 blocks behind, she must produce 4 blocks more than the honest miners in the future. This gives her a roughly 0.10 chance of ever succeeding in this double spend—if she's prepared to try indefinitely. She probably doesn't want to keep trying forever, which gives her a slightly smaller probability of succeeding.

Tom tries to double spend, too

Imagine if Tom attempted a double spend instead of Lisa (figure 7.28). He's only got half of Lisa's hashrate, 100 Mhash/s.

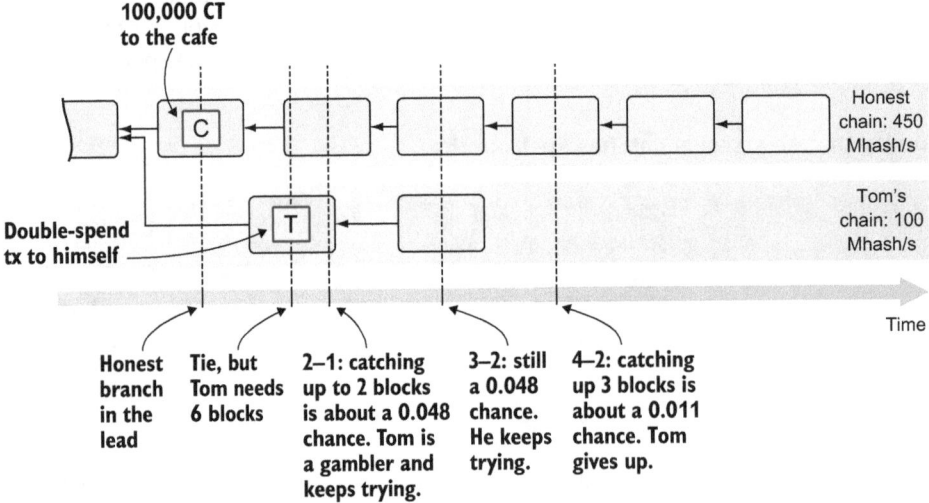

Figure 7.28 Tom attempts to double spend with an 18% hashrate and gives up. He's lucky to find 2 blocks in about the same time the honest miners find 3.

Tom's chances are smaller than Lisa's. He's getting a bit lucky and finds 2 blocks early, but after falling 2 blocks behind the honest miners, he thinks his chances are too small and gives up. Having to produce 3 more blocks than the honest miners at a probability of about 0.011 ($z = 3$) is a terrible thought.

Tom's a smart guy and knows not to try this. He understands that he's far better off securing the blockchain along with everybody else and getting his fair share of the rewards than trying to defeat it. After all, with 18% of the hashrate, he gets almost a fifth of all block rewards. That's more than 50 CT per hour. After 2,000 hours, or 12 weeks, he'd have made 100,000 honest cookie tokens, instead of trying to steal them.

Tom and Lisa collude to double spend

Together, Tom and Lisa have 300 Mhash/s. They control more than 50% (54.5%) of the total hashrate (figure 7.29).

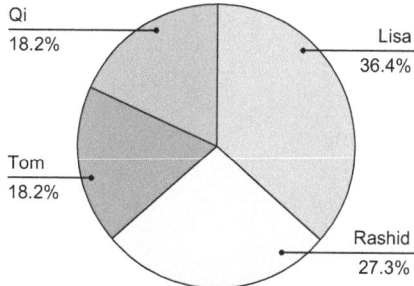

Figure 7.29   Hashrate distribution. Two miners can collude to control a majority of the hashrate.

If they cooperate on a double-spend attack, and if they're willing to try indefinitely, their chances of succeeding are 100% (see table 7.3). If they're only willing to try for, say, 50 blocks, their chances are still very close to 100%.

This scary scenario means Tom and Lisa can rewrite history at will. They run faster than the combined hashrate of all the honest miners. They can create a branch from any block in the blockchain history, work their way up to the honest chain tip, and surpass it. All miners will then move over to Tom and Lisa's branch. Note that they still can't steal anyone's money in the blockchain, but they can make as many double spends as they want.

Let's play with the idea that Tom and Lisa start double spending. For example, they buy the cafe and double spend the transaction so they end up with both the cafe and 100,000 CT. Every now and then, people will notice that the blockchain history has changed. Six confirmation transactions used to be reliable, but now they can't be trusted. What will happen to the cookie token value if the blockchain becomes less reliable? And what happens to the value of cookie tokens when people hear about the double-spend attacks going on?

Panic! People don't want anything to do with this unreliable, insecure cookie token system anymore. Many people will sell all their cookie tokens on the cookie token marketplace outside the cafe. The problem is that there aren't many buyers. What happens to the dollar price of cookie tokens when the demand is low and supply is high? The price tanks.

What happens when the price tanks? More panic! More people want to sell, leading to even bigger price drops.

Tom's, Lisa's, and all other miners' mining business becomes less profitable because the value of their block rewards is so low that they can't sell their cookie tokens to get enough dollars to pay their electricity bill. They need to shut down their mining business because they mine at a net loss.

Tom and Lisa should think twice before starting to attack the system, even though they can. Just the fact that two miners together control more than 50% of the total hashrate could be enough to trigger a price drop because people get nervous about *mining centralization*—when a few people control a large portion of the total hashrate. They don't even have to attack the system to make cookie tokens less valuable.

Mitigating miner centralization

What can people do to counter Tom and Lisa's power? They can start mining at home. Let's say five more people join the mining business, and each adds a computer with 150 Mhash/s. We now have a whole new situation (figure 7.30).

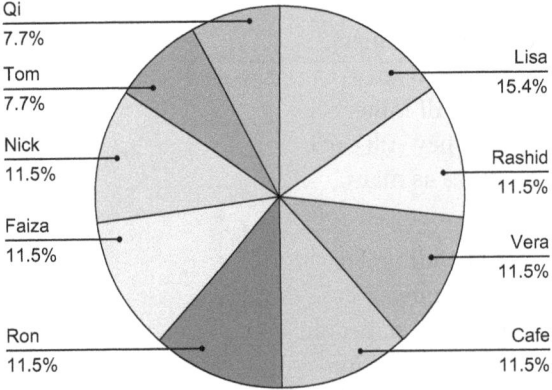

Figure 7.30   New hashrate distribution. It's much harder to get control over a majority of the hashrate.

The total hashrate increases from 550 Mhash/s to 1,300 Mhash/s. The biggest miner, Lisa, with 200 Mhash/s, now has only about 15% of the total hashrate. At least five miners must collude to control a majority of the hashrate because the biggest four miners control 49.9%.

The incentives for people to start mining are strong. They have cookie tokens, and they want the system strong to protect their money from panic price drops due to miner centralization.

Note that as more miners join the race, the rewards per miner will decrease. At some point, some miner—probably an inefficient one—will find that mining isn't worth it anymore and close down its mining computers. The market will push out the inefficient miners in favor of the efficient ones.

Bitcoin's hashrate distribution

As of this writing, Bitcoin's 50 exahash/s are distributed as follows (source: blockchain.info):

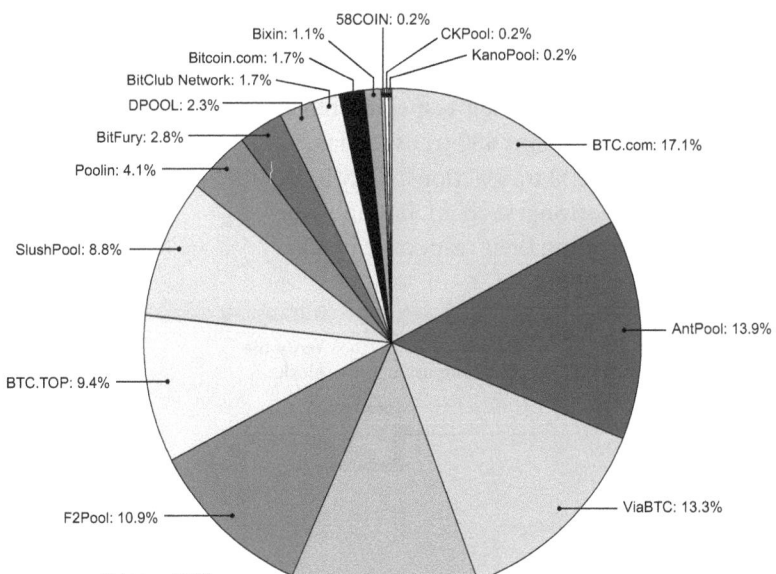

The distribution constantly changes, but this should give you an idea of how it can look in the real world.

Transaction fees

The system now in place has multiple miners that produce blocks independently of each other. This is a massive gain in censorship resistance. All miners must collude to hinder transactions from entering the blockchain. A single miner or a portion of the miners will only be able to make a transaction take longer to confirm, but eventually, one of the noncensoring miners will find a valid proof of work for a block that contains the transaction and publish that block.

All good. But there are two problems:

* Bigger blocks are slower.
* Block size is limited.

These two properties have some implications on miners' transaction selection. Let's start with the first of these two problems and then discuss what effect the block-size limit will have.

Bigger blocks are slower

Suppose Lisa and Tom find valid proof of work for their respective blocks at the same time. Lisa's block is 200 KB and contains 400 transactions, whereas Tom's block is 100 KB and contains 200 transactions. They both want their own block to become part of the strongest chain, but only one of them can take that place. They start uploading their respective blocks to the shared folder at the exact same time (figure 7.31).

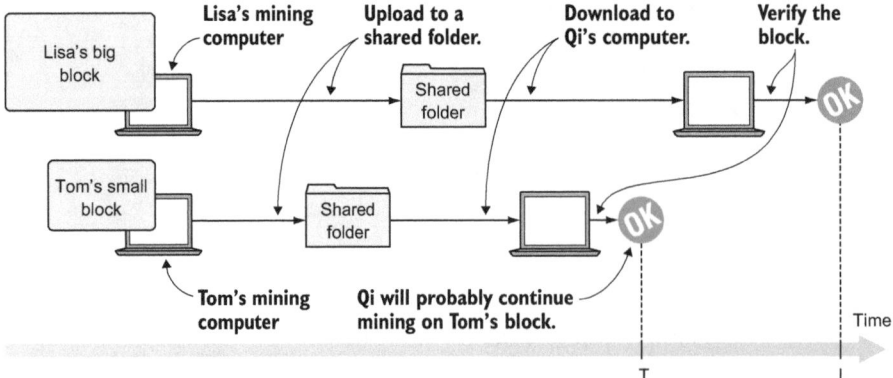

Figure 7.31   Lisa and Tom compete to get Qi and the other miners to mine on top of their block. Tom wins this race because his block was smaller.

Tom's block is smaller than Lisa's. This means Tom will upload his block to the shared folder faster than Lisa uploads hers. It will also be faster for Qi to download Tom's block than it will be to download Lisa's block. Finally, Qi has to verify blocks she downloads before building on them. A smaller block will typically be faster to verify than a big block, so Tom's block is also faster to verify than Lisa's block.

The result is that Qi will, at time T, select Tom's block as the current best chain tip and start mining on top of Tom's block. Lisa's block doesn't really exist for Qi at time T because Qi hasn't verified it yet. She's still downloading Lisa's block from the shared folder. When Qi finally verifies Lisa's block at time L, Qi has already decided to go for Tom's block, and Lisa's block will be stored in case of future chain reorganizations.

Miners have a clear incentive to keep their blocks small. For each extra transaction they add to their blocks, they lose a little competitiveness in the block race.

But wasn't this about transaction fees?

This is where transaction fees come in. If the miner could get paid a little extra for each transaction it adds to its block, that would compensate for the loss of competitiveness.

People making payments are keen on having their transactions confirmed in the blockchain. Wouldn't it be great if John could reserve a little money in his transaction for the miner who includes it? This way, the payer could compensate the miner for the loss of competitiveness.

If you use the transactions a little differently, you can offer this feature. Let's say John wants to buy a cookie. To give miners an incentive to include his transaction, he decides to add a transaction fee. He constructs his transaction as shown in figure 7.32.

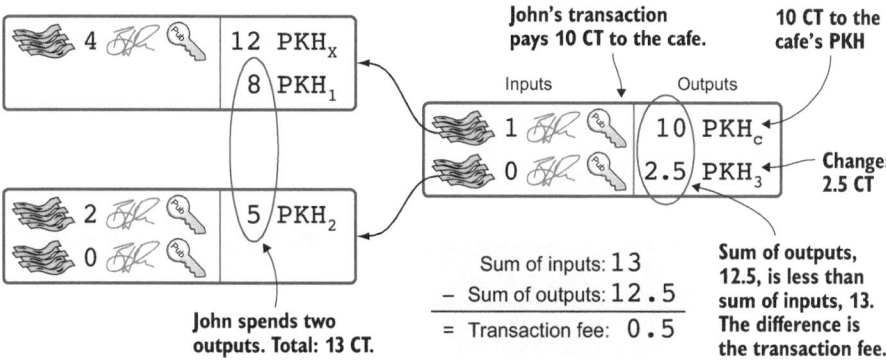

Figure 7.32 John includes a fee for the miner who mines a block with his transaction.

When John created a similar transaction in chapter 5, the sum of the inputs was equal to the sum of the outputs. He didn't pay a transaction fee.

This time, John wants to add a small transaction fee to his transaction. He spends two inputs, totaling 13 CT, and adds an output of 10 CT to the cafe and a change output of 2.5 CT to himself. He then signs the transaction just as he always does and sends it to all the miners.

Lisa, the miner, receives this transaction from John. She notices that there is a transaction fee of 0.5 CT in it. She wants that fee and decides the transaction fee compensates more than enough for the small incremental risk of losing the block race due to including the transaction.

John can tune the incentive for miners to include his transaction. If it's important to him that the transaction be confirmed in one of the next few blocks, he should pay a relatively high fee. If there's no hurry, he can pay a low fee, but he needs to be cautious. If he pays too small a fee, no miner will be willing to confirm his transaction.

We'll talk more about fees, and how you can change a transaction's fee if it gets stuck pending—also known as *fee bumping*—in chapter 9.

For Lisa, when she's deciding whether to include a transaction, all that matters is how big the transaction is and what fee it pays. Basically, it's the *fee per byte* she's interested in. John's transaction is about 400 bytes and pays a 0.5 CT fee. That's 0.00125 CT/byte. This is a simple calculation for Lisa to do, and she does the same for all transactions. If the fee per byte is above a certain threshold, she'll include the transaction.

She can select transactions however she wants, as described in "Transaction selection" in chapter 6. For example, she can include her own transaction without any fee, or she can drop all transactions that pay for cookies no matter how high the fee is. And that's OK. Other miners will have different strategies for selecting transactions. Most will probably make decisions based only on fee per byte.

How does Lisa collect this fee? By using her coinbase transaction (figure 7.33).

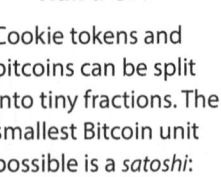

Half a CT?

Cookie tokens and bitcoins can be split into tiny fractions. The smallest Bitcoin unit possible is a *satoshi*: 1 sat = 10^{-8} bitcoin.

Fees in Bitcoin

As of this writing, a transaction fee of 4 sat/byte is normally required to get a transaction into one of the next 6 blocks. A normal transaction, 500 bytes, would cost 0.00002 ₿, or about 20 cents.

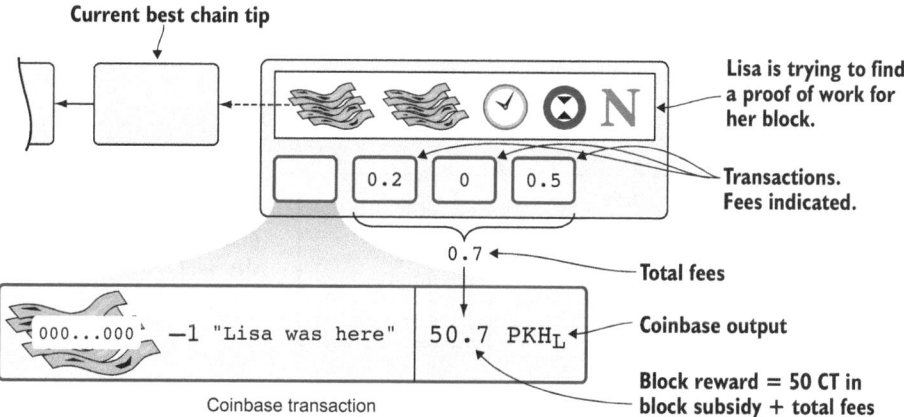

Figure 7.33 Lisa's working on a block, and she's included John's transaction and a few others. She collects the fees in the coinbase output.

Lisa sums up all transaction fees from the transactions in her block and increases the coinbase output with this amount. The amount in the coinbase output—the block reward—is the sum of the block subsidy, the 50 new cookie tokens this block creates, and all transaction fees from the transactions in the block. Note that we've widened the term *block reward* to include both the *block subsidy* (newly created money) and the transaction fees.

When the block is set up correctly, Lisa starts working to find a valid proof of work for this block.

Block size is limited

Blocks aren't allowed to be infinitely large. Simply put, the maximum block size is 1,000,000 bytes, but we'll discuss some nuances of this in the "Block size limit" section in chapter 10. If more transactions are waiting to be confirmed than there is block space available, miners have to choose which transactions to include in the block and which to exclude.

The transaction fee plays an important role in this situation because a higher transaction fee gives miners more incentive to include the transaction in a block instead of other transactions. The fee is used to compete against other transactions for block space, in addition to compensating for the lost competitiveness. This situation is known as a *fee market* (figure 7.34).

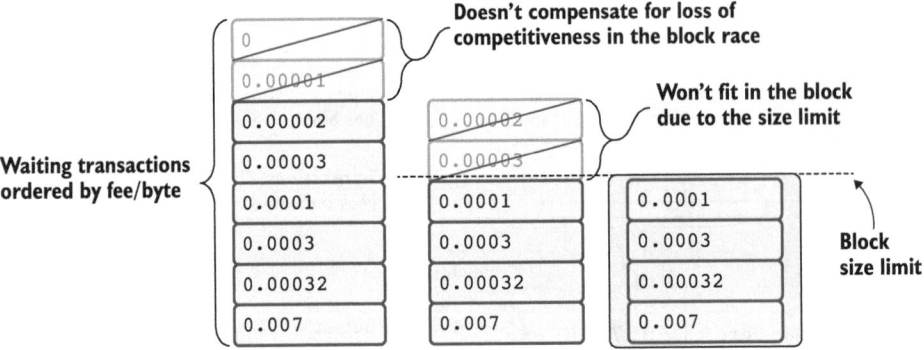

Figure 7.34 In a fee market, transactions compete for block space. The numbers in the transactions denote the fee level in CT/byte.

If more block space is available than there is transaction data waiting to be confirmed, transactions don't compete with each other in the same sense (figure 7.35).

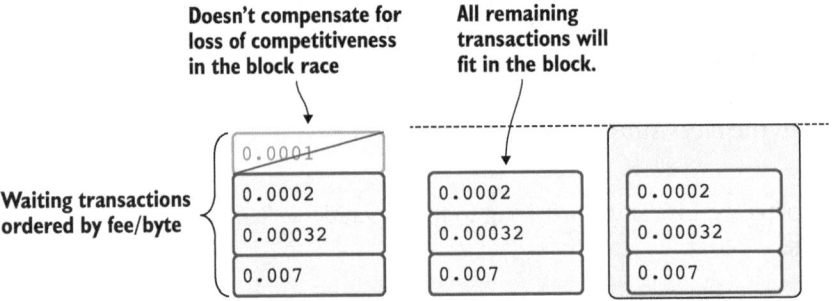

Figure 7.35 When there is no fee market, transactions don't compete with each other. They just have to pay for the lost competitiveness.

In this situation, any transaction that bears the cost of lost competitiveness will be confirmed.

As of this writing, fee markets emerge from time to time during spikes of interest in Bitcoin. But there are still moments with few to no waiting transactions, in which case the fee is low, typically 1 satoshi/byte, or 0.000,000,01 BTC/byte.

When the block subsidy is 0

As we discussed in chapter 2, the block subsidy will be halved roughly every four years. At some point, the block subsidy won't be big enough on its own to give miners incentive to mine. If the value of the block reward is smaller than the electricity bill, what's the point in mining?

Transaction fees will play a bigger and bigger role for miners as the block subsidy decreases. The typical miner wants the income from mining to at least cover their electricity bill (figure 7.36).

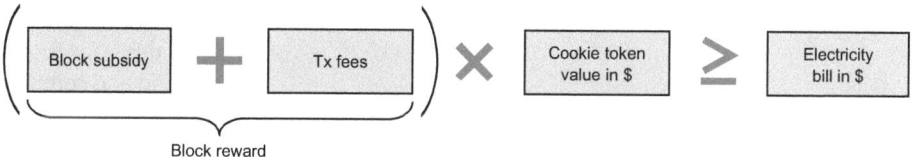

Figure 7.36 **A miner must make at least enough money to pay the electricity bill.**

Note that the *value* of the block subsidy might not always decrease over time. Table 7.4 shows some examples.

Table 7.4 **The block subsidy might be halved, but its value depends on the cookie token value.**

Block subsidy	Value of 1 CT	Value of block subsidy
50 CT	$0.10	$5
25 CT	$0.25	$6.25

This shows that the block subsidy by itself isn't a measurement of mining income. We have to look at the *value* of the block subsidy and the *value* of the transaction fees. One thing is for sure: when the subsidy is zero, the value of the subsidy is also zero. At *some* point, the block subsidy isn't incentive enough to mine.

When this happens, transaction fees will help give efficient miners revenue. If John wants his transaction confirmed, he must pay a fee big enough that one or more miners are willing to include his transaction. This is a market for block space at play.

We can only speculate about where fee levels will be in the future. Some people argue that Bitcoin's fees are already too high for how they want to use Bitcoin today. As transaction fees go up, some current use cases for Bitcoin—for example, payments with tiny amounts—will have to find other ways to work. New systems are being developed on top of Bitcoin that enable people to lump a nearly infinite number of payments together into just one or two transactions. One such system, the Lightning Network, is of particular interest. If a million payments can be made with a single Bitcoin transaction, all those user transactions can share the cost of the transaction fee.

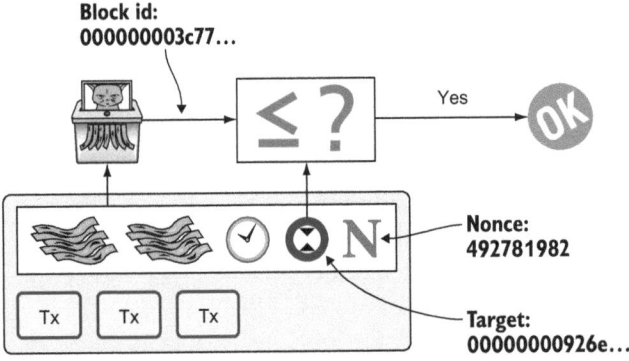

> **Lightning Network**
>
> For more information about the Lightning Network, see web resource 16 (appendix C). Unfortunately, there's no room in this book for this interesting and complex topic.

Recap

This chapter has solved the problem with censorship. Lisa had absolute power over what transactions to include in the blockchain. You solved this by having multiple "Lisas," or miners. By doing so, wallets can send their transactions to any or all miners, and hopefully some of the miners will process the transactions.

The miners compete to produce the next block in the blockchain. They compete to be the first to find a valid proof of work for their block.

The miner that wins the competition will publish its block and collect the block reward, which consists of the block subsidy and the transaction fees. The reward is collected in the coinbase transaction.

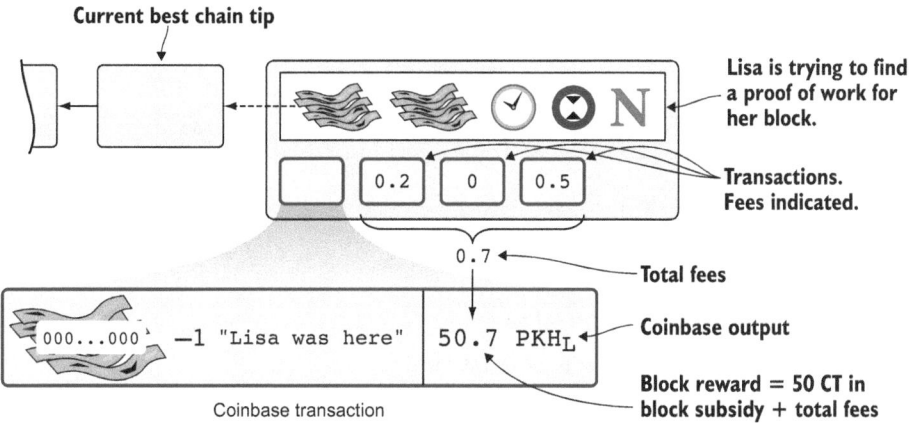

Current best chain tip

Lisa is trying to find a proof of work for her block.

Transactions. Fees indicated.

0.2   0   0.5

0.7 ◄ **Total fees**

000...000   −1 "Lisa was here"   50.7 PKH$_L$ ◄ **Coinbase output**

Block reward = 50 CT in block subsidy + total fees

Coinbase transaction

The block subsidy is used to fairly get new money into circulation in the economy until all 21,000,000 new cookie tokens are minted. The sender of a transaction adds a transaction fee to incentivize miners to include the transaction in their blocks.

This competition will lead to natural splits, when two miners find a block at about the same time. These splits will eventually be resolved.

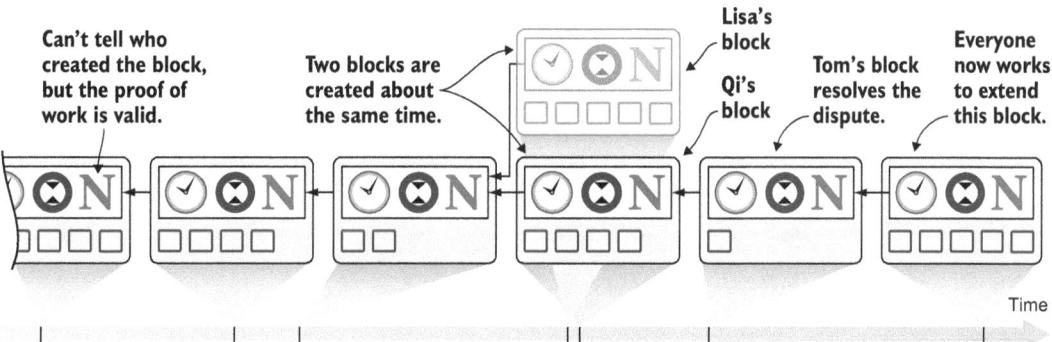

Can't tell who created the block, but the proof of work is valid.

Two blocks are created about the same time.

Lisa's block

Qi's block

Tom's block resolves the dispute.

Everyone now works to extend this block.

Time

The resolution is affected by which branch miners choose to mine on. Miners usually mine on the first valid block they see.

A merchant shouldn't trust a high-value transaction until a sufficiently high number of blocks have been mined on top of the block containing the transaction. This reduces the risk of double spends.

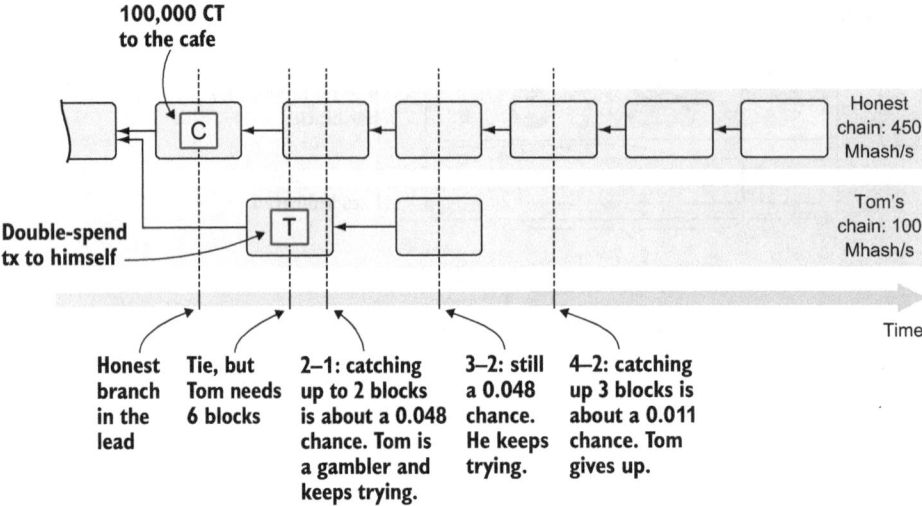

It can be expensive for a miner to try a double spend. If it fails, the miner will have spent a lot of electricity and lost all its block rewards. The choice of the number of required confirmations is up to the merchant and should take into account the transaction value.

System changes

Proof of work replaces the block signatures introduced in chapter 6, and we can remove them from the concept mapping table (table 7.5).

Table 7.5   Block signatures have been replaced by the Bitcoin concept of proof of work. Lisa has transformed into one of several miners.

Cookie tokens	Bitcoin	Covered in
1 cookie token	1 bitcoin	Chapter 2
~~Lisa~~	~~A miner~~	~~Chapter 7~~
~~Block signature~~	~~Proof of work~~	~~Chapter 7~~
The shared folder	The Bitcoin network	Chapter 8

Lisa is now doing the exact same tasks as a Bitcoin miner, which is why we remove Lisa from the table as well. The shared folder will be the last bit of the cookie token system we'll take care of. That's for the next chapter.

It's time to release a shiny new version of the cookie token system (table 7.6).

Table 7.6   Release notes, cookie tokens 7.0

Version	Feature	How
NEW 7.0	Censorship-resistant	Multiple miners, "Lisas," enabled by proof of work
	Anyone can join the mining race	Automatic difficulty adjustments
6.0	Prevent Lisa from deleting transactions	Signed blocks in a blockchain
	Fully validating nodes	Download and verify the entire blockchain
	Lightweight wallet saves data traffic	Bloom filters and merkle proofs
5.0	Spend multiple "coins" in one payment	Multiple inputs in transactions
	Anyone can verify the spreadsheet	Make the signatures publicly available in the transactions
	Sender decides criteria for spending the money	Script programs inside transactions

Exercises

Warm up

7.1 In what way was Lisa a central authority in chapter 6?

7.2 Why would the possibility of censoring transactions decrease with multiple miners, or "Lisas"?

7.3 Drawing random numbers worked quite well, but we abandoned this idea. Why was the idea naive?

7.4 How do you check if a proof of work is valid?

7.5 How does a miner generate a valid proof of work?

7.6 What is meant by *strongest chain*?

7.7 What does it mean when a miner has the hashrate 100 Mhash/s?

7.8 A retarget period has just ended, and the last 2,016 blocks took 15 days to produce. Will the target increase or decrease?

7.9 At what percentage of the hashrate can you be certain to pull off a double spend, if you're willing to try indefinitely?

Dig in

7.10 Suppose a big block and a small block are created at the same time. Why is the big block less likely to become part of the strongest chain compared to the small block?

7.11 Suppose the block rate suddenly doubles exactly in the middle of a retarget period. It goes from 6 blocks per hour to 12 blocks per hour, on average. No other changes happen during the retarget period. What will happen to the target after this period?

7.12 Suppose Selma has 52% of the total hashrate. She decides to change the retarget period of her software program from 2,016 blocks (two weeks) to 144 blocks (one day). No one else thinks this is a good idea, and they keep running the old software. What will happen after her next retarget period of one day when she adjusts her target? Will the rest of the miners and full nodes accept Selma's blocks? Who will suffer from this situation?

7.13 Why would a miner choose not to confirm a transaction that pays a very small transaction fee?

Summary

- Having multiple miners avoids a central authority that can censor transactions.

- Proof of work is used to select who gets to create a block.

- Proof of work enables anyone to start mining without asking for permission.

- The target is automatically calibrated every 2,016 blocks to keep money creation at the predetermined rate.

- A transaction fee gives miners incentive to include the transaction in their block.

- To keep the risk of double spends low, the recipient of cookie tokens, or bitcoins, selects how many confirmations are needed.

- A miner gets as much in block rewards as it deserves. The more hashrate it puts into the system, the bigger share of the rewards it gets.

- The stronger a chain is—the more accumulated proof of work it has—the harder it is to rewrite that chain.

This chapter covers

- Removing the last central authority: the shared folder

- Following a transaction in the peer-to-peer network

- Leaving behind the silly cookie tokens

- Bootstrapping the peer-to-peer network

Let's talk about the elephant in the room: the shared folder. All blocks the miners produce must pass through the shared folder on their way to other full nodes and miners. This chapter will remove the central shared folder and replace it with a decentralized *peer-to-peer network* (figure 8.1). The peer-to-peer network lets full nodes (including miners) send blocks directly to each other. When nodes can talk directly to each other, we no longer need a central point of authority for communication.

Another issue we haven't talked much about is how wallets send transactions via email to the miners. When a new miner joins the system, all wallets need to update their miner list. Not cool. With this nice peer-to-peer network of nodes, wallets can broadcast their transactions to all miners without knowing who or where they are.

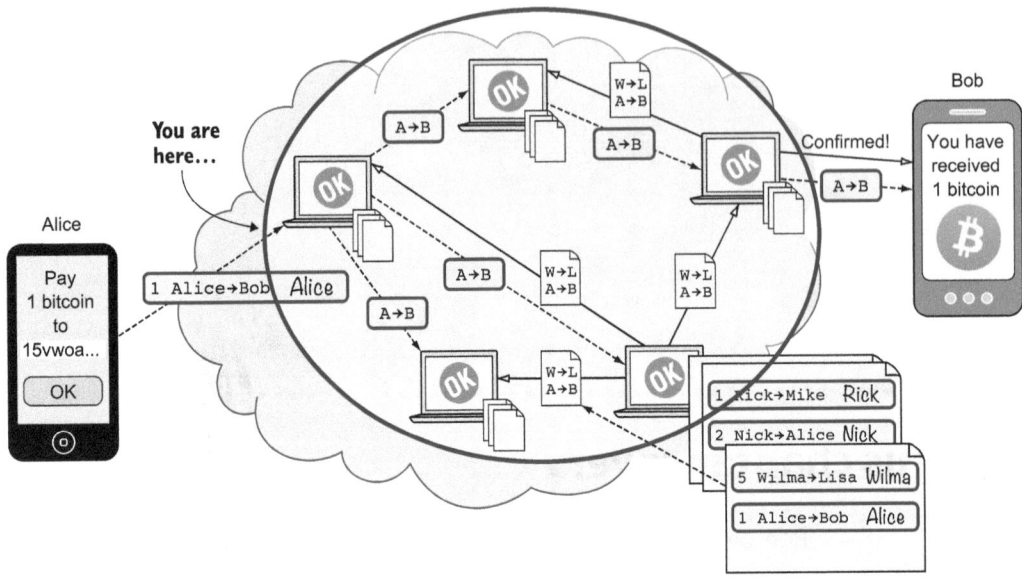

Figure 8.1   Bitcoin's peer-to-peer network

We'll follow a transaction's path through the network, both as an unconfirmed transaction and, eventually, as part of a mined block. The transaction will start in John's wallet and end as a confirmed transaction in the blockchain with Bob's wallet being notified about it.

After following the transaction through the system, you'll no longer need the cookie token system to help you understand Bitcoin. We'll talk only about Bitcoin from that point forward. Practically no differences exist between the cookie token system and Bitcoin anymore, so it doesn't make sense to keep talking about cookie tokens when, in fact, you want to learn about Bitcoin!

The last topic in this chapter will cover how a new node connects to and becomes part of the peer-to-peer network. This is far from trivial. How does it find nodes to connect to? How does it download the blockchain up to the latest block? We'll sort all that out. Toward the end of the chapter, you'll learn how to set up a full node of your own.

The shared folder

The shared folder administrator, Luke, is a central authority (figure 8.2). He ultimately gets to decide which blocks can be stored in the shared folder. He also gets to decide who can read from and write to the shared folder.

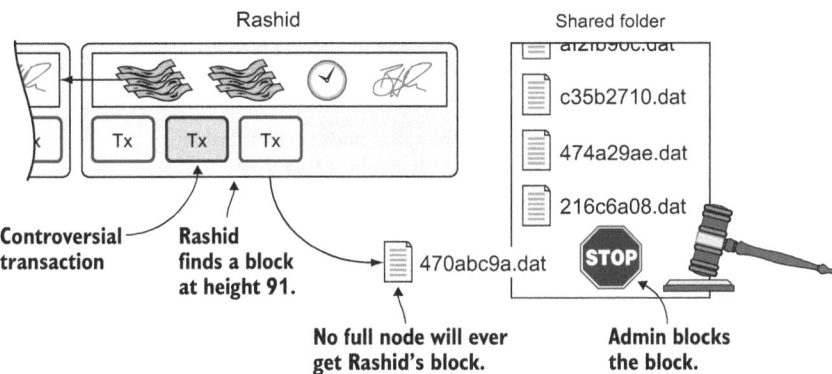

Figure 8.2   The shared folder is a central point of authority.

So far, we've assumed Luke is a totally neutral good guy—but what if he isn't, or what if he's forced by Acme Insurances to reject certain blocks? What's the point of proof of work if the system can be censored at the block level? Proof of work made the *transactions* censorship-resistant because it let users send their transactions to multiple miners. But the *blocks* containing the transactions can still be censored by whoever has administrator privileges over the shared folder. Simply put, the system isn't yet censorship-resistant. As long as a single entity can decide which blocks or transactions to allow, the system isn't censorship-resistant.

The shared folder poses yet another problem. Imagine that Rashid has created a 1 MB block and published it to the shared folder. Everyone watching the shared folder, all full nodes, will download Rashid's block at the same time. If you have 100 full nodes, the total amount of data you need to send from the shared folder to the different nodes is 100 MB. This will cause *block propagation*—the transfer of a block from its creator to all other nodes—to be terribly slow. The more nodes, the slower the block propagation.

Let's build a peer-to-peer network

What if the full nodes and miners could talk directly to each other instead of relying on the central shared folder? They could send the blocks directly to one another in a peer-to-peer network (figure 8.3).

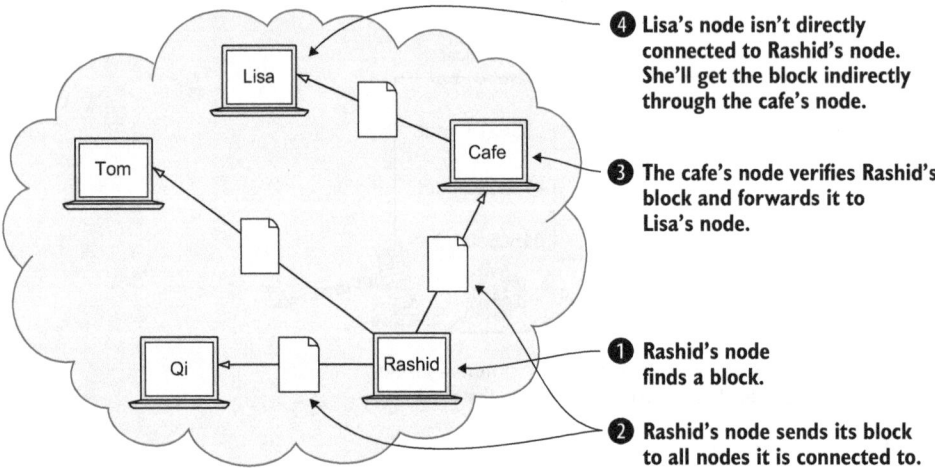

4 Lisa's node isn't directly connected to Rashid's node. She'll get the block indirectly through the cafe's node.

3 The cafe's node verifies Rashid's block and forwards it to Lisa's node.

1 Rashid's node finds a block.

2 Rashid's node sends its block to all nodes it is connected to.

Figure 8.3   In a peer-to-peer network, blocks are passed from one node to another, much as gossip spreads among people.

Think of the peer-to-peer network as a large number of people. One person doesn't know everyone else, but might know three people. When something interesting happens—for example, Rashid finds a block—he tells his three friends about it, who in turn tell all their friends, and so on until everybody knows about this new block. We call such networks *gossip networks* for apparent reasons.

Blocks can no longer be easily stopped. A node can choose not to pass a block on, or *relay* it, to its peers, but the peers are connected to several other peers that will gladly relay the block to them. A single node can't do much to censor information.

Relay

To *relay* a received block means to pass the block on to others.

Suppose Rashid finds a block, and he wants to get this block out to all nodes. Rashid sends his block to Qi, Tom, and the cafe. For some reason, the cafe doesn't forward the block to Lisa (figure 8.4). But Lisa has several peers in this network. She's connected to Tom and Qi. Tom will tell Lisa about this new block and send it to her. The cafe can't hide information from Lisa as long as she's well-connected—that is, has many different peers.

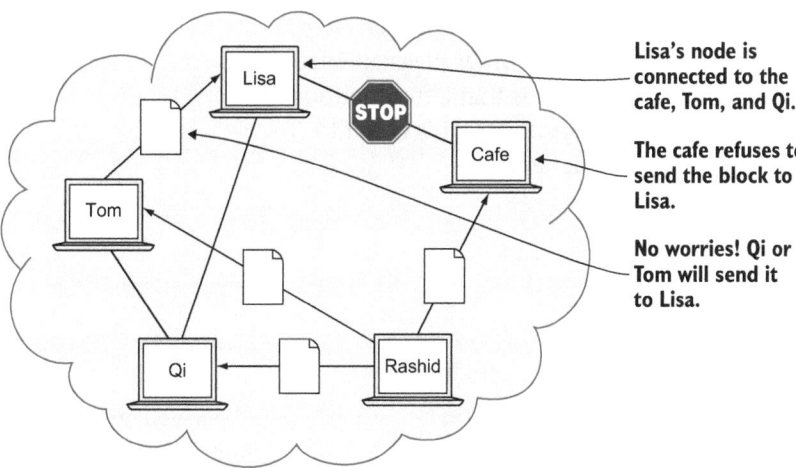

Figure 8.4   If the cafe refuses to relay a block to Lisa, someone else will do it.

Now that you have this nice network, wallets can use it to get their transactions sent to miners. Then they won't have to keep track of miner email addresses anymore. The transactions will be broadcast over the peer-to-peer network and reach all full nodes within seconds. This includes the miners, because they're also full nodes. We covered this briefly in chapter 1, as repeated in figure 8.5.

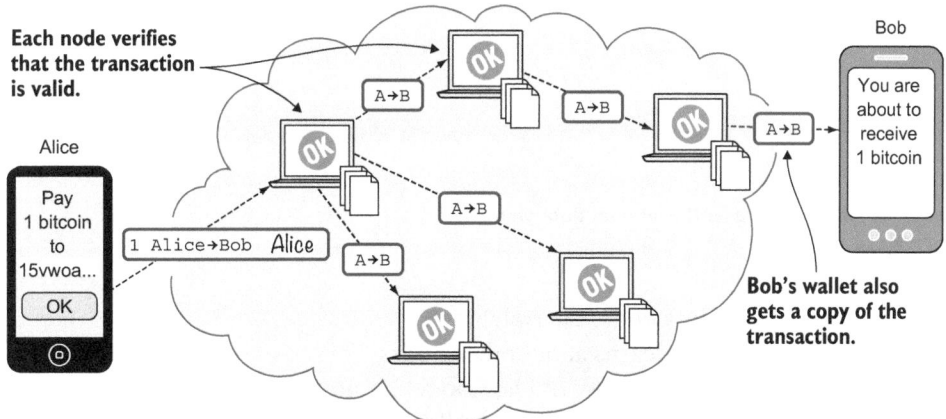

Figure 8.5   Transactions travel the peer-to-peer network just like blocks do. Wallets no longer need to know the miners.

The same thing goes here as for blocks: a single node can't hinder transactions from spreading across the network. Another pleasant effect of using the peer-to-peer network for transactions is that a transaction's recipient can be notified that the transaction is *pending*, or is about to be confirmed. We'll look at how this works a bit later.

How do peers talk?

Let's look at how the communication between two peers happens. We'll look specifically at how Tom connects to Lisa and how they communicate across their communication channel, called a Transmission Control Protocol (TCP) connection (figure 8.6).

TCP

When you open a web page on https://bitcoin.org, your web browser will make a TCP connection to bitcoin.org, download a web page through that connection, and display it to you.

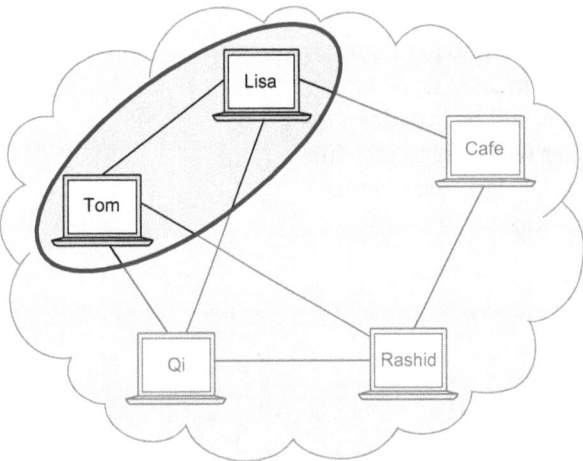

Figure 8.6   Tom and Lisa communicate over the internet through a communication channel.

Suppose Tom's node knows about Lisa's node. I'll explain in "Bootstrapping the network" how Tom learns about other nodes. For now, let's assume he has the *IP address* and *port* of Lisa's node. He now wants to connect to Lisa's node to communicate with it. All computers on the internet have an Internet Protocol (IP) address, which is how one computer can send information to another. A computer program that listens for incoming connections must listen on a specific port number of its computer's IP address. Lisa's computer has the IP address 142.12.233.96 and runs a cookie token program that listens for incoming connections on port 8333.

Tom's node connects to Lisa's node through the IP address
142.12.233.96 and TCP port 8333. His node (computer program) starts
by asking its operating system (OS) to initiate a connection to Lisa
(figure 8.7). The OS sends a message to Lisa's computer saying that Tom
wants to talk to a computer program on Lisa's port 8333. Her computer
knows a program is listening on port 8333, so it sends back a "Sure,
welcome" message. Tom's computer acknowledges this by sending back
an "OK, cool. Let's talk …" message.

> **Port 8333**
>
> Port 8333 is the
> default listening port in
> Bitcoin Core, the most
> widely used full node
> software.

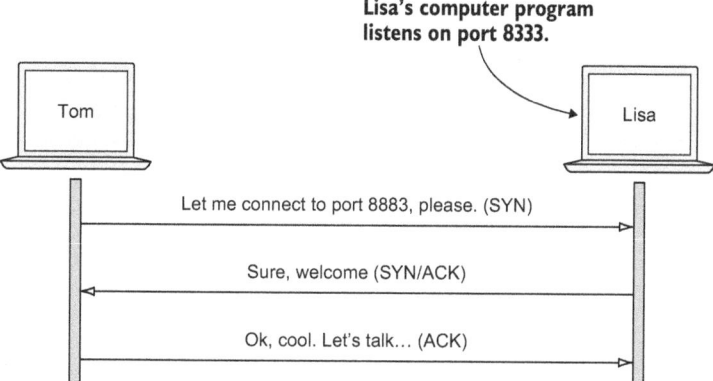

**Figure 8.7   Tom's computer program sets up a TCP connection to Lisa's computer
program. After this, they can send and receive data between each other.**

The node software on Tom's and Lisa's computers wasn't involved in this
exchange—it was carried out by their OSs, such as Linux, Windows,
or macOS. When the message sequence is finished, the OS hands the
connection over to the node software. Lisa's and Tom's nodes can now
speak freely to each other. Tom can send data to Lisa, and Lisa can send
data to Tom over this communication channel, or *TCP connection*.

The network protocol

Tom and Lisa can now send and receive data over a communication
channel. But if Tom's node speaks a language that Lisa's node doesn't
understand, the communication won't be meaningful (figure 8.8). The
nodes must have a common language: a *protocol*.

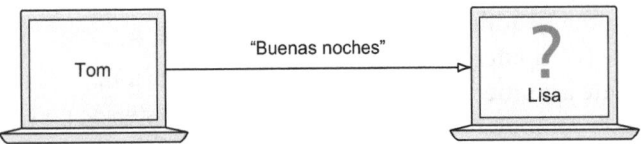

Figure 8.8   Lisa must be able to understand what Tom writes on the channel.

The cookie token network protocol defines a set of message types that are allowed. A typical message in the cookie token (well, Bitcoin) network is the `inv` message (figure 8.9).

Tom tells Lisa that he has two transactions and a block along with their hashes (IDs).

Lisa now knows that she can fetch those items from Tom.

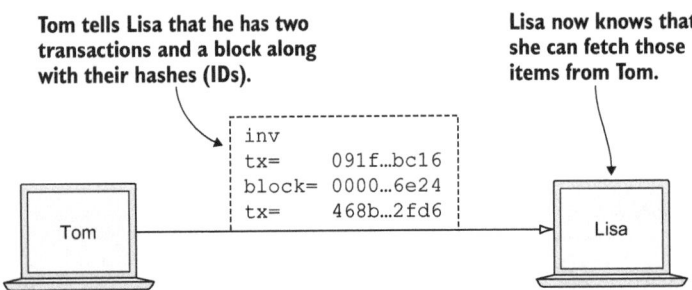

```
inv
tx=       091f…bc16
block=    0000…6e24
tx=       468b…2fd6
```

Figure 8.9   A typical network message

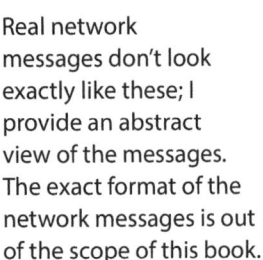

This is an abstraction

Real network messages don't look exactly like these; I provide an abstract view of the messages. The exact format of the network messages is out of the scope of this book.

A node uses the `inv`—short for *inventory*—message to inform other nodes about something it has. In figure 8.9, Tom's node informs Lisa's node that Tom has three things to offer Lisa: two transactions and a block. The message contains an ID for each of these items.

John sends the transaction

Let's follow a transaction through the network from start to end to see what network messages are being used. We'll assume the peer-to-peer network is already set up. We'll come back to how the network is *bootstrapped* later in this chapter.

In the "Lightweight wallets" section of chapter 6, we said that wallets can connect to full nodes and get information about all block headers and transactions concerning them using bloom filters and merkle proofs (figure 8.10).

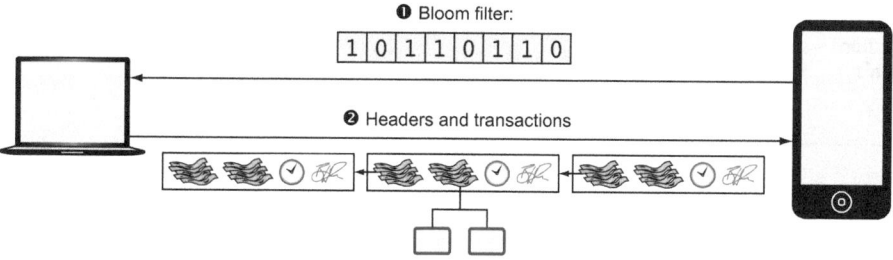

Figure 8.10 Lightweight wallets communicate with nodes using the Bitcoin network protocol.

I didn't go into detail then about how this communication works. It uses the same protocol the nodes use when they communicate with each other. The wallets and the full nodes (including miners) all speak the same "language."

Suppose John wants to buy a cookie from the cafe. John's wallet is connected to Tom's node with a TCP connection. He scans the payment URI from the cafe's wallet. John's wallet creates and signs a transaction. You know the drill. Then it's time to send the transaction to Tom's node (figure 8.11).

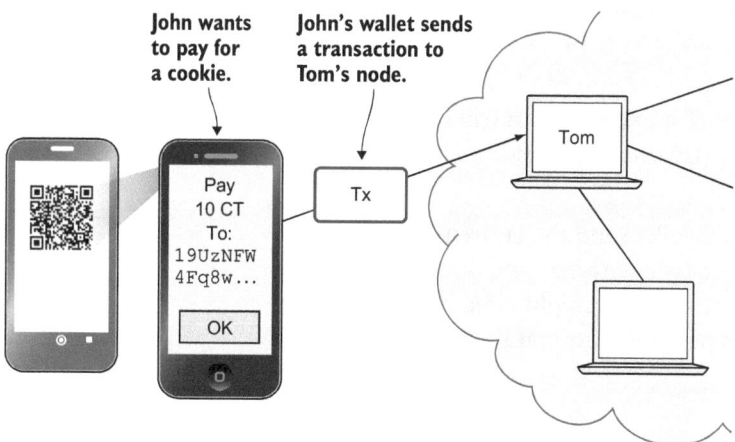

Figure 8.11 The transaction is sent to Tom's node through a TCP connection.

This happens in a three-step process. John's wallet doesn't just send the transaction unsolicited: it first informs Tom's node that there's a transaction to be fetched (figure 8.12).

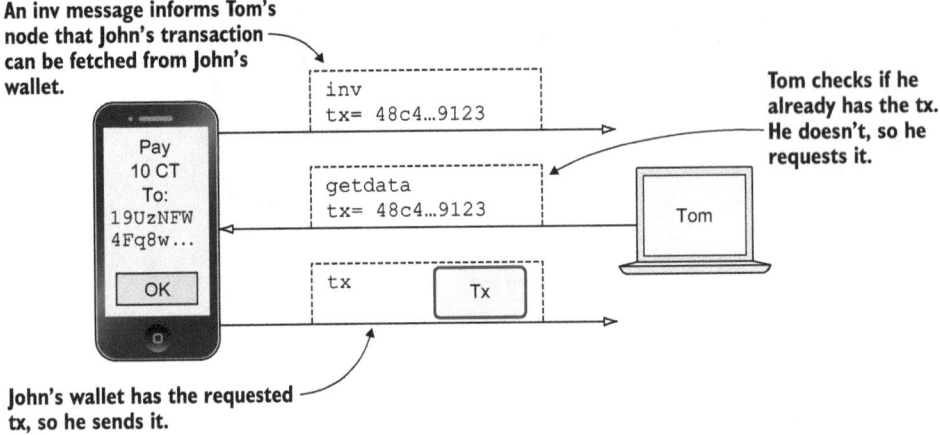

An inv message informs Tom's node that John's transaction can be fetched from John's wallet.

Tom checks if he already has the tx. He doesn't, so he requests it.

John's wallet has the requested tx, so he sends it.

Figure 8.12 Tom's node is informed about John's transaction so that Tom can fetch it.

The first message is an `inv` message, as described in the previous section. John's wallet sends the `inv` to Tom's full node. Tom checks if he already has the transaction. He doesn't, because John's wallet just created it and hasn't sent it to anyone yet. Tom's node wants to get this transaction, so he requests it with a `getdata` message that looks just like an `inv` message but with a different meaning: `getdata` means "I want this stuff," whereas `inv` means "I have this stuff."

John's wallet receives the `getdata` message and sends a `tx` message containing the entire transaction to Tom's node. Tom will verify the transaction and keep it. He'll also relay this transaction to his network neighbors.

You might ask, "Why doesn't John's wallet send the entire transaction immediately? Why go through the hassle with `inv` and `getdata`?" This will become clear later, but it's because nodes might already have the transaction; we save bandwidth by sending only transaction hashes instead of entire transactions.

Tom forwards the transaction

If the transaction is valid, Tom's node will inform his neighbors about it (figure 8.13) using an `inv` message, just like John's wallet did when it informed Tom's node about the transaction.

The process is the same for these three message exchanges as the one John used when he first sent the transaction to Tom (figure 8.14). Lisa, Qi, and Rashid will get an `inv` message from Tom.

Tom's node forwards the transaction to his peers using the same method as John did when he sent it to Tom.

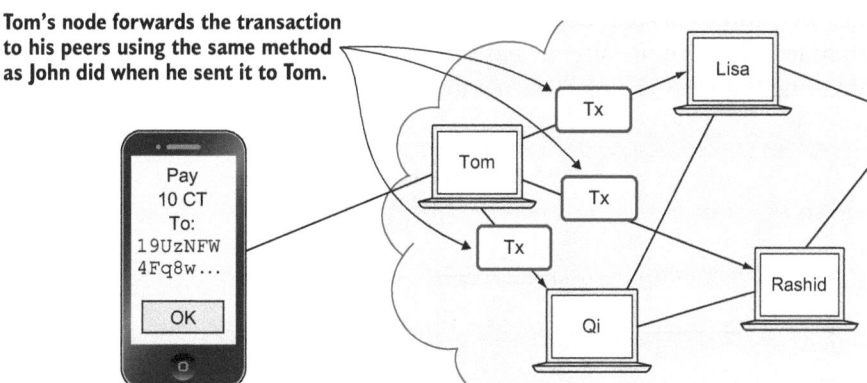

Figure 8.13   Tom forwards the transaction to his peers.

An inv message informs Qi's node that John's transaction can be fetched from Tom's node.

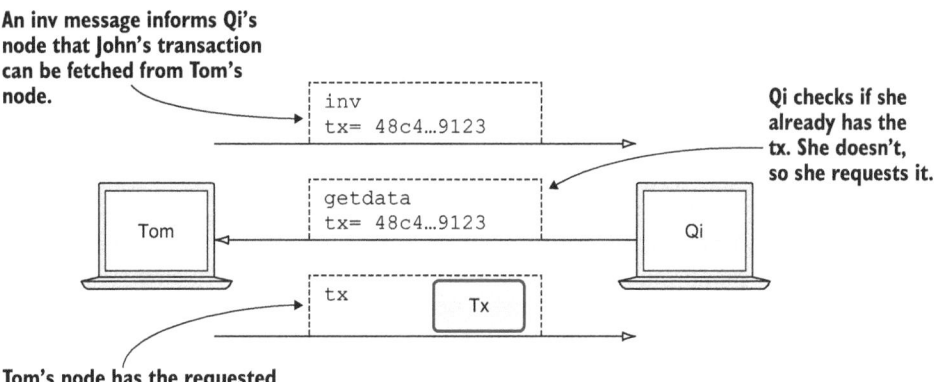

Qi checks if she already has the tx. She doesn't, so she requests it.

Tom's node has the requested tx, so he sends it.

Figure 8.14   Tom's node sends the transaction to Qi's node using the familiar three-step process.

When Lisa, Qi, and Rashid have received the transaction, they too will inform their peers about it after they've verified it. Qi's and Rashid's nodes are a bit slower, so it takes them a while to verify the transaction; we'll get back to them later.

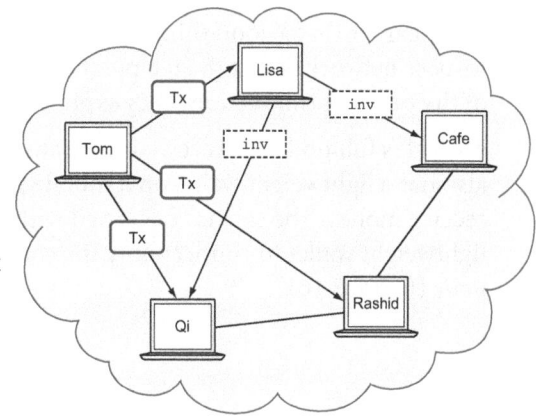

Lisa was quick to verify the transaction, so she'll be the first of the three to relay it. She already knows that she received the transaction from Tom, so she won't inform Tom's node with an `inv` message. But Lisa doesn't know that Qi already has the transaction, and she doesn't know if the cafe has it. She'll send an `inv`

to those two nodes. The cafe's node will send back a `getdata` because it hasn't yet seen this transaction. Qi's node already has this transaction and won't reply with anything (figure 8.15). She'll remember that Lisa has it, though.

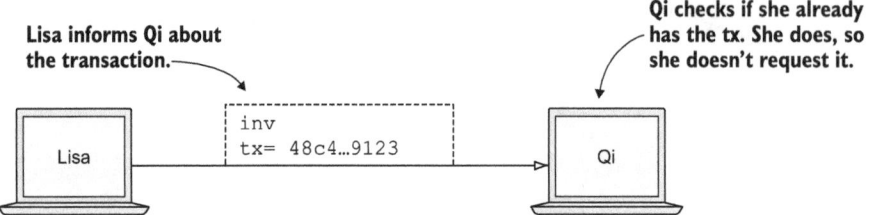

Figure 8.15 Lisa's node sends an `inv` to Qi's node, but Qi's node already has the transaction.

Qi has just finished verifying the transaction. She knows that Lisa's node has it, so she doesn't have to send an `inv` to Lisa's node. But she doesn't know if Rashid has it, so she sends an `inv` to Rashid's node.

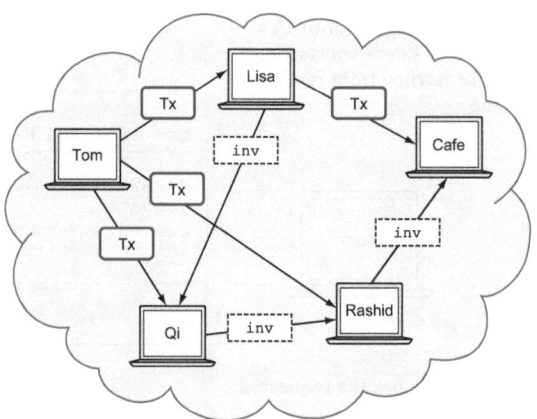

Rashid's was the slowest node when verifying John's transaction, so when it's time for him to send an `inv` to his neighbors, he's already received an `inv` from Qi's node. And he also knows from earlier that Tom already has the transaction. He'll just send an `inv` to the cafe's node, which will ignore the `inv` because it already has the transaction.

The cafe's lightweight wallet is notified

I said earlier that a good thing about letting transactions travel the peer-to-peer network is that the recipient wallet can get a quick notification of the pending transaction. Let's explore this now.

The cafe's full node has received the transaction and verified it. The cafe also has a lightweight wallet on a mobile phone that it uses to send and receive money. The cafe is concerned with security, so it configured this lightweight wallet to connect only the cafe's own full node, its *trusted node* (figure 8.16).

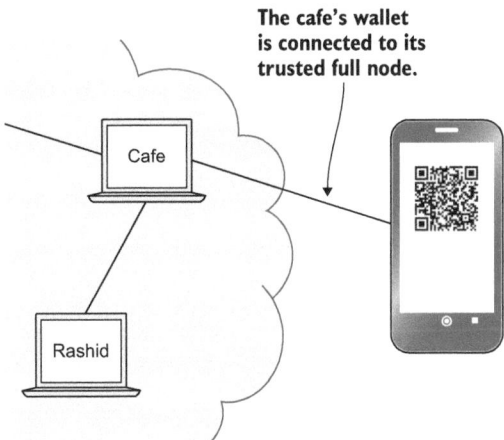

Figure 8.16   The cafe's lightweight wallet has a TCP connection to its own full node.

This common setup gives the cafe the complete security of a full node combined with the flexibility and mobility of a lightweight wallet. I described this setup in the "Security of lightweight wallets" section in chapter 6.

The cafe's full node has just verified John's transaction. It now wants to inform its neighbors about this new transaction. It's connected to Lisa's node, Rashid's node, and the cafe's lightweight wallet. The full node already knows that Lisa's and Rashid's nodes have this transaction, so it doesn't send an `inv` to those two nodes. The full node doesn't know whether the wallet has the transaction, but it won't immediately send an `inv` message to the wallet.

The wallet is a lightweight wallet, which uses bloom filters, described in the "Bloom filters obfuscate addresses" section in chapter 6. The full node will test the transaction against the bloom filter and, if it matches, send an `inv` message to the wallet. If there's no match, it won't send an `inv` message.

John's transaction is for the cafe, so the bloom filter will match the transaction, and the full node will send an `inv`. The wallet will request the actual transaction using `getdata`, as figure 8.17 shows.

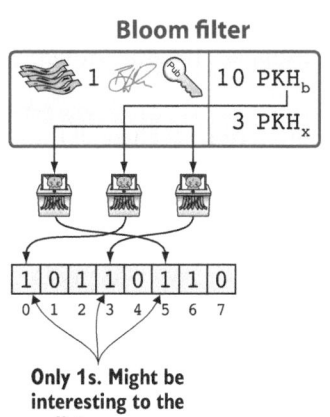

Bloom filter

Only 1s. Might be interesting to the wallet.

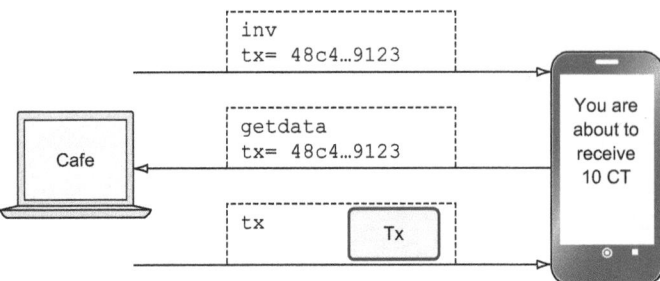

Figure 8.17 **The cafe's wallet gets John's transaction from the cafe's trusted node after the transaction is checked against the bloom filter.**

The wallet has now received the transaction. It can show a message to the cafe owner that a transaction is pending. The cafe owner has a choice: trust that the transaction—a so-called *0-conf transaction*—will be confirmed eventually, or wait until the transaction is confirmed. If the cafe accepts the 0-conf transaction, then it trusts that John has paid a high enough transaction fee and that the transaction won't be double spent.

This time, the cafe decides that it needs to wait until the transaction is included in a valid block. This brings us to the next phase: including the transaction in a block in the blockchain.

Including the transaction in a block

Let's recall some of the miners in this system. At the end of "Mitigating miner centralization" in chapter 7, there were 10 different miners; but let's go back in time and pretend Qi, Tom, Lisa, and Rashid are the only miners in this system right now.

The transaction reached all these miners during transaction propagation. John's wallet used to send the transaction via email to all miners. Now, he sends it to any of the full nodes, and it propagates across the entire peer-to-peer network. Miners can choose to include John's transaction in the blocks

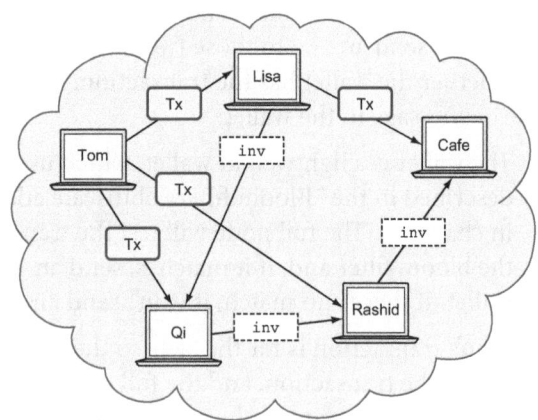

they're mining. Suppose the transaction includes a transaction fee so that some or all miners are willing to include it, and that Rashid is the next miner to find a valid proof of work for his block, which happens to contain John's transaction (figure 8.18).

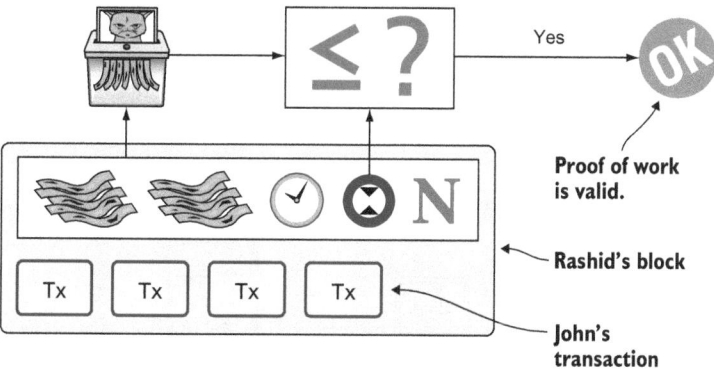

Figure 8.18 Rashid's block containing John's transaction

Rashid wants to get his block to the other miners as quickly as possible to minimize the risk of some other miner getting a block out before Rashid's block.

He creates a `headers` message and sends it to all his peers: Tom, the cafe, and Qi. Rashid's peers will send back a `getdata` message, and Rashid will reply with the actual block. The message exchange between Rashid and Qi will look like the one in figure 8.19.

> **BIP130**
>
> This process is defined in BIP130, which replaces an old block-propagation mechanism that used `inv` messages.

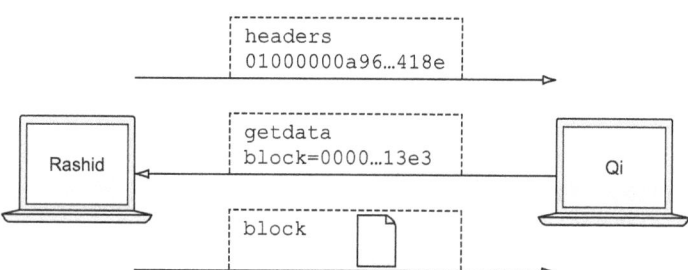

Figure 8.19 Rashid's node sends Rashid's block to Qi's node.

The actual block is sent in a `block` message containing the full block.

Let's continue the block propagation throughout the peer-to-peer network. Rashid has sent his block to Tom, the cafe, and Qi. Now, these three nodes will verify the block and, if it's valid, send out `headers` messages to all their peers who might not already have it (figure 8.20).

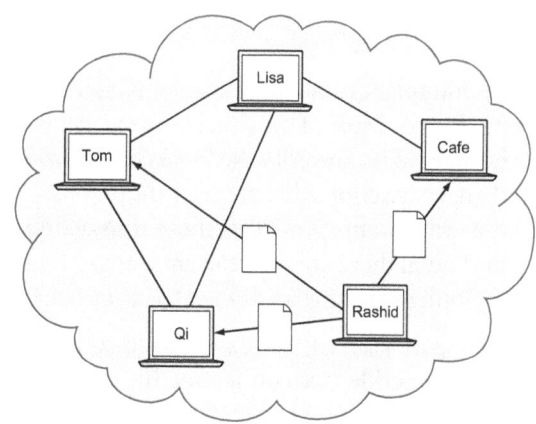

Qi and Tom happen to send their `headers` messages to each other at the same time. This isn't a problem; because they both have the block, they'll ignore the `headers` received from peers. Lisa will request the block from one of her peers just like Qi requested the block from Rashid.

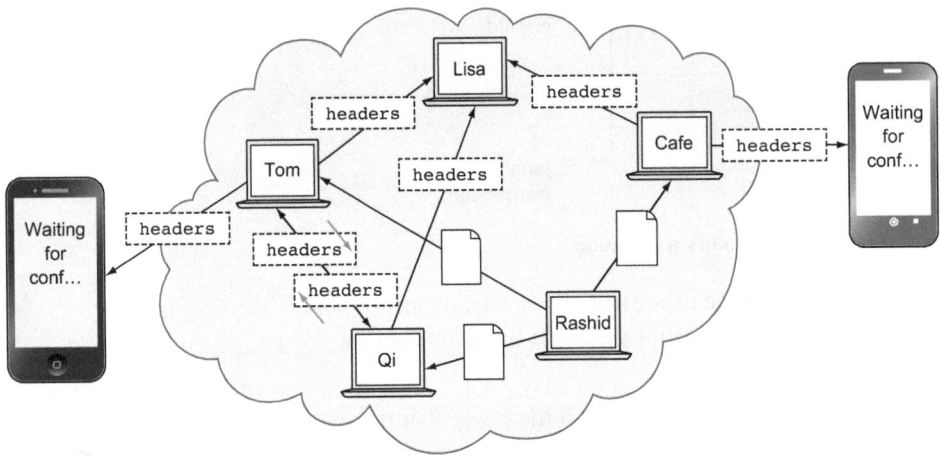

Figure 8.20 All but Lisa have the block. Tom, the cafe, and Qi send `headers` messages.

This concludes the propagation of this block—almost. The lightweight wallets need to be informed about the block.

Notifying wallets

Tom's node is connected to John's wallet, so Tom sends a `headers` message to John. Likewise, the cafe's full node sends a `headers` message to the cafe's lightweight wallet. Tom's and the cafe's full nodes won't test the block against the bloom filters in any way. They will send the `headers` message unconditionally, but the lightweight wallets won't request the full blocks.

As you might recall from chapter 6, lightweight wallets don't download the full blocks. Most of the time, John's wallet is only interested in the block headers so it can verify the blockchain's proof of work. But every now and then, transactions that are relevant to John's wallet are in the blocks, and the wallet wants proof that those transactions are included in the block. To find out if there are any relevant transactions, he sends a `getdata` message to Tom, requesting a `merkleblock` message for the block.

John gets a `merkleblock` message containing the block header and a partial merkle tree connecting his transaction ID (txid) to the merkle root in the block header (figure 8.21).

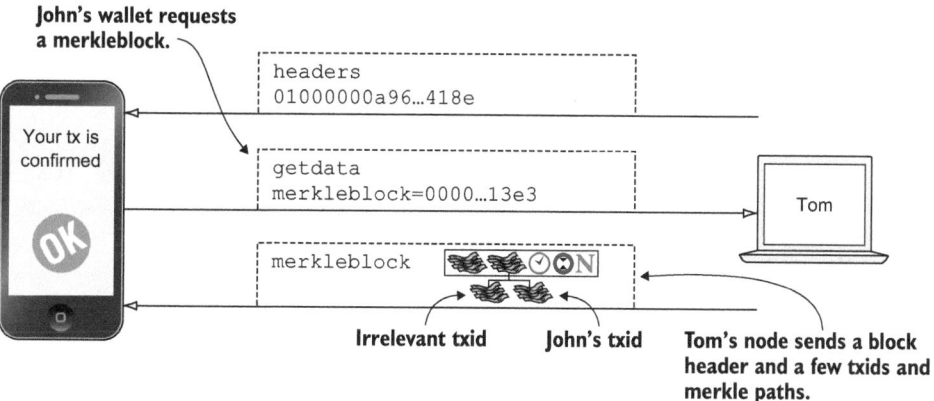

Figure 8.21 Tom sends a `merkleblock` containing a merkle proof that John's transaction is in the block.

Figure 8.22 gives a little repetition from chapter 6.

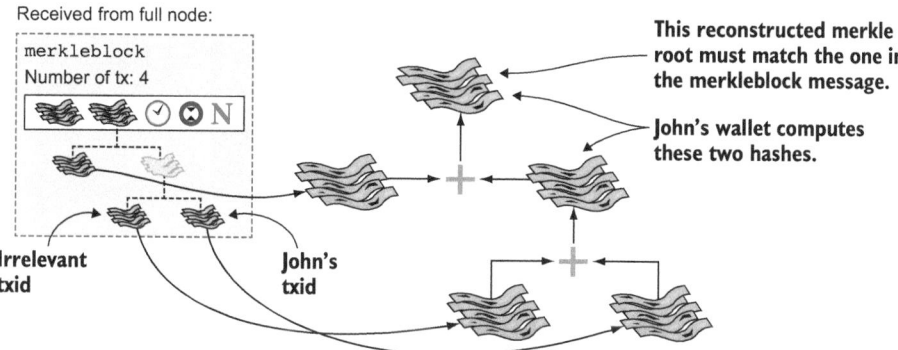

Figure 8.22 The `merkleblock` message contains a block header and a partial merkle tree.

John's wallet will verify that

• The block header is correct and has a valid proof of work.

• The merkle root in the header can be reconstructed using the partial merkle tree.

• The txid of John's transaction is included in the partial merkle tree. He doesn't care about the irrelevant transaction that's used to obfuscate what belongs to John.

John's wallet is now sure his transaction is contained in the new block. The wallet can display a message to John saying, "Your transaction has 1 confirmation."

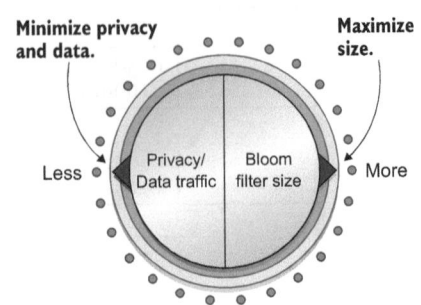

The cafe's lightweight wallet will be notified the same way.

Because the cafe's wallet uses a trusted node, privacy isn't much of an issue (figure 8.23). The wallet can use a big bloom filter to reduce the number of irrelevant transactions, which in turn will reduce mobile data traffic. The sparser the bloom filter, the less extra obfuscation traffic will be sent to the wallet.

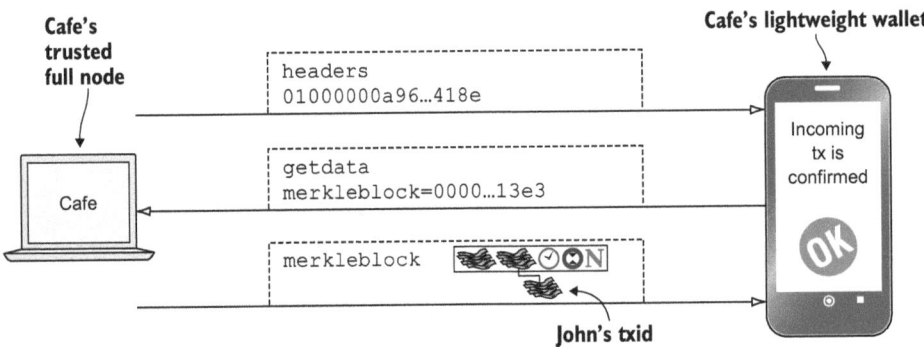

Figure 8.23   The cafe requests a merkle block from its trusted full node.

The cafe's owner feels comfortable handing the cookie over to John now. John eats his cookie. The deal is done.

More confirmations

As time passes, more blocks will be mined by the miners. These blocks will all propagate the network and end up on every full node. The lightweight wallets will get merkle blocks to save bandwidth.

For each new block coming in, John's transaction will be buried under more and more proof of work (figure 8.24). This makes John's transaction harder and harder to double spend. For each new block, the transaction will get one more confirmation.

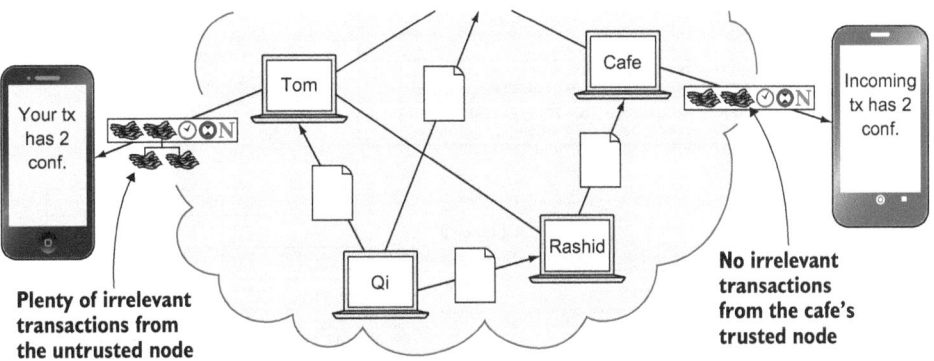

Figure 8.24 As more blocks arrive, John's transaction becomes safer and safer.

Leaving the cookie token system

I don't think the cookie token system will add any more to your understanding of Bitcoin. It's time to let go of the cookie tokens and start talking solely about Bitcoin. We've developed the cookie token system to a point where there are no differences from Bitcoin. Table 8.1 shows the concept mapping table.

Table 8.1 The shared folder is ditched in favor of a peer-to-peer network.

Cookie tokens	Bitcoin	Covered in
1 cookie token	1 bitcoin	Chapter 2
~~The shared folder~~	~~The Bitcoin network~~	~~Chapter 8~~

The last cookie token concept that differs from Bitcoin, the shared folder, has been eliminated. Let's look at how it all happened, in figure 8.25.

We'll keep our friends at the office a while longer. John will probably have to buy a few more cookies, but he'll use Bitcoin to do it.

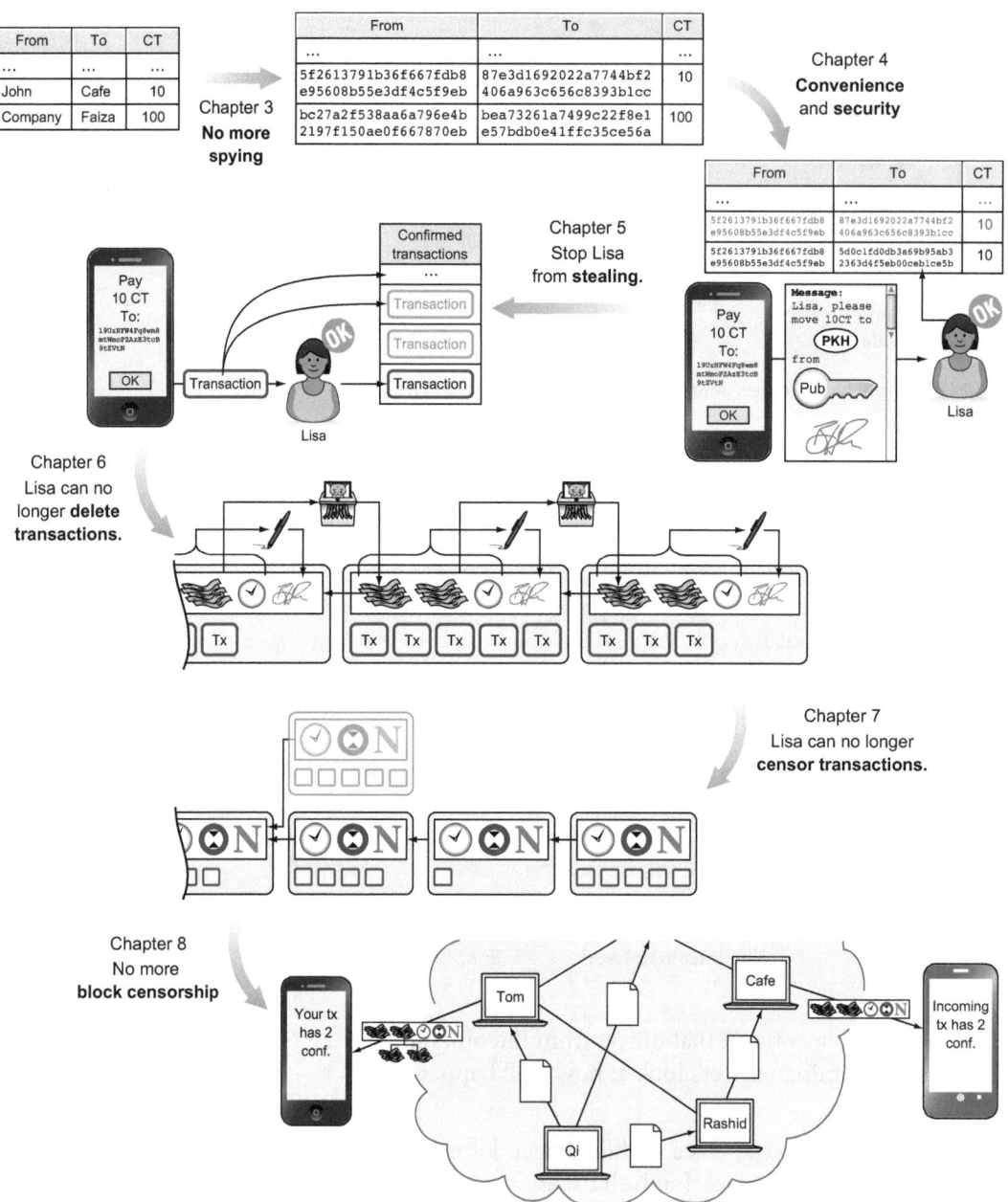

Figure 8.25   The cookie token system's evolution

Bitcoin at a glance

The Bitcoin peer-to-peer network is huge. As of this writing:

- There are about 10,000 publicly accessible full nodes.

- Bitcoin's money supply is about 17,400,000 BTC.

- Each bitcoin is worth around $6,500.

- Bitcoin processes about 250,000 transactions per day.

- An estimate of 100,000 BTC, valued at $630 million, is moved daily.

- The total mining hashrate is about 50 Ehash/s, or 50×10^{18} hash/s.
  A typical desktop computer can do about 25 Mhash/s.

- The transaction fees paid each day total around 17 BTC. This averages
  to 6,800 satoshis per transaction, or about $0.40 per transaction.

- People in all corners of the world use Bitcoin to get around problems
  in their day-to-day lives.

Where were we?

This chapter is about Bitcoin's peer-to-peer network. The first half of
the chapter described the network in action after it's been set up, as
illustrated by figure 8.26, repeated from chapter 1.

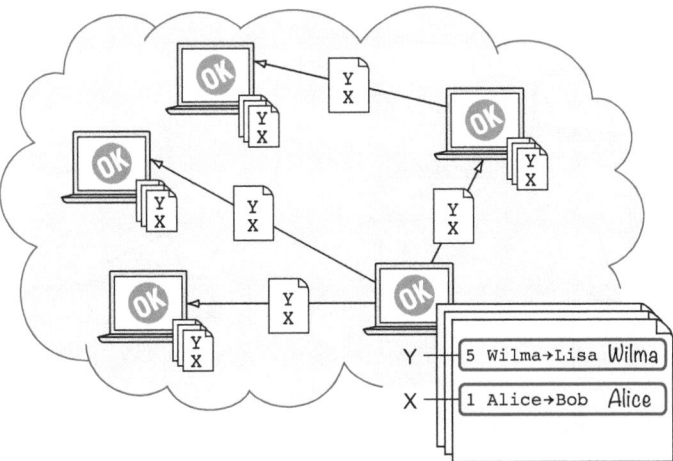

**Figure 8.26 The Bitcoin network distributes blocks (and transactions)
to all participants.**

The second half of this chapter will look at how a new node joins the network.

Bootstrapping the network

The scenario in "The network protocol" assumed that all nodes involved were already connected to each other. But how does a new node start? How would it find other nodes to connect to? How would it download the full blockchain from the genesis block, block 0, up to the latest block? How does it know what the latest block is?

Let's sort it out.

Suppose Selma wants to start her own full node. This is how it would typically happen (figure 8.27):

❶   Selma downloads, verifies, and starts the full node computer program.

❷   The computer program connects to some nodes.

❸   Selma's node downloads blocks from her peers.

❹   Selma's node enters a normal mode of operation.

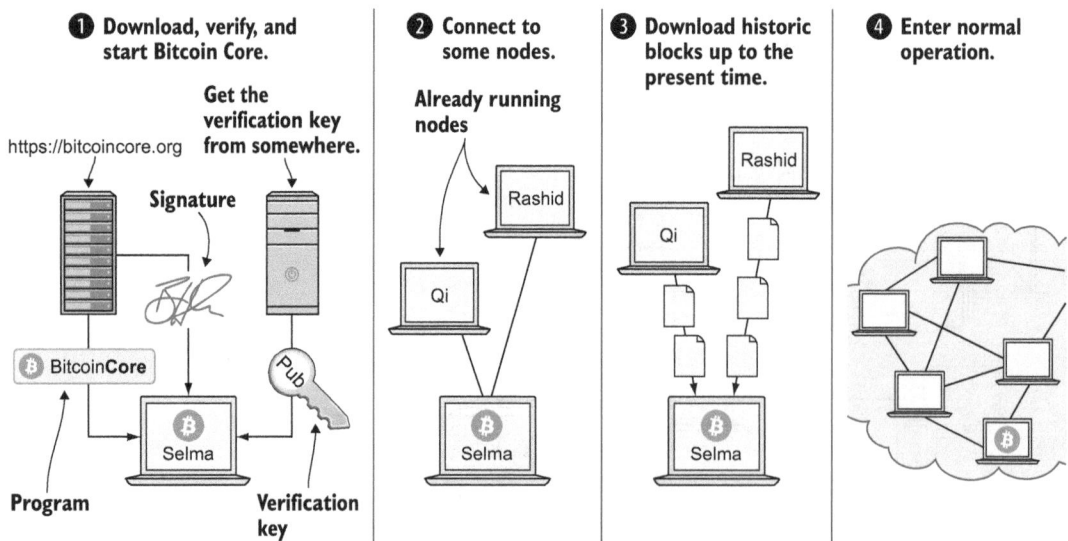

Figure 8.27   Running a full node involves downloading and running the software, connecting to other nodes, downloading old blocks, and entering normal operation.

Step ❶—Run the software

Selma needs a computer program to run a full node. The most commonly used such program is Bitcoin Core. Several others are available, such as libbitcoin, bcoin, bitcoinj, and btcd. We'll focus only on Bitcoin Core, but you're encouraged to explore the others yourself.

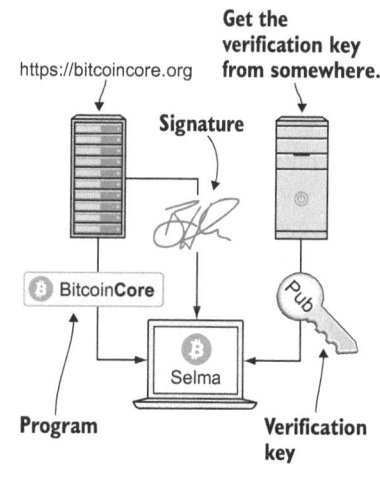

To download Bitcoin Core, Selma visits its web page, https://bitcoincore.org, and finds a download link there. But she encounters a potential problem: Selma isn't sure the program she downloads is actually the version the developers behind Bitcoin Core released. Someone could have fooled Selma into downloading the program from bitconcore.org instead of bitcoincore.org, or someone might have hacked bitcoincore.org and replaced the downloadable files with alternative programs.

The Bitcoin Core team therefore signs all released versions of the program with a private key—let's call it the *Bitcoin Core key*. They provide the signature in a downloadable file, named SHA256SUMS.asc. This file contains the hash value of the released Bitcoin Core software and a signature that signs the contents of the SHA256SUMS.asc file (figure 8.28).

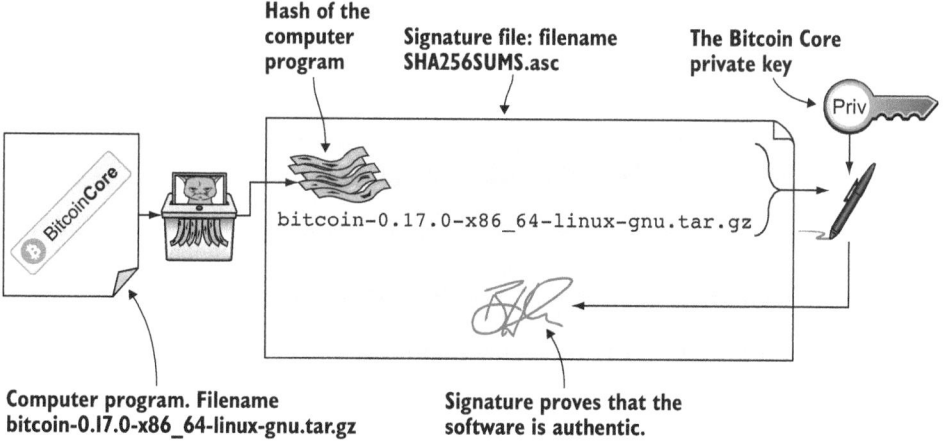

Figure 8.28 The Bitcoin Core team signs the released program with their private key.

Selma has downloaded both the program, in a file called bitcoin-0.17.0-x86_64-linux-gnu.tar.gz, and the signature file, SHA256SUMS.asc. To verify that the program is in fact signed by the Bitcoin Core private key, she needs to know the corresponding public key. But how can she know what this key is?

This is a hard problem. Remember when Lisa used to sign blocks with her private key? How would the full nodes verify that the blocks were actually signed by Lisa? They used multiple sources to fetch Lisa's public key—for example, looking at the bulletin board at the entrance of the office, checking the company's intranet, and asking colleagues. The same applies here; you shouldn't trust a single source, but should use at least two different sources. The key that's currently being used to sign Bitcoin Core releases is named

```
Wladimir J. van der Laan (Bitcoin Core binary release signing key)
<laanwj@gmail.com>
```

and has the following 160-bit SHA1 hash, called *fingerprint*:

```
01EA 5486 DE18 A882 D4C2  6845 90C8 019E 36C2 E964
```

This book can serve as *one* of Selma's sources. She decides to

1. Get the fingerprint of the key from https://bitcoincore.org.

2. Verify the fingerprint with the *Grokking Bitcoin* book.

3. Verify the fingerprint with a friend.

The fingerprints from the three sources match, so Selma downloads the public key from a *key server*. A key server is a computer on the internet that provides a repository of keys. Key servers are commonly used to download keys identified by the key's fingerprint. Selma doesn't trust the key server, so she needs to verify that the fingerprint of the downloaded key matches the expected fingerprint, which it does.

Now, when she has the Bitcoin Core public key, she can verify the signature of the SHA256SUMS.asc file (figure 8.29).

She uses the Bitcoin Core public key to verify the signature in the signature file. She must also verify that the program has the same hash value as stated in SHA256SUMS.asc. The signature is valid, and the hashes match, which means Selma can be sure the software she's about to run is authentic.

Where to get the key

It doesn't really matter where you get the actual public key, but it's important to verify that its fingerprint is what you expect.

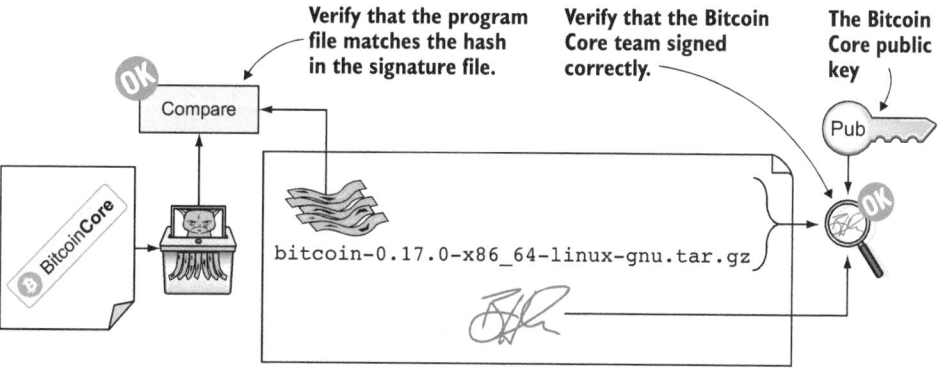

Figure 8.29   Selma verifies the Bitcoin Core signature and that the hash in the signature file matches the hash of the actual program.

Selma starts the program on her computer.

Step ❷—Connect to nodes

When Selma's full node program starts, it isn't connected to any other nodes. She's not part of the Bitcoin network yet. In this step, the node will try to find peers to connect to.

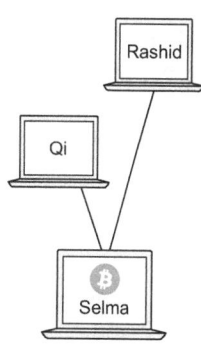

To connect to a peer, the full node needs the IP address and the TCP port for that peer. For example:

```
IP: 142.12.233.96 port: 8333
```

An IP address and port are often written as

```
142.12.233.96:8333
```

Finding initial peers

Where does Selma's node find initial addresses of other peers? Several sources are available (figure 8.30):

* Configure the full node with custom peer addresses. Selma can get an address by asking a friend who's running a full node.

* Use the Domain Name System (DNS) to look up initial peer addresses to connect to.

* Use hardcoded peer addresses in the full node program.

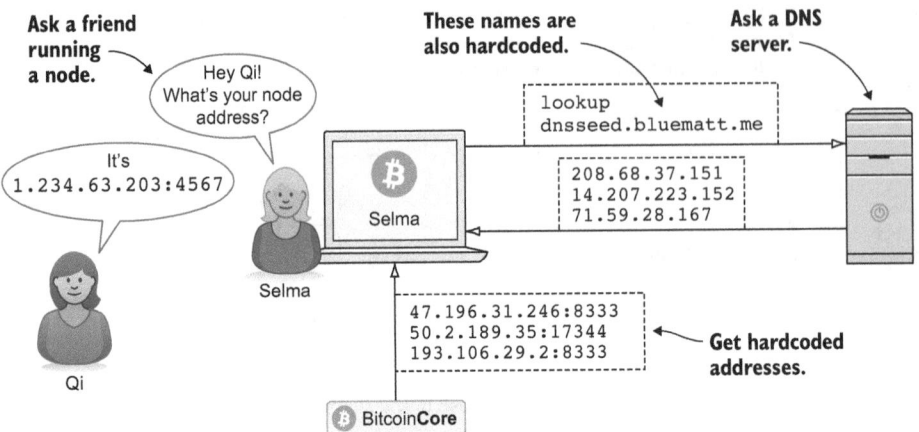

Figure 8.30   Selma's full node has three different types of sources to find initial peers.

Selma's node shouldn't initially connect to just one node. If that single node is malicious, she'd have no way of knowing it. If you connect to multiple nodes initially, you can verify that they all send data consistent with each other. If not, one or more nodes are deliberately lying to you, or they themselves have been fooled.

The default way of finding initial node addresses is to look them up in the DNS system. DNS is a global name lookup system, used to look up IP numbers from computer names. For example, when you visit https://bitcoin.org with your web browser, it will use DNS to look up the IP number of the name bitcoin.org. The Bitcoin Core software does the same. Names to look up are hardcoded into Bitcoin Core, just like the hardcoded IP addresses and ports. Several DNS seeds are coded into the software. A lookup of a DNS seed can return several IP addresses, and every new lookup might return a different set of IP addresses. The final, third option is used as a last resort.

Note from figure 8.30 that DNS lookups don't return port numbers. The other two methods of finding initial peers usually include one, but the DNS response can return only IP addresses. The nodes on these IP addresses are assumed to listen on the default port that Bitcoin Core listens on, which is 8333.

Handshaking

Suppose Selma's node chooses to connect to Qi's node, 1.234.63.203:4567, and to Rashid's node, 47.196.31.246:8333. Selma sets up a TCP connection to each of the two nodes and sends an initial

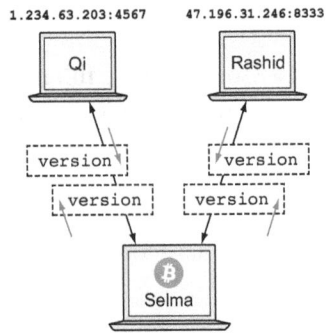

message to both of them on the new TCP connections. Let's look at how she talks to Qi's node (figure 8.31).

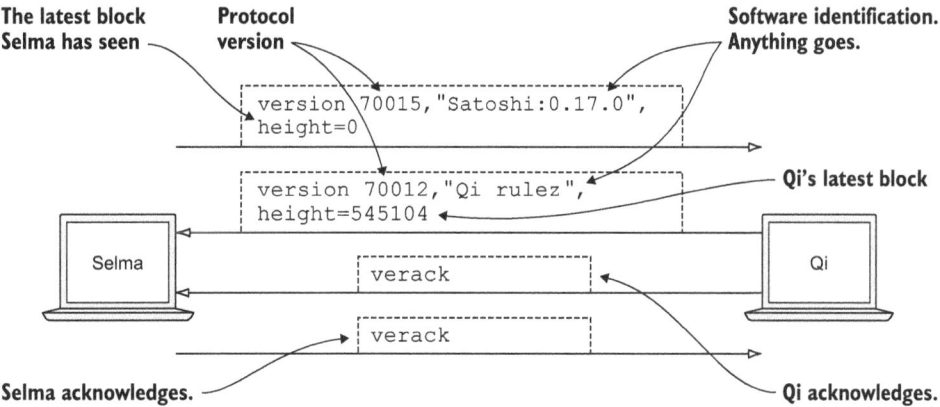

Figure 8.31   Selma exchanges a `version` message with Qi.

The exchange, called a *handshake*, starts with Selma, who sends a `version` message to Qi. The handshake is used to agree on which protocol version to use and tell each other what block heights they have. The `version` message contains a lot of information not shown in the figure, but the most essential stuff is there:

- *Protocol version*—The version of the network protocol, or "language," that peers use to talk to each other. Selma and Qi will use version 70012 because that's the highest version Qi will understand. Selma knows all protocol versions up to her own.

- *User agent*—This is shown as "software identification" in the figure because "user agent" is a bit cryptic. It's used to hint to the other node what software you're running, but it can be anything.

- *Height*—This is the height of the tip of the best chain the node has.

Other useful information in the `version` message includes

- *Services*—A list of features this node supports, such as bloom filtering used by lightweight clients.

- *My address*—The IP address and port of the node sending the `version` message. Without it, Qi wouldn't know what address to connect to if she restarts and wants to reconnect to Selma's node.

When Qi's node receives Selma's `version` message, Qi will reply
with her own `version` message. She'll also send a `verack` message
immediately after the `version` message. The `verack` doesn't contain
any information; rather, it's used to acknowledge to Selma that Qi has
received the `version` message.

As soon as Selma's node receives Qi's `version` message, it will reply
with a `verack` message back to Qi's node. The handshake is done. Selma
also goes through the same procedure with Rashid's node.

Finding peers' peers

When Selma's node is connected to Rashid's node, it will ask that node
for other peer addresses to connect to. This way, Selma will be able to
expand her set of peers (figure 8.32).

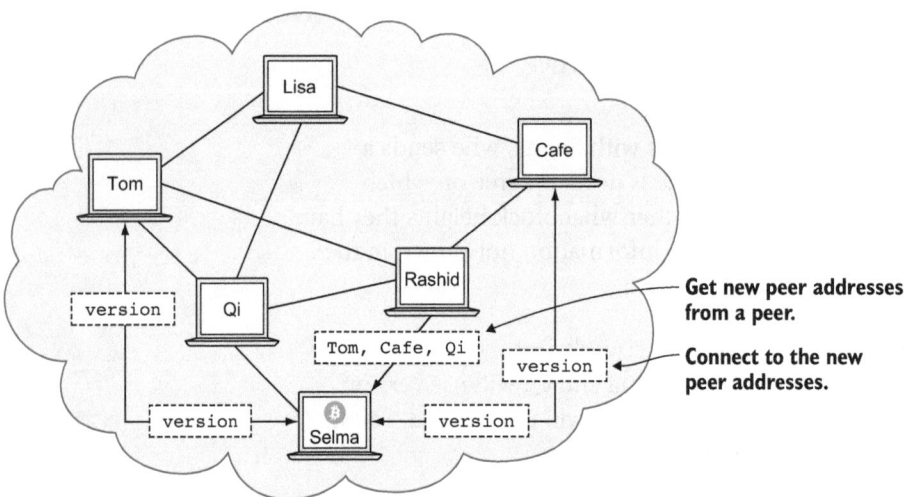

Figure 8.32   Selma asks her peers for more peer addresses to connect to.

Selma is only connected to two peers: Qi's node and Rashid's node. But
she thinks she needs more nodes to connect to. Being connected to only
two nodes has some implications:

- Qi and Rashid can collude to hide transactions and blocks from
  Selma.

- Qi's node may break, leaving Selma with only Rashid's node. Rashid
  can then singlehandedly hide information from Selma.

- Both Qi's and Rashid's nodes may break, in which case Selma will
  be completely disconnected from the network until she connects to
  some other nodes via the initial peer-lookup mechanisms.

Figure 8.33 shows how Selma asks Rashid for more peer addresses to connect to.

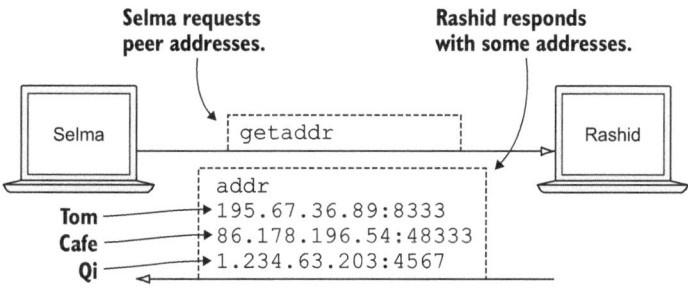

Figure 8.33   Selma requests more peer addresses from Rashid's node. He responds with a bunch.

Selma sends a `getaddr` message to a peer, Rashid's node. Rashid responds with a set of IP addresses and TCP ports that Selma can use to connect to more peers. Rashid chooses which addresses to send to Selma, but it's usually the addresses to which Rashid is already connected and possibly some that Rashid collected from his peers but didn't use himself.

Selma will connect to any number of the received addresses to increase her *connectivity*. The more peers you're connected to, the better your connectivity. A high degree of connectivity decreases the risk of missing out on information due to misbehaving peers. Also, information propagates more quickly if nodes have higher connectivity. A typical full node in Bitcoin has about 100 active connections at the same time. Only eight (by default) of those are *outbound connections*, meaning connections initiated by that node. The rest are *inbound connections* initiated by other nodes. Consequently, a full node that isn't reachable on port 8333 from the internet—for example, due to a firewall—won't get more than eight connections in total.

Initial nodes

After getting an `addr` message, nodes disconnect from initial nodes (except manually configured ones) to avoid overloading them. They're initial nodes for many other nodes.

Step ❸—Synchronize

Now that Selma is well-connected to, and part of, the Bitcoin network, it's time for her to download and verify the full blockchain up to the latest block available. This process is called *synchronization*, *sync*, or *initial blockchain download*.

Selma has only a single block: the genesis block. The genesis block is hardcoded in the Bitcoin Core software, so all nodes have this block when they start.

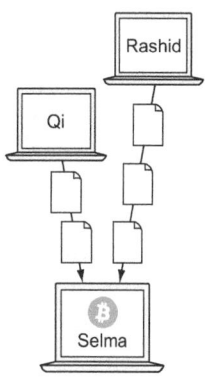

She needs to download all historic blocks from her peers and verify them before she can verify newly created blocks. This is because she has no idea what the current unspent transaction output (UTXO) set looks like. To build the current UTXO set, she needs to start with an empty UTXO set, go through all historic blocks from block 0, and update the UTXO set with the information in the transactions in the blocks.

The process is as follows:

1. Download all historic block headers from one peer, and verify the proof of work.

2. Download all blocks on the strongest chain from multiple peers in parallel.

Selma selects one of her peers, Tom, to download all block headers from. Figure 8.34 shows how Selma's node downloads the block headers from Tom's node.

She sends a `getheaders` message containing Selma's latest block ID, which happens to be the genesis block, block 0. Tom sends back a list of 2,000 block headers; each block header is 80 bytes. Selma verifies each header's proof of work and requests a new batch of headers from Tom. This process continues until Selma receives a batch of fewer than 2,000 headers from Tom, which is a signal that he has no more headers to give her.

Simplified

The `getheaders` message contains a list of some block IDs from Selma's blockchain so that Tom can find a common block they both have in case Tom doesn't have Selma's tip. Let's not bother with that.

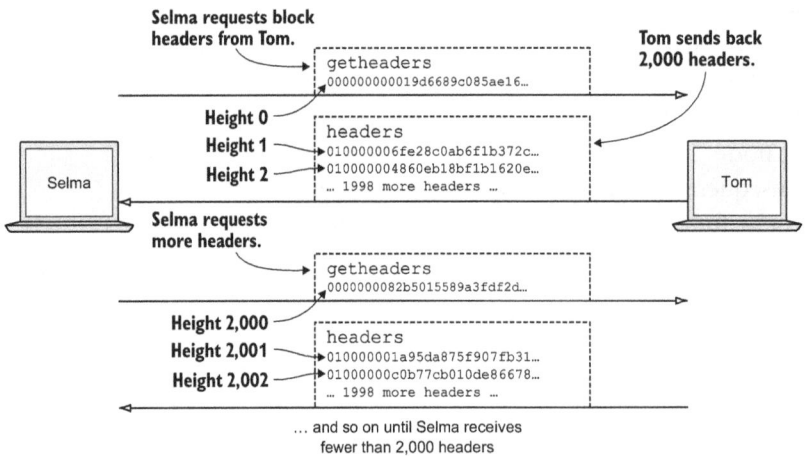

Figure 8.34   Selma downloads block headers from Tom by repeatedly sending a `getheaders` message with her latest block ID.

When Selma has received all the headers from Tom, she determines which branch is the strongest and starts downloading actual block data belonging to that branch from her peers. She can download block data from multiple peers at the same time to speed things up. Figure 8.35 shows her communication with Rashid's node.

It starts with Selma, who sends a `getdata` message to Rashid. This message specifies which blocks she wants to download from Rashid, who sends back the requested blocks in `block` messages, one by one. Note that Selma downloads only some of the blocks from Rashid. She also downloads blocks from Tom in parallel, which is why there are gaps in the sequence of requested blocks. The process repeats until Selma doesn't want any more blocks from Rashid.

Bigger batches ₿

In this example, Selma requests 3 blocks at a time, but in reality, Bitcoin Core would request a list of at most 16 blocks per batch.

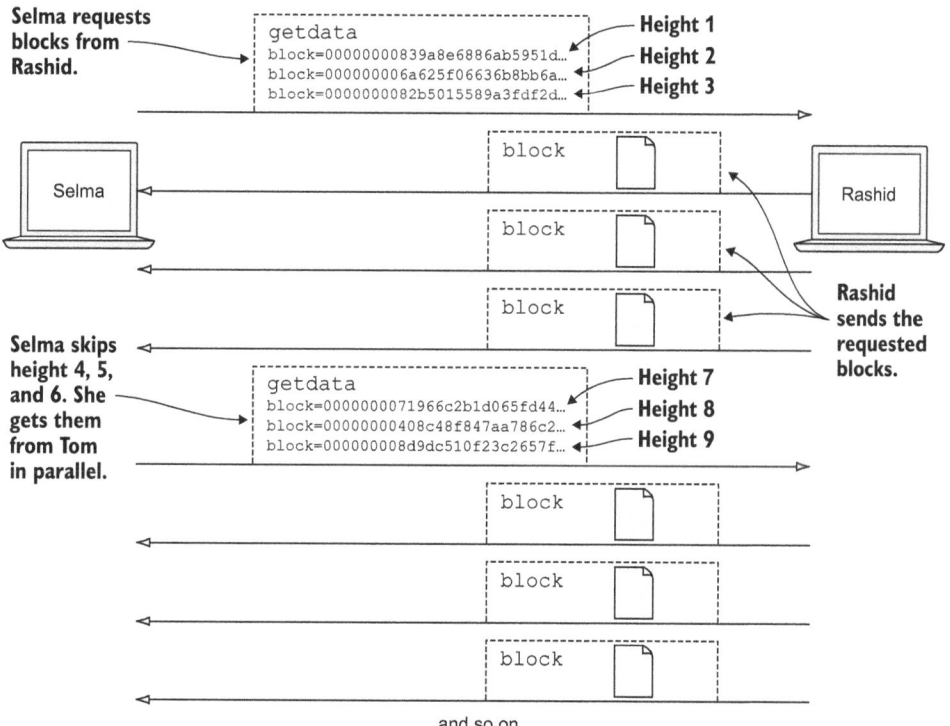

Figure 8.35   Selma downloads blocks from Rashid by repeatedly sending a `getdata` message with a list block IDs she wants the blocks for.

As Selma downloads blocks, Rashid will probably receive more fresh blocks from his peers. Suppose he has received a new block by the time Selma has received the first 100 blocks from Rashid. Rashid will then send out a `headers` message to his peers, including Selma, as described in the section "Including the transaction in a block." This way, Selma will be aware of all new blocks appearing during her initial synchronization and can later request them from any peer.

As Selma receives blocks, she verifies them, updates her UTXO set, and adds them to her own blockchain.

> **Initial download**
>
> The initial blockchain download, about 210 GB as of this writing, takes several hours, even days, depending on your hardware performance and internet speed.

Verifying early blocks

The most time-consuming part of verifying a block is verifying the transaction signatures. If you know of any block ID that's part of a valid blockchain, you can skip verifying the signatures of all blocks prior to and including this block (figure 8.36). This will greatly speed up the initial blockchain download up to that block.

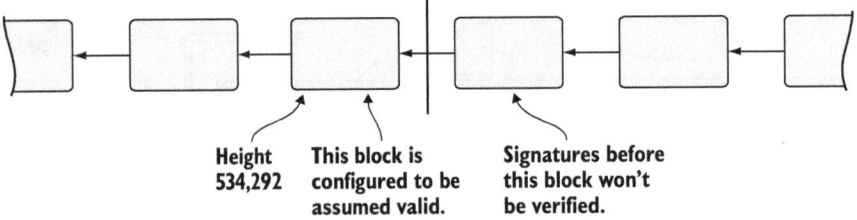

Height 534,292	**This block is configured to be assumed valid.**	**Signatures before this block won't be verified.**

Figure 8.36   To speed up initial block download, signatures of reasonably old transactions won't be verified.

Of course, other stuff, like verifying that no double spends occur or that the block rewards are correct, is still done. The syncing node must build its own UTXO set, so it must still go through all transactions to be able to update the UTXO set accordingly.

Bitcoin Core ships with a preconfigured block ID of a block from some weeks back from the release date. For Bitcoin Core 0.17.0, that block is

```
height: 534292
hash: 0000000000000000002e63058c023a9a1de233554f28c7b21380b6c9003f36a8
```

This is about 10,000 blocks back in the blockchain at release date. This is, of course, a configuration parameter, and the aforementioned block is just a default reasonable value. Selma could have changed this when starting her node, or she could have verified with friends and other sources she trusts that this block is in fact representing an "all valid transactions blockchain." She could also have disabled the feature to verify all transaction signatures since block 0.

After a while, Selma is finally on the same page as the other nodes and ready to enter the normal mode of operation.

Step ❹—Normal operation

This step is easy because we already discussed it in "The network protocol." Selma enters the normal mode of operation. From now on, she'll participate in block propagation and transaction propagation, and verify every transaction and block coming in (figure 8.37).

Selma is now running a full-blown full node.

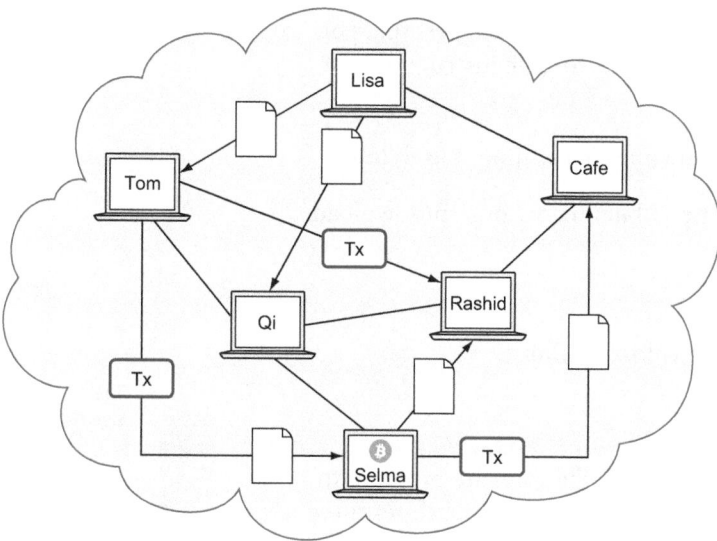

Figure 8.37   Selma is finally an active part of the Bitcoin peer-to-peer network.

Running your own full node

Online instructions

More detailed instructions for all major OSs are available at web resource 18 in appendix C.

WARNING!

This section will walk you through setting up your own Bitcoin Core full node on a Linux OS. It's intended for readers comfortable with the Linux OS and command line.

You've seen how a Bitcoin full node is downloaded, started, and synchronized in theory. This section will help you install your own full node.

This section requires that you

- Have a computer with at least 2 GB of RAM running a Linux OS.

- Have lots of available disk space. As of this writing, about 210 GB is needed.

- Have an internet connection without a limited data plan.

- Know how to start and use a command-line terminal.

If you don't have a Linux OS, you can still use these instructions; but you'll have to install the version of Bitcoin Core that's appropriate for your system, and the commands will look different. I suggest that you visit web resource 18 in appendix C to get up-to-date instructions for your non-Linux OS.

The general process for getting your own node running is as follows:

1. Download Bitcoin Core from https://bitcoincore.org/en/download.

2. Verify the software.

3. Unpack and start.

4. Wait for the initial blockchain download to finish.

Downloading Bitcoin Core

To run your own full Bitcoin node, you need the software program to run. In this example, you'll download Bitcoin Core from web resource 19 in appendix C. As of this writing, the latest version of Bitcoin Core is 0.17.0. Let's download it:

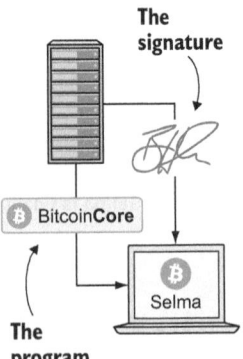

```
$ wget https://bitcoincore.org/bin/bitcoin-core-0.17.0/\
    bitcoin-0.17.0-x86_64-linux-gnu.tar.gz
```

As the filename bitcoin-0.17.0-x86_64-linux-gnu.tar.gz indicates, the command downloads version 0.17.0 for 64-bit (x86_64) Linux (linux-gnu). By the time you read this, new versions of Bitcoin Core will probably have been released. Consult web resource 19 to get the latest version of Bitcoin Core. Also, if you use another OS or computer architecture, please select the file that's right for you.

Verifying the software

WARNING!

This section is hard and requires a fair amount of work on the command line. If you just want to install and run the Bitcoin Core software for experimental purposes, you can skip this section and jump to "Unpacking and starting." If you aren't using it for experimental purposes, please understand the risks explained earlier in this chapter in "Step ❶—Run the software" before skipping this step.

This section will show you how to verify that the downloaded .tar.gz file hasn't been tampered with in any way. This file is digitally signed by the Bitcoin Core team's private key. The verification process involves the following steps:

1. Download the signature file.
2. Verify that the hash of the .tar.gz file matches the hash in the message part of the signature file.
3. Download the Bitcoin Core team's public key.
4. Install the public key as trusted on your computer.
5. Verify the signature.

Let's get started.

Downloading the signature file

To verify that your downloaded Bitcoin Core package is actually from the Bitcoin Core team, you need to download the signature file named SHA256SUMS.asc. Figure 8.38, repeated from "Step 1—Run the software," explains how the SHA256SUMS.asc file is designed.

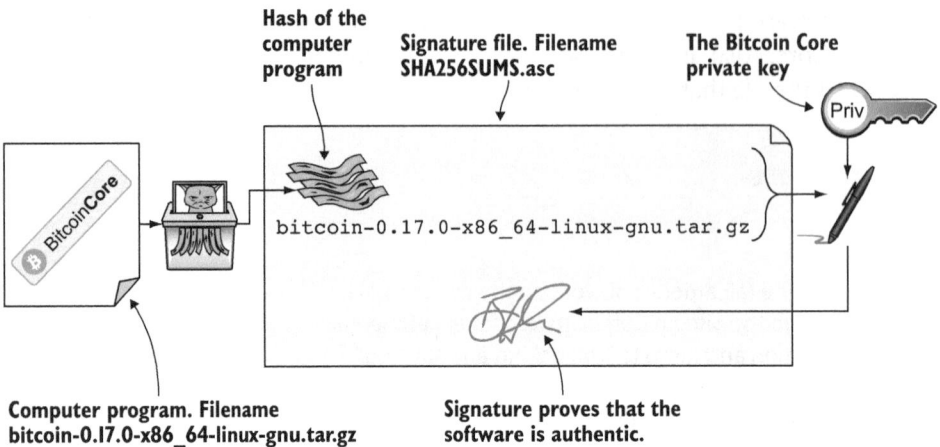

Figure 8.38   The Bitcoin Core team signs the released program with their private key.

Download the signature file SHA256SUMS.asc from the same server you downloaded the program from:

```
$ wget https://bitcoincore.org/bin/bitcoin-core-0.17.0/SHA256SUMS.asc
```

This file will be used to verify that the downloaded .tar.gz file is signed by the Bitcoin Core team. Note that this file is for version 0.17.0 only. If you use another version of Bitcoin Core, please select the correct signature file at web resource 19.

The following listing shows what the contents of this file look like (the actual hashes have been shortened):

```
-----BEGIN PGP SIGNED MESSAGE-----
Hash: SHA256

1e43...35ed  bitcoin-0.17.0-aarch64-linux-gnu.tar.gz
a4ff...7585  bitcoin-0.17.0-arm-linux-gnueabihf.tar.gz
967a...f1b7  bitcoin-0.17.0-i686-pc-linux-gnu.tar.gz
e421...5d61  bitcoin-0.17.0-osx64.tar.gz
0aea...ac58  bitcoin-0.17.0-osx.dmg
98ef...785e  bitcoin-0.17.0.tar.gz
1f40...8ee7  bitcoin-0.17.0-win32-setup.exe
402f...730d  bitcoin-0.17.0-win32.zip
b37f...0b1a  bitcoin-0.17.0-win64-setup.exe
d631...0799  bitcoin-0.17.0-win64.zip
9d6b...5a4f  bitcoin-0.17.0-x86_64-linux-gnu.tar.gz
```

```
-----BEGIN PGP SIGNATURE-----
Version: GnuPG v1.4.11 (GNU/Linux)

iQIcBAEBCAAGBQJbtIOFAAoJEJDIAZ42wulk5aQP/0tQp+EwFQPtSJgtmjYucw8L
SskGHj76SviCBSfCJ0LKjBdnQ4nbrIBsSuw0oKYLVN6OIFIp6hvNSfxin1S8bipo
hCLX8xB0FuG4jVFHAqo8PKmF1XeB7ulfOkYg+qF3VR/qpkrjzQJ6S/nnrgc4bZu+
lXzyUBH+NNqqlMeTRzYW92g0zGMexig/ZEMqigMckTiFDrTUGkQjJGzwlIy73fXI
LZ/KtZYDUw82roZINXlp4oNHDQb8qT5R1L7ACvqmWixbq49Yqgt+MAL1NG5hvCSW
jiVX4fasHUJLlvVbmCH2L42Z+W24VCWYiy691XkZ2D0+bmllz0APMSPtgVEWDFEe
wcUeLXbFGkMtN1EDCLctQ6/DxYk3EM2Ffxkw3o5ehTSD6LczqNC7wG+ysPCjkV1P
O4oT4AyRSm/sP/o4qxvx/cpiRcu1BQU5qgIJDO+sPmCKzPn7wEG7vBoZGOeybxCS
UUPEOSGan1Elc0Jv4/bvbJ0XLVJPVC0AHk1dDE9zg/0PXof9lcFzGffzFBI+WRT3
zf1rBPKqrmQ3hHpybg34WCVmsvG94Zodp/hiJ3mGsxjqrOhCJO3PByk/F5LOyHtP
wjWPoicI2pRin2Xl/YTVAyeqex519XAnYCSDEXRpe+W4BdzFoOJwm5S6eW8Q+wkN
UtaRwoYjFfUsohMZ3Lbt
=H8c2
-----END PGP SIGNATURE-----
```

The signed message in the upper part of the file lists several files along
with their respective SHA256 hashes. The listed files are installation
packages for all OSs and architectures for which Bitcoin Core is
released. The lower part of the file is the signature of the message in the
upper part. The signature commits to the entire message and thus to all
the hashes and files listed in the message.

Verifying the hash of the downloaded file

The file you downloaded is named bitcoin-0.17.0-x86_64-linux-gnu.tar.
gz so you expect that the SHA256 hash of that file matches `9d6b…5a4f`
exactly. Let's check:

```
$ sha256sum bitcoin-0.17.0-x86_64-linux-gnu.tar.gz
9d6b472dc2aceedb1a974b93a3003a81b7e0265963bd2aa0acdcb1759
↳8215a4f  bitcoin-0.17.0-x86_64-linux-gnu.tar.gz
```

This command calculates the SHA256 hash of your downloaded file. It
does indeed match the hash in the SHA256SUMS.asc file. If they don't
match, then something is wrong, and you should halt the installation
and investigate.

Getting the Bitcoin Core signing key

To verify that the signature in the signature file was done using the
Bitcoin Core signing key, you need the corresponding public key. As
noted in "Step 1—Run the software," you should convince yourself
about what fingerprint the Bitcoin Core key has and then download
that key from any source.

Get the
verification
key from
somewhere.

Verification
key

You could, for example,

- Get the fingerprint of the Bitcoin Core team's key from https://bitcoincore.org, the official website of the Bitcoin Core team.

- Consult the book *Grokking Bitcoin* to verify the fingerprint.

- Verify the fingerprint with a friend.

Start by finding the Bitcoin Core team's public key fingerprint on their website. You find the following fingerprint on the downloads page:

```
01EA5486DE18A882D4C2684590C8019E36C2E964
```

Now, consult the book *Grokking Bitcoin* to check if the fingerprint in that book matches the fingerprint from https://bitcoincore.org. Look in the "Step 1—Run the software" section of chapter 8 of that book. It says

```
01EA 5486 DE18 A882 D4C2  6845 90C8 019E 36C2 E964
```

This is the same fingerprint (although formatted slightly differently). The book and the website https://bitcoincore.org both claim that this key belongs to the Bitcoin Core team. Let's not settle for that. You'll also call a friend you trust and have her read the fingerprint to you:

> **You:** "Hello, Donna! What's the fingerprint of the current Bitcoin Core signing key?"
>
> **Donna:** "Hi! I verified that key myself a few months ago, and I know the fingerprint is `01EA 5486 DE18 A882 D4C2 6845 90C8 019E 36C2 E964`."
>
> **You:** "Thank you, it matches mine. Goodbye!"
>
> **Donna:** "You're welcome. Goodbye!"

Donna's statement further strengthens your trust in this key. You think you've collected enough evidence that this is, in fact, the correct key.

Let's start downloading the key. To do this, you can use a tool called gpg, which stands for GnuPG, which in turn stands for Gnu Privacy Guard. This program conforms to a standard called OpenPGP (Pretty Good Privacy). This standard specifies how keys can be exchanged and how to do encryption and digital signatures in an interoperable way.

GnuPG is available on most Linux computers by default. To download a public key with a certain fingerprint, you run the following gpg command:

```
$ gpg --recv-keys 01EA5486DE18A882D4C2684590C8019E36C2E964
gpg: key 90C8019E36C2E964: public key "Wladimir J. van der Laan (Bitcoin
↳Core binary release signing key) <laanwj@gmail.com>" imported
gpg: no ultimately trusted keys found
gpg: Total number processed: 1
gpg:                imported: 1
```

Depending on the version of gpg you use, the output can vary. This command downloads the public key from any available key server and verifies that the downloaded public key in fact has the fingerprint that you requested. The owner of this key is "Wladimir J. van der Laan (Bitcoin Core binary release signing key)."

The prior command downloads the key into gpg and adds it to your list of known keys. But the output of this command mentions "no ultimately trusted keys found." This means this key isn't signed by any key that you trust. You've only imported the key. In gpg, keys can sign other keys to certify that the signed key is legit.

Signing the public key as trusted on your computer

You've verified that the key belongs to the Bitcoin Core team and installed that key onto your system using gpg.

You'll now sign that key with a private key that you own. You do this to remember this key as trusted. The Bitcoin Core team will probably release new versions of Bitcoin Core in the future. If GnuPG remembers this public key as trusted, you won't have to go through all these key-verification steps again when you upgrade.

The process is as follows:

1. Create a key of your own.
2. Sign the Bitcoin Core public key with your own private key.

GnuPG lets you create a key of your own with the following command:

```
$ gpg --gen-key
gpg (GnuPG) 2.1.18; Copyright (C) 2017 Free Software Foundation, Inc.
This is free software: you are free to change and redistribute it.
There is NO WARRANTY, to the extent permitted by law.

Note: Use "gpg --full-generate-key" for a full featured key generation
↳dialog.
GnuPG needs to construct a user ID to identify your key.
```

GnuPG will ask for your name and email address. Answer these questions; they'll be used to identify your key:

```
Real name: Kalle Rosenbaum
Email address: kalle@example.com
You selected this USER-ID:
    "Kalle Rosenbaum <kalle@example.com>"

Change (N)ame, (E)mail, or (O)kay/(Q)uit?
```

Continue by pressing O (capital letter "oh"). You then need to select a password with which to encrypt your private key. Choose a password, and make sure you remember it.

Key generation might take a while, because it takes time to generate good random numbers for your key. When it's finished, you should see output like this:

```
public and secret key created and signed.

pub    rsa2048 2018-04-27 [SC] [expires: 2020-04-26]
       B8C0D19BB7E17E5CEC6D69D487C0AC3FEDA7E796
       B8C0D19BB7E17E5CEC6D69D487C0AC3FEDA7E796
uid                     Kalle Rosenbaum <kalle@example.com>
sub    rsa2048 2018-04-27 [E] [expires: 2020-04-26]
```

You now have a key of your own that you'll use to sign keys that you trust. Let's sign the Bitcoin Core team key:

```
$ gpg --sign-key 01EA5486DE18A882D4C2684590C8019E36C2E964
pub  rsa4096/90C8019E36C2E964
     created: 2015-06-24  expires: 2019-02-14  usage: SC
     trust: unknown       validity: unknown
[ unknown] (1). Wladimir J. van der Laan (Bitcoin Core binary release
↳signing key) <laanwj@gmail.com>
pub  rsa4096/90C8019E36C2E964
     created: 2015-06-24  expires: 2019-02-14  usage: SC
     trust: unknown       validity: unknown
 Primary key fingerprint: 01EA 5486 DE18 A882 D4C2  6845 90C8 019E 36C2
↳E964
     Wladimir J. van der Laan (Bitcoin Core binary release signing key)
↳<laanwj@gmail.com>
This key is due to expire on 2019-02-14.
Are you sure that you want to sign this key with your
key "Kalle Rosenbaum <kalle@example.com>" (8DC7D3846BA6AB5E)

Really sign? (y/N)
```

Enter y. You'll be prompted for your private key password. Enter it, and press Enter. The Bitcoin Core key should now be regarded as trusted by gpg. This will simplify the process when you upgrade your node in the future.

Let's look at your newly signed key:

```
$ gpg --list-keys 01EA5486DE18A882D4C2684590C8019E36C2E964
pub   rsa4096 2015-06-24 [SC] [expires: 2019-02-14]
      01EA5486DE18A882D4C2684590C8019E36C2E964
uid           [ full ] Wladimir J. van der Laan (Bitcoin Core binary release
↳signing key) <laanwj@gmail.com>
```

The word to look for is full in square brackets. This means gpg, and you, fully trust this key.

Verifying the signature

It's time to verify the signature of the SHA256SUMS.asc file:

```
$ gpg --verify SHA256SUMS.asc
gpg: Signature made Wed 03 Oct 2018 10:53:25 AM CEST
gpg:                using RSA key 90C8019E36C2E964
gpg: Good signature from "Wladimir J. van der Laan (Bitcoin Core binary
↳release signing key) <laanwj@gmail.com>" [full]
```

It says that the signature is Good and that it's signed with a key that you fully trust, [full].

To summarize, you've done the following:

1. Downloaded Bitcoin Core and the signature file
2. Verified that the hash of the .tar.gz file matches the stated hash in SHA256SUMS.asc
3. Downloaded a public key and verified that it belongs to Bitcoin Core
4. Signed that key with your own private key so GnuPG and you remember that the Bitcoin Core key is legit
5. Verified the signature of the SHA256SUMS.asc file

When you later upgrade the program, you can skip several of these steps. The process will then be

1. Download Bitcoin Core and the signature file.
2. Verify that the hash of the .tar.gz file matches the stated hash in SHA256SUMS.asc.
3. Verify the signature of the SHA256SUMS.asc file.

Unpacking and starting

Let's unpack the software:

```
$ tar -zxvf bitcoin-0.17.0-x86_64-linux-gnu.tar.gz
```

This will create a directory called bitcoin-0.17.0. Go into the directory bitcoin-0.17.0/bin, and have a look:

```
$ cd bitcoin-0.17.0/bin
$ ls
bitcoin-cli  bitcoind  bitcoin-qt  bitcoin-tx  test_bitcoin
```

Here you have several executable programs:

* bitcoin-cli is a program you can use to extract information about the node you're running as well as manage a built-in wallet that's shipped with Bitcoin Core.

* bitcoind is the program to use if you want to run the node in the background without a graphical user interface (GUI).

* bitcoin-qt is the program to run if you want a GUI for your node. This is mainly useful if you use the built-in wallet.

* bitcoin-tx is a small utility program to create and modify Bitcoin transactions.

* test_bitcoin lets you test run a test suite.

In this tutorial, you'll run bitcoind, which stands for "Bitcoin daemon." In UNIX systems such as Linux, the word *daemon* is used for computer programs that run in the background.

Let's start the Bitcoin Core daemon in the background and see what happens:

```
$ ./bitcoind -daemon
Bitcoin server starting
```

This starts your node. It will automatically begin connecting to peers and downloading the blockchain for you.

Initial blockchain download

This process will take time. Depending on your internet connection, processor, and disk, it can vary from several days down to a few hours.

You can use the bitcoin-cli program to query the running node about the download progress, as in the following:

```
$ ./bitcoin-cli getblockchaininfo
{
  "chain": "main",
  "blocks": 207546,
  "headers": 549398,
  "bestblockhash":
➥"00000000000003a6a5f2f360f02a3b8e4c214d27bd8e079a70f5fb630a0817c5",
  "difficulty": 3304356.392990344,
  "mediantime": 1352672365,
  "verificationprogress": 0.0249296506976196,
  "initialblockdownload": true,
  "chainwork":
➥"000000000000000000000000000000000000000000000202ad90c17ec6ea33c",
  "size_on_disk": 11945130882,
  "pruned": false,
  "softforks": [
    {
      "id": "bip34",
      "version": 2,
      "reject": {
        "status": false
      }
    },
    {
      "id": "bip66",
      "version": 3,
      "reject": {
        "status": false
      }
    },
    {
      "id": "bip65",
      "version": 4,
      "reject": {
        "status": false
      }
    }
  ],
```

```
"bip9_softforks": {
   "csv": {
      "status": "defined",
      "startTime": 1462060800,
      "timeout": 1493596800,
      "since": 0
   },
   "segwit": {
      "status": "defined",
      "startTime": 1479168000,
      "timeout": 1510704000,
      "since": 0
   }
},
"warnings": ""
}
```

This command shows a lot of information about the blockchain. Note that blocks have been downloaded and verified up to height 207546. Bitcoin Core will download block headers prior to the full blocks to verify proof of work. This node has downloaded headers up to height 549398, which are all the headers there are at this time. Another interesting thing is the `initialblockdownload` field, which will remain `true` until the initial block download is finished.

Keep this daemon running. You'll get back to it in appendix A, where I'll give you a small tutorial on how to use bitcoin-cli to examine the blockchain and use your built-in wallet.

If you want to stop the node, issue the following command:

```
$ ./bitcoin-cli stop
```

You can start the node again whenever you like, and the node will begin where it left off.

Recap

We've replaced the last central point of authority, the shared folder, with a peer-to-peer network. In a peer-to-peer network, the full nodes communicate directly with each other. Each node is connected to several (potentially hundreds of) other nodes. This makes it extremely hard to prevent blocks and transactions from propagating the network.

This chapter had two main parts:

* How transactions and blocks flow through the network

* How new nodes join the network

Part 1—Following a transaction

In the first part of the chapter, we followed a transaction through the system. It started with John buying a cookie. His transaction was propagated across the peer-to-peer network and to the cafe's wallet.

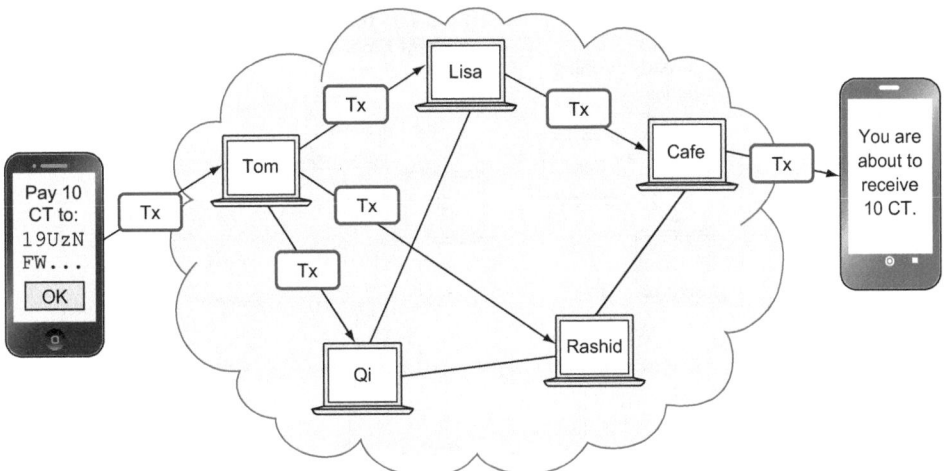

The cafe will almost immediately see that a transaction is incoming, but it's not yet confirmed. The next stage is to mine the block. Rashid is the lucky miner who finds the next block containing John's transaction.

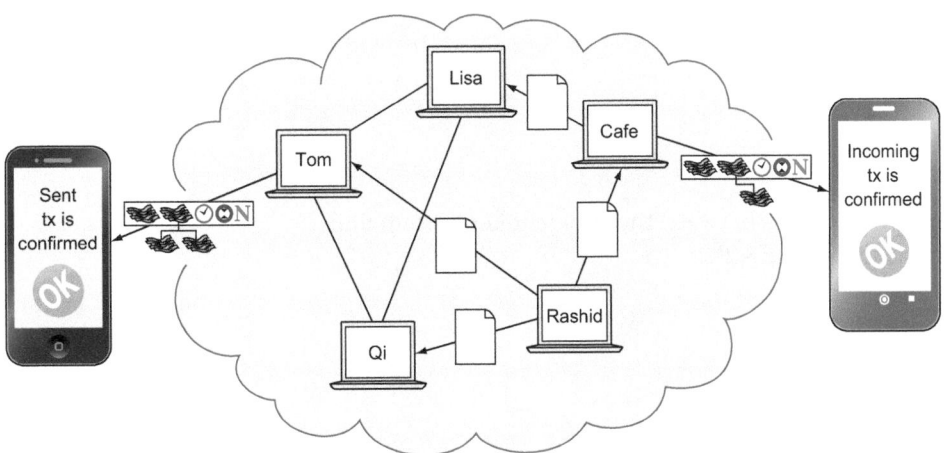

Rashid sends out the block to his peers, who will relay it to their peers and so on until the block has reached the entire network. Part of this propagation includes sending the block to lightweight wallets. These lightweight wallets will request `merkleblock` messages from the full node so they don't have to download the full block.

Part 2—Joining the network

Starting a new node involves fours steps:

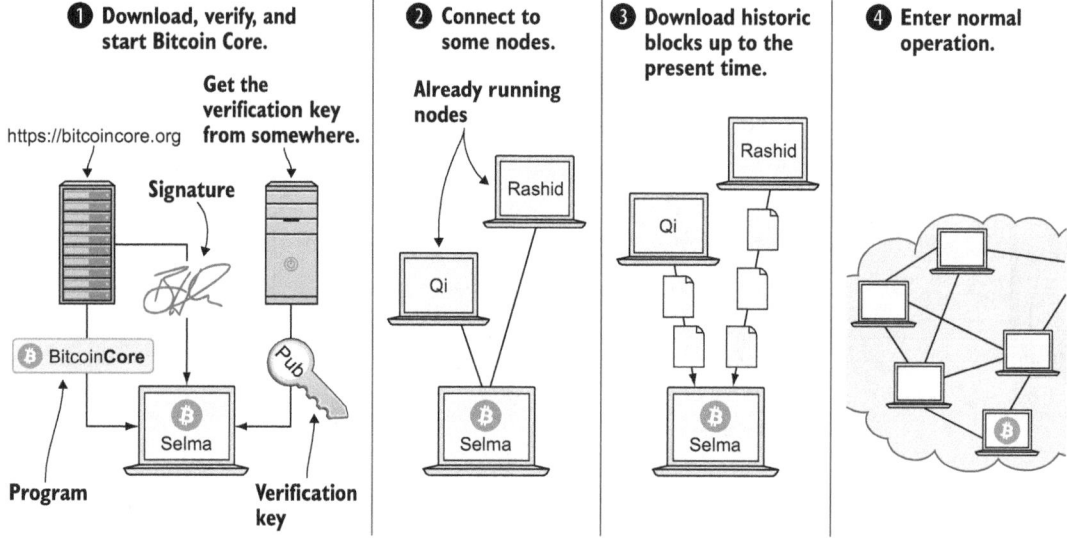

❶ Download and verify, for example, the Bitcoin Core software. Then start it.

❷ Connect to other nodes.

❸ Download historic blocks.

❹ Enter normal operation.

System changes

The table of concept mappings between the cookie token system and Bitcoin has become tiny (table 8.2).

Table 8.2 The shared folder has been ditched in favor of a peer-to-peer network.

Cookie tokens	Bitcoin	Covered in
1 cookie token	1 bitcoin	Chapter 2

Given that there are no longer any technical differences between the cookie token system and the Bitcoin system, we'll drop the cookie tokens and work only with Bitcoin from now on.

This will be the final release of the cookie token system. Another, much more widely used system, Bitcoin, has taken the world by storm, and we've decided to ditch the cookie token project. Enjoy the last version (table 8.3).

Table 8.3. Release notes, cookie tokens 8.0

Version	Feature	How
NEW 8.0	Censorship-resistant; for real this time	Shared folder replaced by a peer-to-peer network
	Transaction broadcasting	Transactions broadcast to miners and others using the peer-to-peer network
7.0	Censorship-resistant	Multiple miners, "Lisas," enabled by proof of work
	Anyone can join the mining race	Automatic difficulty adjustments
6.0	Prevent Lisa from deleting transactions	Signed blocks in a blockchain
	Fully validating nodes	Download and verify the entire blockchain.
	Lightweight wallet saves data traffic	Bloom filters and merkle proofs

Exercises

Warm up

8.1 Why is the shared folder a bad idea?

8.2 What does it mean to relay a transaction or a block?

8.3 What are `inv` messages used for?

8.4 How does the full node decide what transactions to send to lightweight wallets?

8.5 How does a node notify a lightweight wallet about an incoming pending transaction?

8.6 Blocks aren't sent in full to lightweight wallets. What part of the block is always sent to the wallet?

8.7 Why does the cafe send a very big bloom filter to its trusted node?

8.8 What would a security-conscious person do after downloading Bitcoin Core but before starting the software?

8.9 What types of sources for peer addresses are available to a newly started node?

8.10 How would a full node know if any newly created blocks are available for download when it's finished syncing?

8.11 The Bitcoin peer-to-peer network consists of the following nodes:

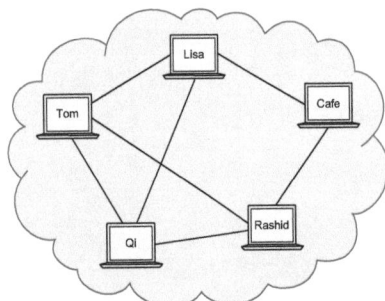

Which node owners do you need to threaten to prevent Lisa from getting any blocks but those she creates herself?

Dig in

8.12 Suppose Qi just received two transactions with transaction IDs $TXID_1$ and $TXID_2$. She now wants to inform Rashid about these new transactions. She doesn't know if Rashid already knows about them. What does she do?

8.13 Suppose you're running a full node and experience a power outage for 18 minutes. When power comes back, you start your node again. During those 18 minutes, two blocks, B_1 and B_2, have been created. Your latest block is B_0. What will your node do after reconnecting to the network? For simplicity, assume that no new blocks are found during synchronization, and that you have only one peer. Use this table of message types to fill out the following template:

Type	Data	Purpose
block	Full block	Sends a block to a peer
getheaders	Block ID	Asks a peer for subsequent block headers after the given block ID
getdata	txids or block IDs	Requests data from a peer
headers	List of headers	Sends a list of headers to a peer

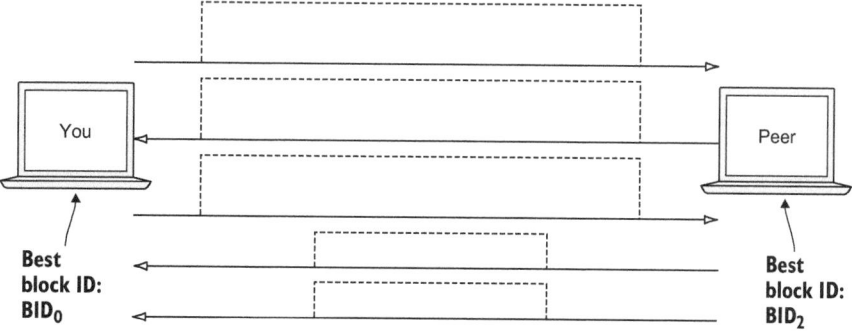

Summary

- The peer-to-peer network makes blocks censorship-resistant.

- A node connects to multiple peers to reduce their vulnerability for information hiding.

- The Bitcoin network protocol is the "language" nodes speak to communicate.

- Transactions are broadcast on the Bitcoin peer-to-peer network to reach both miners and the recipient of the money early.

- New nodes synchronize with the Bitcoin network to get up to date with the other nodes. This takes hours or days.

- Nodes don't need to stay online 24/7. They can drop out and come back and sync up the latest stuff.

- Signature verification can be skipped for older blocks to speed up initial synchronization. This is useful if you know a specific block is valid.

This chapter covers

- Time-locking bitcoins

- Swapping coins between blockchains

- Attaching arbitrary data to transactions

- Bumping the fee of a pending transaction

We're now past the core chapters of the book, in which you learned the Bitcoin basics. In this chapter, we'll dig deeper into the functionality transactions can offer.

We'll start by exploring time locks. A *time lock* is a way to make a transaction invalid until some point in time. This means the transaction can't be confirmed before that time constraint is met. Also, an output of a transaction can be programmed to prevent it from being spent until a time constraint is fulfilled. This is useful for digital contracts, such as atomic swaps, covered later in this chapter.

It's sometimes useful to store a small amount of data in a transaction in the blockchain. For example, a car manufacturer might want to track ownership of a car by putting its chassis number into a Bitcoin transaction, effectively creating a token on the Bitcoin blockchain. The current owner can then transfer ownership of the car by sending that token to the new owner.

As mentioned in the "Other cryptocurrencies" section in chapter 1, several alternative cryptocurrencies are available. Sometimes, you might want to trade, for example, namecoins for bitcoins. The most obvious way to do this is to use an exchange to sell bitcoins and buy namecoins. But there are other, more decentralized ways to do it. *Atomic swaps* let you swap bitcoins directly with someone holding namecoins without a trusted third party, like an exchange.

If you pay a too-small transaction fee, miners might refuse to confirm the transaction within a reasonable time. In this situation, it can be helpful to replace the transaction with another one that pays a little more in fees. This is known as *fee-bumping*.

Finally, we'll explore some intricate details of signatures. You can create signatures in different ways depending on your use case. You can tune what the signature should commit to: in other words, change how the signing algorithm hashes the transaction.

Time-locked transactions

When you create and sign a transaction, it's valid and ready for inclusion in any future block. You can broadcast it immediately and have it mined. This is the normal case.

But in some cases, you may want to sign a transaction with a guarantee that it won't be mined until after at least, say, one year has passed.

Suppose you have 100 bitcoins, and you want your daughter to inherit the money to her address $@_D$, but only after you die. You can create a transaction that's time-locked (figure 9.1).

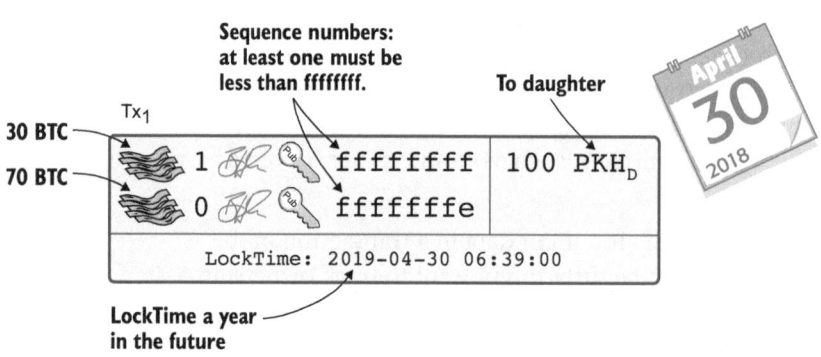

Figure 9.1   **A payment to your daughter that will become valid on 30 April 2019**

> **No fee?**
>
> For the sake of simplicity, most examples in this chapter don't pay any fees.

What makes this transaction special are the inputs' sequence numbers and the transaction lock time. I briefly mentioned sequence numbers in chapter 5. They're used to enable the lock time: if any input has a sequence number less than `ffffffff`—for example, `fffffffe`—the lock time set on the transaction will be effective. If all sequence numbers are `ffffffff`, the lock time won't have any effect.

You give this transaction, Tx₁, to your daughter. It's currently invalid; your daughter stores it on her computer and prints a backup that she keeps in another place. It isn't broadcast; no full node will accept a block containing this transaction yet. The transaction will become valid the morning of 30 April 2019. If you die before that, your daughter must wait until after the lock-time date and then claim the money by broadcasting the transaction, which will have become valid by then.

If you don't die before that date, you want to make sure the time-locked transaction becomes useless so your daughter can't take the money once the date has passed.

You can create, but not yet broadcast, a new transaction, Tx₂, that double spends an output that Tx₁ spends (figure 9.2). You then create a new transaction, time-locked for yet another year, for your daugher. When she's stored the transaction safely, you broadcast Tx2.

> **Sequence numbers**
>
> Sequence numbers are always included in inputs, but I haven't shown them because they didn't matter to the transactions used so far.

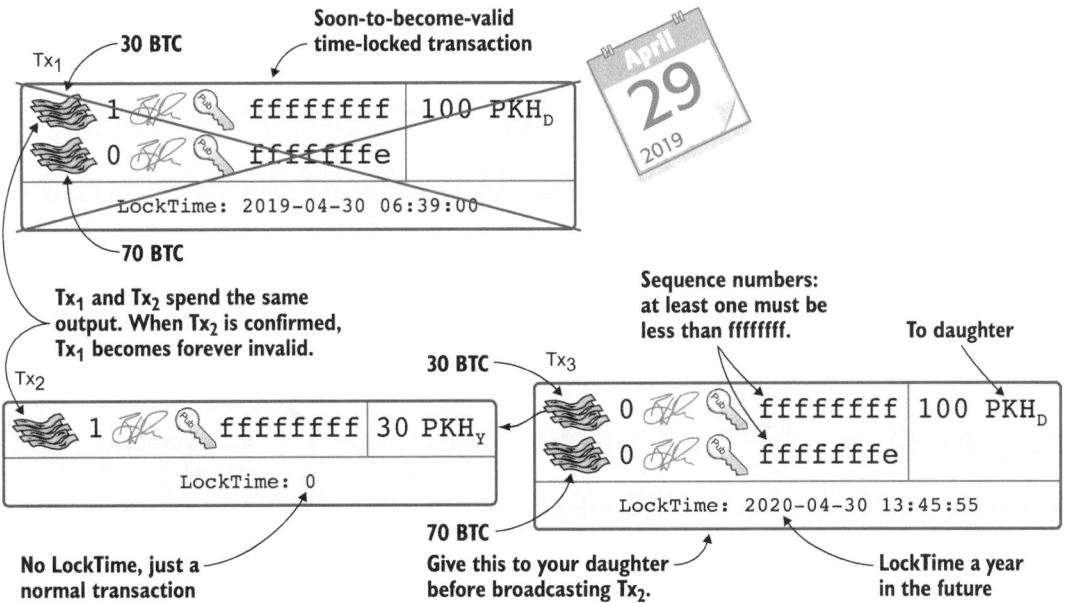

Figure 9.2 Make Tx₁ invalid by spending an output that Tx₁ spends, and create a new time-locked transaction for your daughter.

You need to

1. Create and sign a transaction, Tx_2, that spends at least one of the outputs spent by Tx_1. Tx_2 is a normal, not time-locked, transaction. Don't broadcast this transaction just yet.

2. Create a new time-locked transaction, Tx_3, that spends all your outputs as if Tx_2 was confirmed. Tx_3 is locked for another year. Give it to your daughter.

3. Broadcast Tx_2. Once Tx_2 is mined, Tx_1 will become forever invalid because one of the inputs of Tx_1 is spent by Tx_2.

Note how the order of events is important here. If Tx_2 is broadcast *before* you give Tx_3 to your daughter, there's a chance you'll die before giving her Tx_3. Then, your daughter won't be able to receive the funds because she has no valid transaction to claim them with. Tx_1 is invalidated by Tx_2 in the blockchain, and Tx_3 isn't in your daughter's possession.

>
>
> **Transaction malleability**
>
> There's a problem here. The txid of Tx_2 *can* change while being broadcast, making Tx_3 forever invalid. This is called *transaction malleability* and is fixed by using segregated witness as discussed in chapter 10.

Time measurements

You can express a lock time in two ways. The first is by setting a date and time as in the previous example. The second is to set a block height.

Block time

The first example expressed the lock time as a date and time. This means the *median time past* must be greater than the lock time in the transaction. In chapter 7, I noted that a block's timestamp must be greater than the past 11 blocks' median timestamp, or the *median time past* of the block. We use the median time past to decide whether a transaction is valid as regards the lock time. Suppose you died on 24 January 2019. Your mourning daughter wouldn't be able to claim your money until 30 April 2019. Figure 9.3 illustrates this more precisely.

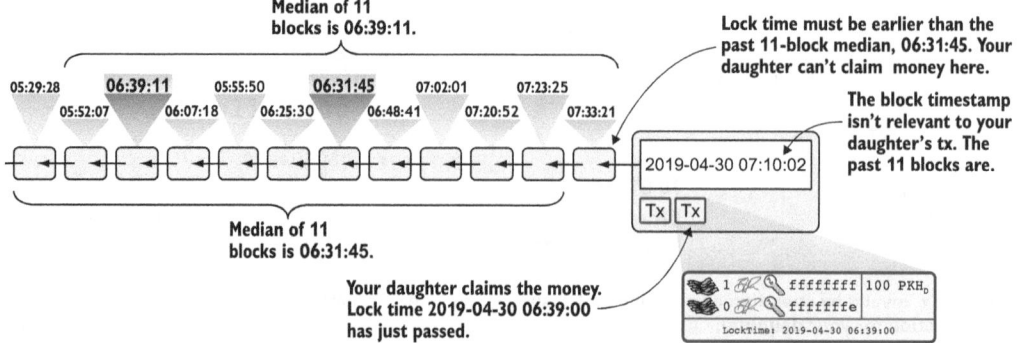

Figure 9.3 Your daughter can claim your money after the median time past is earlier than your lock time.

Your daughter's transaction can't be mined in any block before the last one shown. Before that block, the median time past is too early.

Her transaction won't even propagate through the Bitcoin network until the lock time has passed. The nodes don't want to keep time-locked transactions in their memories because there are better uses for their precious memory space than to fill them up with transactions that aren't even valid (yet). It's up to your daughter to broadcast the transaction after the lock time has passed.

Block height

You can also express time using block height. You can say that a transaction isn't valid, for example, until after block height 571019. This means the transaction shown in figure 9.4 can't be mined until after block 571019 has been mined.

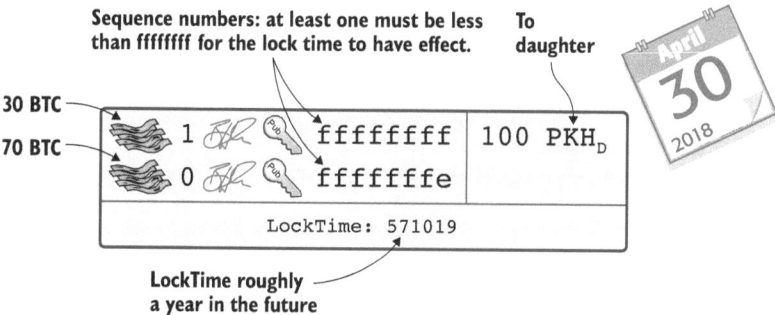

Figure 9.4   A time-locked transaction based on block height. This transaction is first valid at block height 571020.

The earliest block in which the transaction can be included is at height 571020. It's hard to predict exactly when that block will be mined, but thanks to the difficulty adjustments that keep the average block time at about 10 minutes, you can expect about 52,596 blocks per year.

Relative time locks

The earlier example showed a use case for absolute time locks on transactions. But you can also lock an input of a transaction until its spent output is old enough. This is called a *relative time lock*. You do this on a per-input basis (figure 9.5).

BIP68

This Bitcoin Improvement Proposal (BIP) describes how an input can require a certain distance in time or blocks from the spent transaction output. It applies to transactions with a version of at least 2.

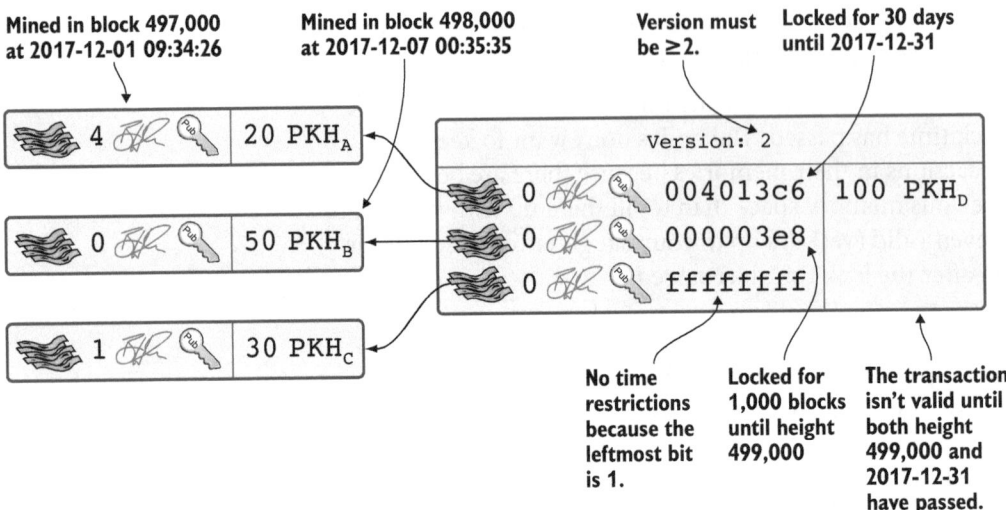

Figure 9.5 Relative time locks can be expressed either as a number of blocks or as a number of time units. You use the inputs' sequence numbers for this.

The transaction's first input has a sequence number of 004013c6. This says the transaction isn't valid until 30 days have passed since the spent output was confirmed (figure 9.6).

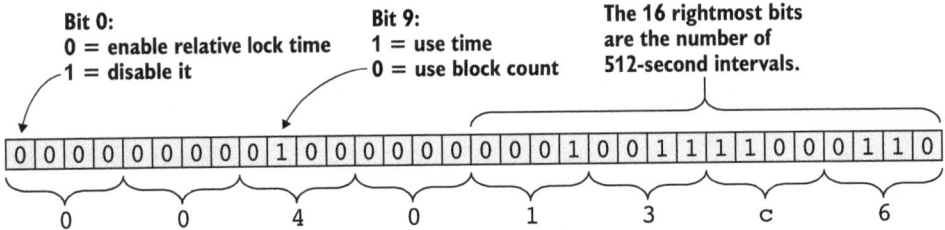

Figure 9.6 The first input locks the transaction for 30 days from the spent output.

The leftmost bit of this sequence number is 0, which means the relative lock time is enabled. The bit at index 9 from the left is 1, which means the rightmost 16 bits should be interpreted as "number of 512-second intervals." The 16 rightmost bits are 13c6, which translates to 5,062 in decimal form; 5,062 intervals of 512 seconds is roughly 30 days.

The second input has a sequence number of 000003e8 (figure 9.7). This means the transaction is invalid until 1,000 blocks have been mined since the spent output was mined.

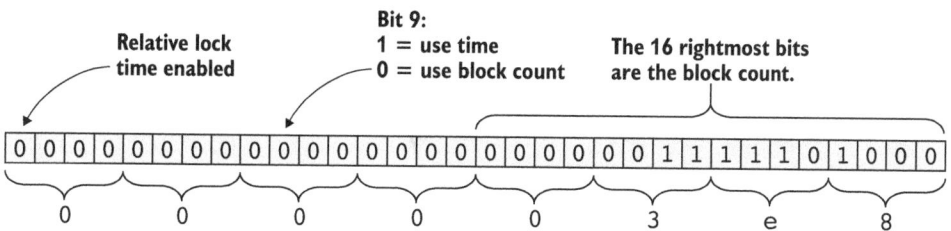

Figure 9.7 The second input locks the transaction for 1,000 blocks from the spent output.

The leftmost bit is 0 here, too, which means the relative lock time is enabled for this input. The bit at index 9 from the left is 0, which means the 16 rightmost bits should be interpreted as the number of blocks; `03e8` is hex code for 1,000.

The transaction's version needs to be at least 2 for relative time locks to work. If the version is 1, the sequence numbers won't have any effect on the relative lock time, but they will affect absolute lock time and the replace-by-fee feature, which I'll discuss later in "Replacing pending transactions."

Time-locked outputs

Time locks aren't particularly useful in themselves. The only thing you can do with them is create a transaction that might eventually become valid.

It might be more useful to say something like, "The money in this output can't be spent before New Year's Eve." This is an example of a *time-locked output*. An output can be locked absolutely or relatively, and locks can be time-based or height-based.

Absolute time-locked outputs

Suppose you want to give your daughter 1 BTC in allowance on 1 May. You can make a transaction as figure 9.8 shows.

> **BIP65**
>
> This BIP describes in detail the script operator `OP_CHECKLOCK-TIMEVERIFY`, which implements the absolute time-locked output.

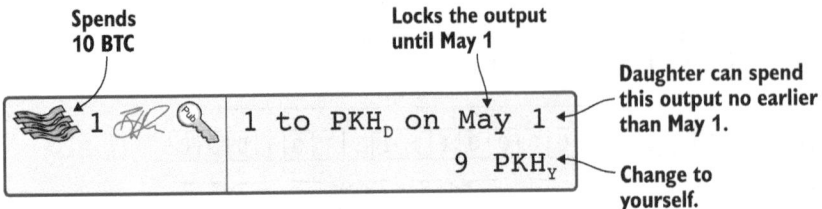

Figure 9.8   Paying allowance in advance to your daughter. She may not spend it before 1 May.

You can broadcast this transaction immediately to the Bitcoin network and have it mined. The first output is the interesting part. It says that this output can't be spent before 1 May. For the curious, the exact pubkey script is

```
<1 may 2019 00:00:00> OP_CHECKLOCKTIMEVERIFY OP_DROP
OP_DUP OP_HASH160 <PKHD> OP_EQUALVERIFY OP_CHECKSIG
```

This script will make sure the transaction spending the output is sufficiently time-locked, as figure 9.9 shows.

> **"OP_DROP?"**
>
> Using OP_CHECKLOCKTIME VERIFY requires a successive OP_DROP due to how the operator was deployed in Bitcoin. You'll learn about that in chapter 10. Ignore it for now.

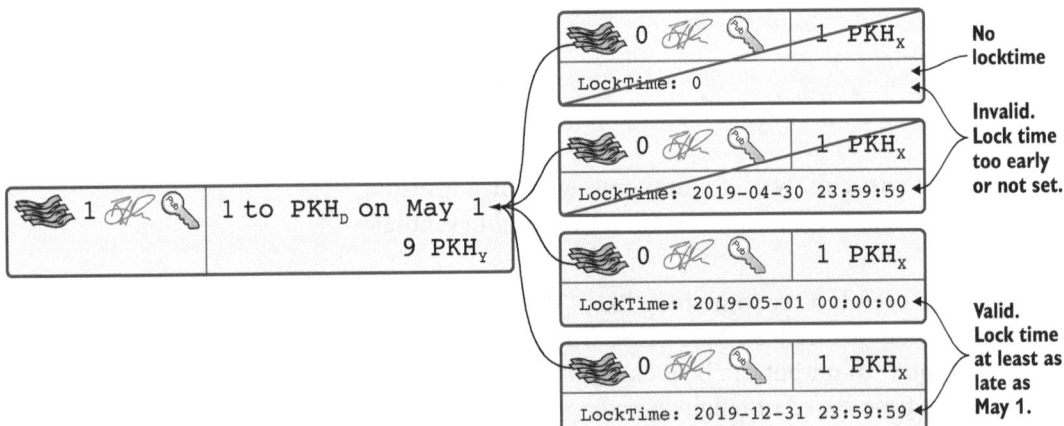

Figure 9.9   Various spending transactions and their validity

The first two transactions will never be valid because their time locks aren't sufficiently late. The first one isn't locked, which is illegal according to the pubkey script. The second one is at least time-locked, but it isn't late enough—1 second before 1 May is too early.

The third transaction is OK because the time lock is at least as high as the time in the pubkey script, 2019-05-01 00:00:00. This transaction will be valid on and after 1 May. The last transaction will be valid on New Year's Eve, right before the fireworks. Note, however, that you can't get both of the last two transactions confirmed—you can get at most one of them confirmed—because they spend the same output.

The result of this example is that your daughter will be able to spend the output as she pleases after 1 May.

Relative time-locked outputs

A relative time-locked output works similarly to an absolute time-locked output, but relative locks require a certain amount of time to *pass* between the block containing the spent output and the block containing the spending transaction (figure 9.10).

> **BIP112**
>
> This BIP describes relative time-locked outputs. The script operator is called `OP_CHECK-SEQUENCEVERIFY`.

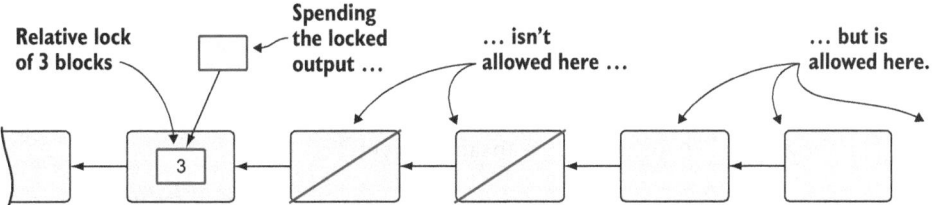

Figure 9.10 Spending a relative time-locked output is allowed after a certain number of blocks have passed.

Relative time locks are most commonly used in *digital contracts*. A digital contract can be regarded as a traditional contract between parties, but it's enforced by the rules of the Bitcoin network rather than national laws. Contracts are expressed as Bitcoin pubkey scripts. We'll illustrate the use of relative time-locked outputs with an atomic swap in the next subsection. An atomic swap means two people swap coins with each other across different cryptocurrencies.

Atomic swaps

A commonly mentioned digital contract is the *atomic swap*, where two parties want to swap coins with each other between different blockchains.

Suppose John is chatting with Fadime on a public forum on the internet. They don't know each other and have no reason to trust one another. But they both want to trade.

They agree that John will trade 2 BTC for 100 of Fadime's namecoins (NMC). Namecoin is an alt-coin used as a decentralized naming system,

>
> **Atomic**
>
> In computer science, the word *atomic* means a process either completes in its entirety or not at all. For atomic swaps, it means either the swap completes or both parties get to keep their old coins. No other outcomes are possible.

like DNS. We talked briefly about alt-coins in chapter 1. It isn't important what Namecoin actually is used for in this example; we only conclude that it's another cryptocurrency on a blockchain other than Bitcoin's.

The conversation between John and Fadime starts as follows:

> **John:** Do you want to swap 100 NMC for my 2 BTC? My Namecoin public key is 02381efd...88ca7f23. I've created a secret random number that has the SHA256 hash value H. I will not tell you the secret number yet.

> **Fadime:** Sure John, let's do it! My Bitcoin public key is 02b0c907...df854ee8

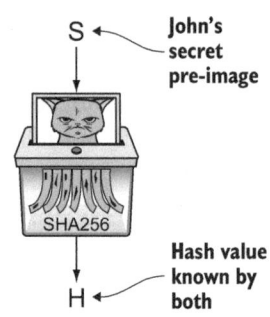

We'll call the secret number S. Only John knows S for now, but he shares the hash of S—which is H—with Fadime. Now, they both have enough information to get started.

They create one transaction each (figure 9.11). John creates a Bitcoin transaction that spends 2 BTC. Fadime creates a Namecoin transaction that spends 100 NMC. They don't broadcast their transactions yet.

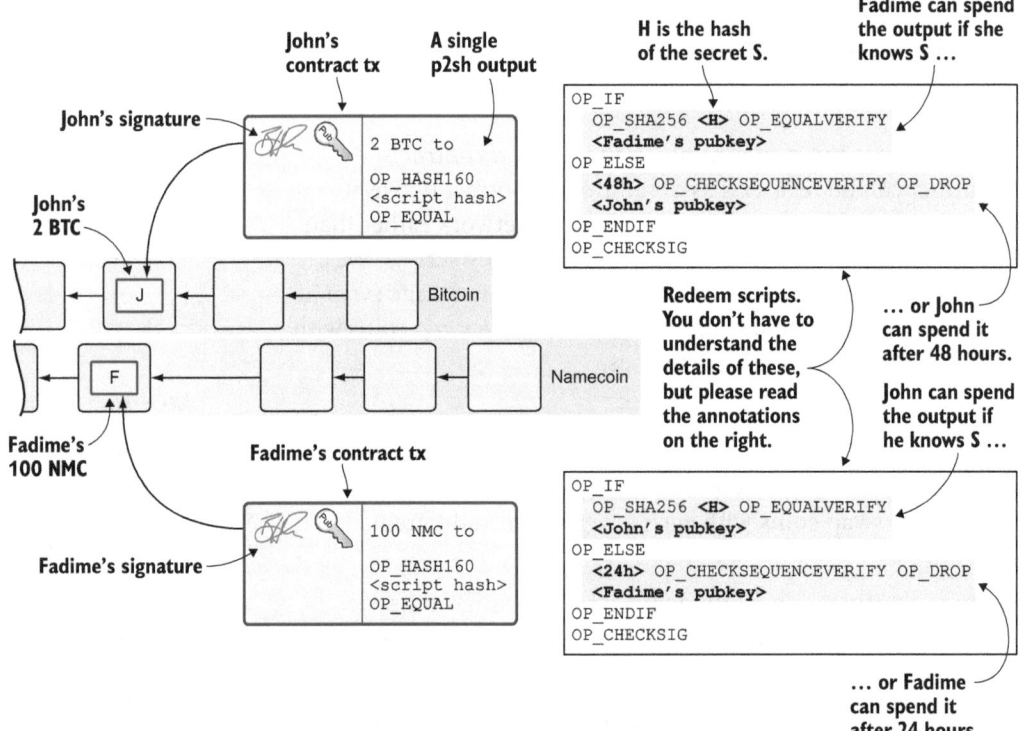

Figure 9.11   John and Fadime create a contract transaction each. The redeem script of the p2sh output contains the contract details.

The output of John's contract transaction can be spent in one
of two ways:

- By providing the pre-image of H and Fadime's signature. John knows
  this pre-image—his secret number S from the conversation described
  earlier—but Fadime doesn't.

- With John's signature after 48 hours.

Likewise, the output of Fadime's contract transaction can be spent in
one of two ways:

- By providing the pre-image of H and John's signature

- With Fadime's signature after 24 hours

The relative lock time is enforced by the script operator
OP_CHECKSEQUENCEVERIFY. This operator ensures that the output of
John's contract transaction can't be spent by John until 48 hours have
passed since the contract transaction was confirmed. In Fadime's
contract transaction, the operator ensures that Fadime doesn't spend
the output until after 24 hours.

Fadime knows John has the secret number. If Fadime broadcasts her
contract transaction now, John can take the money and not fulfill his
part of the deal. For this reason, she won't broadcast her transaction
until she's seen John's transaction safely confirmed in the blockchain.
Because Fadime doesn't know the secret, S, John can safely broadcast
his contract transaction without Fadime running away with
the money.

John broadcasts his contract transaction. Remember
that the output of the contract transaction in this
example is a pay-to-script-hash (p2sh) output. The
output contains a p2sh address that doesn't say anything
about this being John's contract output. For Fadime
to identify John's contract transaction on the Bitcoin
blockchain, she'll construct the same redeem script as
John created for his contract transaction and generate
the p2sh address that John's contract transaction paid
to. She can then look for that p2sh address in the
Bitcoin blockchain.

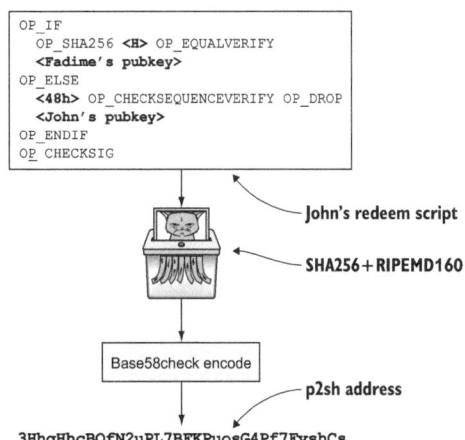

When Fadime finds that John's transaction is confirmed, she broadcasts her own contract transaction. John waits until Fadime's transaction is sufficiently confirmed on the Namecoin blockchain. Then, the actual swap happens in two steps. Figure 9.12 shows the first step.

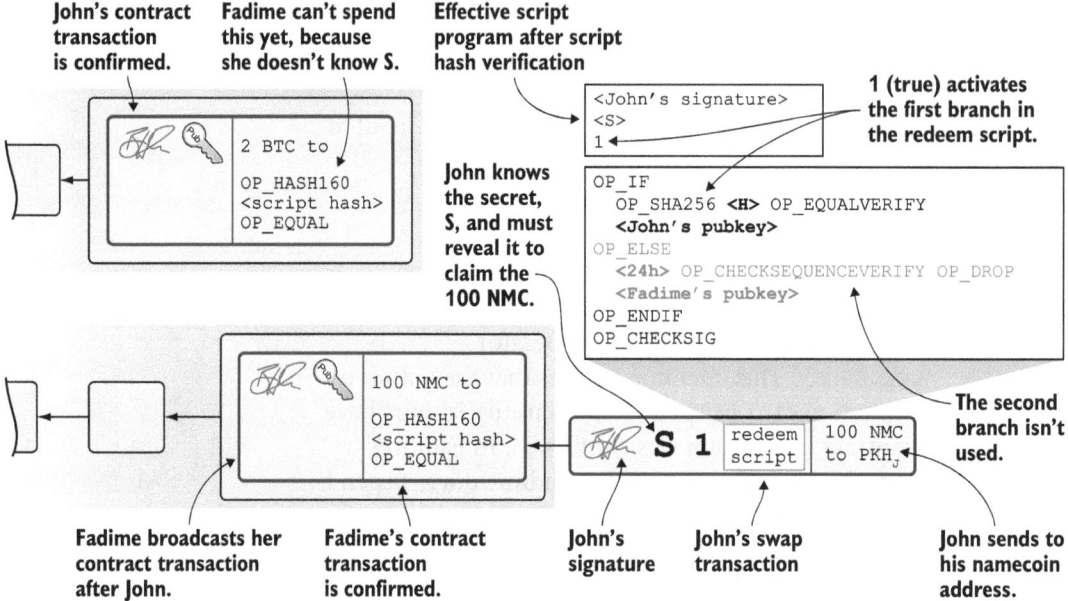

Figure 9.12   The first step of the actual swap. John claims Fadime's 100 NMC by revealing the secret S.

John broadcasts his swap transaction. John's swap transaction spends Fadime's contract transaction output by providing S and his signature. Again, note that John is spending a p2sh output. This means the first thing that happens during script validation is that the redeem script John provided in the signature script will be hashed and compared to the hash in the pubkey script. The actual redeem script will then be run.

We won't go through the program in detail. But when the redeem script starts running, the stack will have 1 on top. This means `true` in Namecoin, just as in Bitcoin. This value will cause the program to run the part of the script that requires a pre-image and John's signature. The other part isn't run at all.

The script will leave the stack with a `true` on top because John provides both required items in the correct order—his signature and the pre-image, `s`. He successfully claims his 100 NMC.

As soon as Fadime sees John's swap transaction on the Namecoin network, she can create her own swap transaction for the Bitcoin blockchain (figure 9.13).

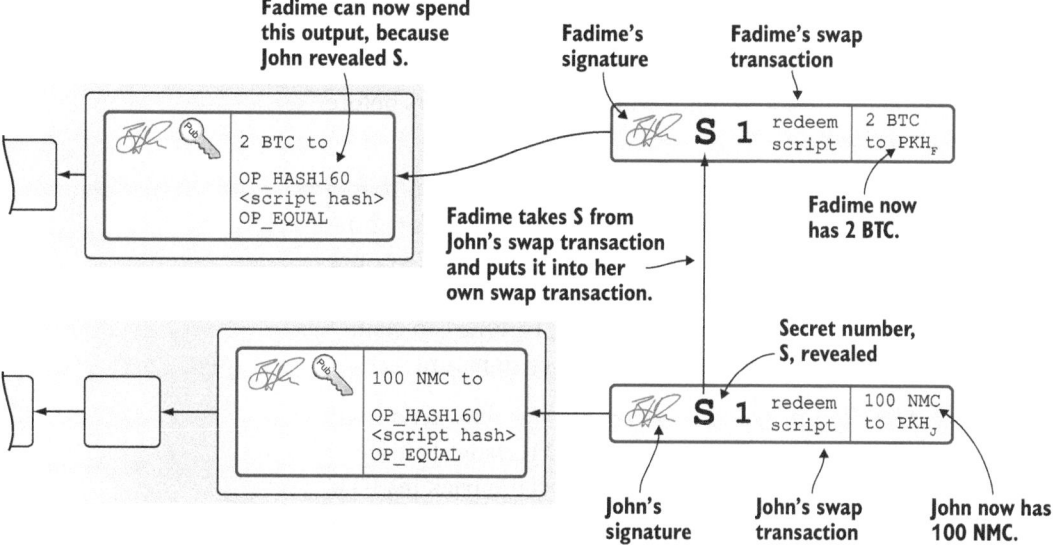

Figure 9.13   Fadime completes the atomic swap by sending her swap transaction to the Bitcoin network.

She takes the pre-image, S, from John's swap transaction and puts it into her own swap transaction, which pays 2 BTC to Fadime's public key hash, PKH$_F$. When the two swap transactions are confirmed, the atomic swap is complete. The effect of all this is that John has sent 2 BTC to Fadime under the condition that Fadime sends 100 NMC to him, and Fadime sends 100 NMC to John under the condition that John sends 2 BTC to her.

Atomic swap failure

The sequence of events in this atomic swap example illustrates a case in which both parties, John and Fadime, play by the rules. No one had to actually use the time-locked branches of the contract transaction outputs. This subsection will go through some ways the swap might fail:

- *Fadime doesn't broadcast her contract transaction.* This means John can't spend the output of Fadime's contract transaction, which means Fadime will never get to see S. Without S, she can't spend John's contract output. The only possible outcome is that John must wait 48 hours for the relative time lock to pass and then reclaim his money.

- *John doesn't spend Fadime's contract output in 24 hours.* Fadime can reclaim her coins, and John must wait another 24 hours before claiming his coins back.

- *John spends Fadime's contract output just after 24 hours has passed but before Fadime claims back her coins.* Fortunately, John's contract output has a 48-hour relative lock time as opposed to the 24 hours in Fadime's contract output, so John can't claim his coins back until he's waited another 24 hours. During this time, Fadime can claim her BTC from John's contract output using S and her signature.

- *Fadime gets hit by a bus just after broadcasting her contract output.* This is no good. John will be able to take his NMC from Fadime's contract output and then wait 48 hours to also claim back his BTC. Fadime loses out on this one.

In the final case, we could argue that the swap wasn't atomic. After all, it didn't go through, and John ended up with all the coins. This is a somewhat philosophical question. But we can think of swaps as being atomic under the condition that Fadime can take action. We don't have this condition for John, though. It's a matter of who creates the secret, S.

Storing stuff in the Bitcoin blockchain

In the early days of Bitcoin, it became clear that people wanted to put stuff in transactions in the Bitcoin blockchain that didn't have anything to do with Bitcoin itself: for example, listing 9.1, which is a blockchain tribute to cryptographer Sassama, allegedly posted by Dan Kaminsky. (The message is wrapped into three columns here to save space.)

Listing 9.1   A tribute in a transaction

```
---BEGIN TRIBUTE---        LEN "rabbi" SASSAMA      P.S.  My apologies,
#./BitLen                       1980-2011         BitCoin people.  He
::::::::::::::::::::        Len was our friend.    also would have
:::::::.::.::.:.:::         A brilliant mind,      LOL'd at BitCoin's
:.: :.' ' ' ' ' : :        a kind soul, and       new dependency upon
:.:'' ,,xiW,"4x, ''        a devious schemer;        ASCII BERNANKE
:  ,dWWWXXXXi,4WX,         husband to Meredith    :':::.:::::.:::.::.:
' dWWWXXX7"       'X,      brother to Calvin,     : :.: ' ' ' ' : :':
 lWWWXX7     __    _ X     son to Jim and         :.:          '.:
:WWWXX7 ,xXX7' "^^X        Dana Hartshorn,        :    _,^"    "^x,  :
lWWWX7, _.+,, _.+.,        coauthor and           '  x7'          '4,
:WWW7,. '^"-" ,^-'         cofounder and          XX7             4XX
 WW",X:         X,         Shmoo and so much      XX               XX
 "7^^Xl.    _(_x7'         more.  We dedicate     Xl ,xxx,    ,xxx,XX
 l ( :X:        __ _       this silly hack to     ( ' _,+o, | ,o+,"
 '. " XX  ,xxWWWWX7        Len, who would have    4   "-^' X "^-'" 7
 )X- "" 4X" .___.          found it absolutely    l,     ( ))      ,X
,W X     :Xi _,,_          hilarious.             :Xx,_ ,xXXXxx,_,XX
WW X      4XiyXWWXd        --Dan Kaminsky,        4XXiX'-___-'XXXX'
"" ,,      4XWWWWXX        Travis Goodspeed       4XXi,_____iXX7'
, R7X,       "^447^                               , '4XXXXXXXXX^ _,
R, "4RXk,        _,',                             Xx,  ""^^^XX7,xX
TWk  "4RXXi,    X',x                              W,"4WWx,_ _,XxWWX7'
lTWk,  "4RRR7' 4 XH                               Xwi, "4WW7""4WW7',W
:lWWWk,  ^"     '4                                TXXWw, ^7 Xk 47 ,WH
::TTXWWi,_  Xll :..                               :TXXXWw,_ "), ,wWT:
=-=-=-=-=-=-=-=-=                                 ::TTXXWWW lXl WWT:
                                                  ----END TRIBUTE----
```

Although this was certainly interesting and funny, it had some implications for Bitcoin's full nodes.

The message in listing 9.1 was written into the blockchain using a single transaction with txid

`930a2114cdaa86e1fac46d15c74e81c09eee1d4150ff9d48e76cb0697d8e1d72`

The author created a transaction with 78 outputs, one for each 20-character line in the message. Each line ends with a space, so only 19 characters are visible.

For example, the last output's pubkey script looks like this:

```
OP_DUP OP_HASH160 2d2d2d2d454e4420545249425554452d2d2d2d20
↳OP_EQUALVERIFY OP_CHECKSIG
```

Blockchain explorer

You can take a closer look at this transaction using a blockchain explorer, such as the one at web resource 17, found in appendix C.

The interesting part is the PKH. This isn't an actual PKH, but a made-up one. Maybe you can see a pattern when you compare it to the line
"`----END TRIBUTE---- `":

```
2d 2d 2d 2d 45 4e 44 20 54 52 49 42 55 54 45 2d 2d 2d 2d 20
 -  -  -  -  E  N  D     T  R  I  B  U  T  E  -  -  -  -
```

This "public key hash" encodes one 20-character line in the message. It uses the *ASCII table* to encode characters. For example, the character - is encoded as the byte `2d`. The characters A–Z are encoded by the bytes `41-5a`, and a space is encoded as byte `20`.

Let's look at the PKHs of the message's last 10 lines along with the ASCII-decoded text:

```
20203458586958272d5f5f5f2d60585858582720    4XXiX'-___-'XXXX'
202020345858692c5f2020205f69585837272020     4XXi,_    _iXX7'
20202c206034585858585858585858585e205f2c20    , '4XXXXXXXXX^ _,
202058782c202022225e5e5e5858372c78582020    Xx,  ""^^^XX7,xX
572c22345757782c5f205f2c5878575758372720 W,"4WWx,_ _,XxWWX7''
5877692c20223457573722234575737272c5720 Xwi, "4WW7""4WW7',W
54585857772c205e3720586b203437202c574820 TXXWw, ^7 Xk 47 ,WH
3a5458585857772c5f2022292c202c7757543a20 :TXXXWw,_ "), ,wWT:
3a3a54545858575757206c586c205757543a2020 ::TTXXWWW lXl WWT:
2d2d2d2d454e44205452494255544520 d2d2d2d20 ----END TRIBUTE----
```

Bloated UTXO set

Because these PKHs are made up, they have no known pre-images. This also means no known public/private key pairs are associated with them, so no one can ever spend the outputs. They're *unspendable*. The last PKH's Bitcoin address is `157sXYpj...QnHB6FGU`. Anyone who pays money to this address is throwing that money in the trash. The money is lost forever. It's the equivalent of burning a dollar bill.

Unspendable outputs like these are indistinguishable from ordinary, spendable outputs. You can't prove that they're unspendable. Full nodes have to treat them as spendable, meaning they have to keep these unspendable outputs in their unspent transaction output (UTXO) set forever. This places an unnecessary burden on nodes, which need to keep all these outputs in memory.

Bitcoin's developers came up with a partial solution to this problem. Instead of sending money to unprovably unspendable outputs, users can create *provably unspendable* outputs. If a full node can determine if an output is unspendable, it doesn't have to insert that output into its UTXO set.

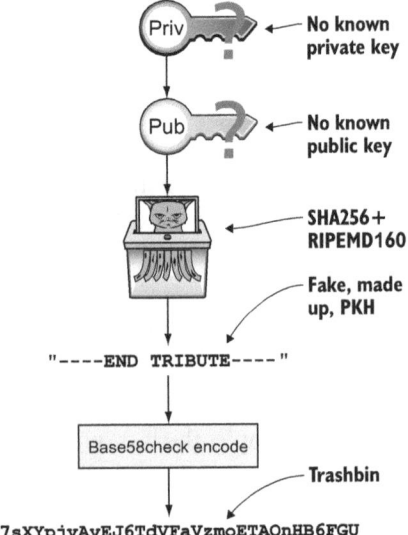

No known private key

No known public key

SHA256 + RIPEMD160

Fake, made up, PKH

"`----END TRIBUTE----`"

Base58check encode

Trashbin

157sXYpjvAyEJ6TdVFaVzmoETAQnHB6FGU

The partial solution involves a new script operator called `OP_RETURN`. This operator immediately fails when executed. A typical `OP_RETURN` pubkey script can look like this:

```
OP_RETURN "I'm Grokking Bitcoin"
```

If someone tried to spend this output, the script would fail once it encountered the `OP_RETURN`. If the pubkey script contains this operator, a full node can determine that the output isn't spendable and ignore it, saving the UTXO set from being forever bloated with this nonsense. A typical `OP_RETURN` output pays 0 BTC, but it can also set a value greater than 0 to "burn" money.

There are a few policies regarding `OP_RETURN`:

* The full pubkey script must not be bigger than 83 bytes.

* There can be only one `OP_RETURN` output per transaction.

These two policies are just that—policies. Full nodes adhering to these policies won't relay transactions that violate them. But if they encounter a block that contains transactions that violate the policies, the block will be accepted and relayed. I'll talk more about policies and *consensus rules*, strict rules that apply to blocks, in chapters 10 and 11.

Creating a token in Bitcoin

I talked briefly about tracking ownership on the blockchain in chapter 1. Suppose a car manufacturer, let's call it Ampere, decides that it wants to digitally track the ownership of its cars on the Bitcoin blockchain. This can be accomplished by creating a token in Bitcoin.

Suppose Ampere wants to create a token for a newly manufactured car with chassis number 123456. It broadcasts a Bitcoin transaction as shown in figure 9.14.

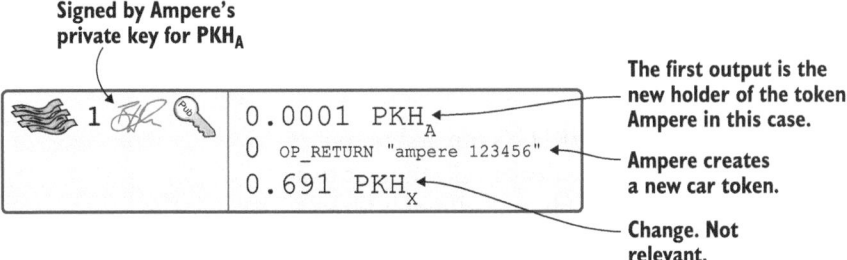

Figure 9.14 Ampere creates a new token for a newly built car. It issues the token to itself because it still owns this car.

This "Ampere token protocol" specifies that a new token is created when

- Ampere spends a coin from PKH_A.
- The transaction contains an `OP_RETURN` output with the text
  `"ampere <chassis number>"`.
- The first output is the initial token owner.

Ampere has a well-known web page at https://www.ampere.example. com, where it has published its public key corresponding to PKH_A. It also pumps out its public key through advertisements and via Facebook and Twitter. It does all this so people can verify that PKH_A actually belongs to Ampere.

Suppose Ampere sells this car to a car dealer. The dealer has a public key hash, PKH_D. Figure 9.15 shows how Ampere will transfer digital ownership to the dealer.

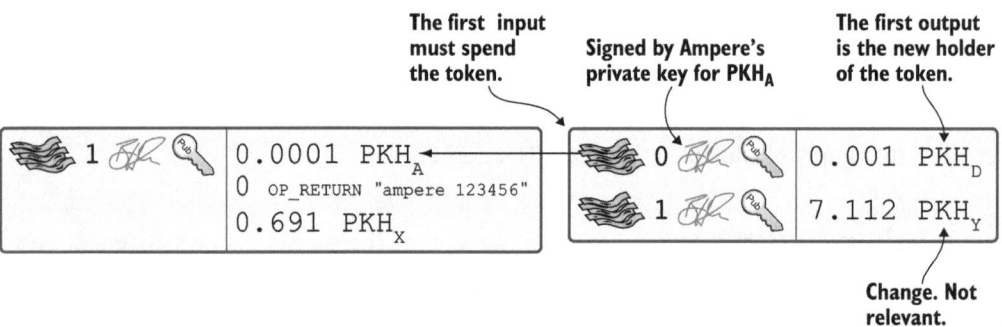

Figure 9.15   Ampere sells the car to a car dealer with public key hash PKH_D.

According to our simple protocol, car ownership is transferred by spending the old owner's output. The following rules apply:

- The spending transaction spends the old owner's output.
- The first output of the spending transaction is the new owner of the car.

The car dealer is now the new owner because PKH_D is the first output of the spending transaction. That's it. When the dealer sells this car to a consumer, Fadime, it transfers the car's ownership to Fadime's address, PKH_F (figure 9.16).

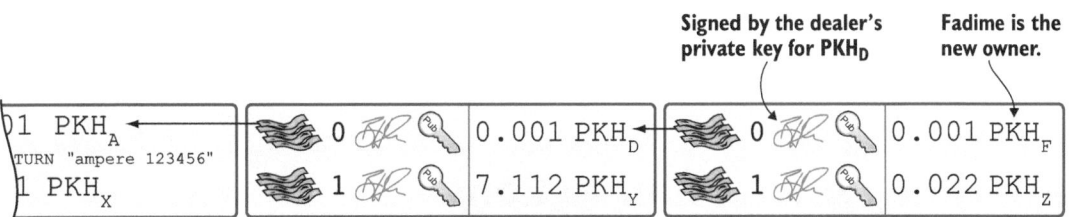

Figure 9.16   The car dealer transfers the car's ownership to Fadime's PKH_F.

Starting the car with proof of ownership

Now that Fadime is the rightful owner of this car, wouldn't it be cool if she could start it by proving she's the owner? She can. The car is equipped with an ignition lock that starts the engine when Fadime sends a proof of ownership to the car (figure 9.17).

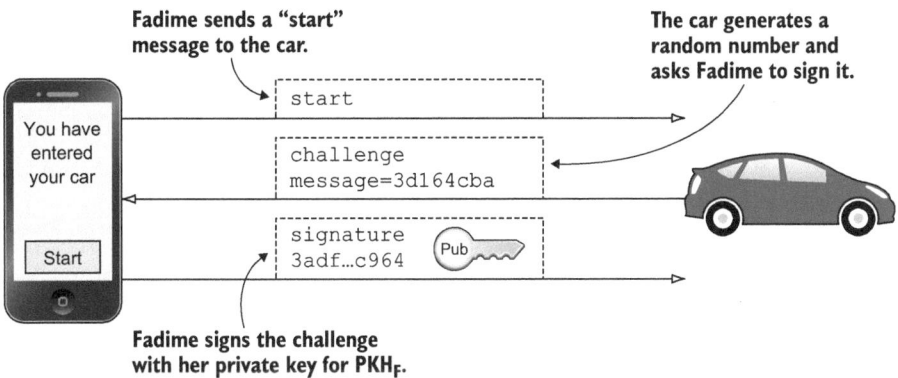

Figure 9.17   Fadime starts her car by signing a challenge with her private key.

Fadime first asks the car to start. The car won't start if it doesn't know that Fadime has the private key belonging to PKH_F. The car generates a big random number and sends it to Fadime, who signs this random number with the private key and sends the signature and her public key to the car.

The car needs the public key to verify that it corresponds to PKH_F as written in the blockchain. The car keeps track of who currently owns it by running a lightweight wallet that understands the Ampere token protocol.

When the car has verified that the signature is valid and from the correct private key, it will start the engine.

Replacing pending transactions

When you send a Bitcoin transaction to buy a book online, the bookstore will wait for the transaction to confirm before it sends the book to you. Usually, your transaction will be confirmed within an hour or so, but what if it isn't? What if no miner ever wants to include your transaction? This can certainly happen if your transaction fee isn't sufficient (figure 9.18).

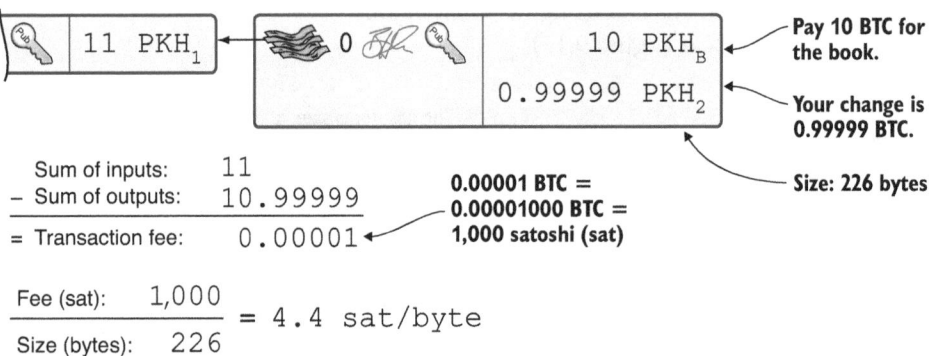

Figure 9.18 **You pay for your book and set the transaction fee to 0.00001 BTC.**

You might recall from "Transaction fees" in chapter 7 that the transaction fee is the sum of the input values minus the sum of the output values. The fee per byte that miners care about is calculated by dividing that fee by the transaction's size—in this case, 1,000 satoshis divided by 226 bytes, which is about 4.4 sat/byte.

If no miner is willing to include the transaction for that fee, your transaction will be stuck waiting for confirmation. If the transaction isn't confirmed, you won't get your book. You probably want to do something about this situation. Maybe you can create a new, similar transaction, but with a higher fee. Let's try (figure 9.19).

That's nice: you've created and signed a new transaction with a fee 20 times higher. This will surely get mined, you think, and broadcast the transaction.

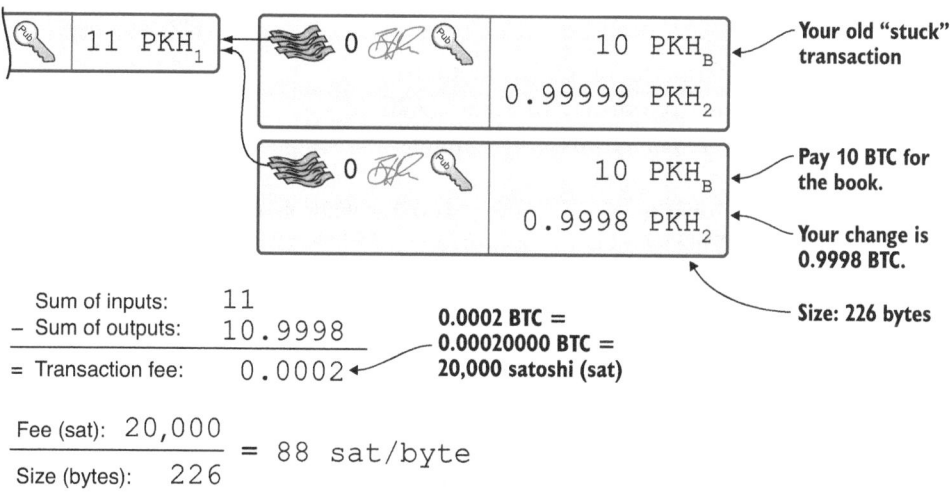

Figure 9.19 You try to replace your old, stuck transaction with a new one with a higher fee.

The problem is that your new transaction will probably be regarded as a double-spend attempt and be dropped by most nodes. They'll think the first transaction is the one that counts, and they'll disregard any further transactions that spend the same output. How to handle the second transaction is completely up to the nodes, but the most common policy is to drop it. This is what Bitcoin Core does, and that's the most widely used Bitcoin software. This policy is known as the *first-seen policy*.

You might be able to circumvent this policy by sending the second transaction directly to one or more miners. Miners have different incentives than full nodes. Mining full nodes want to earn rewards—subsidy + fees—by providing proof of work to the blockchain, whereas non-mining full nodes want to keep their memory and computing resource consumption down. If a miner could get hold of the second, high-fee transaction, it would probably decide to include it despite the fact that the low-fee transaction was the first seen. Replacing transactions in this way is impractical because you don't know any miners' IP addresses unless they're published somehow. You also reveal your IP address to the miners, and the miners then become targets for various surveillance organizations or companies wanting to monetize information about you.

Hint for exercises

Keep this in mind for exercise 11.

Opt-in replace-by-fee

In 2016, a policy was deployed for transaction replacement. It's generally called *opt-in replace-by-fee*, or opt-in RBF (figure 9.20). It works by using the sequence numbers of a transaction's inputs.

BIP125

This BIP describes how transactions can declare themselves replaceable.

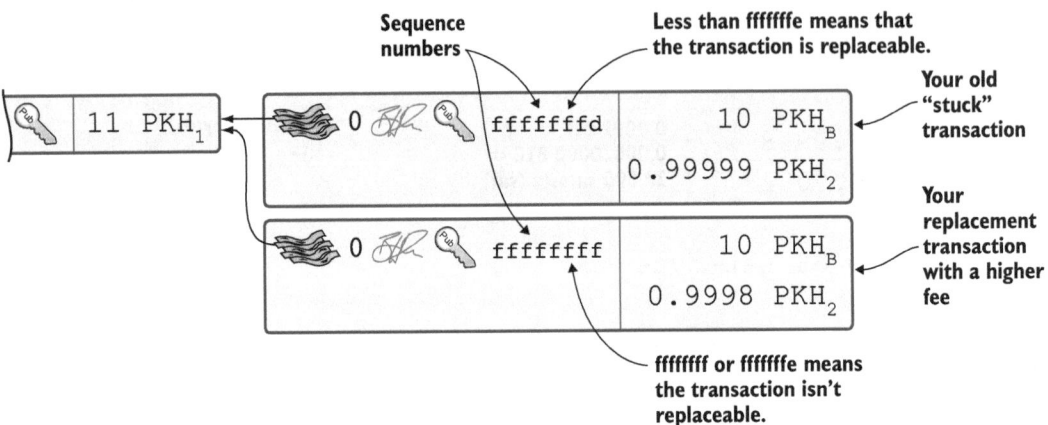

Figure 9.20   Use opt-in RBF to easily replace a transaction before it's confirmed.

Suppose again that you want to pay for a book in an online bookstore. When you create the transaction, you make sure one of the inputs (there's only one in this example) has a sequence number less than `fffffffe`. This signals to nodes that you want this transaction to be replaceable.

When a node receives this transaction, it will be treated as a normal transaction, but the replaceability will be remembered.

When you later notice that your transaction doesn't confirm because of a too-low fee, you can create a new, replacement transaction with a higher fee. When you broadcast the replacement transaction, the nodes receiving it will—if they implement the opt-in RBF policy—kindly replace the old transaction with the new one and relay the new one to their peers. The old transaction will be dropped. This way, the replacement transaction will eventually reach all nodes, including miners, and will hopefully be confirmed within a reasonable time.

In this example, you set the sequence number of the replacement transaction's input to `ffffffff`. This means the replacement transaction is not itself replaceable. If you want the replacement transaction to also be replaceable, you must set its sequence number to `fffffffd` or less, just as you did with the replaced transaction.

You might be wondering where these sequence numbers come from. The intention with sequence numbers from the beginning was to allow for another kind of transaction replacement. The feature was disabled early in Bitcoin, but the sequence numbers remained in the transaction inputs. These sequence numbers have since been repurposed for absolute lock time, relative lock time, and replace-by-fee, as described throughout this chapter. If you feel confused, don't worry; I'll summarize the different uses of sequence numbers in this chapter's "Recap" section.

Child pays for parent

There is yet another way to bump up a fee. Suppose you have the situation depicted earlier in figure 9.18, and you notice that this transaction gets stuck (figure 9.21).

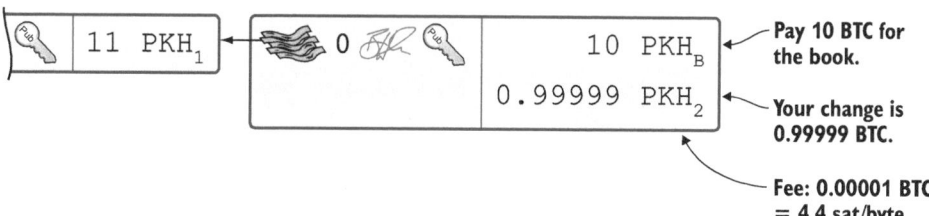

Figure 9.21 You haven't paid a sufficient transaction fee. The transaction is stuck pending because miners don't want to include it in a block.

You can make another transaction that spends your change and pays an extra-high fee to compensate for the low fee in the original transaction (figure 9.22).

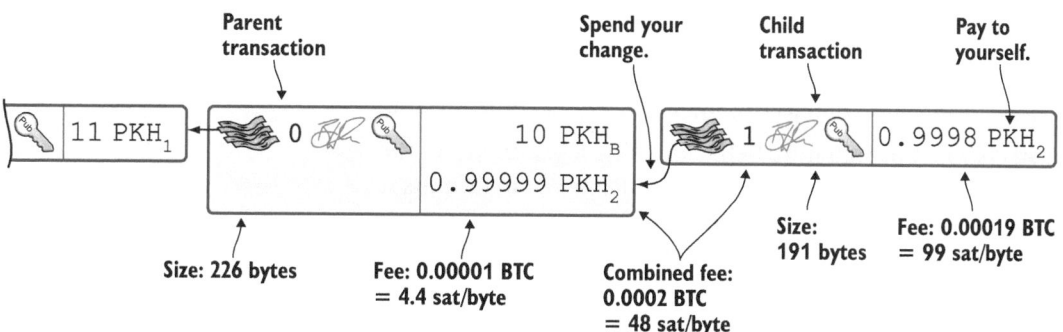

Figure 9.22 Spending your change and paying an extra fee for the "parent" transaction

Suppose a miner sees these two transactions. If the miner wants to collect the fee from the child transaction, it has to include both the parent and the child transactions. If it tries to include only the child transaction, the block won't be valid because the child transaction spends money that doesn't exist in the blockchain.

Both you and the bookstore can perform this trick. If you don't bump the fee, the bookstore can spend its output of 10 BTC and pay itself 9.9998 BTC to add 0.0002 BTC to the combined fee.

Different signature types

When you sign a typical Bitcoin transaction, you sign the entire transaction, excluding the signature script (figure 9.23).

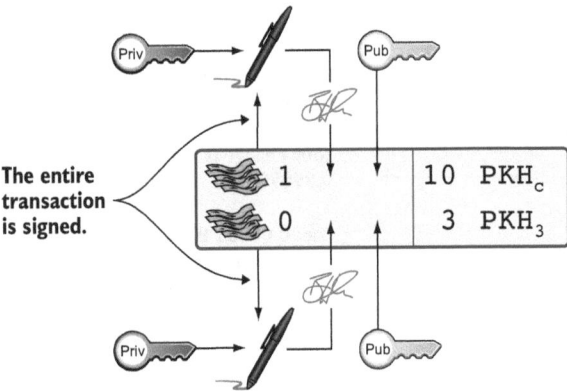

Figure 9.23   Normally, the entire transaction is signed. All inputs and all outputs are covered.

This transaction contains two inputs, and each input signs the complete transaction. A signature *commits to* all inputs and all outputs. If any of the inputs or outputs change, the signature will become invalid.

You can change this signature behavior using a parameter in the signature called the SIGHASH type. You can commit to outputs in three ways (ALL, SINGLE, and NONE) and to inputs in two ways (ANYONECANPAY set or not set). Any combination of an input SIGHASH type and an output SIGHASH type can be used, which makes six different combinations, as figure 9.24 shows.

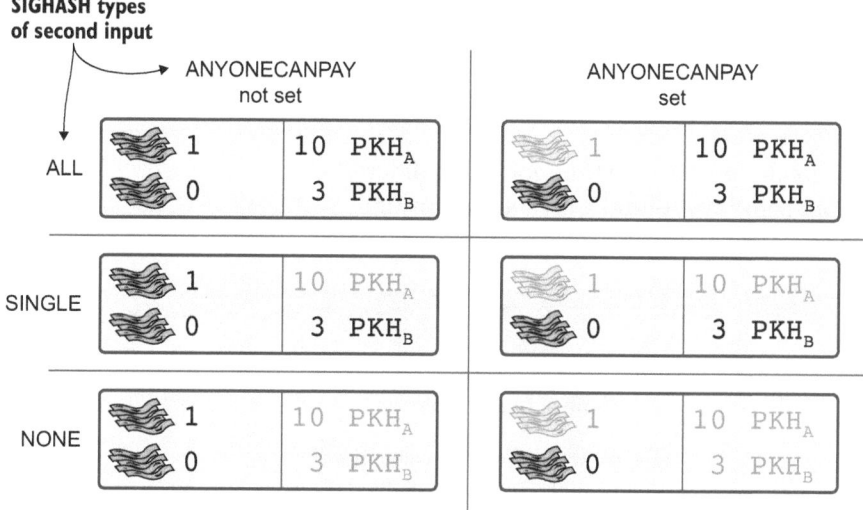

Figure 9.24. A signature can commit to different parts of the transaction depending on the `SIGHASH` types. The signature doesn't include the grayed-out parts.

For the outputs, you can commit to the following:

- *All outputs (`ALL`)*—No one gets to change any outputs.

- *A single output at the same index as the input (`SINGLE`)*—You only care about the specific output. The other outputs can change.

- *No outputs (`NONE`)*—You don't care where the money goes. Anyone can add any outputs without invalidating your signature.

For the inputs, you can commit as follows:

- *All inputs (`ANYONECANPAY` is not set)*—No one can change any input without invalidating your signature.

- *Only the current input (`ANYONECANPAY` is set)*—Other inputs might be changed, removed, or added. You don't care who pays. Anyone can pay.

For the vast majority of signatures, `ALL` combined with an unset `ANYONECANPAY` is used to commit to the whole transaction. This is what you're used to from the earlier chapters in this book. Other types are rare and are used primarily for specialized digital contracts.

Recap

This chapter has been a potpourri of things you can do with transactions.

Transactions and transaction outputs can be time-locked in different ways to prevent funds from being spent until a certain date or time span has occurred, as the following table shows.

Action	Result
Set the lock time of a transaction.	The transaction won't be valid until a certain time or block height.
Set the relative time lock on an input using the sequence number.	The transaction won't be valid until a certain amount of time or number of blocks have passed.
Use `OP_CHECKLOCKTIMEVERIFY` in a pubkey script.	The output can't be spent until a certain time or block height.
Use `OP_CHECKSEQUENCEVERIFY` in a pubkey script.	The output can't be spent until a certain amount of time or number of blocks have passed.

All these variants can be expressed in either block height or time. Time locks are useful mostly in digital contracts, such as atomic swaps. An atomic swap lets people who don't trust each other swap coins without using a trusted third party.

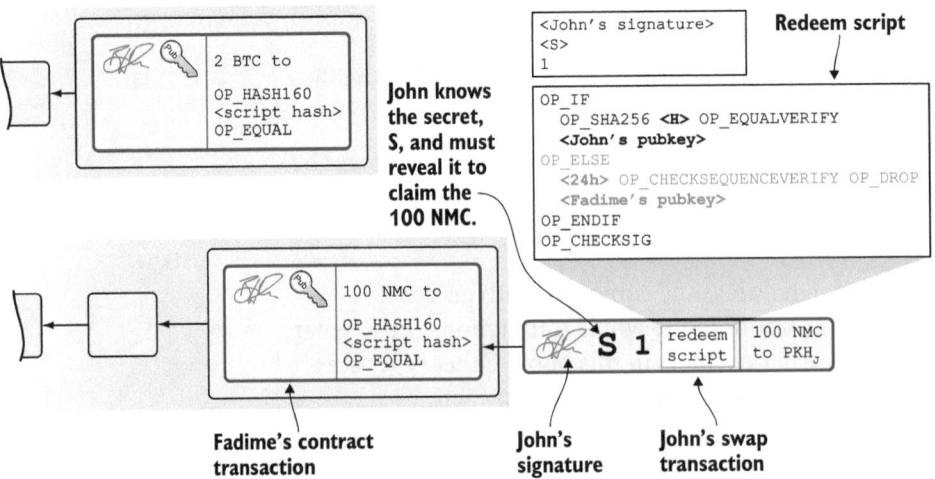

The general idea is that John must reveal the secret, S, to claim his coins. Fadime can then use S to claim her coins.

Arbitrary data can be stored in OP_RETURN outputs without placing a burden on nodes' UTXO sets. You can use this to create tokens. For example, the ownership of a car can be tracked and verified on the Bitcoin blockchain.

A transaction can sometimes get stuck in a pending state because no miners want to include it in their blocks. This usually happens because you've paid a too-small fee. To prepare for this situation, you can mark the transaction as replaceable by setting the sequence number of at least one input to a value lower than fffffffe. If that transaction gets stuck, you can bump the the fee by broadcasting a replacement transaction that pays a higher fee.

Inputs' sequence numbers are used for various purposes. We've discussed many different uses for sequence numbers in this chapter, and it's hard to keep track of them. Table 9.1 summarizes the meaning of different sequence number values.

Table 9.1 Sequence numbers are used to enable or disable various features.

Sequence value	Lock time, any input	Replace-by-fee (BIP125), any input	Relative lock time on input (BIP68)*
00000000–7fffffff	✓	✓	✓
80000000–fffffffd	✓	✓	✗
fffffffe	✓	✗	✗
ffffffff	✗	✗	✗

✓ = enabled, ✗ = disabled
*Tx version 2 required.

Exercises

Warm up

9.1   What's required from a transaction's inputs to enable absolute lock time?

9.2   Suppose a transaction is time-locked (absolute) to 25 December 2019 00:00:00. How does a miner check whether the transaction is OK to put in a block?

9.3   Where is the relative lock time of an input located?

9.4   Suppose Adam and Eve want to swap coins with each other using an atomic swap. How many transactions would be created on each blockchain upon completion?

9.5   Why is it bad for the UTXO set to store arbitrary data such as "HELLO WORLD" as fake PKHs in outputs as opposed to storing them in `OP_RETURN` outputs?

9.6   Why would you want to replace a broadcast transaction that isn't confirmed yet?

Dig in

9.7   Explain the differences between absolute lock time and relative lock time.

9.8   (This exercise is hard; feel free to skip it.) Suppose you want to bet 1 BTC that it's going to snow in London on Christmas Eve, and Ruth bets 1 BTC that it's not. You appoint a person, Beth, whom you both trust to solve any conflicts that might occur. You and Ruth collaborate to create and broadcast a transaction that spends 1 BTC each to an output of 2 BTC with the following redeem script. (The redeem script *can* be made smaller, but to make it simpler to read, I used a slightly bigger version.) Explain how the redeem script works on a conceptual level.

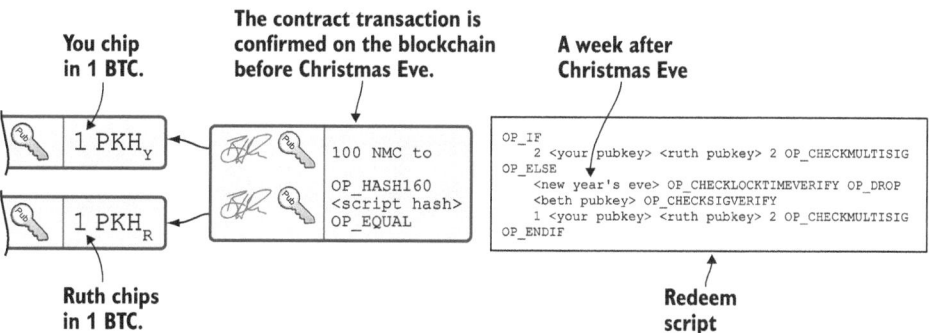

9.9 If a p2sh output pays to the hash of a redeem script that consists solely of an OP_RETURN with 32 random bytes, would full nodes be able to know that the output is unspendable?

```
OP_RETURN 53a1e411...b4e6d949
```

9.10 Explain how the first-seen policy works. Also, are nodes obliged to follow the policy?

9.11 Opt-in RBF offers a method for transaction replacement. Is there any fundamental security difference between a transaction with opt-in RBF enabled and a transaction that doesn't opt in? Explain your reasoning.

Summary

- Transactions can be locked with respect to time or block height depending on your application needs. The locks can be either absolute or relative.

- A transaction output can require the spending transaction to be time-locked. This is useful in many digital contracts.

- Atomic swaps are a useful way to exchange cryptocurrencies between two parties that don't trust each other.

- Arbitrary data—for example, a car ownership token—can be stored in OP_RETURN outputs without burdening the UTXO set.

- A transaction can be marked replaceable. This lets you replace the transaction in case it doesn't confirm within a reasonable time.

- Signatures can commit to different parts of the transaction using six combinations of SIGHASH types. This can be handy in certain digital contracts.

This chapter covers

- Understanding Bitcoin's problems

- Moving signatures out of transactions

Bitcoin is far from perfect. It has several shortcomings that we should address. The first section of this chapter will explain some of these shortcomings. Among the most critical are *transaction malleability* and inefficiencies in signature verification. We've already mentioned transaction malleability in the "Time-locked transactions" section in chapter 9—someone might change a transaction in subtle, but valid, ways while it's being broadcast, which will cause its txid to change.

A solution to these problems was presented at a 2015 conference on Bitcoin scaling. This solution is known as *segregated witness* (segwit), which is a weird name for moving signature data out of transactions. I'll describe this solution in detail: it includes changes in pretty much all parts of Bitcoin, including Bitcoin addresses, transaction format, block format, local storage, and network protocol.

Because segwit was a pretty big change in Bitcoin, it wasn't trivial to deploy without disrupting the network. It was carefully designed so old software would continue working and accepting segwit transactions and blocks, although without verifying certain parts of them.

Problems solved by segwit

In this section, we'll discuss the problems that segwit will solve.

Transaction malleability

To explain transaction malleability, let's go back to the example in chapter 9 in which you gave a time-locked transaction to your daughter. When almost a year has passed since you created your time-locked transaction, you need to invalidate that transaction and create a new time-locked transaction, as figure 10.1 shows.

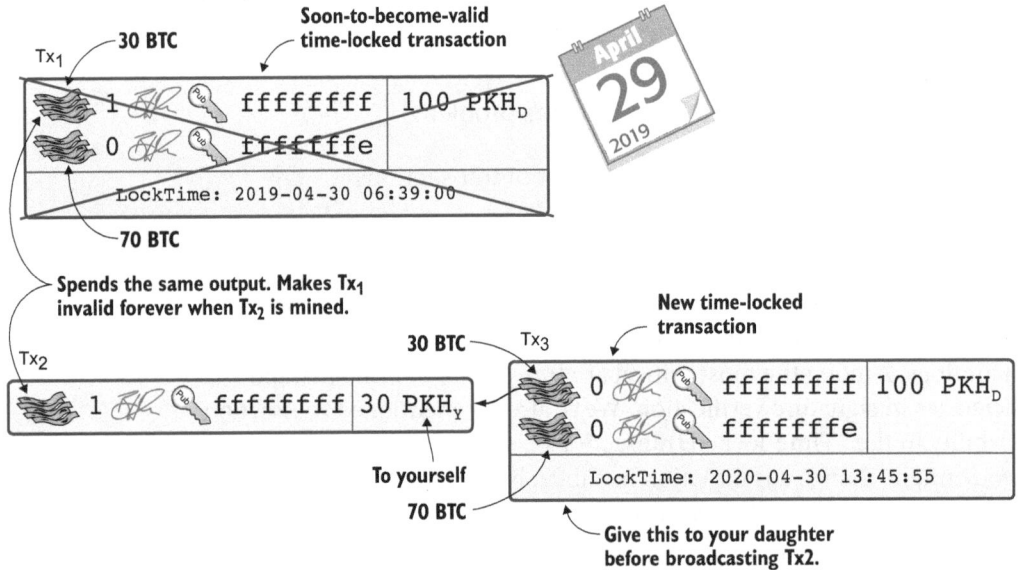

Figure 10.1   You spend one of the outputs that the previous time-locked transaction spends and create a new time-locked transaction that you give to your daughter.

It's important to give the new time-locked transaction, Tx_3, to your daughter before broadcasting Tx_2, which invalidates the previous time-locked transaction, Tx_1. Otherwise, if you do it the other way around and get hit by a bus between the two steps, your daughter won't be able to claim the money.

Suppose you do this correctly and first give Tx_3 to your daughter and then broadcast Tx_2. Tx_3 spends the output of Tx_2, which means Tx_3 contains the txid of Tx_2 in one of its inputs. Let's see what might happen when you broadcast Tx_2 (figure 10.2).

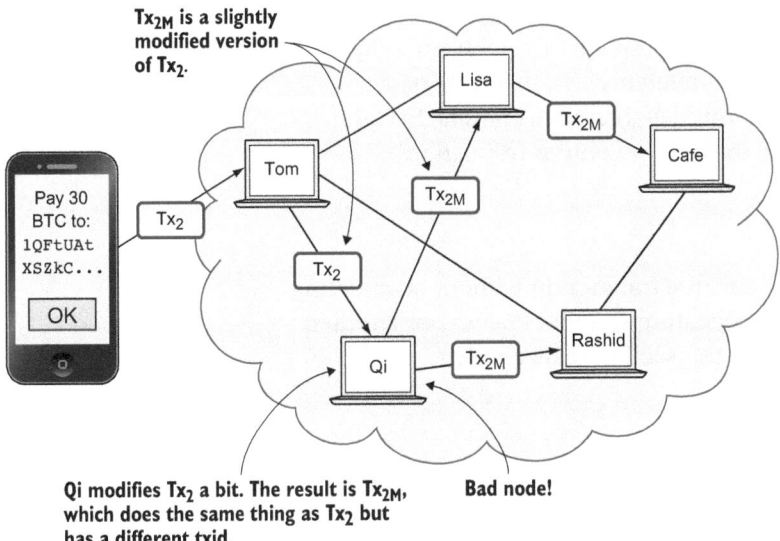

Tx$_{2M}$ is a slightly modified version of Tx$_2$.

Qi modifies Tx$_2$ a bit. The result is Tx$_{2M}$, which does the same thing as Tx$_2$ but has a different txid.

Bad node!

Figure 10.2 Your transaction is being modified by Qi on its way through the network.

Qi wants to mess things up. When she receives your transaction Tx$_2$, she modifies it in a certain way into Tx$_{2M}$, so Tx$_{2M}$ is still valid and has the same effect as the original transaction, Tx$_2$. (You'll see shortly some different ways she can do this.) The result is that two different transactions now flow through the network that spend the same outputs and send the money to the same recipients with the same amounts—but they have *different txids*.

Because Tx$_2$ and Tx$_{2M}$ spend the same outputs, they're in conflict with each other, and at most one of them will be confirmed. Suppose Tx$_{2M}$ is the winner and gets mined in the next block. What happens to your daughter's inheritance? See figure 10.3.

> **Malleability**
>
> The word *malleate* means to form—for example, metal with a hammer. This term is used in cryptography to mean changing a signature without making it invalid or changing an encrypted message without making it totally garbled.

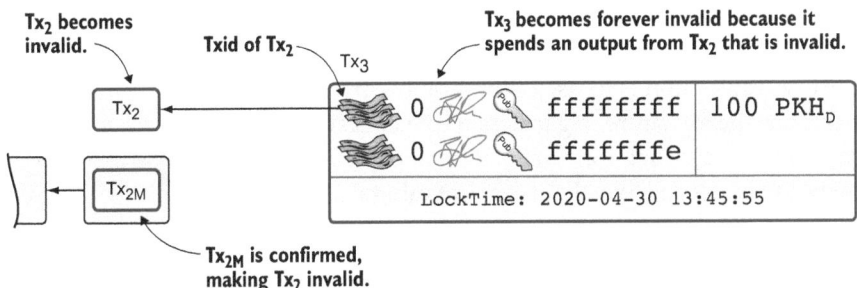

Tx$_2$ becomes invalid. **Txid of Tx$_2$** **Tx$_3$ becomes forever invalid because it spends an output from Tx$_2$ that is invalid.**

Tx$_{2M}$ is confirmed, making Tx$_2$ invalid.

Figure 10.3 The inheritance fails because your daughter's time-locked transaction is forever invalid due to transaction malleability.

The *malleated* transaction, Tx_{2M}, is stored in the blockchain. This makes Tx_2 invalid because it spends the same output as Tx_{2M}. The first input of the time-locked transaction, Tx_3, references Tx_2 using its txid, so when 30 April 2020 has passed, your daughter won't be able to claim her inheritance: she'll be trying to spend an output from an invalid transaction.

How can Qi change the txid?

Qi has several options for changing the transaction without invalidating it. They all involve changing the signature script in one way or another. Figure 10.4 shows three classes of transaction malleability.

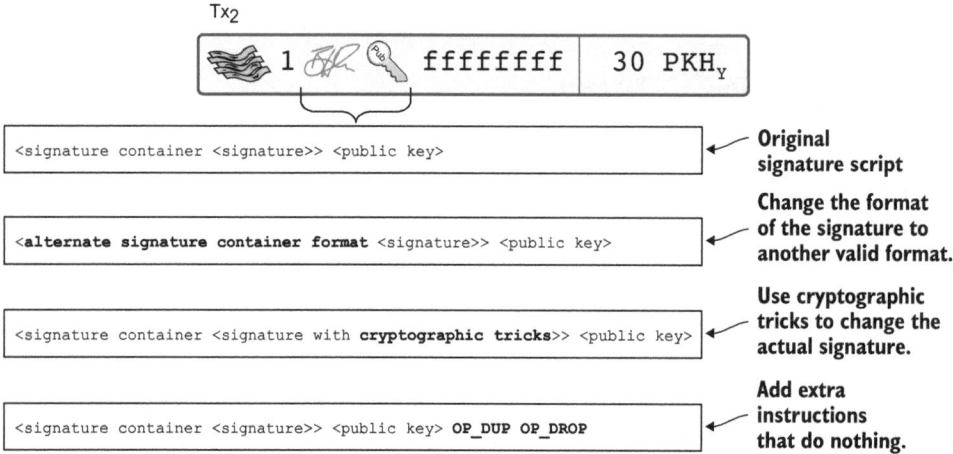

Figure 10.4   Three classes of transaction malleability

The first one modifies the signature container format, which changes how the signature is *encoded* in the signature script. You can encode the signature in a few different ways that are all valid. This issue was fixed in a system upgrade by using BIP66, which requires all signatures to be encoded in a specific way. The fix was activated in block 363724.

> **BIP66**
>
> BIP66 fixes the first class of malleability issues.

The second way to malleate a transaction is to use cryptographic tricks. I won't go into details here, but the signature, regardless of the container format, can be modified in a few ways that don't make it invalid. Only one such trick is known, but we can't rule out that there are others.

The last approach is about changing the script program itself. You can do this in several ways. The one in figure 10.4 first duplicates (OP_DUP) the top item on the stack and then immediately removes (OP_DROP) the duplicate from the stack; effectively, this change does nothing, and the whole program will run just fine.

The second and third forms of transaction malleability are somewhat limited by *relay policies*. This means nodes will require that the signatures conform to specific rules and that no script operators except data pushes be present in the signature script. Otherwise, the node won't relay the transaction. But nothing is stopping a miner from mining malleated transactions. Relay policies are implemented to make transaction malleability harder, but they can't prevent it.

Inefficient signature verification

When a transaction is signed, the signature algorithm hashes the transaction in a certain way.

Remember from "Signing the transaction" in chapter 5 that you clean all signature scripts before signing. But if you did *just* that, all the transaction's signatures would use the exact same hash. If the transaction spent two different outputs that pay to the same address, the signature in one of the inputs could be reused in the other input. That property could be exploited by bad actors.

To avoid this problem, Bitcoin makes each signature commit to a slightly different version of the transaction by copying the spent pubkey script into the signature script of the input that's currently being signed.

Let's zoom in a bit on what's happening. Suppose you want to sign a transaction with two inputs. The first input is signed as illustrated in figure 10.5.

Why not use a dummy byte?

Inserting the pubkey script into the signature script seems unnecessary. It'd be simpler to add a single dummy byte in the signature script to avoid signature reuse. No one really knows why the pubkey script is used for this.

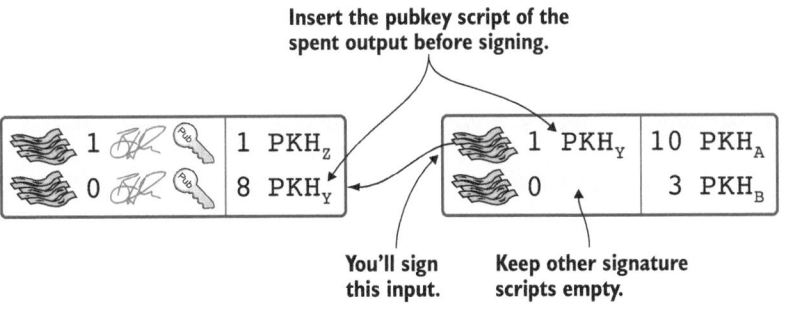

Figure 10.5   Signing the first input. You prepare by copying the pubkey script to the signature script.

The signature scripts of all inputs are empty, but you copy the pubkey script of the spent output and insert it into the signature script of the spending input. You then create the signature for the first input and move on to sign the second input (figure 10.6).

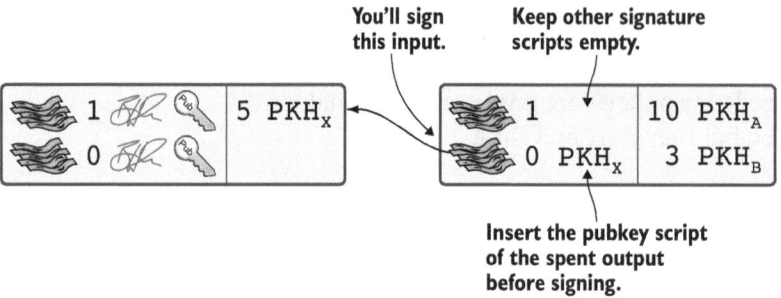

Figure 10.6   Signing the second input

Here, all signature scripts except the second one are empty. The second signature script is populated with the spent output's pubkey script. The signature is then created.

By doing this exercise for each input, you ensure that signatures aren't reusable across inputs if signed by the same private key. But this also introduces a problem: signature verification becomes inefficient.

Suppose you want to verify the signatures of the aforementioned transaction. For every input, you need to perform basically the same procedure as when the transaction was signed: clean all the signature scripts from the transaction and then, one at a time, insert the pubkey script in the signature script of the input you want to verify. Then, verify the signature for that input.

This might seem harmless, but as the number of inputs grows, the amount of data to hash for each signature increases. If you double the number of inputs, you roughly

- Double the number of signatures to verify

- Double the size of the transaction

If the time to verify the transaction with two inputs in figure 10.7 is 1 ms, it will take 4 ms to verify a transaction with four inputs. Double

Why 1 ms?

The 1 ms time is just an example. The actual time to verify a transaction varies among nodes.

the number of inputs again, and you have 16 ms. A transaction with 1,024 inputs would take more than 4 minutes!

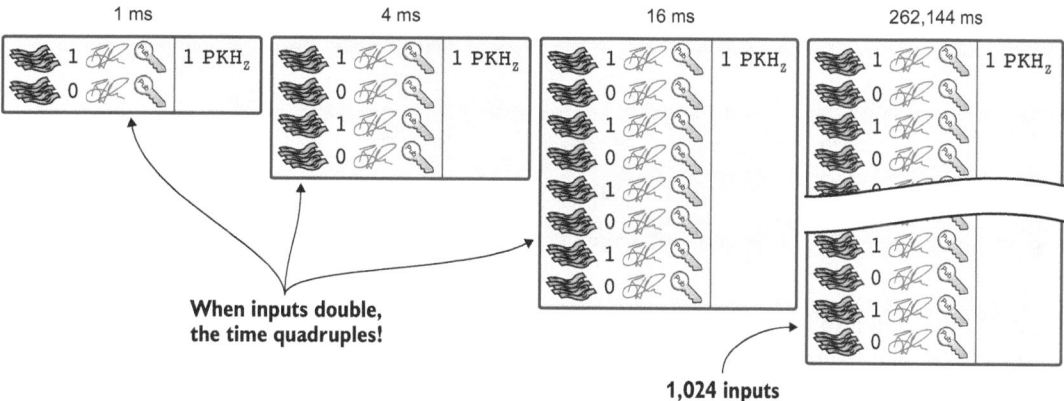

Figure 10.7 Total time for hashing during signature verification. Time roughly quadruples when the number of inputs doubles.

This weakness can be exploited by creating a large transaction with a lot of inputs. All nodes verifying the transaction will be occupied for minutes, making them unable to verify other transactions and blocks during this time. The Bitcoin network as a whole would slow down.

It would be much better if the transaction verification time grew linearly instead of quadratically: the time to verify a transaction would double as the number of inputs doubled. Then, the 1,024 inputs would take roughly 512 ms to verify instead of 4 minutes.

Waste of bandwidth

When a full node sends a transaction to a lightweight wallet, it sends the complete transaction, which includes all signature data. But a lightweight wallet can't verify the signatures because it doesn't have the spent outputs.

The signature scripts constitute a large percentage of the transaction size. A typical signature script spending a p2pkh output takes 107 bytes. Consider a few different transactions with two outputs, as table 10.1 shows.

Table 10.1   Space occupied by signature script data of different typical transactions

Inputs	Total signature script size (bytes)	Tx size (bytes)	Signature script percentage
1	107	224	47%
2	214	373	57%
3	321	521	61%
8	856	1,255	68%

Wouldn't it be nice if a full node didn't have to send the signature script data to the lightweight wallet? You'd probably save more than 50% data traffic. There's just one problem: such data is needed to calculate txids. If you skip sending signature scripts of transactions, the lightweight wallet won't be able to verify that the transaction is included in a block because it can't verify the merkle proof (figure 10.8).

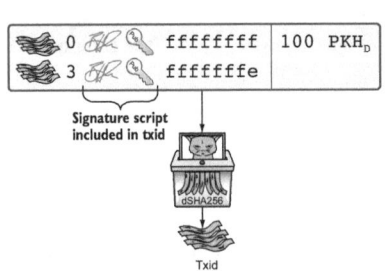

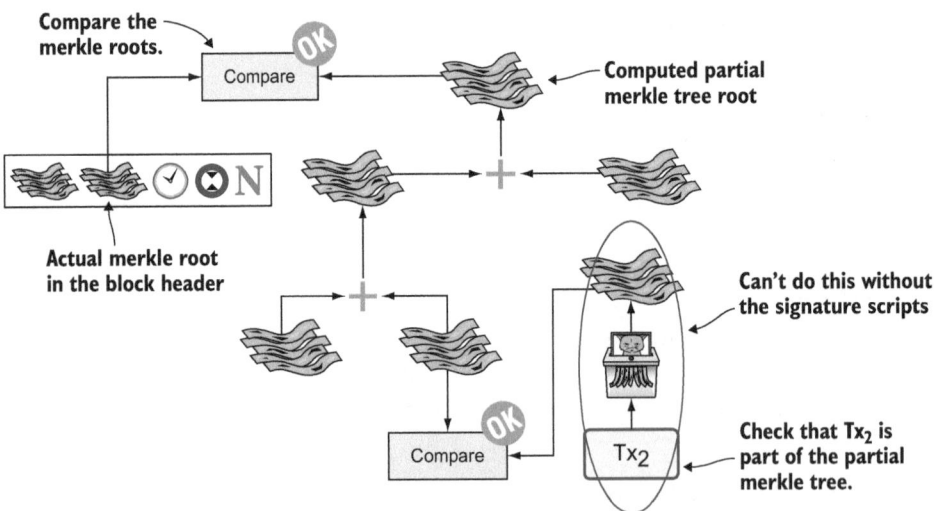

Figure 10.8   Without the signature scripts, a lightweight wallet can't verify that a transaction is included in the block.

We'd definitely like to solve this somehow.

Script upgrades are hard

Sometimes, we want to extend the script language with new operations. For example, OP_CHECKSEQUENCEVERIFY (OP_CSV) and OP_CHECKLOCKTIMEVERIFY (OP_CLTV) were introduced in the language in 2015 and 2016. Let's look at how OP_CLTV was introduced.

We'll start with what op_ codes are. They're nothing but a single byte. OP_EQUAL for example, is represented by the byte 87 in hex code. Every node knows that when it encounters byte 87 in the script program, it needs to compare the top two items on the stack and push the result back on the stack. OP_CHECKMULTISIG is also a single byte, ae. All operators are represented by different bytes.

When Bitcoin was created, several NOP operators, OP_NOP1–OP_NOP10, were specified. These are represented by the bytes b0–b9. They're designed to do nothing. The name NOP comes from No OPeration, which basically means, "When this instruction appears, ignore it and move on."

These NOPs can be used to extend the script language, but only to a certain extent. The OP_CLTV operator is actually OP_NOP2, or byte b1. OP_CLTV was introduced by releasing a version of Bitcoin Core that redefines how OP_NOP2 works. But it needs to be done in a compatible way so we don't break compatibility with old, non-upgraded nodes.

Let's go back to the example from "Absolute time-locked outputs" in chapter 9, where you gave your daughter an allowance in advance that she could cash out on 1 May (see figure 10.9).

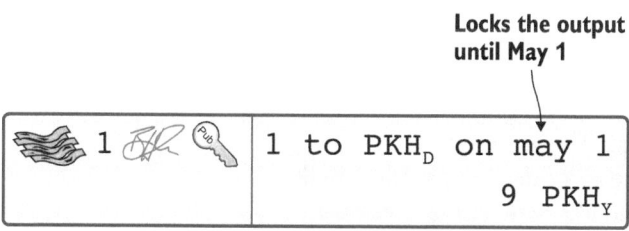

Figure 10.9   Using OP_CLTV to lock an output until 1 May

The pubkey script for this output is

```
<1 may 2019 00:00:00> OP_CHECKLOCKTIMEVERIFY OP_DROP
OP_DUP OP_HASH160 <PKH_D> OP_EQUALVERIFY OP_CHECKSIG
```

This is how a new node—which is aware of the new meaning of byte `b1`—interprets the script. It will do the following:

1. Push the time `<1 may 2019 00:00:00>` to the stack.
2. Check that the spending transaction's lock time has at least the value found on top of the stack, or fail immediately otherwise.
3. Drop the time value from the stack.
4. Continue with normal signature verification.

An old node, on the other hand, will interpret the script as follows:

```
<1 may 2019 00:00:00> OP_NOP2 OP_DROP
OP_DUP OP_HASH160 <PKH_b> OP_EQUALVERIFY OP_CHECKSIG
```

It will

1. Push the time `<1 may 2019 00:00:00>` to the stack.
2. *Do nothing.*
3. Drop the time value from the stack.
4. Continue with normal signature verification.

Old nodes still treat `OP_NOP2` as they used to—by doing nothing and moving on. They aren't aware of the new rules associated with the byte `b1`.

The old and the new nodes will behave the same if the `OP_CLTV` succeeds on the new node. But if the `OP_CLTV` fails on the new node, the old node won't fail, because "do nothing" never fails. The new nodes fail more often than the old nodes because new nodes have stricter rules. The old nodes will always finish the script program with success whenever the new nodes finish with success. This is known as a *soft fork*—a system upgrade that doesn't require all nodes to upgrade. We'll talk more about forks, system upgrades, and alternate currencies born from Bitcoin's blockchain in chapter 11.

You might be wondering what the `OP_DROP` instruction is for. `OP_DROP` takes the top item on the stack and discards it. `OP_CLTV` is designed to behave exactly like `OP_NOP2` when it succeeds. If `OP_CLTV` had been designed without taking old nodes into account, it would probably remove the top item from the stack. But because we need to take old nodes into account, `OP_CLTV` doesn't do that. We must add the extra `OP_DROP` after `OP_CLTV` to get rid of the time item from the stack.

This was an example of how old script operators can be repurposed to do something stricter without disrupting the entire network.

This method of script upgrades has been done for two operators so far:

Byte	Old code	New code	New meaning
b1	OP_NOP2	OP_CLTV	Verify that the spending transaction has a high enough absolute lock time.
b2	OP_NOP3	OP_CSV	Verify that the spending input has a high enough relative lock time.

Only 10 `OP_NOP` operators are available to use for script upgrades, and such upgrades are limited to exactly mimic the `OP_NOP` behavior if they don't fail.

Sooner or later, we'll need another script-upgrade mechanism, both because we'll run out of `OP_NOP`s and because we want the new script operators to behave differently than `OP_NOP` when they succeed.

Solutions

A solution to all these problems was presented at a 2015 conference. The solution was to move the signature scripts out of transactions altogether.

Let's look again at the anatomy of a normal transaction, shown in figure 10.10.

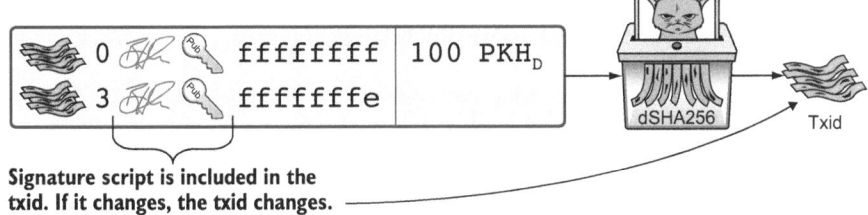

Signature script is included in the txid. If it changes, the txid changes.

Figure 10.10 The txid is calculated from the entire transaction, including signature scripts.

If we could change the system so the txid didn't cover the signature script, we'd remove all known possibilities of unintentional transaction malleability. Unfortunately, if we did this, we'd make old software incompatible because it calculates the txid in the traditional way.

Segwit solves this problem and all the aforementioned problems in a forward- and backward-compatible way:

BIP141

The new rules defined by segregated witness are specified in BIP141, "Segregated Witness (Consensus layer)."

- Forward-compatible because blocks created by new software work with old software

- Backward-compatible because blocks created by old software work with new software

In crypto-lingo, a *witness* basically means a signature. It's something that attests to the authenticity of something. For a Bitcoin transaction, the witness is the contents of the signature scripts, because that's what proves the transaction is authenticated. *Segregated* means parted, so we part the contents of the signature scripts from the transaction, effectively leaving the signature scripts empty, as figure 10.11 shows.

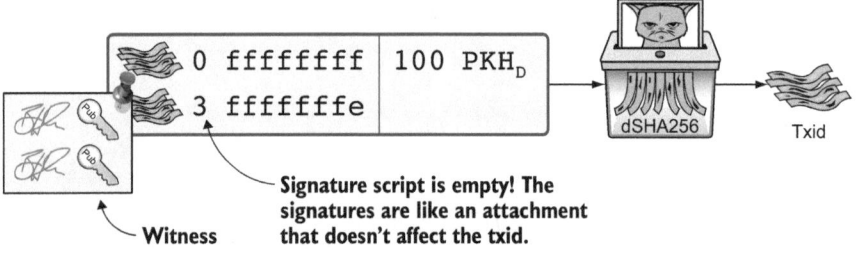

Figure 10.11 A segwit transaction contains no signature data. The signatures are attached, instead. The txid doesn't commit to the signatures.

Segregated witness **thus means the contents of the signature scripts are removed from the transaction and put into an external structure called the witness.**

We'll follow a few segwit transactions to see how they affect the different parts of the Bitcoin system. But first, let's get some bitcoin into a segwit wallet.

Segwit addresses

Suppose your wallet uses segwit, and you're selling a laptop to Amy. Your wallet needs to create an address that you can give to Amy. So far, nothing new.

But segwit defines a new address type that's encoded using *Bech32* instead of base58check. Suppose your wallet creates the following segwit address:

```
bc1qeqzjk7vume5wmrdgz5xyehh54cchdjag6jdmkj
```

This address format provides several improvements compared to the base58check addresses you're used to:

- All characters are of the same case, which means

  - QR codes can be made smaller.

  - Addresses are easier to verbally read out.

- The checksum used in Bech32 will detect up to four character errors with 100% certainty. If there are more character errors, the probability of detection failure is less than one in a billion. This is a major improvement to the 4-byte checksum in base58check, which doesn't provide any guarantee.

Your segwit address consists of two parts. The first two characters, bc (short for bitcoin) is the *human-readable part*. The 1 is a delimiter between the human-readable part and the *data part*, which encodes the actual information that Amy will use to create the transaction output:

- A version, 0 in this case.

- A *witness program*. In this case, the witness program is a PKH, c8052b79...3176cba8.

We'll explain what the witness program is a bit further on. Think about it as a PKH for now. The version and witness program aren't directly extractable from the address because they're encoded using bech32. You give the address bc1qeqzj...ag6jdmkj to Amy by showing her a QR code. She has a modern wallet that understands this address format, so she scans your address and extracts the version and witness program, as figure 10.12 illustrates.

> **BIP173**
>
> This BIP defines the checksummed encoding scheme Bech32 and how segwit addresses are composed and encoded using Bech32.

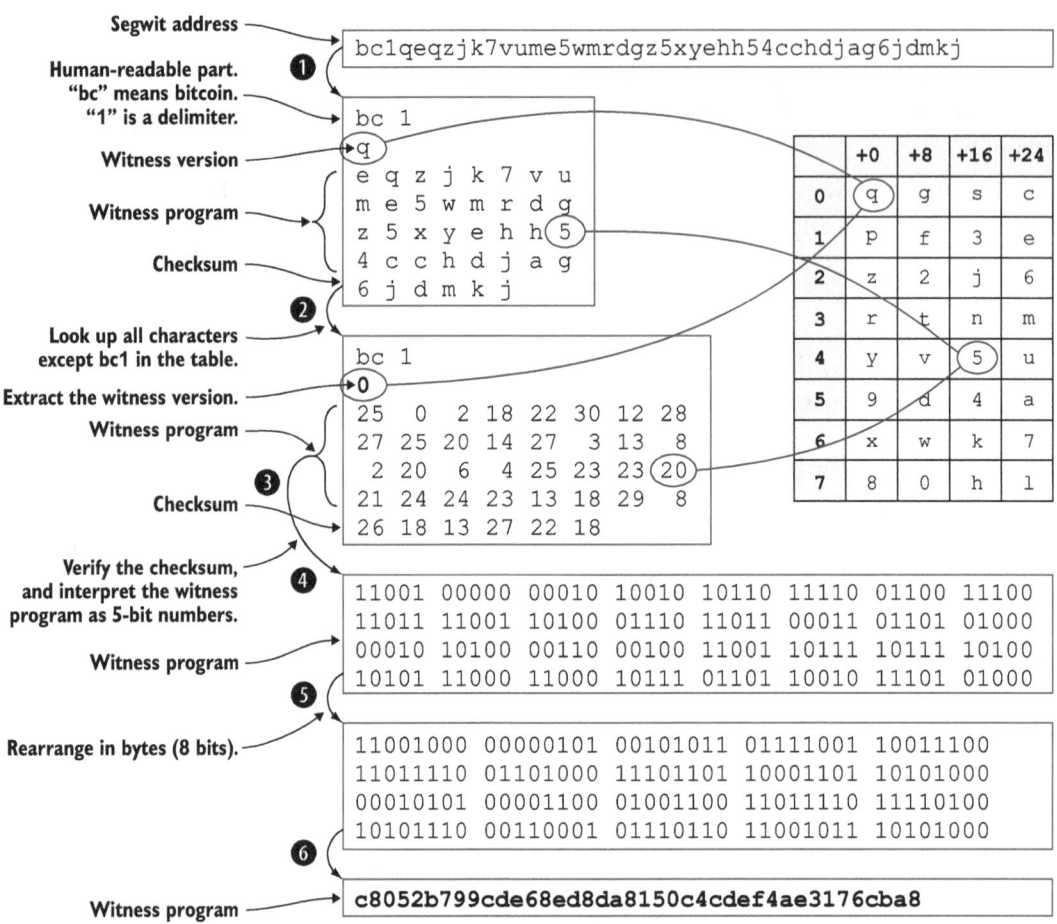

Figure 10.12 Amy decodes the segwit address to get the witness version and the witness program.

This occurs in multiple steps:

❶ The human-readable part and the data part are separated.

❷ The data part of the address is converted, character by character, into numbers using a base32 lookup table. The first of these numbers is the witness version, 0. The following numbers, except the last six, are the witness program. The last six numbers are the checksum.

❸ The checksum is verified; no errors were detected in this example.

❹ The witness program is rewritten by writing each number as a 5-bit number.

> **Checksum**
>
> I won't go into details on the checksum. I encourage the interested reader to read BIP173.

⑤ The bits are rearranged in groups of 8 bits. Each such group represents a byte of the witness program.

⑥ Amy extracts the witness program as `c8052b7…3176cba8`.

Amy creates a transaction with a new kind of pubkey script that you aren't used to (figure 10.13).

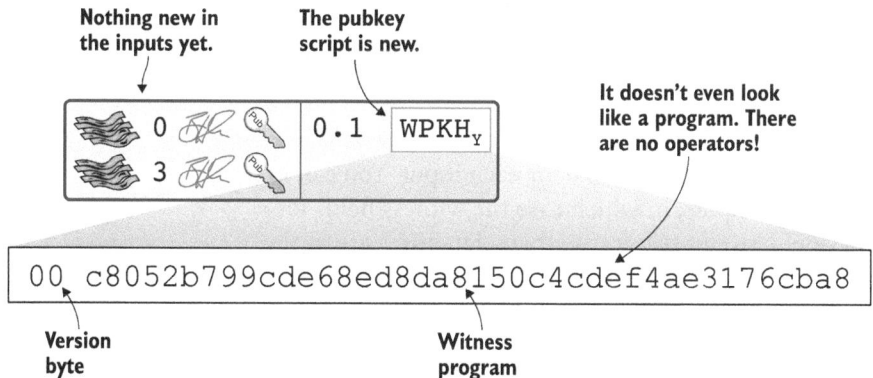

Figure 10.13 Amy sends 0.1 BTC to your segwit address. The pubkey script doesn't contain any script operators, just data.

She broadcasts this transaction on the Bitcoin network. The network will accept the transaction because it's correctly signed in the old-fashioned way. Eventually, it will be confirmed in a block. Your wallet will acknowledge that you've received the money, and you'll give the laptop to Amy.

Spending your segwit output

Now that you've received your money, you want to spend it on a used popcorn machine. It costs only 0.09 BTC. It's a bargain! Suppose the owner of the popcorn machine has the segwit address `bc1qlk34…ul0qwrqp`.

Your transaction sends the money to the popcorn machine owner's segwit address and pays a 0.01 BTC transaction fee (figure 10.14). The input has an empty signature script; the signature data is instead added as a *witness field* in the attached witness.

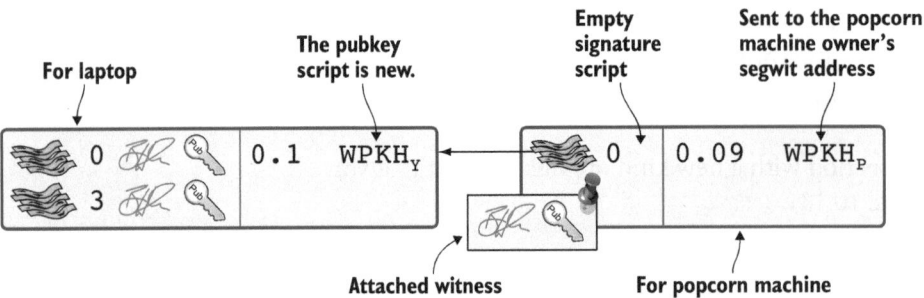

Figure 10.14 You create and broadcast a payment to the popcorn machine owner.

Had there been multiple inputs in this transaction, there would be multiple witness fields in the witness, one for each input. You can mix segwit inputs and legacy inputs, in which case the witness fields for the legacy inputs would be empty because their signatures are in the respective signature script, as they always were.

Verifying the segwit transaction

You've sent your transaction for the popcorn machine to the Bitcoin peer-to-peer network for processing. Let's see how an upgraded full node verifies this transaction before relaying it to other nodes (figure 10.15). Because it's running the latest and greatest software, it knows how to deal with segwit transactions.

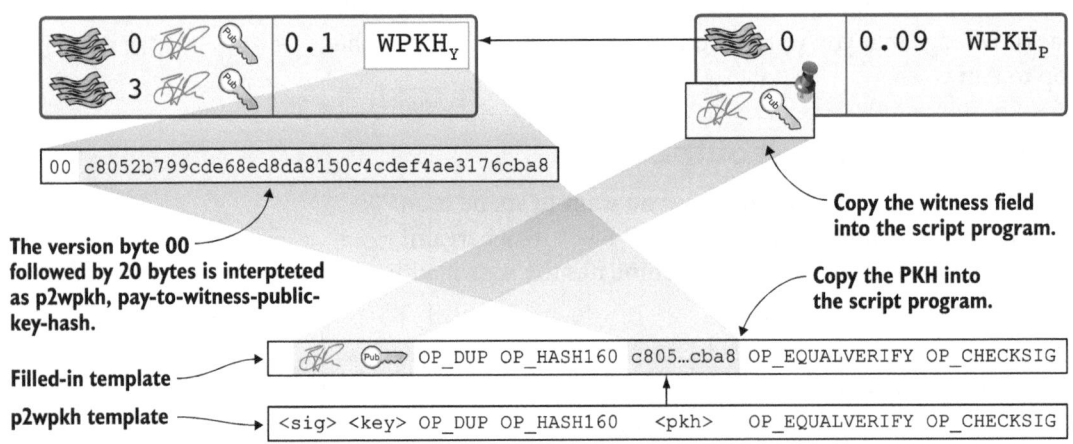

Figure 10.15 A full node verifies your transaction's witness. The pattern 00 followed by exactly 20 bytes gets special treatment.

The full node, which knows about segwit, looks for a pattern in the pubkey script starting with a single version byte followed by a 2- to 40-byte witness program. In this case, the pattern matches, which means this is a segwit output.

The next step for the full node is to understand what *kind* of segwit output it is. As of this writing, there's only one version of segwit output: version 00. This version comes in two different flavors:

- *Pay-to-witness-public-key-hash (p2wpkh)*, identified by a 20-byte witness program, as in this example

- *Pay-to-witness-script-hash (p2wsh)*, identified by a 32-byte witness program. p2wsh will be explained later in this chapter.

In this case, we have the version byte 00 followed by exactly 20 bytes, which means this is a p2wpkh payment. If the version byte is unknown to the node, the node will immediately accept this input without further processing. This acceptance of unknown versions will become useful for future, forward-compatible upgrades of the script language. All segwit nodes will recognize version 00.

The p2wpkh is the simplest of the two types because it's similar to the well-known p2pkh. Let's look at how they both work:

- *p2pkh*—The pubkey script contains the actual script that checks the signature in the signature script.

- *p2wpkh*—The actual script is a predetermined template, and the witness program *is* the PKH to insert into the script template. The signature and the public key are taken from the witness.

In the end, it's seemingly the exact same program that is run for both of these two types. The difference is where the components come from. But other differences exist between segwit scripts and legacy scripts—for example, the meaning of OP_CHECKSIG has changed, as you'll see in "New hashing method for signatures."

Why do p2wpkh at all when we're running the exact same script program as in p2pkh? Recall that we want to solve transaction malleability. We do this by removing the signature data from the transaction inputs so no one can change the txid by making subtle changes to the signature script.

The full node has verified this transaction and sends it to its peers. There's just one problem: one peer has no idea what segwit is. It's an old node that hasn't been upgraded for a while.

Remember p2sh

A segwit output is recognized by pattern matching, just like a p2sh output was in chapter 5.

Why "witness program"?

It's called a witness program because it can be regarded as a program of a weird language. In version 00, the witness program is a single operator whose length defines its behavior.

"Verifying" on old nodes

An old node has just received your transaction and wants to verify it. Old nodes know nothing about segwit or that there are witnesses attached to transactions. The old node downloads the transaction as it always has, which is without the witness attachment. Figure 10.16 shows what the node sees.

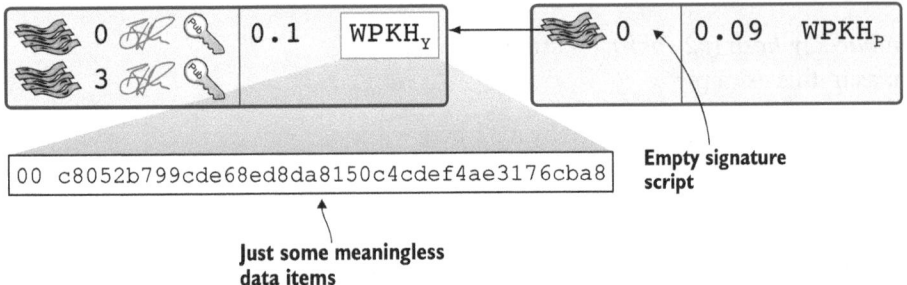

Empty signature script

Just some meaningless data items

Figure 10.16   An old node sees just two data items in the pubkey script and an empty signature script.

Because the node doesn't know anything else, it creates the script program by taking the empty signature script and appending the pubkey script. The resulting program looks like this:

```
00 c8052b799cde68ed8da8150c4cdef4ae3176cba8
```

The node runs this program. The program puts two data items on the stack—first `00`, and then the `c805…cba8`. When it's done, there's nothing left to do but check whether the top item on the stack, `c805…cba8`, is `true`. Bitcoin defines anything that's nonzero to be true, so this script will pass, and the transaction is authorized.

This doesn't seem very secure. This is known as an *anyone-can-spend*, meaning anyone can create a transaction that spends the output. It requires no signature. You just have to create an input with an empty signature script to take the money.

In chapter 11, we'll talk about how to deploy upgrades like segwit safely. For now, you can assume that 95% of the hashrate (miners) run with segwit. If a transaction uses your output as an anyone-can-spend, and a non-segwit miner includes it in a block, then this block will be rejected by 95% of the hashrate and consequently excluded from the strongest chain. The miner will lose its block reward.

Nonstandard transactions

A node that doesn't recognize the spent script type normally doesn't relay the transaction. It's considered nonstandard. This relay policy reduces the risk that a transaction that uses the segwit output as an anyone-can-spend ends up in a block.

Including your segwit transaction in a block

Your segwit transaction has propagated through the network, and all nodes have verified it along the way. Now, a miner wants to insert the transaction into a new block. Suppose the miner runs modern software and thus knows about segwit. Let's look at how it's included in the block (figure 10.17).

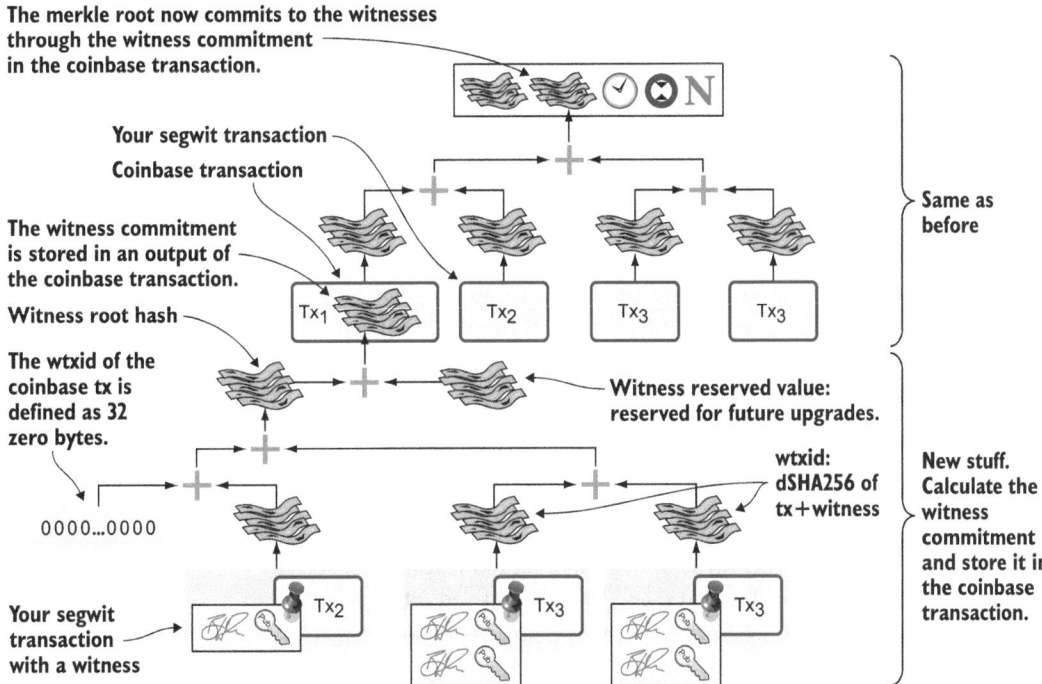

The merkle root now commits to the witnesses through the witness commitment in the coinbase transaction.

Your segwit transaction

Coinbase transaction

The witness commitment is stored in an output of the coinbase transaction.

Witness root hash

The wtxid of the coinbase tx is defined as 32 zero bytes.

0000...0000

Your segwit transaction with a witness

Witness reserved value: reserved for future upgrades.

wtxid: dSHA256 of tx+witness

Same as before

New stuff. Calculate the witness commitment and store it in the coinbase transaction.

Tx₁ Tx₂ Tx₃ Tx₃

Tx₂ Tx₃ Tx₃

Figure 10.17   Your segwit transaction gets included in a block. The block commits to the witnesses by putting the witness commitment into an output of the coinbase transaction.

The block is built as before, but with one important difference. A new block rule is introduced in segwit: if there are segwit transactions in the block, the coinbase transaction must contain an output with a *witness commitment*. This witness commitment is the combined hash of the *witness root hash* and a *witness reserved value*. The witness root hash is the merkle root of the *witness txids* (*wtxids*) of all transactions in the block. The wtxid is the hash of the transaction *including the witness*, if there is one. An exception exists for the coinbase, whose wtxid is always defined as 32 zero bytes. The witness reserved value is dedicated for future system upgrades.

The witness commitment is written in an OP_RETURN output
(figure 10.18).

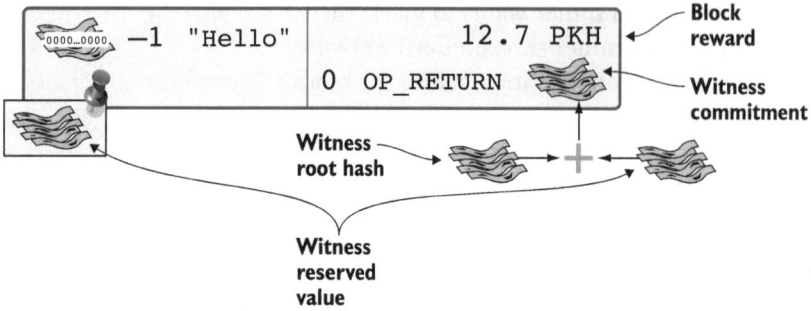

**Figure 10.18   The coinbase transaction's witness contains the witness reserved value,
and an OP_RETURN output contains the witness commitment.**

The witness reserved value can be any value. But a full node verifying
this block needs a way to know what that value is. If the node didn't
know the witness reserved value, it wouldn't be able to reconstruct
the witness commitment for comparison with the OP_RETURN output's
witness commitment. The coinbase transaction's witness contains the
witness reserved value so full nodes can verify the witness commitment.

Old nodes verifying the block

The block in figure 10.17 is valid for new segwit-enabled full nodes, so
it must also be valid for old nodes that don't know what segwit is. An
old node won't download any witnesses from its peers because it doesn't
know they exist (figure 10.19).

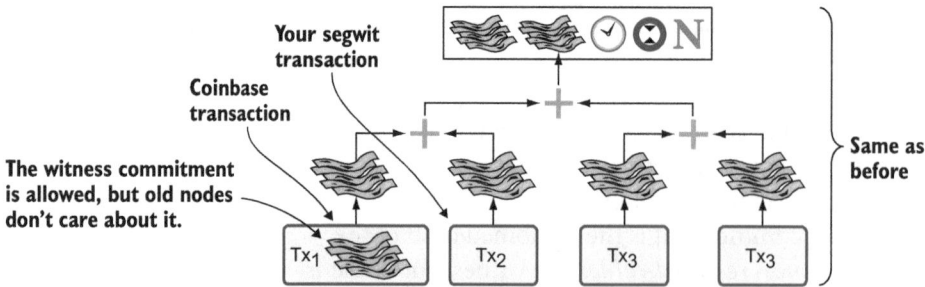

**Figure 10.19   An old node verifies the block with your transaction. It won't verify the
signatures or the witness commitment.**

This node will do what it's always done—run the scripts of the
transactions, which will look like spending anyone-can-spend outputs.

That's OK, move on. If some of the transactions in the block are non-segwit, those transactions will be fully verified.

We've now gone full circle with your transaction to the popcorn machine owner, who hands over the machine to you.

Pay-to-witness-script-hash

Do you remember when we introduced p2sh in the "Pay-to-script-hash" section of chapter 5? p2sh moves the pubkey script part of the program to the spending input. Let's have another look at the charity wallet that John, Ellen, and Faiza set up (figure 10.20).

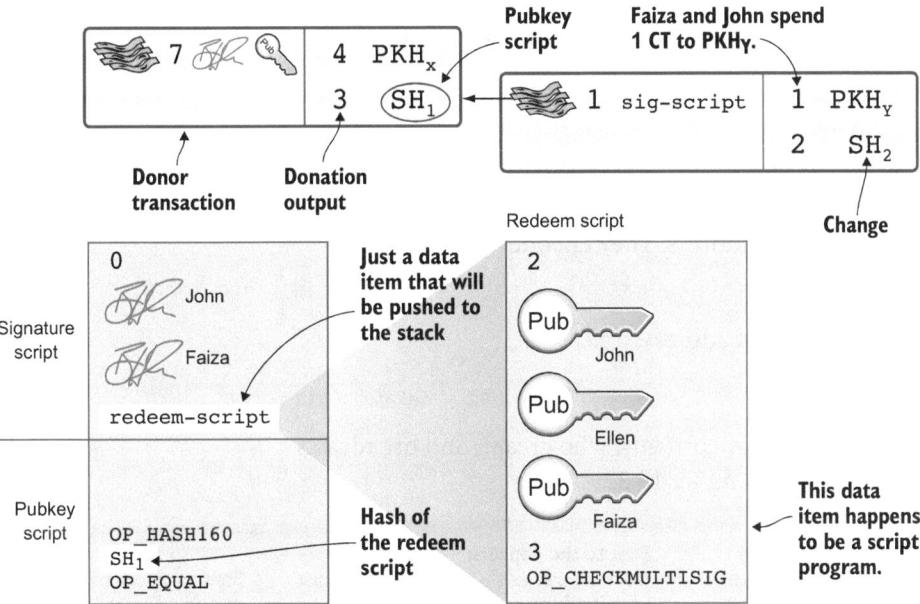

Figure 10.20   John and Faiza spend an output from their multisig wallet.

The idea here was that the payer—the donor, in this case—shouldn't have to pay a higher fee for a big, complex pubkey script. Instead, the recipient wanting to use this fancy scheme will pay for the complexity.

With segwit, you can do about the same thing using pay-to-witness-script-hash, which is the segwit version of p2sh. Isn't naming in Bitcoin fantastic?

Suppose John, Ellen, and Faiza use segwit for their charity wallet and that the previous popcorn machine owner wants to give the money he received for the popcorn machine to the charity.

John, Ellen, and Faiza must provide the popcorn guy with a p2wsh address. Their *witness script* is the same as their p2sh *redeem script* was when they were using p2sh (figure 10.21).

Witness script

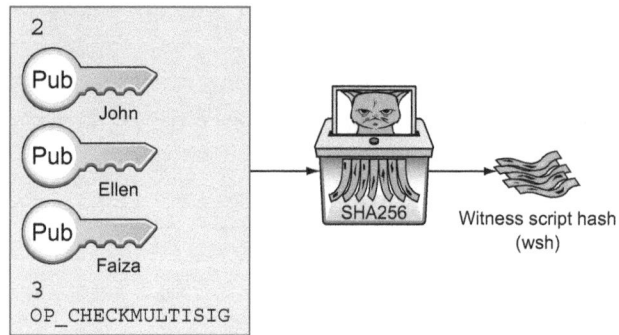

Figure 10.21   The witness script is hashed into a witness script hash.

They use this witness script hash to create a p2wsh address in the same way you created your p2wpkh address. They encode

```
00  983b977f86b9bce124692e68904935f5e562c88226befb8575b4a51e29db9062
```

using Bech32 and get the p2wsh address:

```
bc1qnqaewluxhx7wzfrf9e5fqjf47hjk9jyzy6l0hpt4kjj3u2wmjp3qr3lft8
```

This address is handed to the popcorn guy, who creates and broadcasts a transaction like that shown in figure 10.22.

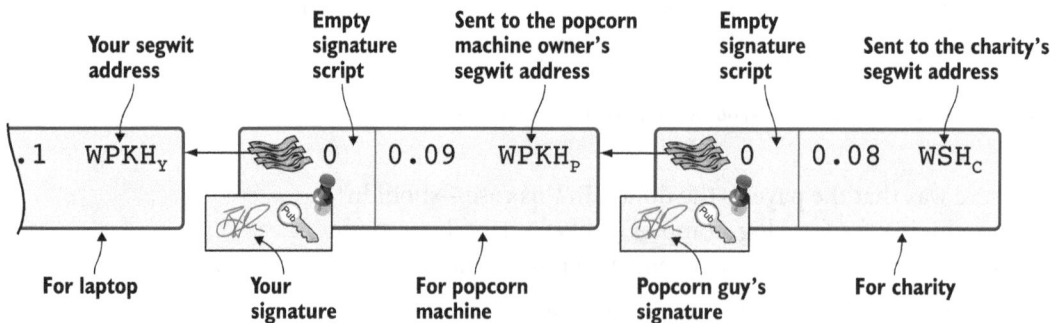

Figure 10.22   The popcorn guy sends the money to the charity's p2wsh address.

The transaction has the witness attached, just like your transaction to the popcorn guy. The only difference between your transaction and the popcorn guy's transaction is that their outputs have a different witness program length. Your transaction had a 20-byte witness program because it was a SHA256+RIPEMD160 hash of a public key, and the popcorn guy's transaction has a 32-byte witness program because that's the SHA256 hash of a witness script.

This transaction will be verified and eventually included in a block.

Spending the p2wsh transaction

Suppose John and Faiza want to spend the 0.08 BTC they got from the popcorn guy by sending it to a shelter for homeless people. The shelter happens to also have a p2wsh address. John and Faiza collaborate to create the transaction figure 10.23 shows.

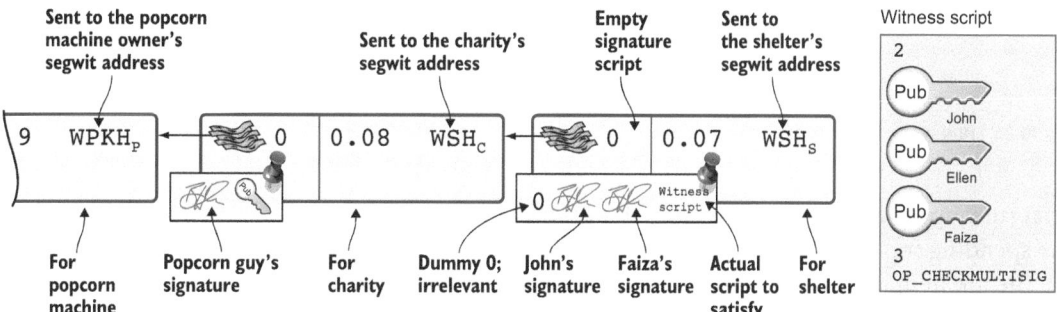

Figure 10.23   The charity pays 0.07 BTC to the shelter's address. The witness is the signatures followed by a data item that contains the actual witness script.

Note how there's nothing in the signature script. When we used p2sh in chapter 5's "Pay-to-script-hash," the signature script got really big because it contained two signatures and the redeem script, which in turn contained three public keys. With segwit, all data is contained in the witness instead.

Verifying the p2wsh input

A full node that wants to verify this transaction needs to determine the type of output being spent (figure 10.24). It looks at the output, finds the pattern `<version byte> <2 to 40 bytes data>`, and concludes that this is a segwit output. The next thing to check is the value of the version byte.

The version byte is `00`. A version `00` segwit output can have two different lengths of the witness program, 20 or 32 bytes. We covered the first one in the previous sections on p2wpkh. The witness program in this example is 32 bytes, which means this is a p2wsh output.

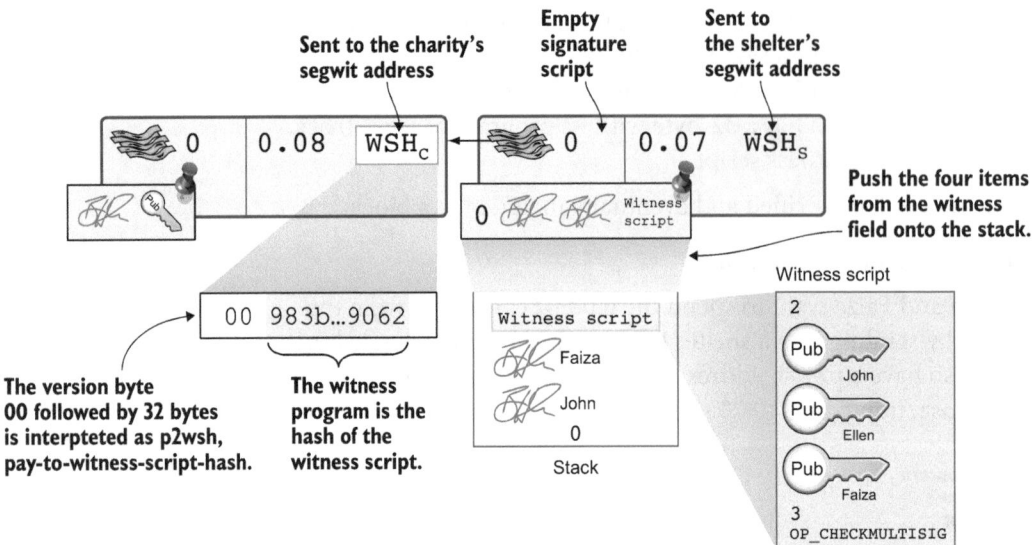

Figure 10.24   Preparing to verify the p2wsh input

Special rules apply when spending a p2wsh output. First, the data items
in the spending input's witness field are pushed onto the program stack.
Then, the top item on the stack, the witness script, is verified against the
witness program in the output (figure 10.25).

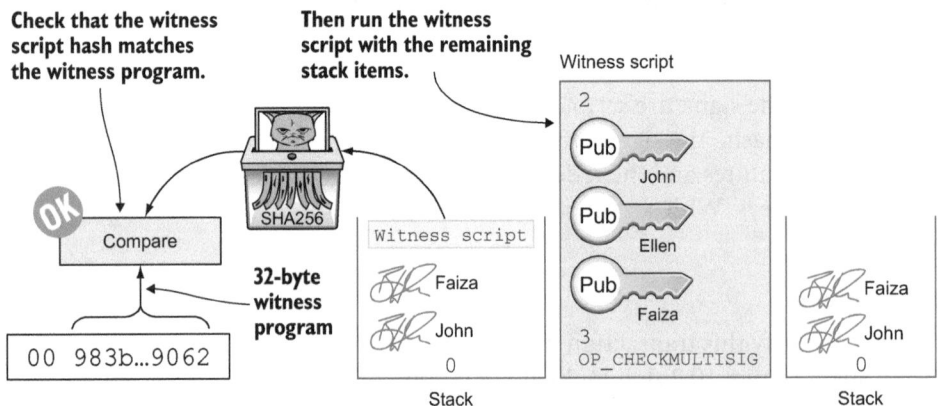

Figure 10.25   Verifying the witness of a p2wsh payment

The witness script is hashed and compared to the witness program
in the spent output before being executed with the three items on the
stack. This process is similar to that of verifying a p2sh payment.

Miners and block verifiers handle all segwit transactions the same way, so there's no difference in how the transaction is included in a block compared to p2wpkh transactions.

New hashing method for signatures

One problem that segwit solves is inefficient signature hashing. As explained in "Inefficient signature verification," if the number of inputs doubles, the time it takes to verify the transaction roughly quadruples. This is because you

- Double the number of signatures to verify

- Double the transaction's size

If you double the number of hashes performed *and* double the amount of data each hash needs to process, you effectively quadruple the total time spent on hashing.

The solution is to make the signatures in steps. Suppose you want to sign all four inputs of a transaction, as figure 10.26 shows.

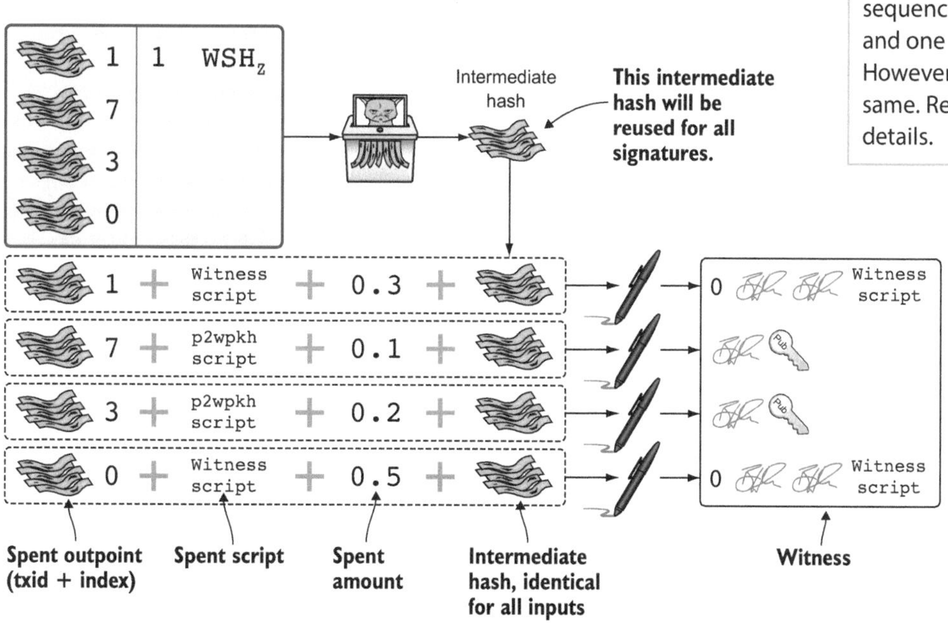

> **BIP143**
>
> This solution is specified in BIP143, "Transaction Signature Verification for Version 0 Witness Program."

> **This algorithm is simplified**
>
> In reality, three different intermediate hashes are created: one for all outpoints, one for all sequence numbers, and one for all outputs. However, the effect is the same. Read BIP143 for details.

Figure 10.26 Hashing is done in two steps. The intermediate hash is reused for each input.

First you create an intermediate hash of the complete transaction. If the transaction contains non-segwit inputs, those signature scripts will be cleaned prior to hashing. The intermediate hash commits to all of that transaction's inputs and outputs. Then, for each input, add the intermediate hash to some input-specific data:

- *Spent outpoint*—The txid and index of the output this input spends
- *Spent script*—The witness script or p2wpkh script corresponding to the spent output
- *Spent amount*—The BTC value of the spent output

The bulk of the transaction is hashed only once to create the intermediate hash. This drastically reduces the amount of hashing needed. When the number of inputs doubles, the needed amount of hashing only doubles. This makes the hashing algorithm perform *linearly with the number of inputs* instead of *quadratically*. The time to verify the transaction with 1,024 inputs discussed in figure 10.7 is reduced from 262,144 ms to 512 ms.

Old hashing

262,144 ms

1,024 inputs →

Signature commits to amount

Why do we include the spent amount? We didn't do that in the old signature-hashing algorithm. This has nothing to do with hashing efficiency, but it fixes yet another problem that offline wallets and some lightweight wallets face.

An offline wallet—for example, a hardware wallet—can't know how much money is being spent. If the offline wallet is to sign a transaction, the wallet can't display the transaction's fee amount to the user because it can't see the values of the outputs it's spending (figure 10.27). It has no access to the blockchain.

> **Hardware wallets**
>
> A *hardware wallet* is an electronic device designed to keep private keys safe. Unsigned transactions are sent to the device for signing. The device usually requires a PIN code to sign.

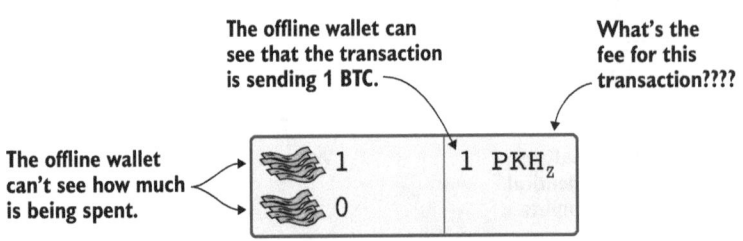

The offline wallet can see that the transaction is sending 1 BTC.

What's the fee for this transaction????

The offline wallet can't see how much is being spent.

Figure 10.27   An offline wallet can't know a transaction's fee.

This is true for both non-segwit and segwit transactions. But with segwit transactions, when the signatures commit to the spent output amounts, the wallet must get the amounts from somewhere to be able to sign. Suppose the input amounts are somehow provided to the offline wallet, alongside the transaction to sign. The wallet can then sign the transaction using those amounts and even show the user what fee is being paid before signing.

If the offline wallet receives the wrong amount, it won't be able to tell. It can't verify the input values. But because the signatures now cover the amounts, the transaction will be invalid. A verifying node will know the correct amounts and use them when verifying the signatures. The signature check will fail. The new signature hashing algorithm makes it impossible to trick a wallet into signing a valid transaction with a fee the user didn't intend.

Bandwidth savings

Segwit removes the signature data from the transaction, so when a lightweight wallet requests a transaction from a full node, the full node can send the transaction without the witness data. This means less data traffic is needed per transaction. This fact can be used to either

- Keep the bloom filter size as is and get about 50% reduction in data traffic

- Improve privacy by decreasing the size of the bloom filter to get more false positives without increasing data traffic

Upgradable script

The version byte is used for future script language upgrades. Before segwit, we had to use the OP_NOPs to introduce new features to the language—for example, OP_CSV. This wasn't optimal for the following reasons:

- We might run out of OP_NOPs—there are eight left.

- The OP_NOPs can't be redefined in arbitrary ways; they still need to behave as OP_NOPs in case the new behavior succeeds.

The version byte allows for much more powerful future upgrades. We can do anything from slight modifications of specific operators to implementing completely new languages.

Wallet compatibility

Most old wallets won't support sending bitcoin to a segwit address. They usually only allow p2pkh and p2sh addresses. So segwit's developers created *p2wsh nested in p2sh* and *p2wpkh nested in p2sh*: ways to trigger the segwit verification instead of the legacy script verification.

Suppose you have a segwit wallet and want to sell your popcorn machine to your neighbor, Nina. But Nina doesn't have a segwit-aware wallet. She can only pay to ordinary addresses, like p2pkh and p2sh. You can make a p2sh address that Nina can pay to (figure 10.28).

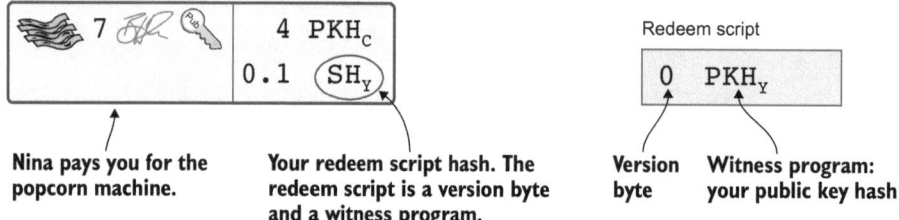

Figure 10.28 Nina sends 0.1 BTC to your segwit wallet using a p2wpkh inside a p2sh address.

Nina pays to 3KsJCgA6…k2G6C1Be, which is an old-style p2sh address that contains the hash of the redeem script 00 bb4d4977…75ff02d1. This redeem script is a version byte 00 followed by a 20-byte witness program. This is the pattern for p2wpkh, which we covered earlier. Nina's wallet knows nothing about this. It sees only a p2sh address and makes a payment to that script hash.

Later, when you want to spend your output, you create a transaction like the one in figure 10.29.

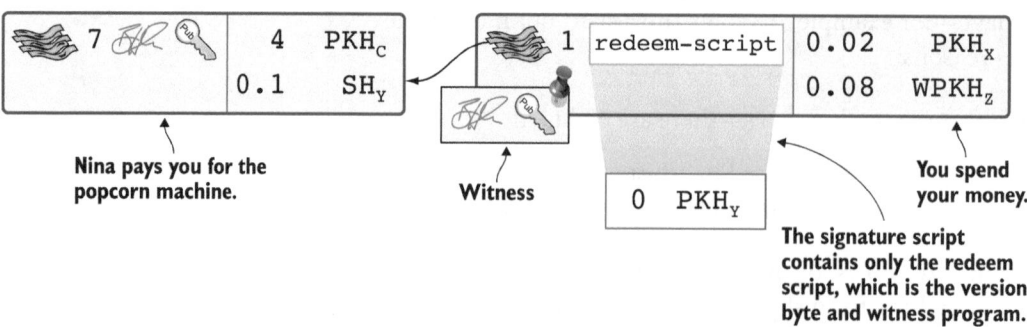

Figure 10.29 You spend the money you got from Nina by setting the version byte and witness program in the redeem script in your input's signature script.

You create a witness, just as you would with a normal p2wpkh input, but you also set the redeem script as a single data item in the signature script. The redeem script happens to be a version byte followed by your 20-byte PKH. Using this signature script, old nodes can verify that the script hash in the spent output matches the hash of the redeem script in the signature script. New nodes will detect that the redeem script is a version byte and a witness program, and verify the witness accordingly.

This way of nesting a segwit payment inside a p2sh payment can also be used for p2wsh payments in a similar fashion: a p2wsh nested in p2sh.

Recap of payment types

We've talked about several types of payments. Figures 10.30–10.35 summarize the most common ones.

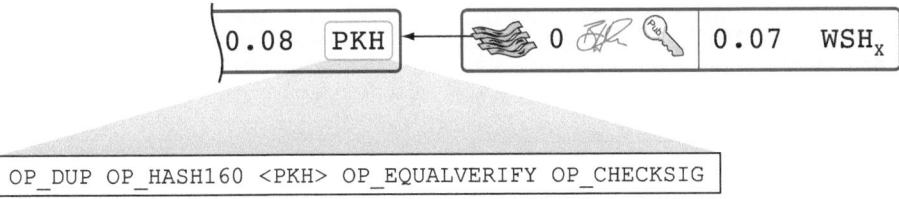

Figure 10.30   p2pkh: address format 1<some base58 characters>

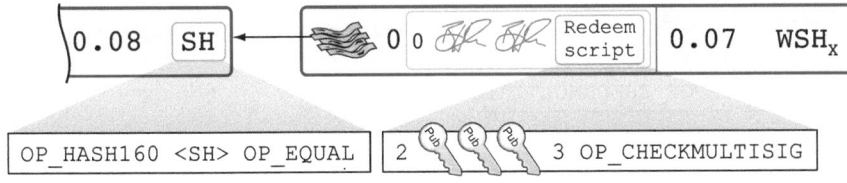

Figure 10.31   p2sh: address format 3<some base58 characters>

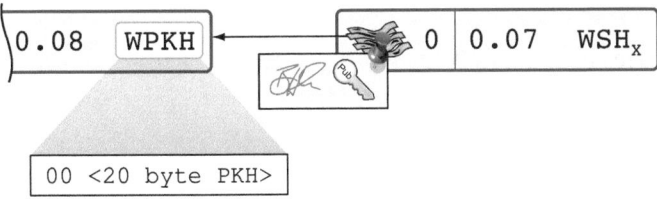

Figure 10.32   p2wpkh: address format bc1q<38 base32 characters>

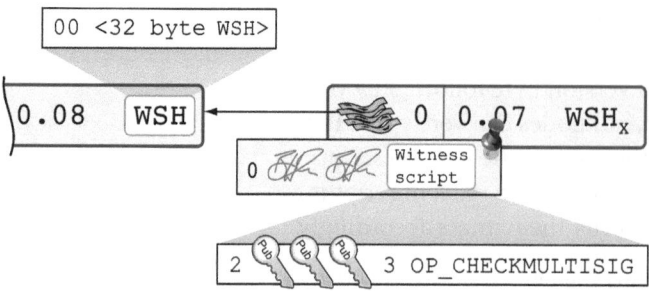

Figure 10.33   p2wsh: address format bc1q<58 base32 characters>

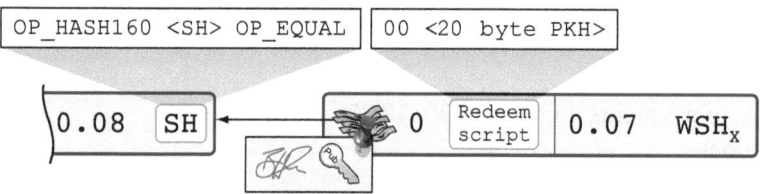

Figure 10.34   p2wpkh nested in p2sh: address format
3<some base58 characters>

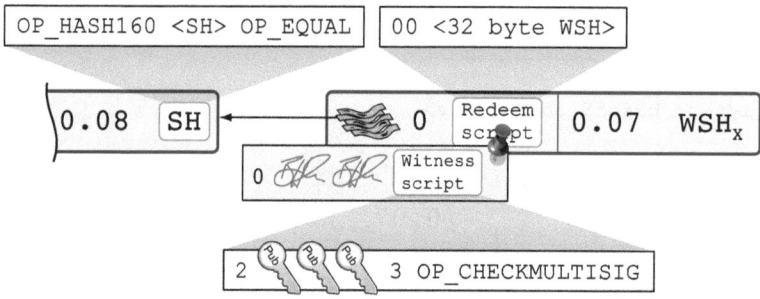

Figure 10.35   p2wsh nested in p2sh: address format 3<some base58 characters>

Block limits

Bitcoin blocks are limited to 1,000,000 bytes in size and 20,000
signature operations.

Block size limit

In 2010, the Bitcoin software was updated with a block size limit of
1,000,000 bytes. It isn't totally clear why this was done, but most people

think the limit was introduced to reduce the impact of certain denial of service (DoS) attacks. DoS attacks aim at stalling or crashing Bitcoin nodes so the network can't function properly.

One way to mess with the network is to create a very large block that takes 10 seconds to download on a good internet connection. This might seem fast enough, but uploading this block to five peers will take 50 seconds. This will cause the block to propagate very slowly across the peer-to-peer network, which will increase the risk of an unintended blockchain split. Unintended splits will resolve with time, as you saw in the section "Drawing lucky numbers" in chapter 7, but Bitcoin's overall security will decrease during such splits.

Another potential problem with big blocks that attackers could exploit is that people with poor internet connections will be left out completely because they can't keep up with the network, or they don't have the required processing power, RAM, or disk storage space needed to run a full node. These people will need to switch to systems with less security, such as lightweight wallets, reducing the security of the whole network.

Regardless of the reason, this limit is in place.

Signature operations limit

The signature operations limit was put in place because signature-verification operations are relatively slow, especially in non-segwit transactions. An attacker could stuff a transaction with a tremendous number of signatures, causing verifying nodes to be busy verifying signatures for a long time. The limit of 20,000 such operations per block was somewhat arbitrarily chosen to prevent such an attack.

Increasing the limits

It will take a *hard fork* to remove or increase these limits. A hard fork is a rule change that causes old nodes and new nodes to disagree on what the strongest valid blockchain is. We'll examine forks and upgrades in chapter 11. For now, suppose new nodes decide that 8,000,000-byte blocks are OK. When a miner publishes a block that's bigger than 1,000,000 bytes, new nodes will accept it, whereas old nodes won't. A permanent blockchain split will occur, and we'll effectively have two different cryptocurrencies.

Segwit offers an opportunity to somewhat increase both these limits without a hard fork.

Increasing the block size limit

The old rule of 1,000,000 bytes remains, so old nodes can continue working as they used to. New nodes will count block size differently, but in a compatible way. Witness bytes will be counted with a "discount" compared to other bytes, such as the block header or transaction outputs. A new measurement, *block weight*, is put in place. A block's maximum weight is 4,000,000 *weight units* (WU; figure 10.36).

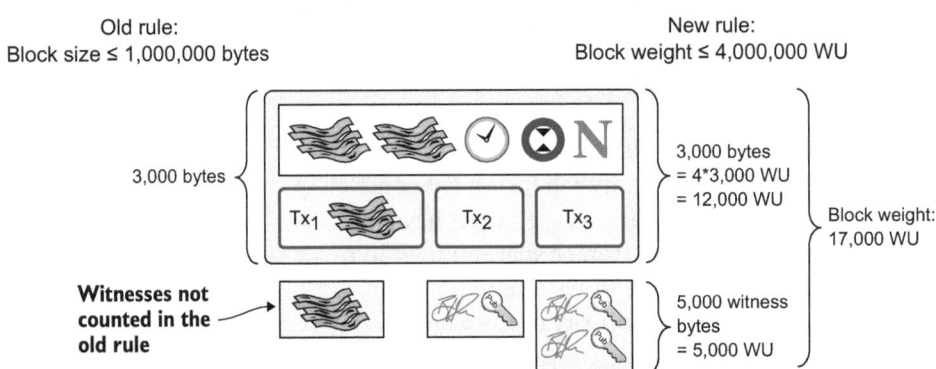

Figure 10.36 Witness bytes and nonwitness bytes are counted differently. Witness bytes contribute less to the block weight and not at all to the traditional block size, the base block size.

Let's call the block excluding the witnesses the *base block*:

- 1 byte of base block data is counted as 4 WU.
- 1 byte of witness data is counted as 1 WU.

The effect is that the old 1,000,000-byte block size limit remains because the new rule and the old rule are effectively the same on the base block. But the more segwit is used, the more data can be moved from the base block to the witnesses, which allows for a bigger total block size.

Suppose the witnesses in a block account for ratio r of the data in a block. The maximum block weight is 4,000,000, and a total block size T gives

$$4(1-r)T + rT \leq 4 * 10^6$$
$$(4 - 3r)T \leq 4 * 10^6$$
$$T \leq \frac{4 * 10^6}{4 - 3r}$$

Inserting various values of *r* into this formula gives different maximum total block sizes, as table 10.2 shows.

Table 10.2   Maximum block sizes for different ratios of witness data

r (witness bytes/total bytes)	Max total block size (bytes)
0	1,000,000
0.1	1,081,081
0.3	1,290,323
0.5	1,600,000
0.6	1,818,182
0.7	2,105,263
0.8	2,500,000

As the relative amount of witness data increases in the block, we can squeeze in more transactions. The effect is an actual maximum block size increase.

The witness discount is implemented for several reasons:

- The signature scripts and witnesses don't go into the UTXO set. Data that goes into the UTXO set has higher costs because the UTXO set should preferably be stored in RAM for fast transaction verification.

- It gives wallet developers, exchanges, and smart contract developers more incentive to make fewer outputs, which reduces the UTXO set's size. For example, an exchange can choose to consolidate its many outputs into a few outputs.

- The witnesses don't have to be sent to a lightweight wallet.

Increasing the signature operations limit

Because we're increasing the block size with segwit, we also need to increase the number of allowed signature operations; allowing more transaction data per block should imply that we also need to allow more signature operations. We can increase the limit in the same manner as we increased the block size limit.

We increase the number of allowed signature operations from 20,000 to 80,000 and count each legacy signature as four operations and each segwit operation as one operation. We count a segwit signature operation less than a legacy operation because the former is more efficient, as discussed in "New hashing method for signatures."

This will have the same effect as the block size increase. If a block contains only legacy inputs, the old limit of 20,000 actual operations remains. If the block contains only segwit inputs, the new limit of 80,000 actual operations is in effect. Any combination of legacy and segwit inputs in a block will result in a limit somewhere between 20,000 and 80,000 actual signature operations.

Recap

This chapter has walked through segregated witness, which solves some problems:

* *Transaction malleability*—A txid might change without changing the effect of its transaction. This can cause broken links between transactions, making the child transaction invalid.

* *Inefficient signature verification*—As the number of inputs doubles in a transaction, the time to verify the transaction increases quadratically. This is because both the transaction's size and the number of signatures to verify doubles.

* *Wasted bandwidth*—Lightweight wallets must download the transactions, including all signatures, to be able to verify the merkle proof, but the signature data is useless to them because they don't have the spent outputs to verify against.

* *Hard to upgrade*—There is limited room for script language upgrades. A handful of `OP_NOP`s are left, and you can't change an `OP_NOP` however you please. If the new operator behavior succeeds, it must behave exactly as an `OP_NOP`.

Solutions

By moving signature data out of the base transaction, that data will no longer be part of the txid.

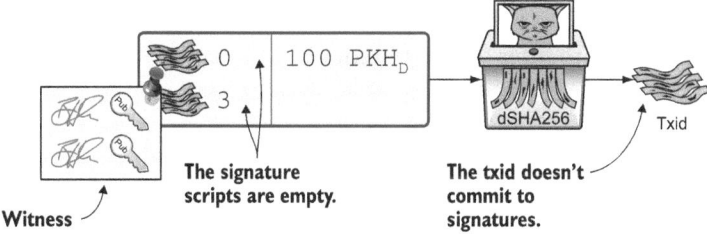

The signature scripts are empty.

The txid doesn't commit to signatures.

Witness

If the signature is malleated, it won't affect the txid. Unconfirmed chains of transactions become unbreakable.

A new signature-hashing algorithm is used that makes the verification time grow *linearly* with the number of inputs. The old signature-hashing algorithm hashes the entire transaction for each signature.

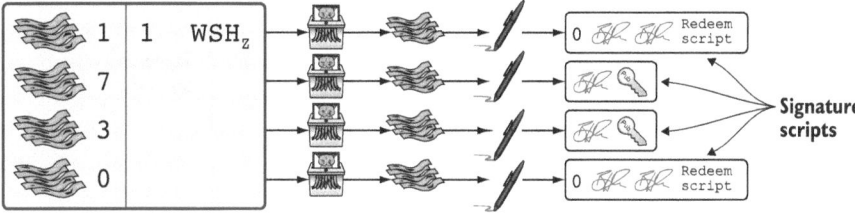

Signature scripts

Signatures in witnesses will hash the transaction only once.

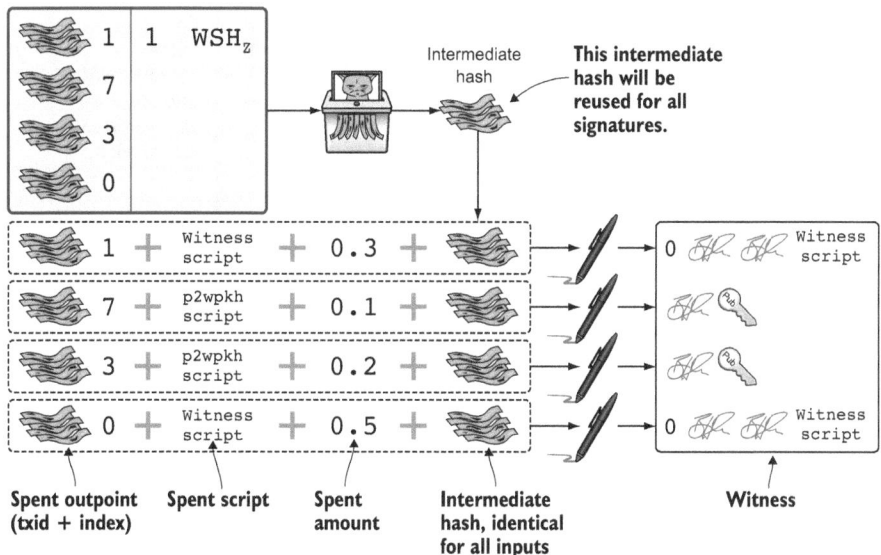

This intermediate hash will be reused for all signatures.

Spent outpoint (txid + index)   **Spent script**   **Spent amount**   **Intermediate hash, identical for all inputs**   **Witness**

The intermediate hash is reused for each signature, which greatly reduces the total amount of hashing.

The bandwidth that lightweight wallets require decreases because they don't have to download the witnesses to verify that a transaction is included in a block. They can use the per-transaction savings to increase their privacy by decreasing their bloom filter size or to reduce data traffic with preserved privacy.

The witness version in the pubkey script allows for future upgrades of the script language. These upgrades can be arbitrarily complex with no restrictions on functionality.

New rules apply for blocks containing segwit transactions. An output in the coinbase transaction must commit to all the block's witnesses.

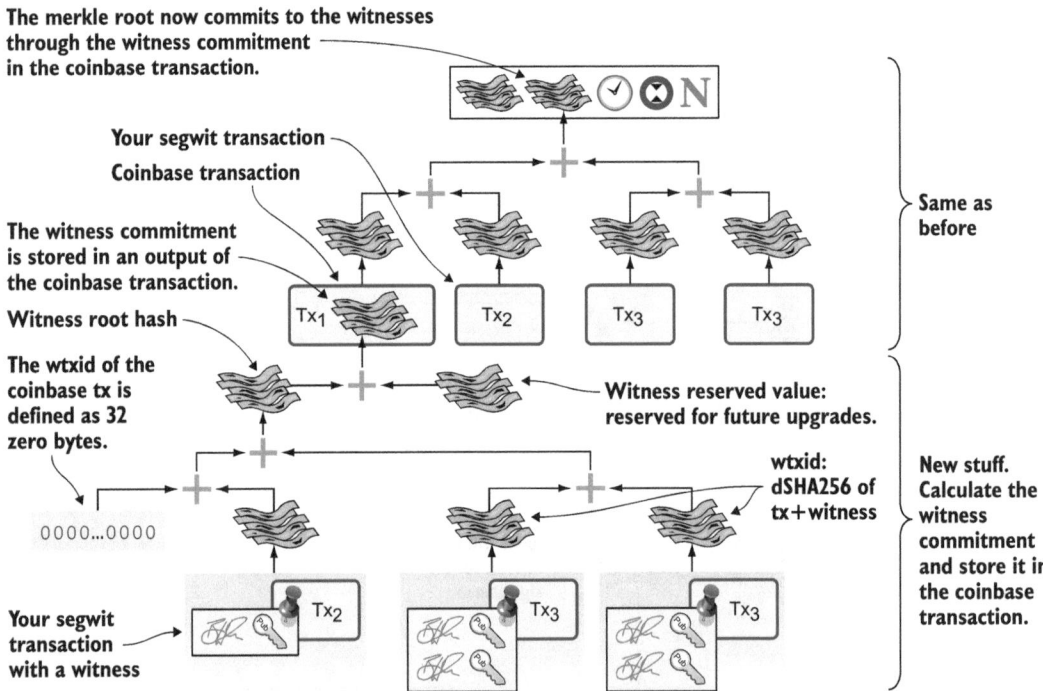

Old nodes will still work because they aren't aware of the commitment in the coinbase transaction. This let us introduce segwit without disrupting, or splitting, the blockchain into two separate cryptocurrencies.

Exercises

Warm up

10.1 What part of the transaction is the cause for transaction malleability?

10.2 Why is transaction malleability a problem?

10.3 Why do we say that legacy transaction verification time increases quadratically with the number of inputs?

10.4 Why do lightweight wallets need the signatures of a legacy transaction to verify that it's included in a block?

10.5 Suppose you want to add a new feature to Bitcoin's Script language, and you want to redefine the behavior of OP_NOP5. What's important to think about when you design the new behavior to avoid a blockchain split (because not all nodes will upgrade simultaneously)?

10.6 Which of the following are segwit addresses? What kind of segwit addresses are they?

    a. `bc1qeqzjk7vume5wmrdgz5xyehh54cchdjag6jdmkj`
    b. `c8052b799cde68ed8da8150c4cdef4ae3176cba8`
    c. `bc1qnqaewluxhx7wzfrf9e5fqjf47hjk9jyzy6l0hpt4kjj3u2wmjp3qr3lft8`
    d. `3KsJCgA6ubxgmmzvZaQYR485tsk2G6C1Be`
    e. `00 bb4d49777d981096a75215ccdba8dc8675ff02d1`

10.7 What's the witness version used for? The witness version is the first number in a segwit output—for example, `00` in

`00 bb4d49777d981096a75215ccdba8dc8675ff02d1`

Dig in

10.8 Explain how a segwit transaction is valid according to an old node that knows nothing about segwit. This is what the old node sees:

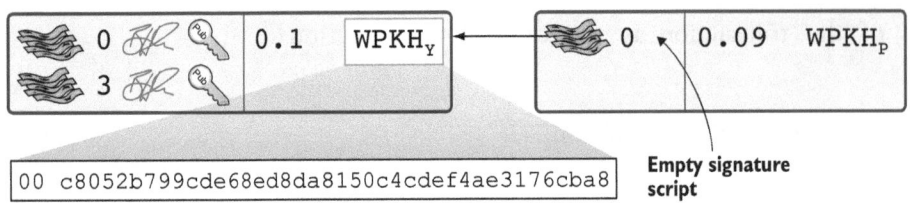

10.9 Explain how a segwit transaction is verified by a new node that knows about segwit. This is what it sees:

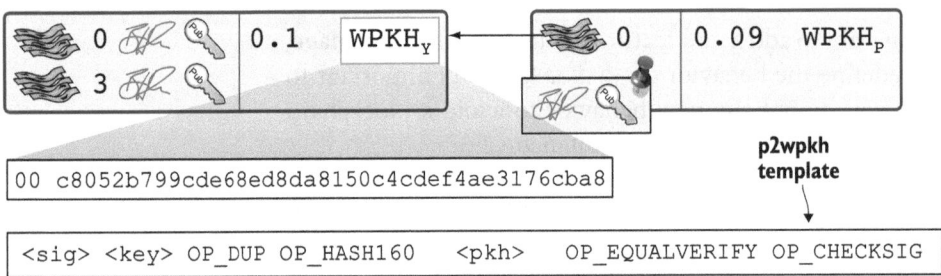

10.10 Suppose you want to upgrade the Bitcoin system. You want the witness commitment to commit to the transaction fees in the block, in addition to the witness root hash, by making a merkle tree of all transaction fees. Suggest how the fee merkle root could be committed to in the block without breaking compatibility with old nodes. You don't have to think about future upgradability after this change, because that's more complex. Use the following figure as a hint:

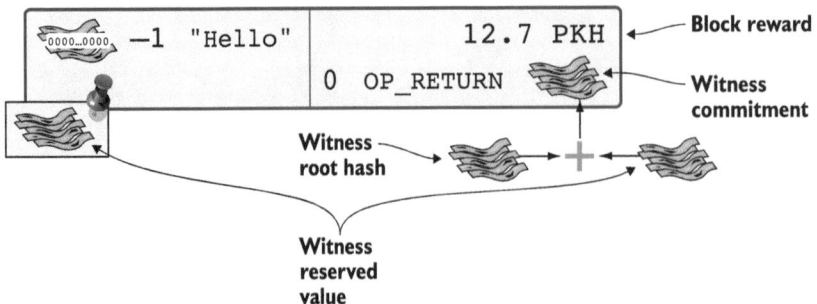

10.11   How would old nodes and new nodes verify blocks that contain the commitment in the previous exercise?

Summary

- Segwit moves signature script data out of transactions to solve transaction malleability issues.

- Segwit uses a new signature-hashing algorithm that makes transaction verification faster. This helps nodes stay up to date with less resources.

- Lightweight wallets get better privacy with preserved data traffic by not downloading witness data.

- The witness version byte of the pubkey script makes upgrading the script language easier.

- We can increase the maximum block size somewhat by counting witness bytes with a discount.

- A new address format helps wallets distinguish between legacy payments and segwit payments.

- Segwit can be "embedded" in old-style p2sh addresses to let old wallets send money to segwit wallets.

This chapter covers

- Understanding hard forks and soft forks

- Upgrading Bitcoin safely

- Understanding that users make the rules

To understand this chapter, you should be comfortable with concepts like the blockchain (chapter 6), proof of work (chapter 7), and the peer-to-peer network (chapter 8). If you had difficulties with those chapters, I suggest you revisit them before continuing with this chapter. Of course, you can also just try to read on anyway.

Bitcoin's consensus rules can change in two ways: via either a soft fork or via a hard fork. These two types of changes are fundamentally different. In "Bitcoin forks," you'll learn about the differences between hard and soft forks and about what happens when different nodes run different consensus rules. You'll need to understand this before learning how to safely upgrade Bitcoin's consensus rules..

Rolling out a consensus rule change over the Bitcoin network can be difficult. Each Bitcoin node is sovereign, and no one dictates what software people should run—users decide for themselves. This makes it hard to roll out, or *deploy*, consensus rule changes without having broad user and miner support. The *deployment mechanisms* have evolved over time, and we'll go through this evolution and explore the current state of deployment mechanisms.

As of this writing, most (noncritical) updates to Bitcoin's consensus rules have been made via *miner-activated soft forks*, in which miners signal support and eventually start enforcing the new rules. But this approach presents some issues—for example, a big miner can veto an upgrade despite broad user adoption. People are looking to solve this with *user-activated soft forks*. This means power is where power belongs: with the people using Bitcoin, the *economic majority*. It's the economic majority that ultimately and collectively decides the consensus rules, and this insight is put into practice with user-activated soft forks.

Bitcoin forks

Open source software is software that you're free to download, use, inspect, change, and redistribute as you please. A lot of the software you use on a daily basis is probably open source. Maybe you use the Google Chrome web browser or an Android mobile phone. These are examples of software built on open source projects.

Open source projects can be *forked*. If you make a copy of the source code for Linux, make some changes to it, and distribute your new version of the Linux source code, you have created a *fork* of the project.

Bitcoin is an open source project that can be forked just like any other open source project, such as Linux. But in this book, *fork* will mean something different.

In the Bitcoin context, the term *fork* means a change in the consensus rules. The consensus rules define what a valid blockchain is. When some set of nodes uses the same consensus rules, consensus emerges among them about what the current unspent transaction output (UTXO) set—"who owns what"—is. In short, a fork changes the definition of a valid blockchain.

> **Differing definitions**
>
> People define the term *fork* in different ways. In this book, I use the definition that I find best, which is "a change in the consensus rules."

For example, the rule that limits the block weight to 4,000,000 WU is a consensus rule. Changing that limit would be a fork. But a relay policy that prevents transactions with tiny fees from being relayed isn't part of the consensus rules. Changing that policy isn't a fork.

You can change the consensus rules in Bitcoin Core, in a copied version of Bitcoin Core, or in any alternative Bitcoin full-node software program. If someone runs your modified program, that person is running a fork.

We generally categorize forks in Bitcoin as follows (figure 11.1):

- *Hard forks*—A hard fork relaxes the consensus rules. Some blocks that are considered invalid by nodes running the old version of the software program will be considered valid by nodes running the new version. Doubling the maximum allowed block weight would be a hard fork.

- *Soft forks*—A soft fork tightens the consensus rules. All blocks that nodes running the new version of the program consider valid will also be considered valid by those running the old version. But some blocks considered valid by nodes running the old version will be considered invalid by those running the new version. Reducing the maximum allowed block weight would be a soft fork.

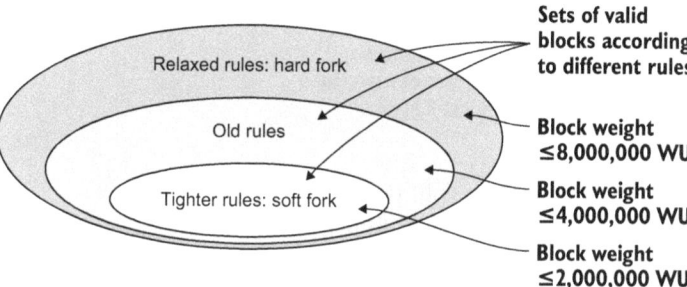

Figure 11.1 Soft forks tighten the consensus rules, whereas hard forks widen them—for example, decreasing the maximum block weight or increasing it, respectively.

Changes that don't change the consensus rules, such as modifying the color of the graphical user interface or adding a new feature to the peer-to-peer networking protocol, aren't Bitcoin forks. But they could be considered forks of a software project in the traditional sense. From now on, I'll use the term *fork* only to mean a change of consensus rules.

As an analogy for soft and hard forks, imagine a popular vegetarian restaurant where lots of vegetarians go to eat. This restaurant has only one dish on its menu. Think of the restaurant as a miner,

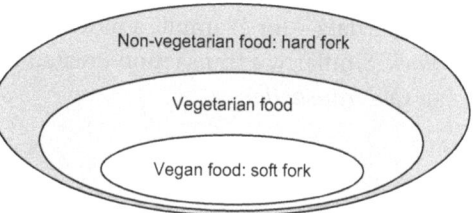

the guests as full nodes, and the meals served as blocks. The restaurant produces meals that guests eat—the miner produces blocks that full nodes accept.

Imagine that the restaurant changes its dish, as table 11.1 shows.

Table 11.1 The restaurant can make a hard fork by adding meat to its dish or a soft fork by restricting the food to vegan.

Vegetarian restaurant serves ...	Will guests accept it?	Fork type	Why
Vegetarian food	Yes	None	Vegetarians eat vegetarian food.
Nonvegetarian food	No	Hard fork	The rules are *relaxed*. Vegetarians can't eat here any more.
Vegan food	Yes	Soft fork	The rules are *tightened*. Vegetarian rules still apply.

If you create a fork, soft or hard, you risk having a chain split if anyone runs your forked computer program. Some nodes will follow the strongest chain that's valid according to the old rules, and some nodes—those running your software—will follow the strongest chain that's valid according to your new rules. The result might be a split in the blockchain.

We'll work through a few examples to illustrate what happens in different scenarios. We'll start with the simplest case: a change that doesn't affect the consensus rules. The name *Bitcoin Old* will refer to the previous version of the program, and *Bitcoin New* will refer to the changed version of the program. A node running Bitcoin Old is called an *Old node*, and a *New node* is a node running Bitcoin New. We'll denote data—for example, a block—created by a New node as *a New block*. Similarly, a transaction created by an Old node will be denoted as an *Old transaction*.

Nonconsensus rule changes

Suppose you want to add a new "feature" to Bitcoin Core's networking code. You want to add a new network message type called `kill` that one Bitcoin node can send to another Bitcoin node. This message's recipient node will immediately shut itself down. Only New nodes will know how to deal with an incoming `kill` message. Old nodes will ignore the—for them—unknown message (figure 11.2).

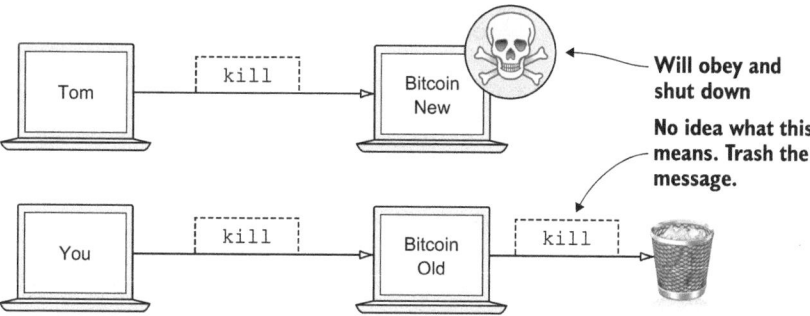

Figure 11.2 **Your new message will be accepted by New nodes and ignored by Old nodes.**

Most people consider your change a huge security risk. They don't want their nodes shut down by a random stranger on the internet. You'll have a hard time convincing them to use Bitcoin New. You can't force this software on anyone; people will have to actively want it and install it for Bitcoin New to get network-wide adoption.

Stupid changes like the `kill` message won't make it in the world of open source.

Making something useful instead

Suppose you invent something useful instead: *compact blocks.* Compact blocks let a peer send a block to another peer, but without sending the full block. Instead, this technique uses the fact that the recipient node has already received most of the transactions in the block. Remember that a transaction first travels the network during transaction propagation, then travels the network again during block propagation once the transaction is confirmed.

When Rashid sends a block to Qi (figure 11.3), wouldn't it be great if the block didn't have to contain the transactions Qi already has? Bandwidth requirements would drop dramatically.

BIP152

This was implemented in Bitcoin Core in 2016 and greatly improved the block-propagation time in the Bitcoin network. BIP152, "Compact Block Relay," describes this in detail. I describe only a simplified version here.

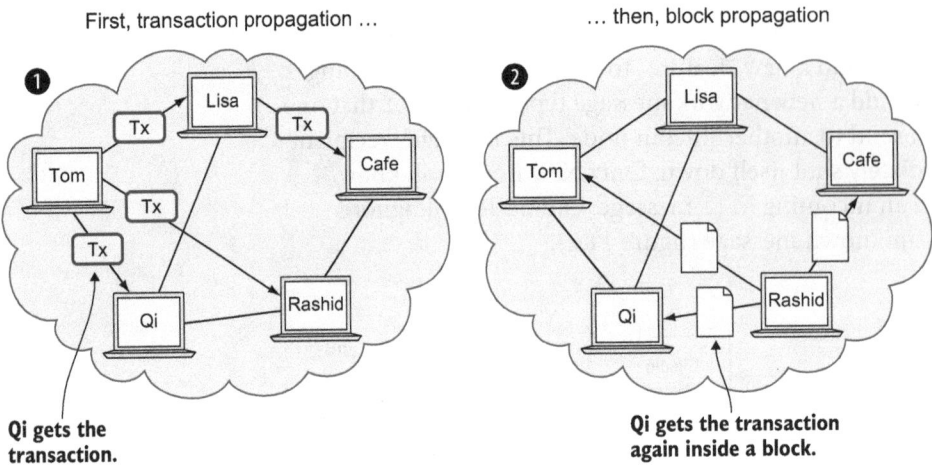

First, transaction propagation ...   ... then, block propagation

Qi gets the transaction.

Qi gets the transaction again inside a block.

Figure 11.3   Qi gets a transaction twice: first during transaction propagation, and then during block propagation.

Rashid can instead send just the block header and a list of txids (figure 11.4). Qi can then reconstruct the block from the transactions she already has in memory and the message from Rashid. In case Qi doesn't have one of the transactions, she'll request them from Rashid.

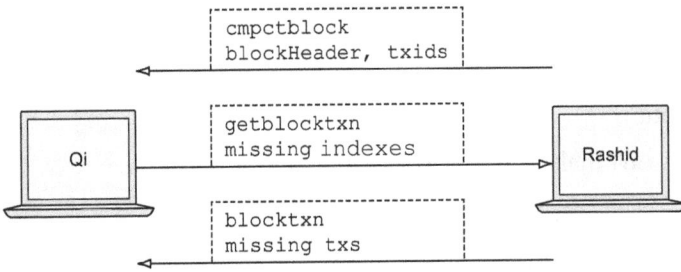

Figure 11.4   Compact blocks in action. Rashid sends just the necessary data to Qi.

The protocol starts with Rashid sending Qi a `cmpctblock` message. Qi will use this message to re-create the block using the transactions she already has in memory. If she succeeds, she's done and can start verifying the block. If she's missing some transactions, she'll request them from Rashid using a `getblocktxn` message containing a list of those transactions' indexes. Rashid will then reply with a `blocktxn` message containing the missing transactions.

Note that this is a simplified version of how it actually works. The main differences are as follows:

- The `cmpctblock` message can also include some complete transactions—for example, the block's coinbase transaction.

- Compact blocks can work in two different modes:

  - In high-bandwidth mode, `cmpctblock` messages are sent unsolicited instead of first using an `inv` or `headers`.

  - In low-bandwidth mode, the `cmpctblock` is sent only on request after an `inv` or `headers` has been received.

- The list of txids sent in the `cmpctblock` messages aren't full txids, but shortened versions to save data traffic. They're still long enough to almost always uniquely identify the actual transactions used.

This is a really useful change that many people find valuable. You release your software, and people start using it. Not everybody has to upgrade to this version. If only one of your peers uses it, you'll benefit by running it yourself because the bandwidth requirements between you and that one peer will decrease. As more and more nodes start adopting compact blocks, your total bandwidth requirement will drop even more.

You haven't made any changes to the consensus rules. Blocks are verified using your software exactly as before. Old nodes will accept New blocks and vice versa.

Hard forks

As described in "Bitcoin forks," a hard fork is a software change that relaxes the consensus rules. New blocks, created by New nodes, might be rejected by Old nodes. In the example with the vegetarian restaurant, a hard fork would be when the vegetarian restaurant starts to serve meat.

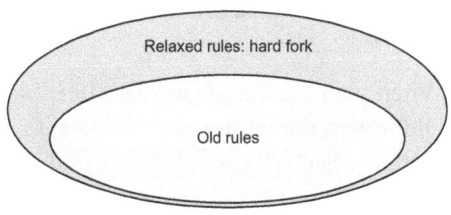

Suppose you create a fork that changes the maximum allowed block weight—discussed in "Increasing the block size limit" in chapter 10—from 4,000,000 WU to 8,000,000 WU. This would allow for more transactions to be stuffed into each block. On the other hand, a higher limit could negatively affect some nodes in the Bitcoin network, as we talked about in chapter 10.

Anyhow, you make this change and start using it in the Bitcoin network. When your node receives a block from a Bitcoin Old node, you'll accept it because the block is definitely ≤ 8,000,000 WU; the Old node won't create or relay blocks larger than 4,000,000 WU.

Suppose you're a miner running Bitcoin New. You're lucky enough to find a valid proof of work, and you publish your block. This block will definitely be ≤ 8,000,000 WU, but it might or might not be ≤ 4,000,000 WU. If it is ≤ 4,000,000 WU, it will be accepted by Old nodes. But if not, Old nodes will reject your block. Your blockchain will diverge from the Bitcoin Old blockchain. You've caused a blockchain split (figure 11.5).

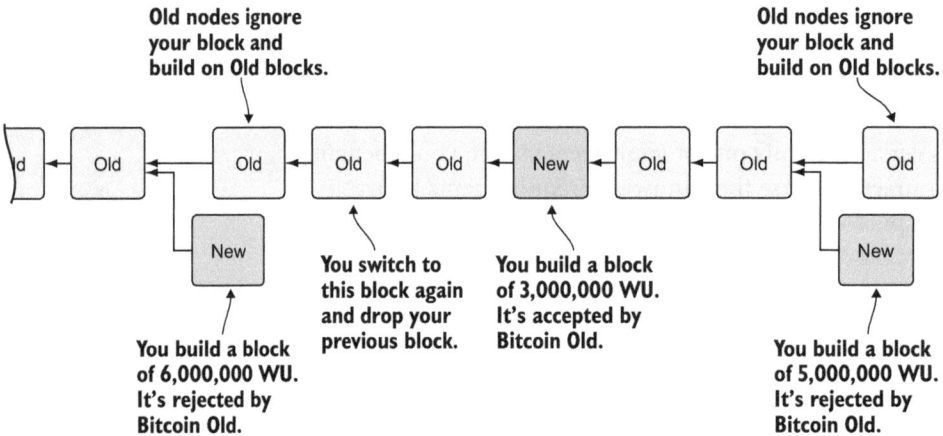

Figure 11.5 Your node running Bitcoin New is a loser against the Bitcoin Old nodes. Bitcoin Old will discard all of your blocks that violate the ≤ 4,000,000 WU rule.

When your New node mines a new block, it might get rejected by the Old nodes, depending on whether it's ≤ 4,000,000 WU. For the blocks that are rejected, you'll have wasted a lot of electricity and time mining blocks that don't make it into the main chain.

But suppose a majority of the hashrate likes your Bitcoin New program and starts using it instead of Bitcoin Old. What happens then? Let's see how it plays out (figure 11.6).

When a New node mines a big block, all New nodes will try to extend that block, but all Old nodes will keep on trying to extend the latest— valid, according to Old rules—block.

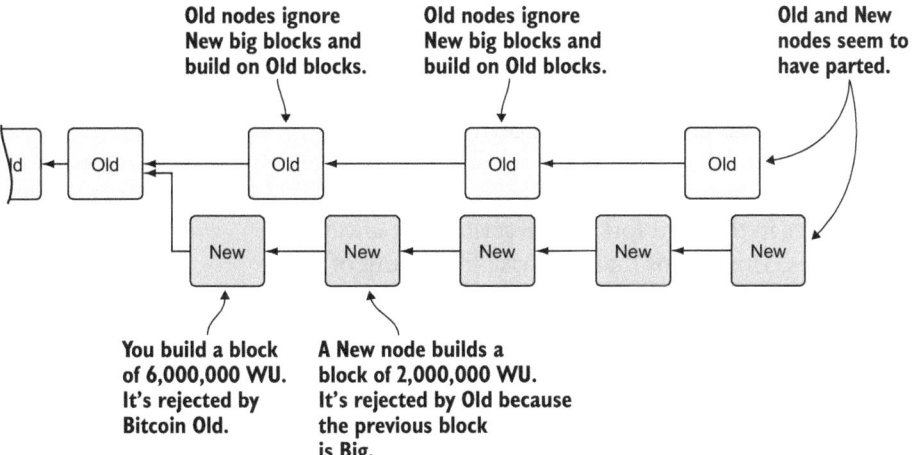

Figure 11.6 A majority of the hashrate runs Bitcoin New. It seems to have caused a permanent chain split.

New nodes win more blocks over time than Old nodes because they collectively have more hashrate than Old nodes. It seems like the New nodes' branch will stay intact because it gets a reassuring lead in accumulated proof of work.

New nodes have apparently created a lasting chain split. But if some miners decide to go back to running Bitcoin Old, or if additional miners enter the race using Old nodes so that Old gets a majority of the hashrate again, the New chain might face problems, as figure 11.7 shows.

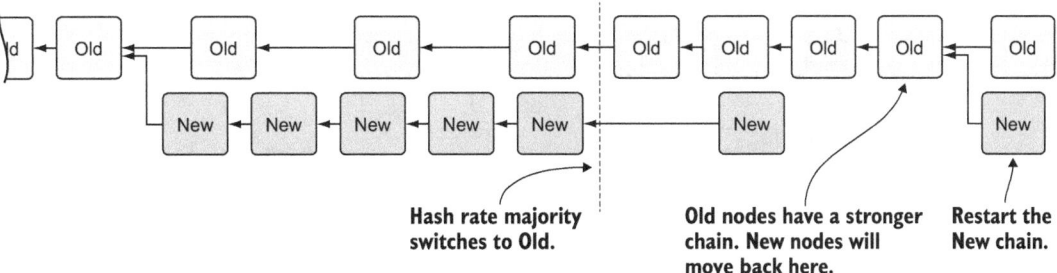

Figure 11.7 The Bitcoin New chain is wiped out because the Bitcoin Old chain becomes stronger.

When Old nodes have a hashrate majority, they will outperform the New nodes and eventually catch up with the New nodes and surpass them. New nodes acknowledge this fact by switching back to mining on the Old chain. We say that the branch created by the New nodes was wiped out by a chain reorganization, commonly known as a *reorg*.

Wipeout protection

Blocks created by Old nodes in the hard fork just described are always compatible with New nodes. This means there is a risk for a reorg of the New chain.

This isn't the case with all hard forks. Suppose, for example, that you want to change the proof of work hash function from double SHA256 to single SHA256. Your New blocks will always be rejected by Old nodes; and, conversely, Old blocks will always be rejected by New nodes. A change like this is therefore guaranteed to avoid a reorg by the Old branch. It's wipeout-protected by nature—but many changes aren't.

An example of a change that isn't wipeout-protected by nature is an alternative cryptocurrency called *Bitcoin Cash*. It was created through a hard fork of Bitcoin Core at block height 478559 on 1 August 2017. The main thing Bitcoin Cash did was increase the maximum base block size and remove segwit from the code. This made the Old chain compatible with New nodes and vulnerable to wipeout. To protect against Bitcoin New being wiped out in a reorg, Bitcoin Cash added *wipeout protection* by requiring the first block of the split to be bigger than 1,000,000 bytes (1 MB). See figure 11.8.

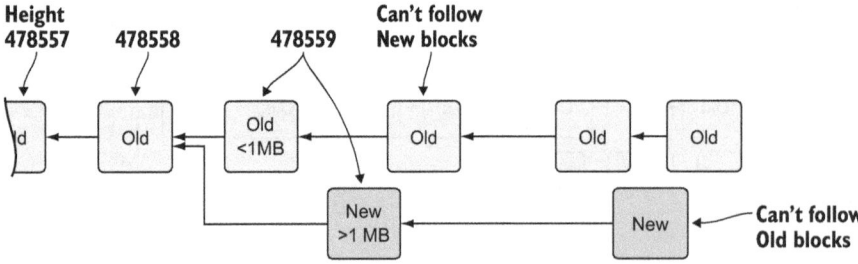

Figure 11.8   Bitcoin Cash protects against wipeout by requiring the first block after the chain split to be >1 MB.

The result is that Bitcoin New nodes *cannot* move back to the Bitcoin Old branch because that branch has a block less than or equal to 1 MB at height 478559.

Soft forks

We've discussed soft forks several times throughout this book. A soft fork is a change in the consensus rules in which New blocks are accepted by Old nodes. The consensus rules are tightened. In the case with the vegetarian restaurant, a soft fork would be when the restaurant changes its food to vegan.

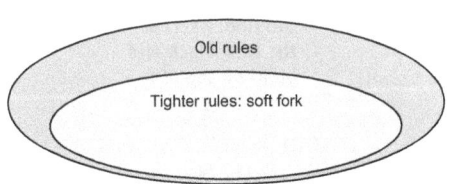

Segwit is an example of a soft fork. The change was carefully designed so that Old nodes won't fail in verifying blocks that contain segwit transactions. All Old nodes will accept any valid New blocks and incorporate them into the blockchain.

On the other hand, an Old node *could* create a block that isn't valid according to Bitcoin New. For example, a non-segwit miner could include in its block a transaction that spends a segwit output as if it were an anyone-can-spend output (figure 11.9).

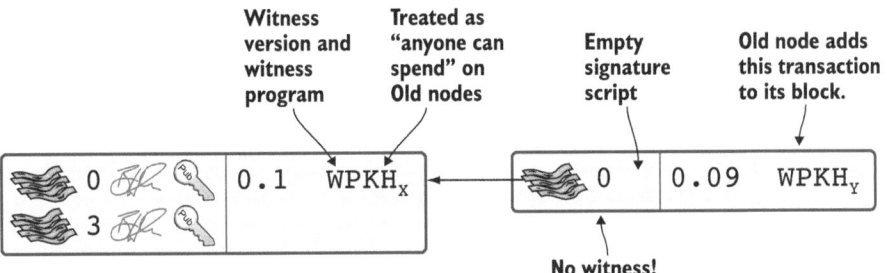

Figure 11.9   An Old miner regards a segwit output as anyone-can-spend and adds to the block a transaction that spends it as such.

Suppose there is only a single miner with a small hashrate running Bitcoin New. Also assume that the Old miners produce a block that's invalid according to New nodes, as in the earlier example with the non-segwit transaction. The result would be that the Old nodes build a block that's not accepted by the New miner. The New miner would reject the invalid Old block. This is the point where the blockchain splits in two (figure 11.10).

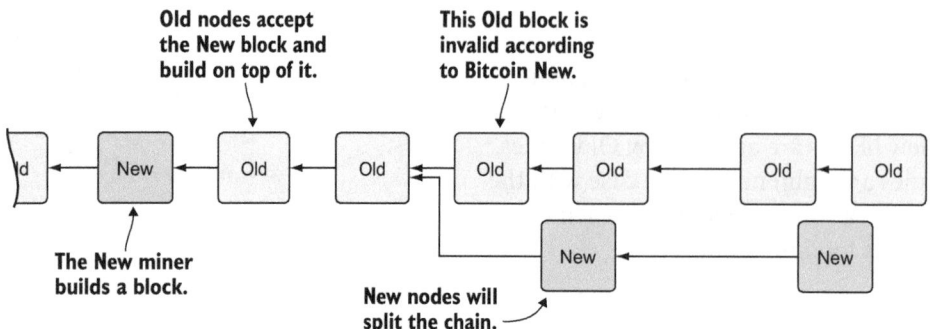

Figure 11.10   The soft fork might cause a chain split if the Bitcoin Old nodes produce a block that Bitcoin New miners don't accept.

In this situation, the Old chain is at risk of being wiped out by a reorg. Suppose more miners decide to upgrade to Bitcoin New, causing a hashrate majority to support the New blockchain. After a while, we'll probably see a reorg (figure 11.11).

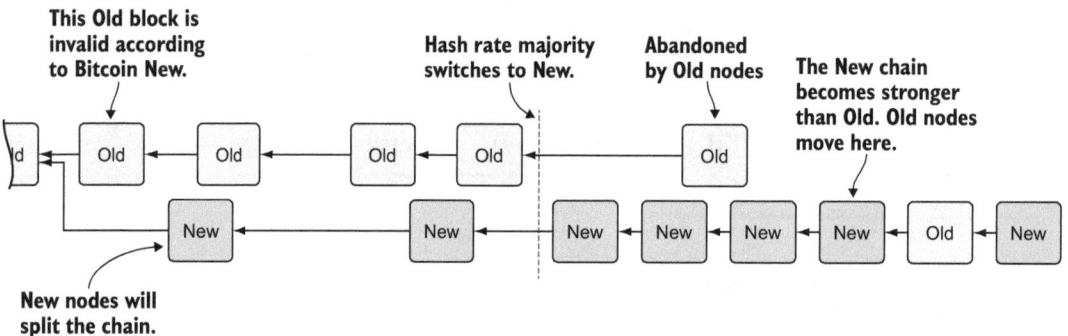

Figure 11.11   As people adopt Bitcoin New, the branch will cause a reorg for Old nodes.

The Bitcoin New branch will become the stronger branch, so the remaining Old miners will abandon their branch and start working on the same branch as the New nodes. But as soon as an Old node creates a block that's invalid on New nodes, it will lose out on the block reward because it won't be accepted on the New branch.

Differences between hard and soft forks

Let's look again at what differentiates soft forks from hard forks, as a general rule:

- A hard fork *relaxes* the rules. Increasing the maximum block weight is a hard fork.

- A soft fork *tightens* the rules. Segwit is a soft fork.

This is a simple, yet true, distinction. We can summarize the effects of a chain split caused by a hard fork versus a soft fork as follows:

- *Hard fork*—The New branch might get wiped out in a reorg. Use wipeout protection to avoid this. The Old branch can't be wiped out.

- *Soft fork*—The Old branch might get wiped out in a reorg. You can't protect the Old branch from a wipeout because that would make this fork a hard fork. Remember that the definition of a soft fork is that Old nodes accept New blocks.

Transaction replay

Regardless of what causes a chain split, its effects are the same. Users end up with two versions of their UTXO: one spendable on the Old chain, and one spendable on the New chain. We effectively have two cryptocurrencies, Bitcoin Old and Bitcoin New (figure 11.12).

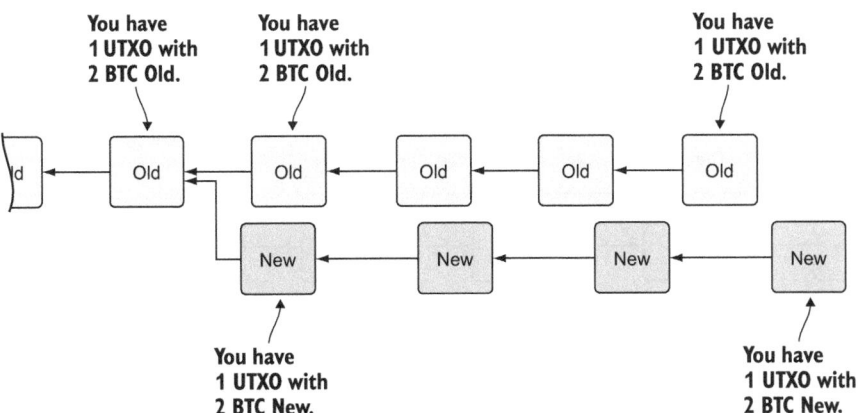

Figure 11.12   After a chain split, you effectively have two versions of your UTXOs.

Suppose the chain split in figure 11.12 has occurred, and you want to pay for a book at an online bookstore. You want to do this using Bitcoin Old because that's what the bookstore wants.

You create your transaction and broadcast it. The Old nodes in the network will accept your transaction because you spend a UTXO that exists on those nodes. But your transaction is *also valid on New nodes* because those nodes have the same UTXOs as well (figure 11.13).

Value swings

If a chain split occurs, it might have a severe impact on the value of the bitcoins on the Old branch. The value per coin on the New branch might or might not be known; it depends on whether those coins are widely traded yet.

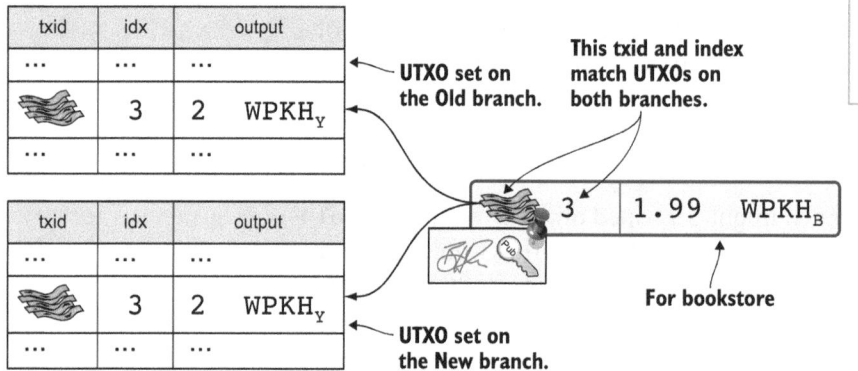

Figure 11.13 Your transaction to the bookstore is valid on both the Bitcoin Old and the Bitcoin New branches.

If your transaction propagates to both a New miner and an Old miner, it will probably end up in both branches of the blockchain. This isn't what you intended. Your transactions have been *replayed* on the Bitcoin New branch (figure 11.14).

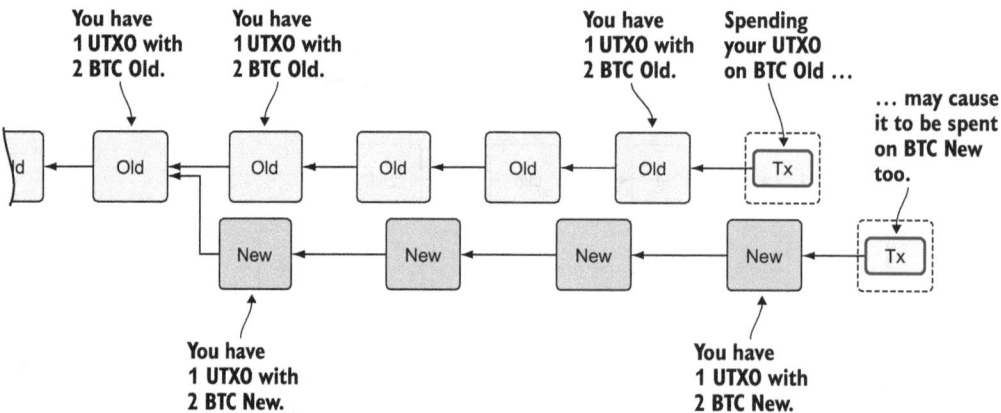

Figure 11.14 Transaction replay causes you to pay in both currencies.

Replay protection

To protect users against replay during a chain split due to a hard fork, the transaction format on the New chain can be changed in such a way that the transaction is valid on at most one branch.

When Bitcoin Cash did its chain split, it made sure Old transactions weren't valid on New nodes and New transactions weren't valid on Old nodes (figure 11.15).

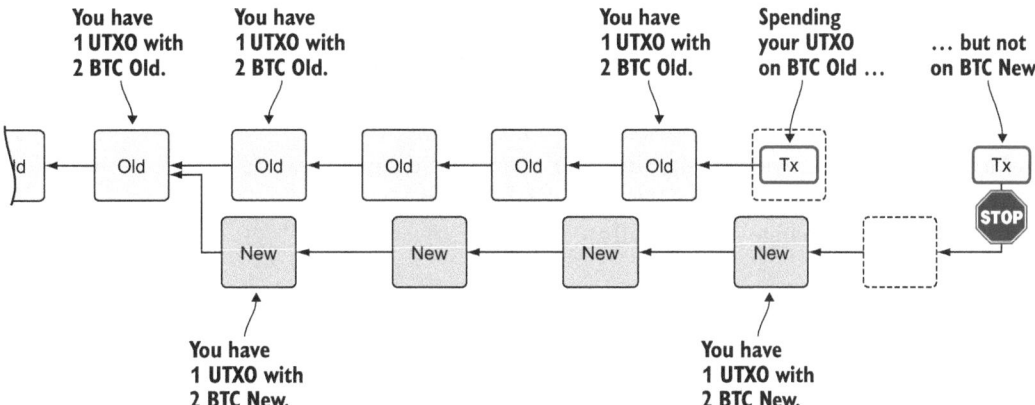

Figure 11.15 With replay protection, a transaction is valid on only one of the branches.

To achieve this, a transaction on the New branch must use a new SIGHASH type, FORKID, in transaction signatures. This type doesn't do anything, but using it makes the transaction invalid on the Old chain and valid on the New chain. If a transaction doesn't use FORKID, the transaction is valid on the Old chain and invalid on the New chain.

Using a new SIGHASH type for signatures is, of course, not the only way to achieve replay protection. Any change that makes transactions valid on at most one chain will do. You can, for example, require that New transactions subtract 1 from the input txid. Suppose the UTXO you want to spend has this txid:

```
6bde18fff1a6d465de1e88b3e84edfe8db7daa1b1f7b8443965f389d8decac08
```

If you want to spend the UTXO on the Old chain, you use this hash in the input of your transaction. If you want to spend the UTXO on the New chain, you use this instead:

```
6bde18fff1a6d465de1e88b3e84edfe8db7daa1b1f7b8443965f389d8decac07
```

Note that this is just a silly example, not a full-fledged proposal.

Upgrade mechanisms

All non-urgent upgrades of Bitcoin so far have been made using soft forks. Doing a soft fork safely is a hard problem, and the mechanisms used to do them have evolved over time.

The main worry when doing a soft fork is that the blockchain will split in two and stay that way over a significant time period. If this happened, we would effectively have two cryptocurrencies.

This would cause confusion: Exchanges would need to decide which branch they considered to be "Bitcoin" and which branches to support for their exchange service. Users would need to be made aware that a split had happened so they could avoid sending money on the wrong branch. Merchants would have to make sure they charged the currency or currencies they intended to. A blockchain split might also cause the cryptocurrency value to change dramatically.

Using coinbase signaling—BIP16

When p2sh was introduced in 2012, the Bitcoin community had no experience in upgrading. It had to come up with a way to avoid a blockchain split. The community implemented soft-fork *signaling* using the coinbase. New miners signaled support for p2sh by putting the string /P2SH/ into the coinbase of the blocks they produced (figure 11.16).

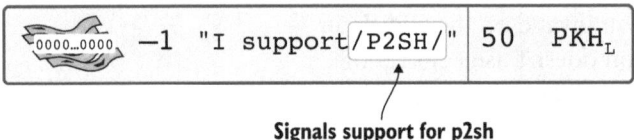

Signals support for p2sh

Figure 11.16   A miner signals support for p2sh by writing /P2SH/ **in the coinbase's signature script.**

On a specific day, the Bitcoin developers checked if at least 550 of the last 1,000 blocks contained /P2SH/. They did, so the developers made a new software release that would start enforcing the p2sh rules on 1 April 2012, a flag day.

This worked out well; miners quickly adopted the soft fork, and the entire network upgraded within a reasonable time. No split occurred because at least 50% of the hashrate had upgraded prior to the flag day.

User-activated soft fork

A deployment method in which users, not just miners, start enforcing rules has become known as a *user-activated soft fork*. We'll talk about this later in this chapter.

Using incremented block version number signaling—BIP34, 66, and 65

I haven't talked about it much before, but the block header comes with a version (figure 11.17). This version is encoded in the first 4 bytes before the previous block hash.

Version is 1

Figure 11.17   The block header contains a block version. The first blocks used version 1.

The version is the only thing missing from our previous block headers. This is the actual 80-byte Bitcoin block header:

```
4 bytes version
32 bytes previous block id
32 bytes merkle root
4 bytes timestamp
4 bytes target
4 bytes nonce

Total 80 bytes
```

The block version can be used to signal support for certain new features.

The first soft fork deployment using block-version signaling was done in 2013. This soft fork added a rule that all new blocks must contain the block's height in their coinbase transaction (figure 11.18).

The *activation* of the soft fork was performed in steps using block-version signaling to avoid a blockchain split:

1. New miners increase the block version from 1 to 2 (figure 11.19). Note that this happens gradually as more and more nodes switch to Bitcoin New over time.

BIP34

This BIP, "Block v2, Height in coinbase," describes both how to store the height in the coinbase and how to deploy the change using version numbers.

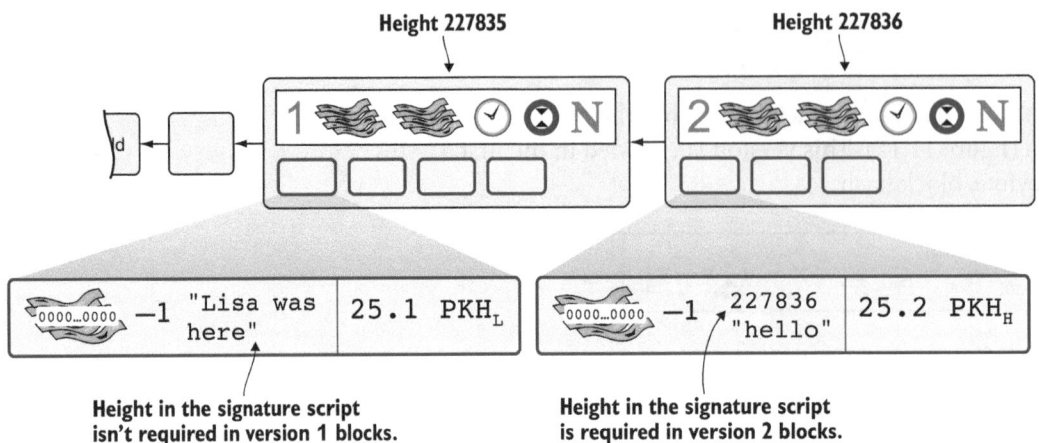

Height 227835

Height 227836

Height in the signature script
isn't required in version 1 blocks.

Height in the signature script
is required in version 2 blocks.

Figure 11.18   BIP34 requires that all blocks contain the block height in the coinbase.

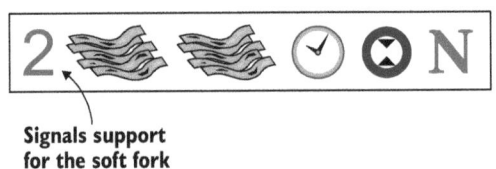

Signals support
for the soft fork

Figure 11.19   Miners that run the soft fork signal support for it
by increasing their block version.

2. Wait until 750 of the last 1,000 blocks have a version of at least 2.
   When this threshold is reached, the New miners probably have
   about 75% of the hashrate.

3. Start rejecting newly produced version 2 blocks that don't contain
   the height in the coinbase. These blocks are falsely signaling
   for BIP34.

4. Wait until 950 of the last 1,000 blocks have version ≥2. When this
   happens, the New miners have about 95% of the hashrate.

5. Start rejecting all new blocks with version 1. All miners producing
   version 1 blocks will be losers because 95% of the hashrate rejects
   those blocks. The hope is that miners that still haven't upgraded
   will do so quickly to avoid losing too much money on mining
   worthless blocks.

During step 1, nothing has changed. Only Bitcoin Old rules are in effect. But when 750 of the last 1,000 blocks have version 2, we enter the next step. Here, nodes running the soft fork start ensuring that every new block of version 2 has the height in the coinbase. If not, the block is dropped. One reason is that nodes might be deliberately or accidentally using block version 2 for other purposes than this soft fork. The 75% rule removes false positives before evaluating the 95% rule.

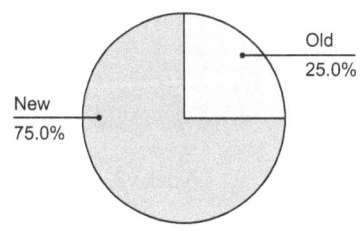

From this point, some Old miner *could* cause a chain split by creating a block of version 2 that violates the "height in coinbase" rule (figure 11.20).

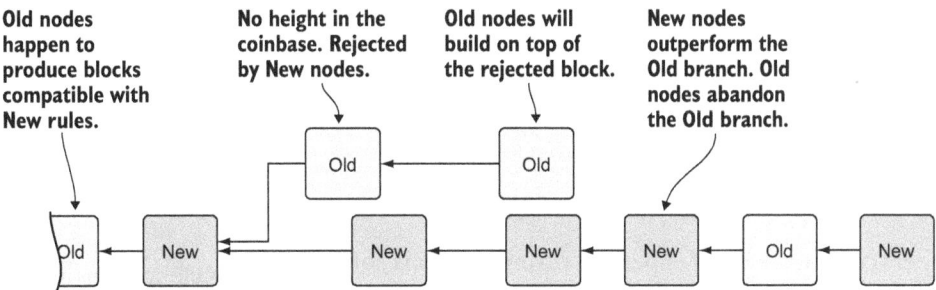

Figure 11.20 The Old nodes could cause a chain split, but it probably won't last for long.

The Old miners would build on top of that block, whereas the New miners would build on top of the previous block. But the New miners *probably*—depending on the amount of "false" version 2 signaling—have more hashrate and will outperform the Old miners and wipe out the Bitcoin Old branch.

When a greater portion of the blocks—95% of the last 1,000—signals support with version 2 blocks, we enter the last step, step 5. From this point forward, all blocks with versions < 2 will be dropped.

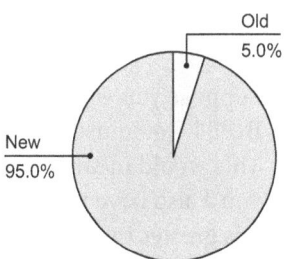

Why did we go through these stages? It isn't entirely clear why the 75% rule was used, but it does remove false positives, as described. The deployment might have worked fine with the 95% rule only. We won't explore the rationale behind the 75% rule—just accept that it was used for this deployment and a few others. Table 11.2 lists soft forks that were introduced using this mechanism.

Table 11.2   Features deployed an using incremented block version

BIP	Name	Date	Block version
BIP34	Block v2, Height in Coinbase	March 2013	2
BIP66	Strict DER Encoding	July 2015	3
BIP65	OP_CHECKLOCKTIMEVERIFY	December 2015	4

The upgrade mechanism just described is called a *miner-activated* soft fork. The miners start enforcing the new rules, and all or most full nodes will follow because the New blocks are accepted by both Old and New full nodes.

Using block version bits signaling—BIP9

Bitcoin's developers collected a lot of experience from previous soft forks. A few problems needed to be addressed:

- You can only deploy one soft fork at a time.

- Used block versions can't be reused for new purposes.

The most annoying problem is that you can't roll out multiple soft forks at once. This is because previous deployment mechanisms, such as the one used for BIP34, checked whether a block version was greater than or equal to a certain number, for example, 2.

Suppose you wanted to deploy both BIP34 and BIP66 simultaneously. BIP34 would use block version 2, and BIP66 would use block version 3. This would mean you couldn't selectively signal support for only BIP66; you'd also have to signal support for BIP34 because your block's version 3 is greater than or equal to 2.

The developers came up with a bitcoin improvement proposal, BIP9, that describes a process for how to deploy several soft forks simultaneously.

This process also uses the block version, but in a different way. The developers decided to change the way block version bytes are

> **BIP9**
>
> This BIP specifies a standard for how to use the block header's version field to perform multiple simultaneous deployments.

interpreted. Block versions that have the top 3 bits set to exactly `001` are treated differently.

First, all such block versions are greater than 4 because the smallest such block version is `20000000`, which is a lot bigger than `00000004`. So, blocks using BIP9 will always support the already-deployed BIP34, 66, and 65. Good.

Next, the 29 bits to the right of the leftmost `001` bits can be used to signal support for at most 29 simultaneous soft forks. Each of the 29 rightmost version bits can be used to independently deploy a single feature or group of features (figure 11.21). If a bit is set to `1`, then the miner that produced the block supports the feature represented by that bit number.

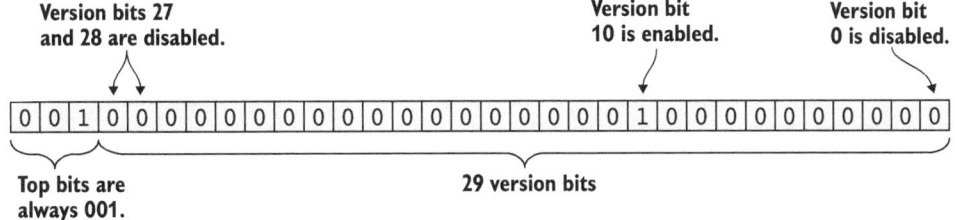

Figure 11.21 The block version is treated differently. Each of the right 29 bits can signal for different proposals.

Several parameters need to be defined for each deployable feature:

- *Name*—A short but descriptive name for the feature
- *Bit*—The number of the bit to use for signaling
- *Start time*—What time to start monitoring for miner support
- *Timeout*—A time when the deployment will be considered failed

The deployment goes through a number of *states* (see figure 11.22). The state is updated *after each retarget period*.

- DEFINED—The starting state. It means a retarget hasn't yet happened after the start time.
- STARTED—Wait until at least 1,916 (95%) blocks in the last retarget period signal support.

- LOCKED_IN—A grace period to give the remaining nonsignaling miners a chance to upgrade. If they don't, their blocks might be rejected.

- ACTIVE—The new rules are in effect.

- FAILED—The timeout occurred before the deployment got LOCKED_IN. If conditions happen simultaneously, timeout has precedence over other conditions, such as the 95% rule.

Comparing times

When comparing block times to the start time and timeout, we always use median time past, as described in "Rules for timestamps" in chapter 7.

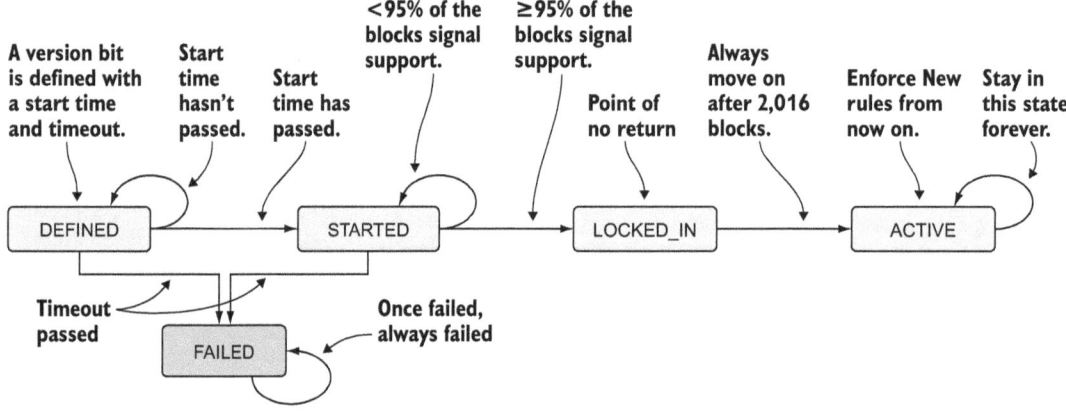

Figure 11.22   State transitions happen every 2,016 blocks.

When the deployment is ACTIVE or FAILED, the bit used to signal support should be reset to 0 so that it can then be reused for other deployments.

Using BIP9 to deploy relative lock time

Let's look at an example of how a deployment using version bits can play out. We'll look at how relative lock time was deployed. The developers of this new feature defined the following BIP9 parameters:

BIPs 68, 112, and 113

This "feature" is actually a group of BIPs that collectively make the relative lock time work.

```
name:       csv
bit:        0
start time: 2016-05-01 00:00:00
timeout:    2017-05-01 00:00:00
```

The timeout was one year after the start time, which gave the miners about one year to upgrade to the soft fork implementing this feature.

Figure 11.23 shows the state transitions that occurred.

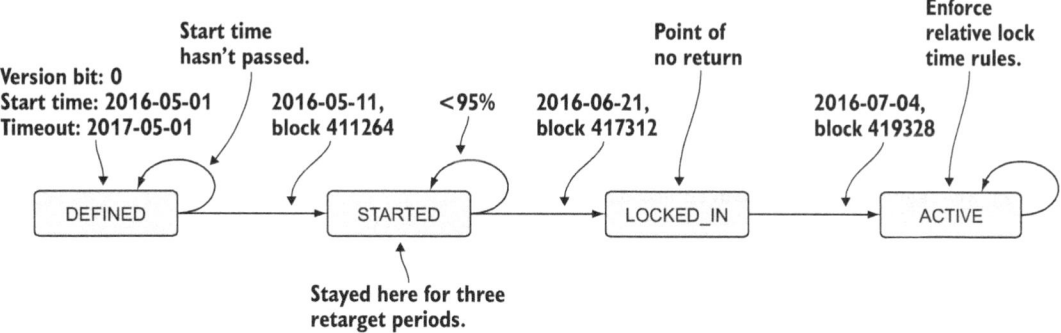

Figure 11.23   BIP9 deployment of `csv`. It went well.

This deployment went quickly and smoothly. It took only three retarget periods for 95% of the miners to upgrade to the new software.

Unfortunately, all deployments aren't as smooth.

Using BIP9 to deploy segwit

Segwit, described in chapter 10, also used BIP9 for its deployment, but things didn't work out as anticipated. It started out the same way `csv` deployment did. The parameters selected for this deployment were as follows:

```
name:       segwit
bit:        1
start time: 2016-11-15 00:00:00
timeout:    2017-11-15 00:00:00
```

A new version of Bitcoin Core was released with these segwit deployment parameters. Users adopted this new version pretty quickly, but for some reason, miners seemed hesitant. The signaling plateaued at around 30%, and the deployment process got stuck in the `STARTED` state, as figure 11.24 shows.

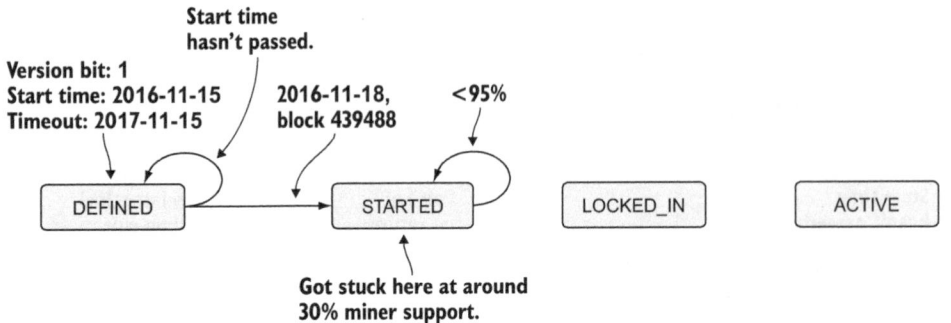

Figure 11.24   The segwit deployment didn't proceed as anticipated.

The segwit deployment was at risk of failing—entering the `FAILED` state after timeout. If this happens, a whole new deployment cycle must be put in place and executed, which could take another year.

Conflicts of interest

Another proposal was discussed in parallel. This proposal was known as *Segwit2x*. It was a proposal to first activate segwit *and then* increase the maximum block weight via a hard fork, in addition to the maximum block size increase segwit itself provides. This proposal would use BIP9 with version bit 4 to signal support. Bitcoin Core didn't show any interest in this proposal, but the Bitcoin

Core software repository was copied under the name btc1 by a group of people who used it to implement the proposal. The threshold would be 80% of the last 2,016 blocks to lock in segwit. This proposal got a lot of traction among miners.

A discrepancy seemed to exist between what full nodes wanted and what miners wanted. Rumors and theories floated around about what caused this discrepancy. We won't go into that here, but will stick to what we know.

A user-activated soft fork

In the midst of all this, another proposal, BIP148, surfaced that would start dropping blocks that didn't signal bit 1 (segwit) on 1 August 2017. The effect would be that nodes running BIP148 would experience a 100% adoption of BIP141, which would cause BIP141 to lock in after at most

two retargets. This is what's known as a *user-activated soft fork*. Users—those running full nodes—collectively decide that they'll start applying new rules, and if miners don't comply, their blocks will be discarded. We'll talk a bit more about user-activated soft forks toward the end of this chapter.

BIP148 was an attempt at forcing segwit deployment despite hesitant miners.

Some groups, especially the Bitcoin Core team, thought this proposal was too risky. It would cause a chain split if a miner published a non-segwit-signalling block. But there was also a group of people wanting to move forward with BIP148 regardless. This caused some worry in the Bitcoin community.

A proposal to bridge the groups

We had a stalled segwit deployment, an alternate segwit2x fork coming that many miners seemed to want, and a group of impatient users wanting to enforce segwit using BIP148.

To avoid a timeout of the segwit deployment—which would further delay segwit—and to avoid a possible blockchain split by BIP148, and to please the segwit2x crowd, a new BIP was written. BIP91 would satisfy all of these groups. It would use BIP9 with a custom threshold:

```
name:       segsignal
bit:        4
start time: 2017-06-01 00:00:00
timeout:    2017-11-15 00:00:00
Period:     336 blocks
Threshold:  269 blocks (80%)
Ceases to be active when segwit (bit 1) is LOCKED_IN or FAILED.
```

This BIP did things a bit differently than normal BIP9 deployments. It used a shorter period—336 blocks instead of 2,016 blocks—and a lower threshold—80% instead of 95%.

While active, this BIP behaved like BIP148. All blocks that didn't signal bit 1 (segwit) were rejected. Note how this was compatible with both BIP148 and segwit2x. It signaled using bit 4, the same bit segwit2x would use, and it enforced segwit lock-in by rejecting non-bit-1-signaling blocks.

This BIP wasn't implemented in Bitcoin Core, but in a copied version of Bitcoin Core. This version quickly got broad adoption among miners, and on 21 July 2017, the BIP got LOCKED_IN. See figure 11.25.

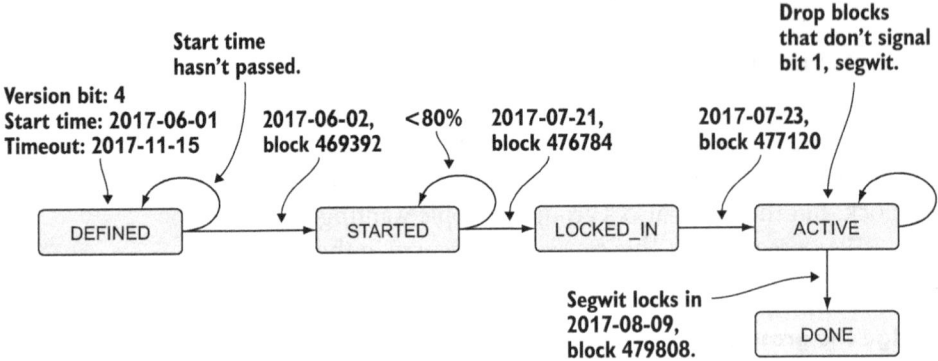

Figure 11.25 BIP91 updates its state every 336 blocks instead of the usual 2,016. This went quickly.

It activated three days after LOCKED_IN. Note that it was mainly miners that adopted BIP91. Normal users typically used Bitcoin Core, which didn't implement BIP91.

When miners activated BIP91, they started dropping blocks that didn't signal bit 1, which is the bit for the segwit deployment. The result was that non-bit-1 blocks didn't make it into the strongest chain, which quickly forced the remaining miners to upgrade to segwit to avoid mining invalid blocks.

Miners were starting to signal segwit, the original segwit proposal using bit 1 for its deployment, and it got LOCKED_IN on 9 August 2017 and became ACTIVE on 24 August 2017, as figure 11.26 shows.

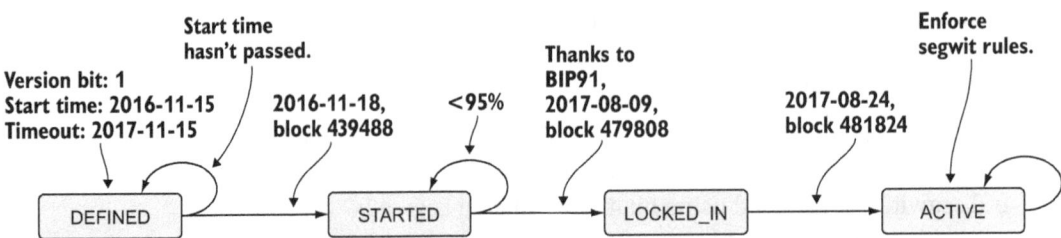

Figure 11.26 Segwit finally activates thanks to BIP91.

Normal nonmining users, merchants, and exchanges didn't have to do anything in particular to stay on the strongest chain because their software (normal segwit-enabled software) follows the strongest valid chain. This meant BIP141 got `LOCKED_IN` and then `ACTIVE` for all users and miners at the same time.

Lessons learned

The events that occurred during segwit deployment weren't anticipated. Few people thought that miners would refuse to adopt BIP141. Yet that's what happened.

It became clear that BIP9 isn't an ideal way to deploy a soft fork. It gives 5% of the hashrate a veto against it. Given that several miners each control more than 5% of the total hashrate, any one of those individual entities can block a system upgrade.

As noted in "Trust in Lisa" in chapter 5, we pay miners to perform correct, honest transaction confirmations. We don't pay them to *decide* the rules, we pay them to *follow* the rules. The rules are decided collectively by everyone, you and me, by running our Bitcoin software of choice.

Think about that.

User-activated soft forks

To underscore the importance of the economic majority (you, me, and everyone else using Bitcoin), and to avoid having miners vetoing proposals that the economic majority wants, people started thinking more about user-activated soft forks.

Let's look at a fictitious example of a user-activated soft fork.

Suppose 99% of Bitcoin users (end users, exchanges, merchants, and so on) want a rule change—for example, smaller blocks—that would be a soft fork. Also suppose no miner wants smaller blocks, so they all refuse to comply. Assume also that 99% of the nonmining full nodes change their software to reject all big blocks after a certain block height.

What will happen when that block height passes? Miners that produce big blocks will build a blockchain that users will deem invalid (figure 11.27).

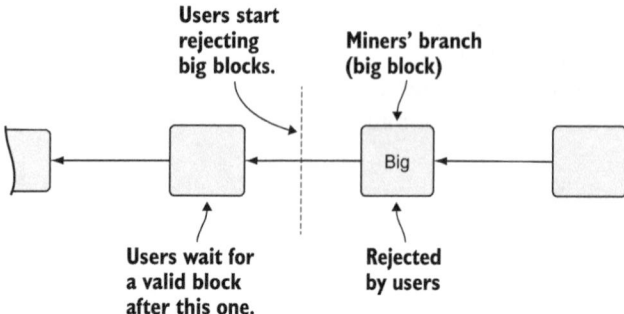

Figure 11.27   Users start rejecting big blocks. They see no new valid blocks, but plenty of invalid (too-big) blocks.

The value of the block rewards in the "miner" chain will be unknown because the exchanges don't deal with the miner chain. Miners won't be able to exchange their block rewards to pay their electricity bills. Even if the electricity provider takes Bitcoin, the miners won't be able to pay with their block rewards because the electricity provider won't accept the miner's blocks as valid. The electricity provider is also a Bitcoin user, remember?

But if a single miner decides to comply with users' demands, the blocks that miner produces will be the only blocks users actually accept (figure 11.28).

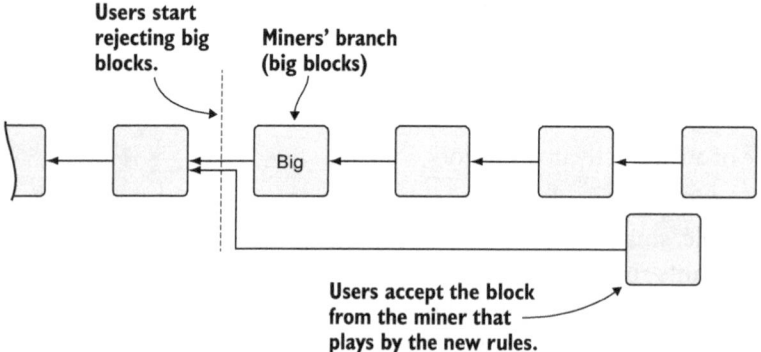

Figure 11.28   One miner decides to go with the users' will and only build small blocks. This miner will be able to pay the bills.

This single miner will be rewarded for the block it created because the economic majority accepts the block. The blocks on the miner (big-block) chain are still pretty worthless because no users accept them. On top of this, the single small-block miner will be able to charge more fees than before because the total amount of block space is smaller—both because the maximum block weight is smaller and because the total number of blocks is smaller.

Some more big-block miners will probably realize they're quickly running out of money and decide to switch to the user-accepted branch (figure 11.29).

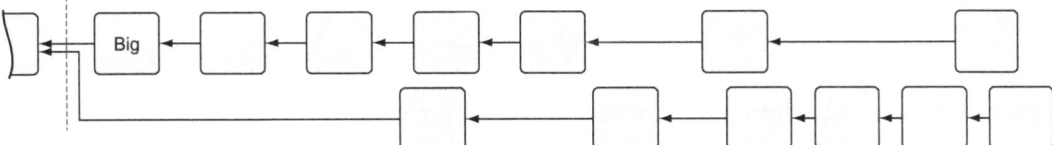

Figure 11.29   A few more miners realize it's more profitable to work on the users' branch.

When more miners move over to the users' branch, that branch will eventually grow stronger than the big-blocks branch. When this happens, the big-blocks branch will get wiped out (figure 11.30), and the remaining miners will automatically switch to the small-blocks branch because the change is a soft fork.

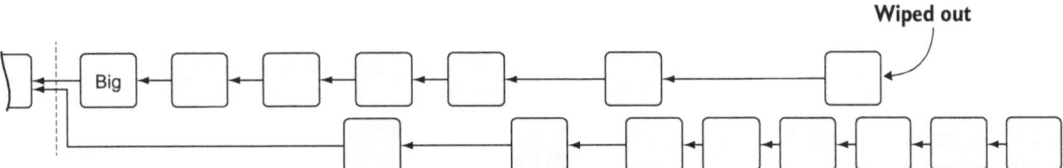

Figure 11.30   The users' branch is stronger and wipes out the big-blocks branch.

Users win.

One of the first soft forks in Bitcoin, the deployment of BIP16 (p2sh), was a user-activated soft fork. The deployment was manual in the sense that developers, on a specific day, manually counted the number of blocks that signaled support and then decided on a flag day that they put in the next release of the Bitcoin software. After this date, all blocks that didn't comply with the new rules were rejected by nodes running this software.

To use the insights from the recent segwit deployment, a new deployment mechanism is in the making as of this writing. It's generally called a user-activated soft fork. The idea is to start with a BIP9-like

deployment, but with the exception that if the deployment doesn't get
LOCKED_IN well before the timeout, blocks that don't signal for the
fork will be dropped. This will effectively cause 100% support because
noncompliant blocks won't count anymore, and the deployment will
soon get LOCKED_IN.

Recap

This chapter has taught you about hard forks and soft forks, and how to
deploy soft forks without splitting the blockchain. We've talked about
several miner-activated soft forks and a few user-activated soft forks.

We can illustrate hard forks and soft forks as shown here.

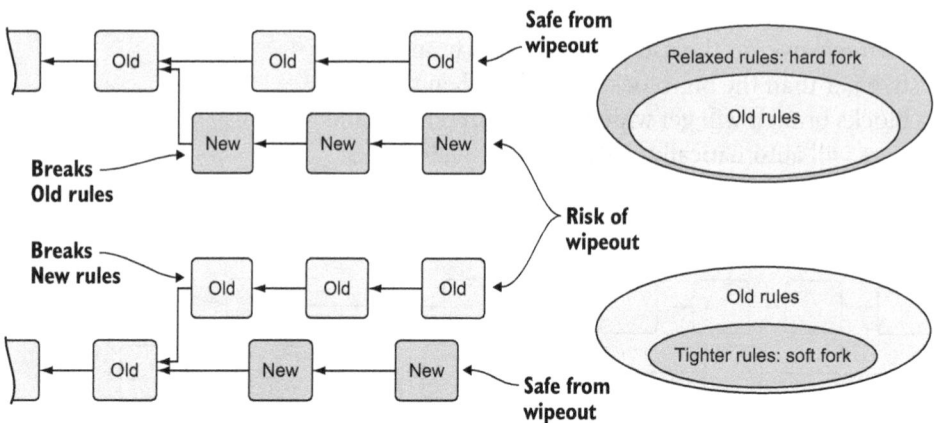

In a *hard fork,* the rules are *relaxed* so that a New block might be
invalid according to Old rules. In the event of a blockchain split, the
New branch might get wiped out by the Old branch.

In a *soft fork,* the rules are *tightened.* Old blocks might be invalid
according to New rules. In case of a blockchain split, the Old branch
risks a wipeout.

You can protect a hard fork against a wipeout by deliberately making
the New branch incompatible with the Old branch. For example,
Bitcoin Cash requires the first block after the split to have a base size
> 1,000,000 bytes, which is invalid according to the Old rules. You can't
protect the Old branch in a soft fork from wipeout.

To roll out a soft fork, care must be taken not to split the blockchain. If a split happens, and both branches remain active over a significant amount of time, it will cause a lot of pain for users, exchanges, miners, and so on.

In a *miner-activated soft fork*, miners signal their support; when, for example, 95% of the blocks signal support, the new rules start being enforced after a grace period. BIP9 standardized this process.

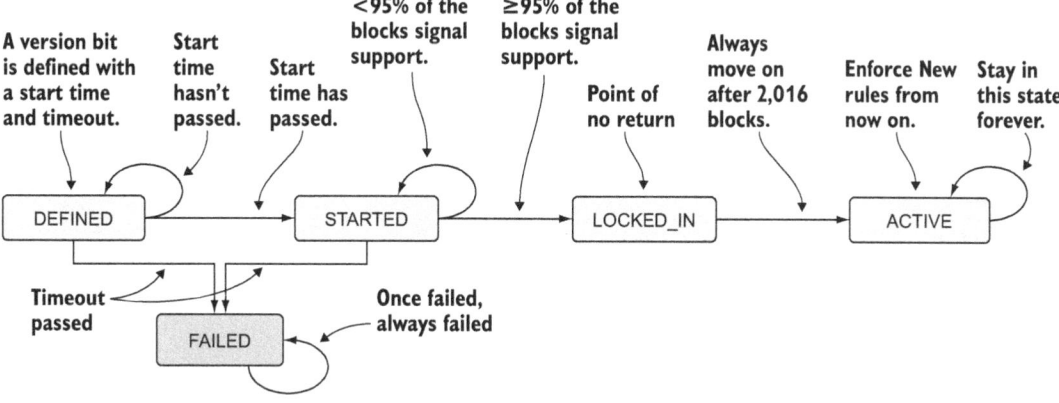

In a *user-activated soft fork*, users start enforcing the rules on a specific day (or block height). A standard for this is being developed as of this writing, and it will probably be a hybrid of BIP9 and user-activated soft fork.

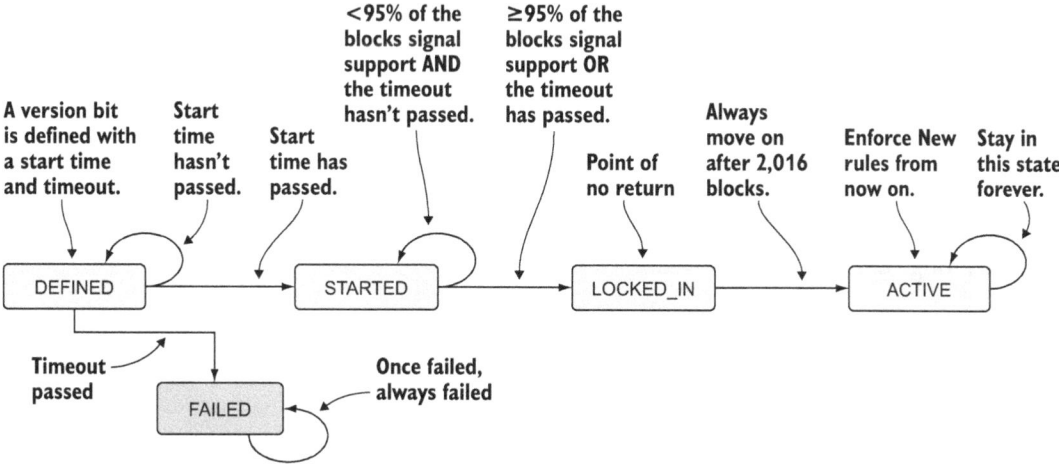

The difference from a pure BIP9 deployment is that the user-activated soft fork process is guaranteed to proceed to `ACTIVE` once the node has entered the `STARTED` state. In the `STARTED` state, miners have a chance to move the deployment to a `LOCKED_IN` state; but if they don't, and the timeout has passed, then the supporting full nodes (including miners that support the upgrade) will start enforcing the rules anyway.

A user-activated soft fork was used to deploy BIP16, p2sh, but it was done manually. Other than this, the community has no real-world experience with user-activated soft forks.

Exercises

Warm up

11.1   A soft fork is a change of the consensus rules, but what characterizes the changes made in a soft fork?

11.2   Suppose a hard fork causes a blockchain split, and the New branch has 51% of the hashrate. Furthermore, suppose the hashrate on the New branch drops to about 45%.

   a.   What event will eventually happen?

   b.   Why did I say that the event will *eventually* happen? When does the event occur?

   c.   What can the developers of Bitcoin New do to prevent the event from happening?

11.3   Suppose an Old node causes a blockchain split due to a soft fork in which 80% of the hashrate runs Bitcoin New. Will the Old branch of the split last long? Explain your answer.

11.4   Suppose you try to deploy a soft fork using BIP9. Your deployment has just reached the `LOCKED_IN` state. How long do you have to wait before your rules start being enforced?

Dig in

11.5 Suppose a fork changes the consensus rules such that Old nodes can create blocks invalid to New nodes, and New nodes can create blocks invalid to Old nodes.

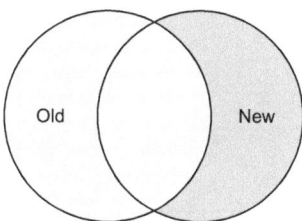

What nodes (New, Old, both, or none), would be able to cause a blockchain split when this fork is deployed?

11.6 Why is it desirable to have a reassuring majority of the hashrate supporting Bitcoin New in a soft fork before starting to enforce the New rules?

11.7 Suppose a hard fork has caused a permanent blockchain split and you're about to make a payment using Bitcoin New. Why is replay protection desirable in this scenario?

11.8 Suppose you want to deploy a soft fork using BIP9 with the following parameters:

```
bit:         12
start time: 2027-01-01 00:00:00
timeout:    2028-01-01 00:00:00
```

Also assume that the deployment is in STARTED state, all 2016 blocks in the current retarget period have been mined, and all of them signal support using bit 12. The last (2016th) block, B_1, in the current retarget period has the following properties:

```
timestamp T₁:          2027-12-31 23:59:59
median time past MTP₁: 2027-12-31 23:59:58
```

Will this deployment eventually get to the ACTIVE state?

11.9   Suppose you want to make a user-activated soft fork. You find it hard to convince other users to install your software. What would happen on the flag day if just a small percentage (<30%) of the economy chose to run your software?

11.10   Suppose you want to make a user-activated soft fork. Lots of other users seem to like your soft fork. Say that 80% of the economy installs your fork. Why would miners (even those that don't like your change) probably switch to the New rules during this user-activated soft fork?

11.11   In the previous exercise, your soft fork had support from 80% of the economy. Suppose also that a majority of the hashrate decides to follow your New rules. What happens with the nonmining nodes that don't run your fork?

Summary

- You don't want a blockchain split when deploying a fork because this would cause disruption in the Bitcoin economy.

- A hard fork is a consensus rule change that requires every miner to upgrade. Otherwise, the blockchain will split.

- A soft fork is a consensus rule change that doesn't require simultaneous upgrade of the entire network.

- During a blockchain split due to a hard fork, you want wipeout protection to make sure the New branch isn't reorged by Old nodes.

- In a blockchain split, you want replay protection to let you select what branch your transactions are applied to.

- A miner-activated soft fork—for example, one using BIP9 for deployment—lets miners deploy a noncontroversial soft fork.

- A user-activated soft fork lets users enforce a soft fork deployment. If a hashrate majority eventually follows, the soft fork succeeds without a lasting blockchain split.

This appendix continues from "Running your own full node" in chapter 8. I'll show you how to set up a Bitcoin wallet, receive and send bitcoins, and explore the Bitcoin blockchain using `bitcoin-cli`, Bitcoin Core's command-line tool.

Note that this appendix won't go into great depth on `bitcoin-cli`. This should only be regarded as a source of inspiration; it will provide you with the basics to get started. You're encouraged to explore further.

Communicating with bitcoind

When `bitcoind` starts, it also starts a web server that listens on TCP port 8332 by default. When you use `bitcoin-cli`, it will connect to the web server, send your command to the web server over HTTP, and display relevant parts of the response to you.

For example, suppose I want to know the block ID of the genesis block (the block at height 0), and I issue the following command:

```
$ ./bitcoin-cli getblockhash 0
```

`bitcoin-cli` creates an HTTP POST request with the body

```
{"method":"getblockhash","params":[0],"id":1}
```

and sends it to the web server that `bitcoind` runs. The request body's `method` property is the command you want to execute, and the argument `0` is passed to the web server as an array with a single element.

The web server processes the HTTP request by looking up the block hash in the blockchain and replies with an HTTP response with the following body:

```
{"result":"000000000019d6689c085ae165831e934ff763ae46a2a6c172b3f1b60a8ce26f",
↳"error":null,"id":"1"}
```

`bitcoin-cli` then displays the value of the `result` property on the terminal:

```
000000000019d6689c085ae165831e934ff763ae46a2a6c172b3f1b60a8ce26f
```

This body of the HTTP request follows a standard called JSON-RPC, which describes how a client can call functions on a remote process using JavaScript Object Notation (JSON).

Using curl

Because the communication with `bitcoind` happens through `HTTP`, any program that can send `HTTP POST` requests, such as the command-line tool `curl`, can be used to communicate with `bitcoind`. But to use tools other than `bitcoin-cli`, you need to set up a username and password to use as authentication to the web server.

Stop the node with `./bitcoin-cli stop`. Open—or create, if it doesn't exist—Bitcoin Core's configuration file ~/.bitcoin/bitcoin.conf, and add these lines:

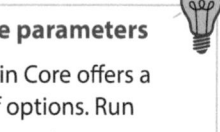

More parameters
Bitcoin Core offers a lot of options. Run `./bitcoind --help` to get a complete list.

```
rpcuser=<a username that you select>
rpcpassword=<a password that you select>
```

After you've modified and saved the ~/.bitcoin/bitcoin.conf file, start your node using `./bitcoind -daemon`, to make the changes effective.

Here's how I called `getblockhash` using `curl` (the backslash \ character means the command continues on the next line):

```
curl --user kalle --data-binary \
    '{"method":"getblockhash","params":[0],"id":1}' \
    -H 'content-type: text/plain;' http://127.0.0.1:8332/
Enter host password for user 'kalle':
{"result":"000000000019d6689c085ae165831e934ff763ae46a2a6c172b3f1b60a8ce26f",
↳"error":null,"id":1}
```

Remember to change the username from `kalle` to the username you configured in bitcoin.conf.

This command will prompt you for the password. Enter the password, and press Enter. The reply from the web server will be the same as when you used `bitcoin-cli`, but you'll need to scan through the response body to spot the result, which is the hash of block 0.

Graphical user interface

Bitcoin Core comes with a graphical user interface (GUI). This appendix mainly deals with the command-line interface `bitcoin-cli` for controlling and querying your running `bitcoind`. But if you want to use Bitcoin Core as a Bitcoin wallet (and not just as a full node), it can be useful to familiarize yourself with the GUI version. The GUI version of Bitcoin Core lets you perform most common tasks expected from a Bitcoin wallet, but to access Bitcoin Core's full set of features, you'll need to use `bitcoin-cli`.

To use the GUI version of Bitcoin Core, you need to stop the current node and start the GUI version, called `bitcoin-qt`:

```
$ ./bitcoin-cli stop
Bitcoin server stopping
$ ./bitcoin-qt &
```

If `bitcoind` didn't have time to finish shutting down before you started `bitcoin-qt`, you'll get an error message from `bitcoin-qt`. If so, click OK and try running `./bitcoin-qt &` again in a few seconds.

`bitcoin-qt` uses the same data directory, ~/.bitcoin/, as `bitcoind`, which means `bitcoin-qt` will use the already downloaded and verified blockchain and the same wallet as `bitcoind`. It's just the user interface that differs.

By default, `bitcoin-qt` won't start the web server to accept JSON-RPC requests as `bitcoind` does. To use `bitcoin-cli` with `bitcoin-qt`, start `bitcoin-qt` as follows, instead:

```
$ ./bitcoin-qt -server &
```

Why -qt?

The Bitcoin Core GUI is built using a GUI programming library called QT. Hence the name, `bitcoin-qt`.

Getting to know bitcoin-cli

You've started Bitcoin Core in the background by running

```
$ ./bitcoind -daemon
```

The most important command to know is the `help` command. Run it without any arguments to get a list of all available commands:

```
$ ./bitcoin-cli help
```

You'll get a long list of commands grouped by subject—for example, `Blockchain`, `Mining`, and `Wallet`. Some commands are self-explanatory, but if you want to know more about a specific command, you can run `help` with the command name as an argument.
For example:

```
$ ./bitcoin-cli help getblockhash
getblockhash height

Returns hash of block in best-block-chain at height provided.

Arguments:
1. height           (numeric, required) The height index

Result:
"hash"          (string) The block hash

Examples:
> bitcoin-cli getblockhash 1000
> curl --user myusername --data-binary '{"jsonrpc": [CA]"1.0", "id":"curltest",
"method": "getblockhash", "params": [1000] }' -H 'content-type: text/plain;'
http://127.0.0.1:8332/
```

You can invoke `bitcoin-cli` in two ways:

- *Using positional arguments*—The meanings of the arguments are based on their relative positions: for example, `./bitcoin-cli getblockhash 1000`. This is the most common way to use `bitcoin-cli`.

- *Using named arguments*—The arguments are named on the command line: for example, `./bitcoin-cli -named getblockhash height=1000`. This is sometimes useful when the command takes optional arguments and you want to specify the second optional argument but not the first. You'll see examples later.

Getting to work

Let's create an encrypted wallet and back it up. You'll then receive some bitcoins and pass that money on to another address while dissecting the transactions for details—all using `bitcoin-cli`.

Creating an encrypted wallet

When `bitcoind` (or `bitcoin-qt`) starts, it will automatically create a wallet for you and store it in the file ~/.bitcoin/wallet.dat. But this wallet isn't encrypted, which means its private keys and its seed, used to derive key pairs as discussed in chapter 4, are stored in the clear on your hard drive. Let's look at some data for such a wallet:

```
$ ./bitcoin-cli getwalletinfo
{
  "walletname": "",
  "walletversion": 169900,
  "balance": 0.00000000,
  "unconfirmed_balance": 0.00000000,
  "immature_balance": 0.00000000,
  "txcount": 0,
  "keypoololdest": 1541941001,
  "keypoolsize": 1000,
  "keypoolsize_hd_internal": 1000,
  "paytxfee": 0.00000000,
  "hdseedid": "bb989ad4e23f7bb713eab0a272eaef3d4857f5e3",
  "hdmasterkeyid": "bb989ad4e23f7bb713eab0a272eaef3d4857f5e3",
  "private_keys_enabled": true
}
```

The output from the `getwalletinfo` command shows various information about the wallet currently being used. This automatically created wallet is unnamed, which is why `walletname` is empty.

`balance` is how many confirmed bitcoins you have (including unconfirmed outgoing transactions), and `unconfirmed_balance` is the sum of incoming unconfirmed payments. `immature_balance` is relevant only for miners and denotes the number of newly created bitcoins, which can't be spent until after 100 blocks passed. Refer to the help section on `getwalletinfo` for more details about the output.

To create an encrypted wallet, you need to create a *new* wallet using the
command encryptwallet:

```
$ ./bitcoin-cli -stdin encryptwallet
secretpassword<ENTER>
<CTRL-D>
wallet encrypted; Bitcoin server stopping, restart to run with encrypted wallet.
↳The keypool has been flushed and a new HD seed was generated (if you are using HD).
↳You need to make a new backup.
```

This command creates a new encrypted wallet. The -stdin option is
used to read the password argument from standard input, which in
this case means you type the password in your terminal window after
starting the command. End your input by pressing Enter and Ctrl-D.
The reason for using -stdin is that you don't want the password to be
written in the command itself, because most shell interpreters, such as
bash, keep a history of commands in a file. The -stdin option ensures
that the password doesn't end up in any such history files.

It's important to create a new encrypted wallet instead of just encrypting
the existing wallet, because the old wallet might already have been
compromised on your hard drive. As noted by the output, bitcoind
has stopped. Bitcoin Core can't currently switch to a new wallet file
while running.

Let's start bitcoind again and look at the wallet. You'll see something
similar to this:

```
$ ./bitcoind -daemon
Bitcoin server starting
$ ./bitcoin-cli getwalletinfo
{
  "walletname": "",
  "walletversion": 169900,
  "balance": 0.00000000,
  "unconfirmed_balance": 0.00000000,
  "immature_balance": 0.00000000,
  "txcount": 0,
  "keypoololdest": 1541941063,
  "keypoolsize": 1000,
  "keypoolsize_hd_internal": 1000,
  "unlocked_until": 0,
  "paytxfee": 0.00000000,
  "hdseedid": "590ec0fa4cec43d9179e5b6f7b2cdefaa35ed282",
  "hdmasterkeyid": "590ec0fa4cec43d9179e5b6f7b2cdefaa35ed282",
  "private_keys_enabled": true
}
```

Your old, unencrypted wallet.dat has been overwritten by the new, encrypted wallet.dat. For safety, however, your old seed is kept in the new encrypted wallet, in case you had actual funds in the old wallet or accidentally receive funds to that old wallet in the future. The `unlocked_until` value of `0` means your private keys are encrypted with the password you entered when you encrypted your wallet. From now on, you need to decrypt your private keys to access them. You'll do that when you send bitcoin later.

Backing up the wallet

You've created an encrypted wallet, and before you start using it, you need to back it up. In chapter 4, we talked about mnemonic sentences, as defined in BIP39, which made backing up hierarchical deterministic (HD) wallet seeds simple. But this feature is *not* implemented in Bitcoin Core, for a few reasons—mainly, that the mnemonic sentence lacks information about the following:

- The version of the seed format.

- The *birthday*, which is when the seed was created. Without a birthday, you have to scan the entire blockchain to find your old transactions. With a birthday, you only have to scan the blockchain from the birthday onward.

- The derivation paths to use for restoration. This is somewhat remedied by using standard derivation paths, but not all wallets implement the standard.

- Other arbitrary metadata, such as labels on addresses.

To back up your Bitcoin Core wallet, you need to make a copy of the wallet.dat file. Be careful not to copy the file using your operating system's copy facilities while `bitcoind` or `bitcoin-qt` is running. If you do this, your backup might be in an inconsistent state because `bitcoind` might be writing data to it while you copy. To make sure you get a consistent copy of the file while Bitcoin Core is running, run the following command:

```
$ ./bitcoin-cli backupwallet ~/walletbackup.dat
```

This will instruct `bitcoind` to save a copy of the wallet file to walletbackup.dat in your home directory (you can change the name and path of the file to anything you like). The backup file will be an exact copy of the original wallet.dat file. Move the walletbackup.dat file to a safe place—for example, a USB memory stick in a bank safe-deposit box or on a computer at your brother's apartment.

Receiving money

You've created an encrypted, backed-up wallet. Great! Let's put some bitcoins into it. To do this, you need a Bitcoin address to receive the bitcoins to, so let's get one:

```
$ ./bitcoin-cli -named getnewaddress address_type=bech32
bc1q2r9mql4mkz3z7yfxvef76yxjd637r429620j75
```

This command creates a bech32 p2wpkh address for you. If you prefer another type of address, you can change `bech32` to `legacy` to get a p2pkh address or to `p2sh-segwit` to get a p2wpkh nested in p2sh address. Head back to the "Recap of payment types" section in chapter 10 to refresh your memory on the different payment and address types.

Now, let's send bitcoin to that address. Be careful not to send money to the address printed in this book (although I'll happily accept it), but rather to an address you generate yourself with your own full node wallet.

This raises the question of how to get bitcoins to send to your wallet. You can get bitcoins in several ways:

- Buy bitcoins on an exchange.

- Ask friends who have bitcoins if they can give or sell you some.

- Earn bitcoins as payment for your labor.

- Mine bitcoins.

> **On the web**
>
> Visit web resource 20 in appendix C to find out more about how to get bitcoins where you live.

I'll leave it up to you how you obtain bitcoins and assume that you somehow will get bitcoins into the address you created previously.

I made a payment to my new address and then checked my wallet:

```
$ ./bitcoin-cli getunconfirmedbalance
0.00500000
```

This shows a pending incoming payment of 5 mBTC (0.005 BTC). I now have to wait until it's confirmed in the blockchain. Meanwhile, you can dig into the transaction by running the `listtransactions` command. Here are my results:

```
$ ./bitcoin-cli listtransactions
[
  {
    "address": "bc1q2r9mql4mkz3z7yfxvef76yxjd637r429620j75",
    "category": "receive",
    "amount": 0.00500000,
    "label": "",
    "vout": 1,
    "confirmations": 0,
    "trusted": false,
    "txid": "ebfd0d14c2ea74ce408d01d5ea79636b8dee88fe06625f5d4842d2a0ba45c195",
    "walletconflicts": [
    ],
    "time": 1541941483,
    "timereceived": 1541941483,
    "bip125-replaceable": "yes"
  }
]
```

This transaction has 0 confirmations and pays 0.005 BTC. You can also see that this transaction's txid is ebfd0d14...ba45c195.

Let's take a closer look at the transaction using the command `getrawtransaction`:

```
$ ./bitcoin-cli getrawtransaction \
    ebfd0d14c2ea74ce408d01d5ea79636b8dee88fe06625f5d4842d2a0ba45c195 1
{
  "txid": "ebfd0d14c2ea74ce408d01d5ea79636b8dee88fe06625f5d4842d2a0ba45c195",
  "hash": "ebfd0d14c2ea74ce408d01d5ea79636b8dee88fe06625f5d4842d2a0ba45c195",
  "version": 1,
  "size": 223,
  "vsize": 223,
  "weight": 892,
  "locktime": 549655,
  "vin": [
    {
      "txid": "8a4023dbcf57dc7f51d368606055e47636fc625a512d3481352a1eec909ab22f",
      "vout": 0,
      "scriptSig": {
        "asm": "3045022100cc095e6b7c0d4c42a1741371cfdda4f1b518590f1af
        ↳0915578d3966fee7e34ea02205fc1e976edcf4fe62f16035a5389c661844f7189
        ↳a9eb45adf59e061ac8cc6fd3[ALL]
        ↳030ace35cc192cedfe2a730244945f1699ea2f6b7ee77c65c83a2d7a37440e3dae",
```

```
            "hex":
          "483045022100cc095e6b7c0d4c42a1741371cfdda4f1b518590f1af0915578d3966
↳fee7e34ea02205fc1e976edcf4fe62f16035a5389c661844f7189a9eb45adf59e061
↳ac8cc6fd 30121030ace35cc192cedfe2a730244945f1699ea2f6b7ee77c65c83a2d7
↳a37440e3dae"
        },
        "sequence": 4294967293
      }
  ],
  "vout": [
    {
      "value": 0.00313955,
      "n": 0,
      "scriptPubKey": {
        "asm": "OP_DUP OP_HASH160 6da68d8f89dced72d4339959c94a4fcc872fa089
↳  OP_EQUALVERIFY OP_CHECKSIG",
        "hex": "76a9146da68d8f89dced72d4339959c94a4fcc872fa08988ac",
        "reqSigs": 1,
        "type": "pubkeyhash",
        "addresses": [
          "1AznBDM2ZfjYNoRw3DLSR9NL2cwwqDHJY6"
        ]
      }
    },
    {
      "value": 0.00500000,
      "n": 1,
      "scriptPubKey": {
        "asm": "0 50cbb07ebbb0a22f11266653ed10d26ea3e1d545",
        "hex": "001450cbb07ebbb0a22f11266653ed10d26ea3e1d545",
        "reqSigs": 1,
        "type": "witness_v0_keyhash",
        "addresses": [
          "bc1q2r9mql4mkz3z7yfxvef76yxjd637r429620j75"
        ]
      }
    }
  ],
  "hex":
"01000000012fb29a90ec1e2a3581342d515a62fc3676e455606068d3517fdc57cfdb
↳23408a000000006b483045022100cc095e6b7c0d4c42a1741371cfdda4f1b518590f1af0915578
↳d3966fee7e34ea02205fc1e976edcf4fe62f16035a5389c661844f7189a9eb45adf59e061ac8
↳cc6fd30121030ace35cc192cedfe2a730244945f1699ea2f6b7ee77c65c83a2d7a37440e3
↳daefdffffff0263ca0400000000001976a9146da68d8f89dced72d4339959c94a4fcc872fa08988
↳20a1070000000000016001450cbb07ebbb0a22f11266653ed10d26ea3e1d54517630800"
}
```

This command prints the entire transaction in a human-readable (well, at least developer-readable) form. Let's start from the top and go through the most relevant parts of this transaction. The `txid` is the transaction id. The `hash` is the double SHA256 hash of the whole transaction, including the witness. For non-segwit transactions, `hash` is equal to `txid`.

The `size` of the transaction is 223 bytes, and `vsize` (the virtual size) is also 223 vbytes; `vsize` is the transaction's number of weight units (`892`) divided by 4, so the virtual size of a non-segwit transaction (which this is, because it only spends non-segwit outputs) is equal to its actual `size`.

The locktime of this transaction is set to `549655`, which was the height of the strongest chain at the time of the transaction's creation. Thus the transaction can't be mined until block height 549656. This reduces the attractiveness of an attack in which a miner deliberately tries to reorg the blockchain and include the transaction into a block height that's already been mined.

Next comes the list of inputs. This transaction has a single input that spends output at index `0` (`vout`) of the transaction with `txid` `8a4023db…909ab22f`. The input spends a p2pkh output.

The input's sequence number is `4294967293`, which is `fffffffd` in hex code. This means the lock time is enabled ($\leq$`fffffffe`) and the transaction is replaceable ($\leq$`fffffffd`) according to BIP125. The meaning of the sequence number was summarized in table 9.1.

After the list of inputs comes the list of transaction outputs. This transaction has a list of two outputs. The first pays 0.00313955 BTC to a p2pkh address you haven't seen before. This is *probably* a change output. The second output sends 0.005 BTC to the p2wpkh address created earlier.

Let's see if the transaction is confirmed yet. You can check, for example, with `getbalance`. In my case, if it shows `0.00500000`, then the transaction has confirmed:

```
$ ./bitcoin-cli getbalance
0.00500000
```

Cool, the money is confirmed! Let's move on.

Sending money

You've received some bitcoins. Now, you want to send bitcoins to someone else. To send bitcoins, you can use the `sendtoaddress` command. You need to make a few decisions first:

- Address to send to

- How much money to send: 0.001 BTC

- How urgent the transaction is: not urgent (you'll be happy if it confirms within 20 blocks)

I'll send the bitcoins to address `bc1qu456…5t7uulqm`, but you should get another address to send to. If you have no other wallet, you can create a new address in Bitcoin Core to send to just for experimental purposes. I've obfuscated my address below so that you don't send to my address by mistake:

```
$ ./bitcoin-cli -named sendtoaddress \
    address="bc1qu456w7a5mawlgXXXXXXu03wp8wc7d65t7uulqm" \
    amount=0.001 conf_target=20 estimate_mode=ECONOMICAL
error code: -13
error message:
Error: Please enter the wallet passphrase with walletpassphrase first.
```

Oh, dear! An error. As indicated by the error message, the private keys are encrypted in the wallet.dat file. Bitcoin Core needs the private keys to sign the transaction. To make the private keys accessible, you need to decrypt them. You do this using the `walletpassphrase` command with the `-stdin` option to prevent the passphrase from being stored by your command-line interpreter, such as bash:

```
$ ./bitcoin-cli -stdin walletpassphrase
secretpassword<ENTER>
300<ENTER>
<CTRL-D>
```

The last argument, `300`, is the number of seconds you should keep the wallet unlocked. After 300 seconds, the wallet will be automatically locked again in case you forget to lock it manually. Let's retry the `sendtoaddress` command:

```
$ ./bitcoin-cli -named sendtoaddress \
    address="bc1qu456w7a5mawlgXXXXXXu03wp8wc7d65t7uulqm" \
    amount=0.001 conf_target=20 estimate_mode=ECONOMICAL
a13bcb16d8f41851cab8e939c017f1e05cc3e2a3c7735bf72f3dc5ef4a5893a2
```

The command output a txid for the newly created transaction. This means it
went well. You can relock the wallet using the `walletlock` command:

```
$ ./bitcoin-cli walletlock
```

The wallet is now locked. I'll list my transactions again:

```
$ ./bitcoin-cli listtransactions
[
  {
    "address": "bc1q2r9mql4mkz3z7yfxvef76yxjd637r429620j75",
    "category": "receive",
    "amount": 0.00500000,
    "label": "",
    "vout": 1,
    "confirmations": 1,
    "blockhash": "000000000000000000000240eec03ac7499805b0f3df34a7d5005670f3a8fa836ca",
    "blockindex": 311,
    "blocktime": 1541946325,
    "txid": "ebfd0d14c2ea74ce408d01d5ea79636b8dee88fe06625f5d4842d2a0ba45c195",
    "walletconflicts": [
    ],
    "time": 1541941483,
    "timereceived": 1541941483,
    "bip125-replaceable": "no"
  },
  {
    "address": "bc1qu456w7a5mawlg35y00xu03wp8wc7d65t7uulqm",
    "category": "send",
    "amount": -0.00100000,
    "vout": 1,
    "fee": -0.00000141,
    "confirmations": 0,
    "trusted": true,
    "txid": "a13bcb16d8f41851cab8e939c017f1e05cc3e2a3c7735bf72f3dc5ef4a5893a2",
    "walletconflicts": [
    ],
    "time": 1541946631,
    "timereceived": 1541946631,
    "bip125-replaceable": "no",
    "abandoned": false
  }
]
```

The new transaction is the last one of the two. It isn't yet confirmed, as indicated by `"confirmations"`: 0. The fee paid was 141 satoshis. Let's look into this transaction in detail:

```
$ ./bitcoin-cli getrawtransaction \
    a13bcb16d8f41851cab8e939c017f1e05cc3e2a3c7735bf72f3dc5ef4a5893a2 1
{
  "txid": "a13bcb16d8f41851cab8e939c017f1e05cc3e2a3c7735bf72f3dc5ef4a5893a2",
  "hash": "554a3a3e57dcd07185414d981af5fd272515d7f2159cf9ed9808d52b7d852ead",
  "version": 2,
  "size": 222,
  "vsize": 141,
  "weight": 561,
  "locktime": 549665,
  "vin": [
    {
      "txid": "ebfd0d14c2ea74ce408d01d5ea79636b8dee88fe06625f5d4842d2a0ba45c195",
      "vout": 1,
      "scriptSig": {
        "asm": "",
        "hex": ""
      },
        "txinwitness": [
        "30440220212043afeaf70a97ea0aa09a15749ab94e09c6fad427677610286666a3
decf0b022076818b2b2dc64b1599fd6b39bb8c249efbf4c546e334bcd7e1874115
da4dfd0c01",

        "020127d82280a939add393ddbb1b8d08f0371fffbde776874cd69740b59e098866"
      ],
      "sequence": 4294967294
    }
  ],
  "vout": [
    {
      "value": 0.00399859,
      "n": 0,
      "scriptPubKey": {
        "asm": "0 4bf041f271bd94385d6bcac8487adf6c9a862d10",
        "hex": "00144bf041f271bd94385d6bcac8487adf6c9a862d10",
        "reqSigs": 1,
        "type": "witness_v0_keyhash",
        "addresses": [
          "bc1qf0cyrun3hk2rshttetyys7kldjdgvtgs6ymhzz"
        ]
      }
    },
```

```
    {
      "value": 0.00100000,
      "n": 1,
      "scriptPubKey": {
        "asm": "0 e569a77bb4df5df446847bcdc7c5c13bb1e6ea8b",
        "hex": "0014e569a77bb4df5df446847bcdc7c5c13bb1e6ea8b",
        "reqSigs": 1,
        "type": "witness_v0_keyhash",
        "addresses": [
          "bc1qu456w7a5mawlg35y00xu03wp8wc7d65t7uulqm"
        ]
      }
    }
  ],
  "hex":
```

"0200000000010195c145baa0d242485d5f6206fe88ee8d6b6379ead5018d40
↳ce74eac2140dfdeb0100000000feffffff02f319060000000001600144bf041f27
↳1bd94385d6bcac8487adf6c9a862d10a086010000000000160014e569a77bb4
↳df5df446847bcdc7c5c13bb1e6ea8b024730440220212043afeaf70a97ea0aa09
↳a15749ab94e09c6fad427677610286666a3decf0b022076818b2b2dc64b1599
↳fd6b39bb8c249efbf4c546e334bcd7e1874115da4dfd0c0121020127d82280a
↳939add393ddbb1b8d08f0371fffbde776874cd69740b59e09886621630800"

```
}
```

The first thing to note is that txid and hash differ. That's because this is a segwit transaction. As you may recall from chapter 10, the witness isn't included in the txid—that's how you avoid transaction malleability—but the hash in the output includes it. Note that size and vsize differ, too, which is expected from a segwit transaction. The fee was 141 satoshis, as shown by the listtransactions command, and the vsize was 141 vbytes. The fee rate was thus selected by Bitcoin Core to be 1 sat/vbyte.

The transaction has a single input that spends output 1 of transaction ebfd0d14...ba45c195. You should recognize this output from the section where I paid 0.005 BTC to my Bitcoin Core wallet. Because that output was a p2wpkh output, the signature script (scriptSig) is empty, and the txinwitness contains the signature and pubkey.

The sequence number of the input is 4294967294, which equals fffffffe. This means the transaction has lock time enabled but isn't replaceable using BIP125 (opt-in replace-by-fee).

I have two outputs. The first is the change of 0.00399859 BTC back to an address I own. The other is the actual payment of 0.001 BTC. Let's check the balance again:

```
./bitcoin-cli getbalance
0.00399859
```

Yep, there it is. I didn't have to wait for confirmation to see the new balance, because `getbalance` always includes my own *outgoing* unconfirmed transactions. I've spent my only UTXO (of 0.005 BTC) and created a new UTXO of 0.00399859 to myself:

```
Spent:    0.005
Pay:     -0.001
Fee:     -0.00000141
====================
Change:  0.00399859
```

It sums up perfectly.

I've shown a few commands you can use to wing your Bitcoin Core node, but there's a lot more to it. Explore `./bitcoin-cli help` to find out more.

Chapter 2

2.1 256 bits.

2.2 32 bytes.

2.3 A cryptographic hash function.

2.4 `061a` is `6*256 + (16 + 10) = 1,536 + 26 = 1,562` in decimal form. The binary form of `06` is `0000 0110`, and the binary form of `1a` is `0001 1010`, so the full binary representation is `0000 0110 0001 1010`.

2.5 No. If it was possible, the function wouldn't be second-pre-image-resistant.

2.6 Properties 2 and 4 are lacking.

2.7 Second-pre-image resistance is stopping the attacker. The attacker needs to find an input that gives the same hash as a certain other input: the cat picture.

2.8 The money supply increase rate will decrease over time because the reward to Lisa halves every 4 years. This means the total amount of CT to ever be created will be about 21,000,000.

2.9 The coworkers have read access to the spreadsheet. They can watch the spreadsheet and verify that Lisa doesn't reward herself too much or too often.

2.10   The private key is created using a random number generator of some sort. A simple one is a coin that you flip 256 times to generate your 256-bit private key. You can also use your operating system's built-in random number generator.

2.11   The private key.

2.12   The message is hashed because you want signatures to be small and fixed in size. You don't want the signatures to be big just because the signed message is big.

2.13   Mallory would need John's private key to steal cookies from him. She would also need his name, John, to write into the email to Lisa, but that's easily available in the spreadsheet.

2.14   Fred can use your public key to encrypt the message and send the encrypted message to you. You can then decrypt that message using your private key.

2.15   You sign the message using your private key and write the digital signature onto the note in the bottle. Fred can then verify that the signature is in fact made with your private key. He does this by using your public key to decrypt the signature and comparing the decrypted hash with the actual hash of the message. If they match, he can be sure the message is from you.

Chapter 3

3.1   The PKH is made short because a) it makes the spreadsheet smaller in size and b) it makes cookie token addresses (and Bitcoin addresses) shorter to write for a user.

3.2   Yes, you can. There's a base58check decoding algorithm that does this.

3.3   It's used by a payer to translate the recipient's address into a PKH. The payer needs to write the recipient's PKH in the email to Lisa.

3.4   Let's base58-encode 0047 step by step:

1. Remove leading 00 bytes. There is one, which leaves you with 47.

2. Convert to a decimal number: 47 in hex is $4 \times 16 + 7 = 71$ in decimal.

3. Divide 71 by 58: $71 = 1 \times 58 + 13$. The quotient is 1, and the remainder is 13.

4. Divide the quotient, 1, by 58: $1 = 0 \times 58 + 1$. The quotient is 0, and the remainder is 1.

5. Look up the remainders 13 and 1. Result: E and 2.

6. Add a 1 for the removed 00 byte in step 1, which results in E21.

7. Reverse it: 12E. Done.

3.5   The 4-byte checksum.

3.6   He must make two separate payments. For example: payment 1 pays 2 CT from $@_1$ to the cafe, and payment 2 pays 8 CT from $@_2$ to the cafe. Another way is to first pay 2 CT from $@_1$ to $@_2$ and then pay 10 CT from $@_2$ to the cafe.

3.7   Yes it is. Base58check-encode the PKHs to get the addresses.

3.8   No, because the spreadsheet contains PKHs. Because cryptographic hash functions are one-way functions, you can't go from PKH to public key.

3.9   They can look at the amounts. Many of the 10 CT payments are probably cookie purchases.

3.10   The bad guy can't steal cookie tokens because he needs the public key to exploit the flaw in the public key derivation function. The spreadsheet contains PKHs; the bad guy can't get the public key from it.

3.11   The bad guy needs the private key to sign fraudulent emails to Lisa. Even though he can reverse RIPEMD160, he'd still need to pre-image attack SHA256 and reverse the public key derivation function to get to a working private key.

Chapter 4

4.1 `bitcoin:155gWNamPrwKwu5D6JZdaLVKvxbpoKsp5S?amount=50`

4.2   Each character corresponds to 6 bits of entropy because $2^6 = 64$.
Ten such characters make 60 bits of entropy, which corresponds to 60
coin flips.

4.3   The four problems:

- Passwords are easily forgotten.

- Randomness is hard.

- The security of a password decreases as technology improves.

- You need to keep track of two items: the backup *and* the
  password. This increases the risk that the backup is lost.

4.4   The seed is created by first generating a huge random number,
then the random number is encoded as a mnemonic sentence, and
lastly, the mnemonic sentence is used to generate the seed.

4.5   An xprv consists of a private key and a chain code.

4.6   An xpub consists of a public key and a chain code.

4.7   The xprv at path `m/2/1` and the wanted index `7`.

4.8   No, you would need xprv `m/2/1` to derive xpub `M/2/1/7'`. You
first derive hardened xprv `m/2/1/7'` from `m/2/1` using hardened xprv
derivation and then calculate the xpub `M/2/1/7'` from `m/2/1/7'`.

4.9   You can use the following procedure to get the master xprv:
  1. Use master xpub `M` to derive xpub `M/4` and remember the left-
      half hash, L_4.
  2. Use `M/4` to derive the left-half hash L_{41} at index 1.
  3. Subtract L_{41} from the private key `m/4/1` to get private key `m/4`.
  4. Subtract L_4 from the private key `m/4` to get private key `m`.
  5. `m` together with the chain code of xpub `M` is the master xprv.

4.10   Yes, you'd be able to steal all funds in any addresses because you can calculate the master xprv.

4.11   The victim could have used hardening to generate `m/4'` instead. This way, you wouldn't be able to get the master xprv. If you stole `m/4'/1` and the master xpub, you would only be able to steal funds on the `m/4'/1` key. You wouldn't be able to calculate the `M/4'` xpub.

4.12   The employees can import the xpub for the counter sales account. They will then be able to generate any public keys under that account and thus generate as many addresses as they need without ever having to know any private keys.

4.13   Your (and Anita's) wallet can generate 10 addresses ahead of time and monitor the spreadsheet for those addresses. If Anita gets paid to one of these addresses—probably the first of those 10—then your wallet won't reuse that address when you request a payment from a customer. You would instead take the next unused address.

Chapter 5

5.1   You would spend the 4 CT and the 7 CT outputs. The new outputs would be 10 CT to the cafe and 1 CT in change to an address you control.

5.2   They're used in inputs to reference transactions from which to spend outputs.

5.3   Because you can't spend part of a transaction output. You either spend the output or you don't. If the spent output contains more value than you're paying, you need to give back change to yourself.

5.4   In the signature scripts in the inputs.

5.5   Because the verifiers need to know what public key to verify the signature with. You can't verify the signature with a PKH, so you need to explicitly reveal the public key in the signature script.

5.6   The signature scripts are cleaned so that verifiers don't have to know the order in which the inputs are signed.

5.7   Each output of a transaction contains a pubkey script. It contains the second part of a script program. The first part will be provided later, when the output is spent.

5.8   The Script program must end with OK on top of the stack.

5.9   A p2sh address always starts with a 3. You can also recognize it by base58check-decoding it and looking at the first byte. If that byte is 05, it's a p2sh address.

5.10   You'll create a transaction with one input and three outputs:

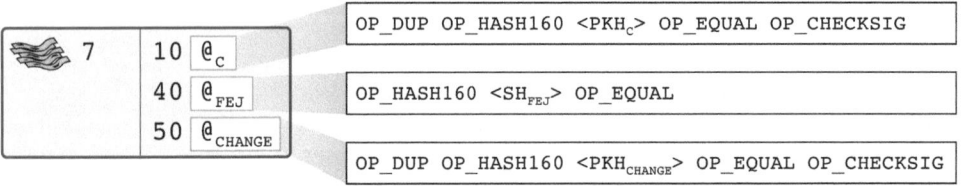

5.11   10,003 UTXOs. You remove two UTXOs by spending two outputs, and you add five new UTXOs. The net effect on the UTXO set is thus +3 UTXOs.

5.12   The pubkey script can be, for example, 1. The spending input can have an empty signature script. The full Script program just puts a 1 on the stack. A result stack with non-zero on top means OK.

5.13   OP_ADD 10 OP_EQUAL. This will first add the two top items on the stack and put the result back on top. Then, you'll push the number 10 to the stack and compare the two top items. If they're equal, OK will be pushed to the stack.

5.14   Yes. Your full node verifies everything in the spreadsheet from the very first transaction up to the transaction containing your money from Faiza. It verifies (among other things) the following:

- Lisa created the expected number of coinbase transactions with the correct amounts in them.

- For each transaction in the spreadsheet, the value sum of outputs doesn't exceed the value sum of inputs.

- All signatures from Faiza's payment back to all coinbase transactions are OK.

5.15 If there are several UTXOs to the same PKH, then as soon as one of them is spent, the security of the other UTXOs to the same PKH will be degraded. This is because you remove a layer of security, the cryptographic hash function. From this point, you rely solely on the public key derivation function to be secure. You can avoid this problem by using unique addresses for all your incoming payments. Then, all your UTXOs will have different PKHs.

Chapter 6

6.1 By the previous block's block ID, which is the hash of the previous block's header.

6.2 The merkle root of a block commits to all transactions in that block.

6.3 Lisa's block signature commits to the timestamp, the merkle root (and indirectly all transactions in this block), and the previous block ID (and indirectly the whole blockchain before this block).

6.4 The first transaction in each block is a coinbase transaction. This coinbase transaction creates 50 new cookie tokens and sends them to Lisa's cookie token address.

6.5 All transactions. The hash functions will all result in an index containing 1 because there are no zeroes in the bloom filter. Any item in the transaction that you test will be a positive.

6.6 The following are tested:

- The txid together with the index that identifies the output to spend

- All data items in the signature scripts

- All data items in the pubkey scripts

- The txid of the transaction

6.7 They aren't pre-image resistant, collision resistant, or second-pre-image resistant. The output space is small—typically just a few hundred to a few thousand numbers. It will take only a fraction of a second to find a pre-image of, for example, `172`.

6.8 The rightmost leaf must be copied to make an even number of leaves. The same goes for the next level, where the third hash needs to be copied.

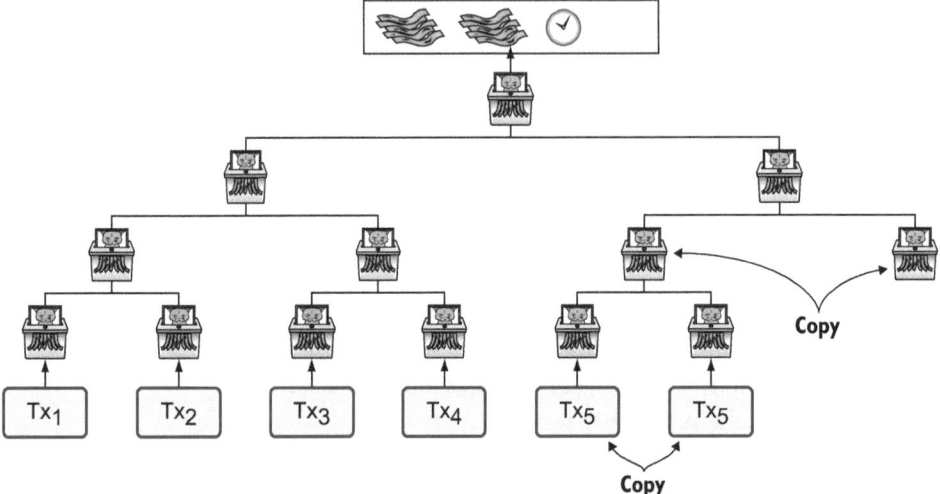

6.9 If Lisa's private block-signing key is stolen, the thief can create blocks in Lisa's name. Also, if a bad guy replaces Lisa's block-signing public key on one or more sources, such as the bulletin board or the intranet, the bad guy can fool people into accepting blocks not signed by Lisa.

6.10 Lisa can censor transactions, and the shared folder administrator can censor blocks.

6.11 a) Yes, a new node that downloads all blocks from the shared folder will notice that there are two versions of the block. b) Yes, an old node that has already downloaded the original block will detect that there is an alternate version of the block.

6.12 The bits at indexes `1`, `5`, `6`, and `7` are set to 1 and the other to 0. The full node would *not* send this transaction to the lightweight wallet. Nothing that's tested hashes to only indexes where the bits are `1`. This was something of a trick question, because the spent txid and the output index of the spent transaction aren't tested individually, so 1,6,6 will never be considered by the full node.

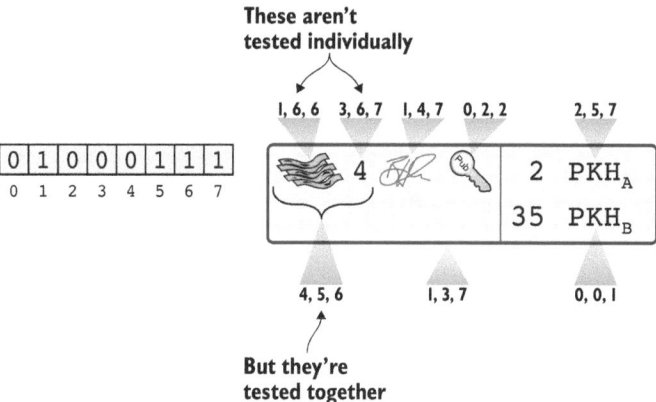

6.13 The partial merkle tree is

```
Number of tx: 3
Flags:  ✓ ✓ ✗ ✓ ✓ ✓
Hashes 3 4 6
```

6.14 The interesting transactions are numbers 7 and 13, or leaf numbers 6 and 10 from the left. You've already seen the solution in the section "Handling thousands of transactions in a block" in chapter 6, but I provide it here as well for reference.

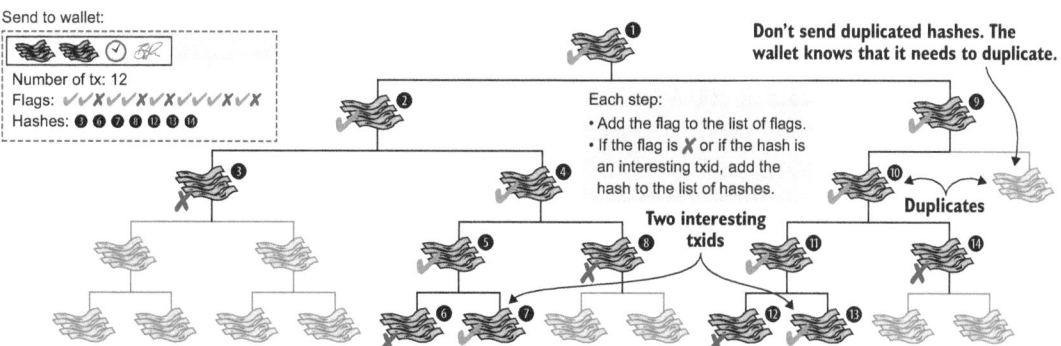

6.15 You need to verify the following:

- The transaction's txid is in the list of hashes.

- The root of the partial merkle tree matches the merkle root in the block header.

- The block header is correctly signed.

Chapter 7

7.1 She single-handedly decides what transactions get confirmed.

7.2 The probability of censorship will decrease because all miners must cooperatively decide to censor a transaction to succeed. Otherwise, your transactions will eventually be confirmed by some noncolluding miner.

7.3 Miners can cheat with random numbers. You can't prove whether a miner cheated.

7.4 Verify that the block ID of a block is lower than the target in the block header, and that the target is the agreed-on target.

7.5 By repeatedly changing the nonce and hashing (double SHA256) the block header until the block ID (the block header hash) is lower than the target.

7.6 The branch with the most accumulated proof of work. This isn't necessarily the same as the branch with the most blocks.

7.7 A miner with a hashrate of 100 Mhash/s can perform 100,000,000 tries per second to find a valid proof of work.

7.8 The target will increase. If the 2,016 blocks take 15 days instead of the goal of 14 days, then it's too hard to find blocks, so you need to decrease the difficulty, which means increasing the target.

7.9 50%. But if you plan to give up at some point, your chances will decrease.

7.10 The small block will reach the other miners more quickly than the big block because a smaller block travels a computer network faster than a big block. The small block is probably also quicker to verify than the big block. Miners will probably download and verify the small block faster than the big block and continue their mining activity on top of the small block, which gives the small block a higher probability of becoming part of the strongest chain.

7.11 The target will decrease by a factor of 3/4. The time to produce 2,016 blocks is 1.5 weeks; the first 1,008 blocks take 1 week, and the next 1,008 blocks take 0.5 weeks. So, the new target becomes

$$N = O * \begin{cases} \frac{1}{4} & \text{if } T < 0.5 \\ \frac{T}{2} & \text{if } 0.5 \leq T \leq 8 \\ 4 & \text{if } 8 < T \end{cases} = O * \frac{1.5}{2} = O * \frac{3}{4}$$

7.12 Selma has the majority of the hashrate. As long as she plays by the same rules as everyone else, she's going to earn a lot of block rewards. When she breaks the rules by changing the target prematurely, all full nodes except Selma's will discard her blocks. Selma will continue working on her own branch of the blockchain with her new rules, while all the rest will work on the branch with the old rules. The branches will be mutually incompatible. The hashrate of the old branch will drop to 48%, but the system will tick on, and everyone will continue their daily lives as normal. Selma, on the other hand, will spend a lot of electricity and time on her new branch, and no one will buy her block rewards. The value of her mined coins will probably be close to zero because she's not following the rules. Selma is a loser.

7.13 The fee-per-byte metric used by most miners will be very low. For every byte of transaction data the miner puts in its block, it will lose a little competitiveness because the block will get bigger and thus slower to transport over the network and to verify. If the fee per byte for the transaction isn't high enough to compensate for the lost competitiveness, the miner probably won't include it.

Chapter 8

8.1   The shared folder is a bad idea because it gives the shared folder administrator absolute power over what blocks to allow. Also, if the administrator decides to start mining, he can shut off all competition and have complete power of the system.

8.2   To relay a block or a transaction means to pass it on to peers.

8.3   An `inv` message is used to announce to peers that you have a certain block or transaction; `inv` stands for inventory.

8.4   It will run the transaction through the bloom filter it got from the wallet. If any tested item in the transaction matches the filter, the node will send the transaction to the lightweight wallet.

8.5   The full node sends an `inv` to the lightweight wallet after consulting the bloom filter. The wallet can then fetch the transaction if it doesn't already have it.

8.6   The block header.

8.7   Because the cafe doesn't have to obfuscate to its trusted node what addresses belong to the wallet. It sends a very big bloom filter to save data traffic on its mobile phone; a bloom filter that contains mostly zeroes will send almost no false positives.

8.8   She would verify the signature of the program using the public key she knows belongs to the Bitcoin Core development team. She does this to avoid being tricked into running malicious software.

8.9   Using a DNS server to get a list of IP addresses for a DNS seed (a DNS name) configured in Bitcoin Core, asking trusted friends, and using hardcoded addresses shipped with Bitcoin Core.

8.10   The node's peers will announce any new blocks by sending `headers` messages to the node, even during its synchronization process.

8.11   You need to convince the cafe, Qi, and Tom to hide blocks from Lisa. You can bribe them or threaten them.

8.12 She sends an `inv` message to Rashid's node containing the two transaction IDs.

8.13 Your node starts the synchronization process, which will look like this:

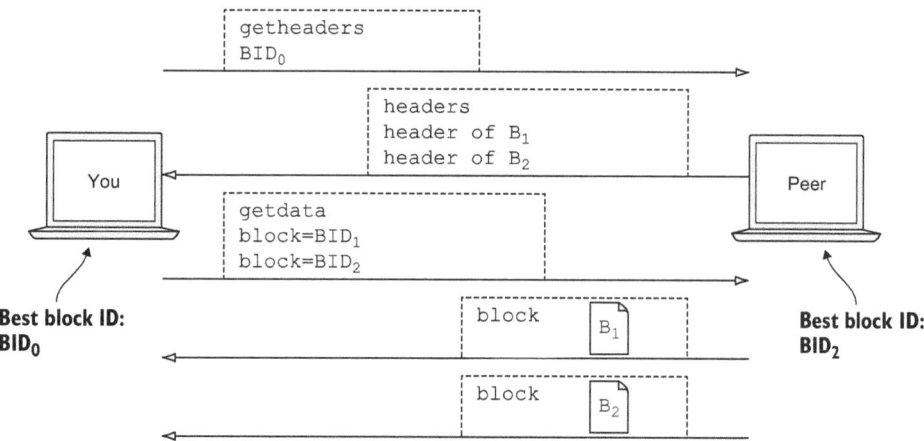

Chapter 9

9.1 At least one of the inputs must have a sequence number strictly less than `ffffffff`.

9.2 The median of the timestamps of the 11 previous blocks must be strictly later than 2019-12-25 00:00:00.

9.3 In the rightmost 16 bits of the sequence number.

9.4 Two transactions on each blockchain: one for the contract transaction and one for the swap transaction.

9.5 With fake PKHs, the data must be stored forever in the UTXO set because Bitcoin nodes can't distinguish between fake PKHs and real ones. The nodes won't be able to tell if the output is unspendable or not. With an `OP_RETURN` output, the node knows that the output is unspendable and thus doesn't have to keep it in the UTXO set.

9.6   Your first transaction paid a too-small fee and got stuck pending. You then want to replace it with a new transaction that pays a higher fee.

9.7   Absolute lock time: a transaction is invalid until a certain block height or time. Relative lock time: an input of a transaction is invalid until the spent output has been confirmed for a certain number of blocks or a certain time period.

9.8   The redeem script contains two branches of code. The first branch will require that both you and Ruth sign to spend the 2 BTC. This can be done at any time. To spend the 2 BTC using the second branch requires that all of the following conditions are met:

- You have waited until New Year's Eve.

- Beth has signed the transaction.

- You or Ruth signs the transaction.

To be precise, you and Ruth can spend using the first branch with the following signature script (excluding the redeem script):

```
0 <your sig> <ruth sig> 1
```

The second branch can be spent at the earliest on New Year's Eve with

```
0 <your or ruths sig> <beth sig> 0
```

The rightmost digit in both these signature scripts will select what branch to use; the rest fulfill the requirement in the respective branch.

The time-locked branch ensures that Beth has no power to collude with either you or Ruth before New Year's Eve.

9.9   No. The redeem script isn't known to the nodes until the output is spent. And because you can't spend an OP_RETURN redeem script, nodes will never know about the redeem script. The node will thus never know that this is an unspendable output.

9.10   A full node that receives a transaction will keep it in memory until it's included in a block. If a second, conflicting transaction arrives, the node will drop that second transaction and not relay it. It will consider the first-seen transaction as the "real" one and the second transaction as a double-spend attempt. Nodes (including miners) aren't required to follow this policy because it's just a policy.

9.11   Miners can always select whatever valid transactions they want to include in their blocks. Thus all transactions are in a way replaceable. A miner can offer replacement as a service—that is, upload a double-spend transaction with a high fee via the miner's website to have it confirmed in the miner's next winning block.

It is, of course, simpler for normal users to replace a transaction that has opted in to RBF. But using services like the aforementioned one is simple enough for a motivated thief. The difference in security therefore isn't as big as you might think.

Chapter 10

10.1   The signature scripts.

10.2   A transaction, T_2, that spends an output of an unconfirmed transaction, T_1, can become invalid if T_1 is changed into T_{1M} while being broadcast, and T_{1M} gets confirmed. This causes a lot of problems for contracts.

10.3   The time to verify a legacy transaction increases four times when the number of inputs doubles. This is because

- You need to verify twice the number of signatures.
- Each signature takes double the time to verify because the transaction to hash has doubled in size.

10.4   To verify that the transaction is included in a block, the lightweight wallet needs to calculate the transaction's txid. The wallet needs the signatures to calculate the txid because they're included in the txid.

10.5   The new behavior of `OP_NOP5` must, if it succeeds, be exactly like the old behavior of `OP_NOP5`. This means it should have no effect on the stack if it succeeds.

10.6   a (p2wpkh) and c (p2wsh) are segwit addresses. d is a p2sh address, but it might contain a nested p2wpkh or p2wsh payment in the redeem script. We can't say for sure. But the address is a p2sh address, not a segwit address.

10.7   The witness version is used to make future upgrades easier. The rule is that unknown witness versions are accepted. When a new witness version is deployed, old nodes will accept any payment that spends outputs with that new witness version. This avoids causing old and new nodes to follow different branches of the blockchain.

10.8   All data items in the signature script are pushed to the stack. No such items exist in the signature script, so there's nothing to do there. Then, `00` will be pushed followed by `c805…cba8`. The Script program is then finished, and the top item on the stack is checked. It's not zero, which means the spending is valid.

10.9   The new node will notice that the output has the segwit pattern. It will also notice that the witness version is `00` and that the witness program is 20 bytes. That means this is a p2wpkh output. To spend such an output, the signature script must be empty, and the witness must contain exactly a signature and the pubkey corresponding to the witness program, PKH_Y. The p2wpkh template is filled in using the signature and public key from the witness field and the PKH from the pubkey script (the witness program). The filled-in template is then run normally.

10.10   The fee merkle root can be placed in the right branch under the witness commitment. But you also need to put the fee merkle root in the witness for the coinbase input so that old segwit nodes can verify the witness root hash.

10.11   An old segwit node will verify the block exactly as before. The witness reserved value will be taken from the witness of the coinbase input. Using the hash from the witness lets the old node build the witness commitment and compare it with the hash in the OP_RETURN output, but it won't know that the witness reserved value is a fee merkle root. Old nodes thus won't be able to verify the fee merkle tree.

A new node will do the same verification as an old node, but it will also calculate the fee merkle root and compare it to the hash in the coinbase's witness.

Chapter 11

11.1   A soft fork tightens the consensus rules. This means blocks created by Bitcoin New nodes are guaranteed to be accepted by Bitcoin Old nodes.

11.2   **(a)**   The New branch will get wiped out by the Old branch.

(b)   It will *eventually* get wiped out when the Old branch catches up with the New branch and surpasses it. This can take quite a few blocks, depending on the initial deficit.

(c)   Bitcoin New could be equipped with wipeout protection—for example, by requiring that the first block in the split have a certain property that's not valid in the Old chain. Bitcoin Cash, for example, required that the first block be >1,000,000 bytes.

11.3   No, it will be outperformed by the New branch, and the Old branch will pretty quickly be wiped out, or reorged.

11.4   2,016 blocks. The LOCKED_IN state is always one retarget period.

11.5   Both. Old nodes can create a block that's not valid according to New nodes. Conversely, New nodes can create a block that's not valid according to Old nodes.

11.6   If the New nodes don't have a majority of the hashrate, the Old nodes can cause a lasting blockchain split. This would effectively result in two cryptocurrencies.

11.7   Replay protection is desirable because a transaction intended for one branch of the split shouldn't risk ending up on the other branch.

11.8   Yes. Suppose the 11 timestamps before B_1, sorted by value, are

```
a ≤ b ≤ c ≤ d ≤ e ≤ MTP₁ ≤ g ≤ h ≤ i ≤ j ≤ k
```

To calculate MTP_2 of block B_2 following B_1, add T_1 to this list. Because a timestamp of a block needs to be strictly later than the MTP of the block, T_1 must be sorted to the right of MTP_1 in the list. For example:

```
a ≤ b ≤ c ≤ d ≤ e ≤ MTP₁ ≤ g ≤ h ≤ T₁ ≤ i ≤ j ≤ k
```

You must also remove the timestamp of the block with lowest height from the list of timestamps. No matter what timestamp you remove, MTP_2 will be either MTP_1 (if you remove a timestamp to the right of it), or the timestamp immediately to the right of MTP_1 (if you remove a timestamp to the left of it) which can be either g or T_1:

If $MTP_2 = MTP_1$, then $MTP_2 <$ timeout because $MTP_1 <$ timeout.

If $MTP_2 = g$, then $MTP_2 \leq T_1 <$ timeout.

If $MTP_2 = T_1$ then $MTP_2 <$ timeout because $T_1 <$ timeout.

So, the MTP of B_2 is less than timeout in all cases, and all blocks (>95%) of the last 2,016 blocks signal support, which means the deployment will move to LOCKED_IN and—2,016 blocks later—to ACTIVE.

11.9   A portion (<30%) of the economy starts rejecting blocks that don't comply with your soft fork. This means you'll cause a blockchain split that will remain as long as a majority of miners support the Old branch.

11.10   When most of the economy starts rejecting Old blocks, miners probably won't want to mine Old blocks because the block rewards will become nearly worthless for them. It would be hard for miners to sell their Old coins on an exchange or pay for electricity with them. If they switch to mine New blocks instead, plenty of options exist for exchanging their block rewards for goods, services, or other currencies.

11.11   The nonmining users using Old software will automatically switch to the New branch once that branch is stronger than the Old branch. This is because, in a soft fork, the New branch is valid according to the Old software.

1. Satoshi Nakamoto, "Bitcoin: A Peer-to-Peer Electronic Cash System," 2008, http://mng.bz/lppR.

2. Bitcoin Stack Exchange, http://mng.bz/BDDl.

3. Bitcoin Developer Reference, http://mng.bz/dPP1.

4. Bitcoin source code repository, http://mng.bz/rBBj.

5. Kalle Rosenbaum, source code for *Grokking Bitcoin*, http://mng.bz/qBO2.

6. "Financial Inclusion Data / Global Findex," The World Bank, 2014, http://mng.bz/Vqqx.

7. "Reception of WikiLeaks: Response from the financial industry," Wikipedia, http://mng.bz/gYnV.

8. Menelaos Hadjicostis, "Bank of Cyprus Depositors Lose 47.5% of Savings," USA Today, July 29, 2013, http://mng.bz/pEez.

9. Bitcoin improvement proposals (BIPs), GitHub, http://mng.bz/OA0E.

10. Choose Your Bitcoin Wallet, http://mng.bz/xJJ6.

11. Andrea Corbellini, "Elliptic Curve Point Addition," http://mng.bz/YOBA.

12. Discussion of why double SHA256 is used in Bitcoin, Stack Exchange Cryptography, http://mng.bz/G2aO.

13. Complete list of Script operators in Bitcoin, Bitcoin Wiki, http://mng.bz/A22Q.

14. Arthur Gervais, Ghassan O. Karame, Damian Gruber, and Srdjan Capkun, "On the Privacy Provisions of Bloom Filters in Lightweight Bitcoin Clients," Cryptology ePrint Archive, http://mng.bz/ZZZ9.

15. Peter Todd, "What Attack Does the Difficulty Drop Rate Limiter Prevent?", http://mng.bz/zgWQ.

16. Lightning Labs, Lightning Resources, http://mng.bz/RGGa.

17. A blockchain explorer showing the ascii-art transaction discussed in chapter 9, http://mng.bz/J88Q.

18. Running a Full Node, http://mng.bz/2AAw.

19. Bitcoin Core download page, http://mng.bz/177R.

20. Getting Started with Bitcoin, http://mng.bz/P885.

index

RELATED MANNING TITLES

Building Ethereum Dapps
Decentralized applications on the Ethereum blockchain
by Roberto Infante

> ISBN: 9781617295157
> 504 pages, $39.99
> March 2019

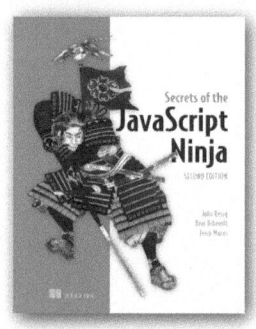

Secrets of the JavaScript Ninja, Second Edition
by John Resig, Bear Bibeault, and Josip Maras

> ISBN: 9781617292859
> 464 pages, $44.99
> August 2016

The Quick Python Book, Third Edition
by Naomi Ceder

> ISBN: 9781617294037
> 472 pages, $39.99
> May 2018

Grokking Deep Learning
by Andrew W. Trask

> ISBN: 9781617293702
> 336 pages, $49.99
> January 2019

For ordering information go to www.manning.com